Connect Trade Union, A History 1920-2020
Towards one big Irish Engineering Union

GW00701907

Written by
Luke Dineen

Edited by
Peter Rigney and *Sean Heading*

Hardback ISBN 978-1-8381112-8-1

Paperback ISBN 978-1-9164489-9-5

A limited edition of
100 Hardbacks and 1000 Paperbacks

Typeset in 10.5pt New Baskerville on 13.5 body.

Layout and Printing by
CRM Design + Print Ltd
Dublin 12

Produced by trade union labour in Ireland

Permission to reproduce copyright material is gratefully acknowledged.
Every effort has been made to trace copyright holders but if any have been inadvertently
overlooked the necessary arrangements will be made at the first opportunity

Table of Contents

List of Tables

Dedication

This book is dedicated to all Connect Trade Union members, past & present, who through their selfless actions in promoting the cause of craft & engineering workers have brought the union through one hndred years to be the union it is today.

Acknowledgements

No matter what the topic, academic histories are not the product of one person's sole input; they are a collective effort. Many people provided me with invaluable help without which this book could not have been written. My primary debts are to Francis Devine, Paddy Kavanagh and Seán Heading. Francis was an invaluable mentor throughout the writing of this book, and I greatly appreciate his confidence in me from the beginning. Special thanks to Paddy, Seán and Brian Donnelly for the faith they showed in me and for their belief in the value of a history of the Connect Trade Union. Peter Rigney and Mary Muldowney kindly proof read my work, for which I thank them both. I am similarly grateful to Eamon Devoy for his help throughout this project. Special thanks also go as to the ever-obliging staffs of the National Library; Berkeley Library, TCD; the UCC and Cork City and County Archives; and the Guinness, ESB and CIÉ private archives. I especially want to thank Brian Donnelly of the National Archives of Ireland who was wonderfully helpful to me. We are all obliged to the staff of the Military Archives, whose trojan work in digitising the witness statements of the Bureau of Military and the military pension application files has illuminated much about the Irish revolution.

This book is a record of those who sustained Connect's predecessors through trial and tribulation. Recording this was possible because of those who agreed to sit down with me and be interviewed. Their insight and personal experience of events gave me a more holistic understanding of Connect's union's history. The volunteers of the Irish Labour History Society and the Irish Railway Records Society deserve special credit. Without their dedication, many illuminating records would have been lost. I am also indebted to Jacqui Kirk, who conducted research on my behalf in the UK National Archives and at the Modern Records Centre at Warwick University. The personal aid given to me by friends and family over the years has been as important as any academic guidance, and you all have my utmost gratitude.

Foreword

Anyone walking up Gardiner Row will be aware of the plaque commemorating the occupancy of our building 6 Gardiner Row by the squad, or the Intelligence unit of the Dublin IRA. In recent years the release of material by the military archives has revealed a much deeper connection between our union and the struggle for independence. The decade 1913 to 1923 saw the foundation of three of the unions that eventually went on to become Connect Trade Union.

The state was founded a century ago and we are now commemorating the momentous historical and social events of a hundred years ago. Until recently we spoke of the war of independence. We now refer to the struggle for independence. This is because we know that civil resistance was a key part of the struggle. This is in no way to disrespect the role of the men and women who fought for Irish independence (my grandfather was one of them) but it recognises that there was a very comprehensive struggle in which unions and their members played a central role. This was not fully portrayed in mainstream historical works.

This book aims to redress the balance, at least in part. Skilfully written by Luke Dineen, it shows how Irish trade unionists assisted the national struggle but also struggled for independent unions and it outlines the role of the Irish republican brotherhood in founding our union and how two iconic figures of the struggle Michael Collins and Countess Markiewicz, supported this process. Later these two people found themselves on opposite sides of the tragic split that led to the Civil War.

The union is proud of our history, even more so given its role in the struggle for independence, however the main struggle continues to this very day and that is the fight for workers' rights, decent pay and secure employment in return for their labour and the preservation and enhancement of the skilled trades. With this book we also remember all past officials, activists and members who through their work and belief in collectivism made this union what it is today.

Pride alone is insufficient to preserve memory and therefore the EMC decided to commission this centenary work while being a fine example of the historians craft it is also a record of the contribution of craft and engineering workers to the development of the state. I hope it will be read not just by union members but by those interested in Irish social and political history.

Paddy Kavanagh
General Secretary

Message from President Michael D. Higgins

The best outcomes for workers, their defence and their prospects, are achieved by being a trade union member. The world of work is on the cusp of great changes. Remote working and hybrid or blended working, along with changes resulting from ongoing trends in digitalisation and automation, are presenting real challenges in terms of organisation of work. Some are new and some are familiar. In both, the principle is the upholding of labour rights and the achieving and sustaining of decent work conditions – such has been the *raison d'être* of the trade union movement in this country since the State's foundation and long before.

Work, we must never forget, represents the expression of our human essence. This is reflected in the way we work, what it means to us, and how we balance the lives we live together. In so many ways, work and what it means defines the society of which we are a part, its aspirations and mores, its democratic or authoritarian character.

Current challenges in technology and its application challenges us to define a new period of leadership within the trade union movement if we are to achieve democratic outcomes. In facing these challenges, it is to the trade union movement that workers can look for both ambition and realism, learn how to focus on what might be termed 'the art of the possible' that is embedded in the international vision that unions have historically exemplified, envisioned in terms of what we can achieve together, tapping humans' endless capabilities within a framework of protective, inclusive labour rights, rights that safeguard workers, particularly the most vulnerable. That protection is surely urgent in terms of the recent, often regressive, trends in the world of work. Such trends, often termed 'innovations', frequently merely represent advances insofar as they maximise productivity, efficiency, profitability, often at the expense of workers' hard-won rights.

Ireland boasts a long and proud tradition of trade unionism, a movement that has endured relentless struggles to secure human rights in often epic, hard-fought battles; a movement inextricably interlinked in our nation's struggle for independence or giving a lead in opposition to the waste of human life that is war.

This thoroughly researched book, Connect Trade Union
A History 1920-2020 – "Towards one big Irish Engineering Union" which traces the full 100-year history of Connect and its predecessors, provides an illuminating and comprehensive account of a full century of trade union activity, indeed going back further, tracing the origins of modern unions to the medieval guilds. In explaining the fascinating history of the Irish Engineering, Shipbuilding and Foundry Trades Union (IESFTU), as it was originally called, launched in May 1920 by a group of craftsmen imbued with an extraordinary sense of dedication to the cause of Irish independence in every sphere, the book demonstrates how

craft consciousness and conflict, and the interplay between the two, were constant themes throughout the history of Connect's predecessors; so too were conflicts with British unions, a manifestation of the Anglo-Irish conflict.

The politicisation of the Irish working class was a long and complex process, as is noted in the book. Fenianism was liberal, internationalist, secular, anti-sectarian and even, at times, socialistic, while locally interpreted or invoked republicanism could be curtailed into being more nationalistic, with a strong Catholic vein, as it sought to avoid the tags of Bolshevism or of being anti-Clerical, but as well as having weaker socialist or egalitarian tendencies, its braver elements confronted power. Such contradictory dynamics gave the independence struggle a cross-class appeal and composition, strengthening radical instincts among the working class.

The Irish Engineering, Shipbuilding and Foundry Trades Union was the result of the turbulence that Ireland endured between 1907 and 1921. Of course Jim Larkin helped to lay the groundwork for the establishment of the Irish Engineering, Shipbuilding and Foundry Trades Union, his foundation of the Irish Transport and General Workers Union (ITGWU) in 1909 representing a decisive break with the established (British) mode of trade unionism in Ireland. The creation of an independent, national union in Ireland not beholden to an executive council in London was a partial decolonisation of Irish labour. The ITGWU led the way for Irish workers to pursue a brand of trade unionism that they saw as more applicable to Irish political and material conditions. This was taken as an inspiration to the men who launched the IESFTU, whose complaints that British craft unions had little sympathy with, or understanding of, Irish needs had much validity by 1920.

The union's role in alleviating a succession of financial and economic crises, in alleviating the hardship being experienced by workers in this island over the decades is well-expounded in this book.

I have so often been struck by the reluctance of those who claim to be fervent enthusiasts of democratic institutions to acknowledge the contribution of trade unions over the decades – to acknowledge, to take account of what they have secured, what they have protected us from, indeed to see how they are our best advocates for our enduring bond to democracy.

Too rarely is it asked to what level society would have sank without such a movement, one that secures and protects the irreducible right to dignity in the workplace and in society. Now unions and union members must reclaim and speak out on their role as the best source of new forms of socially just, sustainable, ecologically responsible forms of economy and society.

Experiencing the pandemic has informed a heightened recognition of the role of the State, a realisation which, I believe, now exists across society regarding how labour issues are inextricable related. I refer to work-life balance, employer flexibility, remote working and, most importantly, the need to value our essential workers and the essential role of frontline workers who have been undervalued, and, in so many instances, underpaid, sometimes egregiously, for too long.

It was such workers, many of whom are represented by unions such as Connect, who secured the public good, kept society and economy operating at an essential, basic level while we attempted together to suppress the virus's spread.

Now is the time to challenge how we think about the world of work, and the delivery of new technology, so that we can identify and unleash human potential and flourishing, make work and employment as satisfying and rewarding as it should be for everyone in every sector of the economy and society, how we can protect those who, for whatever reason, are outside the basic protections and possibilities of what is narrowly called "the labour market", from falling into poverty and exclusion. We must demand that all work, for example, in the caring area is recognised, remunerated properly and valued.

The task now at hand – to create a society that is more equal, one in which all work is valued, without discrimination or narrowly defined by the market, and all jobs are decent, fulfilling and secure, together with adequate social protection – is far from easy to achieve given current geopolitics and the recent, if now thankfully fading, fixation with a neoliberalism that was not open to critique in terms of its assumptions, practices or consequences.

So much is possible, and can be made possible now. The battle for decent work and all it entails continues to be one of the defining struggles of our times, one that can be genuinely inclusive and emancipatory and joyful for all who participate in the cause. It is one in which, I know, Connect will play a central role.

Let us all commit to ongoing to increasing our activism in what is an international campaign for decent work, to playing our part in the creation of a society that removes the hurdles standing between so many of our people and their personal and social fulfilment. Let us commit to valuing all of those heroic workers, wherever they may be, who risk their lives and their security to support us, defending their rights, in these new circumstances, as the founders of the trade union movement did over a century ago. Let us play our part together in our times advocating a vital transition to a renewed political economy of hope, of a sustainable, just, inclusive future on our shared, vulnerable planet. Let us hear it loud and clear. Join the union, and in protecting and redefining the world of work, we build a decent, fulfilling world.

Le cheile is feidir sin a dhéanamh, ár feidireachtaí a gabháil. Beir beannacht.

Michael D. Higgins
Uachtarán na hÉireann
October 2022

Background
and Context

The nineteenth century was one of decline for most Irish craftsmen. The Act of Union had integrated the Irish and British economies, culminating in the removal of the last tariffs between the two countries in 1824. Free trade with the 'workshop of the world' devastated an economy still based on traditional crafts, many of which went into terminal decline. But modernity did benefit some. Modern engineering is a by-product of the Industrial Revolution, with Belfast becoming Ireland's major industrial success story of the nineteenth century. New trades, such as boiler-making and electrical work, were born while others, such as metalwork, experienced a vast expansion. Their importance to the new economy gave these workers real bargaining power, making them a 'labour aristocracy' – a well-paid stratum of craftsmen characterised by their conservatism, hostility to labourers and amicable rapport with their employers.[1] In Ireland, these workers had a standard of living comparable to their British peers. The pre-industrial crafts struggled to maintain a centuries' old culture against rapid economic change. Mechanisation eroded traditional control over work, as did the employers' use of machines to maximise profits. It fell to the trade unions to defend the craftsman against such an onslaught. Industrialisation paralleled the introduction of modern state services. The National Schools slashed illiteracy rates from 53 per cent in 1841 to 18 per cent in 1891.[2] A better educated working class was a more politically engaged one, which aided the spread of republican and radical ideas. The leadership of the Fenians was notably more proletarian and Catholic than previous revolutionary republican organisations, which contributed immensely to the democratisation of Irish nationalism.[3] The Irish economy, which was one of the poorest in Europe in the mid-nineteenth century, compared favourably with the continental average by 1900. Though social services remained woefully inadequate, 'the material quality of working-class life had advanced more in the previous 40 years than over the previous 400.'[4]

The birth of modern engineering

Engineering has existed for as long as humans have forged metal objects. Millwrights, the precursors of modern engineers, existed in Saxon times.[5] From then until the mid-eighteenth century, technologies to derive power from water, wind and animals developed gradually. The Industrial Revolution led to major improvements in mechanical technology, especially in the generation and transition of power by machines. By the mid-nineteenth century, iron machinery was used extensively in most branches of European manufacture.[6] The Industrial Revolution shaped modern capitalism in two phases. The first transformed the centre of production from workshop to factory and introduced methods and processes applicable to an industrial economy. The second involved the application of these methods across more areas of industry, which forced a reorganisation of traditional crafts. The engineer was the lynchpin of development in this second phase. In the first phase, however, civil and

1

mechanical engineers did not yet exist. In the eighteenth century, capitalists and inventors turned primarily to millwrights, the closest approximation of both, to develop the new machines. Millwrights' proficiency and experience with flourmill, waterwheel and windmill construction built the early Industrial Revolution.[7]

But the revolution would soon leave the millwrights' handicraft behind. From the 1790s, as iron became more important in machine-making, millwrights lost their predominance as new machines (such as steam engines) created a demand that they could not meet. If the Industrial Revolution was going to transform the world, then the engineering industry would have to take the lead. 'A revolution in … machine-making was necessary – a transformation from making machines by hand to making machines by machines.'[8] This happened between 1800 and 1840. The lathe and planer, the parents of all machine-tools, and modern taps and dies took shape during these years. Enough cast iron became available to enable machines, shafts, pulleys and gears to replace wood.[9] This facilitated an enormous industrial expansion between 1850 and 1875 which created the modern engineering industry. In 1850, textile machinery, locomotives and steam engines were the main engineering products. There was a vast expansion of engineering technology over the following decades, led by developments in marine engineering, armaments manufacture, machine tools and agricultural machinery. By 1890, the industry had expanded to include bicycle manufacture and electrical engineering. Marine engineering was revolutionised by the replacement of sail by steam as the method of propulsion and the replacement of wood by iron, and later by steel, as the material of construction.

Advancements in tools and machinery changed the typical engineering firm from a general shop to a specialised unit. Inevitably, workers had no choice but to become more adept as machines, materials and castings became more complex. By the 1850s, most engineering grades had assumed their modern form. Specialisation deepened differentiation in the metal trades, which was reflected in the respective places of work. The general shop where all worked together was replaced by separate shops for the individual trades in the same firm.[10] Between 1890 and 1914, these shops were convulsed by the 'Second Industrial Revolution', a renewed period of rapid technological development. Many important technologies were invented – electricity, the telephone, the internal combustion engine and the assembly line – and existing ones improved. Planning now took precedence over improvisation: complex machines were liabilities unless plans and discipline were strictly obeyed, making timekeeping vital.[11] Workers became known not by their name but by the numbers on their clock-cards. Employers tried to exploit mechanisation to drive down wages (see Chapter 2). Piecework was introduced to most shipbuilding and engineering trades, much to the craftsmen's chagrin. By the eve of the First World War, the British engineering industry had been completely transformed over the previous century. It would experience a similar convulsion during the war years, which crystallised the fundamental differences between the British and Irish industries.

Economy and deindustrialisation in nineteenth-century Ireland
In the nineteenth century, Irish manufacturing crumbled in the face of competition from British products that were cheaper and/or of superior

quality. The Irish working class was among the first in Europe to experience deindustrialisation. By 1914, every Irish city outside Ulster had reached an economic nadir with a thinner industrial base than what had existed in 1800.[12] Across Ireland and Britain, employers assailed the craftsmen's traditional independence by cutting costs through subdividing labour, introducing technical change and casualisation, and employing women and boys instead of craftsmen.[13] In 1841, of the 3.2 million Irish workers, only 240,000 were craftsmen. By 1911, deindustrialisation had made the figures even starker. Of some nine hundred thousand employees, seven out of every nine were in subsistence employment. Fewer than thirty thousand worked in shipbuilding while construction employed just under fifty thousand tradesmen.[14] Shipbuilding in the capital survived perilously after a century of regression. The industry was extinct in Waterford and had been declining in Cork since the 1860s. In Derry, four different shipyards existed between 1830 and 1924. The last was the most successful, employing 2,600 in 1922.[15]

In contrast to the south, shipbuilding's expansion in Ulster was seismic. Consequently, shipbuilding was one of the few Irish industries to grow overall. Belfast's 'big' and 'wee' shipyards of Harland & Wolff and Workman Clark employed over thirty-six thousand at their 1919 peak.[16] There were other industrial successes. The construction of the Irish railway network created a new type of demand for heavy engineering and ironwork. The railway companies had their own workshops for the construction and maintenance of rolling stock, giving permanent employment to many craftsmen. In Ireland, railway work began in 1834 in Dublin, which became the hub of the national network. The railway workshops dominated southern engineering: by the end of the nineteenth century, most of Dublin's 2,650 engineering workers were employed in the railways. The Great Southern and Western Railway's (GSWR) works at Inchicore developed into the largest engineering works outside Ulster. By 1913, it employed about 1,400 men and the Great Northern Railway's (GNR) Dundalk shop employed at least one thousand. Surprisingly, Belfast never emerged as a major centre of railway engineering.[17] Tramways opened in Dublin and Belfast (1872), Derry (1897) and Cork (1898), which also had domestic workshops. The growth of modern transportation had the knock-on effect of increasing the number of iron foundries, as did the need for machinery. Dublin, Belfast and Cork became major centres of ironwork, while Pierce's of Wexford became Ireland's biggest foundry, employing one thousand by 1914.[18]

Modernisation was a mixed blessing for workers. Artisans waged a desperate, often violent struggle against machinery wherever it was introduced. Mechanisation eroded traditional work patterns and sometimes even changed the composition of a workforce. In Passage West, for example, local shipwrights were swapped for men from Scotland and Belfast when iron became the primary shipbuilding material.[19] Table 1 demonstrates how deindustrialisation affected the Cork crafts. The city's ropemaking, nail making and cork cutting trades were decimated, and there were no weavers or hatters left by 1901. Most trades survived, however, though their numbers were considerably reduced. In contrast, the number of farriers, engineers and coachbuilders increased while the number of printers, bakers and building tradesmen held firm.[20] Decline was therefore not universal.

3

Table 1: Numbers in the Principal Trades in Cork, 1841-1901[21]

Trade	1841	1851	1861	1871	1881	1891	1901
Farriers	3	24	34	27	28	32	32
Printers	116	143	181	191	189	227	184
Engineers	183	142	116	333	242	232	298
Coachmakers	76	68	147	158	161	139	179
Saddlers	140	99	117	97	97	81	76
Shipwrights	91	153	166	111	74	44	43
Carpenters	603	500	645	603	522	612	586
Masons	241	324	300	256	250	284	214
Stonecutters	98	114	117	116	154	93	98
Slaters	150	125	123	90	50	60	35
Plasterers	101	49	55	88	121	111	135
Plumbers	259	226	282	301	102	146	201
Painters	-	-	-	-	247	276	341
Cabinetmakers	218	175	227	142	124	129	120
Weavers	325	160	113	25	7	7	0
Hatters	98	63	56	37	26	18	0
Tailors	748	551	638	564	442	397	275
Shoemakers	1,398	1,216	1,078	702	590	510	425
Bakers	253	367	353	348	322	290	274
Ropemakers	109	90	-	64	34	23	14
Tobacco workers	20	63	77	140	106	254	216
Tanners	288	258	89	137	96	101	36
Brushmakers	45	59	55	39	25	25	11
Coopers	725	551	638	564	442	397	275
Blacksmiths	316	231	322	273	213	172	147
Nailors	131	105	98	78	49	23	7
Sawyers	163	173	172	95	65	55	93

Trade unionism and craft consciousness

Many nineteenth-century craft unions – especially those representing pre-industrial trades – traced their origins to the medieval guilds. The guilds' establishment followed the Norman conquest of Ireland when royal charters for trade representation were issued. They were a principal component of the medieval social, economic and legal systems. Their primary function was to control labour by regulating working practices and restricted apprenticeships. They could even set wages and prices via the Corporation and assizes. Significantly, guilds also functioned as a mutual benefit society that assisted members in times of distress. In theory, the guild system benefitted everyone: masters benefitted by the control of wages; journeymen by the control of prices and apprenticeships; and consumers by the maintenance of high workmanship standards. Guilds went into serious decline in the eighteenth century.[22] As the zeitgeist moved towards laissez-faire, they fell victim to capitalism, mechanisation and specialisation. Parliament began to appropriate their functions and dismantle statutory restrictions on trade that regulated the market. Accordingly, journeymen began to combine in defence of their interests. This process began in Dublin in the 1670s and had reached the provinces by the early eighteenth century. From 1729, the Irish parliament passed a series of laws outlawing combination and heavily punishing guilty offenders. A particularly draconian Act of 1780 authorised the death penalty for those convicted of attacks on workshops, tools or materials. In 1824, Westminster finally decriminalised trade unionism, which launched the modern labour movement.[23]

Nineteenth-century craft unionism was a defensive movement based on mutuality, community and solidarity. Unlike labourers, tradesmen could expect regular employment and decent pay and conditions. Though unions often paid lip-service to craft unity, they ensured that narrow interests triumphed every time. Unions existed to safeguard members by exercising strict control over the labour market, beginning with their own rank-and-file. High membership fees and severe limits on apprenticeship numbers were the first lines of defence. While these tactics became increasingly redundant with time, they 'confirmed the collective identity of the trade and individual artisan's position within it.'[24]

> The closed-shop tradition of the trade, with its emphasis on family links between journeymen, masters and apprentices, ensured that economic defensiveness was strengthened by ties of blood. Nor was this simply the blood tie between the journeyman as father and the apprentice as son, but also an implied relationship between the trade as parent and the individual journeyman or apprentice as offspring of the craft.[25]

Craft consciousness compelled artisans to come together and form trades councils in Cork (1880), Belfast (1881) and Dublin (1885), all of which are direct predecessors of the present-day bodies.[26] The 'closed-shop' highlighted artisan's exclusiveness and skill in contrast to who he feared most: the labourer. The division between the two was so deep that it even influenced their respective attire. No self-respecting tradesman would have felt properly dressed without his bowler hat, a 'symbol of his prosperity and his thoroughgoing respectability... Behind the symbol there lay a certain air of superiority over the ordinary 'five-eight', an expression used to describe the labourer', who typically wore the cloth cap.[27]

Completing an apprenticeship was perhaps the central component of craft identity. A boy typically started his apprenticeship aged fourteen. He was bound by a seven-year written indenture that tightly controlled his wages and behaviour on and off the job.[28] Apprenticeships had existed from ancient times and indentures from the Middle Ages. By the eighteenth century, the seven-year period was universal across Europe.[29] Most trades only paid 'encouragement money' of a few shillings for the first year, gradually reaching half a journeyman's rate by the final year. Medieval indentures were still used by many pre-industrial trades up to the 1960s in the Dublin building trades.[30] Modern apprenticeships were operative in the Belfast shipyards. There, boys typically started aged sixteen and served five to seven years (five being the most common) depending on the trade.[31] These apprenticeships were also draconian in nature. Harland & Wolff, for example, compelled an apprentice to obey all company orders and 'diligently and faithfully serve his employers.'[32] A nineteenth-century engineering apprenticeship was poor training for the modern industry.

It was largely the apprentice's responsibility to learn what he could by watching and assisting journeymen. Few employers considered it their duty to make sure apprentices gained a knowledge of all aspects of their craft, and semi-skilled workers were often left to gain experience as best they could, with little help from supervisors and craftsmen. [33]

Unions opposed any attempt by the state or middle-class philanthropists to teach the craft. Despite pressure from employers, attendance at state-sponsored technical education classes was sparse for years after their establishment in 1899.[34] Attendance at these classes was voluntary and apprentices were trained on the job. The state's role was limited to instruction in science and art where they applied to industry.[35]

The apprenticeship was not just 'the means of transmitting skills to a younger generation', it was 'the badge of the craftsman … proud of his identity as 'a seven-years' man.'[36] The apprenticeship inculcated 'values concerning status and tradition, pride not just in one's craft but in one's personal worth.'[37] The values espoused by craftsman were a mixture of new and old. Traditional pride in one's craftsmanship was joined by a yearning for 'respectability' which defined the Victorian bourgeoisie. Thrift, self-improvement, self-education, industriousness and temperance were common aspirations among the British 'aristocrats of labour' and the middle classes. In Ireland, these features were joined by more disciplined religious observation.[38]

By the mid-nineteenth century, shipbuilding and engineering, with their need for skilled labour, had made Belfast one of the leading centres of trade unionism in the UK. Immigration of tradesmen from Britain encouraged the growth of British unions in the city, often their first Irish branches. The Iron Moulders' Society set up shop in 1826 and the Boilermakers' Society in 1841. The United Patternmakers' Association also established a sturdy base in the north-east. Most significant of all was the inception of the Amalgamated Society of Engineers (ASE) in 1851. Belfast and Dublin were represented at its foundational meeting. By 1891, it had fourteen Irish branches with 2,228 members, 1,515 of them in Belfast.[39] The ASE introduced a 'new model' to British trade unionism. Established throughout the 1850s and 1860s, new model unions were centralised, national organisations with full-time general secretaries. They levied high rates of contributions which enabled them to pay generous benefits. They too reflected craft conservatism and prided themselves on their respectability, as exemplified by their mottos of 'defence not defiance' and 'a fair day's pay for a fair day's work.' They recoiled at strikes and instead used moral force and public pressure to make their case. They also preserved strict control of apprenticeships and enforcement of restrictive practices.[40]

New model unionism re-orientated the values and outlook of the Irish labour movement towards Britain. Its importation was accompanied by a (largely successful) drive to subsume local societies. Workers in the new industries joined the 'amalgamateds' (as British unions were known in Ireland). Born of other industries, the electrical trade was one of the youngest in Ireland. Gasfitters were the first craftsmen to work in it and their sons became Ireland's first qualified electricians.[41] In 1889, Irishmen participated in the launch of the Electrical Trades Union (ETU) to cater for UK electricians. Seven years later, Irish electricians inaugurated their own union, the Irish Electrical Workers; it barely lasted a year.[42] To an Irish craftsman, the advantages of joining the bigger, British unions were obvious. Unions still had important benefit functions, giving the British a major advantage. Should an Irishman seek work in Britain, a recognised card of a British union was of enormous assistance. By 1900, three-quarters of Ireland's seventy thousand trade unionists were in British unions. Assimilation into the British movement was, Emmet O'Connor believes, British labour's contribution to the Anglicisation of Ireland. This was a broad colonial process reflected most clearly in the language shift from Irish to English, the adoption of English social culture and sports, and the increasing Anglo-centrism of the Irish media. Since the 1850s, Irish labour had applied the methodology of British trade unionism despite its unsuitability to an unindustrialised economy with high unemployment, few tradesmen and a vast pool of unskilled labour.[43] This, O'Connor argues, was the ultimate manifestation of how Irish labour had been 'mentally colonised' by its British counterpart:

> Mental colonisation is what happens when a people reject their own values as 'backward' and try to fit themselves into the 'modern' paradigms of the metropolitan country. It is not the same as external influence. The mentally colonised do not adapt ideas to their own reality: they try to live in other people's reality.[44]

Labourers suffered more than artisans from the malaise. From the late 1880s, they began to organise on a mass scale under the banner of 'new unionism' (1889-92). In Ireland, British unions led this phenomenon. Armed with the weapon of trade unionism, labourers began to demand better wages and conditions from employers and some 'new unions' even flirted (however mildly) with socialism. A combination of employer aggression and state violence crushed most new unions, although some survived to live a precarious existence. The fierce hostility new unionism received from the trades also aided its demise. Labour returned to the conservative, craft unionism of old. Tradesmen remained fearful that a unionised labourer could become the despised 'handyman', allowing him to displace skilled labour and undercut the craft rate.[45] With workers so deeply divided, labour could make only limited gains. New unionism was the first of the three stages of Irish labour's modernisation and 'Larkinism' (1907-14) was the second. Syndicalism (1917-23) was the third, and most enduring, wave of modernisation. Each stage involved an evolution of tactics: labour unions evolved into industrial unions, then general unions and finally the One Big Union; blacking became the sympathetic strike and finally generalised action. Labour also progressed politically: the formation of the Irish Trades Union Congress (ITUC) in 1894 presaged the establishment of an Irish Labour Party in 1912 as well as its adoption of a socialist constitution in 1918.[46] Until Larkinites took control of it in 1911, Congress had been a 'craft union talking shop with little or no political significance' which represented only about 5 per cent of Irish workers (typically the pre-industrial trades).[47] It made little positive impact before 1918.

Class conflict

The Irish economy was a paradox of development and decline in the post-Famine era. Huge levels of emigration caused a massive 25 per cent population decline between 1851 and 1911, which had the unintended consequence of significantly raising wages by reducing under- and unemployment and sapping labour supply.[48] As Table 2 shows, Irish craft wages converged with British rates, reaching a respectable level of parity by 1914.[49] From 1874 to 1898, pay grew in tandem with a decline in the cost of living, thereby significantly improving workers' living standards.[50]

As the south slipped into industrial abyss, the north boomed. By 1911, Belfast's population had burgeoned to 387,000, making it Ireland's biggest city. With 8.8 per cent of the island's population, Belfast contained 21 per cent of its industrial workforce. Like every part of Belfast society, labour was plagued by sectarian divisions.[51] In the shipyards, Protestants were disproportionately represented in the crafts while Catholics were grossly underrepresented, being predominantly labourers.[52] Sectarianism and politics bound Protestant workers to their employers, creating an alliance that diffused class conflict.[53] In 1893, the ASE had told the Royal Commission on Labour that it was happy with conditions in Belfast, though it did complain of poor safety practices, lighting and sanitation in the shipyards. The union maintained that industrial disputes were rare because 'employers generally meet their employees in a fair manner' and because it had not 'pushed demands to extreme.' The Boilermakers' Society told the commission that they were 'getting on very nicely ... with our employers.'[54]

Table 2: Craft Wages in Ireland and Britain, 1914 (shillings per week). [55]

Industry	Ireland	Britain
Railways	35.0	36.6
Cycle manufacture	36.2	43.0
Construction & engineering	34.7	38.1
Agricultural machinery	23.8	33.3
Printing & binding	33.3	35.3
Furniture	38.1	38.9
Coachbuilding	35.8	38.7
Average	34.9	37.7

Table 3: Metal Craftsmen's Strikes in Ireland, 1888-1913.[56]

Cause	Dublin	Leinster (exc. Dub.)	Munster	Belfast (exc. Bel.)	Ulster	Ireland
Wages & Conditions	2	2	-	21	1	26
Demarcation59	-	-	2	8	1	11
Other60	2	1	2	5	-	10
Total	4	2	4	36	2	47

But the yards were not the centres of harmony that the unions claimed. While strikes were uncommon relative to the numbers employed, several minor stoppages occurred An analysis of why craftsmen downed tools, and how often they did so, is illuminating here (see Table 3). Between 1888 and 1914, Belfast accounted for three-quarters of disputes involving Irish engineering and shipbuilding craftsmen; Dublin and Munster combined only accounted for one-sixth. This is not surprising given the metalworkers' strength in Belfast and their weakness in the south. Just over half of Irish metal strikes were about wages and conditions while employment of non-unionists made up less than 10 per cent.[59] Work was not just an artisan's economic livelihood; it was the ultimate expression of his worth as a man, making him extremely sensitive to encroachment from employers, labourers and his fellow craftsmen alike. Shipbuilding was a highly complex process that employed a multitude of crafts (as many as ninety).[60] With such a diverse workforce, shipyards were prone to demarcation disputes between different trades about who did what work, which was not always clear to either the unions or the employers.[61] Trades in decline due to modernisation were especially eager to save what was left of their trade, an example being the shipwrights' constant disputes with the carpenters and/or joiners.

The Belfast shipyards experienced only one major stoppage in this era. In 1895, 1,300 engineering workers and ironfounders downed tools for a wage increase, prompting employers to join with their Clydeside colleagues in a common front. In a deeply resented move, Belfast shipbuilders locked out ten thousand men. The engineering workers accepted compromise while the ironfounders pushed for, and secured, their full demand. Left-wing radicals tried to mobilise a cross-channel response to the strike, but Belfast's insular mentality prohibited this happening. Sectionalism was reinforced by the 1897 UK engineering trades agreement, the first to include Belfast, which left wages to be decided locally. Although they embroiled Belfast engineering workers in the general lockouts of 1897-98 and 1922, UK-wide agreements had a stabilising influence in the long-term. They did not, as the radicals had hoped, bring Belfast into the current of labour politics.[62] It was not until 1919 that another major stoppage occurred in the Belfast shipyards.[63] The city's sectionalism choked any possibility of a non-sectarian labour movement.

> The Belfast shipyards were the sites for the development of both sectarian consciousness and a limited craft awareness… the development of a *class* consciousness… was fundamentally impeded by the developed sectional awareness of the shipyard craftsmen. The skilled workers need not have been militant Orangemen … only a minority … were, but their sectionalism was a prime material condition that allowed externally produced sectarian ideologies to be established and reproduced.[64]

A symbiotic relationship existed between the deepening of sectarianism and the expansion of the shipyards. Shipyardmen were prominent in the sectarian riots of 1857, 1864 and 1901; in the workplace expulsions of 1886, 1893, 1912 and 1920; and in worker opposition to the anti-conscription movement in 1918 and to Irish nationalism generally. In 1912, the police estimated that about 30 per cent of them were active in unionist clubs and/or Orange lodges in their workplaces.[65]

Overall, the shipyardmen had good reason to be happy. Between 1860 and 1900, skilled wages rose faster in Belfast than in Britain, though actual earnings may have been lower because of the absence of piecework.[66] Metal craft wages in Belfast were the best in Ireland and among the best in the UK.[67] At the turn of the century, Belfast engineering craftsmen earned 37s. to 39s., whereas peak rates were 38s. to 40s. in England and 36s. in Scotland. Likewise, shipwrights' and ironfounders' wages were at or near those paid at the leading British centres.[68] Taking London as one hundred, skilled engineering wages were ninety-four in Belfast, eighty-eight in Dublin and eighty-seven in Cork in 1905;

the mean figure for Ireland was ninety. Taking Dublin as one hundred, they were 103 in Belfast and ninety-six in Cork.[69] The working week was fifty-four hours for most Irish metalworkers, though for some it was as high as 56½. Between 1905 and 1912, Irish food prices jumped by 25 per cent while unemployment soared to 20 per cent. Engineering wages remained static outside Belfast, ensuring that workers' living standards diminished in real terms.[70] Maintaining high wages was made easier by the concentration of workers in a few large firms and the close circuit between the Belfast and the major British centres. It was an arrangement with significant consequences:

> When each stage in the construction of a ship ended, it was usual for the workers engaged on it to move to another centre if work was not available in the home port... A further consequence is of sociological and indeed, in an Irish setting, political interest; the high proportion of Protestants in the Belfast shipyards was reinforced by immigration of Glasgow workers sharing the same fiercely partisan sectarian outlook and the same hostility toward Irish Catholics.[71]

However, it would be wrong to exaggerate the metal craftsman's 'privileges.' The work was dangerous and conditions harsh, making accidents, even death, common. Craftsmen had to be in excellent health to cope with the physical demands. Even myopia was not accepted, leading to many otherwise healthy workers being sacked when their eyesight declined.[72] Their life expectancy was low, averaging only thirty-eight in the 1860s and forty-eight in the late 1880s.[73] In 1907, forty-eight foundrymen in every thousand suffered injury. In 1912, in the Belfast, Clyde and Tyne shipyards, 1,448 were injured and sixty-two killed in falls, while 1,400 were injured and fifteen killed by objects falling on them.[74] Sanitary conditions were worse in Dublin than in Belfast; in Limerick, they were among the worst in Europe.[75]

The cost of living began to rise again at the turn of the century. Only in Belfast did wage growth match inflation until 1914.[76] Nevertheless, southern craftsmen were quiescent, making strikes a 'rare occurrence.'[77] An unsuccessful stoppage of Dublin shopmen in 1902 for a wage increase and against the introduction of piecework was indicative of labour's weakness in the first decade of the twentieth century. There are several reasons for the lack of militancy. The defeat of new unionism was one, as was the lack of collective bargaining structures. The most salient was the 1902 Taff Vale judgement, the result of a lawsuit taken against the Amalgamated Society of Railway Servants by the Taff Vale Railway Company in south Wales after a prolonged strike there. The judge found in favour of the employers, ruling that trade unions were liable for the loss of profits accruing from strikes, effectively killing labour militancy across the UK. The 1906 Trades Disputes Act, which explicitly stated that unions were not liable for profits lost, reversed the ruling. Craftsmen were impacted by employer aggression towards labourers, leading to a rapprochement between trade and spade. The 1911 lockout at Pierce's and the 1913-14 Dublin lockout were cases in point.[78]

Table 4: Irish Engineering Wages, 1900.[79]

Locality	Fitters	Turners	Smiths	Millwrights	Pattern makers	Copper-smiths	Brass finishers
Belfast	37s.	38s.	37s.	38s.	39s.	-	38s. 3d.
Dublin	33s.	33s.	34s.	35s.	35s.	-	-
Cork	34s.	34s.	34s.	34s.	36s.	36s.	-
Drogheda	30s.	30s.	32s.	30s.	30s.	-	-
Dundalk	33s.	33s.	33s.	33s.	36s.	-	-
Limerick	32s.	34s.	32s.	34s.	34s.	-	-
Derry	28s.	29s.	29s.	28s.	28s.	-	-
Newry	30s.	30s.	30s.	30s.	30s.	-	-
Portadown	30s.	30s.	30s.	30s.	-	-	-
Waterford	32s.	32s.	30s.	-	32s.	-	-

In January 1907, labour's fortune began to transform when Big Jim Larkin disembarked from a cross-channel ferry at Belfast Harbour to reorganise labourers, leading to a renaissance of militancy until 1914. His efforts culminated in the creation of the ITGWU in 1909, a partial decolonisation of Irish labour and a turning point in its history, and the 1913-14 Dublin lockout, when Irish labour was engulfed in a titanic struggle against William Martin Murphy and the Dublin Employers' Federation. Anti-labourer snobbery remained a feature of craft unionism in the Larkinite years. It was a major factor in the 1909 split in the Cork Trades Council following a disastrous lockout of labourers that summer. Sick of Larkinite militancy, fourteen craft unions broke away and founded the Cork District Trades Council, giving Cork two trades councils. Unlike its rival, the breakaway council refused to support the ITGWU during the 1913 lockout. Both councils reunified in 1916. Fitters had been attached to the District Trades Council throughout its existence.[80]

'Larkinism', as employers disparagingly christened it, exalted the 'irrational' aspect of the human condition. In other words, it infused new moral, rather than material, values into Irish trade unionism. As Ireland's contribution to the rebirth of militancy taking place across Europe and North America, Larkinism had much in common with contemporary Western syndicalism. But unlike syndicalism, Larkinism resulted from the absence of radical alternatives, not from disenchantment with them. As an agitator, Larkin projected the workers as moral heroes and presented himself as the embodiment of their spiritual resurrection. Larkinism was a radical ideology that instilled new ethical values of working-class solidarity into the mechanics of class conflict. It achieved this by ennobling methods which facilitated the unionisation of the unskilled as part of a morality of struggle. Its defining feature was the sympathetic strike – its most efficacious weapon against employers. Its three central characteristics were a glorification of the working class, sympathetic action and class solidarity. The values Larkin infused into labour provided the basis for generalised action from 1918, the only tactic capable of winning concessions in a poorly industrialised economy with a vast pool of unskilled labour. Larkinism thus laid the foundation for Irish syndicalism, the ideological and methodological basis for Irish labour between 1917 and 1923, its most successful period.[81]

Table 5: Irish Engineering Wages, October 1913.[82]

Locality	Fitters	Turners	Smiths	Millwrights	Pattern makers	Copper-smiths	Brass finishers
Belfast							
General	41s.	41s.	40s.	-	43s.	41s. 6d.	-
Mills & Machine shops	40s.	40s.	40s.	-	-	-	-
Dublin							
General	36s.	36s.	36s.	38s.	38s.	36s.	33s.
Railway	33s.	33s.	33s.	34s.	36s.	38s.	36s.
Cork	34s.	34s.	34s.	34s.	36s.	36s.	-
Drogheda	30s.	30s.	32s.	30s.	30s.	-	-
Dundalk	33s.	33s.	33s.	33s.	36s.	-	-
Limerick	34s.	32s.	32s.	34s.	34s.	-	-
Derry	34s.	34s.	34s.	34s.	34s.	-	-
Newry	32s.	32s.	32s.	32s.	30s.	-	-
Passage	36s.	36s.	36s.	-	-	-	-
Portadown	32s.	32s.	32s.	32s.	32s.	-	-
Waterford	30s.	30s.	30s.	-	32s.	-	-

Housing, health and prices

Southern reliance on cheap, unskilled labour – and the lack of skilled jobs in the metal trades in particular – had atrocious social consequences, especially when comparisons with industrialised Belfast are made. The famous red bricked houses that dotted the northern city's terraces were a world apart from the notorious Dublin slums, described by a contemporary English commentator as 'a thing apart in the inferno of degradation.'[83] Of the 59,263 Dublin families recorded in the 1901 Census, 37 per cent lived in a one-roomed tenement and 23 per cent in a two-roomed one.[84] By contrast, one-room tenements housed 13 per cent of the population of Glasgow and only 0.03 per cent in Belfast.[85] Over 40 per cent of Dubliners lived in overcrowded dwellings – more than anywhere else in the UK – whereas just 5 per cent of inhabited houses in Belfast were considered overcrowded.[86] Accordingly, Dublin had an average density of 38.53 people per acre while Belfast had an average of 25.91.[87]

Filth and overcrowding inevitably led to major public health problems in Dublin, which had the worst child mortality rates in Europe. At the turn of the centenary, Belfast's infant mortality rate was 136 per thousand births as against 246 in Dublin. The capital's death rate from contagious diseases dwarfed its northern counterpart – 4.05 per thousand compared to 2.1 – and its death rate from sexually transmitted diseases was 1.4 per ten thousand as against 0.51 in Belfast (0.76 in London). Such diseases accounted for one third of mortalities in Dublin. In 1913, the city's overall mortality rate per thousand was 23.1; the figure was 18.4 in Belfast, 14.3 in London and 12.8 in Bristol.[88] While mortality rates began to fall in Dublin from 1914, they soared during the influenza pandemic of 1918-19, when such deaths far exceeded those from political violence. Influenza killed 1,767 in County Dublin in 1918 (37 per thousand)

and 1,099 in 1919 (23 per thousand). Unsurprisingly, the flu ravaged the slums the hardest: the death rate in the inner city peaked at 56 per thousand during the third and final wave (in Ireland) of the virus in the first quarter of 1919. Mortality rates resumed their downward trend once was the pandemic was over. Infecting about a fifth of the population, there were approximately eight hundred thousand flu cases in Ireland and about twenty-three thousand deaths.[89]

Not only did the Belfast engineer enjoy higher wages than his southern colleagues in 1905 but his rent was also much lower, as Table 6 illustrates. Retail prices in Ireland were strikingly high compared to Britain, although rents were markedly lower. In Dublin, however, slum rents were exorbitant by Irish standards, ranging from 2s. to 4s. 6d. a week – 11 to 28 per cent of an engineering labourer's wage. A craftsman usually lived in a four or five room house with a rent of 6s. to 10s, or 17 to 30 per cent of a week's wages. In Belfast, a typical working-class family resided in a two-storeyed dwelling with four rooms and a small scullery. A standard craftsman's house had a sitting room and a kitchen on the ground floor and two bedrooms on the upper floor, the fifth room being a bedroom over the scullery. Rents ranged from 2s. 6d. to 6s. 3d., with 3s. 6d. being the most common.[90] A fitter could expect to pay 8 to 17 per cent of his income on rent.

Table 6: Rents and Retail Prices in Ireland, 1905.[91]

Index	Dublin	Belfast	Cork	Limerick	Derry	Waterford	Mean for Ireland
Dublin=100	-	-	-	-	-	-	-
Rent	-	61	66	69	54	53	-
Prices	-	101	95	96	97	92	-
Rent & prices	-	93	85	91	88	84	-
London=100	-	-	-	-	-	-	-
Rent	71	46	48	55	39	38	50
Prices	100	101	95	96	97	92	97
Rent & prices	94	90	86	88	86	81	87

Table 7: Craftworkers residing in Dublin tenements, 1918.[92]

Trade	Number	Wage
Blacksmiths	29	15s. to 43s.
Boilermakers	12	20s. to 43s.
Carpenters	159	15s. to 50s.
Electricians	20	20s. to 45s.
Engineers	13	36s. to 50s.
Fitters	61	15s. to 60s.
Painters	155	15s. to 47s. 6d.
Plumbers	51	20s. to 50s.

The First World War sparked a brief surge in the numbers receiving indoor or outdoor relief (paupers). In January 1915, there were 272 paupers per every ten thousand people in Dublin but only ninety-five per ten thousand in Belfast. Dublin's fourteen thousand slums continued to fester. A 1918 survey found that 5,506 tenement lettings in Dublin were for one room, housing 15,930 people; 2,087 were for two rooms, housing 8,361; and 909 were for three or more rooms, housing 4,348. An average of just under three people resided in each one-roomed tenements. Each two-roomed tenement housed just over four people on average, while those with three of more rooms averaged just under five people in each. At least 1,599 lettings, accommodating 8,503 families, were classified as unfit for human habitation. Weekly rents ranged from 1s. to 13s. 6d. depending on the number of rooms. While unskilled workers made up the vast bulk of those in the north city tenements, Table 7 shows that they included some craftsmen too. The wide variation in wages within trades is due to the inclusion of apprentices.[93] The most spacious tenements cost qualified craftsmen 22.5 to 31 per cent of their weekly income to rent.

Unaffordable prices were a constant burden for working-class families in Ireland. In 1922, the Free State government set up the Commission on Prices to examine ways in which the cost of living could be lowered. Its report is a revealing insight into working-class life in early twentieth-century Ireland. ITGWU general president Thomas Foran told the commission that 'porter and stout could not be regarded as luxuries for a workingman but part of his diet' – a more important part of his diet than milk![94] Bread and potatoes were also dietary staples. A typical Dublin worker consumed three pints of the black stuff a day, making the pub his major social outlet; widespread alcoholism was the result.[95] It was an expensive pastime due to profiteering publicans: the price of a pint had jumped by an astonishing 396 per cent in Dublin between 1914 and 1922. A pint of porter or a bottle of stout were usually 8d. each whereas the latter was usually 7d. in the north of England and as low as 6d. in London. A pint of Guinness cost 10d. in Lucan and Leixlip and 9d. in Cork and Mallow, but only 6d. in Manchester. In Dublin, milk was sold at less than half the price of a pint of beer. In both Britain and Ireland, the proportion of family income spent on food and rent had fallen while that spent on clothing, fuel, light and sundries had risen between 1914 and 1922, suggesting significantly higher disposable income. The greatest differential was in rents, with British families paying a higher proportion of their income on housing.[96]

Table 8: Percentage of household expenditure spent on essentials in the Irish Free State and the United Kingdom, 1914 & 1922.[97]

	Irish Free State		United Kingdom	
Items	July 1914	June 1922	July 1914	June 1922
Food	56	57	60	59
Clothing	17	18	12	16
Rent	8	5	16	13
Fuel and light	7	7	8	8
Sundries	12	13	4	4

Table 9: Annual Death Rate per 1,000 of the Population, 1922-24.[98]

City	1922	1923	1924
Dublin	17.6	15.0	16.7
Cork	18.0	14.0	19.3
Limerick	19.3	17.2	14.5
Waterford	15.3	15.2	16.4

Political engagement

Politicisation of the Irish working class was a long and complex process. It began in the 1830s with the manufacture revival campaigns, where workers and employers joined together for the restoration of native industry and repeal of the Union.[99] From the mid-century, politicisation became less dependent on the middle classes when greater education and a shorter week gave workers the time and the ability to participate politically. Ulster loyalism was one such outlet (Belfast shipyardmen were its most notorious vanguard), revolutionary republicanism was another. Craftsmen were a key stratum of the Irish Republican Brotherhood (IRB) in the 1860s, as they had been for the Young Irelanders in 1848. In Dublin, about 60 per cent of those arrested for Fenianism were artisans. It was similar in Cork, where craftsmen comprised 46 per cent of the Fenian rank-and-file and 32 per cent of its leadership.[100]

Republicanisation coincided with periods of economic depression. Politics was more alluring to artisans than trade unionism. Deindustrialisation fuelled anti-establishment, and therefore anti-British, sentiment, strengthening nationalism's appeal. As with other European centres, a well-established middle class was a vital prerequisite to luring craftsmen into nationalist politics. The workplace was crucial in the politicisation process. Fenianism was also popular among the petit bourgeoisie, who supplied many of its leaders. Via close, daily contact, workers' politics were moulded by their employers whilst working alongside them in small establishments. Conversely, factories and large workshops, where considerable numbers of men were concentrated, were also breeding grounds for Fenianism. Fitters and shipwrights, who worked in such establishments, made up a sizeable chunk of the Cork Fenians. The trade union was another vehicle for the expression of political consciousness. From the nineteenth century, Irish trade unionists became increasingly politicised and politically homogenous. Their unions were determined to protect this unity from fragmentation and imposed a similar discipline on their political activities as they did in the workplace. Politicisation was interwoven with leisure time. Pubs, musical bands, temperance societies, the GAA, educational establishments and cultural organisations became fora where workers met and ideas spread in a convivial setting.[101] These outlets were attractive because they allowed class differences to temporarily disappear; all were equal on a sports field, employer and worker, craftsman and labourer. 'So closely enmeshed did the social and political become that not alone was politicisation accelerated by popular social activities, but social life was itself politicised.'[102] Publicans, many of whom were strongly nationalist, were especially influential in swaying the politics of artisans. Publicans could influence their clients in a spirit of camaraderie fostered by alcohol and the singing of seditious songs. It is not facetious to say that porter fuelled patriotism.[103]

Irish republicanism was an odd blend of the old and the new. Though it romanticised the past, it was born of modernity. Fenianism, for example, was liberal, internationalist, secular, anti-sectarian and even socialistic. On the other hand, republicanism could also be insular, nationalistic, Anglophobic and overtly Catholic and anti-socialist. Its contradictory dynamics gave it a cross-class appeal and composition. Many workers who became republicans were devout Catholics and vocally anti-socialist and illiberal.[104] Nonetheless, republican involvement intensified radical instincts among the working class.[105] While Fenianism survived after 1867, its composition became more rural and less proletarian. Only one-sixth of the eighty-one IRB organisers watched by Dublin Castle between 1880 and 1902 were craftsmen.[106] Between 1858 and 1923, republicanism's social makeup and outlook changed as Ireland suffered the dialectical forces of modernisation and degeneration. Republicans received much passive sympathy from the working class, even before the Great War and Easter Week changed the political paradigm. Under the right material and political conditions, that sympathy could easily become active support and participation, as it eventually did.

Chapter Notes and References

1   Eric Hobsbawm, 'The Labour Aristocracy in Nineteenth-Century Britain', in *Labouring Men* (London: Weidenfeld & Nicolson, 1964), pp. 272-315.

2   Emmet O'Connor, *A Labour History of Ireland, 1824-2000* (2nd Edition) (Dublin: UCD Press, 2011), p. 31.

3   Cronin, *Country, Class or Craft?*, p. 140.

4   O'Connor, *A Labour History of Ireland*, p. 31

5   James B. Jeffreys, *The Story of the Engineers, 1800-1945* (London: Lawrence & Wishart Ltd., 1945), p. 9.

6   Andy Bielenberg, *Cork's Industrial Revolution, 1780-1880: Development or Decline?* (Cork: Cork University Press, 1991), p. 1.

7   Jeffreys, *The Story of the Engineers*, pp. 9-10; Andy Bielenberg, *Ireland and the Industrial Revolution: The impact of the industrial revolution on Irish industry, 1801-1922* (Abingdon: Routledge, 2009), p. 119.

8   Jeffreys, *The Story of the Engineers*, p. 12.

9   Ibid., pp. 12-15.

10   Ibid., pp. 15, 57.

11   Ibid., pp. 122-127.

12   Bielenberg, *Cork's Industrial Revolution*, p. 116; Cormac Ó Gráda, *Ireland: A New Economic History, 1780-1939* (Oxford: Clarendon Press, 1994), pp. 306-313.

13   Cronin, *Country, Class or Craft?*, p. 17; R.J. Morris, 'The labour aristocracy and the British class structure', in Anne Digby & Charles Feinstein (eds.), *New Directions in Economic and Social History* (London: Gill & Macmillan, 1989), pp. 170-181.

14   O'Connor, *A Labour History of Ireland*, p. 7, 75.

15   John Smellie, *Shipbuilding and Repairing in Dublin: A Record of Work Carried Out by the Dublin Dockyard Co., 1901-1923* (Glasgow: McCorquodale & Co., 1935), pp. 139-150; O'Mahony, *Maritime Gateway*, p. 114; Gerald Hassan, *Thunder & Clatter: The History of Shipbuilding in Derry* (Derry: Guildhall Press, 1997); Bill Irish, *Shipbuilding in Waterford, 1820-1882: a historical, technical and pictorial study* (Bray: Wordwell, 2001).

16   O'Connor, *A Labour History of Ireland*, pp. 36-37. The figure of thirty-six thousand includes clerks and women. By 1919, Harland & Wolff employed twenty-seven to twenty-eight thousand men. By 1920, Workman Clark employed twenty thousand. See John Lynch, 'The Belfast Shipyards and the Industrial Working Class', in Francis Devine, Fintan Lane, & Niamh Purséil, (eds.), *Essays in Irish Labour History: A Festschrift for Elizabeth and John W. Boyle* (Dublin: Irish Academic Press, 2008), pp. 135-137; and E.J. Riordan, *Modern Irish Trade and Industry* (London: Methuen, 1920), pp. 99-100.

17 Bielenberg, *Ireland and the Industrial Revolution*, pp. 116-119.

18 Ibid., pp. 111-116.

19 Cronin, *Country, Class or Craft?*, pp. 35-36, 42

20 Ibid., pp. 17-22.

21 Maura Cronin, *Country, Class or Craft? The Politicisation of the Skilled Artisan in Nineteenth Century Cork* (Cork: Cork University Press, 1994). p. 21.

22 Emmet O'Connor, *A Labour History of Waterford* (Waterford: Waterford Trades Council, 1989), pp. xxv, xxxiii.

23 O'Connor, *A Labour History of Ireland, 1824-2000*, pp. 1-6.

24 Cronin, *Country, Class of Craft?*, p. 207.

25 Ibid.

26 For a history of the Dublin Trades Council, see Seamus Cody, John O'Dowd, Peter Rigney, *The Parliament of Labour: 100 Years of the Dublin Council of Trade Unions* (Dublin: Dublin Council of Trade Unions, 1986).

27 Dermot Keogh, *The Rise of the Irish Working Class: The Dublin Trade Union Movement and the Labour Leadership, 1890-1914* (Belfast: Appletree Press, 1982), pp. 31-32.

28 Indentures typically stipulated that an apprentice had to obey his master, be loyal to him, keep his secrets and not waste or steal his goods; could not frequent taverns, alehouses or playhouses; could not play dice, cards or other games; could not sleep away from his master's house; and could not marry or 'fornicate.'

29 Though the reason for the seven-year period is unclear, it may have been fixed to mirror the time it took to prepare for the priesthood. See John Gerald Ryan, 'Apprenticeships in Ireland: An Historical Perspective' (NUI Maynooth: PhD, 1993), pp. 1-66.

30 See, for example, Indenture of Henry Marsh to the Painting Trade, June 1916, U233, UCC Manuscripts Collection, UCC Archives.

31 Lynch, 'Belfast Shipyards', p. 141. The five-year apprenticeship was the standard in the metal trades. Carpenters, joiners and painters served six years and plumbers served seven.

32 This taken from a 1922 indenture cited in Stephen Cameron, *Belfast Shipbuilders: A Titanic Tale* (Newtownards: Colourpoint, 2011), p. 59.

33 W.E. Coe, *The Engineering Industry of the North of Ireland* (Newton Abbot: David & Charles, 1969), p. 175.

34 Ryan, 'Apprenticeships in Ireland', pp. 115-139. State technical education began in Ireland in with the Department of Agriculture and Technical Instruction.

35 Thomas McCarthy, *Apprenticeships in Ireland*, Commission of the European Communities, Social Policy Series, No. 33, 1977, p. 5

36 Cronin, *Country, Class of Craft?*, p. 208.

37 Dick Geary, *European Labour Protest, 1848-1939* (New York: St. Martin's Press, 1981), p. 73.

38 Cronin, *Country, Class of Craft?*, pp. 209-218.

39 Henry Patterson, 'Industrial Labour and the Labour Movement, 1820-1914', in Liam Kennedy & Philip Ollerenshaw (eds.), *An Economic History of Ulster* (Manchester: Manchester University Press, 1985), p. 176. This figure is cited in Sidney Pollard and Paul Robertson, *The British Shipbuilding Industry, 1870-1914* (Massachusetts: Harvard University Press, 1979), p. 154.

40 John W. Boyle, *The Irish Labour Movement in the Nineteenth Century* (Washington D.C.: The Catholic University of America Press, 1988), pp. 92-95.

41 Electrical Trades Union (Ireland) National Executive Committee (NEC) minutes, 5, 6, 7 Mar. 1946. All primary source material is in the Connect archives unless stated otherwise.

42 Boyle, *The Irish Labor Movement in the Nineteenth Century*, p. 99.

43 O'Connor, *A Labour History of Ireland*, pp. 47-49. New model unions derive their name from Sidney and Beatrice Webb's characterisation of them in their famous 1894 book *The History of Trade Unionism*.

44 Emmet O'Connor, 'Labour and politics, 1830–1945: colonisation and mental colonisation', in Fintan Lane & Donal Ó Drisceoil (eds.), *Politics and the Irish Working Class, 1830-1945* (Basingstoke: Palgrave Macmillan, 2005), p. 27.

45 Maura Murphy, 'The working classes of nineteenth-century Cork', *Cork Historical and Archaeological Society Journal*, LXXX, 1980, p. 43. A 'handyman' was a labourer who turned his hand to a skilled worker's job. For new unionism in Ireland, see O'Connor, *A Labour History of Ireland*, pp. 50-59.

46 Emmet O'Connor, *Syndicalism in Ireland, 1917-1923* (Cork: Cork University Press, 1988), pp. 182-185, 191.

47 Puirséil, Niamh, 'War, work and labour', in Horne, John (ed.), *Our War: Ireland and the Great War* (Dublin: Royal Irish Academy, 2008), p. 183. See also Emmet O'Connor, 'Problems of Reform in the Irish Trade Union Congress, 1894-1914', *Historical Studies in Industrial Relations*, Vol. 23-24, Apr. 2007, pp. 37-59.

48 Kevin O'Rourke, 'Did the Great Irish Famine Matter?', *The Journal of Economic History*, Vol. 51, No. 1, Mar. 1991, pp. 1-22; Kevin O'Rourke, George Boyer & Timothy J. Hatton, 'The impact of emigration on real wages in Ireland, 1850-1914', in Timothy J. Hatton & Jeffrey G. Williamson (eds.) *Migration and the international labour market, 1850-1993* (London: Routledge, 1994), pp. 221-239; and Jeffrey G. Williamson, 'Economic convergence: placing post-famine Ireland in comparative perspective', *Irish Economic and Social History*, Vol. 21, 1994, pp. 5-27.

49 Until 1971, Irish and British currencies comprised of pounds (£), shillings (s.) and pence (d.). The penny was subdivided into ½d. (halfpenny) and ¼d. (farthing). There were twenty shillings in a pound and twelve pence in a shilling. This 'pre-decimalisation' system remained in place until 1971 when the British and Irish pounds were decimalised, making pounds and pence the two units. Throughout this book, shillings will be used up to describe anything up to 100s., after which pounds will be used.

50 H.D. Gribbon, 'Economic and social history, 1850-1921', in W.E. Vaughan (ed.), *A New History of Ireland: VI, Ireland under the Union, II, 1870-1921* (Oxford: Clarendon Press, 1996), pp. 317-318, 339-340.

51 O'Connor, *A Labour History of Ireland*, pp. 36-37, 40-41.

52 Though Catholics were 24 per cent of Belfast's population in 1901, they made up only 8 per cent of ship, boat and barge builders; 6 per cent of shipwrights; 10 per cent of engine and machine workers; 11 per cent of fitters and turners; and 10 per cent of boilermakers. See Patterson, 'Industrial Labour and the Labour Movement', p. 178. Alastair Reid, 'Skilled Workers in the Shipbuilding Industry, 1880-1920: A Labour Aristocracy?', in Austen Morgan & Bob Purdie (eds.), *Ireland: Divided Nation, Divided Class* (London: Ink Links, 1980), pp. 111-124.

53 Coe, *The Engineering Industry in the North of Ireland*, p. 181.

54 Cited in Patterson, 'Industrial Labour and the Labour Movement', p. 167.

55 Ó Gráda, *A New Economic History*, p. 238.

56 *Reports on strikes and lock-outs in the United Kingdom, 1888-1913*, 1889-1916, UK Parliamentary Papers (UKPP).

57 This includes protection of work: attempts by employers to replace craftsmen with labourers and/or boys

58 This includes refusal to scab, refusal to work with non-trade unionists, and for or against the dismissal of colleagues.

59 These percentages are based on calculation on information extracted from *Reports on strikes and lock-outs in the United Kingdom*, 1889-1916, UKPP

60 This figure is cited in Sidney Pollard and Paul Robertson, *The British Shipbuilding Industry, 1870-1914* (Massachusetts: Harvard University Press, 1979), p. 154.

61 This percentage is based on calculation on information extracted from *Reports on strikes and lock-outs in the United Kingdom*, 1889-1916, UKPP. See also Henry Patterson, 'Industrial Labour and the Labour Movement, 1820-1914', in Liam Kennedy & Philip Ollerenshaw (eds.), *An Economic History of Ulster* (Manchester: Manchester University Press, 1985), p. 176

62 O'Connor, *A Labour History of Ireland*, p. 59; Coe, *The Engineering Industry in the North of Ireland*, pp. 184-185; Henry Patterson, *Class Conflict and Sectarianism: The Protestant Working Class and the Belfast Labour Movement, 1868-1920* (Belfast: Blackstaff Press, 1980), pp. 33-37.

63 John R Hume and Michael S. Moss, *Shipbuilders to the World: 125 Years of Harland and Wolff, Belfast, 1861-1986* (Belfast: Blackstaff Press, 1986), p. 168. Though John Lynch disputes the scale of the harmoniousness, he concedes that industrial relations were good at Harland and Wolff.

64 Patterson, *Class Conflict and Sectarianism*, p. 41.

65 Ibid., p. 42; Emmet O'Connor, 'Sheep in Wolves' Clothing: Labour and Politics in Belfast, 1881-1914', in Devine, Lane & Purséil (eds.), *Essays in Irish Labour History*, p. 67.

66 Coe, *The Engineering Industry in the North of Ireland*, pp. 177-179.

67 *Report on Standard Time-Rates of Wages in United Kingdom, 1900*, 1900, Cd. 317, LXXXII, UKPP.

68 Boyle, *The Irish Labor Movement in the Nineteenth Century*, pp. 93-94.

69 *Cost of Living of the Working Classes. Report of an Enquiry by the Board of Trade into Working-Class Rents, Housing and Retail Prices Together with Standard Rates of Wages Prevailing in Certain Occupations in Principal Industrial Towns in the United Kingdom*, Cd. 3864, CVII, 1908, UKPP, pp. xxxvii, xxxix.

70 T.R. Gourvish, 'The Standard of Living, 1890-1914', in Alan O'Day (ed.), *The Edwardian Age: Conflict and Stability, 1900-1914* (London: Archon Books, 1979), pp. 14-15; *Cost of Living of the Working Classes. Report of an Enquiry by the Board of Trade into Working-Class Rents, Housing and Retail Prices Together with the Rates of Wages Prevailing in Certain Occupations in Industrial Towns in the United Kingdom in 1912*, Cd. 6955, LXVI, 1913, UKPP, pp. 451, 493. The aggregated augmentation in prices between 1905 and 1912 ranged from 7 per cent in Dublin to 17 per cent in Waterford.

71 Boyle, *The Irish Labor Movement in the Nineteenth Century*, p. 94.

72 *Royal Commission on Labour, Minutes of Evidence, Appendices (Group A) Volume III. Mining, Iron, Engineering and Hardware*, 1893, C.6894-VII, XXXII, UKPP, p. 92. The Irish organiser of the ASE claimed that this policy was an 'unwritten rule' in Belfast.

73 Lynch, 'Belfast Shipyards', p. 140.

74 Lynch, 'Belfast Shipyards', p. 140.

75 *Royal Commission on Labour, Minutes of Evidence, Appendices (Group A) Volume III. Mining, Iron, Engineering and Hardware*, UKPP, p. 92.

76 *Report of an enquiry by the Board of Trade into working-class rents and retail prices, together with the rates of wages in certain occupations in industrial towns of the United Kingdom in 1912*, 1913, CD. 6955, LXVI, UKPP pp. 286, 288.

77 *Royal Commission on Labour, Minutes of Evidence, Appendices (Group A) Volume III. Mining, Iron, Engineering and Hardware*, UKPP, p. 186.

78 For the 1902 strike, see Hugh Geraghty & Peter Rigney, 'The Engineers' Strike in Inchicore Railway Work, 1902', *Saothar*, Vol. 9, 1983, pp. 20-31; for the 1911 Wexford foundry dispute, see Michael Enright, *Men of Iron: Wexford Foundry Disputes of 1890 & 1911* (Wexford: Wexford Council of Trade Unions, 1987); for the 1913 Dublin lockout, see Pádraig Yeates, *Lockout: Dublin 1913* (Dublin: Gill & Macmillan, 2000).

79 *Report on Standard Time-Rates of Wages in United Kingdom, 1900*, 1900, Cd. 317, LXXXII, UKPP.

80 Stephen McQuay Reddick, 'Political and Industrial Labour in Cork, 1899-1914' (UCC: MA, 1984); *Cork Examiner*, 11 June-13 Aug. 1909.

81 O'Connor, *Syndicalism in Ireland*, pp. 1-13.

82 *Standard time rates of wages in the United Kingdom at 1st October, 1913*, 1914, Cd. 7194, LXXX, UKPP.

83 Arnold Wright, *Disturbed Dublin: The Story of the Great Strike of 1913-14* (London: Longman, 1914), p. 29.

84 *Cost of Living of the Working Classes*, 1908, p. 560. For a history of the Dublin tenements, see Jacinta Prunty, *Dublin Slums, 1800-1925: a study in urban geography* (Newbridge: Irish Academic Press, 1998).

85 Pádraig Yeates, *A City in Wartime: Dublin, 1914-18* (Dublin: Gill and Macmillan, 2011), p. 10. These figures pertain to 1913.

86 *Cost of Living of the Working Classes*, 1908, p. 568. These figures pertain to 1901. In 1911, just 0.6 per cent of tenements in Belfast were one roomed and 5 per cent were two roomed.

87 William J. Thompson, 'The Census of Ireland, 1911', *Journal of the Royal Statistical Society*, June 1913, Vol. 76, No. 7, p. 640.

88   *Supplement to the Twenty-Nineth Annual Report of the Local Government Board for Ireland*, Cd.
     1260, 1902, XXXVIII, UKPP, pp. 6, 22; *Cost of Living of the Working Classes*, 1908, pp. 562,
     568. Yeates, *A City in Wartime*, pp. 10, 276. Contagious diseases refer to the likes of
     smallpox, typhus, measles, scarlet fever and whooping cough.
89   Pádraig Yeates, *A City in Turmoil: Dublin, 1919-21* (Dublin: Gill & Macmillan, 2012), pp.
     23-24; Yeates, *A City in Wartime*, pp. 10, 270-299; Ida Milne, *Stacking the Coffins: Influenza,
     War and Revolution in Ireland, 1918-19* (Manchester: Manchester University Press, 2018).
90   *Cost of Living of the Working Classes*, 1908, pp. 560-562, 567-568.
91   Ibid., pp. xxxiii, xxxviii.
92   Ibid., p. 217. This table is just a sample. For more of the survey's findings, including a
     fuller list of craftsmen residing in the Dublin tenements, see Ibid., pp. 214-220.
93   Yeates, *A City in Wartime*, pp. 214-216, 264.
94   Cited in Pádraig Yeates, *A City in Civil War: Dublin, 1921-4* (Dublin: Gill & Macmillan,
     2015), p. 166.
95   Documentation found in TSCH/3/S1802, Department of An Taoiseach records, NAI.
96   Yeates, *A City in Civil War*, pp. 162-171.
97   Ibid., p. 171.
98   Aodh Quinlivan, *Dissolved: The remarkable story of how Cork lost its Corporation in 1924* (Cork:
     Cork City Library, 2017), p. 114.
99   For the manufacturing revival campaign, see Paul A. Pickering, '"Irish First": Daniel
     O'Connell, the Native Manufacture Campaign, and Economic Nationalism, 1840-44',
     Albion: A Quarterly Journal Concerned with British Studies, Vol. 32, No. 4, Winter, 2000, pp.
     598-616.
100 John B. O'Brien, 'Population, Politics and Society in Cork, 1780-1900', in O'Flanagan &
     Buttimer (eds.), *Cork: History and Society*, p. 715; Murphy, 'The working classes of
     nineteenth-century Cork', p. 47; Tom Garvin, *The Evolution of Irish Nationalist Politics*
     (Dublin: Gill and Macmillan, 1981), pp. 53-57. According to Garvin, one-third of the
     265 Fenians tried before the Dublin Special Commission in 1867 were artisans.
101 Cronin, *Country, Class or Craft?*, pp. 133-159; Geary, *European Labour Protest*, pp. 16, 68.
     See also RV Comerford, 'Patriotism as pastime: the appeal of Fenianism in the mid-
     1860s', *Irish Historical Studies*, Vol. 82, No. 86, Sept. 1980, pp. 239-250.
102 Cronin, *Country, Class or Craft?*, p. 149.
103 Ibid., pp. 148-150.
104 Tom Garvin, *Nationalist Revolutionaries in Ireland, 1858-1928* (Oxford: Oxford University
     Press, 1987), pp. 33-40, 125-126; Garvin, *The Evolution of Irish Nationalist Politics*, pp. 59-
     65.
105 For example, Fenians were heavily involved in the wave of labour unrest that swept Cork
     in 1870. See Seán Daly, *Cork: a city in crisis: a history of labour conflict and social conflict,
     1870-1872* (Cork: Tower Books, 1978).
106 Garvin, *Nationalist Revolutionaries*, p. 38.

1

The Birth of the Union, 1914-20

By 1914, Irish labour had little to show for the previous twenty-five years of struggle.[1] Still reeling from its defeat in the Dublin lockout, it was poorly placed to counter the First World War's impact on workers. The war fundamentally altered the state's role in industrial relations, especially in the metal trades. Engineering workers were vital to the war effort, giving the ASE unprecedented power. The conflict further expanded Britain's already vast engineering, metal and munitions industries, benefitting British craftworkers more than Irish ones. Cooperation with the government brought the ASE into the political establishment, making it more hostile to republican subversion. British and Irish craftsmen were now on divergent paths. It was a war of two halves for the working classes of both countries. Food shortages and mass inflation accentuated latent class tensions from 1914-16 and subsequently created new ones, resulting in an explosion of labour militancy from 1917. The war created hardship for workers, but farmers, employers and shopkeepers exploited the situation to profiteer. In July 1918, a Westminster-appointed committee estimated that the cost of living was 74 per cent higher for working-class families than in 1914. Labourers suffered most: their living costs had jumped by 81 per cent compared to 67 per cent for craftsmen.[2] People's eagerness to buy products unavailable in wartime triggered an economic boom in 1919 and 1920 that fuelled more drastic inflation and, consequently, even more intense labour militancy. Wage increases failed to match spiralling prices until 1919, when syndicalism gave workers the upper hand in the class war.

By then, the Irish political climate had been transformed, with workers in the south firmly behind Sinn Féin. Across Europe, fury towards the ruling elites for sleepwalking the continent into a pointless, catastrophic war had destabilised conservative politics which created the space for radicalism to flourish. Revolutions in Russia, attempted revolutions in Germany, Italy and Hungary, and civil wars in Russia and Finland were the most vivid manifestations of the tumult. The crisis reached a crescendo in 1919 and 1920 when 'two red years' of violent class conflict rocked the Western World. The upheaval gave credence to the widespread belief that the collapse of capitalism was imminent, portending a socialist future. In Ireland, the Easter Rising was a product of the same forces of destabilisation. The martyrdom of 1916 began an irreversible political re-alignment in nationalist Ireland. Ulster unionists responded by tightening inter-class bonds among northern Protestants, quashing radical impetuses in the process. Republican revolution and Ulster unionist counterrevolution pushed southern labour to the left, towards syndicalism. Of all the breakaways, a native union for craftsmen was one of the most enduring.

The impact of the First World War
The outbreak of the First World War in July 1914 brought adversities to the working class that were novel in nature and unparalleled in scale. Chief among

them was mass inflation, the result of Germany's devastating U-Boat campaign against British merchant ships.[3] But inflation was just one reason for the move away from the laissez-faire economic model. During the war, the British economy was geared towards the production of munitions and food, so workers in these industries had a relatively 'good' war. The government developed an industrial policy aimed at tackling four key issues: controlling the cost of living, maintaining essential war supplies, addressing labour shortages (resulting from military recruitment) and maintaining industrial peace. The state was thus forced to adopt labour-friendly policies. In February 1915, the government established the Committee on Production to regulate wages, output and labour supply in the shipbuilding and engineering industries. The Munitions of War Act 1915 prohibited strikes and lockouts in war industries and introduced compulsory state arbitration of industrial disputes. As it facilitated the application of this ban to other industries, the Act was far more consequential than intended and compulsory arbitration soon became the norm across the economy. Although the legislation frightened the unions at first, its benefits soon became obvious. Previously, employers could grind out a victory in an industrial dispute by issuing a pre-emptive lockout and simply waiting for strike pay to run out. Now, they had to bargain with the unions, who were practically guaranteed to secure a pay increase if they issued strike notice. Binding arbitration thus encouraged workers to unionise. Unsurprisingly, employers bitterly resented the Act and regularly complained of state intrusion into their businesses.[4] However, the new regime was not completely favourable to workers, who could be prosecuted if they withdrew their labour in industries covered by the legislation.[5]

Table 10: UK Retail Price & Cost-of-Living Indices, 1915-21 (July 1914=100).[6]

Year	Food	All Items	Cost of living
1915	131	123	125
1916	160	146	145
1917	198½	176	180
1918	215	203	205
1919	219	215	210
1920	256	249	252
1921	229½	226	

Southern cities had fewer war industries than Ulster and their workforces contained much unskilled labour. Workers in the south were therefore less affected by the new atmosphere of co-operation with employers and missed the benefits that accrued. They increasingly locked horns with employers who were reluctant to share massive wartime profits in the form of wage rises. Employers grudgingly gave 'war bonuses' – a name given to highlight the temporary nature of the payment – to placate workers, but it was not enough. Ireland's relatively low level of military recruitment removed another hindrance to industrial action.[7] Forty to fifty thousand people, the vast of them men, migrated to Britain for work during the war. From 1916, however, the southern economy began to benefit from the war, which temporarily reversed the fortunes of long-declining industries such as shipbuilding. Numbers at the Rushbrooke and Passage Dockyards doubled to eight hundred, while employment at the Dublin Dockyard Company had swelled to one thousand by 1920.[8] After much nationalist campaigning, munitions factories were opened in Dublin, Cork, Waterford and Galway, employing 2,148 (mostly women) in total.[9]

The total mobilisation of the economy slashed levels of pauperism across the Kingdom by lacerating unemployment to near zero. Numbers on relief fell from 191 per ten thousand in January 1915 to 125 in December 1918. The return of the peace economy reversed this development. Unlike Belfast, which was more deeply integrated into the British war machine, southern economies suffered little from the advent of peace, just as they had benefitted little from the outbreak of war. Accordingly, rates of pauperism rose less severely in Dublin than in Belfast. From a low of sixty-nine per ten thousand in December 1918, pauperism had reached eighty-nine per ten thousand in Belfast by November 1919, when the average rate for the UK was 130; in Dublin, pauperism rose from 261 to 263 over the same period. Cork, Limerick and Waterford performed as poorly as Dublin in tackling pauperism.[10]

Table 11: Craft Wages in Harland & Wolff, 1913 vs. 1919.[11]

	Patternmakers	Fitters	Shipwrights	Sailmakers
1913	44s.	41s.	40s.	36s.
1919	73s. 6d.	70s. 6d.	72s. 6d.	65s. 6d.
Percentage increase	67	72	79	82

The war had acute long-term effects for engineering craftsmen. It rapidly accelerated the 'dilution' of the craft, ongoing since the Second Industrial Revolution. Dilution refers to the replacement of craftsmen with machines operated by labourers, the semiskilled or women, who could all be paid below the craft rate. The recruitment of craftsmen into the army, which created a skills shortage in munitions factories, was another reason for dilution. Employers argued that dilution was unavoidable if war demands were to be met.[12] Metalworkers initially considered operating machinery below their dignity as craftsmen but were eventually forced to change tack. While the new policy protected numbers and wages, it sacrificed craft bargaining power and made craftsmen susceptible to blacklegging. Dilution also degraded the quality of the apprenticeship. Employers exploited apprentices' low wages to give them jobs on machines instead of instructing them in the craft. On 'Red Clydeside', a revolutionary shop stewards' movement for workers' control of industry emerged in response to the incursion. It forced the ASE to abandon craft exclusiveness and accept dilution as an irreversible, even progressive development that could raise the labourers' lot. Dilution, the stewards argued, should be met in a way that reconciled the interests of both the craftsman and the dilutee. The result was a radicalism among craftsmen that undermines the argument that such workers are inherently conservative.[13]

Dilution also touched Irish craftsmen. In December 1916, the Dublin Trades Council complained that labour exchanges were denying benefits to unemployed craftworkers unless they take jobs as labourers in war industries.[14] Though dilution was supposed to be temporary, the clock could not be completely turned back when the war was over. The new milieu fuelled anti-British sentiment. Irishmen resented the ease at which union cards were issued in England, a consequence of dilution. British men (including ex-soldiers) with union cards could arrive in Ireland to take engineering and shipbuilding jobs. There were also cases of Irish labourers emigrating to England and returning a few months later to work in the same workshop with an ASE card even though they had never served an apprenticeship.[15] Wartime upheavals laid the basis for an Irish craft union and produced Irish labour's final, and most intense, wave of agitation: syndicalism.

Syndicalism and the rebirth of militancy

Originating in France in the early 1890s, syndicalism can be broadly defined as revolutionary trade unionism. It was born out of the perceived failure of existing socialist politics and reformist trade unionism. Syndicalists maintained that political parties create an unaccountable elite that will inevitably betray the base. Parties grouped their members according to their beliefs and not their class, whereas trade unions grouped workers according to their material interests irrespective of belief. As political power simply reflected economic power, trade unions, syndicalists believed, were the most authentic manifestation of the class struggle. Not only were they the agents for the overthrow of capitalism, but they also contained the embryo of a truly democratic society. In the new age of the people, the workers themselves – not professional politicians, intellectuals or bureaucrats – would be the ruling class. Syndicalists maintained that industrial harmony was an illusion because the interests of employers and workers were irreconcilable. They sought to use trade unions to replace expressions of industrial grievances with revolutionary class consciousness; the organisation of all workers into One Big Union was the logical conclusion of this process. The proletariat could then utilise its most effective weapon, the general strike, to seize power at the point of production.[16] Syndicalists also strove to create a proletarian counterculture to replace the perceived decadence of capitalist society: economic revolution would herald a moral transformation. They were critical of Marxism's presentation of itself as a 'value-free', rational science and instead fused moral and material goals to mass mobilise. Like Larkin, they did this by appealing to the 'irrational' traits of the human psyche: faith, will, intuition and morality. The creation of myths was central to both ideology and action, and an exaltation of the workers as a virtuous, risen people on the cusp of moral grandeur existed in the syndicalist current. Syndicalism was the world's most popular brand of revolutionary socialism from the 1890s until the Bolshevik revolution, when it lost that honour to communism, and captivated both Larkin and James Connolly.[17] In Ireland, it influenced most unions in Ireland to some extent, but was embodied most strongly in the ITGWU, followed by the National Union of Railwaymen (NUR), a British union.

A global phenomenon, the emergence of syndicalism coincided with the Second Industrial Revolution and dilution. Syndicalism not only swept Europe and North America but also reached Australia, New Zealand, South Africa and even South America.[18] Like British shipyardmen, French artisans turned en masse to syndicalism when mechanisation, deskilling and absorption into the factory system threatened control over work.[19]

> New management techniques were introduced, which resulted in the replacement of systems of internal contract and indirect employment whereby skilled workers hired, paid and supervised their own assistants,

or ... assembled, monitored and paid their own teams... In addition to increasing direct supervision, employers experimented with ... piecework, premium bonuses, internal promotion and job ladders, to elicit greater worker effort, docility and loyalty ... a common feature ... was the consolidation of control... which involved transferring production expertise from workers to the employers, and which inevitably drew resistance.20

Any attack on work practices was an attack on the craftsman himself. Work was more than the means to a wage: it had spiritual rewards that aroused intense self-pride. Control over work had been long-established and doggedly maintained to resist the degeneration of craft labour to commodity status. 'The craft worker always retained ... the creative psychology of the producer.'[21] He believed he had as much right to his trade as a capitalist had to his business, making him hypersensitive to any increase in industrial discipline and social control. Craftsmen resisted every attempt by employers to supervise, mechanise or simplify their work. The factory workshop was his fiefdom – a corner of freedom in a place defined by employer tyranny. Dilution threatened not only job security but personal values, which helps to explain the intensity of craft militancy between 1914 and 1923 as well as the allure of syndicalism.[22]

The product of structural factors, Irish syndicalism was a native expression of the international unrest. Syndicalism tended to be strongest in backward parts of advanced countries where labourers were neglected by the established unions. As an area heavily reliant on primary production where industrial tactics had to be militant, southern Ireland was a typical centre of syndicalism.[23] 'Syndicalism made a big impact on Ireland because it was less industrialised, had a less developed system of conciliation and arbitration and relatively militant employers, and was a marginal area of trade unionism within the United Kingdom, neglected by the British trade unions.'[24] The proliferation of syndicalism was a major reason for the rebirth of militancy from 1917. Until then, the pattern of industrial conflict had reflected war needs consequent to the evolution of bargaining power. Workers in sectors relevant to the war effort, especially shipyard craftsmen, dominated strikes. Because British and Irish craftsmen were members of the same unions, British militancy inevitably influenced Irish members and spilled over into Ireland. Strikes increased every year between 1915 and 1918. Ireland accounted for 12.2 per cent of UK stoppages during the war, compared to just 1.8 per cent from 1910-13. In the metal trades, Ireland's percentage share of UK strike activity rose from 1.9 per cent before the war to 9 per cent during it. There were 534 recorded strikes in Ireland during the war, including 109 (20 per cent) in the metal trades.[25]

The militancy was necessary. Inflation surpassed wage increases throughout the war, leading to many workers' living standards declining in real terms. From 1919, however, craftsmen would experience vast improvements in their standards of living. Indeed, the most significant industrial struggle in Irish history occurred in the engineering and shipbuilding trades. On 25 January 1919, forty thousand Belfast engineering workers and shipyardmen struck unofficially for a forty-four-hour week (from fifty-four). The unrest spread to the Corporation, giving the strike committee control of the power supply, enabling it to issue permits. Because the action was almost general, journalists dubbed the city the 'Belfast soviet.' The stoppage lasted for three weeks until the unions accepted a forty-seven-hour week. Directly and indirectly, the strike affected sixty thousand workers at its height. The strike committee included Catholics and Protestants, nationalists and unionists, united in struggle. This display of 'Bolshevism' alarmed Dublin Castle, which sent up troops to crush it.[26] Trouble spread to Dublin, and engineering and shipyard unions were galvanised to secure a reduction in the working week from fifty hours to forty-seven. Craftsmen at Corporation workshops and the municipal power station also obtained the shorter week.[27]

Sympathetic strikes had been mooted in support of the Belfast action, but the ITUC urged caution, arguing that any action would have to be national – but a national movement did not exist. Most Ulster Protestants were overtly hostile to a Congress now openly identifying with the republicans. Besides, the hours' movement was born in British shipyards, not Irish ones. Metal unions in Ulster wanted nothing to do with Dublin. Although thirty thousand northern trade unionists, mainly in the engineering and shipbuilding industries, remained unaffiliated for political reasons, Congress was experiencing stunning growth. By 1920, it represented 225,000 workers, a far cry from its 1916 figure of one hundred thousand. Its 1917 conference had revealed the emerging gulf between north and south. Northerners strongly had opposed a motion calling for an 'Irish Federation of Labour', fearing it would wipe out the amalgamateds.[28] The following year, Congress nailed its republican colours to the mast by not contesting the general election, giving Sinn Féin a free run in most constituencies. Any pretence of political impartiality was gone, as was any hope of retaining northern loyalists. By 1920, Dublin had overtaken Belfast to become the chief centre of Irish labour.

Table 12: Craftsmen's Wages at Guinness, 1914 & 1920.[29]

Trade	1 Aug. 1914	25 Oct. 1920	Increase (%)
Pipelayers	34s.	97s.	185
Sheet metal workers, whitesmiths & tinsmiths	39s.	£5. 1s. 6d.	160
Electricians	39s.	£5	156
Gasfitters	37s.	95s.	156
Shipwrights	39s.	97s. 6d.	150
Metal machinists	33s.	82s. 6d.	150
Boilermakers	40s.	99s. 6d.	149
Plumbers	39s.	97s.	148
Coppersmiths	39s.	97s.	148
Blacksmiths	39s.	95s.	143
Patternmakers	39s.	94s. 6d.	142
Fitters & turners	39s.	92s. 6d.	137
Millwrights	39s.	92s. 6d.	137
Wiremen	37s.	-	-
Sawyers	33s.	-	-
Electrical linesmen	-	97s.	-
Woodcutting machinists	-	96s.	-
Coachbuilders	-	£5. 0s. 8d.	-

Table 13: Strikes in Ireland, 1914-21.[30]

Engineering	48
Shipbuilding	56
Other Metal	5
Total	**109**

Table 14: Number of Strikes in Ireland by Region and Sector, 1914-18.[31]

Era/Industry	Dublin	Rest of Leinster	Munster	Belfast	Rest of Ulster	Connacht	Ireland
Metals	12	8	7	19	6	-	52
Shipbuilding	7	-	5	29	15	-	56
Total	**32**	**8**	**12**	**48**	**21**	-	**108**

Labour and the Republic

As the war dragged on, opposition to recruitment became a rallying cry which united republicans, socialists and militant trade unionists. The 1916 Rising was a turning point. As with most of Irish society, the working class had been radicalised by the executions of the leaders and quickly converted to Sinn Féin. By March 1918, hostility to British rule was ready to be set alight. The Germans provided the spark when their Spring Offensive made the threat of conscription, spoken of since 1915, a reality. All strands of nationalist Ireland came together to fight it. The ITUC took the lead in the most riveting demonstration of proletarian power of the revolutionary era: the one-day general strike on 23 April, the first of its kind in Ireland. Hundreds of thousands gathered across the country to listen to anti-war speeches and sign pledges to resist conscription. In Cork, for example, thirty thousand attended the city's largest ever protest.[32] The stoppage was remarkably successful and took place everywhere outside of Belfast. The conscription crisis further discredited the British government and, consequently, did much to facilitate labour's move from constitutional nationalism to republicanism.

The outbreak of the War of Independence on 21 January 1919 hastened this process. Inevitably, the national struggle was paramount to workers, even amid unprecedented class conflict. Although labourers were much more likely to enlist in the National Army during the Civil War, craftsmen provided the plurality of activists in all categories outside Dublin until 1922. Nearly all were apprentices or journeymen rather than masters with their own shop. Craftsmen made up forty per cent of 1916 internees in Dublin and nineteen per cent of internees outside the capital. Twenty-seven per cent of those court martialled in Dublin were craftsmen.[33] During the War of Independence, two-thirds of Dublin Volunteers were craftsmen, professionals and white-collar workers. The Dublin and Passage shipyards and the Ford's factory in Cork became hotbeds of militant republicanism. While the proportion of craftsmen who were Volunteers declined in Dublin and Cork as the revolution progressed, they were still two or three times as likely to join the IRA as the general population. Though upper middle- or upper-class people rarely joined the IRA, the same was true of casual labourers and the unemployed. In Cork city, a quarter of the Sinn Féin leadership were craftsmen. Volunteers were disproportionately young: most, even the officers, were in their twenties.[34]

On 15 November 1919, Dublin Castle issued the Motor Permits Order, which stipulated that motor vehicles could only be used with a permit. It was hoped that permits would assist the monitoring of private transport as the IRA was increasingly using cars to carry weapons. Apart from inconveniencing their work, drivers deplored the order's political ramifications. The Irish Automobile Drivers' and Mechanics' Union (IADAMU) refused to apply for permits and called its members out on strike. As one member put it, the order would turn his union into a 'semi-spy organisation.' The stoppage was labour's first instance of direct support for the national struggle. Republican involvement in it was minor and, where it did occur, a product of local initiative rather than national endeavour. Fitters and toolmakers came out in sympathy and were duly victimised. The stoppage lasted from November 1919 to January 1920, when the ASE executive withdrew its support for this 'political' strike; other amalgamateds soon followed suit, depriving their Irish members of strike pay.[35] The strike quickly crumbled as a result. The British unions then negotiated an unfavourable settlement with the employers and the Dublin Metropolitan Police behind the strikers' backs. The motor permits' affair further soured relations between Irish craftsmen and their British unions. There are direct links between it and the eventual breakaway: John (Jack) James Redmond, ASE Dublin district secretary, served on the strike committee. Though supported by the ITUC, the stoppage secured only minor concessions. But as labour's first instance of direct support for the republicans, it deepened the commitment to independence, industrial as well as political.[36]

Far more successful was the ITUC's two-day general strike from 13-14 April 1920 for the release of republican prisoners on hunger strike in Mountjoy Jail. For the second time in two years, labour had brought the economy to a halt everywhere outside Belfast for a political and moral goal – a vivid demonstration of its power. Trades councils across the country moved into the vanguard by enforcing this semi-revolutionary strike with 'red guard' worker militias. Alarmed by the contagion of Bolshevism, the government capitulated and released the prisoners three days later.[37] The War of Independence created the political conditions in which unions could thrive. By subverting British rule and establishing rival institutions of state, the republicans undermined the legitimacy of heretofore recognised authority, with the IRA's campaign crippling the military and the police. The struggle's revolutionary nature and popular support further radicalised labour. Political strikes aided working-class interests by cultivating an impression among trade unionists that they were acting outside the law, fostering an atmosphere of class warfare. Though unions were willing to engage in direct action and even violence to express an authentically anti-capitalist strain, the British government's portrayal of Irish labour as a Bolshevik-Republican front demonstrate how detached from reality it had become. The *Cork Constitution* – a right-wing, unionist daily – reflected the paranoia when it declared that 'Labour and Sinn Féin … are so closely associated as to be indistinguishable.'[38] The establishment often presented agitation as a part of an insidious Bolshevist plot (which employers also widely believed) and political strikes as the work of Sinn Féin. The City and County of Dublin Conservative Workingmen's Club, a prominent social outlet for Dublin's dwindling Protestant working class, similarly liked to depict Sinn Féin as crypto-

Bolshevists.[39] In fact, political stoppages 'stemmed from labour initiative and retained an independent character' throughout.[40] The Dáil neither initiated these strikes nor sought to control them.

Table 15: Craftsmen as a Percentage of IRA Volunteers, 1917-23.[41]

Area	Officers			Men			1926 Census
	1917-19	1920-21	1922-23	1917-19	1920-21	1922-23	-
Dublin	24	23	21	33	23	23	23
Cork	33	39	41	45	37	34	-
Munster	21	26	28	18	20	23	10
Connaught	17	3	-	12	17	10	5
Ulster	40	16	-	29	18	-	20
Leinster	32	23	-	12	16	17	13
Provincial Ireland	23	26	28	16	19	23	9

The union in gestation

By mid-1920, Irish disenchantment with the amalgamateds had been augmenting for seven years. Like many Irish craftsmen, Jack Redmond believed that the British had not done enough to support their Dublin comrades during the 1913 lockout. Although was ASE Dublin district secretary by 1914, he had been alienated by what he perceived as the leadership's indifference to Irish affairs. He told delegates to the 1914 ITUC that Irish engineers were representing themselves at their own expense. Redmond was born in 1879 and grew up in a Corporation house at Ross Road, Wood Quay. An engine fitter by trade, he served his time on the Merseyside with Cammel Laird before being employed at a Dublin United Tramway Company workshop. He became critical of how close to the British government his union became during the First World War.[42]

During the war, the idea for a separate Irish craft union began to circulate among trade unionists within the IRB. Thomas Leahy of the Boilermakers' Society and Joseph Toomey, ASE district delegate, are good examples of the kind of republicans who spearheaded the project. Leahy was born in 1890 in England but later moved to Dublin. In 1912, as was common for his generation of craftsmen, he returned to England to work as a riveter at Vickers' Shipyard. There, he immersed himself in Irish republicanism and founded a branch of the Irish Volunteers. He also became an active trade unionist. In 1914, Leahy returned to Ireland to avoid conscription and found work at the Dublin Dockyard – a future hotbed of republicanism where craftsmen used their skills to covertly make explosives for the cause. As a Volunteer (2nd Battalion, E Company, Dublin Brigade), he took part in the 1916 Rising under the command of future Fianna Fáil TD Oscar Traynor. After the surrender, he was imprisoned at Knutsford before being transferred to Frongoch. He was released under the December 1916 general amnesty.[43]

Toomey was born in 1884 in Co. Wexford, but his family moved to Dublin shortly afterwards. He worked first for Ashenhurst and then for Williams Motor Engineers as a fitter. A committed republican from his teenage years, he joined the Volunteers (2nd Batt., B Coy., Dublin Brigade) at their foundation in 1913. He was also a member of the IRB and took part in the Rising. Brigade Officer Micheál Ó Murchú recalled that Toomey 'could be relied on in any emergency. He was known as one of the most reliable men in B Coy., always supporting the movement by every means in his power.' Peter Pursfield considered him 'a most willing and efficient Volunteer.'[44] After the December 1916 amnesty, Toomey re-joined the Volunteers. Militarily, his craft was of vital importance. From early 1918, he manufactured hand grenades for his battalion, continuing to do so until late 1919 when that work was taken over by General Headquarters. In December 1919, he partook in the IRA's attack on the *Irish Independent*'s printing presses. He was arrested on 31 July 1920 and imprisoned until 6 June 1921. Upon his release he immediately reported back to his Company for duty.[45]

Since her release from prison in 1917, Constance Markievicz had championed the establishment of a craft union modelled on the ITGWU embracing all Irish craftworkers. Her opportunity came when Sinn Féin held its historic October 1917 ardfheis at Dublin's Mansion House. On top of making Sinn Féin a fully separatist party, delegates adopted Markievicz's resolution to support Irish workers severing their connection with British unions. Tadhg Barry of Cork had intended to put forward an amendment that a committee of trade unionists be formed to bring the idea to fruition, but he was inadvertently absent for the vote and so the amendment was never moved. Luckily for Barry, the amendment was not necessary: in late 1917 or early 1918, the IRB established such a committee within its ranks.[46] Tasked with infiltrating the amalgamateds and ending their presence in Ireland, the committee met weekly to report progress and plan more activity. In Autumn 1919, Michael Collins established a 'Secret Service Unit' to secure influential positions for republicans within the labour movement.[47] Collins was determined that Dublin Castle would not infiltrate labour, warning ITGWU general treasurer William O'Brien of the likelihood of spies joining his union.[48] The unit's objectives were to gather intelligence for the IRA and secure control over key economic sectors so that workers there could be called out on strike if necessary. Engineering and powerhouse workers were especially valuable. In early 1918, the executive of the Volunteers had established an engineering department, drawing from the building and engineering trades, electrical and railway workers, quarrymen (for their explosives experience) and engineering students. In 1919, the department was reorganised into the 5th (Engineers) Battalion of the IRA, consisting of four companies under Rory O'Connor's leadership.[49] Toomey had a significant role in the project to recruit engineering craftsmen, as he explained to the Military Service Pension Board in 1936:

> I was a member of an intelligence, or Secret Service Unit under the control of … Michael Collins… the Labour Board was formed under this Unit; and about the Autumn of 1919, I was detailed for special duty on this Labour Board by order of the Army Council.

> Our duty was to use our influence in our various trade unions, and in the labour movement generally, on behalf of the Republic; to get hold of men in important key positions, such as power stations, railways, and transport dockworkers, etc; and most important of all, to undermine the amalgamated and cross channel unions, and where possible to organise

a breakaway from these unions, and establish purely Irish unions instead; manned and controlled by men with republican and national tendencies. In other words, we were republican agents within the trade union movement. This was regarded as very important work by both the Army Council and the Dáil at the time.

We were in direct communication with Michael Collins, both as Minister of Finance and Chief Intelligence Officer of the Army, and ... were supplied with financial assistance to carry on the work. As members of the IRA ... We worked under active service conditions, and our Company Officers were instructed to excuse us from ordinary parades, while still ... liable for mobilisation at any time.[50]

The unit – which was started at an IRB meeting chaired by Joseph McGrath, future Minister for Labour and Industry and Commerce – operated under a codename, the 'Labour Board.' Martin Conlon – an IRB man and an official with the Municipal Employees' Trade Union – was another central Labour Board figure. Toomey worked for the Board while serving in 2nd Coy., 5th Batt. of the Dublin Brigade during the War of Independence.[51] Another notable Board member was Thomas Maguire of the Irish Stationary Engine Drivers' Society, a former Dublin branch secretary of the Associated Society of Locomotive Engineers and Firemen. Maguire later attested that the Board existed 'to influence the trade unions so that they would assist the IRA engaged in active opposition to the army of occupation.'[52] Born in 1882, Maguire had been an IRB member since 1902 and an Irish Volunteer since the movement's inauguration in 1913. He was stationed at the Four Courts during the 1916 Rising with A Coy., 1st Batt. of the Dublin Brigade, with whom he also served during the War of Independence. Before the Rising, he used his job (MGWR fireman) to carry dispatches to Volunteers. He lost his job for his role in the Rising and was subsequently employed at Dublin Corporation's power station. He helped Toomey manufacture grenades and ammunition at secret munitions plants in Dublin organised by Seán Russell and was solely responsible for bringing the Stationary Engine Drivers under Labour Board control.[53]

Martin Conlon chaired the Labour Board. He had a link to the craft unions through his deputy Luke Kennedy, an electrician and former mechanical fitter. Both were members of the IRB's Supreme Council. Patrick McGuirk, a Dublin IRA officer, was appointed Board secretary. Having served on the executive on the Irish Volunteers from its inception until 1917, Kennedy 'took a very important part in the preparations for the Rising' and saw service at the GPO.[54] He subsequently claimed that he would have been entitled to sign the Proclamation had he been present while it was being signed. As chairman of the Dublin Arms Committee, Collins employed him to repair and acquire weapons and wire bombs. In 1919, he took over from Conlon as chairman of the Labour Board after its first meeting. Collins considered the Board's work so important that its members were excused from regular military activity and worked fulltime, meeting five or six times a week. Active in the ETU, Kennedy later became an official of the Electrical Section of the engineering union created by the Labour Board, having taken many of his fellow electricians with him.[55] Christopher Farrelly was another Board member and 1916 veteran who saw active service at Jacob's biscuit factory on Bishop's Street with C Coy., 2nd Battalion, with whom he also served during the War of Independence. A superior officer described him as 'an exceptionally good volunteer' who 'carried out all the duties assigned to him.'[56]

In early 1920, the Board recruited a committee to organise the breakaway, of which Redmond was made president and Patrick McIntyre secretary. McIntyre was already secretary of the southern district of the Iron Moulders' Society, an area covering Dundalk to Cork. The organising committee also included Michael Slater, brass finisher; Rowland Bent, fitter; John J. Rooney, coachbuilder; Farrelly, iron moulder; Michael Doyle, shipwright; and Robert Donohoe, electrician. McIntyre had been elected to Dublin Corporation for Sinn Féin in the municipal elections, held on 15 January 1920; Toomey and Slater were unsuccessful candidates for the party.[57] Liam de Róiste, Sinn Féin TD for Cork City, believed that 'Labour, official or otherwise, has done very badly. These elections clearly show that the appeal to a war between classes is not a very moving one in Ireland.'[58] The results contradict this assertion. Nationally, the Labour Party had its best municipal election and returned 324 candidates. Sinn Féin returned 422, compared to 213 nationalists and 297 Unionists. Labour secured one-quarter of the vote, second only to Sinn Féin, which secured one-third of it.[59] Slater had been a member of the IRB since his youth and an Irish Volunteer from the beginning, helping to establish a rifle club at Father Matthew Park to train republicans. In 1914, he was involved in gun-runnings at Howth and Kilcoole. During the Rising, he had served with B Coy., 2nd Batt, escaping arrest by going on the run. He served with 2 Coy., 5th Batt. during the War of Independence and took no part in the Civil War. He worked for the Corporation workshop at Stanley Street where, until Sinn Féin secured a majority on the Corporation in January 1920, he had to camouflage his republican activities. Slater brought the Dublin United Brass Founders', Finishers' and Gas Fitters' Society, of which he was president, under Labour Board control.[60]

Capturing the electricians owed much to Donohoe, another Labour Board member and 1916 veteran. With B Coy., 1st Batt. he saw action on Chancery and Greek Streets and helped to defend the Four Courts. From 1919, he served with 1 Coy., 5th Batt., with whom he oversaw armed guard for brigade council meetings. Donohoe's main task was to instruct his fellow Volunteers in drilling and cable joining to manufacture grenades. Anxious to see more combat, he did not enjoy his time on the Labour Board and went 'under protest', only participating because GHQ ordered him to. He worked for Dublin Corporation and later for the Electricity Supply Board (ESB).[61] Rooney similarly used his influence at the Inchicore workshop – where Volunteers surreptitiously built grenades and repaired arms – to convince his colleagues in the National Union of Vehicle Builders to transfer to the planned Irish union. Like Slater, he was skilled at organising breakaways, having founded the Irish Society of Vehicle Builders in 1918, which merged with the Irish engineering union two years later. Born in 1877 in a tenement on Mabbot Street, Dublin, Rooney was steeped in the independence struggle from childhood. He was the younger brother of William Rooney – the prominent Irish nationalist, poet, journalist and Gaelic revivalist – and his father had partaken in the 1867 Fenian uprising. An Irish Volunteer since its inception, during the Rising he fought from Jacob's and the Royal College of Surgeons with E Coy., 2nd Batt. He served with the same unit until mid-1919 when he was appointed to the Labour Board. Rooney was ordered to infiltrate the NUR but was unsuccessful. He played no part in the Civil War. A keen sportsman and cultural revivalist, he later served as secretary and president of Faughs Hurling Club.[62]

Yeates considers the creation of the Labour Board 'the most important single initiative undertaken by the Government of the Irish Republic in the industrial relations arena' with 'lasting consequences' for Irish trade unionism.[63] Its significance is undeniable given that Connect Trade Union can trace its origins directly back to it. The Board reflected Sinn Féin's belief that national unity, especially in wartime, was sacrosanct. This view was especially prominent among the Catholic clergy and right-wing republicans, some of whom were employers. But the national climate was conducive to radicalism. Industrial regeneration was central to Sinn Féin's vision, which could support some left-wing policies. Many republicans were sympathetic to a vague notion of a 'co-operative commonwealth' as an alternative to capitalism, socialism and class conflict. As Republican Courts offered prompt settlements of disputes, both employers and unions utilised them instead of their British competitors. They were formally established by Dáil decree in June 1920, having been operational since June 1919.[64] In September 1920, the Dáil instituted the Labour Arbitration Tribunal – on which trade unionists like Maguire served – which considers a forerunner to the Labour Court and the Labour Relations Commission. Thus, the Irish state's industrial relations policy has its origins in the foundation of the state itself.[65]

With such strong links to Sinn Féin, Redmond's committee had little difficulty in establishing channels of communication. Joseph McDonagh – TD for North Tipperary and brother of 1916 leader Thomas McDonagh – acted as the intermediary between the committee and the government of the First Dáil. In March 1920, he met the committee for talks. Setting up the union would be expensive – and only the Dáil could effort it. The men sought a £2,000 bank loan – equivalent to €104,000 in today's money – an enormous sum for the fledgling Department of Labour whose running costs for 1920 were well under half that. The figure was largely a reserve fund to match the financial power of the amalgamateds, whose large membership allowed them to provide generous benefits. The men knew that 'if they could show to the older and more conservative members that demands for sick and unemployment benefits could be met, the greatest obstacle to the success of the movement could be overcome.'[66] Appeals to patriotism alone were not enough to compete with material realities. A major reason for dissatisfaction was delays in the payment of unemployment and sickness benefits to Irish members from London.[67] However, disillusion with the British was the primary catalyst for the separatist sentiment, as the men made clear in a letter to McDonagh:

> For some years it has been the opinion of ... members belonging to Amalgamated Societies, particularly in the engineering trades, that it was advisable to have one large Irish union for these trades... we believe that this is a favourable opportunity for starting such a project... for some time past the attitude of the English executives has been one in keeping with the attitude of the English government towards this country... For instance the attitude taken up by the executive of the Amalgamated Society of Engineers in Easter Week was in keeping with the policy of the Government of the day... [as was] their attitude on the Conscription Act, and ... the Motor Permit Order pointing out that this was a political question, and [refusing] to grant their members strike pay ... the time

had arrived when we should have a union of our own, governed and controlled in Ireland by Irishmen... the only binding link between Ireland and England is that of the amalgamated unions, whose executives ... are in league with the British government.[68]

Though Irish breakaways had a poor track record, the men believed that the new political landscape made the mighty British metal unions vulnerable. More significantly, they claimed that the ramifications would not be confined to the engineering trade, as the new body would 'spell the death knell for English unions in this country.'[69]

McDonagh was impressed by the men's proposal and forwarded it to the Department of Labour. On 13 April, Diarmaid Ó hÉigeartaigh, an IRB man and department secretary, passed the letter to Collins, who wanted more information before committing to such an endeavour. He asked Markievicz, now Minister for Labour in the republican government, to meet the men. On 5 May, she did so with TDs Art O'Connor and Seán Etchingham, who had been working with her to establish rudimentary institutions of mediation and arbitration. The craftsmen again requested that the government guarantee the £2,000, including a £100 (€2,100) advance to cover the union's inauguration. The ASE was the chief target for poaching. While the committee accepted that few of the ASE's twenty-two thousand Ulster members would join, it predicted that at least a thousand of its eight thousand southern members would join immediately with most of the others following suit shortly afterwards. The men believed that most of the ASE's Dublin, Cork, Waterford, Dundalk, Passage and Cobh branches would transfer. They even believed that recruiting in Derry was possible, a misguided belief born of southern ignorance of northern conditions (see Chapter 3). They were so confident of success that they told Markievicz that there was no need to appoint a permanent organiser because there would be enough local activists to recruit members. The committee estimated that membership dues would generate £3,900 a year while running costs would only be £500. The money was also necessitated by the prospect of British unions invoking existing agreements with employers to crush the nascent Irish union.[70] Importantly, the men stressed that they would 'use every means in their power to induce their members to accept ... arbitration.'[71] Markievicz was convinced. On 7 May, her department forwarded £100 for a public meeting to launch the union. The wheels were now firmly in motion.

The union is born

In early May, a circular explaining the reasons for the breakaway was issued to trade unionists across the island, including Belfast. This allowed the *Northern Whig*, a liberal unionist daily, to get hold of it. After denouncing the initiative as 'the latest move of Sinn Féin,' the paper published excerpts from the circular:

> This decision [to breakaway] has been arrived at as a result of the actions of the different English executives in connection with the treatment meted out to their Irish members on several occasions. It is undoubted fact that we have in Ireland the material for a fighting and militant union that will cater for the men engaged in this industry, not only in accordance with the wishes of the great majority, but which will act itself out not to hamper but to help our efforts in every possible way.[72]

The *Whig* speculated that 'a few nationalists and Red Flaggers' would give the new union 'their benediction,' and that 'Sinn Féin … hope that by this manoeuvre they may frighten the officials of the leading trade unions across the water into giving more active support to the Irish revolutionary movement.'[73] The paper was more accurate than it may have realised. Separatism and sectarianism had become indivisible in a labour movement which did not challenge Sinn Féin or Ulster unionism.[74] On 7 May, adverts appeared in the Dublin newspapers advertising the inaugural meeting of an Irish union for the metal trades. Two days later, over seven hundred craftsmen packed into the Abbey Theatre to witness a truly historic event: the launch of Ireland's first national engineering craft union. Delegates attended from Cork, Drogheda, Wexford, Enniscorthy and northeast Ulster. Republican fervour was palpable at the meeting as the War of Independence raged outside. On that day alone, republicans at Wormwood Scrubs demanding political status were on their nineteenth day of hunger strike and the IRA attacked police barracks in Counties Cork and Armagh. The day before, the IRA shot Richard Revell, Detective Sergeant with the Dublin Metropolitan Police (DMP). Revelle was a member of G Division, the DMP's special branch, and had been a notetaker at trade union and Sinn Féin meetings for years.[75] Earlier that week, Volunteers in Kerry had assassinated a policeman who had helped to arrest Roger Casement in 1916.[76]

Unsurprisingly, anti-British sentiment was strongly and repeatedly expressed at the Abbey. Toomey, who presided, was the main speaker:

> Their interests and the interests of the people across the Channel clashed. They were two separate and distinct peoples and could not always view matters from the same standpoint. Some people might say that the interests of all workers were common. That might be so, but workers in different countries saw things in a different light. They were progressing in the labour movement in Ireland far quicker than in … England … and the question was whether they were going to be held back by … England… That meeting was the beginning of the end of amalgamated unions … they were prepared to … deal with any opposition from whatever quarter it came, although they had no animosity towards the men from whom they were breaking away.[77]

Redmond gave financial reasons for the breakaway, claiming that remittance sent to the British far exceeded what they were spending on Irish branches. Like Toomey, he ridiculed the *Whig*'s allegations.[78] McIntyre maintained that while the new union was 'out for no trouble' with the amalgamateds, it would 'fight them here on Irish soil' if they refused to recognise it.[79] A Cork ASE man claimed that seventy-five per cent of the young members of his branch would join the new union. A Belfast representative told the meeting that if they wanted to have a 'real industrial union in the shipping trade' then they should organise his city. Delegates from other parts of Ulster and Wexford also spoke.[80] The meeting christened the new union the 'Irish Engineering, Shipbuilding and Foundry Trades Union' (IESFTU) and appointed the organising committee as the Provisional Executive Committee. The ASE and ETU picketed the proceedings and announced that any member who attended would lose his job and be expelled from his union.[81] One ETU man stormed out of the meeting after he was laughed at for relaying the threat.[82]

The conservative and unionist press roundly assailed the new 'Fenian' union. The *Londonderry Sentinel* noted with suspicion the formation of this 'Sinn Féin engineering industries' union', while *The Scotsman* abhorred that 'the Labour wing of the Sinn Féin movement' had issued 'a declaration of war on the English unions in the engineering and foundry trades.'[83] Most vituperatively of all, the *Belfast Newsletter* condemned this 'anti-English union' as 'another development of the anti-English spirit among the Sinn Féiners and Bolshevists.'

> They allege that they are "progressing" in the labour movement in Ireland far quicker than … England… their "progress" is like that of Lenin and Trotsky in Russia, which has brought indescribable misery upon many millions of people… the trade unions in Great Britain are opposed to a movement of that kind, and they are altogether out of sympathy with the Irish Bolshevists. That is why the latter are breaking away from them… They prefer the Red Flag… The objects of the new organisation are plain, and no man who is not a rebel should think of joining it… the trade unionists of Belfast are neither Bolshevists nor rebels, and they will have nothing to do with the new anti-English organisation.[84]

On 15 May, the IESFTU was officially launched in Dublin with 420 members. It declared its intention to represent all Irish engineering craftsmen, a confidence that reflected labour's swagger in 1920.[85] But forces outside the workers' control were conspiring against them. The First World War had caused a massive expansion in output that, by mid-1920, had created a capitalist crisis of overproduction; a deep recession had begun. Wages stagnated across Ireland, and it would be many years before workers saw advances again. Employers sought a return to pre-1914 pay and conditions and shed surplus labour in response to plummeting prices and demand. Defending hard earned gains was now the imperative. It was here, in the industrial sphere, that the new union would have to prove itself.

Chapter Notes and References

1   David Fitzpatrick, 'Strikes in Ireland, 1914-1921', *Saothar*, no. 6, 1980, p. 26; A.E. Malone, 'Irish Labour in War Time, *Studies*, Vol. 7, June 1918, p. 320.

2   Emmet O'Connor, *Derry Labour in the age of agitation, 1889-1923, 2: Larkinism and syndicalism, 1907-23* (Dublin: Four Courts Press, 2016), p. 24. The committee only examined Britain.

3   A.L. Bowley, *Prices and Wages in United Kingdom, 1914-1920* (Oxford: Oxford University Press, 1921), pp. 3, 35-36, 43. Liam Kennedy has cited the government's suspension of the gold standard, huge deficit spending and the belated implementation of price control as the reasons for wartime inflation. See Liam Kennedy, 'The Cost of Living in Ireland, 1698-1998', in David Dickson & Cormac Ó Gráda (eds.), *Refiguring Ireland: Essays in Honour of L.M. Cullen* (Dublin: The Lilliput Press, 2003), p. 262.

4   Stephen Broadberry & Peter Howlett, 'The United Kingdom during World War One: Business as Usual?', in Stephen Broadberry and Mark Harrison (eds.), *The Economics of World War One* (Cambridge: Cambridge University Press), pp. 213-215, 222-226; Theresa Moriarty, 'Work, warfare and wages: industrial controls and Irish trade unionism in the First World War', in Adrian Gregory & Senia Pašeta (eds.), *Ireland and the Great War: 'A War to Unite Us All'?* (Manchester: Manchester University Press, 2002), pp. 76-77; Puirséil, 'War, work and labour', p. 188.

5   In 1915, for example, this happened to electricians at Edmundson's, Dublin. See *Freeman's Journal*, 28 Sept. 1915.

6   B.R. Mitchell, *British Historical Statistics* (Cambridge: Cambridge University Press, 1988), p. 739; Bowley, *Prices and Wages*, p 106.

7   Fitzpatrick, 'Strikes in Ireland', p. 28.

8   O'Mahony, *Maritime Gateway*, p. 114; Riordan, *Modern Irish Trade and Industry*, pp. 99-100; Yeates, *A City in Wartime*, p. 148.

9   Riordan, *Modern Irish Trade and Industry*, pp. 207-211.

10   Yeates, *A City in Wartime*, pp. 264-265.

11   Lynch, 'Belfast Shipyards', p. 134.

12   Humbert Wolfe, *Labour Supply and Regulation* (Oxford: Clarendon Press, 1923), pp. 148-172.

13   James Hinton, *The First Shop Stewards' Movement* (London: George Allen & Unwin, 1973), pp. 56-75.

14   Yeates, *A City in Wartime*, p. 149.

15   'Memorandum of discussion at conference of representatives of joint committee re. scheme for the formation of one Irish union compromising 'all branches of engineering trades in Ireland', DE 2/116, Dáil Éireann collection, National Archives of Ireland (NAI).

16   Ralph Darlington, *Radical Unionism: The Rise and Fall of Revolutionary Syndicalism* (Chicago: Haymarket Book, 2008).

17   O'Connor, *A Labour History of Ireland, 1824-1960*, pp. 67-68; O'Connor, *Syndicalism in Ireland*, pp. 6-8

18   For global syndicalism, see Marcel Van der Linden & Wayne Thorpe (eds.), *Revolutionary Syndicalism: An International Perspective* (Aldershot: Scolar Press, 1990); and Marcel Van der Linden, *Transnational Labour History: Explorations* (Aldershot: Ashgate Publishing Ltd., 2003).

19   Bob Holton, *British Syndicalism, 1900-14: Myths and Realities* (London: Pluto Press, 1976); Hinton, *The First Shop Stewards' Movement*; Joseph White, 'Syndicalism in a Mature Industrial Setting: The Case of Britain', *International Syndicalism*, pp. 101-117.

20   Van der Linden & Thorpe, 'The Rise and Fall of Revolutionary Syndicalism', pp. 57-58.

21   Hinton, *The first shop stewards' movement*, pp. 93-94.

22   Ibid., pp. 93-100.

23   Emmet O'Connor, 'War and Syndicalism, 1914-1923', in Donal Nevin (ed.), *Trade Union Century* (Cork: Mercier Press, 1994), pp. 56-58.

24   Emmet O'Connor, 'Old Wine in New Bottles? Syndicalism and 'Fakirism' in the Great Labour Unrest, 1911-1914', *Labour History Review*, Vol 17, No. 1, 2014, p. 35.

25   Fitzpatrick, 'Strikes in Ireland', pp. 36-37.

26   For accounts of the strike, see Austen Morgan, *Labour and partition; the Belfast working class, 1905-23* (London: Pluto Press, 1991), pp. 148-190; and Patterson, *Class conflict and sectarianism*, pp. 92-114.

27   Yeates, *A City in Turmoil*, pp. 10-11.

28   ITUC, *Report of the Twenty-Fourth annual Congress*, 1918, ILHM, pp. 114-115.

29   'Comparative statement of the wages of workmen on 1st August 1914 and 25th October 1920', GDB/C004.06/0027.05, Guinness archives.

30   Fitzpatrick, 'Strikes in Ireland', p. 37.

31   Ibid.

32   Borgonovo, *Dynamics*, p. 194.

33   Peter Hart, 'The Social Structure of the IRA, 1916-23', *The Historical Journal*, Vol. 42, No. 1, Mar. 1999, p. 220.

34   Yeates, *A City in Wartime*, p. 43; Peter Hart, *The IRA at War, 1916-23* (Oxford: Oxford University Press, 2005), pp. 118-119; Borgonovo, *War and Revolution*, p. 80; Peter Hart, *The I.R.A. and Its Enemies: Violence and Community in Cork, 1916-1923* (Oxford: Oxford University Press, 1998), pp. 156-157; Hart, 'Social Structure, pp. 207-231.

35   *Irish Independent*, Nov. 1919-Feb. 1920; ITUC, *Twenty-sixth annual report*, 1920, pp. 58-59.

36   The only concession obtained was that drivers who had a permit would not have to reapply when changing employment. See ITUC, *Twenty-sixth annual report*, 1920, NLI, pp. 11-18, 89-90, Yeates, *A City in Turmoil*, pp. 66-68.

37   *Irish Independent*, 14, 15 Apr. 1920.

38   *Cork Constitution*, 29 Oct. 1920.

39 O'Connor, *Syndicalism in Ireland*, pp. 71-72, 87-88; *Intercourse between Bolshevism and Sinn Féin*, 1921, Cmd. 1326, XXIX, UKPP; and Richard Dawson Bates, *Red Terror and Green: The Sinn Féin Bolshevist Movement* (London: Murray, 1920). For the Conservative Workingmen's Club, see Martin Maguire, 'The Organisation and Activism of Dublin's Protestant Working Class, 1883-1935', *Irish Historical Studies*, Vol. 29, No. 113, May 1994, pp. 65-87.

40 O'Connor, *Syndicalism in Ireland*, pp. 87-88.

41 Hart, 'Social Structure', pp. 207-231.

42 Pádraig Yeates, 'Craft workers during the Irish revolution, 1922-22', *Saothar*, No. 33, 2008, p. 38; 1911 Census. George Barnes, former ASE general secretary, served as Minister of Pensions in the British cabinet between 1916 and 1917 and as a minister without portfolio between 1917 and 1920.

43 Thomas Leahy, Witness Statement (WS) 660, Bureau of Military History (BMH); Thomas Leahy, Military Service Pension (MSP) Application, MSP34REF321, MSP collection, both found in Military Archives (MA); Yeates, *A City in Civil War*, pp. 318-319

44 Micheál Ó Murchú, 9 Nov. 1936 to MSP Board; Peter Pursfield to MSP Board, 9 Dec. 1936; both found in Thomas Maguire, MSP Application, MSP collection, MSP34REF24358, MA.

45 Joseph Toomey, 'Application to the Minister for Defence for a Service Certificate', MSP Application, MSP34REF21715, MSP collection, MA; Frank Henderson, WS 821, BMH, MA, pp. 22-24. The *Independent* was targeted because of its denunciation of the IRA's attempted assassination of Sir John French, Lord Lieutenant of Ireland, on 20 December 1919.

46 *Freeman's Journal*, 26 Oct. 1917; Seán Kennedy, WS 885, BMH, MA, pp. 18-19; Donal Ó Drisceoil, *Utter Disloyalist: Tadhg Barry and the Irish Revolution* (Cork: Mercier Press, 2021), pp. 169-170.

47 Pádraig Yeates, *Irish Craft Workers in a Time of Revolution* (Dublin: TEEU, 2016), p. 3.

48 Michael Collins to William O'Brien, 6 July 1921, MS. 15,687/3, William O'Brien Papers, NLI. O'Brien was also a member of the IRB.

49 Aaron Ó Maonaigh, 'The death of Volunteer Seán Doyle: 'A conflict of testimony'', 7 June 2019, *The Irish Story*, retrieved 29 Mar. 2020 from https://www.theirishstory.com/2019/06/07/the-death-of-volunteer-sean-doyle-a-conflict-of-testimony/#_ednref12.

50 Cited in Yeates, *Irish Craft Workers*, p. 3. Several Labour Board members submitted this exact statement in their application for an MSP. For the original, see Christopher Farrelly, MSP application, MSP34REF20605, MSP collection, MA.

51 This Battalion was formed in early 1919 under Commandant Liam Archer. Most craftsmen in the IRA, including metal craftsmen, were members of it. See Harry Colley, WS 1,687, BMH, MA, p. 40.

52 Cited in Yeates, 'Craft workers during the Irish revolution', p. 40.

53 Sworn statement by Tomás Maguire, sworn statement to MSP Advisory Committee, 10 Dec. 1937, Maguire, MSP collection, MA.

54 'Piaras Béaslaí to MSP Board, 22 Dec. 1935', Luke Kennedy, MSP Application, MSP34REF21389, MSP collection, MA.

55 'Sworn statement made before Advisory Committee by Luke Kennedy, 10 Dec. 1937', Kennedy, MSP Application, MA; Luke Kennedy, WS 165, BMH, MA.

56 T. MacMahon to MSP Board, 21 Nov. 1935, Farrelly, MSP Application, MA.

57 Yeates, *Irish Craft Workers*, pp. 3-4.

58 Liam de Róiste diaries, 18 Jan. 1920, U271/A/26, Cork City and County Archives.

59 Arthur Mitchell, *Labour in Irish politics, 1890-1930: the Irish labour movement in an age of revolution* (Dublin: Irish University Press, 1974), pp. 126-127.

60 Michael Slater, Application for MSP, MSP34REF21845, MA. Founded in 1817, the Dublin Brass Founders' Society would become the oldest constituent body of the planned breakaway engineering union.

61 Sworn Statement made by Robert Donohoe before Advisory Committee, 13 Nov. 1936', Robert Donohoe MSP Application, MSP collection, MSP34REF20487, MA; *Irish Press*, 11 Jan. 1938

62 *Irish Press*, 14 Dec. 1945; John J. Rooney, MSP Application, MSP34REF21793, MSP collection, MA; 1911 Census.

63 Yeates, *Irish Craft Workers*, p. 4.

64 Michael Laffan, *The Resurrection of Ireland: The Sinn Féin Party, 1916-1923* (Cambridge: Cambridge University Press, 1999), pp. 252-259.

65 Yeates, *Irish Craft Workers in a Time of Revolution*, p. 5.

66 Joint committee to Joe McDonagh, 9 Mar. 1920, Report on the new Irish Engineering Society, DE/2/116, Dáil Éireann collection, NAI.

67 Yeates, *A City in Turmoil*, p. 131.

68 Cited in Yeates, *Irish Craft Workers*, p. 6.

69 Cited in ibid., p. 7.

70 Ibid., pp. 7-9.

71 Cited in ibid., p. 9.

72 *Northern Whig*, 6 May 1920.

73 *Wicklow People*, 29 May 1920.

74 Yeates, *A City in Turmoil*, p. 132.

75 *Irish Independent*, 7 May 1920; Yeates, 'Craft workers during the Irish revolution', p. 37.

76 Ibid., 5 May 1920.

77 Ibid., 10 May 1920.

78 Ibid.

79 Cited in Yeates, *Irish Craft Workers*, p. 10.

80 *Irish Independent*, 10 May 1920.

81 'Sworn statement made before advisory committee by Luke Kennedy, 10 Dec. 1937', MSP Application, MA.

82 *Watchword of Labour*, 15 May 1920.

83 *The Scotsman*, 7 May 1920; *Londonderry Sentinel*, 11 May 1920.

84 *Belfast Newsletter*, 11 May 1920.

85 IESFTU inaugural meeting minutes, 9 June 1920. Specifically, the union intended to represent fitters, turners, patternmakers, blacksmiths, machinists, iron moulders, brass moulders and finishers, electricians, boilermakers and allied workers.

2

The Early Years, 1920-22

Born amid intense class and national conflict, the IESFTU had a baptism of fire. Nevertheless, its belief that the turmoil would pave the way for a better future for workers was not groundless. The War of Independence had made the prospect of British withdrawal a reality and many trade unionists expected kinder treatment from an independent Irish state. Both Sinn Féin and the IESFTU considered the breakaway an industrial expression of the independence struggle, helping to cement an alliance that was vital to the union's survival. It incurred 'bitter opposition' from some of Britain's biggest and most powerful unions, who attempted to strangle it at birth.[1] But the British were not the only threat that the union faced. As the slump took hold, employers clamoured for a return to pre-1914 wages. The Irish manufacturing trade almost halved in 1921 and by December, unemployment had reached over 26 per cent. Across Europe, the economic slump degenerated into violent class conflict and political reaction against proletarian radicalism in 1920. Likewise, industrial disputes in Ireland would increasingly end in defeat for workers as the employers regained the upper hand in the class war. However, the slump coincided with the height of the War of Independence, the Anglo-Irish Truce (11 July 1921) and the Anglo-Irish Treaty split. The resulting political instability forced most employers to delay their counterattack against wages. Those in the metal trades had cross-channel support, allowing them to cut pay immediately. If the union were to achieve long-term growth, it would have to prove its worth against some of Ireland's most intransigent employers.

Establishing an Irish craft union

The day after the Abbey meeting, the provisional executive met for the first time. Redmond presided and Donohoe acted as secretary. The ETU asked for support for Dublin cinema operatives on strike, but the committee declined lest it be distracted from the immediate task of organising. It was the beginning of a long and tumultuous relationship between the new union and electricians. The committee also decided to order a thousand contribution cards and to hold a recruitment meeting at the National Foresters' Hall at 41 Parnell Square – previously used for drilling by the IRB and Volunteers – the following week. The Hall became the union's first headquarters. The recruitment drive was remarkably successful: the union enrolled 440, all members of British unions, on the first night. At its second meeting, the executive began to establish branches and sent recruiters to the major southern centres. McIntyre, who was made fulltime general secretary, was tasked with overseeing the union's expansion. He would earn 60s. a week for this, which was lower than most Irish craft wages.[2] Gaining Sinn Féin's trust was vital for both recognition and growth. Although the Department of Labour remained reluctant to grant the £2,000, Markievicz convinced her fellow TDs of the men's bona fide and ability. 'The men were sincere republicans and capable of the work that they were undertaking,' she reported.[3] The money was granted and lodged in the National Land Bank, a Dáil-backed friendly society established in 1919. Links between the union and the national movement continued to deepen. The Gaelic League allowed the union to move into Colmcille Hall on Blackhall Street as a temporary office. Other tenants included the 1st Battalion of the Dublin Brigade of the IRA and a local unit of Cumann na mBan, the IRA's women's auxiliary.[4]

The union's executive committee wrote to their organisers in the provinces telling them to organise meetings of engineering workers to set up branches. Establishing a presence at the Dublin, Cork and Passage shipyards was problematic because some men there were loyalists from Belfast and the Clyde. Nevertheless, the union made fast progress. Branches were opened in Wexford on 20 May, in Limerick on 21 May, in Enniscorthy on 26 May and in Dundalk on 2 June. Brendan Corish, the Labour Party mayor of the town, helped to establish the Wexford branch. On 1 June, Sinn Féin mayor of Limerick Michael O'Callaghan – later murdered by the Black and Tans on 7 March 1921 – launched the Limerick branch from City Hall with Redmond, McIntyre and Leahy in attendance. James Carr, president of the trades council, became branch chairman.[5] The *Limerick Leader* hailed the establishment of the union as another advance in the march for independence. On 5 August 1920, a Drogheda branch was formed under the auspices of Christopher Burke, a Drogheda-born IRA volunteer. Speaking in the town's mayoralty rooms, Redmond announced that the union now controlled the railway workshops in Dublin and had 1,641 members, up from nine hundred the previous month.

On 9 August, Rooney, Redmond and Terence MacSwiney – Cork's lord mayor, IRA commander and future republican martyr – launched the Cork branch from Cork City Hall with money from Collins.[6] MacSwiney argued the Connollyite case that 'industrial freedom' and 'political freedom' were 'allied in Ireland … by joining and strengthening the union they were also helping on the work of Irish independence.' Redmond informed the attendees that membership stood at 1,745 by then – 1,206 of whom were Dubliners – as dozens joined every day.[7] Three days later, MacSwiney was arrested for possessing 'seditious' literature after a raid on Cork City Hall. A military court sentenced him to two years in Brixton Prison, where he immediately went on hunger strike in protest. After seventy-four days without food, MacSwiney died on 25 October. The Cork Trades Council had called three local general strikes for his release and on 29 October, the ITUC conducted a national general strike in his honour.[8] The IESFTU, which had 4,500 members on MacSwiney's death, paid its respects by partaking in the stoppages.[9] That the Cork, Limerick and Drogheda branches were sponsored by prominent local republicans shows that the union's links to the independence movement were not confined to Dublin. Members in Cork were quickly given an ultimatum by the AUE: re-join within twenty-four hours or be forced to leave the country. The threat was ignored. With such appeal, it is little wonder that the IESFTU continued to spread rapidly. By the year's end, it also had branches in Galway, Clonmel, Sligo, Wicklow, Passage West, Arklow, Blackrock, Clondalkin, Kildare, Cobh, Portarlington and Waterford, and had one planned for Meath. Dublin had ten branches: six were meeting in 6 Gardiner Row, three in 10 Upper Abbey Street and one in Inchicore.[10] Farrelly recalled that, at its zenith, the union was strong enough to bring Dublin to a 'complete standstill' because it had the enginemen at the power stations.[11]

The IESFTU informed the amalgamateds of its intention to secure recognition from the employers and other unions, which the British were not going to grant without a fight. Accordingly, the Irish union sought support from the ITUC for the battle. Craftsmen poured into the IESFTU. Within a few weeks of its establishment, woodcutting machinists, motor mechanics and shovel finishers expressed interest in joining.[12] Even the IADAMU, heavily in debt and in decline, sought to merge. The IESFTU was lukewarm about the approach, possibly because some members, as former ASE men, were still bitter towards the IADAMU after the motor permit strike. This animosity was shared by the ITGWU, which meant that taking over the IADAMU risked damaging relations with Ireland's most powerful union. A clever compromise was agreed: the IESFTU took the mechanics while the Transport Union took the drivers.[13] Sensing its popularity, the provisional executive agreed to allow plumbers, machine riveters, stationary engine drivers, blacksmiths and iron machinists to become members. The weekly subscription rate was set at 1s. 6d.[14]

Electricians were a key target for the union. With 1,341 members and eleven branches in Ireland, there was no shortage of ETU men to poach.[15] Though it admitted semiskilled members such as smiths' helpers and holders-up (boilermakers' helpers), the IESFTU resolved to leave the electricians' helpers alone for fear of aggravating their union, the ITGWU. On 20 June, most ETU members in Dublin joined the IESFTU in a body, making it the premier electrical union outside Ulster: 99 per cent of electricians at the Corporation's Ringsend power station signed up.[16] The plumbers also came over that month. The ETU executive had been under pressure from its Irish members to call a general strike to force the British army to leave the country. In his union's journal, Jack Ball, its general president, expressed his disgust at Black and Tan terror. In July, a UK-wide ETU ballot on a general strike was defeated 5,640-1,408, causing quick disintegration of the union in Ireland. The following month, John Joseph (Jack) Collins, a prominent Irish member of the ETU executive, resigned. He claimed that he 'had no other course left owing to the action of the members on the question of the withdrawal of the army of occupation.' Meanwhile, Seán O'Duffy, its fulltime Dublin district secretary, was using his position to secretly transfer members to the IESFTU. The executive stopped his salary in late 1920 when it learned of his actions. But the IESFTU did not completely reap the rewards of the ETU's downfall in Ireland: The Cork and Drogheda branches transferred to the ITGWU, as did cinema operators in Dublin. In October 1920, the ETU had 274 members in its three remaining Dublin branches, all refusing to pay contributions and amassing huge arrears. It sent no delegates to the 1921 ITUC because of the 'unsettled' conditions. That September, the inevitable happened: the union closed in Dublin.[17] By August 1920, the IESFTU had renamed itself the 'Irish Engineering, Electrical, Shipbuilding and Foundry Trade Union' to reflect its near monopoly on electricians outside of Ulster. It changed its name again to the 'Irish Engineering, Industrial and Electrical Trade Union' for a few months in 1921.[18] In accordance with its new rulebook, it became the Irish Engineering Industrial Union (IEIU) on 1 August, a name it kept until 1948.

On 24 July 1920, the IESFTU held a rules conference at Dublin City Hall's Council Chambers, which produced a rulebook that closely mirrored the ASE's. Allowing the union to use the Chambers was an important acknowledgement of its legitimacy by Sinn Féin, who had a majority on Dublin Corporation. The provisional executive had their positions formalised. Redmond was appointed as president as McIntyre as secretary, Toomey as vice-president, Slater as treasurer and Leahy, Bent and Rooney as trustees. With some other members, they formed the first National Executive Committee (NEC), the union's supreme governing body. A separate Resident Executive Committee (REC) would handle the week-to-week running of the IESFTU. The union employed a fulltime office staff whom it paid 75s. for a forty-four-hour week, a good wage by Dublin standards.[19] At the IRB's behest, Maguire became more involved with the Stationary Engine Drivers to expedite its merger with the IEIU to give the IRA control over Dublin's power and lighting stations.[20] After much wrangling, they joined that November. But the recruiting drive was not without some failures. After seven months of consideration, the Limerick Stationary Engine Drivers' and Firemen's Society rejected amalgamation in 1921.[21] An opportunity to bring over the Dublin tinsmiths and sheet metal workers, who had just ended their affiliation with the British, was squandered in 1920 when they formed their own union. In August 1921, Toomey was elected IEIU assistant general secretary, a new position which replaced the vice presidency. Maguire was subsequently elected to the executive, which comprised a multiplicity of crafts: moulders, steam engine drivers, boilermakers, electricians, fitters, smiths, vehicle builders, shipwrights, machinists, brass finishers and plumbers.[22]

Table 16: Unions that joined the IESFTU/IEIU, 1920-21.[23]

Ironfounders' Society (Dublin branch)	June 1920
Dublin Brassfinishers' Society	June 1920
ETU (Dublin membership)	June 1920
'Irish Vehicle Workers' Society'	Aug. 1920
Operative Society of Mechanical Heating & Domestic Engineers, Whitesmiths, Ironworkers & Pipefitters	Aug. 1920
Irish Stationary Engine Drivers' Society	Nov. 1920
Cork NUR no. 4 branch	Dec. 1921

Obtaining head office

The lack of a permanent headquarters was incurring significant costs and holding back plans to open as many as five branches in Dublin.[24] In May 1920, the union had unsuccessfully negotiated with the Boilermakers' Society about purchasing their hall on Lower Gardiner Street. After the deal fell through, the executive continued meeting at 41 Parnell Square. At a meeting of the executive in September, Redmond and Toomey suggested 6 Gardiner Row, then the Plaza Hotel, as a permanent headquarters. When a mass meeting of Dublin members agreed to a levy to meet the costs, the rest of the executive quickly warmed to the proposal. On 7 November, the union officially purchased the building, taking possession of it the next day. On 13 November, the executive held its first meeting in its new headquarters, which it renamed the 'Irish Engineering Hall.' It has been the union's home ever since. The building cost £2,583 (€89,000 in today's money, an enormous sum for the union), paid for by a loan from the National Land Bank. Nevertheless, the IEIU continued to contribute to the Belfast Victims' Fund. This fund helped the eight thousand Catholics and left-wing Protestants expelled from the Belfast shipyards in July

1920 by loyalist mobs in response to IRA activity in the south.[25] Some of the cost of Gardiner Row was met by transferring the deeds of Upper Abbey Street – leased, but not owned, by Maguire's Stationary Engine Drivers – to the union's solicitor James O'Connor. But given that Collins was the Minister for Finance, it is likely that he provided some of the money, or at least security, for the purchase. Not to alienate Collins, the union executive subscribed generously to the Belfast and munitions' strike funds despite opposition from the membership, suggesting that the leadership was more committed to following Sinn Féin policy than its rank-and-file.[26]

The union had other connections with The Big Fella: The Squad, most of whom were craftworkers, operated from 10 Upper Abbey Street under the front of George Moreland cabinetmakers. After McKee's capture and execution in late 1920, Traynor took control of the Dublin Brigade. Traynor was worried that the British might discover the brigade's headquarters, the Dublin Typographical Provident Society's premises at 35 Lower Gardiner Street. Slater arranged that the brigade and the Army Council make 6 Gardiner Row their new home. Soon afterwards leading IRA men began to regularly pass through its doors, including Traynor, Emmet Dalton and Todd Andrews. The brigade acquired many of its premises from the craft unions, reflecting the longstanding links between the latter and militant republicanism. Officially registered as the No. 1 Branch of the Irish Clerical Workers' Union, Gardiner Row remained the brigade's headquarters throughout the War of Independence. The Active Service Unit (ASU), which the brigade established in December 1920 for targeted attacks, also met at Gardiner Row. Like the Squad, the ASU comprised fulltime, paid Volunteers who always carried weapons. Members of both were 90s. a week, rates based on skilled wages in Dublin. It was a 'statement about the social status of soldiers of the Republic.'[27] Farrelly later attested that Gardiner Row – the acquisition of which was 'an activity of the IRA' – was an ideal location for the brigade because 'they were able to carry on army work behind the screen of the trades union activity.' He also claimed that the IEIU was 'controlled by the IRA' and its executive was 'composed of all active IRA men.'[28] While these are overstatements, the republican movement undoubtedly exerted a strong influence over the union. For instance, Gardiner Row hosted bombmaking classes for Volunteers.[29] Delegates to the IRA convention held on 26 March 1922, which repudiated the Dáil's right to dissolve the Republic and rejected the legitimacy of the Free State, had to present their credentials at 6 Gardiner's Row.[30]

Relations with other unions

The amalgamateds' response to the foundation of the IEIU was predictably antagonistic. When the dissidents met at the Abbey, British union officials warned against joining a 'political organisation.' Even *Forward*, the left-wing, Glasgow-based newspaper, was hostile. But other trade unionists were favourable, highlighting the divide between radicals and moderates on the British left. One supporter was Willie Gallacher, a radical leader of the shop stewards' movement who had travelled to Dublin to review the Citizen Army of which he was an honorary member.[31] Vocally pro-republican and Bolshevik, Gallacher had been a founding member of the recently formed Communist Party of Great Britain and would become its first MP in 1935. He supported the anti-Treatyites during the Civil War.

The amalgamateds would not give up without a fight. On 6 June 1920, the ASE's Dublin branch held a public meeting to dissuade members from defecting to the IESFTU. It hoped that the forthcoming merger of the British engineering unions – which would give the resulting Amalgamated Engineering Union (AEU) a membership of 350,000 – would help its case. The ASE had over eleven thousand Irish members, two-thirds of whom were in Belfast. The meeting was addressed by its renowned general secretary Tom Mann, who criticised 'sectionalism' and argued that 'men should be prepared to forget the county or country in which they were born and look to the international question of organised labour.'[32] Similarly, Belfast loyalist James Freeland, the ASE's Irish organiser and Toomey's replacement as district delegate, believed that 'the only hope of solving the Irish problem was in keeping the workers together in one common union.'[33] It was the wrong message at the wrong time for Ireland. With such a poor understanding of the reasons for the breakaway, the ASE stood little chance of stopping the haemorrhage.[34] In response to the meeting, Toomey boasted that 'the seed sown by Connolly is already bearing fruit and the … IESFTU will … forge ahead until they have every worker engaged in the industry in the four corners of Ireland … for the attainment of Connolly's ambition – the Co-operative Commonwealth.'[35]

A clear political divide existed between the two engineering unions operating in Ireland. As republicans flocked to the new organisation, moderate nationalists stayed with the ASE; some ASE men, like Albert Pennycook, were even unionists. A Dublin-born Orangeman, Pennycook was a fitter by trade and a chargehand at the Inchicore works. Political and sectarian tensions inevitably surfaced in the workplace, especially during the War of Independence: many of Pennycook's workmates believed that he had been promoted to piecework checker at just twenty-two because he was a Protestant. After he repeatedly refused to sign timesheets for employees whom he believed were leaving work to carry out 'murderous acts against the British Crown,' the men warned him of the deadly consequences of failing to pay them. In August 1921, the IRA ransacked his home and gave him his final warning at gunpoint. Facing assassination and ostracised by his co-workers and neighbours, he subsequently emigrated.[36] Many mechanical craftsmen on the Irish railways were, like Pennycook's father, immigrants from Britain who had arrived in the nineteenth century. Accordingly, 40 per cent of skilled workers in Inchicore were Protestant in 1911 and a third of Protestants were British-born or had British parents. Protestants were 26 per cent of the national population. Of the 92,000 Protestants in Dublin city and county, ten thousand were working-class men. In the city, 22 per cent of occupied Protestant males were craftsmen. As late as 1922, a fifth of Dublin's population were Protestants, the vast majority of whom were unionist.[37]

Leahy later asserted that taking on some of Britain's most powerful unions was made easier by the 'full support' of the ITGWU, 'who never refused any help when asked.' Kennedy, however, alleged that the ITGWU 'was not very favourable to us at all' because it shared the amalgamateds' hostility towards political unions![38] In reality, the Transport Union initially supported the IEIU and subsequently viewed it as a rival. The IEIU knew that if Congress and the Dáil were to recognise it, then friendly rapport with the ITGWU – whose republican credentials were impeccable – was vital. The IEIU also needed the Transport Union's support to affiliate to the ITUC, which it had done by August 1920. With a membership of 229,000 in 1920, Congress had experienced a spectacular renaissance since 1916, when membership had slumped to 120,000. The ITGWU had benefitted more than any other union from the labour revival. From a nadir of five thousand in 1916, its membership had mushroomed to 130,000 by 1920. The founding of the IEIU and the expansion of the ITGWU were manifestations of the concurrent revival of Irish trade unionism. When Congress met in 1916, nineteen of its thirty-seven affiliates were British. Five years later, the number of affiliates had risen to forty-two but the number of amalgamateds had fallen to thirteen and they now represented less than a quarter of total membership.[39]

As the ITGWU was the sole representative of labourers in the southern metal trades, the IEIU knew it would have to work closely with it on the industrial front. Relations were strong at the beginning but soon deteriorated when workers defected from one union to the other. The ITUC and republican courts often arbitrated the resultant disputes. Nevertheless, the IEIU thought highly of the Transport Union. In late 1921, it tried to institute a joint council to better coordinate negotiations in companies and sectors where both unions had an interest. Full autonomy would be retained under the plan, which the IEIU believed would help it gain recognition for its card. Talks collapsed because the ITGWU would entertain only one proposition: the IEIU join it as a craft section. Relations between the two deteriorated after that. The Transport Union began to actively encourage IEIU shop stewards to join it, citing the IEIU's financial problems as a reason it should merge with its larger counterpart. ITGWU poaching, especially of the disgruntled Inchicore shopmen, also damaged relations.[40] Fights between the two over who should do what jobs had the same effect. The most intractable of these were rows at the Dublin Steam Shipping Company over who should operate a steam lorry and who should represent fitters at the Waterford gasworks. The fitters had left the ITGWU to join the IEIU, provoking the other gas workers to go on strike. The ITUC had to intervene after the unions could not reach agreement. The Steamship Company issue ended up in the courts and both disputes were ongoing in 1922. While the IEIU won the right to represent the lorry driver, it lost an appeal to keep the Waterford gasfitters who had defected from the ITGWU. Neither union was happy with the result. In March 1922, disgruntled former IEIU men helped to inaugurate the ITGWU's Engineering Section.[41]

The IEIU's close relationship with Sinn Féin and the IRA, which helped it secure recognition from employers, deterred British unions from refusing to work alongside it. At Gallagher's tobacco factory in Dublin, however, an IEIU blacksmith was sacked after pressure from the Blacksmiths' Society. A job was found for him at the Corporation workshop. There, the blacksmiths joined the IEIU when instructed by their British union not to work with him. The IEIU confronted similar attempts at the Dublin Tramway's Inchicore works by threatening to down tools at the Ringsend and Ballsbridge depots.[42] The damage done to the chief victim of the breakaway, the AEU, is gleaned from its annual report for 1920. Britain's largest union had lost its Arklow and Wexford branches, and its prospects in Dublin, Cobh and Cork were 'bad.' Limerick and Passage were 'moderate' and 'fair' respectively, while the position in Ulster and Drogheda was 'good.' By the year's end, the AEU had only 1,762 members outside of Ulster, a loss of 6,300 since May.[43] Nevertheless, Freeland found the union's prospects in Ireland 'reassuring' and was confident that 'matters will continue as heretofore.' He foolishly predicted that the 'Irish Engineering and Foundry Trades Union is foredoomed to failure.'[44] The exodus had de facto partitioned the AEU's Irish membership, which its executive implicitly endorsed in July 1920 when it divided its Irish Organising District into Ulster and the 'rest of Ireland.' Realising its weakness, the southern district pleaded with the executive to reconnect the two, but to no avail.[45]

In August 1921, the IEIU affiliated to the Dublin Workers' Council (DWC), which had broken away from the Dublin Trades Council the previous month. The DWC, to which most unions in Dublin defected, was the result of a split within the ITGWU when O'Brien fell out with P.T. Daly, head of the union's insurance section. Most unions went with O'Brien and joined the more radical DWC. The IEIU probably believed that its interests would be best served by aligning with O'Brien, who had used his position on Dublin Corporation to ensure that the DWC had privileges over its rival. For example, the Corporation recognised the DWC as the tradesmen's sole nominating body to the city's Arbitration Board. As in other Irish centres (such as Cork), trade unionists and Sinn Féiners governed Dublin together in a coalition arrangement.[46]

The IEIU embodied the conflict between class and nation with which Irish labour grappled during the revolution. A clear example was the union's campaign to have public authorities give preference to Irish unions when filling vacancies. In August 1921, the Cork Harbour Board followed the example of Limerick Corporation and instituted this policy. The same resolution had failed to pass Dublin Corporation because of Labour Party objections. The AEU was outraged. It had allies in the ITUC and several trades councils, who believed the policy violated the principle of labour solidarity.[47] At a Cork Trades Council meeting, a Shipwrights' Association delegate denounced the IEIU as a 'destructive body that had sprung up and called itself a trade union.'[48] Relations between both unions had long been poor. The Shipwrights had previously threatened drastic action against those who defected to the IEIU, prompting a counterthreat, 'a practical demonstration of the influence wielded by the IEIU.'[49] The preference dispute even made it to the floor of the 1921 ITUC annual conference:

> A complaint reached us from the Amalgamated Engineering Union … that the Corporation of Limerick had passed a resolution that no skilled mechanic be employed by that body unless he were a member of the Irish Engineering Union… as a Corporation, they were dictating to the workman which of the several recognised trade unions he was to become a member of… This is an attitude which the trade union movement in Ireland has strenuously set its face against … it is not the province of the employer to patronise or give character certificates to one union over another.[50]

It was an implicit criticism of the IEIU. The attacks became explicit the following year when the issue again made the ITUC's agenda. Carr put forward a resolution that Congress should take 'concerted action' to ensure that Irish workers were 'catered for by Irish unions.'[51] He withdrew it following staunch opposition from several delegates.[52] After intense lobbying, the preference resolutions were eventually rescinded.[53] The episode damaged the IEIU's relationship with the ITUC and its British affiliates which may have convinced it to improve relations with its rivals. In September 1921, it tried to reach agreement with the ETU on mutual recognition of cards and transfer of members.[54]

Class conflict, 1920-22

Class conflict climaxed in Ireland in 1919 and 1920. The war years had been conspicuous for the frequency and diversity of the wage movements (as pay claims were called), but by 1919, there was but a single 'wages movement.'[55] Strikes and/or lockouts became a near-daily occurrence as class conflict became extraordinarily diffuse, embroiling everyone from the docker to the doctor. Like the war years, the chief cause of unrest was rampant inflation. Syndicalism gave unions the ideology to be militant and the methodology to succeed. Republican insurrection oxygenated a pugnaciousness that made historic gains for workers. A tremendous synergy existed between labour and the republicans. International unrest also helped to radicalise unions. For example, they widely celebrated the Bolshevik Revolution as a blow to imperialism that would advance the cause of small nations such as Ireland in their struggle for self-determination. Irish syndicalism peaked in February 1919 when Congress demanded the forty-four-hour week for all workers, as well as a 50s. minimum wage and an increase of at least 150 per cent on pre-war rates. Congress also voted to become a single 'Irish Workers' Union' inclusive of all sectors, but this was never put into effect and would have been disastrous for labour unity.[56]

By the IESFTU's foundation in May 1920, Irish wages had nearly peaked. From the outset, the union had to secure improvements for its members, either through direct negotiation or state arbitration. Class conflict was so intense that the British government retained wartime structures to arbitrate disputes. Although it did not recognise their legitimacy, the IESFTU pragmatically utilised these institutions when it stood to gain. In October 1920, it obtained higher rates for iron machinists at the Dublin railways via arbitration under the Ministry of Labour, which had opened an Irish Department in Dublin in July 1919 to mitigate the constant deluge of strikes and lockouts.[57] In December 1920, the IESFTU secured wages of 89s. 6d. for electricians (the 'downtown' fitters' rate) and 64s. 8d. for holders-up at the Midland Great Western's (MGWR) works at Broadstone.[58] Inspired by syndicalism, southern craftsmen set aside their traditional suspicion of labourers and joined with them to secure their bargaining power. The results were spectacular (see Table 17). What is most striking is how much better southerners fared than their Belfast equivalents. Not only was the gap narrowed in many places, but by late 1920 engineering wages were higher in Dublin and Cork than in the northern city. In fact, wages in Irish cities, especially Cork, were above most British centres.[59] In 1919, engineering craftsmen in Cork became the best paid in the Kingdom when they obtained a rate of 80s. a week, an honour they would retain for many years thereafter. In mid-1920, they secured £5 5s., their peak rate, after a successful strike for 25s. The city's shipwrights had their wage fixed at £5 3s. 9½d., also among the best in the UK. At their peak, Cork electricians were on £5. 1s. 10d., coachbuilders 94s. and boilermakers 89s. 6d.[60] Weekly wages for metalworkers in the Dublin building trade reached nearly £5.[61] For the first time since the 1890s, the unions had obtained a significantly shorter week. In most places, the fifty-four-hour week had been sliced to forty-seven, forty-four in Dublin. The shorter week allowed for greater leisure and family time for many working-class families, vastly improving their quality of life. As a measure of the IESTU's success, engineering wages were now considerably above what Cork Corporation had determined to be a living wage: 70s.[62]

With 552 strikes, Ireland accounted for 13.4 per cent of UK stoppages recorded between 1919 and 1921. Militancy among metalworkers during this period can be similarly gauged. Nine per cent of strikes in Ireland were in the metal trades and the country accounted for 6 per cent of UK strike activity in the sectors. During the First World War, Belfast had experienced twice as many metal strikes as Dublin: thirty-eight compared to nineteen.[63] Table 19 shows how syndicalism had made Dublin, not Belfast, the chief centre of Irish craft militancy after the war. It helped the IEIU to secure some major triumphs. One was the first working rule agreement with the Dublin Building Trades' Employers' Association, agreed on 31 March 1922, which fixed an 80s. 8d. wage for a forty-four-hour week. By then, however, the pendulum had swung decidedly in favour of the employers. On top of cutting wages, they used the slump to employ labourers and boys instead of tradesmen to pay below the fixed rate, leaving many IEIU members unemployed. For example, the Corporation denied its shopmen overtime for three years because it was secretly bringing in messenger boys at night to do the work.[64] Three major strikes laid the basis for the union's future woes.

Table 17: Craft wages in Ireland as a percentage higher, 1920 vs. 1913.[65]

Locality	*Fitters*	*Blacksmiths*	*Shipwrights*	*Electricians*
Dublin	148	148	102.5,103	134
Belfast	105	110	98,106	-
Cork	209	192	-	-
Cobh	-	-	124	-
Newry	166	166	119	-
Drogheda	167	150	-	-
Derry	134	-	-	-

Table 18: Irish Engineering Wages & Hours, 1920.[66]

Locality	Turners	Fitters	Smiths	Millwrights	Pattern-makers	Hours
Belfast (including Lisburn)	86s. 3d.	84s. 3d.	84s. 3d.	-	87s.	47 & 48
Newry	85s. 3d.	85s. 3d.	85s. 3d.	85s. 3d.	85s. 3d.	48
Larne	84s. 3d.	84s. 3d.	84s. 3d.	84s. 3d.	-	-
Derry	81s. 6d.	79s. 6d.	-	-	-	-
Drogheda	80s	80s.	80s.	-	-	48
Ballymena	72s.	72s.	72s.	-	-	48

Table 19: Number of Strikes in Ireland by Region and Sector, 1919-21.[67]

Industry	Dublin	Rest of Leinster	Munster	Belfast	Rest of Ulster	Connacht	Several provinces	Ireland
Metals	10	5	6	2	6	-	1	30
Shipbuilding	2	1	4	2	12	-	-	21
Total	**12**	**6**	**10**	**4**	**18**	-	**1**	**51**

The 1920 boilermakers' strike

Via its Railway Executive Committee, the British government had controlled the Irish railway network since December 1916 to aid the war effort. Government control had given railway workers many wage advances to keep industrial peace. In mid-1920, the AEU put in a demand for a leapfrogging increase of 23s. 6d., which was rejected. But boilermakers and blacksmiths at the Dublin railway shops persisted with the claim. The IEIU was initially hostile to the threat of strike. Redmond denounced it as a British ploy to crush his union to help 'the army of occupation and the government to close down all railways in Ireland in reprisal for the fight Irish railway workers were making against handling munitions.' He also claimed that a Scottish general secretary had threatened that the amalgamateds would smash their Irish rival even if it cost them £1,000. Despite the bad blood, the IEIU had succeeded in having its card recognised in London, Liverpool and on the Clyde. Moreover, Redmond described the union's membership and funding situations as 'very satisfactory.'[68]

On 30 August, 150 AEU and IEIU shopmen at the Dublin and Limerick railways downed tools for the 23s. 6d. advance. The numbers eventually swelled to three hundred. The desired wage would make them the best paid metalworkers in the UK. The men already earned more than their English counterparts, who had recently had the same claim rejected by an industrial court. Undoubtedly influenced by this decision, the Irishmen declined arbitration. The strike caused the companies severe financial hardship, forcing the MGWR to give notice to its 3,800 staff. As engines could not be repaired, food could not be transported, leaving provincial Ireland on the brink of starvation. The strike prevented a general resumption of railway services from 22 December when the ITUC called off the munitions embargo after appeals from isolated communities facing economic collapse. On 31 January 1921, the boilermakers returned to work after intervention from the Dublin Lord Mayor. They grudgingly accepted a miserly 1s. 9d. increase granted by an industrial court, having previously rejected its award. Their wage was now 81s. 3d. plus the 12½ per cent bonus.[69] The boilermakers' and munitions' strikes had cost the IEIU over £1,000.[70] The strike crystallised the dilemma facing republican trade unionists: the conflicting politics of nation and class. The REC was aloof throughout, and the strike was not supported by the ITUC which had declared that sectional action should not take place until the munitions embargo was over. The stoppage led to internal divisions between the IEIU leadership and branch militants. Patrick O'Hagan argued that when 'members take the reins into their own hands, they should not be paid benefits' and that the NEC should have 'the courage to stand out against the men.'[71] More significant, however, was strike's broader implication which would soon afflict all Irish workers. The railway managers had held out for five months and won a great victory, illustrating how employer attitudes were hardening as the recession deepened.

Table 20: Metal & Shipbuilding Wages in Dublin and Belfast, 1920.[72]

Craft	Dublin	Belfast
Shipwrights	82s., 84s. 6d.	83s. 6d., 85s. 9d.
Ship plumbers	86s. 2d., 88s. 5d.	85s. 10d., 87s. 10d.
Ship joiners	-	83s. 3d.
Ship painters	-	83s. 3d.
Iron founders	83s.	82s. 6d., 84s. 6d., 86s. 6d.
Patternmakers	81s. 6d.	87s. 3d.
Brass moulders	82s. 3d.	85s. 3d., 89s. 3d.
Brass finishers	82s. 3d.	84s. 3d.
Coppersmiths	78s.	-

The 1921 engineering strike

The union's next major strike was one of the most significant in its history. On 27 July 1921, the Engineering Employers' Federation announced a 6s. reduction and the elimination of the 12.5 per cent bonus for Irish engineers.[73] The timing is noteworthy because the cessation of hostilities between the IRA and Crown Forces allowed employers to embark upon their counterattack. Employers would not accept localised negotiations because of the 'unsettled political situation' in Ireland. Those who had been open to localised talks had been superseded by hardliners inspired by events in Britain on 15 April 1921. That day, Britain's 'Triple Alliance' of the Miners' Federation, the NUR and the National Transport Workers' Federation collapsed when the latter two refused to strike against wage cuts in the mines, leaving the miners to fend for themselves. A general assault on British wages followed, emboldening Irish employers to do the same. Whereas many engineering workers juggled their commitments to the national and industrial struggles, their bosses had no such problem. They told Redmond that until the political question was settled, they considered Dublin 'an integral part of the United Kingdom.' Employers in Cork and other centres soon followed suit.[74] This went to the core of the dispute: the IEIU considered Ireland a distinct country with a distinct economy which necessitated a separate agreement. It opted to liaise with the ITGWU in adopting a strategy for dealing with the employers' offensive in areas engineering and other areas. On 2 August, the IEIU called out its Dublin members. It was joined by the AEU, the Boilermakers, National Union of Foundry Workers (NUFW), the Patternmakers' Association and the ITGWU, bringing numbers to almost seven hundred. The dispute could not have come at a worst time financially for the IEIU, which could only issue strike pay to paid up members. Nonetheless, the dispute was a defining moment for the IEIU because it crystallised the benefits of independence from the amalgameds. These unions had been placed in an awkward position because their executives had already accepted reductions in Britain. Nonetheless, their Irish shop stewards vowed to unofficially support the strike.[75]

The ITUC pledged unconditional support for the men. Congress executives knew that the strike's ramifications would be profound. Victory would galvanise all workers to resist the counterattack on wages and force concessions; defeat would embolden employers not to give an inch. Small businessmen still felt inhibited by the political instability and looked to large employers, like engineering firms, for inspiration. Employers in the flour mills, railways, fertiliser industries and shipping and carrying trades also wanted to cut pay.[76] Though the metal unions presented a united front, tensions ran high behind the scenes. The Dublin Dockyard, where the amalgamateds were strongest, was not part of the strike even though IEIU drillers took industrial action there. Despite being in a perilous financial state, the IEIU established a £60 emergency float after complaints that it had not anticipated the widespread hardship the strike had caused. The REC was divided on how to conduct the stoppage and the strike committee, with Redmond as secretary, was blasted by some.[77] The criticisms were not unmerited. On 22 October, the strike ended in a resounding victory for the employers. The union assented to the full reduction, although there would be no victimisation.[78] Corkmen would suffer an additional 5s. cut from December.[79] The strike had cost the cash-strapped union over £1,600. Though it had fought much harder than its British counterparts, the IEIU's failure to secure workplace bargaining was a major and consequential setback. Pay cuts soon followed at the Irish Glass Bottle Company, the Port and Docks Board and in the motor, building, plumbing and hardware trades, many of which took effect in January 1922.[80]

A sensational event occurred in Drogheda during the engineering strike, illuminating the tension between the IEIU rank-and-file and the leadership. On 14 September, strikers seized the town foundry and declared a 'soviet' – a worker-managed enterprise. After the men had restarted production and announced plans for further seizures in Drogheda and Dublin, the police compelled them to hand back the property after only a few hours and without resistance.[81] Soviets were one of the era's defining features, the most salient representation of labour's syndicalist swagger. Conor Kostick estimates that over a hundred soviets materialised in Ireland between 1919 and 1920.[82] After the Limerick Soviet against British militarism – when the local trades council seized control of the city – tactics of workplace occupations were applied to the industrial struggle.[83] Soviets functioned as radical auxiliaries to the wages movement but did not threaten official strategy. They were strike tactics of last resort for a favourable settlement. Labour officials opposed soviets because they were clearly illegal and left unions open to criminal charges and civil damages. The IEIU executive had no intention of supporting, much less directing and spreading, the Drogheda soviet. As Yeates put it, 'the IEIU was in the business of defending members' pay and conditions, not seizing state power.'[84]

To employers, the proliferation of soviets was irrefutable proof that labour had become irredeemably Bolshevist and was now attacking the very basis of capitalism. Feeling isolated, they were horrified by the government's inability to crack down on soviets and other manifestations of labour lawbreaking. Wartime state intervention had reinvigorated employer federations and had hardened their attitudes; the growth of trade unionism had a similar effect. In March 1919, employers from across Ireland had met in Dublin and launched the Irish Associated Employers, the progenitor of the Irish Business and Employers' Confederation. As its founders explicitly stated, the new federation was a direct response to labour militancy. Its goals were to secure government recognition, to counter labour and to combat socialism and nationalisation. Though most employers grudgingly recognised unions by then, they remained implacably opposed to direct action.[85] In 1923, a Cork employer even publicly lamented that there was no Irish Mussolini to punish labour for its flirtations with Bolshevism.[86]

Table 21: Irish Engineering Wages & Hours, December 1921.[87]

City	Fitters & Turners	Blacksmiths	Iron Moulders	Hours
Dublin	83s. 3d.	83s. 3d.	83s. 3d.	47
Cork	94s.	94s.	94s.	47
Waterford	65s. to 70s.	68s.	75s.	50
Limerick	92s. 6d.	92s. 6d.	92s. 6d.	47

The 1921 railway strike and unrest at Inchicore

By autumn 1921, the IEIU was under attack from all quarters. On 15 August, the Irish railway companies announced their own 6s. decrease and abolition of the 12.5 per cent bonus for shopmen. This followed on from the British government's relinquishing control of the Irish railway network. The companies had been receiving subsidies to pay higher wages and operate an eight-hour day to maintain industrial peace. But the new arrangement had not altered the employers' attitudes. As Redmond observed, 'the reason put forward by the managers for reductions was that they must look after dividends for shareholders, but they didn't give a damn about the men who made the dividends.'[88] Here too, the unions put up a united front in public but were hamstrung by internal feuding. The AEU broke ranks and accepted the reductions, further harming relations between it and the IEIU. While Northerners assented to cuts, the syndicalist influence emboldened southerners to fight.[89] The *Irish Independent* correctly reported that the IEIU did not want a strike.[90] The Irish union was teetering on the brink of bankruptcy and could not afford another prolonged stoppage; it pushed for arbitration instead. On 19 September, 1,600 shopmen at Inchicore, Broadstone and Grand Canal Street (the Dublin and South Eastern Railway works) went out. The sudden halting of railway traffic paralysed the economy. Robert Barton, Minister for Economic Affairs, successfully arbitrated the dispute, leading the Broadstone and Grand Canal Street men to resume work after seven days. The conference ratified the 6s. cut from 17 September, not 15 August. The IEIU did not attend the conference due to a communication breakdown. Employers exploited its non-attendance to withhold the application of the modified agreement to its members. With the reduction now a reality, the GSWR men ended their stoppage. As its shop was in Dundalk and therefore subject to the higher Belfast district rate, the GNR was unaffected by the settlement.[91]

The outcome was deeply unpopular. Many IEIU members, especially in Inchicore, felt that they had been roped into a settlement. A mass meeting between them and representatives of the executive in the Banba Hall on 18 September was highly acrimonious. The men had already rejected arbitration by 273 votes to 222 but failed to secure the required two-thirds majority and so the minority view passed. They ignored the result and picketed Broadstone, which the executive deplored. Like most unions, the IEIU took a hard-line against unofficial action on the ground. Afterwards, a deputation told the REC that a determined effort was under way to split the union and set up a new body for railway shopmen. To avert this scenario, the delegation advised that Inchicore be given more autonomy over its affairs. In response, the REC offered to support Inchicore being given a similar level of autonomy as the provincial branches on condition that it accept union rules, including fines and other penalties. This could not happen until the next NEC meeting (only the NEC could grant this). But this was not enough for the GSWR men, who wanted one of the four Dublin seats on the NEC. While the REC was anxious for harmony, it would not sacrifice discipline and was keen to assert its authority. Representatives of other branches and sections, already alienated by the men's behaviour, considered it unfair that Inchicore receive preferential treatment. A provincial delegate told Dubliners that 'reductions at the present time were inevitable' and that the shopmen would be 'attempting the impossible' were they to strike'; in the process, they would 'ruin the future of the union.'[92]

The situation was so bad that Redmond suggested that the REC consider collectively resigning over the crisis. In its defence, the REC was in an unenviable position, having to balance the desire for more local autonomy with the danger of fragmentation. It was determined to keep the fractured union together and rejected a motion to expel the Inchicore men. Nevertheless, it 'strongly condemned' their 'illegal strike' and denied them strike and unemployment pay. It also fined some of the picketers for intimidation of members and suspended Joseph Quinn – Inchicore's representative on the REC and the leader of the dissidents – as general treasurer. Within a week, the REC had learned from a loyal member at the GSWR that the dissidents had refused its offer and would no longer forward contributions or recognise the NEC. The NEC would later agree to give them provincial branch status but not representation on the REC or NEC, which would have given Inchicore disproportionate influence at national level. Even though they faced expulsion, the men continued their push for full representation on both the REC and NEC, as other provincial branches had. The REC decided not to issue cards or pay benefits to the dissidents.[93]

The affair demonstrates the difficulty of organising craftsmen across different industries in one union. 'Ironically … relations between the warring sections had often been better when they were represented by separate unions.'[94] It was also not the first instance of Inchicore's rebelliousness. Shortly beforehand, iron moulders there had objected to their shop steward being a brass moulder. Some refused to show him their union cards and made a point of paying their contributions at Gardiner Row rather than give them to him.[95] At the heart of the railway dispute was the Inchicore men's belief that they had not received the same level of support as had their colleagues in the general shops. They had a point. For example, strike pay was only issued after the AEU began promising benefits to anyone who defected. The REC believed that the engineering shops were in a better financial position than the railways and could afford to continue to pay existing rates, or at least inflict less stringent cuts. Plus, there were more engineering than railway companies and their economic circumstances varied more drastically. Accordingly, the union sought local bargaining on cuts rather than total opposition to them; this it tried, but failed, to explain to the Inchicore men.[96] The episode laid the basis for the first major split in the IEIU.

But even this cloud had a silver lining. The shops of three Cork railways – the

Bandon, the Muskerry and the Macroom – were not a party to the national settlement and cuts were imposed without negotiation. Strikes broke out in October and November as a result. Unhappy with the support from their British unions, shopmen came out in sympathy and promised to join the IEIU; to not be a financial burden, they would join after the dispute. In October, a Cork NUR branch came over; subsequently, members of the National Union of Vehicle Builders and the Associated Society of Locomotive Engineers and Firemen also defected. The AEU's acceptance of the reduction had lost it much support in Cork – and the IEIU Cork branch sought to take full advantage. It asked the NEC to authorise a withdrawal of labour on the GSWR to damage the AEU (and other British unions) and recruit the disillusioned shopmen. The NEC refused because doing so would involve Inchicore where wounds were still raw. The Cork branch grew from 320 to 358 because of its stance. In December, Dáil-sponsored arbitration removed the 12.5 per cent bonus but reinstated the 6s. It was a great victory at a time when unions were very much in retreat. The Cork success was also due to Redmond, who had visited the city to aid recruitment. It was his last great service to the union he had been instrumental in founding. He resigned in October because he was about to start a business and felt that there would be a conflict of interests if an employer was president of a trade union. His union's finances were so bad at the time of his departure that it could not afford to give him a testimonial. Slater became president on a temporary basis before Toomey took over in June 1922. James Byrne replaced Toomey as assistant general secretary.[97]

The first financial crisis

The mortgage for Gardiner Row and the cost of supporting strikes were major reasons for the financial crisis that rocked the IEIU from mid-1921 to early 1922. By July 1921, debts topped £3,500. By the year's end, the union owed the National Land Bank over £3,100 and could not afford to cover the funeral costs of members who had died. In a particularly distressing case, the REC did not even have £10 due to the wife of a Guinness worker who had died from tuberculosis of the larynx. Though Redmond believed that the situation was not 'hopeless,' he regarded it as 'extremely critical' and a threat to the union's very existence. Dubliners had their weekly contributions raised by 1s. Funds were also raised by upping rent on tenants and collecting from those in arrears. The latter included the Dublin Brigade, the James Connolly Labour College (whose rent was 12s. a week) and Hampton Leedon Ltd. (the worst offender).[98] The REC held bingo nights (later dropped after they began making a loss) and halted benefits to unemployed members and those interned by the authorities. The union's support for the James Connolly Labour College is symptomatic of the syndicalist influence, which championed a proletarian counterculture to replace the perceived decadence of capitalist society.[99] The situation was so bad that the union considered applying for a bar licence from the Dáil's Ministry for Home Affairs. At the height of the crisis in October, the REC had only £50 on hand to pay for current expenses of £303. On New Year's Day 1922, members met to discuss the crisis. Redmond agreed to chair the proceedings in the absence of an elected successor. Members agreed to up weekly contributions to 2s. 6d. and to impose levies ranging from 10s. to £10. The generous response is especially noteworthy considering that officials could not give a proper financial report because Quinn was refusing to hand over the books. The executive's case was aided by the fact that shopmen at other railways strongly opposed Quinn's group. The meeting ended with a demand for the nationalisation of the railways, which was forwarded to the ITUC.[100]

The sacrifices yielded results. By late January, the IEIU had a balance of £579 as against outstanding debts of £434.[101] 'It was an outstanding performance for a small, new-born union ... in the midst of economic recession.'[102] In a burst of extravagance, the executive allowed McIntyre to put down linoleum in his office and decided to organise a collection for the Dublin Destitute Children's Committee. More significantly, stronger finances allowed the appointment of a southern organiser – Cork NEC representative Patrick Fitzgerald – in February on a trial basis for 80s. a week. He had declined a wage of £5. Even though Fitzgerald had enrolled thirty members into the Cork branch and brought the union to Bandon, the NEC discontinued his position from 29 April 1922 because funds remained tight. The economic downturn had resulted in unemployment in the engineering industry running at over 20 per cent by early 1922, leading thousands of ordinary members across the country to turn to the REC to save them from destitution. The REC decided to only pay benefit to members who could prove they were unemployed due to victimisation for trade union activity. Not only did it refuse the application of a member in Clonmel seeking assistance because he had been 'on the run', but it decreed that being on the run did not constitute victimisation or prevent a member from taking up work.[103] The executive had taken pay cuts and Redmond had worked without a wage, but most of the credit for resolving the crisis must go to the rank-and-file, whose sacrifices ensured the union's survival. But the railway shopmen had rejected the cuts in benefits, resulting in a flow of defections to the NUR and ITGWU whose weekly contributions were much lower. Both accepted the shopmen even though they were in arrears. The anomaly of the defectors joining a British (NUR) or a general union (ITGWU) reflects the internal divisions within the IEIU that would subsequently cripple it.[104]

The IEIU and the War of Independence

The establishment of an Irish craft union was but one outcome of separatist sentiment and disillusion with British unions. Between 1917 and 1923, eleven Irish unions were founded as breakaways, with four adopting an industrial union structure. The rise of Irish unions shifted labour's centre of gravity from Belfast to Dublin.[105] Many trade unionists were also active republicans, an interaction that accentuated radical impulses and pushed labour to the left. Republicans forced labour to consider the issue of state power for the first time, politicising it as never before. Sinn Féin's parallel administration demonstrated to labour the political nature of the state, something especially apparent in revolutionary times. Labour's political rhetoric evolved from militant trade unionist to social democratic and finally to revolutionary. It began to champion vague concepts of a 'workers' republic' and/or a 'co-operative commonwealth' as alternatives to the capitalist state, even if it never properly defined them. Its radicalisation and the consolidation of the republican consensus had made Labour an open though unofficial ally of Sinn Féin. Direct action from unions helped to consolidate the revolution. Sinn Féin never sought labour's support but nonetheless received it. By the Truce, Irish labour was stronger and more socialist and republican than ever before.[106]

Republicanism permeated the IEIU at every level. In both ideology and membership, it was much closer to Sinn Féin than to the Labour Party, which craftsmen widely regarded as representing labourers and the low-paid. At least four of those on the union executive were or had been Sinn Féin members, including Leahy, a socialist who saw Sinn Féin as the vanguard party of the Irish revolution.[107] Even the union's caretaker, Thomas Hannigan, was an IRB and IRA man, having gotten the job in January 1921 through Dick McKee, Commandant of the Dublin Brigade. A Volunteer since 1913, Hannigan had been sacked as a MGWR clerk for participating in the Rising and had been evicted from his house, which his employer owned. He was not the only one to suffer victimisation. The GSWR, one of Ireland's largest employers with nine thousand workers, had a long history of hostility to trade unionism and anything resembling radical politics. It sacked some of its employees for participating in the Rising and, despite years of agitation by their families, never rehired them. The Dublin and South Eastern Railway rewarded those who worked as normal during the Rising with bonuses.[108]

Hannigan served with B Coy., 1st Batt. during the War of Independence with whom he mobilised after Bloody Sunday in November 1920. He lived at 6 Gardiners Row from 1920 until his death in 1957. But there was more to his role than maintaining the premises. Traynor deputed him as a 'warning scout' who would stand for hours at the entrance by a hidden buzzer and sound the alarm in the event of a raid, giving the staff time to hide all traces of their work. Hannigan was also tasked with vetting strangers before they could contact IRA men.[109] The *Irish Press* subsequently claimed that the 'Engineers' Hall' was one of the IRA's best guarded secret meeting places and that the British never raided it throughout the War of Independence, although the National Army did so incessantly during the War Civil. Subsequent testimony from Dublin Brigade members does not support this assertion.[110] The IEIU had a martyr, one of the Forgotten Ten, in Thomas Bryan, a twenty-two-year-old electrician hanged with nine other Volunteers on 14 March 1921. Bryan had been captured after an abortive attempt to ambush an Auxiliary patrol near Tolka Bridge in Drumcondra on 21 January 1921. He was barely out of his apprenticeship with Hanley & Robinson electrical contractors when he was recruited to the ASU. He had served with Na Fianna Éireann in 1916 and had gone on hunger strike with Thomas Ashe in 1917.[111] The ITUC and the two Dublin trades councils called a half-day general strike in the city to protest the hangings. Another example of the IEIU's republicanism came in September 1921 when the REC received an income tax bill from the authorities. It referred the letter to the Dáil.[112]

Bryan personified where his union had succeeded. At its second meeting, the provisional committee decided to admit apprentices, who they were especially eager to enrol, on the same terms as journeymen. It was an important decision. The IEIU proved especially successful in organising apprentices, a major reason for its growth. Apprentices were typically more radical and more likely to become Volunteers than journeymen; many were active in Na Fianna, whose members typically came from skilled working-class or lower middle-class backgrounds. Leahy later testified that nearly all apprentices in Dublin were in the Volunteers or Sinn Féin.[113] The Irish Revolution was a revolution of the young and apprentices were prominent in many IRA brigades. In Cork, at least one-third of IRA members were tradesmen, with building workers and motor drivers conspicuous. In particular, the trades of the city's Ford's factory became a hotbed of militant separatism.[114] Upper-middle- or upper-class men rarely joined the IRA; neither did general labourers or the unemployed, even though they strongly supported it.[115] Tradesmen were even more prominent among IRA officers, who primarily consisted of 'the upwardly mobile members of the skilled working class, white-collar workers and lower professions among whom the IRB was based.'[116] The close relationship between the Dublin Brigade and the craft unions reflected the enduring legacy of the Fenian tradition in the city. Both the Labour Board and the IEIU were often used as fronts to recruit for the IRA. The union badge was specifically designed as a way for volunteers to covertly recognise each other unbeknownst to the authorities. As a result, some of those who wore it were not union members or even trade unionists.[117]

The IEIU also actively supported labour's last major action for the Republic, the most audacious and effective to date: the refusal of dockers and railwaymen to carry British munitions or army personnel. Beginning on 24 May 1920, the stoppage was inspired by British dockers' refusal to load the *Jolly Roger* with weapons destined for Poland (then at war with Bolshevik Russia). On 21 December, with funds stretched and over five hundred railwaymen sacked, the NUR ended the embargo.[118] The ASE executive once again repudiated what it considered a political action. Its Cork branch was accused of scabbing by the city's trades council for repairing military vehicles at Victoria (now Collins) Barracks.[119] In contrast, the IEIU contributed generously to the Munitions of War Fund, helping to sustain a strike that seriously harmed British counterinsurgency efforts.[120] The Anglo-Irish Truce of July 1921 was a relief to the union. For Sinn Féin, labour had served its purpose and there was no longer a need for cross-class, national unity. The result was a breakdown in the republican-labour alliance and the re-emergence of unrest. As the Royal Irish Constabulary (RIC) noted in October 1921, 'the Labour Party are not so much interested in Sinn Féin as heretofore; their attitude towards it has changed considerably.'[121]

The IEIU and the North

Though the IEIU still had no Ulster branches by late 1920, it had maintained links with northern labour. On 7 November, it hosted James Baird, one of Belfast's most famous trade unionists, who addressed a mass meeting of the union's Dublin membership. An Ulster Protestant, a Boilermakers' Society organiser and a socialist republican to boot, Baird denounced Irish representatives on British union executives as 'Carsonites from Belfast who acted as their Carsonite unionism was concerned.' He believed that the sooner all Irish craftsmen, north and south, were in one union the better, because 'the religious bogey was stirred up to divide the workers.'[122] In November 1921, the IEIU deferred a previous decision to form a Belfast branch because poor finances meant that the timing was 'hardly opportune.'[123] The addition of Belfast would have added to its existing branches in Dublin, Cork, Dundalk, Drogheda, Cobh, Passage West, Limerick, Wicklow, Galway, Sligo and Wexford.[124] Despite its lack of presence in Ulster, events there would soon impact the IEIU.

By late 1921, Dublin foundrymen had adopted a policy of refusing union cards to, or working with, non-IEIU members. The aim was to ensure that employers recruited locally. It was a policy fraught with pitfalls and eventually sparked a lockout in the foundries when a Belfast man, a Catholic victim of Orange pogroms, was given a job at Ross and Walpole. The firm agreed to take him after meeting the Belfast Victims' Committee. He was an NUFW member and, though he was willing to join the IEIU, local men refused to work with him. They wanted the job to go to a Dubliner who, ironically, was also an NUFW member. The REC backed the men and even appealed for Dáil intervention, a foolish move given that the Dáil was the chief sponsor of the Belfast Victims' Committee.[125] Besides, Sinn Féin was socially and economically conservative and therefore unwilling to threaten private property or the economic status quo. The party's social composition may explain why: even though only ten per cent of the general population came from the commercial and professional classes, these groups made up 65 per cent of the First Dáil and 58 per cent of the Second Dáil.[126]

McIntyre correctly believed that the lockout had injured the union's prospects of organising north of Dundalk. Regardless, it stood no chance of establishing a northern base because the sectarian barrier was too strong for an overtly republican organisation to overcome, especially in these tumultuous times. The amalgamateds never lost their foothold in Ulster, even among nationalists. What was remarkable about northern trade unionism is how little, not how much, it was coloured by sectarianism.

> Ulster had a fractured society, tormented by religion and politics ... These diversities were pressed together into a single economy with ... mixed workforces... people coped with the density of difference by compartmentalising their mentalities and adjusting the response code in each. That learned behaviour made it easier to detach the trade unions from sectarianism, though the separation could never be complete. In a society in which religion mattered ubiquitously, including in the workplace and the unions themselves, sectarianism invariably curbed solidarity... behaviour was determined simply by an instinct for survival.[127]

Eighty per cent of trade unionists in the six counties belonged to British, 15 per cent to local and 5 per cent to Dublin-based unions.[128] Efforts to avoid sectarian splits detached the amalgamateds from politics, ensuring that militancy was less likely to mature into radicalism in the north than in the south or Britain. It was enough for them that nationalists and unionists could unite on wages and conditions. 'With one economy and so many mixed workforces ... solidarity was not only the norm, it was an operational necessity.'[129] Irish unions like the IEIU were too tainted by their 'Fenianism' to compete and unionism was too conservative an ideology to produce a labour movement of worth. The leaders of the 'apolitical' British unions offered an enduring resolution to the sectarian conundrum that their republican or loyalist counterparts could not: wage militancy while conveniently avoiding the Ulster question. This strategy was especially attractive to unionists, but it was enough for most nationalists too. Some left-wing radicals recognised the Ulster Protestant's ability to be simultaneously wage militant and politically conservative. They were convinced that Protestants could only be won over to the Republic if it were a workers' republic: only socialism could transform class consciousness into class unity and anti-imperialism.[130] But their argument failed to see the rational basis for cross-class Protestant homogeneity. In the short-term, Protestants did better by embracing sectarian (rather than class) politics as it maintained an economic dominance over Catholics that reinforced a psychological feeling of communal superiority. British unions were willing to uphold this inequality. The result was a tenuous unity across the sectarian divide masked by the veneer of class rhetoric – a provincial, insular movement whose foremost goal was to track cross-channel wages.[131] Like all unions in the Free State, the IEIU fared only marginally better for the rest of the decade.

Chapter Notes and References

1   Leahy, WS 660, BMH, pp. 36-38.
2   IESFTU Provisional Executive Committee (PEC) minutes, 10, 11 May, 1 June 1920; Redmond to Markievicz, 18 May 1920, DE 2/116, Dáil Éireann collection, NAI. The IESFTU's inaction may have been influenced by the nature of the strike: the ITGWU had refused to work with the ETU. The IESFTU would not have wanted to perturb the ITGWU so early in its existence.
3   Cited in Yeates, 'Craft workers during the Irish Revolution', p. 41.
4   Yeates, *Craft Workers*, p. 11.
5   Minutes of the openings of the Wexford, Limerick, Enniscorthy and Dundalk branches, 20, 21, 26 May, 2 June 1920; *Wicklow People*, 29 May 1920; *Limerick Leader*, 2 June, 12 July 1920.
6   Rooney helped to start the branch with funds given to him by Dick Stokes who, Rooney believed, received it from Collins. See Rooney, MSP Application, MA.
7   IESFTU PEC minutes, 11, 15 May, 1 July 1920; *Freeman's Journal* 5 July 1920; *Drogheda Independent*, 7 Aug. 1920; *Cork Examiner*, 10 Aug. 1920. Seán Mac Eoin, commandant of the 1st Battalion of the Longford Brigade, made Christopher Burke officer in command of the IRA Arsenal at Bailieborough, County Cavan.
8   The local general strikes took place on 24 August, 22 September and 15 October. See *Cork Examiner*, 25 Aug., 23 Sept, 16, 29 Oct. 1920.
9   *Forward*, 9 Oct. 1920.
10 'Sworn statement made before advisory committee by Luke Kennedy, 10 Dec. 1937', MSP Application, MA, p. 8; IESFTU PEC minutes, 16, 22 Nov. 1920; Sarah Ward-Perkins, *Select Guide to Trade Union Records: With Details of Unions Operating in Ireland to 1970* (Dublin: Irish Manuscripts Commission, 1996), p. 201; Yeates, *Craft Workers*, p. 17; *Meath Herald and Cavan Advertiser*, 31 July 1920.
11 Sown statement, Farrelly, MSP Application, MA.
12 IESFTU PEC minutes, 4, 6, 18, 19, 21, 26 June, 7 July 1920.
13 Devine, 'Division, Disillusion and Dissolution', p. 31; IEIU REC minutes, 5, 7 Sept., 24 Oct. 1921. See also IADAMU management committee minutes, 11 Feb. 1920-13 Dec. 1922, Ms. 7,302, NLI. Having been in decline since the motor permits' strike, the IADAMU joined the ITGWU in late 1922.
14 IESFTU PEC minutes, 11 Aug. 1920.
15 ITUC, *Twenty-sixth annual report*, 1920, p. 147.
16 Yeates, *Craft Workers*, p. 13; IESFTU PEC minutes, 29 May 1920.
17 John Lloyd, *Light & Liberty: The History of the EETPU* (London: Weidenfeld & Nicolson, 1990), pp. 155-156.
18 *Irish Independent*, 30 Aug., 7 Oct., 13 Nov. 1920, 5, 12, 26 Mar. 1921. A 1921 union document says it consists of the following trades: 'boilermakers, engineers, shipwrights, blacksmiths, electricians, iron and brass moulders, brass finishers, plumbers, iron machinists, patternmakers and iron dressers, stationary engine drivers, coppersmiths, whitesmiths, vehicle workers, etc.' The union had a few different names in its early years. For brevity's sake, from this point it will be referred to as the IEIU.
19 Yeates, *Craft Workers*, p. 21.
20 Maguire, sworn statement, MA.
21 This was a local union, not a branch of the Irish Stationary Engine Drivers' Society. See Limerick Stationary Engine Drivers' and Firemen's Society minutes, 7 Sept. 1919, 15 Aug., 26 Sept. 1920, 23 Jan., 17 Apr. 1921, TU/98/40/1, NAI.
22 Ibid., p. 22.
23 IESFTU/IEIU minutes, 1920-22.
24 The executive had originally proposed that the No. 1 Branch meet at 41 Parnell Square; No. 2 meet somewhere at Inchicore; No. 3 meet at Colmcille Hall, where the office for unemployed members seeking positions was; No. 4 meet at Oriel Hall; and No. 5 meet at Great Brunswick (now Pearse) Street. All these places had strong connections to the republican movement. See Yeates, *A City in Turmoil*, pp. 307-308.

25 In response, the Dáil initiated the Belfast Boycott, an embargo on goods coming from the city co-ordinated by the Department of Labour and backed by the ITUC. See Kevin Johnstone, *In The Shadows of Giants: A Social History of the Belfast Shipyards* (Dublin: Gill & Macmillan, 2008), pp. 199-203; and D.S. Johnson, 'The Belfast boycott, 1920-1922', in J.M. Goldstrom and L.A. Clarkson (eds.), *Irish population, economy, and society: essays in honour of the late K.H. Connell* (Oxford: Oxford University Press, 1981), pp. 287-307.

26 Yeates, *Craft Workers*, pp. 13-16; Yeates, *A City in Turmoil*, pp. 144-145. James O'Connor also worked for Sinn Féin.

27 Yeates, *A City in Turmoil*, p. 267.

28 Sown statement made before advisory committee by Christopher Farrelly, 15 May 1936, Military Pension Application, MA.

29 'Sworn statement made by Joseph Murray before Advisory Committee, 13 Dec. 1935, Joseph Murray, MSP Application, MSP34REF1403, MA.

30 Ibid., p. 15; Harry Colley, WS, 1687, BMH, MA, p. 71; Yeates, *A City in Turmoil*, p. 144. The Squad was an IRA united Collins established in 1919 to assassinate G Division detectives.

31 *Forward*, 18 Sept., 9 Oct. 1920; Yeates, *A City in Civil War*, p. 9; Leahy, WS 660, BMH, p. 36.

32 *Irish Independent*, 7 June 1920.

33 Ibid.

34 IESFTU Engineering Section minutes, 5 June 1920.

35 *Watchword of Labour*, 19 June 1920.

36 Yeates, *A City in Civil War*, p. 19.

37 Martin Maguire, 'A socio-economic analysis of the Dublin Protestant working class, 1870-1926', *Irish Economic and Social History*, Vol. 20, 1993, pp. 35-61; Martin Maguire, 'The Church of Ireland and the problem of the Protestant working class of Dublin, 1870s-1930s', in Alan Ford, James McGuire & Kenneth Milne (eds.) *As by Law Established: The Church of Ireland since the Reformation* (Dublin: Lilliput Press, 1995), pp. 195-203..

38 Leahy, WS 660, BMH, p. 38; 'Sworn statement made before advisory committee by Luke Kennedy, 10 Dec. 1937', Military Service Pension Application, MA.

39 Francis Devine, *Organising History: A Centenary of SIPTU, 1909-2009* (Dublin: Gill & Macmillan, 2009), p. 93; O'Connor, 'Colonisation and Mental Colonisation', p. 34.

40 Devine, *Organising History*, pp. 106-107. ITGWU poaching of brass finishers in Dublin enraged the IEIU. See IEIU REC minutes, 5 Apr. 1922; and IEIU NEC minutes, 21 Apr. 1922.

41 IEIU REC minutes, 8 Aug.-7 Dec. 1921; *Cork Examiner*, 5 Sept. 1921; *Irish Independent*, 29 Mar. 1922; Yeates, *Craft Workers*, pp. 22, 48.

42 Yeates, *Craft Workers*, pp. 11-12.

43 Cited in Ibid., p. 12.

44 Ibid.

45 Keith Harding, 'The Irish Issue in The British Labour Movement, 1900-1922' (University of Sussex: PhD, 1983), pp. 188-189

46 *Evening Herald*, 18 July 1921; Seamus Cody, John O'Dowd & Peter Rigney, *The parliament of labour: 100 years of the Dublin Council of Trade Unions* (Dublin: Dublin Council of Trade Unions, 1986), pp. 134-138; Yeates, *Craft Workers*, pp. 22-23; Conor McCabe, 'The Irish Labour Party and the 1920 local elections, *Saothar*, no. 35, 2010, pp. 7-20.

47 Thomas Crean, 'The Labour Movement in Kerry and Limerick, 1914-21', (TCD: PhD, 1994), pp. 237-238. The IEIU tried, and failed, to get Cork Corporation to adopt the same policy as the Harbour Board.

48 *Cork Examiner*, 7 Jan. 1922. The IEIU affiliated to the Cork Trades Council in May 1922. See *Cork Examiner*, 13 May 1922.

49 Cited in Yeates, *Craft Workers*, p. 21.

50 ITUC, *Report of twenty-seventh annual meeting*, 1921, ILHM, pp. 20-21.

51 ITUC, *Report of the twenty-eighth annual meeting*, 1922, ILHM, p. 239.

52 Ibid., pp. 239-243.

53 IEIU REC minutes, 22 July 1921; *Cork Examiner*, 30 Aug., 10 Nov. 1921, 13 May 1922.

54 Yeates, *Craft Workers*, p. 23.

55 O'Connor, *2: Larkinism and syndicalism*, p. 33.

56 ITUC, *Twenty-fifth annual report*, 1919, pp. 44-45; *Freeman's Journal*, 10 Feb. 1919; O'Connor, 'Colonisation and Mental Colonisation', p. 35.

57 See *Report on conciliation and arbitration, being particulars of proceedings under the Industrial*

Courts Act, 1919 [including the Wages (Temporary Regulation) Acts, as amended], the Conciliation Act, 1896, and the Restoration of Pre-War Practices Act, 1919, 1921, 185, XIV, UKPP, pp. 76, 77. In 1916, with industrial disputes spreading rapidly across Britain, the Ministry of Labour was carved out of the Board of Trade's Labour Department.

58 *Freeman's Journal,* 18, 22 Dec. 1920. These wages include a war bonus of 26s. 6d.

59 *Standard time rates of wages in the United Kingdom at 1st October, 1913,* 1914, Cd. 7194, LXXX; and *Standard time rates of wages and hours of labour in the United Kingdom at 31st December, 1920,* 1921, Cd. 1253, UKPP.

60 *Cork Examiner,* 9 July 1919, 3 June, 15 July 1920; *Workmen's Register,* 1913-24, BL/BC/MB/334, Murphy's brewery collection, University College Cork Archives.

61 By mid-1920, weekly wages in the Dublin building trade were 89s. 10d. for heating engineers, 92s. 7d. for gasfitters and brass founders and finishers, 96s. 3d. for electricians and 99s. for sheet metal workers. See *Labour Gazette,* Jan., June 1920.

62 *Watchword of Labour,* 2 Oct. 1920.

63 Fitzpatrick, 'Strikes in Ireland', pp. 36-37.

64 Yeates, *Craft Workers,* pp. 13, 19. The Dublin Building Trades Employers' Association was the predecessor of the National Joint Industrial Council for the electrical contracting industry.

65 *Standard time rates of wages in the United Kingdom at 1st October, 1913,* UKPP; ibid. Where two rates are given, the lower rate is for new work and the higher one for repair work.

66 *Standard time rates of wages and hours of labour in the United Kingdom at 31st December, 1920,* UKPP, p. 40.

67 Fitzpatrick, 'Strikes in Ireland', p. 37.

68 *Irish Independent,* 30 Aug. 1920.

69 *Freeman's Journal,* 2 Sept., 8 Nov., 22 Dec. 1920-31 Jan. 1921; *Labour Gazette,* Feb., Mar. 1921. Apprentices, who had sought a 11s. 9d. increase, do not appear to have gotten any increase.

70 Yeates, *Craft Workers,* p. 18.

71 IEIU NEC minutes, 21 July 1921.

72 *Standard time rates of wages and hours of labour in the United Kingdom at 31st December, 1920,* UKPP. Some trades offered different rates for the same work in different industries: shipbuilding vs. railway engineering, for example.

73 The 12½ per cent bonus had granted to Irish craftsmen by the Committee on Production. See *Irish Independent,* 20 Sept. 1918.

74 Yeates, *A City in Civil War,* pp. 8-9.

75 *Freeman's Journal,* 30 July-3 Aug. 1921.

76 Ibid., 8, 11, 24, 26, 31 Aug., 1 Sept. 1921.

77 Yeates, *Craft Workers,* pp. 20-21; Yeates, *A City in Civil War,* p. 9. The drillers' action was not supported by the REC, which instructed the men to resume work. It was too little too late, and three men were victimised.

78 *Freeman's Journal,* 17 Sept., 24 Oct. 1921.

79 *Cork Examiner,* 10 Nov. 1921.

80 Yeates, *Craft Workers,* pp. 29, 31.

81 *Irish Independent,* 15, 16 Sept. 1921; *Drogheda Independent,* 17, 24 Sept. 1921.

82 Conor Kostick, *Revolution in Ireland: Popular Militancy, 1917-23* (London: Pluto Press, 1996), p. 70.

83 David Lee, 'The Munster Soviets and the Fall of the House of Cleeve', in David Lee and Debbie Jacobs (eds.), *Made in Limerick: History of Industries, Trade and Commerce,* vol. 1 (Limerick: Limerick Civic Trust, 2003), pp. 295-300; Mike Milotte, *Communism in Modern Ireland: The Pursuit of the Workers' Republic since 1916* (Dublin: Gill & Macmillan, 1984), p. 33. Though primarily triggered by wage grievances, Irish soviets were also partially inspired by syndicalism, the Bolshevik Revolution and events in Europe: workplace occupations were a central feature of revolutionary movements in Germany, Italy and Hungary.

84 Yeates, *Craft Workers,* p. 25.

85 O'Connor, *Syndicalism in Ireland,* pp. 74-76.

86 Ibid., pp. 105-106.

87 *Cork Examiner,* 10 Nov. 1921.

88 IEIU, minutes of the railway shopmen's meeting, 14 Aug. 1921.

89 *Irish Independent,* 17, 20 Aug. 1921.

90 Ibid., 21 Sept. 1921.

91 Ibid., 17-22 Sept.-4 Oct. 1921.

92 Cited in Yeates, *A City in Civil War*, p. 11.

93 Yeates, *Craft Workers*, pp. 28-29, 33-36.

94 Ibid., p. 24.

95 Ibid.

96 Ibid., pp. 28, 41-42.

97 *Cork Examiner*, 17 Oct., 4, 5, 17, 24 Nov., 3-9 Dec. 1921; IEIU REC minutes, 2 June, 7, 12, 28 Oct., 16 Nov., 16 Feb., 16, 23 Oct. 1922; IEIU NEC minutes, 31 Dec. 1921. Redmond subsequently established a successful business making metal bed frames. See Seán Redmond, 'family memoir', 17 Dec. 2007.

98 Yeates, *Craft Workers*, pp. 18, 28, 30-31, 36-37; Yeates, *A City in Civil War*, p. 9. The Irish Bookbinders' Union was among the IEIU's tenants. For the foundation of the Communist Party of Ireland, see Emmet O'Connor, *Reds and the Green: Ireland, Russia and the Communist International* (Dublin: UCD Press, 2004), pp. 16-92. For the Socialist Party of Ireland see Emmet O'Connor, 'True Bolsheviks? The Rise and Fall of the Socialist Party of Ireland, 1917-21', in George Boyce & Alan O'Day (eds.), *Ireland in Transition, 1867-1921* (London: Routledge, 2004), pp. 209-222.

99 IEIU REC minutes, 26 Nov. 1921. The first undertaking of its kind, the James Connolly Labour College was founded in 1919 as an explicitly working-class educational institution. It provided lectures and courses in economics, history, law, public speaking and general studies. It was sponsored by the pro-Bolshevik Socialist Party of Ireland, which became the Communist Party of Ireland in 1924. See O'Connor, *Syndicalism in Ireland*, pp. 6-8

100 Yeates, *A City in Civil War*, pp. 11, 44.

101 Ibid., p. 44.

102 Yeates, 'Craft' Workers', p. 40.

103 Yeates, *A City in Civil War*, pp. 43-45; IEIU NEC minutes, 23 Feb., 21 Apr. 1922.

104 Yeates, *Craft Workers*, p. 37. In February, for example, many IEIU men at Broadstone joined the ITGWU.

105 O'Connor, *Syndicalism in Ireland*, p. 68.

106 Ibid., pp. 73, 87, 89. In this context, 'active republicans' refers to members of Sinn Féin and/or the IRB and/or the IRA.

107 Yeates, *Craft Workers*, p. 39.

108 Yeates, *A City in Wartime*, pp. 173-175. The GSWR's director, Sir William Goulding, was a prominent member of the southern unionist establishment.

109 'Oscar Traynor to Military Pension Board, 20 Oct. 1936', Thomas Hannigan MSP application, MSP34REF15588, MSP Collection, MA.

110 *Irish Press*, 9 May 1935. Oscar Traynor later recalled that he and Dalton were confronted by a British soldier during a raid on 6 Gardiner Row. See Oscar Traynor, WS 340, BHM, MA, pp. 80-81.

111 Yeates, *Craft Workers*, pp. 16-17; Thomas Bryan MSP Application, MSP collection, MA; *Irish Press*, 9 May 1935, 4 Jan. 1949, 30 May 1957

112 Yeates, *Craft Workers*, p. 23; Yeates, *A City in Turmoil*, pp. 233-234

113 Leahy, WS 660, BMH, p. 38.

114 Michael V. Donoghue, WS 1,741, BMH, MA.

115 Peter Hart, *The I.R.A. and its Enemies: Violence and Community in Cork, 1916-1923* (Oxford: Clarendon Press, 1998), pp. 155-157.

116 Yeates, *A City in Turmoil*, p. 229

117 'Sworn statement made before advisory committee by Luke Kennedy, 10 Dec. 1937', MSP Application, MA.

118 Charles Townshend, 'The Irish railway strike of 1920: Industrial action and civil resistance in the struggle for independence', *Irish Historical Studies*, vol. 21, 1978, pp. 265-282; Arthur Mitchell, *Labour in Irish politics, 1890-1930: The Irish Labour Party in an Age of Revolution* (New York: Barnes & Noble, 1974), pp. 120-122

119 *Cork Examiner*, 3, 10 July 1920.

120 *Freeman's Journal*, 17, 29, 30 June, 10, 29 July, 18 Sept. 1920; ITUC, *Munitions of war fund: receipts and disbursements* (Dublin: Word Printing Works, 1921), LO P 94, NLI.

121 Cited in O'Connor, *Syndicalism in Ireland*, pp. 72-3.

122 *Sligo Champion*, 13 Nov. 1920.

123 IEIU NEC minutes, 16 Nov. 1921.

124 Yeates, *A City in Turmoil*, p. 134.

125 IEIU REC minutes, 23, 28, 30 Nov., 1, 21 Dec. 1921; *Freeman's Journal*, 2, 5, 6, 7 Dec. 1921; *Evening Herald*, 8 Dec. 1921; Yeates, *Craft Workers*, pp. 32-34, 50.
126 Brian Hanley, "The Layers of an Onion': Reflections on 1913, Class and the Memory of the Irish Revolution', in Conor McNamara & Pádraig Yeates (eds.), *The Dublin Lockout 1913: New Perspective on Class War & its Legacy* (Newbridge: Irish Academic Press, 2017), p. 152.
127 O'Connor, *2: Larkinism and syndicalism*, p. 53.
128 O'Connor, 'Sheep in Wolves' Clothing', p. 67.
129 O'Connor, *2: Larkinism and syndicalism*, p. 53.
130 Ibid, pp. 53-54.
131 Joseph Lee, *Ireland, 1912-1985: Politics and Society* (Cambridge: Cambridge University Press, 1989), p. 5; Ibid., pp. 53-54.

3

Craftsmen and the Free State, 1922-29

Syndicalism bequeathed to us the modern Irish labour movement. Between 1917 and 1923, the principle of trade unionism for every worker – labourer, craftsmen and clerk – was finally established. By 1922, labour in the South was bigger, stronger and much more Irish. Although the amalgamateds had not been destroyed, there was now a viable alternative to them. Employers across the state breathed a collective sigh of relief when the Irish Civil War ended in a decisive victory for the National Army. Their long-awaited counterattack against labour's post-1917 gains ensued, leaving much destruction in its wake. Wages were slashed and conditions decimated. Labourers suffered the most and general unionism on the land and in small towns collapsed. Craft unionism suffered too, albeit less severely, as engineering workers had been the first to suffer the aggression. ITUC membership melted to 175,000 by 1924; by 1929, it had tumbled to ninety-two thousand, a contraction of nearly 150 per cent from its 1920 pinnacle.[1] Employers justified their actions by reference to prices. Weighed at 100 in July 1914, the cost-of-living index had peaked at 276 in November 1920 before plunging to 169 by March 1923.[2] The counterattack's greatest casualty was syndicalism, which would never be revived. Irish labour's radical years were over, and it progressively moved rightwards for the rest of the decade.

This too was a general trend. Labour's prospects were bleak across Europe in the early 1920s. The continent had been engulfed by class conflict as the propertied middle classes who dominated policy making fought to re-assert their hegemony. Ireland's proprietorial sector, especially on the land, was stronger than in most European countries. In 1922, the Treatyites formed their own party, Cumman na nGaedheal, which had close links to farmer and employer organisations. The party had an unenviable task in consolidating the state in the aftermath of the Civil War. Although the worst of the recession had ended by 1924, trade was still lethargic. The Free State economy was rural, poor, unindustrialised and strongly tied to Britain (agricultural shipments to the UK constituted 90 per cent of Free State exports). According to the 1926 census, industry employed only 8 per cent of the workforce, agriculture 53 per cent; 61 per cent lived outside towns or villages. The statistics for the cities told their own story. Over eight hundred thousand people resided in overcrowded conditions (defined as more than two persons per room). There were 22,915 families living in one-room dwellings and 39,615 families living in two rooms; of the latter group, 2,761 families consisted of nine persons or more. The consequences were often fatal. In working-class, north inner-city Dublin, the average death rate per one thousand children aged one to five was 25.6; in middle-class Drumcondra, it was 7.7.[3]

Unions faced deep hostility and stone-hearted conservatism from the Treatyites. The government was unwilling to upset the British and was ideologically beholden to large farmers and a few major capitalists. It saw agricultural exports as the motor of economic development and had a dogmatic commitment to laissez-faire, making it opposed to state intervention and public enterprise. The major exception, the Shannon hydroelectric scheme, exposed the weakness of private enterprise and the lack of engineering expertise in Ireland. Trade unions were irrelevant to public policy. In 1922, the Department of Labour and the British Ministry of Labour were replaced by the Department of Industry and Commerce. The new department, along with the Department of Finance, was dominated by conservative, middle-class men who opposed strong union influence over the economy. The government did little to tackle the social problem, ensuring that high unemployment and emigration remained central features of the Irish economy.[4] Thus, the unions had a bleak decade in the 1920s under Cumman na nGaedheal. The IEIU's experience was better than most, its internal ruptures notwithstanding.

The IEIU and the Civil War

On 7 January 1922, Dáil Éireann ratified the Anglo-Irish Treaty (signed on 6 December 1921), creating the twenty-six county Irish Free State. A Provisional Government was in power until 6 December 1922. The Treaty presented a major dilemma for Irish labour as the national struggle which had previously united it now threatened to divide it. The ITUC abstained from the Treaty debate and urged its affiliates to remain neutral. After reiterating its commitment to a 'workers' republic', a call for a plebiscite on the issue was all that Congress could muster.[5] Even the leadership of the famously militant and republican ITGWU urged neutrality.[6] The Irish bourgeoisie had no such predicament. Employers' federations, Chambers of Commerce and farmers' associations across the twenty-six counties pleaded for the Treaty's ratification for several reasons, one being was an impatience to launch the counterattack, on hold pending resolution of the political situation. Like labour, employers had been internally fractured on the constitutional question during the Great War but were now firmly united behind the Free State.[7] While the Treaty split was not a socio-economic one, components of a class-based division were evident. The support given to it by the 'men of property' gave the embryonic state some badly-needed legitimacy and created a solid nexus of interests between employers and Treatyites.[8] The Free State government regularly ascribed its highest levels of support to shopkeepers, commercial and farming elements, clergy, doctors and bankers; the working class, on the other hand, was perceived as more susceptible to 'Irregularism.'[9] Conversely, the government's beliefs about its own middle-class support were also held by its anti-Treatyite opponents.[10] The political situation spiralled out of control in the early months of 1922, with lawlessness prevailing in the absence of an operational state. On 24 April, the ITUC brought out Free State workers in a one-day general strike (in which the IEIU participated) against 'the spirit of militarism.'[11] While the stoppage was ostensibly against both sides, it was clearly aimed at the anti-Treatyites, who funded their armed struggle by looting and robbery.

Like most Irish trade unions, the IEIU was anxious to avoid a split and kept quiet on the Treaty. But some internal tension was unavoidable, as Leahy recalled to the Bureau of Military History:

> The fight for independence … failed to break that friendship and loyalty to each other, but on the fatal vote for the Treaty we found ourselves in opposite camps… I will never forget the day at 6 Gardiner's Row when

the news came through on the vote. Our E.C. had arranged a meeting that evening on other matters and advantage was taken after business to test members' feeling on it... Most of them supported the decision of Collins and Griffith on the vote; those of us who thought of ourselves as a Labour Union within the Republic came away with sad hearts but determined to ... carry on the complete separation of our country from England.[12]

Leahy had joined the Irish Citizen Army (ICA) in 1917, around the time that he got a job at the Dublin Dockyard. The Citizen Army was a Dublin-centric organisation. During the War of Independence, it was organised into two battalions in the city – north and south. By then, however, it had still not recovered from the destruction of Liberty Hall in 1916, allowing the IRA to surpass it and become a far more effective force against the British. Poor organisation and inertia also hurt the ICA. It assisted the IRA by acquiring rifles, watching suspect persons and houses, collecting arms and ammunition, and helping deserters from the British Army. Other work included gathering intelligence, carrying arms, guarding IRA meetings and surveying the British military and police.[13] The ICA participated in some notable military operations, like the burning of the Custom House in May 1921.[14]

Leahy had been appointed ICA Intelligence Officer and sat on its Army Council. He used his influence in the Dockyard to secure employment for IRA men and to procure weapons through Wales and Scotland. Like most ICA members, Leahy opposed the Treaty during the Civil War. He was arrested in April 1923 – when he was unemployed – on Talbot Street while doing union work. On his release that September, he was employed as a boilermaker at the Inchicore Works until 1925 when he was sacked after the southern railway companies amalgamated. Leahy emigrated to Britain and worked in several cities before eventually finding employment on the Clyde. He re-joined the Boilermakers' Society after it refused to recognise his IEIU card. Though he considered himself a socialist, Leahy was primarily a separatist who prayed for the day when 'all of our people, north, south, east and west' could live 'under the flag of a united and Gaelic, free Ireland.'[15] His mention of Gaelicism suggests that Irish workers had a similar outlook to their middle-class colleagues.

> Many of the revolutionary generation grew to adulthood on a diet of propaganda and writing which strongly emphasised Ireland's exclusivity in the annals of history and suffering; a tortured history that was merely a prelude to a new chapter of independence... a Gaelic and Catholic nation that was distinct.[16]

On 27 June 1922, Free State troops began shelling the Four Courts to dislodge the IRA units that had occupied it since 13 April. The Irish Civil War had begun. By then, the Dublin Brigade had already moved its headquarters next door to Barry's Hotel at 7 Gardiner Row. The switch possibly took place between January and March when the IEIU and IRA GHQ exchanged correspondence, although this remains unclear. The union was fortunate because, after the attack on the Four Courts, Barry's was heavily damaged by a Free State artillery bombardment that may otherwise have visited 6 Gardiner Row. The IEIU was not unaffected, however: the attack damaged head office, for which the union sought £878 in compensation from Dublin Corporation and £377 from the Provisional Government.[17] The REC wanted to stay out of the war and focus purely on the employers' counterattack. On 14 September, it began to officially register the IEIU as a trade union, which was finalised on 19 December. The minutes record few references to the fratricide upending the country. But the executive did reduce the weekly contribution rate for those in 'the army' (it is unclear which one) to 9d. until their return to civilian life (the standard rate was 1s. 6d.). It also tried to ensure that men looking to join the union were not fighting for either side.[18] These efforts were bound to fail, and it was only a matter of time before the union was dragged into the conflict. Tom Hannigan had helped to defend Barry's and, in August 1922, took part in an IRA operation to destroy bridges around Dublin. That month, a mental breakdown forced him to withdraw from the war.[19]

The Civil War cruelly took several union members. On 26 August, members of the National Army stopped and searched nineteen-year-old Seán Cole – the commanding officer of the 2nd Batt. of Na Fianna in Dublin – at Newcomen Bridge before taking him away in a car. Later that day, his lifeless body was found at Yellow Road, Whitehall, perforated by four bullet holes. An apprentice electrician with Thomas Dockrell & Sons, he had served with Na Fianna from 1917 until his death. On 18 November 1922, Thomas Maguire – not to be confused with Tomás Maguire – died. Thomas Maguire served his time as a fitter with the MGWR. He had participated in 1916 with Na Fianna and was an active Volunteer from 1918, serving as Company Intelligence Officer for the 5th Batt. He got a job at the Pigeon House after being sacked from Broadstone. Having opposed the Treaty, Maguire was promoted to the rank of IRA captain during the Civil War. Aged just twenty-three, he was killed in Inchicore by a mine that exploded prematurely.[20] Another union member to take the anti-Treatyite side was Noel Lemass (brother of Seán), an apprentice fitter, who had also taken part in the Rising. Like Maguire, he worked at the Stanley Street workshop but spent most of the War of Independence in prison or on the run. He was abducted at gunpoint in July 1923 and brutally murdered. A memorial stone now marks the spot in the Dublin Mountains where his mutilated body was discovered in October of that year. Possibly the last IRA man to fall victim to the Black and Tans was also an IEIU member. On 29 May 1922, Staff Captain James Flanagan, a moulder at the Drogheda Ironworks, had been gunned down at Gormanston railway station during a shootout between the IRA and the Tans. Aged just twenty-two, he had served as an engineer with the Drogheda Batt., South Louth Brigade since 1920.[21]

For the IEIU, Maguire's death began a period of introspection about how it should treat members participating in the Civil War. It opted to pay no mortality benefit to anyone killed, injured or made sick by their involvement in it, supplementing its previous decision to not pay benefits to those victimised or unemployed because they were 'on the run' or wanted by the authorities.[22] The REC was clearly afraid of being harassed by Free State forces for perceived 'Irregular' sympathies. Carr had already been arrested but was released shortly afterwards.[23] The executive was forced to pay Maguire's bereaved mother benefit when solicitors warned that it was open to legal action because 'no executive body had power to go outside its rules … without the authority of the general body of the members'[24] The executive also had to get legal advice when a member serving in the National Army applied for funeral benefit for his wife's recent death. The solicitor advised payment of the benefit and the man was duly supported.[25] The REC balloted its members on whether benefit should be paid to the families affected by the Civil War. The membership agreed with the

REC's original position, overwhelmingly voting to deny financial support to any man or his family should he suffer a tragic fate because of his enlistment in either 'Irish army.' No member would receive any kind of support during his enlistment – and that enlistment would have to be for eight weeks before he was again eligible for benefit.[26] Members had effectively voted to sever the union's previous association with the republican movement. Despite, or perhaps because of, its neutrality, the union incurred hostility from both sides. On 3 August 1922, the anti-Treatyites informed it that they considered railway workers who 'assisted' the Free State by repairing and maintaining carriages and armoured cars to be legitimate targets for assassination, a threat they forwarded to other unions two days later.[27] The IRA's destruction of railway infrastructure had a deleterious effect on shopmen. It forced many of the smaller, less profitable companies to cut pay, issue redundancies and close for periods during the Civil War.[28]

On 24 May 1923, the Civil War officially ended when IRA Chief of Staff Frank Aiken ordered his men to dump arms and to offer no further resistance to the Free State. The unions' 'neutrality' on the Treaty was partially a product of syndicalism, whose failure to develop a thorough analysis on the class nature of the state was notorious. Syndicalism had nurtured a belief among trade unionists that proletarian power could be attained by solely industrial means. The strike against 'militarism' underscores labour's failure to develop a coherent policy on the class nature of the Treaty settlement and the state it produced. Whilst labour was undoubtedly politicised by the independence struggle, its refusal to politically engage with the Republic confined radicalism to the industrial arena. Consequently, labour inadvertently facilitated the degeneration of Sinn Féin's embryonic state into the reactionary Irish Free State.[29] The Labour Party had also remained aloof from the Civil War, completing its estrangement from Sinn Féin. The republican-labour alliance was dead, never to be revived.

On 21 February 1922, the ITUC gathered for a special delegate conference on whether the Labour Party should take part in the coming general election, to be held on 16 June.[30] The meeting voted 104-49 that Labour should contest the election on social and economic issues. The IEIU sided with the minority, arguing that Congress should ballot unions on the question before any decision be made. Its delegates may have felt, as many republicans did, that the election should be a straightforward referendum on the Treaty. The conference also voted 128-12 that a separate plebiscite be held on the Treaty, but it is unclear how the IEIU voted on this. The union continued to oppose the Labour's participation in the election in the aftermath of the conference. When, at an REC meeting, Carr proposed that they donate £50 to the Labour Party's election fund in Dublin and £50 to any union members who ran for the Dáil and signed the party's election pledge, he found no seconder.[31]

Nevertheless, the Labour Party was ready to pursue class politics again against both pro- and anti-Treaty Sinn Féin factions. The party felt that the slump, high unemployment and the employer counterattack had crystallised to workers where their interests lay. The Labour Party surpassed all expectations in the election as it benefited from anti-Treaty losses: parties who did not oppose the Treaty gained over 78 per cent of the popular vote. Labour won seventeen out of the eighteen seats it contested, only narrowly losing out on the final seat. But the party had misinterpreted the reasons for its success. Its campaign in the 1923 general election, to which the IEIU financially contributed, was a major disappointment. The party had hoped that government conservatism and anti-Treatyite indifference to workers would create the space for it to flourish; instead, it lost three seats. Held on 27 August, the press attributed the party's poor performance to the strikes and lockouts that were raging across the country, but this was not the case. Although workers were unhappy with how Labour had distanced itself from the industrial struggle, the Civil War had ensured that the national question would once again upstage class politics. Furthermore, Labour's 1922 vote had been artificially high, inflated by the pro-Treaty protest vote it received.[32] An employers' party had contested both elections. It had close links to Cumman na nGaedheal with whom it formed an electoral pact.[33]

Working-class support for, or at least acceptance of, the Treaty presented an awkward reality for republicans because much of their class-infused rhetoric was aimed at the Free State's bourgeois character. It also refutes simplistic Marxist arguments of a clear class basis to the conflict. The recession had spurred great working-class recruitment into the National Army, a useful solution for the government to the social problems created by high unemployment. The republican response vacillated between sympathy for the workers and a moralistic, puritanical hostility typical of Irish middle-class prejudice. Recruits were often denounced in explicitly classist terms: 'undesirables', 'criminals', 'low caste hirelings', 'gutter scoundrels', 'tramps', 'tinkers' and 'Soupers.'[34] Free State rhetoric was no better and similarly suffused with an anti-working-class bias. Republican volunteers were dismissed as 'of pot-house derivation', 'city scum', 'tramps and wasters', 'corner boys' and 'the dregs of society' – lazy, feckless individuals with a parasitic relationship to the 'respectable.' This outlook manifested itself in Treatyite fears that republicans posed an incipient threat to the social order itself, implicitly revealing the Free State's reactionary nature. It also suggests a post-colonial dynamic of mental colonisation where the attitudes of the departing power are embraced by the nationalist revolutionaries who displaced it.[35]

Cumann na nGaedheal's alliance with the employers helped to embed the 'conservative consensus' into the Irish body politic. By the decade's end, the Free State served the interests of employers far more than workers.[36] Fianna Fáil's entry into the Dáil in 1927 killed any possibility of a strong Labour Party in Ireland during this era. Fianna Fáil stole many Labour Party votes by fusing mild social democracy with a commitment to industrial and political independence. Labour's ongoing drift to the centre also facilitated its upstaging by Fianna Fáil. Between 1923 and 1927, Labour's rhetoric on the Treaty's unpopular elements, like the Oath of Allegiance, was compromising because the party baulked at any 'embrace' of 'nationalism.' It supported Fianna Fáil's entry into the Dáil as a stabilising influence that would 'normalise' politics. The result was a weak, ineffective party that prided itself on being the only constitutional opposition to Cumman na nGaedheal, an honour it had now lost. The IEIU was one of the few unions to view 'normal' politics as deleterious to Labour and urged it to take a firmer stand against the right-wing government.[37] At the 1925 ITUC, it had proposed that Congress withdraw Labour TDs from the Dáil unless the government stopped cutting public sector wages.[38]

Class conflict, 1922-29

With the economy still in deep recession 1922, industrial disputes increasingly ended in defeat for workers. In January 1922, the IEIU had no choice but to accede to an 8s. 3d. cut in the Dublin vehicle building trade after the ITGWU accepted it. And in April, coachbuilders in Cork had their pay slashed by 25 per cent after a seventeen-week strike.[39] Nevertheless, the IEIU could still secure the occasional victory. Although the arbitrator had confirmed reductions in the railway workshops in 1921, he recommended that the question of whether shopmen were entitled to the district rates, which were much higher, be explored. Accordingly, the unions served the companies with a claim for rate, which the companies eventually agreed to refer to arbitration. In July 1922, James McNeill awarded shopmen the district rates in a terrific victory for the unions. Although some lost out, most craftsmen received generous improvements. In Dublin, the weekly increases ranged from 6s. 8d. to 26s. while in Limerick, the average was 19s.[40] It was an important victory at a time when the IEIU was suffering heavy losses. Militancy remained a potent force on the ground liable to ignite into unofficial action, much to the chagrin of the REC. In January, IEIU apprentices at the Ringsend Shipbuilding Company walked off the job in support of the Boilermakers' Society over the employment of boy labourers. Six months later, coachbuilders in Cork again downed tools without sanction to combat a wage reduction.[41]

Even deeper reductions were imposed at Passage and Rushbrooke, amounting to 36s. 6d. in some trades. In Dublin, the Dockyard was the scene for one of the most important strikes of the era in Dublin. On 1 September 1922, the yard closed when five hundred men downed tools after refusing to accept a sizable weekly cut of 16s. 6d. Employers wanted to harmonise wages in Dublin and on the Clyde. Local rates had traditionally tracked the Clyde, leading to a 18s. reduction in 1921; however, Dublin rates remained 55-60 per cent higher than on the Clyde.[42] After the Dublin Dockyard proposed to phase out the 26s. 6d. war bonus – which would reduce craftsmen's pay to 48s., far below other industries – its men went out on strike. They returned to work after a Department of Labour conference led to the withdrawal of the notice of reductions. The IEIU was rewarded for its stand with defections from the AEU.[43] On 26 August, the strike resumed after the reductions were reintroduced. During the First World War, the Dockyard had expanded substantially due to lucrative Royal Navy contracts. From 1921, however, the navy's reversion to a peacetime programme had caused a dramatic contraction in demand that had made many smaller British and Irish yards unviable. The IEIU was aware of this and, along with the yard's directors, proposed that the Provisional Government subsidise the industry, arguing the strategic importance of shipbuilding to an island economy. The government rejected this idea because it was 'against the spirit of the Treaty ... to try to compel the owners of vessels using Irish ports to get repairs done in Irish yards.'[44] The Dockyard went into voluntary liquidation in 1923, blaming it on labour disputes. Vickers Ltd. bought the yard that Autumn and reopened it in October 1924.[45] However, the unions continued to black the yard, leading Vickers to employ scabs. Even employing these men on lower rates failed to revive its fortunes and Vickers struggled on until 1938, when the yard closed again.[46]

Table 22: Wages at Passage West and Rushbrooke Dockyards, 1922.[47]

Workers	Feb. 1922	Dec. 1922
Boilermakers	96s. 6d.	79s. 6d.
Joiners	87s.	70s. 6d.
Shipwrights	86s. 3d.	67s. 8d.
Fitters & Smiths	83s. 6d.	67s.
Painters	82s.	65s. 6d.

The *Evening Herald* blamed the IEIU and the ITGWU, who had 'defied economic facts', for the Dockyard's prolonged closure and praised the Boilermakers' and Shipwrights' Societies for accepting cuts.[48] The amalgamateds had agreed with employers behind the backs of their fellow trade unionists, which infuriated the IEIU. At the 1924 ITUC annual conference, the IEIU tried to effectively ban British unions from affiliating to Congress. During the debate, it proposed an addendum denying affiliation to any union that supported wages and conditions being governed by agreements in another country. Patrick O'Hagan, IEIU general secretary since 1923, cited the British unions' acceptance of the Clyde rates in the Dublin yards as an example of their perfidy. J.T. O'Farrell, leader of the Railway Clerks' Association (a British union) and a Labour Party senator, strongly opposed the addendum because it came from an organisation which he considered a 'flapper' (breakaway) union, one that 'had split trade union organisation among engineers.' Other British unions, which had clearly not yet forgiven the IEIU, also opposed the addendum. After a rancorous debate, Congress narrowly voted to move onto other business. The IEIU delegates stormed out in protest. The union rescinded its affiliation and did not attend the 1925 Congress.[49]

Employers in the building trade were also flexing their muscles. The IEIU had a toehold in the trade through its organisation of electricians and metalworkers. In 1922, Dublin's master builders sought their own 16s. 6d. decrease as well as cuts to the 'country allowance' travel expense. They had initially wanted a 29s. 4d. cut and to increase the working week to forty-seven hours but backed down after strong union opposition. The IEIU bartered the cut down to 8s. 3d.[50] Though most Free State workers were still on peak wages in late 1922, a crisis was in gestation. The end of the Civil War allowed effective policing to be enforced. Employers no longer feared violent retaliation against their property and could now wage all-out war. The government set an example by crushing a strike of postal workers in autumn 1922.[51] It was a portent of things to come.

According to Francis Devine, 1923 may well be 'the worst year in the history of Irish trade unionism.'[52] Employers across the Free State waged all-out war against wages and conditions. They believed that the slump had empowered radicals by drastically reducing the room for compromise between what was necessary and what unions were willing to accept. They found labour's willingness to countenance economic catastrophe chilling.[53] Workers fought back across the Free State: about twenty thousand were on strike at the height of the industrial crisis. They were as galvanised by a moral drive for justice as economic rationale, a testament to syndicalism's allure and a fitting farewell to it. Among the more protracted disputes were a three-month national dockers' strike and a seven-month lockout of three thousand farm labourers in Waterford that descended into violent class conflict. Having suffered the counterattack earlier than most, the IEIU was not as affected as other unions by employer aggression in 1923 and even won some concessions. With the AEU's assistance, it negotiated the 18s. 6d reduction sought by engineering employers in Limerick to 10s. and ensured that there would be fewer apprentices at the railway works (taking journeymen off short time). At the Dundalk railway works, it bartered down a 16s. decrease to 5s. Craftsmen at Dublin Corporation and the Boards of Guardians also faced cuts.[54] Although the IEIU ameliorated the reduction imposed in Dublin's vehicle building firms, its members suffered cuts across the country in 1923 and 1924, with no industry or trade being spared.[55] Reductions were not the only malady the union had to deal with, as some employers used the poor economy as a pretext to try and dislodge it. In October 1922, Hadden's foundry employed a Scottish heating engineer instead of a local one and threatened to only employ AEU men to fill vacancies. Citing 'managerial rights', it subsequently sacked an IEIU foreman and would only re-employ him if he assented to a decrease. The man refused and his colleagues went out in solidarity. He was reinstated after arbitration under the Department of Industry and Commerce.[56]

Employer aggression led to a rapprochement between the IEIU and its British rivals. For example, in mid-1923, the IEIU refused to scab when the National Union of Vehicle Builders downed tools at O'Gorman's, Clonmel against the presence of non-union labour.[57] Simultaneously, relations with the ITGWU deteriorated. In early 1923, the ITGWU had adopted a 'very threatening attitude' towards the IEIU during a lockout of flourmill labourers. The Transport Union 'refused to allow the members of other unions employed in the Limerick mills to go into their work', but the IEIU put up a 'firm stand' and the ITGWU relented. An ITGWU effort to recruit fitters from the IEIU to its Engineers' Section, operational since March 1922, also failed. ITGWU poaching remained a constant source of friction. The IEIU responded in kind, taking many members from its rivals, most notably at Rushbrooke Dockyard where relations between it and the ITGWU were especially tense.[58] The bad blood had begun in May 1922 when the *Voice of Labour*, the ITGWU's weekly, published an article falsely alleging that the IEIU and the newly founded Amalgamated Transport and General Workers' Union (ATGWU) had agreed to work together to crush the ITGWU. The paper had previously attacked the IEIU over its conduct during the 1921 railway strike.[59]

Nowhere were aggressive than in Cork. From 15 August to 12 November, the city was crippled by a general lockout of ten thousand workers, including its metal craftsmen. The settlement slashed wages from 94s. to 88s. 1½d for engineering craftsmen and to 82s. 3d. for building tradesmen and coachbuilders.[60] In most places, labour doggedness and unity had forced employers to accept only half the reductions they had sought. The ITUC had pleaded with the government for a national settlement of disputes but made no effort to co-ordinate unrest. O'Connor regards the autumn crisis of 1923 as a 'watershed' because it marks the point when labour degenerated from a movement 'with a capacity to defend living standards and an ambition to change class relations' into 'a destructive force with no vision beyond immediate sectional interests.'[61] The struggle had exhausted Irish labour, killing militancy in most of the Free State. In the long-term, the movement had been soundly defeated and the employers' hegemony assured. It would be many years before workers began to receive increases again. From 1924, the number of strikes fell steadily, as did union membership and strength. By 1929, the ITGWU, the biggest Irish union, had only 15,500 members, an astonishing collapse from its 1920 peak of 130,000 members. The number of trades councils, indicative of the geographic spread of trade unionism, had multiplied from fifteen in 1918 to forty-six in 1921 before plunging to just ten by 1930.[62]

Table 23: Strikes, Trade Union Membership and Emigration, 1923-30.[63]

Year	No. of strikes	No. involved	No. of days lost	Trade union membership	Emigration
1923	131	20,635	1,208,734	130,735	-
1924	104	16,403	301,705	126,522	19,077
1925	86	6,855	293,792	98,986	30,180
1926	57	3,455	85,345	95,002	30,041
1927	53	2,312	64,020	89,013	27,148
1928	52	2,190	54,292	87,696	24,691
1929	53	4,533	101,397	85,600	20,802
1930	83	3,410	77,417	70,573	15,966

Table 24: Cost of Living in the Free State, 1922-30 (July 1914=100).[64]

Year (Jan.)	Cost of Living	Year (Jan.)	Cost of Living
1922 (Apr.)	191	1927	182
1923	190	1928	177
1924	188	1929	177
1925	195	1930	179
1926	188	-	-

The IEIU, 1922-30

Membership of all unions declined steadily between 1924 and 1930, when the ITUC launched its (unsuccessful) 'Back to the Unions' campaign in which the IEIU participated.[65] Congress had hoped to capitalise on the spike in class consciousness generated by the British general strike of 1926.[66] But recovery was a long way off. Decline was aided by division and several notable splits took place, with the IEIU and ITGWU more affected than most. Unlike other Irish unions, IEIU membership had expanded in 1922. However, from a peak of 4,700 in 1923, Tables 25 & 26 show the decline in membership and branches the union suffered thereafter.[67] Weakened by the counterattack, it had focussed on consolidation and recovery instead. It had engaged in a few, mostly unsuccessful industrial actions. Like all Irish unions, the IEIU was becoming increasingly hostile to Cumman na nGaedheal. In July 1924, the Irish Municipal Employees' Trade Union struck against a wage cut at Dublin Corporation. The government backed the Corporation and rumour spread that it was about to grant the use of 'military labour' to break the strike. In such an event, the IEIU and AEU announced that they would withdraw their members from the Pigeon House power station.[68]

Table 25: IEIU Membership, 1921-29.[69]

Date	Membership	Date	Membership
1 Jan. 1921	4,500	27 Mar. 1926	3,251
1 Jan. 1922	4,000	Mar. 1927	2,500
1 Jan. 1923	4,700	31 Dec. 1927	1,785
31 Mar. 1924	3,158	31 Dec. 1928	1,774
31 Dec. 1924	3,131	31 Dec. 1929	1,594

Table 26: IEIU Branches, 1924, 1927 & 1930.[70]

Date	Branches
31 Mar. 1924	Clonmel, Cobh, Drogheda, Dublin, Dundalk, Limerick, Passage, Tralee, Waterford, Wexford
Mar. 1927	Dundalk, Cork, Cobh, Passage, Limerick, Tralee, Wexford, Drogheda
31 Dec. 1927	Dublin, Dundalk, Cork, Cobh, Passage, Limerick, Tralee, Wexford, Drogheda
31 Dec. 1930	Ibid

Railway shopmen fared better than most of their colleagues. From 1925, Free State railway workers were employed by the Great Southern Railway (GSR), a merger of all the railway companies wholly within the Free State.[71] Although hundreds lost their jobs upon the amalgamation, those with long service were entitled to compensation. Shopmen were not included when, as per a Central Wages Board ruling, the GSR cut its employees pay in 1926.[72] Railway managers had always resented the 1922 MacNeill award and in April 1929, they openly violated it by issuing cuts at in Dublin. Strike was threatened, prompting state intervention. Arbitration under the Department of Industry and Commerce produced a settlement: a 10 per cent reduction. Shopmen may have found some consolation in their 42½-hour week, one of the shortest in operation anywhere in Ireland.[73] By the late 1920s, the IEIU remained the most effective engineering union in Ireland, which caused consternation among its rivals. In January 1928, AEU men at Pierce's foundry went out. The firm had sought wage cuts and had been negotiating with the British union for weeks when the IEIU learned of it. The Irish union entered the fray and forced a concession: the wages question would be deferred until August. Both unions had agreed to take joint action if the cut was enforced, but the AEU was unhappy that management had gone over their heads. The decision to withdraw labour backfired as the IEIU – who believed that 'jealousy on the part of the AEU' was the reason for the strike – gained members from its rival.[74] In March, the AEU launched another lightning stoppage, this time against the employment of a non-union man, forcing the firm to close; afterwards, the man joined the IEIU.[75]

An IEIU rules conference in 1925 gave delegates an opportunity to reflect on working life, and the lack thereof, in the Free State. Toomey, still the general president, addressed the gathering, which was held in 6 Gardiner Row. After spuriously claiming that the IEIU was 'stronger today' than in 1921, 'when the first onslaught was made upon them by the employers', Toomey conceded that 'unemployment continued rampant in their industries with no possible prospect of an improvement in the near future.' Foundries were closing because of the unrestricted importation of cheap, untaxed materials, while railway shopmen were being fired due to poor trade, reduction of freight tariffs and increasing competition from motor traffic. The situation was no better for craftsmen in the public sector, he maintained, where 'business-minded' local authorities followed the government's example by cutting wages.[76] The IEIU was also grappling with internal problems. In 1926, it received a letter from the Department of Finance informing the union that it was £2,000 overdrawn on the 'grant' it received in 1920 to pay for 6 Gardiner Row. The union was not aware of the scale of its liabilities and was in no position to pay anything off the principal, just the interest accumulated. But once again the union paid back its debts in an efficient manner. This time it did so without levying members or slashing their benefits. Instead, expenditure was reduced elsewhere. By 1929, the overdraft had been reduced to £1,000 and was subsequently cleared with monthly payments of £10.[77] The REC knew it had to manage its finances better. 'Several of our members had met with reductions in their wages and certainly something must be done to curtail the expenses of the union if we are to carry on in the future.'[78] Something was indeed done when another financial scandal rocked the union.

In June 1928, the REC was shocked to discover that O'Hagan had falsified its accounts and had misappropriated funds. Rooney, the senior trustee, was the one to unearth O'Hagan's misdeeds. He became suspicious when he noticed a discrepancy in accounts and decided to investigate. He visited the bank to ascertain the facts regarding lodgements from the union and learned that O'Hagan's cash books did not match the bank's records. Subsequent auditing of the accounts revealed that eight lodgements had been recorded between December 1927 and May 1928 when only four had been made, resulting in a £46 deficiency. The REC accused O'Hagan of defrauding the union, charges he vehemently denied, claiming that there was nothing sinister about what had happened. It was, he said, simple human error on his part as he had tried to lodge the money but arrived at the bank too late. Afterwards, he went for a drink and either lost or spent the money. 'For I can only admit that I am careless with money, either my own or anyone else's, which has been my curse for the past couple of years.'[79] He claimed to have tried to take out a loan from the bank but was refused because he was a guarantor for someone who was not making repayments. O'Hagan was sacked as general secretary for incompetence, deceit, falsification of accounts and misappropriation of funds, although he was not expelled from the union. John O'Brien, assistant general secretary, replaced him in an acting capacity. O'Brien proved far more capable than his predecessor and was elected general secretary in September 1929. Having succeeded Toomey in the role, James Bell was re-elected general president.[80] The position of assistant general secretary was abolished.[81]

Splits and internal divisions

The IEIU had set itself a monumental task in organising across trades. Metal work, especially shipbuilding, encompassed a complex differentiation in the workforce that went far beyond the simple division between craftsman and labourer. Craftsmen were themselves divided into 'advantaged' and 'disadvantaged' trades; even within trades there were internal hierarchies. Craftwork's complex division of labour produced overlaps in the applicability of skills, often leading to conflict between craftsmen over who did what work. Although shipbuilding was the most notorious for these demarcation disputes, they were also common in the building trade. The most persistent disputes were between boilermakers and shipwrights, boilermakers and drillers, fitters and plumbers, shipwrights and joiners, and iron and brass moulders.[82]

The IEIU was assiduous in ensuring that members adhered to agreements with employers and observed demarcation lines. In 1920, the secessionists brought with them these inter-craft frictions from their old organisations. And demarcation disputes were not always external. Immediately after its foundation, they became a constant problem within the IEIU. As they threatened the economy, the courts – first the republican and later the Free State – often arbitrated these disputes if the REC could not resolve them. There were disputes between fitters and stationary engine drivers and between brass finishers and vehicle builders.[83] Internal and external arbitration made most of these disputes 'manageable' for the union, but some had disastrous consequence. The union responded to the employers' counterattack with rear-guard actions that made unity between the different trades difficult. As the *Woman's Dreadnaught* observed, 'sectionalism is very strong in this so-called industrial union.' Fitzgerald had verified this claim when he asserted that the IEIU operated on 'anything but industrial lines.'[84]

In 1923, most of the union's electricians broke away because they were unhappy with how the REC had handled their disputes with plumbers, brass finishers and other trades. A significant minority of electricians remained in the IEIU, however, including Donohoe, the Electrical Section's secretary. The electricians' fight with the plumbers was especially acrimonious. Both groups clashed over who should joint electrical cables: as lead was involved, the plumbers claimed the work; as the cables were electrical, the electricians claimed it. The REC had spent more than six months in 1921 and 1922 mulling over the issue before siding with the plumbers; however, it could not find a lasting census. Further, the electricians felt that the IEIU had not done enough on the wages front, either to defend the 12.5 per cent bonus in 1921 or to support the Electrical Section's claim for a wage increase in 1923. The secessionists formed the Electrical Trades Union (Dublin).[85]

Demarcation was not the only challenge of organising a cross-craft union. Sometimes tensions between men of the same trade who worked in different industries could also have calamitous results. By October 1921, the Inchicore shopmen were irate at how the executive was treating their wage dispute compared to how it was simultaneously treating disputes in other sectors. By February 1922, a rumour was circulating in Inchicore that £1,600 could not be accounted for in the IEIU funds. The REC investigated the matter and decided to take a case to the republican courts to recoup the money. The REC was proven to be unfounded – but it was too late, the damage had been done. 'The £1,600 was suspiciously similar to the cost of the engineering strike so much resented by the (Inchicore) railwaymen.'[86] By then, many Inchicore men had ceased contact with the IEIU. All attempts at reconciliation had failed and the REC knew that they intended to leave. The old No. 2 branch, which had been suspended because of its activities during the 1921 railway dispute, was apparently meeting without notifying the executive and was not sending contributions to head office, prompting the union to pursue legal action.[87] But the IEIU was about to lose something much more significant than money.

The Irish General Railway and Engineering Union

On 11 March 1922, the IEIU Inchicore branch officially broke away and formed the Irish General Railway Engineering Union (IGREU), which had existed on paper since 4 October 1921. The IEIU had lost one of its most important branches. The new union had 567 members between two branches: Inchicore and Dublin. It was formally launched on 1 October 1922 and received official recognition as a trade union on 9 June 1923. It had experienced steady growth in 1922, notwithstanding the poor economic climate.[88] Quinn became its first general secretary before handing over to Thomas Balfe in 1923. Edward Gaynor took over the role two years later and John McCormack was general president in 1924. The IGREU initially met at the Inchicore Workman's Club but later opened offices at 56 Blackhall Street and 67 Dame Street.[89] Its aims were more conservative than its rival: 'to regulate the relations between its members and their employers; to promote the welfare and safeguard the interests of its members; to guarantee protection to its members in case of oppression and to assist them to obtain adequate remuneration in return for their labour.'[90] Reflecting the influence of syndicalism, the IEIU sought 'to organise the workers in the industry on industrial lines, with a view of obtaining control, and abolish the present capitalists' control.'[91]

The IGREU had its own republican martyrs. John Monks, a twenty-one-year-old apprentice blacksmith at the Inchicore works, was killed during an engagement between the anti-Treaty IRA and the National Army at Red Cow, Clondalkin on 28 June 1922, the first day of the Civil War. He had served with F Coy., 4 Batt., Dublin Brigade since 1919, with whom he fought against Free State forces during the Civil War. His older Patrick, a boilermaker at the works, had fought alongside him. Patrick had served as quartermaster of the unit (which he had joined in October 1917) throughout the War of Independence and Civil War. In September 1922, he was captured by National Army forces and interned until March 1923. His uncle Richard Monks, a chargehand at the works, served in the same unit as his nephews during the Civil War, which he joined in 1920. Another IGREU member, Patrick Hickey, a brass finisher at the works, died on 30 August 1922 aged twenty-one at Portlaoise Prison after a soldier had shot him the previous day. It is unclear whether the shooting occurred during the attempted burning of the building by IRA prisoners or shortly afterwards as a reprisal. Having joined the Volunteers in 1918, Hickey had served with the 5th Batt. until his death.[92]

Other union men died for the Free State cause. One was Patrick O'Hara, a mechanical engineer and National Army soldier who was wounded on 22 July 1922 at Lower Abbey Street, Dublin after being accidently shot by a drunken fellow soldier. He died from his injuries two days later. He was not the only one to accidently die at the hands of his own men. On 20 January 1923, Private Leo Beahan, an engine fitter, was killed in a motor accident while travelling towards the Curragh.[93] Perhaps the most famous Treatyite who had an IGREU card was Peadar Doyle, a Cumann na nGaedheal (and later Fine Gael) TD for the Inchicore area from 1923 until 1954 and a Corporation councillor from 1918 to 1955 (twice serving as lord mayor). Previously a fitter at the railway works,

Doyle was also a 1916 veteran. On Easter Monday, Con Colbert had made him quartermaster of F Coy., 4th Batt., which had occupied the South Dublin Union under Éamonn Ceannt's command. On 19 September 1920, Doyle's nineteen-year-old son Seán, an apprentice fitter at Stanley Street and an IESFTU member, was killed at Kilmashogue in the Dublin Mountains while on duty with 4 Coy., 5th Batt. during a skirmish with a mixed party of plain-clothes soldiers and Auxiliaries. His funeral procession was one of the largest ever held in Inchicore. His comrade William Luddy, an apprentice at the Inchicore works and a fellow IESFTU member, was arrested at Kilmashogue after Doyle had been killed. He was released on 20 May 1921 and died on 10 April 1922 from appendicitis, pneumonia and cardiac failure.[94]

The splits within the IEIU were probably unavoidable. The idea of a single Irish craft union would not have emerged but for syndicalism, the national struggle, and the work of revolutionaries like Markievicz and Collins. Able and enthusiastic trade unionists like Redmond, McIntyre, Leahy and Toomey also deserve enormous credit for making the 'one big engineering union' a reality. The IEIU's foundational ideology endured among the Inchicore men and the ETU:

> The most striking aspect of the splits is not the wrangling over demarcation lines, internal power struggles or accusations of poaching, but the fact that the members of these various warring groups did not return to the British amalgamated bodies. Having tasted freedom they did not intend to relinquish it.[95]

Relations between the IEIU and both breakaway unions were poor from the beginning. In June 1922, only a month after its first public advertisement, the IGREU took over two IEIU iron dressers at Tonge & Taggart's foundry. It was the beginning of a prolonged dispute between the two unions. The IEIU immediately threatened to call out its members at the foundry unless the two men re-join it.[96] There was another dimension to the affair. The REC had heard that, on behalf of the Inchicore men, Quinn had told the manager that the IGREU would accept into the foundry an influx of Belfast refugees fleeing loyalist attacks. The IEIU suspected that Quinn's promise was a plot to end the IEIU's presence at Tonge & Taggart's. As 'the threat of the Belfast refugees' was 'a dangerous one', the IEIU informed the Department of Labour that 'under no circumstance' would it negotiate with 'representatives of Mr. Quinn's union' or accept Belfast men into the foundry.[97] But it did subsequently participate in a conference with Quinn and accused him of adopting an 'impossible position' and engaging in 'unscrupulous methods.'[98] The dispute dragged on for several months and involved threats of strike, but these were withdrawn after DWC and government intervention. It is unclear which union won the right to represent the two men.[99] What is clear, however, is that the hostility between the unions was deep and neither had any interest in reunification. Despite poaching, there was a regular exchange of members between both unions.[100]

A product of the syndicalist years, the IGREU was quickly swept up by the zeitgeist of militancy. In October and November 1922, hundreds of its shopmen at Inchicore joined ITGWU and NUR men in striking against the GSWR's reduction of the working week from six days to five in the passenger and goods departments; twenty IEIU members also downed tools.[101] The following year, the IGREU opened a Waterford branch and, with AEU support, affiliated to the Dublin Trades Council.[102] Though it had iron moulders, fitters and the semiskilled in many Dublin contract shops, it remained unaffiliated to Congress, which it applied to join in 1926. Though the AEU was again supportive, affiliation was refused because of IEIU objections.[103] The IGREU soon became acquainted with another new union: The Workers' Union of Ireland. In April 1923, Larkin had returned to Ireland after nine years in the United States, three of which were spent in New York's Sing Sing prison for 'criminal anarchism.' In May 1924, Larkinites broke away from the ITGWU and formed the WUI, taking sixteen thousand Dubliners (two-thirds of the city membership) and twenty-three of the three hundred provincial branches with them.[104] In stark contrast to the WUI, the Inchicore Union's impact in its early years was negligible. From 1924, its membership declined as many re-joined the IEIU. A strike at the GSWR is a major reason for this.[105]

There were two components to the stoppage. The first was a WUI claim for a 3s. rise for semiskilled workers, which the company could not grant without violating its existing agreement with the IGREU.[106] The second was a demarcation dispute between WUI vicemen (also semiskilled) and IGREU fitters.[107] Both disputes were long-standing. The semiskilled men had been negotiating intermittently with the GSWR for six months but to no avail. The demarcation dispute went back to the war years and had been given fresh impetus by the establishment of the WUI. The GSWR had recently negotiated an agreement with the IGREU which redrew the line of demarcation further in the fitters' favour, though it did guarantee that there would be no reduction in the number of vicemen.[108] On 12 August, the vicemen withdrew their labour. WUI labourers then went out in sympathy, bringing numbers involved to nine hundred.[109] The fitters, however, remained at work. Relations between both unions had been poor from the start. Like the GSWR and the ITGWU, the IGREU had a stake in defeating Larkin's militant union. On 25 August, Seán McLoughlin, the WUI's socialist-republican Inchicore branch secretary, approached the GSWR and the IGREU with a plan to end the dispute. He proposed a conference to fix an acceptable line of demarcation; that the semiskilled men get their increase; and that there be no victimisation. That evening, the IGREU informed the press, not the WUI, that it had rejected the proposal because it had no dispute with either the company or the WUI.[110] The strike dragged on until 15 September when the WUI was forced to accept a humiliating defeat. Many were victimised and replaced by the scabs who had taken their place, and the demarcation agreement was set in stone.[111] Crushing the strike was made easier by the tacit support the GSWR received from the IGREU and the ITGWU. The Dublin Trades Council expelled the IGREU for its part in the dispute.[112] As late as 1928, the IEIU had 'great hope' that it and 'the Inchicore Union' would soon be reunited.[113] But the IGRWU had no interest in reunion. Divisions between the two ran deep, so it would take decades before reunification could take place.

Table 27: IGREU Branches & Membership, 1922-30.[114]

Year	Branches	Membership
1922	Inchicore, Dublin	612
1923	Inchicore, Waterford, Dublin 1 & 2	595
1924	Inchicore, Waterford, Dublin 1-4	575
1925	Ibid	563
1926	Ibid	439
1927	Ibid	396
1928	Inchicore, Dublin 1-4	393
1929	Ibid	406
1930	Ibid	381

The Electrical Trades Union (Ireland)

On 11 June 1924, the Electrical Trades Union (Dublin) was officially registered. The following year, it changed its name to the Electrical Trades Union (Ireland) (hereafter called the ETU) to distinguish it from its British namesake. In 1928, its registration was cancelled when it failed to submit an annual return for 1926.[115] Shortly after 1921, the British ETU attempted to reorganise in Ireland but was immediately crushed by its Irish namesake. The ETU (Ireland) made 41 Parnell Square its first headquarters, later moving to 27 Adelaide Road. Its first president was John Joseph Shallow and Matthew Patten its first general secretary. In 1927, it opened a Cork branch and affiliated to the Cork Workers' Council, giving it a monopoly on electricians in the Munster capital.[116] The ETU was explicitly conservative from the beginning. Its 1941 rulebook recalled how it was founded to 'raise our standard of living to … conform with Christian principles.'[117] In 1943, the ETU moved its head offices to 5 Cavendish Row where it would remain until its dissolution.

Relations between the ETU and the IEIU were poor at first. The IEIU, which had over four hundred electricians in Dublin before the split, claimed that the ETU had been started by members in arrears who broke away because they wanted better conditions than other workers in the building trade. The ETU had thus acted 'against the principles of trade unionism', allegations the young union rejected.[118] In its nascent years, the ETU tried to consolidate its position in Dublin. In fact, the ETU's first major strike was not for better wages or conditions but against the IEIU. The former objected to the latter's presence in the contract shops and obtained from the employers a commitment to not employ any IEIU electrician. It soon became clear that this was not practicable and the IEIU men remained; on 17 April 1925, one hundred ETU men downed tools in response. While the IEIU had considerable numbers at the Pigeon House, the ETU dominated the private sector. Having infuriated employers and the press, and having alienated their fellow trade unionists, the ETU called off the strike in May. It had no option but to work alongside its rival.[119] Compounding matters, some ETU members were convicted for conduct likely to lead to a breach of the peace and fined.[120] Relations between the two unions were poor for many years thereafter. In 1926 and 1927, the IEIU successfully blocked the ETU's affiliation to the ITUC. It was not until 1937 that the ETU could affiliate.[121]

Like the IEIU, the ETU had a strong republican pedigree. Its first secretary, Seán O'Duffy, is a prime example. Born in Mayo in 1886, O'Duffy moved to Dublin in 1900 and subsequently immersed himself in republican politics and in the GAA. He was Dublin's only indentured electrical apprentice of 1904, when there were only seventy-five qualified electricians in the city. He developed a deep admiration for Jim Larkin during the 1913 lockout. Having joined the Irish Volunteers (A Coy., 1st Batt., Dublin Brigade) that year, O'Duffy paraded at the funeral of Jeremiah O'Donovan-Rossa in August 1915. During the Easter Rising, he served in the area from King Street North to Church Street. After his release from Stafford Jail, he re-joined the Volunteers and reached the rank of captain. He helped Collins establish his espionage and intelligence networks and obtained a pass for Collins that allowed him to pose as an electrician should Dublin Castle learn of his whereabouts. O'Duffy worked as a chargehand at Collinstown Aerodrome (now Dublin Airport), which was being built for the Royal Air Force, at this time.[122] Consequently, he and other Volunteers knew where its arsenal was kept, information they passed on to their superiors. On 20 March 1919, Volunteers raided the arsenal and took seventy-five rifles and over four thousand rounds of ammunition. It was the Dublin Brigade's first major operation since 1916.[123] In September 1921, Austin Stack appointed O'Duffy as a fulltime organiser of the republican courts in counties Wicklow, Wexford, Kildare, Carlow, Laois and Kilkenny. He worked as a court registrar until October 1922 and took no part in the Civil War, although he opposed the Treaty.[124] Having served as a secretary of the IESFTU's Electrical Section, O'Duffy became general secretary of the ETU (Ireland) in 1925. He resigned in 1936 to take up a post as a civil servant in the Department of Industry and Commerce. He had also previously served on the executive committee of the Dublin Trades Council. William Meehan replaced him as ETU general secretary.[125]

The apprenticeship system in the 1920s

The Free State government was very conscious of the low level of craft skill in the Saorstát. More and better-quality craftsmen were needed to industrialise, especially considering the impending opening of the Shannon Scheme. In 1926, the government established the Commission on Technical Education, which reported a year later. It heard evidence from the IEIU, the AEU and the ETU, who were all were scathing about the quality of apprenticeships.

Employers were also highly critical of the system, complaining that it was deeply inefficient and failed to produce an adequate number of craftsmen.[126] The commission agreed, arguing that the present system 'has ceased to be effective' because there was 'no guarantee either for the efficient technical training of the apprentice or for employment after apprenticeship.' There was a particularly serious shortage of skilled workers in the 'newer industries' – engineering and electrical work. The Department of Education believed that part of the problem was that 'the craft spirit was strong in Ireland.' Trade unions were 'as jealous of guarding their privileges in … conditions of entry into their trades as protecting their conditions of employment.'[127] The unions disagreed. O'Duffy told the commission that it was vital that the trades remained closed, but he accepted that the existing apprenticeship system had to change because it was 'nothing short of a fraud on the parents and boys alike.'[128] He quoted a letter from a father alleging that the quality of the training was so bad that the money spent 'might as well have been thrown into the Liffey':

My son served (or wasted) his time in a shop which has become notorious for the number of boys employed. During most of his time, he played cards in a cellar and is now an expert in pontoon etc... little interest was taken in the boy.[129]

The system had hardly changed since the Industrial Revolution and bore 'little relationship to contemporary requirements.'[130] Technical education, in existence in Ireland since 1824, remained voluntary. In 1925, there were sixty-five technical schools with an average enrolment of 240 (excluding the large schools in Dublin and Cork). Instruction was mainly conducted via two-hour evening classes two or three times a week. Even this was difficult to achieve as many apprentices could not or did not attend classes due to work. Links between the centre of employment and the technical schools were haphazard as few employers appreciated the importance of technical education to industrial development.[131] Apprentices therefore received little technical schooling and continued to heavily rely on the indentureship, i.e., learning on-the-job by watching a qualified craftsman. Although employers favoured apprentices attending evening classes, the unions wanted time-off so they could attend day courses. With little state regulation, employers flagrantly abused the apprenticeship system. Some took premiums (sometimes as high as £100) from parents to have their son apprenticed, leading to inequality and preferential treatment. In the engineering trade, those who paid a premium got a holistic education in the trade, not just a subset of it (fitting, turning, patternmaking etc.). Although the engineering unions wanted a ratio of five craftsmen for every two apprentices, the actual figures were 7:1 in Dublin and 10:1 in the state overall. The number of skilled workers in the Free State fell by 16 per cent between 1923 and 1926, from 12,146 to 10,193. There was an even sharper contraction in the number of apprentices because many employers did not take their quota.[132] The trades remained closed throughout the 1920s, accessible only to the sons of craftsmen. As it gave them control over the supply of labour, unions had no intention of ceding the training of apprentices to the state, ensuring that apprenticeships would remain fundamentally unchanged for decades thereafter.

Craftsmen and the Shannon Scheme

The government knew that if the longstanding republican dream of Irish industrial regeneration was to become a reality, then the state would have to be electrified. It soon became apparent that the Irish private sector was unable to undertake such an enormous endeavour in a country as underdeveloped as the Irish Free State. Even the highly conservative Cumman na nGaedheal yielded on its free-market dogma and passed the Shannon Electricity Act 1925. As the longest river in Ireland, the Shannon was an obvious location for a dam. A major hydroelectricity station would be built at Ardnacrusha, Co. Clare from which electricity could be harnessed and distributed around the country. Having had so little to cheer about under the Free State, the unions enthusiastically welcomed the Shannon Scheme. It was a visionary and futuristic plan with brilliant potential to transform the lives of the working class. No union welcomed the Scheme more than the IEIU, which had a stake in its construction. But the project soon became notorious for terrible pay and working and living conditions, with labourers bearing the brunt.[133]

In August 1925, Siemens Schuckert was contracted to build the dam. Thomas McLaughlin, professor of electrical engineering at UCG, was the link between

Siemens and the government, having previously worked for the company. Construction would last for three-and-a-half years and cost £55.2 million, over twice the state's annual budget and a more expensive endeavour than the Civil War. Siemens offered labourers only subsistence wages: 36s. for a fifty-four-hour week. Their colleagues outside the scheme fared better. Labourers employed to convert the Strand Barracks into a storage depot for Siemens were being paid 50s. for a fifty-hour week, while the Limerick city rate was 58s. 9d. for a forty-seven-hour week. The district rate for farm labourers in Limerick and Clare was 54s. 2d. There was widespread dismay at, and condemnation of, the poor pay on offer. In September, the labourers struck, holding out until February 1926. Although the IEIU obeyed the Limerick Trades Council's call not to blackleg, it was not enough. The combined might of Siemens and the government, which provided ex-servicemen as strike-breakers, prevailed. But the labourers did secure a minor concession: a wage of 38s. 3d.[134] Low wages were not the workers' only malady. For the thousands who arrived at Ardnacrusha, living conditions were appalling and caused public outrage. Siemens built wooden huts at a camp for the men, but these quickly became completely inadequate. In 1928, the camp accommodated only 720 when over five thousand were employment. Many had to lodge in Limerick city; others resorted to living in nearby barns, stables and pigsties.[135]

Craftsmen had a better experience. Unlike labourers, they were paid the district rates: 78s. 4d. for fitters and 82s. 3d. for electricians. Riveters did even better: 86s. 2d. and 90s. 1d. All worked a forty-seven-hour week.[136] But craftsmen had their own travails. Some worked twelve to fourteen hours a day and were paid ordinary rates for overtime.[137] The backwardness of the Irish economy meant that there were not enough craftsmen to complete such a project. Those who were employed had no experience of building a project of such magnitude, making accidents common. The incompetence of the Irish craftsman was a constant grievance for Siemens and so it had eight hundred Germans shipped to Ardnacrusha. Throughout, Siemens tried to exploit the superior quality of German labour to displace Irishmen. It claimed that the Irish were very unpunctual, never arriving before 8:30am and never working more than forty-seven to fifty hours a week. The Irish often took 'two to three times as long' to compete jobs as the Germans, who were more productive and had a higher output.[138] The Irish were also prone to poor concentration and malice. Irish jobs were protected by the government. If any Irish worker were threatened with dismissal for reasons that Patrick McGilligan, Minister for Industry and Commerce, considered inadequate, it did not take place as the minister could revoke his replacement's permit.[139] The IEIU also had to work alongside AEU men, as per a government stipulation that metalwork be split 50:50 between both unions.[140]

The division of labour between the Irish and the Germans was a contentious issue throughout the project. On the one hand, the government was under pressure from the IEIU and others to provide jobs for their members, many of whom had been unemployed for a considerable period; on the other, Siemens wanted more of their own experienced men taken on to finish within the deadline.[141] There were twenty Irish foremen employed on the job. Foremen fitters and electricians earned a maximum of £5 for a fifty-hour week, giving them a better wage than most Irish workers. But the Germans ridiculed them more than any other group. 'Firstly, the foremen have little knowledge of their trade, and secondly, they do not induce the men to work. On the contrary, they loll around with their hands in their pockets near their gangs of workmen.'[142] In mid-1927, Siemens presented the Scheme's chief engineer, Professor F.S. Rishworth, with a report containing with a further litany of complaints about the quality of Irish labour. It told how Joseph McGrath – former Minister for Industry and Commerce and now labour advisor to Siemens – counselled the company to get more Germans because it was impossible to get suitably qualified foremen for excavation work or supervision of crane operations. Carelessness and inexperience had caused a disturbingly high number of accidents. Intense damage had been done to machines: locomotives burnt out and running repairs neglected; a massive dredger destroyed because the stoker forgot to fill the boiler with water; and a boring plant rendered useless through senseless continual boring. As Siemens themselves recognised, 'no large civil engineering work having ever been undertaken in Ireland and the lack of development of industry in the country up to the present time' meant that Irishmen had 'no experience in driving engines on building sites and did not know how to look after their machines.' 'Irish workmen are not accustomed to put any energy into their work which we expect, and it is not possible to find skilled men in Ireland of the quality which we need.'[143]

Ireland's huge levels of emigration also hampered construction. A staggering 43 per cent of Irish-born people were living abroad, over one million in the US. Between March 1926 and May 1927, 184 men, most of them trained by Siemens, left the Scheme. Many went to the United States, as evidenced by the number of American firms who had contacted Siemens for references. The report commented that these men were the best of those employed. Siemens were undoubtedly bewildered and frustrated by a phenomenon much more common in Ireland than in Germany. The report also alleged that 'many Irishmen, skilled and unskilled, often do not turn up for work. The excuse is always that they are ill. We however believe that they simply want to take a holiday.' A survey showed that German craftsmen worked an average of 64.5 hours a week over a 23-week period, whereas the Irish worked 55.5 hours a week – a 14 per cent difference. Siemens also calculated absenteeism during a five-week period. They found that fifty-one Germans were absent for a total of thirty days, while 109 Irishmen were absent for a total of 222 days over the same period. The report calculated that, on average, each German was absent for 0.6 days during that period while each Irishman was missing for two days.[144] Siemens followed up the report with an experiment conducted on the transmission lines between Dublin and Kildare: whether gangs of Irish foremen and fitters could work at similar speed to German gangs. They could not. Siemens rightly attributed this failure to inexperience. Under the circumstances, the company believed that the Irish fitters had acquitted themselves quite well.[145]

Conditions on the Shannon Scheme were extremely dangerous. Fifty-two men died during its construction, a figure that would appal many today. Inevitably, there were hundreds of accidents, some causing severe injury. Electricians were at a higher risk than most. The ETU, which had won the sole right to supply electricians, had to support some members permanently injured by the work.[146] In June 1927, an Irish electrician called Patterson was working on the high-tension wires when a German electrician accidentally turned on the current. Patterson was severely burned and was rushed to hospital where an arm and both feet had to be amputated.[147] This accident might have been caused by the language barrier, which inevitably caused friction between the Irish and the

Germans. In an environment where miscommunication could be fatal, frustration sometimes boiled over. Although relations were quite good overall, animosity always lingered beneath the surface. Both groups harboured prejudices typical of an era when racism and xenophobia were widespread. Discrimination fuelled the mutual suspicion. Germans received preferential treatment from the management, even when they were less competent, and there were several cases of unfair dismissals of Irish craftsmen. The five thousand-strong Irish workforce resented being controlled by the Germans, who were paid far above what the Irish got for the same work. German foremen, who had only a few words of English, subjected the Irish to regular verbal abuse.[148]

By late 1928, most of the excavating and concreting work had been completed. From March 1929, craftsmen began to be discharged due to 'slackness of work.' Carpenters were the first to go, followed by train drivers and stokers, blacksmiths, fitters and others who had become redundant.[149] On 22 July 1929, William T. Cosgrave, President of the Executive Council of the Free State, officially opened Ardnacrusha hydro-electric power station. It was the biggest of its kind in the world, though in 1936 it lost that honour to the Hoover Dam on the Colorado River. By 1935, Ardnacrusha was producing 80 per cent of the Free State's electricity.[150] It is still in use today, a testimony to the skill, courage and dedication of those who built it.

Chapter Notes and References

1   McCarthy, *Trade Unions in Ireland, 1894-1960* (Dublin: Institute of Public Administration, 1977), p. 635.
2   James Meenan, *The Irish economy since 1922* (Liverpool: Liverpool University Press, 1970), p. 66.
3   Terence Brown, *Ireland: A Social and Cultural History, 1922-79* (Fontana: Fontana Press, 1981), pp. 16-17.
4   Cormac Ó Gráda, *A Rocky Road: The Irish Economy since the 1920s* (Manchester: Manchester University Press, 1997); Andy Bielenberg & Raymond Ryan, *An Economic History of Ireland since Independence* (Oxford: Routledge, 2013); Brian Girvin, 'Trade Unions and Economic Development', in Donal Nevin (ed.), *Trade Union Century* (Cork: Mercier Press, 1994), pp. 118-120
5   Borgonovo, *The Battle for Cork, July-August 1922* (Cork: Mercier Press, 2012), pp. 26, 30.
6   *Cork Examiner*, 14 Dec. 1921, 2 Jan. 1922.
7   Borgonovo, *Battle for Cork*, pp. 24-26; Yeates, *A City in Wartime*, p. 305.
8   John M. Regan, *The Irish Counter-Revolution, 1921-1936: Treatyite Politics and Settlement in Independent Ireland* (Dublin: Gill & Macmillan, 1999), pp. 82-84; Tom Garvin, 'The Anatomy of a Nationalist Revolution: Ireland, 1858-1928', *Comparative Studies in Society and History*, Vol. 28, No. 3, July 1986, pp. 484-491.
9   Gavin Foster, *The Irish Civil War and Society: Politics, Class, and Conflict* (Basingstoke: Palgrave Macmillan, 2014), p. 55.
10 Cited in Ibid., p. 56.
11 *Irish Independent*, 25 Apr. 1922.
12 Leahy, WS 660, BMH, MA, p. 39.
13 Ann Matthews, *The Irish Citizen Army* (Cork: Mercier Press, 2014), pp. 169-170.
14 R.M. Fox, *The History of the Irish Citizen Army* (Dublin: J. Duffy & Co., 1944), pp. 208-210; Brian Hanley, 'The Irish Citizen Army After 1916', *Saothar*, Vol. 28, 2003, pp. 37-47; Jeffrey Leddin, *The 'Labour Hercules': The Irish Citizen Army and Irish Republicanism, 1913-23* (Dublin: Irish Academic Press, 2019).
15 Leahy, WS 660, BMH, MA, p. 42.
16 Diarmaid Ferriter, *The Transformation of Ireland, 1900-2000* (London: Profile Books, 2004), p. 191.

17 IEIU REC minutes, 10 July 1922; IEIU NEC minutes, 14 Sept. 1922; Yeates, *Craft Workers*, p. 42; *Irish Independent*, 25, 28 July 1922.
18 IEIU REC minutes, 6, 12, 13 Nov. 1922; Yeates, *A City in Civil War*, p. 317.
19 Hannigan, MSP Application, MA.
20 Thomas Maguire, MSP Application, MSP Collection, DP5958, MA.
21 Yeats, *Craft Workers*, pp. 42-43; Seán Cole, MSP Application, MSP Collection, DP3749, MA; James Flanagan, MSP Application, MSP Collection, DP3509, MA.
22 IEIU REC minutes, 27 Nov., 4 Dec. 1922. Faced with a litany of victimisation claims, the NEC had agreed that benefits should only be paid to those who could prove they were dismissed for doing union work or having a union card, and/or blacklisted by an employer or employer association. See Yeates, *Craft Workers*, p. 31.
23 Ibid., 22 Jan. 1923.
24 Ibid., 15 Jan. 1923.
25 Ibid., 7 May 1923; IEIU NEC minutes 26 July 1923.
26 IEIU REC minutes, 22 Jan., 5, 12 Mar. 1923.
27 *Freeman's Journal*, 10 Aug. 1922; T. O'S. to secretary of Irish Engineering Union, TSCH/3/S1573, Dept. of An Taoiseach records, NAI.
28 Brendan Share, *In Time of Civil War: The Conflict on the Irish Railways, 1922-23* (Cork: Collins Press, 2006).
29 O'Connor, *Syndicalism in Ireland*, pp. 91, 94, 185-186; Gavin Foster, 'Class dismissed? The debate over a social basis to the Treaty split and the Irish Civil War', *Saothar*, no. 33, 2008, pp. 73-88.
30 Between 1912 and 1930, the ITUC and the Labour Party were officially part of the one organisation, known as the Irish Labour Party and Trades Union Congress. For simplicity's sake, the organisation will be referred to as the ITUC throughout.
31 Yeates, *A City in Civil War*, p. 54; Yeates, *Craft Workers*, pp. 39-40; ITUC, *Report of the twenty-eight annual meeting, 1922*, ILHM, pp. 66-87.
32 IEIU NEC minutes, 19, 20 May 1923; Arthur Mitchell, *Labour in Irish Politics*, pp. 186-191; Niamh Puirséil, *The Irish Labour Party, 1922-73* (Dublin: University College Dublin Press, 2007), pp. 11, 16-18; *Irish Times*, 31 Aug. 1923. The *Irish Times* alleged that the 19 August incident at a funeral – where drivers of hearses were ordered off their cars – contributed to the Labour Party's poor result in Cork. See *CE*, 20 Aug. 1923.
33 Regan, *The Irish Counter-Revolution*, p. 238.
34 Foster, *The Irish Civil War*, pp. 58-63.
35 Ibid., pp. 36-39.
36 O'Connor, *A Labour History of Ireland*, p. 139.
37 Ibid., pp. 141-142.
38 *Thirtieth annual report of the ITUC*, 1924, pp. 193-194. The amendment was not moved because the IEIU delegates had by then withdrawn. The original resolution was thus passed unamended instead.
39 *Cork Examiner*, 30 Nov., 7 Dec. 1921, 8 Apr., 4, 19 July, 3 Aug. 1922; Yeates, *Craft Workers*, p. 38.
40 *Voice of Labour*, 9 Sept., 14 Oct., 9, 16 Dec. 1922. James McNeill served as Governor General of the Irish Free State from 1928 to 1932. He was the brother of Minister for Education Eoin McNeill.
41 Yeates, *Craft Workers*, p. 38; *Irish Independent*, 21 Jan. 1922; *Evening Echo*, 7 July 1922.
42 *Irish Independent*, 30 Nov., 15 Dec. 1922, 6 Feb. 1923.
43 IEIU REC minutes, 13 Dec. 1921, 19, 23 Jan., 6 Feb., 9 Mar., 10, 18 Apr., 1, 9, 15 May, 19 June, 14 July, 11, 21 Aug. 1922.
44 Ibid., 11 Aug. 1922.
45 *Freeman's Journal*, 7, 10, 11 Oct. 1922, 5, 23 Jan., 16, 22 Mar., 2 June 1923; *Irish Independent*, 15 June 1923, 29 Sept., 3 Oct. 1924; Smellie, *Shipbuilding and repairing in Dublin*; Pat Sweeney, *Liffey Ships and Shipbuilding* (Cork: Mercier Press, 2010), pp. 122-137.
46 Yeates, *A City in Civil War*, pp. 272-273.
47 Colman O'Mahony, *The Maritime Gateway to Cork: A History of the Outports of Passage West and Monkstown, 1754-1942* (Cork: Tower Books, 1986), p. 114; *Cork Examiner*, 14 Feb. 1922.
48 *Evening Herald*, 16 June 1924.
49 *Thirtieth annual report of the ITUC*, 1924, pp. 180-183; *thirty-first annual report of the ITUC*, 1925,
50 IEIU REC minutes, 2, 7 Dec. 1921, 3, 17, 19 Jan., 19 June, 10, 17, 31 July, 11, 21 Aug., 4, 18 Sept., 3 Oct. 1922.

51 Cathal Brennan, 'The Postal Strike of 1922', 8 June 2012, *The Irish Story*, http://www.theirishstory.com/2012/06/08/the-postal-strike-of-1922/#.UhTd-5LVBvl, (retrieved 11 Mar. 2019).

52 Devine, *Organising History*, Chapter 9.

53 O'Connor, *Syndicalism in Ireland*, p. 76.

54 IEIU NEC minutes, 14 Sept. 1922, 16, 17 Feb. 1923; IEIU REC minutes, 27 Nov. 1922

55 IEIU REC minutes, 30 July 1923. It is not clear what the reduction was as the minutes for the period are missing. The employers wanted a 4½d. per hour cut, while the union was willing to accept an hourly cut of 2¼d.

56 Ibid., 30 Oct. 1922, 19, 23, 26 Feb., 5 Mar. 1923; *Freeman's Journal*, 27 Feb. 1923. A foreman is the supervisor responsible for a job and those assigned to it if the workforce exceeds six. Ranking above chargehands, foremen typically earn 20 per cent above the going rate.

57 *Freeman's Journal*, 19, 23 May, 23 June, 26 July 1923; *Nenagh Guardian*, 2, 30 June 1923; IEIU REC minutes, 2, 10, 12, 13 Dec. 1921, 7, 14, 23 May, 27 June, 26 July 1923.

58 IEIU NEC minutes, 16, 17 Feb., 19, 20 May 1923; IEIU REC minutes, 8, 22 Jan., 16 Apr., 14 May 1923. Competition for jobs also contributed to the poor relations between the two unions.

59 IEIU REC minutes, 13, 22 May, 2 June, 14, 17, 31 July, 30 Oct. 1922; *Voice of Labour*, 22, 29 Oct. 1921, 13, 20 May 1922. The alleged agreement to combat the ITGWU came from a dispute between the ATGWU and the IEIU regarding which workers could join which union at the Dublin Tramways workshop.

60 *Cork Examiner*, 15, 22, 24, 29 Nov., 1, 3, 4 Dec. 1923. A figure of eight to ten thousand is stated in *Irish Times*, 31 Aug. 1923. O'Connor claims that about six thousand were locked out. See O'Connor, *Syndicalism in Ireland*, p. 108.

61 O'Connor, *A Labour History of Waterford*, p. 194

62 O'Connor, *Labour History of Ireland* (2nd Ed.), p. 146.

63 Mike Milotte, *Communism in Modern Ireland: The Pursuit of the Workers' Republic since 1916* (Dublin: Gill and Macmillan, 1984), p. 72.

64 Department of Industry and Commerce, *Statistical Abstract* (Dublin: Stationary Office, 1932).

65 Cody, O'Dowd & Rigney, *The Parliament of Labour*, pp. 157-158; IEIU REC minutes, 9, 30 Mar. 1928; *Irish Independent*, 18 Feb. 1929.

66 O'Connor, *A Labour History of Ireland*, p. 146.

67 ITUC, *Twenty-ninth annual report*, 1923, p. 109.

68 *Freeman's Journal*, 31 July, 1 Aug. 1924.

69 IEIU annual returns, 1924-29, T358, RFS records, NAI; ITUC, *annual reports*, 1921-25, NLI.

70 IEIU annual returns, 1924-30, T358, RFS records, NAI.

71 In July 1924, the Dáil passed the Railways Act 1924. The Act merged every Free State railway company into one privately-owned body that came into existence on 1 January 1925: The Great Southern Railway Company. See J.C. Conroy, *A History of Railways in Ireland* (New York: Longmans, Green and Co. Ltd, 1928), pp. 310-315, 325.

72 *Irish Independent*, 18 Sept. 1925, 9 Mar., 22, 23 Apr., 10, 18, 24, 28 May 1926. In December 1923, railway directors, unions and the government had agreed to establish a comprehensive machinery of arbitration for wage and conditions. A hierarchical scheme of five institutions was put in place: local departmental committees, sectional railway councils, railway councils, the Central Wages Board and the Irish Railway Board. Directors, trade unionists, businessmen and members of the public would sit on these bodies.

73 *Irish Independent*, 21, 22 Jan., 25, 31 Feb., 9 Mar., 18, 24 May, 5, 17, 19, 20, 27 June 1929.

74 IEIU REC minutes, 20 Jan. 1928.

75 Ibid., 20, 21, 24, 25 Jan., 30 Mar. 1928; *Cork Examiner*, 23 Mar. 1928; IEIU NEC minutes, 26 Jan. 1928.

76 *Irish Independent*, 14 July 1925.

77 IEIU REC minutes, 16 Mar., 17 May 1928, 14 Apr. 1929; IEIU NEC & REC joint meeting, 13 July 1928; IEIU NEC minutes, 16, 17 Feb., 19, 20 1923, 18, 19, 20 Apr. 1929.

78 IEIU REC minutes, 14 Apr. 1929.

79 Ibid., 7 June 1928.

80 Ibid., 22 Feb., 8, 15, 22, 27 June 1928, 12 Sept. 1929; minutes of meeting of IEIU Dublin membership, 2 July 1928.

81   IEIU NEC minutes, 18-20 Apr. 1929; IEIU REC minutes, 27 June 1929.

82   Patterson, 'Industrial labour and the labour movement', p. 177.

83   IEIU REC minutes, 13 Dec. 1921, 9, 15 May, 10 July, 23 Oct., 20 Nov. 1922, 23 Jan., 5 Mar., 5 Apr., 26 June 1923; IEIU NEC minutes, 21 Apr. 1922, 26 June, 26 July 1923.

84   *Woman's Dreadnaught*, 24 Mar. 1923; IEIU NEC minutes, 31 Dec. 1921.

85   Yeates, *Craft Workers*, p. 44; *Irish Press*, 11 Jan. 1938.

86   Ibid., p. 40.

87   Ibid., p. 41. See also Investigation Committee minutes, 24 Feb-21 Mar. 1922.

88   IEIU REC minutes, 12 Oct. 1921; IGREU, 'annual return for 1922', T357, Registry of Friendly Societies (RFS) records, NAI; *Evening Herald*, 19 May 1922.

89   *Evening Herald*, 26 Aug. 1924, 15 Feb. 1928; Ward-Perkins, *Trade Union Records*, p. 202.

90   IGREU, 'Rules', 1922, p. 3.

91   IEIU, 'Rules' (Dublin: Dollard Printing House Ltd., 1922), p. 5.

92   Patrick Joseph Hickey, MSP application, DP4395, MSP Collection, MA; John Monks, MSP application, DP7433, MSP collection, MA. *Irish Independent*, 13 July 1922; *Freeman's Journal*, 8 Sept. 1922. See also Patrick Joseph Monks, MSP34REF11741; and Richard Monks, MSP application, MSP34REF1491, both found in MSP collection, MA. In his military service pension application, Richard Monks claims that that he lost his job for his republican activity and was unemployed for the next ten years.

93   Patrick O'Hara, MSP application, 2D417, MSP collection, MA; Leo Francis Beahan, MSP application, 3D218, MSP collection, MA; *Freeman's Journal*, 26 July 1922; *Irish Independent*, 12 Jan., 14 Feb. 1923.

94   *Irish Worker*, 21 Mar. 1925; Peadar Seán Doyle, MSP application, MSP34REF2335, MSP Collection, MA; John Doyle, MSP application, 1D28, MSP collection, MA; William Luddy, MSP application, 1D76, MSP collection, MA; Peadar Doyle, WS 155, BMH, MA; Yeates, *A City in Turmoil*, pp. 169-170; *Irish Independent*, 19 Apr. 1922.

95   Yeates, *Craft Workers*, p. 44.

96   IEIU REC minutes, 2 June 1922.

97   Ibid., 14 June 1922.

98   Ibid., 10 July 1922.

99   Ibid., 2, 14, 15 June, 10, 17, 31 July, 4 Sept, 20 Nov. 1922; IEIU NEC minutes, 19 June 1922.

100 IEIU REC minutes, 21 Aug., 4 Sept., 4, 18 Dec. 1922; IEIU NEC minutes, 14 Sept 1922.

101 *Evening Herald*, 16 Oct.-11 Nov. 1922. The sixteen hundred shopmen had been on a three-day week (halftime) since September 1922.

102 IEIU REC minutes, 22 Jan., 14 May, 26 June 1923.

103 ITUC executive committee minutes, 19, 26 Apr., 31 May, 17, 7 June, 5 July 1926, ICTU/Box 100, ICTU collection, NAI.

104 R.M. Fox, *Jim Larkin: The Rise of the Underman* (London: Lawrence & Wishart, 1957), p. 160.

105 For a detailed account of the strike, see Charlie, McGuire, "The strike that 'never should have taken place'? The Inchicore rail dispute of 1924', *History Ireland*, Issue 2, Vol. 17, Mar./Apr. 2009.

106 These included oilers, tubers and helpers. The 3s. increase would bring their wages to 80s., which the vicemen earned. See *Freeman's Journal*, 26 Aug. 1924

107 At the GSWR, vicemen worked in the carriage and wagon shops. The introduction of steel framed carriages reduced the need for vicemen and created conflict between them and the fitters. See *Freeman's Journal*, 16 Aug. 1924.

108 Under the agreement, vicemen would repair coaches and carriages, and have jurisdiction over rebuilt stock and work consequent of alteration to same. All ironwork was the vicemen's domain. The fitters would undertake all new work on coaches and carriages except for ironwork. *Irish Independent*, 25 Aug. 1924.

109 *Freeman's Journal*, 11, 16, 18 Aug. 1924.

110 McGuire, "The strike that 'never should have taken place." See *Freeman's Journal*, 26 Aug. 1924 for a copy of the IGREU's statement to the press.

111 McGuire, 'The strike that 'never should have taken place."

112 *The Irish Worker*, 27 Sept. 1924, 21 Mar. 1925.

113 IEIU REC minutes, 6 Jan. 1928.

114 IGREU, annual returns, 1922-30, T357, RFS records, NAI.

115 ETU (Ireland), annual returns, T366, RFS records, NAI.

116 *Cork Examiner*, 15 Jan. 1927.

117 ETU, *Rulebook* (1941), p. 2.
118 IEIU REC minutes, 9 Mar. 1928.
119 *Evening Herald*, 22 May 1924, 17, 18, 20, 28, 29 Apr., 4 May 1925; *Irish Independent*, 28 Apr. 1925.
120 *Evening Herald*, 23 May 1925.
121 ITUC executive minutes, 8 Nov., 20 Dec. 1926, 17 Jan., 21, 28 Mar., 25 Apr., 27 June 1927, ICTU/Box 100, ICTU collection, NAI; ETU REC minutes, 14 June 1937.
122 A chargehand is the supervisor responsible for a job and those assigned to it if the workforce is between three and six. Ranking below foremen, chargehands typically earn 10 per cent above the going rate.
123 Seán O'Duffy, WS 618, BMH, MA, p. 19-20; 'Seán O'Duffy, sworn statement to Advisory Committee, 1 November 1937', MSP Collection, MSP34REF20489, MA; *Irish Press*, 30 July, 21 Oct. 1981.
124 Seán O'Duffy, WS 313, 618 & 619, BMH, MA. O'Duffy gave three separate testimonies to the Bureau of Military History: one on 30 September 1949 and two on 13 November 1951.
125 *Evening Herald*, 27 Aug. 1925; *Irish Press*, 3 Dec. 1936.
126 *Irish Independent*, 20 Jan. 1927
127 Ibid., 25 Nov. 1926.
128 *Evening Herald*, 22 Jan. 1927.
129 Cited in Ryan, *Apprenticeships in Ireland*, p. 157
130 Ibid., p. 158.
131 Ibid., pp. 151-153.
132 Commission on Technical Education, *Report* (Dublin: Stationary Office, 1927), pp. 88-89; Ibid., pp. 158-160.
133 Michael McCarthy, *High Tension: Life on the Shannon Scheme* (Dublin: Lilliput Press, 2004).
134 Herr Heintze to Professor Frank S. Rishworth, 16 Feb. 1926, SS 13929, Siemens collection, NAI; *Irish Independent*, 20, 22 Jan. 1926.
135 McCarthy, *High Tension*, pp. 77-94.
136 'AEU No. 2 Divisional Committee meeting, 11 Mar. 1926', Shannon Scheme dispute file, ICTU/1/13, ICTU collection, NAI; IEIU REC minutes, 23 Mar. 1928.
137 *Irish Independent*, 3 Aug. 1927; ITUC, *Thirty-third annual meeting of the ITUC*.
138 Heintze to Rishworth, 11 July 1929, SS 13929, Siemens collection, NAI.
139 Rishworth to Siemens, 21 July 1927, SS 13929, Siemens collection, NAI.
140 IEIU REC minutes, 2, 16, 23 Mar. 1928.
141 McCarthy, *High Tension*, pp. 68-69.
142 Cited in McCarthy, *High Tension*, p. 69.
143 Siemens to Rishworth, 12 July 1927, SS 13929, Siemens collection, NAI.
144 Heintze to Rishworth, 12 July 1927 SS 13929, NAI; McCarthy, *High Tension*, pp. 70-71.
145 'Report of the Trial of Irish Gangs on the Dublin-Kildare 38KV Line', SS 13929, Siemens collection, NAI; McCarthy, *High Tension*, p. 71.
146 Heintze to Rishworth, 31 Mar. 1926, SS 13929, NAI.
147 McCarthy, *High Tension*, pp. 65-68, 110, 120-121.
148 Ibid., pp. 65-69, 131.
149 Ibid., pp. 73-75.
150 *Irish Independent*, 23 July 1929; Ronald C. Cox & Michael H. Gould, *Civil Engineering Heritage: Ireland* (London: Thomas Telford, 1998), p. 272.

6 Gardiner Row

(Credit: *Connect Archive*)

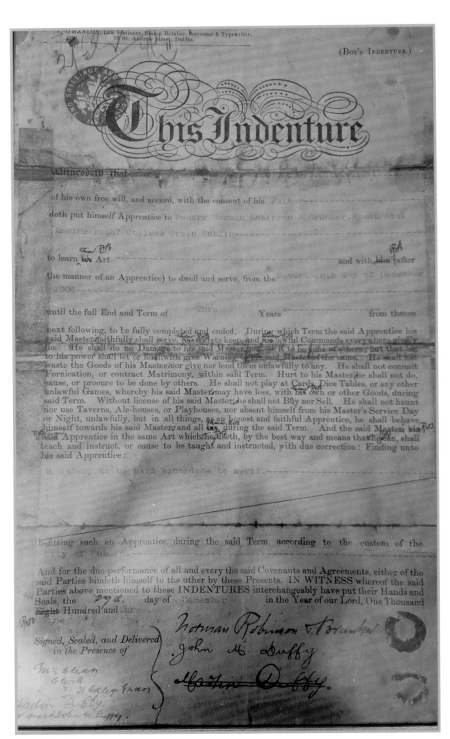

Apprentice Indenture 1908

(Credit: *Connect Archive*)

Photo Section 2

Countess Markievicz
(Credit: *Connect Archive*)

Dublin Electricians, photo taken at the Ardnacrusha Works.
(Credit: *Connect Archive*)

Early National Executive Council of the Union at the back of head office.
(Credit: *Connect Archive*)

ETU Labour Day 1930

(Credit: *Connect Archive*)

View of the construction works at Ardnacrusha, 1920's

(Credit: *ESB Archive*)

Locals observing the process of rural electrification.
(Credit: *ESB Archive*)

Early correspondence from the union to Clontarf pumping station
re manning levels.

(Credit: *Connect Archive*)

Electrical member inspecting panel, Ardnacrusha
(Credit: *ESB Archive*)

"CLASH OF INTERESTS"

Reason for New Irish Trade Union

A largely attended meeting was held in the Abbey Theatre, Dublin, yesterday, for the formation of a trade union to embrace all workers in the engineering and foundry trades in Ireland.

The proposal was the outcome of the treatment received from unions in Great Britain by Irish workers on several occasions, notably in the Conscription crisis of 1918 and the recent Motor Permits strike.

Messrs J. J. Redmond and P. MacIntire, hon. president and secretary, in an appeal stated that there was material in Ireland for th' new union in the engineering, shipbuilding and foundry trades.

Fitters, turners, patternmakers, boilermakers, blacksmiths, brass-finishers, moulders, electricians, machinists, and kindred workers were represented at the meeting.

Red-Tape of British Unions.

Mr. Joseph Toomey, A.S.E., who presided, explained the necessity for the proposed Union. He said the clash of Irish workers' interests with those cross-Channel arose from their being, after all, two separate and distinct peoples. It was true that the interests of all workers were common, but workers in different countries saw things in a different light.

Two Examples.

He referred to the action of the Amalgamated Unions' Executive towards Irish conscription and the motor permits strike, as examples of the London wiseacres' attitude of regarding questions affecting Irishmen as political.

Mr. J. J. Redmond, A.S.E., in dealing with the financial position of the new Union, declared that business experts had pronounced it as sound while a Dublin bank had promised an over-draft. The Executives of British unions in the past 5 years, he said, had been anti-Irish and he could prove it.

Suggestions Repudiated.

The Unions Executive would consist of delegates drawn from different sections with power to compose differences. He denied that the Irish Transport Union or a Sinn Fein plot had any responsibility for the new Union. The English Executives had failed. The new Union would cater for all workers in the Irish Engineering trade. In Dublin and the South of Ireland, the moulders were with them to a man. The old system of amalgamated unions had kept the workers apart. They hoped for fewer and simpler rules and better ideas of organisation and men all round.

Formation Proposal Passed.

Messrs. Leahy, boilermakers; P. MacIntire, moulders; O'Neill, moulders' secretary, Wexford; McGuggin, A.S.E., Cork; Robert Donoghoe, electrical union, Dublin, took part in the subsequent discussion.

Mr. O'Leary, moulders, formally proposed the formation of the new Union. It was seconded by Mr. P. McGran, Belfast, and passed. The organising committee was appointed to act as the Executive, being given power to frame rules and to add to its numbers.

Report of Initial meeting for founding new Irish Engineering Union.

(Credit: *Connect Archive*)

Mr. J. J. Redmond, Pres., presiding at first quarterly meeting of Dublin district of the newly-formed Irish Engineering Electrical Shipbuilding and Foundry Trade Union, referred to the persistent attempts of British trade union emissaries to disrupt the organisation, and the threat of a Scottish general secretary that if it cost the English unions £1,000 they would smash their Irish union. Their union was in a very satisfactory condition as regards membership and funds, and their cards had been recognised on the Clyde, in Liverpool, and in London.

The present attempt to create a strike in the Irish railway shops by members of British trade unions he described as actuated with the objects of breaking the new Irish trade union organisation, and also helping the army of occupation and the Government to close down all the railways in Ireland in reprisal for the fight the Irish railway workers were making against handling munitions.

Evidence of concerns of the behaviour of British based unions towards the new Irish Engineering Union.

(Credit: *Connect Archive*)

THE IRISH ENGINEERING, ELECTRICAL, SHIPBUILDING, AND FOUNDRY TRADE UNION.

A SPECIAL MEETING OF SHOP STEWARDS

Of the Above Union will be Held on TO-MORROW (SUNDAY), 6th Inst., at 6 GARDINER'S ROW. SPECIAL GENERAL MEETING OF MEMBERS OF NO. 4 and 6 BRANCHES will also be Held at Same Address on SUNDAY NEXT, Starting at 12 Sharp.

When very important business will come up for consideration. Punctual attendance is requested. Members of No. 6 Branch please note that during present Curfew Regulations Financial Meeting for the Branch will be held from 8 to 7 p.m.

Notice for Shop Stewards meeting 1920, Head office.

(Credit: *Connect Archive*)

SMITHY 1944

Inchicore Works 1944, Steam Hammer at work
(Credit: *Irish Rail Archive*)

John Redmond, Union's founding President.
(Credit: *Connect Archive*)

Terrance MacSweeney

Michael Collins

REGISTER No. ....   TABLE No. ....

No. 6 Area : MOUNTJOY WARD—M.B.

Polling 8 a.m. to 8 p.m.

KINDLY MARK YOUR BALLOT PAPER FOR THE FOLLOWING SEVEN

Sinn Fein & Labour Candidates

	BYRNE, JOHN, Electrician.
	CLARKE, KATHLEEN, Widow.
	O'SHEA-LEAMY, LILLIE, Shopkeeper
	MAHON, PATRICK, General Printer.
	O'MAOILFHINN, JAMES, Provision Merchant.
	SLATER, MICHAEL, Brass Finisher.
	TOOMEY, JOSEPH, Engineer.

HOW TO VOTE.

Do not put a **X** or your Name on Ballot Paper.

Place the figure **1** opposite the name of the Candidate you like best.
Place the figure **2** opposite the name of the Candidate you like second best.
Place the figure **3** opposite the name of the Candidate you like third best.
Place the figure **4** opposite the name of the Candidate you like fourth best.
Place the figure **5** opposite the name of the Candidate you like fifth best.
Place the figure **6** opposite the name of the Candidate you like sixth best.
Place the figure **7** opposite the name of the Candidate you like seventh best.

Your Paper is spoiled if the figure **1** does not appear opposite the name of one of the Candidates.

Your Paper is spoiled if the figure **1** appears opposite the names of more than one Candidate.

If a Ballot Paper were marked thus : **2, 5, 1, 4,** such paper is only valid up to and including number **2**—because the figure **3** has been omitted.

If you Spoil a Ballot Paper, ask for another.

BRING THIS PAPER TO THE POLLING BOOTH AND HAND IT TO THE SINN FEIN AGENT.

Irish Paper.]   Printed by Patrick Mahon, Yarnhall St.

Sinn Fein handbill 1920

(Credit: *National Library of Ireland*)

Mountjoy Ward Municipal Election
15th JANUARY, 1920.

STRIKE A BLOW FOR

IRISH INDEPENDENCE

BY SUPPORTING THE FOLLOWING

SINN FEIN AND LABOUR CANDIDATES

BYRNE, JOHN, Electrician, 582 North Circular Road.

CLARKE, KATHLEEN, Richmond Ave., Fairview (Widow of late Tom Clarke, who was executed Easter, 1916).

O'SHEA-LEAMY, LILLIE, Shopkeeper, 78a Summerhill.

MAHON, PATRICK, Printer, 71 Summerhill (Chairman City of Dublin Technical Education Committee).

O'MAOILFHINN, JAMES, Provision Merchant, 107 Summerhill.

SLATER, MICHAEL, Brass Finisher, 41 Summerhill Parade (President Brassfounders' Society).

TOOMEY, JOSEPH, Engineer, 31 Clonliffe Avenue (Member Amalgamated Society of Engineers).

THE ABOVE CANDIDATES ARE PLEDGED TO CARRY OUT THE SINN FEIN MUNICIPAL PROGRAMME:—
(1) TO SECURE THE EXPENDITURE INSIDE IRELAND OF THE RATES RAISED IN IRELAND.
(2) TO SECURE EFFICIENCY AND PURITY OF ADMINISTRATION.
(3) TO ESTABLISH THE PRINCIPLE OF FREE AND OPEN COMPETITION FOR PUBLIC APPOINTMENTS.
(4) TO CARRY INTO EFFECT THE DEMOCRATIC PROGRAMME APPROVED BY THE ELECTED REPRESENTATIVES OF IRELAND.

Vote Early and Solid for this Republican Ticket.

DIA SAOIR éIRE.

IRISH PAPER.]   [TRADE UNION LABOUR.

Sinn Fein handbill 1920 – Toomey and Slater
(Credit: *National Library of Ireland*)

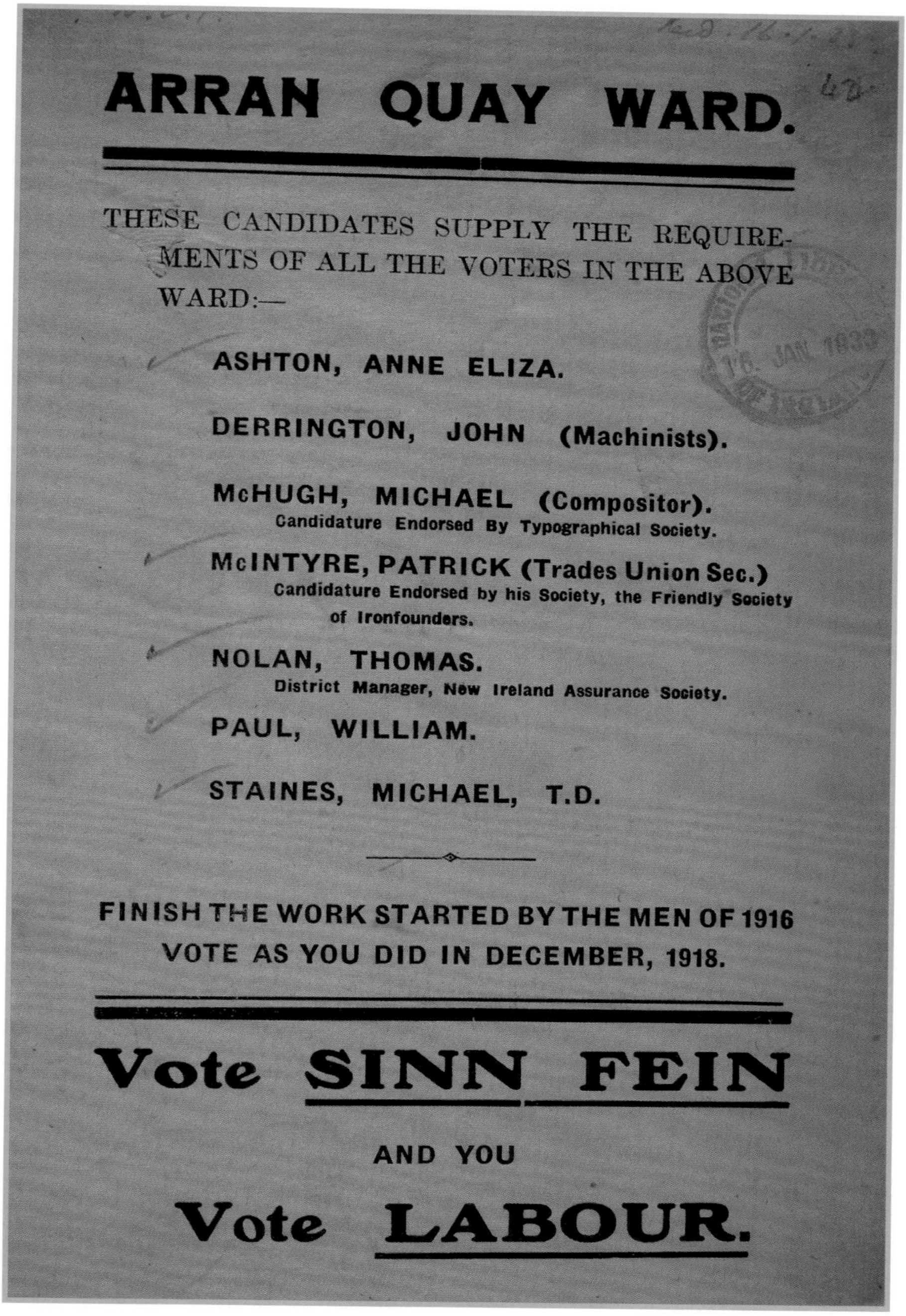

ARRAN QUAY WARD.

THESE CANDIDATES SUPPLY THE REQUIRE-
MENTS OF ALL THE VOTERS IN THE ABOVE
WARD:—

ASHTON, ANNE ELIZA.

DERRINGTON, JOHN (Machinists).

McHUGH, MICHAEL (Compositor).
Candidature Endorsed By Typographical Society.

McINTYRE, PATRICK (Trades Union Sec.)
Candidature Endorsed by his Society, the Friendly Society
of Ironfounders.

NOLAN, THOMAS.
District Manager, New Ireland Assurance Society.

PAUL, WILLIAM.

STAINES, MICHAEL, T.D.

FINISH THE WORK STARTED BY THE MEN OF 1916
VOTE AS YOU DID IN DECEMBER, 1918.

Vote SINN FEIN

AND YOU

Vote LABOUR.

Sinn Fein & Labour Handbill 1920
(Credit: *National Library of Ireland*)

Some of the organisers at the founding meeting in the Abbey Theatre.
(Credit: *Connect Archive*)

Steam Locomotive Works, Inchicore
(Credit: *Irish Rail Archive*)

4

Craftsmen in the Tumultuous Thirties, 1930-39

The Wall Street Crash of 1929 did not initially have any pronounced effects on the Irish Free State. Globally, however, the ensuing economic depression, the deepest and most prolonged in history, devastated economies across the world. The terms of trade favoured the Free State to begin with. The price of grain and animal feeding stuff – which it imported – fell much more rapidly than its major exports of livestock and their products. Because industry in the Free State primarily served the domestic market, it was not as sensitive to an externally depressed economy.[1] But Ireland was not entirely immune to the worldwide economic and political turmoil. In 1932, the election of the first Fianna Fáil government ended a decade of despondency for trade unionists. By then, Cumman na nGaedheal had drifted so far to the right that its reactionary, neo-colonial politics had effectively made the state a beef ranch of Britain. The absurd 'red scare' it had launched against Fianna Fáil had confirmed its status as a bourgeois party that offered nothing to workers. But genuine reds would little solace under the new government. Fianna Fáil in the 1930s was a 'complex coalition of traditionalists, modernisers, visionaries, conservatives, radicals, cranks and optimists; a party which denied it was a sectional grouping, asserting on the contrary that it was a national movement.'[2] The new government heralded a new political consensus from which the craftsman stood to gain. The phase 'de Valera's Ireland' is often used to describe this new milieu. It should be avoided as a simplistic caricature that has been undermined by successive historical research. Contradictions abounded during the 1930s, especially between what Fianna Fáil claimed it would achieve and what it succeeded in doing. There was much continuity between 1922 and 1939. Endeavours to maximise stability, security and political and cultural sovereignty were extensions of the state-building of the 1920s.[3] The results for the craftsman were equally as complex and contradictory.

Trade unionists widely shared de Valera's romantic notion of a self-sufficient nation living in 'frugal comfort.' Fianna Fáil immediately erected a wall of protective tariffs for which unions had long agitated. The party's industrialisation programme yielded impressive results: industrial employment grew from 110,558 in 1931 to 166,513 in 1938 and industrial output rose by 40 per cent between 1931 and 1936. Using 1953 as one hundred, the index of industrial production was 35.2 in 1925 and only 37.6 in 1931; by 1939, the figure had climbed to 56.0.[4] Emmet O'Connor and Mary Daly contend that, proportionately speaking, this performance rivals the Soviet Union's massive industrialisation under Joseph Stalin's second five-year plan (1933-37). Industrialisation gave trade unions, especially craft unions, a new importance. So too did the Control of Manufacture Acts of 1932 and 1934 which promoted native ownership of industry, from which Irish-based unions would benefit. State intervention in the economy increased significantly and several new semi-state companies were established. For the IEIU, the Turf Development Board (1933), Irish Sugar Company (1933) and Aer Lingus (1936) were especially

93

relevant. But there were limits to the success, and Fianna Fáil ran out of ideas after an initial wave of industrial development. The total growth in employment was insignificant: 1,220,284 in 1926 to 1,235,424 in 1936. There were simply not enough new jobs to absorb rural depopulation. Between 1926 and 1931, over 120,000 had taken the traditional solution to unemployment and emigrated. But the global depression had made emigration, especially to the United States, unattractive. High industrial input costs in a small domestic market meant high retail prices for Irish workers. Unemployment reached a high of 133,000 in January 1936, double the 1926 rate.[5] Wages remained quite static: using the 1953 index, they only rose from 44.5 in 1930 to 47.9 in 1939.[6]

However, there were also tangible social improvements that had material benefits for working-class families. The introduction of Joint Industrial Councils and the Conditions of Employment Act 1936 improved working conditions. The former facilitated union and employer representatives to meet under the auspices of the Department of Industry and Commerce; the latter capped working hours at forty-eight for adults and forty for juveniles. The Act also provided for the registration and legal enforcement of agreements agreed through collective bargaining.[7] Although gross national income was made stagnant by the Economic War with Britain, industrial incomes rose. Progress was also made on housing and slum clearance. In 1926, 27 per cent of the population lived in housing with a density of more than two people per room; in Dublin, it was 35 per cent. By 1936, the national figure had fallen to 23 per cent. A new Housing Act helped to build twelve thousand houses annually with public subsidy between 1932 and 1942, compared to two thousand a year under Cumman na nGaedheal. The State credit schemes allowed 17,680 Corporation houses to be built between 1932 and 1936, over twice the number completed under the previous government. The housing programme took many craftsmen off the scrapheap of unemployment. In 1926, there were 9,852 building trade workers; by 1936, the number had nearly doubled to 18,207.[8] The Unemployment Assistance Act 1933 introduced the dole and the passing of the Control of Prices Act 1937 would have been unthinkable a decade prior. Fianna Fáil also made it easier to qualify for blind and old age pensions, and widows' and orphans' pensions were introduced in 1935.[9] Spending on social services rose from 36 per cent of the government's budget to 40 per cent in 1939.[10]

The new political and economic environment gave Irish trade unionism a bargaining power it had not had since 1923. Strike activity and inter-union competition experienced a renaissance. Between 1926 and 1930, the annual number of workdays lost exceeded 100,000 just once. From 1933-38, it was consistently around double that figure save for 1937 when it reached over 1.5 million. But agitation did not reach the level of the early 1920s, when 300,000 days a year were lost on average. From a nadir of ninety-two thousand in 1929, ITUC membership had recovered to 162,000 by 1939.[11] Fianna Fáil introduced novel difficulties for trade unionists. The government believed that multiplicity, wherein two or more unions competed for the same members, was the root cause of militancy and called for union rationalisation. It took advantage of the weakness of class politics in Ireland to employ a language which was sometimes socialist – but practices which were comfortably capitalist – to steal working-class votes from the Labour Party. In presenting themselves as champions of the proletariat, Fianna Fáil simultaneously portrayed those who advocated class politics as purveyors of an exploitation that would hinder the development of a strong, autonomous labour movement.[12] Trade unionists were divided between traditionalists favouring the established mode of sectionalist trade unionism and an antagonistic labour-state relationship, and reformists favouring industrial unionism and a collaborative relationship with the new government. Nowhere would this division have a greater impact than in the engineering trade, where the British remained strong and where the Irish unions were growing.[13]

The IEIU in the 1930s: decline, crisis and renaissance

The 1923-32 period, when the Free State and employers consolidated their authority, was bleak for every union. But few had as terrible a time as the IEIU, which was teetering on the brink of collapse by the early 1930s. Reeling from splits and plummeting membership, the union entered the decade mired in crisis. As members left, so did their contributions, starving the union of desperately needed funds. It had still not paid off its overdraft from the National City Bank for 6 Gardiner Row and needed to pay generous benefits if it wanted to compete with the AEU. Furthermore, the IEIU had a new threat to its existence: its old, breakaway Inchicore branch. The IGREU grew spectacularly in the 1930s. A major reason for this was its adroit ability to poach IEIU men, which it did with considerable success. That the IEIU not only survived the 1930s but emerged stronger than ever is a testament to calibre and dedication of its leaders and rank-and-file.

On 1 October 1930, the IEIU's REC met to hear the result of an internal audit of accounts and heard the first unmistakable evidence of the fiscal crisis that would engulf it for the next five years. The report made for disturbing listening, making clear that the union had no choice but to raise contributions, impose levies and slash benefits, expenses and wages or there would soon be union at all. Assets such as its billiard table and its hall in Dundalk would have to be sold and there would have to strict economies of scale in the payment of superannuation benefit. Controversially, the report argued that either 'unnecessary' positions like general president, lady typist and billiard room assistant should be abolished, or the union be run by parttime officials. The report dominated the next REC meeting which also assessed the union's financial situation. All branches outside of Dublin were in heavy arrears to the REC. The Cork branch owed £125, and its membership had declined rapidly from 368 in 1924 to 144 in January 1930. This was not unique to Cork: The Limerick branch was in its worst shape since its foundation, having been hit hard by ending of the Shannon Scheme.[14] The auditors believed that there was no hope of gaining members in Limerick, Cobh, Dundalk or Passage. With just thirteen members and extensive debts, they advised the REC to close the Cobh branch. The Passage shipyard could only yield thirty-two members for the union. As bad as they were, these figures do not convey the scale of the crisis. As one REC member put it, 'we would not have half as many members if they knew the true position of the union's funds.'[15] In total, the IEIU had only £101 to its name and was losing £14 a week.[16] Most egregious of all was that certain branch officials had contributed to the crisis by paying benefits when they should not have and subsequently lied about it: the caretaker of the Dundalk hall had misappropriated over £100 of union money. One contribution collector had stolen some of the money he had collected and falsified the books to cover it up.[17]

Table 28: IEIU Membership, 1930-39.[18]

Year (31 Dec.)	Membership	Year (31 Dec.)	Membership
1930	1,225	1935	1,637
1931	1,404	1936	1,659
1932	1,238	1937	1,685
1933	1,230	1938	1,771
1934	1.467	1939	1,684

The situation was even worse when the NEC met that November. The IEIU's balance was only £9. The union would have been bankrupt were it not for the £81 it had in the bank that was unaccounted for, which it transferred to its current account. The NEC initiated a series of cost-cutting measures, but it was not enough. Three months later, Bro. Fray told his REC colleagues that, 'if we go on for another week or two there would be no fund there at all.'[19] Rooney agreed, telling them that, 'if they want to keep the union afloat, they would have to put their hands into their pockets.' By then, the union could not afford to pay its staff.[20] The REC cut the wages of its general secretary, president, caretaker and lady typist; sacked the billiard room assistant; and ended the payment given to REC members to attend meetings.[21] By mid-1931, the union had reached a 'low ebb' financially and could not afford to pay its branches, who had to be paid by other branches. The general secretary even had to work without pay.[22]

The crisis continued in 1933, meaning that the union had no choice but to inflict more austerity. Contributions were raised; the president's wage was halved; the lady typist was sacked; and the caretaker's pay was slashed to 50s., less than the wage received by most Dublin labourers.[23] Benefits were reduced once more while eligibility was made more stringent. The measures provoked outrage, but the REC had little option. 'It was no pleasure for the executive at any time to alter the scales of benefits … were it not for the Dublin branch and the assistance given by the executive there would not by any union here at all.'[24] The predicament was compounded by the avarice of some branch officials. As well as claiming exorbitant expenses, Frank Meade, the Limerick branch secretary, refused to implement the reduced rates of benefits and issued benefits to those who were not entitled to them. When the REC demanded to see the branch's receipts, it received threats of a solicitor's letter.[25] At the height of the bad blood, the REC even told the branch to break away if it would not enforce union rules.[26] Although Limerick refused and pledged its loyalty to the union, it was not enough to satisfy the REC. 'The Limerick branch was only hanging on by a thread as far as this executive is concerned, and it was only quite recently that they had officials of that branch before them, and gave them to the end of the quarter to pull themselves together with a view to working the branch properly.'[27] The conflict ended when the REC suspended the Limerick branch secretary for 'refusing to produce the branch books to the general officials for inspection when required, and also for intimidation and insolence to the union officials.'[28]

The crisis was a godsend for the IGREU. Austerity begot discontent among the IEIU rank-and-file, leading to an avalanche of defections that perpetuated the crisis. The Inchicore union smelt blood and went on the attack to finish off its beleaguered rival. To do this, it was happy to violate inter-union agreements prohibiting the poaching of members. Many IEIU members were exasperated that their union had been allowed to fall into such a state and that they had to pay the price for such incompetence.[29] From the beginning of the crisis, prominent IEIU officials were openly calling for their union to amalgamate with the IGREU. One such man was Richard Moore of the Boilermakers' Section, who announced in March 1931 that he was 'in conference' with the General Railway Union. The Inchicore union was willing to take over the IEIU's debts (nearly £4,000 in August 1931) should amalgamation take place.[30] His fellow boilermaker, Thomas Whelan, told the IEIU's Dublin membership that he, 'could not see how this union was going to exist as there was no young men joining' because of 'the exorbitant entrance fee they have to pay.' At the same meeting, Patrick O'Hagan encouraged those present to 'think very carefully what it would mean by going over to this union (the IGREU). It would mean they would be in a union with funds.' He was not wrong. The Inchicore union was endowed with a balance of over £3,000.[31] The IEIU only held onto its Iron Moulders' Section because the fee to join the IGREU was too high.[32] But most moulders transferred, with only twelve remaining loyal. The loss of the moulders was an especially bitter pill for the IEIU to swallow given that 'it was the moulders who practically started the union.'[33]

Whole sections of the union were in open revolt and in secret negotiations to join the IGREU or raise enough money to launch breakaway unions.[34] Bro. Davis 'could see no hope for the future of this union.'[35] Peter Coates, secretary of the Stationary Engine Drivers' Section, agreed. 'He could not see any hope for us, only fusion with the Railway and General Engineering Union', the possibility of which he wanted the membership to discuss. In May 1931, another prominent stationary engine driver informed the REC that he was 'absolutely finished with the union' and had gone over to IGREU, taking much of his section, like Coates, with him. Other stationary engine drivers joined the ITGWU and WUI; others left to form their own union. The IEIU's Stationary Engine Drivers' Section was severely weakened, but not destroyed.[36] Railway shopmen were the next to leave and join the IGREU.[37] The most prominent was O'Hagan, the disgraced former general secretary, who confidently predicted the IEIU's impending demise, telling a Dundalk member that his union was 'on its last legs.'[38] By July 1932, O'Hagan had joined the Inchicore Union and had taken most of the Broadstone shopmen with him. In 1937, he was elected 'trades secretary' of the Irish Engineering and Foundry Union (IEFU) – the successor to the IGREU – tasked with negotiating with employers and looking after members' industrial interests. Thomas Fleming, who had served as general secretary between 1933 and 1937, became the union's 'financial secretary.' Coates, Whelan and Davis would all serve on the REC of the IGREU/IEFU, and Moore became its general president. O'Hagan retained his position until 1941 when poor health forced him to step aside. Coates took over as acting industrial general secretary before Jack Cassidy was elected to the role in 1943, the year O'Hagan died after a lengthy illness.[39]

Though wounded by the losses, the IEIU persevered. Austerity and prudent management of funds helped to turn the situation around. By early 1934, the worst of the crisis was over. The IEIU had finally paid off its overdraft with the National City Bank.[40] But cutbacks were not the primary reason for the clearance of debt. Industrialisation was causing an explosion in membership that greatly improved the union's finances, the building of the sugar factories being a case in point. Accordingly, in 1934 the IEIU opened branches in Thurles, Tuam and Carlow.[41] The crisis forced a significant long-term change in the union's philosophy, one that would have been unthinkable in the 1920s: labourers would now be accepted as members. This decision was undoubtedly influenced by the fact that the Foundry Union had recently started organising labourers. By mid-1936, that union had also been 'recognised' at the sugar factories.[42] Economic necessity and the will to survive influenced the IEIU's change of policy more than anything else. It needed contributions and the unskilled were an untapped source of cash, especially in the burgeoning industries. Though the crisis spurred a growth of class consciousness, the IEIU had not abandoned the snobbery towards labourers typical of craft unions in twentieth-century Ireland. The chairman of the Carlow branch resigned when his union began admitting builders' labourers, assistants, railway porters and motor drivers. Simultaneously, when the Irish Municipal Employees' Union claimed work at Dublin Corporation traditionally reserved for tradesmen, the IEIU joined with the IEFU and the United Stationary Engine Drivers' Union to 'defeat the labourers' union in their onslaught against our status.'[43]

Unionising labourers risked starting a major confrontation with the ITGWU, still the biggest union in Ireland. It wrote to the REC to protest that a 'craft union' was organising these men. But the IEIU was now a truly industrial union, and thus claimed 'the right to organise all workers, skilled, semiskilled and unskilled in the sugar beet and similar factories.' It considered the sugar factories to be part of the engineering industry because sugar is a commodity produced by 'mechanical means.'[44] Transport Union protests forced the ITUC to settle the dispute. While accepting the IEIU's right to organise engineering labourers, Congress denied its right to organise any other kind, including those employed by the Irish Sugar Company whose unionisation by the IEIU was 'entirely extravagant.'[45] After initial non-compliance, the IEIU eventually accepted the recommendation. Nevertheless, both unions remained rivals in the engineering trade thereafter, which strained relations between them.[46]

By the IEIU's fifteenth anniversary on 20 May 1935, the union was 'prospering and making great progress.' That year's annual report made for extraordinary reading. The union was 'very proud' to have paid off its debt on the Dundalk Hall and on Gardiner Row, making both union property. These buildings, 'along with the large balance of cash, places our union in the strongest financial position it has ever been in since its foundation. This achievement is a great tribute to those members who remained loyal to the Irish Engineering Industrial Union.'[47] The union could once more secure major concessions for workers, obtaining better wages for members in Tuam and Thurles than what men in Dublin received. It now had two halls (with facilities that very few other unions had) and an annual income of over £3,000. For the first time in fifteen years, it could boast that if things continued as they were, 'we would be one of the strongest organisations in the country… We had gone through a very rough time in recent years, now we are on the right road … those who had left our union could only realise their mistake and they would regret it.'[48] That November, the REC violated its own rules by partially restoring the wages of its general secretary and caretaker. The general president, Michael Albert Connolly, resigned in protest that officials' pay was upped before rank-and-file benefits, but resumed his position shortly afterwards.[49]

Throughout the 1930s, the IEIU struggled to overcome a problem that tormented it since its birth: how to organise on a cross-craft basis when the lines of demarcation of craftwork were sometimes unclear. When the union was unable establish an agreeable division of work, disaster sometimes ensued. The heating engineers, over whom the IEIU had a monopoly, were at the heart of the union's biggest conflicts over demarcation in the 1930s. Their dispute with the union's fitters set in motion a process which culminated in their estrangement from the IEIU.[50] The REC sided with the fitters, which the Heating Engineers' Section denounced as 'highly unsatisfactory.'[51] In September 1932, an agreement was reached between both that brought a tentative peace.[52]

The affair was a portent of something much more serious and consequential: the dispute between the heating engineers and the plumbers. Across Dublin, plumbers were fixing radiators and running pipes, work which the heating engineers claimed was theirs; both asserted their sole right to copperwork. The feud even spread to the privileged surroundings of the Papal Nuncio's residence and Clongowes Wood College, and to Grangegorman Mental Hospital.[53] The REC struggled with this 'very complicated question.'[54] The issue poisoned relations between the executive and the heating engineers throughout 1931. When the section did not inform the REC that it had allowed a member to work at Clongowes, the general secretary decried it as 'a terrible slap in the teeth', claiming that 'he never got such a take back in all his life.'[55] The heating engineers were vocally critical of how their union was representing their interests. The REC's inability to stop the use of semiskilled and unskilled labour on heating work was another bone of contention.[56] By mid-1932, the heating engineers were pondering 'the future attitude of the section to the Irish Engineering Union.'[57]

The dispute with the plumbers reached its boiling point during the reconstruction of Cork City Hall in 1933-34. The Brightside Engineering Company, which had secured the contract for the job, had not only employed plumbers to do heating work but had also brought over English fitters. The heating engineers were furious and demanded immediate action from their union. They were also unhappy with how the REC had negotiated with the company. Bro Beattie, the section's chairman and representative on the REC, told the executive that his section 'thought there was something very crooked going on in Cork as the general secretary, who has a brother working for this firm, could not give any information as to whether plumbers were employed or not.'[58] The heating engineers wanted the REC to withdraw labour, but the REC were reluctant and claimed that authority to call a strike solely resided with Beattie's section. Relations had been irreparably damaged. Beattie resigned from the REC in protest and the heating engineers censured the general secretary for his conduct.[59] But worse was to come. In 1934, McCann's Ltd. were tasked with the construction of the fifth and final incarnation of Dublin's Theatre Royal on Hawkins Street. It employed an English chargehand whom the heating engineers wanted dismissed, or strike would be called. When the REC ignored the demand, the section had had enough.[60] In September 1934, it left the IEIU 'which of late had been a menace to our trade and our members.' All but one voted to withdraw because their 'contributions weren't used to the interests of the heating section.' Beattie had had a 'friendly chat' with the 'organiser' of the IEFU, which was 'quite prepared' to take over the heating engineers – and so they did.[61] The section became the IEFU's Dublin No. 7 branch with fifty-eight members. The new branch wasted no time in calling a stoppage at the Theatre Royal to force McCann's to sack the English chargehand.[62]

The IEIU, Fianna Fáil and the British

On 1 July 1932, the Fianna Fáil government launched the Economic War by refusing to pay the half-yearly land annuities to Britain, one of the most radical moves ever taken by an Irish government. The British responded with a 20 per cent tariff on Irish imports. Fianna Fáil replied in kind and British imports were heavily taxed. The war was part of a broader economic agenda of developing industry and self-sufficiency by fiscal protection; by 1936, there were over 1,900 tariffs in operation. The war ended in 1938 with the ending of the annuities, the mutual lifting of tariffs and the return the Treaty ports (Spike Island, Berehaven and Lough Swilly).[63] Like the Labour Party, the IEIU supported the government during the Economic War. It actively lobbied the government on protection for its trades from the time it took office.[64] In July 1932, less than three weeks after the outbreak of the Economic War, its Heating Engineers' Section met and congratulated the Labour Party 'on the national and manly support given by them to the government in their effort to restore the industries which have been strangled by England and her faithful allies in the present opposition.'[65] The IEIU also supported Fianna Fáil's protectionist agenda. In fact, the tariff imposed by the government on imported coachbuilding material was higher than what was sought by the IEIU or the Irish Coachbuilders' Association in 1928 (60 per cent).[66]

Many historians have commented upon the 'radical' elements of Fianna Fáil's ideology, but one should be careful not to exaggerate this 'radicalism.' Fianna Fáil was primarily a nationalist party dedicated to developing an indigenous capitalism which, it believed, would benefit both workers and employers. It was far more influenced by Catholic social teaching – which sought class harmony – than socialism. Kieran Allen argues that the underlying philosophy of the Conditions of Employment Act was 'to wean the unions away from militancy and towards a greater reliance on the state.'[67] Where strikes, wage increases or shorter hours 'compromised' the growth of indigenous industry, they were vociferously condemned. Seán Lemass, Minister for Industry and Commerce, even considered introducing compulsory arbitration of disputes but later rejected the idea as too dangerous. Nevertheless, that Fianna Fáil could mobilise working-class voters far more effectively that the Labour Party could is a stark illustration of the weakness of class politics in Ireland in the 1930s.

> Fianna Fáil blended economic and political nationalism with an amorphous social radicalism. Politics now assumed a classic post-colonial format, with Cumman na nGaedheal representing the compradors – those with a material interest in existing economic relations with Britain – and Fianna Fáil appealing to those who wished to reduce ties with the metropole. In Labour's mindset, this was just an irrational continuation of the civil war divide.[68]

Like the ITUC, the IEIU shared much of the government's vision of future industrial relations. Another area of agreement was the thorny issue of British unions, the ending of whose presence in Ireland both Fianna Fáil and the IEIU had wanted to see since their respective inceptions. Both saw them as relics of imperialism, and both were suspicious that such unions were more loyal to class and internationalism than nation.[69] In 1936 Lemass approached the ITUC to persuade them to rationalise its forty-nine affiliated unions. In response, Congress set up a commission to examine five principal areas, the most important of which was how best to reorganise the Irish labour movement. William O'Brien, general secretary of the ITGWU, dominated its thinking. His memorandum, which featured in the commission's final report (1939), proposed that all trade unionists be grouped into ten industrial unions. Out of a total of 134,000, the engineering, shipbuilding and vehicle building group would have six thousand members. In effect, it meant breaking up the larger unions. Although Irish unions were receptive, the amalgamateds were aghast at this 'attack.' Such was the resistance that Congress rejected the proposal; Fianna Fáil, however, did not. With Congress unwilling to grasp the nettle, the government felt compelled to do so instead. O'Brien's memorandum formed the basis for the controversial Trade Union Act 1941 (see Chapter 6).[70] Equally significant was the formation of a lobby group within the ITUC, the Council of Irish Unions, which would break away from Congress on the same issue in 1945. 'Fissures criss-crossed trade unionism at various angles, but the fault line was now the divide between Irish and British conceptions of strategy.'[71]

In 1932, the IEIU and ETU (Ireland) strongly opposed the British ETU's application for affiliation to the ITUC, which had officially separate from the Irish Labour Party since 1930. The British union was offered membership on the strict condition that it confine its activities to the North. Though there was a bitter reaction from northern delegates – who saw it as a rejection of all British unions and northern branches – the decision was a sensible one given the depth of tensions between British and Irish unions.[72] The Foundry Union repeatedly applied for affiliation but was vetoed every time by the IEIU and the Operative Plumbers, who could not countenance the possibility of the heating engineers having ITUC backing in their war with the plumbers. As Congress could not see any way in which the IEIU and IEFU could both be affiliated, it tried (unsuccessfully) to set up a conference to discuss amalgamation.[73] Though nothing came of it, the ITUC had initiated a process which eventually led to the successful merger of both unions.

Many unions agreed with the principle of rationalisation. The AEU had told the 1930 meeting of Congress that one-sixth of engineers had been replaced by semiskilled and boy labour who utilise 'the simplified working of up-to-date machines.'[74] It believed that the best weapon to fight mechanisation was fewer engineering unions. The AEU had not given up on seeing the IEIU re-join it. It was a misguided belief born of the enduring mentality of craft union privilege:

> The unions that were able to defend themselves against a lowering of skill and a reduction of wages were tightly organised not on an industry basis but on the basis of the skill itself ... the groups ... were tribal in character, each person giving a swift and unquestioned loyalty to the other members, and forming thereby the basis of the workgroup's economic power... competing unions ... within the skill ... (were) inhibiting the development of a craft loyalty in a trade which did not have as strong traditions as the others had... here ... is a central feature gives the Irish situation its special character, because the multiplicity of unions ... sprang ... from nationalist-inspired groups who ... would view a merger not as an amalgamation but as domination, both numerically and politically.[75]

Radical politics: republicanism, communism and fascism

As in many other countries, Irish politics diverged in the 1930s, a product of the decade's economic turbulence. A plethora of socialist-republican groups arose, horrifying the authorities, clergy and right-wing vigilantes.[76] The Communist Party of Ireland was relaunched in 1933, with IRA man Seán Redmond (son of John James) joining at its foundation. Some socialists spearheaded Connollyite efforts to ally class politics and republicanism, maintaining that 'class conflict and the national struggle were *necessarily* complimentary.'[77] The IRA Army Council's refusal to combat the fascistic Blueshirts or clearly distinguish itself from Fianna Fáil convinced left republicans that a new political movement was necessary. They launched the Republican Congress in 1934 which, at its peak, brought together eight thousand trade unionists, leftists and republicans including Seán Redmond. The Republican Congress revived the Irish Citizen Army to serve as its military ancillary. But the Republican Congress went into serious decline after a damaging split later in 1934 and by 1936 it was moribund.[78]

The communists had picked an unfortune time to re-emerge. Between 1917 and 1930, the Catholic Church had been quite indifferent to the left and quiet on communism. This changed utterly in late 1929 when Stalin imposed severe limitations on religious freedom and toleration in the Soviet Union. Pope Pius XI responded by excommunicating communists and reiterating that no Catholic could be a communist or vote communist. The Irish Church then launched a ferocious campaign against the communists, resulting in constant denunciations from the pulpits and conservative press. To the hierarchy, the struggle between Christianity and communism went beyond the material world because 'one stands for Christ, the other for Anti-Christ.'[79] The bishops had finally realised the true scale of their power in the young Irish state and were determined to flaunt and solidify their all-pervasive authority, which anti-communism could do. Their demagogy was immediately effective and created a climate extremely hostile to the radical left, helping Cumman na nGaedheal slide deeper into reaction.[80] In 1931, the government established a military tribunal with the power to inflict the death penalty and gave itself the authority to proscribe any organisation thought to pose a security threat to the state. With clerical support, several left-wing and/or republican organisations and demonstrations were banned – the first of the Church's many symbolic victories over the left. Over the next three decades, left republicans, communists and welfare reform initiatives, most notoriously the Mother and Child Scheme in 1951, all suffered the belt of the crozier.[81]

In mid-1929, communists had gained their first industrial foothold at the Inchicore railway works. Militant shopmen there printed a rank-and-file paper, the *Steam Hammer*, 'the first workshop paper in Ireland that based its politics on the clear-cut principles of class against class/'[82] That June, several of the Inchicore militants were sacked after an abortive, unofficial two-day sit-in strike against a wage decrease. The *Steam Hammer* belonged to the Irish Defence League, a constituent of the International Class War Prisoners' Aid (a Comintern front group), giving it a toxic communist image. Because the League held its meetings at 6 Gardiner Row, it had an indirect link to the IEIU. In February 1930, the Special Branch raided one such meeting for arms and documents and arrested twenty-five (half the membership).[83] The detainees received no sympathy from the IEIU which considered the League to be 'discredited by every organisation in Dublin.'[84] The union 'would not stand for the Irish Labour Defence League occupying this house' and demanded they leave.[85] 'If they did not get out then a notice of quit would be served on them… The less publicity the matter got the better.'[86] The League crumbled later that year due to public indifference, internal rifts, clerical hostility and state repression.[87]

In July 1929, the sacked Inchicore men revived the Irish National Unemployed Movement with Christopher Ferguson – a Marxist, shopman and IGREU member – as chief organiser. It acquired rooms from the Dublin Trades Council and began an intense campaign of street meetings and demonstrations in early 1930, some of which ended in violent clashes with the Gardaí. Ferguson himself was arrested at one such demonstration. As an organisation committed to class politics, the Movement inevitably came into conflict with the official labour leadership. It broke up a Labour Party rally and disrupted the party's annual Connolly commemoration. The Movement began to disintegrate shortly after the trades council expelled it.[88] As late as November 1930, communists had a presence among shopmen at Inchicore and Broadstone through the Revolutionary Workers' Group.[89] Anti-communism quickly spread throughout the Irish left and labour movement. In 1935, the Dublin Trades Council told the Communist Party that 'under no circumstance' would they co-operate or have anything to do with it.[90]

The growth of radical politics had had no discernible impact on the IEIU. Its links to the Labour Party had always been weak and since 1921 it had shunned political activism outside mainstream trade unionism. In early 1932, the REC resisted pressure from its Stationary Engine Drivers' Section to join the short-lived 'All-In Workers' Delegate Council' – a conference of left-wing trade unionists under the auspices of the WUI – because Jim Larkin had founded it. Larkin, the REC believed, was an egomaniacal wrecker who did not have the interests of the working class at heart. If he had, 'he would not have split the labour movement when he returned from America when he was refused his job in the union he founded.'[91] It considered him personally responsible for the sorry state in which organised labour found itself in Ireland in the early 1930s. While the IEFU had more radicals than the IEIU, it too had fervent anti-communists as members. Its yearly report for 1937 contained an article warning that communism would be the perilous result of leaving Christianity outside the workshop, as evidenced by recent events in Spain, Mexico and the Soviet Union. 'Beware of communism. It is like the wolf of old in lamb's clothing. It may be in the form of a demand for wages, conditions.' The article provoked an angry response from Thomas Malone, the union's Waterford branch secretary, who announced himself to be a communist and a disciple of James Connolly under such a definition.[92]

The IEIU and the wages movement

The early 1930s was a particularly difficult period for the average IEIU member. His union's financial crisis was accompanied by an economic downturn that emboldened employers to cut wages. Since 1923, pay for most of the Free State's railway workers had been decided by the Irish Railway Wages Board, the outcome of the railway crisis of 1921-23. Between 1923 and 1939, it discussed nothing but wage cuts. When the GNR announced that Dundalk shopmen's pay would be cut, it took all the IEIU's skill to barter down the reduction and avert a strike.[93] But it was only a temporary settlement of what would be a prolonged dispute. On 1 August 1932, over eight hundred shopmen struck against a reduction of hours without a corresponding wage increase. They had already had their weekly wages slashed by about 20s. The proposed change would lead to another cut of approximately one-third (17s.). Every craft union at the works was involved. The IEIU had about eighty members at Dundalk whom it supported with a levy. The strike also encompassed the IGREU, which by then had spread from Inchicore to the Dundalk works.[94] The Department of Industry and Commerce intervened but struggled to produce a settlement agreeable to both sides. Luckily for the department, Dundalk Urban District Council successfully persuaded the men to return to work after a three-week stoppage. Shopmen would work forty-seven hours for a full week and then work two weeks in every seven thereafter.[95]

The state's other railway company, the Great Southern, was also waging war against its workers. In 1932, rumours circulated through Broadstone and Inchicore that the GSR would attack conditions, lengthen hours and sack workers. In September 1932, the IGREU made clear that it would go out if this happened. Another grievance was that the Great Southern had also violated its 1929 agreement with shopmen (which cut earnings by 10 per cent). The men had agreed to the reduction on the condition that the money saved would be invested in improving the workshops. Strike notice was issued but not followed through. In June 1933, the company enforced the decrease on craftsmen outside of Dublin and Limerick. It also made each shopman take three weeks compulsory, unpaid holiday between December and March.[96] The ETU had struck in vain against the measure.[97] The 10 per cent cut remained an abiding grievance for much of the 1930s. With the support of the Dublin Trades Council, the unions agitated intensely for its restoration. They also claimed a revocation of deductions for shopmen at the GNR, which amounted to 11s.[98] They were partially successful: in May 1936, the GSR restored pay by 5 per cent, a considerable victory considering prices were rising after a period of decline.[99] But the IEIU and the Foundry Union were unhappy about the agreement's shortcomings and rejected the company's offer to restore the deduction in full on a staggered basis. They pushed for greater concessions, for which some craftsmen went on unofficial strike in early 1938. Shortly afterwards, the unions secured the full restoration of the 10 per cent deduction.[100] But not everything was going the shopmen's way: the GSR continued to sack hundreds and cut the working week from four days (which the men had worked since 1924) to three. Poor trade, the result of the global depression, was to blame.[101] Disunity and tension between the engineering unions remained intense: The Foundry Union accused the IEIU of using the settlement as a pretext to poach sixty of its members, lodging a formal complaint with the Dublin Trades Council on the matter. The Engineering Group of Unions condemned and censured the IEIU for its behaviour. The hours' issue remained contentious: In September 1938, shopmen in Dublin (1,900 in number), Limerick and Waterford withdrew their labour to demand a full working week.[102]

Industrial relations remained poor at the ESB throughout the 1930s. Working conditions was just one of several complaints that electricians had with the company. The IEIU and ETU were at odds with the Board from its foundation, leading to several joint meetings and a rapprochement between the two unions at the ESB. Both alleged that the ESB did not fully implement an agreement reached with them on 7 August 1931. Electricians had five major grievances: victimisation, employing labourers as electricians, importing electricians, not employing men through unions, and utilising non-union labour. Employment of labourer was the most powerful grievance and led to a 'stay-in strike' in September 1932 when the ETU and IEIU refused to handle cookers at the ESB's Fleet Street department. From December 1923 to January 1933, the ETU men at the ESB's Dundalk station struck after the company continued to employ labourers on electrical work. The ITUC refused the ETU's request that it withdraw all ESB workers.[103] In March 1937, ESB electricians downed tools against the requirement that they drive themselves to their jobs, something which no other employer required. After a week, the Board largely conceded the claim. Electricians would now only have to drive cars in emergencies.[104] The issue of electricians driving themselves to jobs remained contentious for decades afterwards.

Table 29: Cost of Living in the Irish Free State/Éire, 1930-39 (July 1914 = 100).[105]

Year (Feb.)	All Items
1930 (Jan.)	179
1931 (Jan.)	166
1932	162
1933	151
1934	152
1935	153
1936	159
1937	167
1938	173
1939	174

Electrical work maintained its status as among the dangerous types of work one could perform. In fact, it was becoming hazardous as technology progressed and the work became more complex. James Jenkinson, a nineteen-year-old apprentice and IEIU member, was fatally electrocuted on 29 July 1932 while connecting wires to a private house for the ESB. An inquest heard that his death was caused by cardiac paralysis, the third death from such in recent times. The incident highlights the perilous nature of electrical work in the early days of electrification of the country. It also illuminates the power that foremen, even incompetent ones, exercised over their gangs. The foreman on the job believed that his gang would be finished the job before he arrived to direct them to turn off the current.[106]

The sugar industry's growth in the 1930s made it an important part of the Irish economy by the decade's end, which enhanced labour's bargaining power. But the Sugar Company was often unreceptive to union demands, straining industrial relations at the factories for several years after nationalisation. Three major strikes took place at the factories in the 1930s. The first, in 1934, was one of the most inglorious moments in the IEIU's history. The union had sought better wages and conditions for members there since June of that year. When the ITGWU had its request for a wage improvement refused, it immediately threatened a stoppage. Every union at the factory, including the IEIU, pledged to join, which would embroil eight hundred workers. The IEIU and ITGWU also wanted the Sugar Company to only employ members of unions affiliated to Congress. On 21 October, strike was officially called but crumbled just four days later after intervention from Lemass.[107] The government had viewed the strike as an act of economic subversion. The workers, de Valera asserted, had held farmers and consumers 'to ransom' by their 'unpatriotic and unfair attitude.'[108] Hourly wages at the Carlow factory compared well to craft rates in other Irish industries. Fitters and welders in Carlow, for example, earned 1s. 10½d. and electricians 2s.[109] The IEIU was the only union not to withdraw its members, claiming it could not do so because its Carlow branch had voted against going on strike.[110] The ITUC was 'grievously disappointed' with the IEIU, which had 'committed a serious breach of solidarity' and 'acted in a very blameworthy manner.'[111] The IEIU had effectively scabbed. In the end, the company agreed to only employ members of unions *recognised by*, but not necessarily affiliated to, Congress.[112] The ITUC demanded that the IEIU explain why it should not be expelled for misleading the other unions, but the REC was defiant and gave no apology for conforming with its own rules. Congress did not expel the IEIU, but it did censure it.[113]

The next action came in October 1936 when all four factories were implicated. This time, the IEIU was much more steadfast in its support of the ITGWU and issued a joint strike notice with it. As with 1934, the origins of this dispute lie in a request for a wage increase for which both unions had been agitating for a year. The IEIU wanted tradesmen to receive a 1½d. per hour increase, which would give them an hourly rate of 1s. 10d. During the off-season, fitters and welders had a wage of 82s., and electricians 88s. During beet season, wages jumped to £5. 12s. 9d. for the former and £5. 19s. 5d. for the latter. On the surface, tradesmen in the factories were far better off than any of his compatriots. In Cork, for example, the craft rate was 79s. 4d., putting it within most common wage quartile for craftsmen (60-80s.). In 1937, only 3 per cent of workers in the state earned above £5.[114] But looks can be deceptive and wage rates should not be the only metric by which living standards should be analysed. At fifty-six hours, the sugar worker's week was significantly longer than the average of forty-eight, forty-seven or forty-four hours. Unions always put forward wage demands in October in the runup to beet season, the busiest time of year for the factories when the most disruption could be caused.

Strike began on 15 October 1936 at Mallow after the company snubbed the unions. The other factories fell in line shortly afterwards, bringing numbers out to over two thousand. The AEU, ETU and the Amalgamated Society of Woodworkers joined the stoppage. The company refused to negotiate unless there was an immediate resumption of work, making the strike a struggle for a principle – union recognition. The men also wanted to rid the factories of non-union men. The strike ended after two weeks thanks again to Lemass, who left his sick bed to arbitrate the dispute. Work was resumed and the notices of dismissal withdrawn. There was no victimisation. A court of inquiry was set up to examine wages and conditions in the factories, the recommendations of which would be accepted by all. The inquiry lasted just two months – only two meetings were held. It collapsed when the workers' representative withdrew after the court decided to hear evidence from 'yellow unions' not recognised by Congress.[115]

The IEIU led the next action at the factories, which took place in October 1937. When the company declined the Tuam men's request for a wage increase, the branch demanded that the REC serve seven-days' notice. The ITGWU put forward separate claims. However, it eventually concluded that a stoppage was doomed to failure and instead agitated for the creation of a joint conciliation board for the industry. The IEIU's four 'sugar' branches met to discuss the situation and voted to serve strike notice, prompting the company to agree to the formation of a conciliation board. Mallow, Carlow and Thurles supported such a board, but Tuam did not and remained committed to going on strike. The REC sided with the majority and wanted to see the board founded before the campaign began. Though both sides agreed to establish it at a conference under the Department of Industry and Commerce, the talks hit a roadblock. There was disagreement over who the chairman should be, which nearly caused Tuam to pull out of the negotiations. But the conciliation board was eventually established with, as per their wish, the ITGWU and IEIU as the workers' sole representatives.[116] The board was unable to stop a cessation of work in the Tuam factory, in which the IEIU participated, in April 1938 for a rise. An industrial court subsequently investigated the wage question and delivered a settlement favourable to the men. Like the ESB, the Sugar Company also tried to utilise non-union labour when it felt it could get away with it, which provoked another short strike of IEIU men at the Carlow factory just before the 1939 campaign.[117]

The IEIU's embrace of industrial unionism spurred a growth of class consciousness within the union. For example, despite having shopmen to support, the union levied its Dublin membership 1s. per man to support those affected by the 1935 tramway strike and lockout, one of the decade's most significant industrial disputes. The ATGWU and the ITGWU took out the tramwaymen following the dismissal of a driver; the company responded with an eleven-week lockout of all workers, including shopmen.[118] More directly, IEIU brass finishers and moulders were engulfed by the biggest labour dispute since the state's foundation: the 1937 Dublin building trade strike, which involved fifteen unions and eleven thousand men. More working days were lost to strikes in 1937 than any year since 1923: 26,734 people were involved in disputes and 1,754,940 workdays were lost. It was not until 1979 that the country experienced more strikes than in 1937. It was also the most enduring, lasting from April to October 1937.[119] Having sought a wage of 2s. per hour and a new working arrangement, the brass workers stayed out until late May when they accepted a 1½d per hour advance and better conditions. They had been supported by the imposition of a 2s. 6d. on every IEIU member.[120] The brass finishers' demands reflected a broader clamour for wage increases by Irish workers. From 1936, the IEIU put forth a litany of claims for better pay: at Dublin Corporation, the ESB, the railways, the post office, the mental hospitals and the Irish Lights' Commissioners to name but a few.[121] Joint action between the ITGWU and IEIU triggered a major lockout in Tralee in 1936. The following year, a similar move with the AEU for a 15 per cent increase at Pierce's resulted in an unofficial strike by the British union.[122]

Table 30: Industrial Disputes in the Free State/Éire, 1922-46.[123]

Years	Nos.	Days lost	Workers involved	Days lost per worker
1922-26	94	519,000	15,826	33
1927-31	60	121,000	3,575	34
1932-36	93	179,000	8,305	22
1937-41	108	460,000	13,949	33
1942-46	85	122,000	7,024	17

The ETU in the 1930s

Like the IEIU and Foundry Union, the ETU expanded from its Dublin base in the 1930s, though not as extensively as the others. By 1937, the ETU had spread to Cork, Limerick, Waterford and Dun Laoghaire, and had affiliated to the Dublin Trades Council. Apart from electricians, the ETU also organised other electrical workers such as jointers' mates.[124] It experienced bereavement and personnel change in its leadership, losing P. Power to pneumonia and Alfred Orpen to heart illness in 1930 and 1933, respectively. Power was a member of the executive and a trustee; Orpen a former volunteer with the 5th Batt. Orpen joined the IRA in 1920 and fought with the anti-Treaty forces during the Civil War.[125] In April 1934, Shallow died. He was replaced by Jack Collins, who held the position until his own death in 1942.[126] In 1939, Meehan died aged forty-four.[127] Gerard Owens replaced him.

In 1931, the ETU and IEIU joined with the ESB, the Association of Electrical Contractors and the Society of Irish Electrical Traders to form a National Joint Industrial Council (ENJIC) to fix 'down-town rates in the electrical trade. The new council formalised the voluntary collective agreements that had heretofore dictated wages in the sector.[128] Like the IEIU, the ETU had many disputes with the ESB in the 1930s. The employment of non-union labour was a grievance throughout the decade, as was the importation of foreign electricians.[129] But the union also made some significant breakthroughs. At its foundation in 1929, the Electricity Supply Board (ESB) publicly offered electricians a £5. 10s. wage for a sixty-hour week. The ETU and IEIU rejected the proposal and refused to supply the Board with electricians until it implemented the going rates and conditions. The embargo ended in July 1931 when both sides to wage of 80s. 9d. for a forty-four-hour week in Dublin. In January 1936, after months of negotiations, the ETU reached a seminal agreement with the ECA which granted contract electricians in Dublin the same wage and hours. The working week would be 60¼ hours on country contracts. The union had originally sought a forty-hour week in Dublin but postponed the application a general shortening of hours. The agreement was wide-ranging, encompassing country money, apprentice quotas and demarcation.[130] On 26 January 1938, the union signed another far-reaching national agreement with the ESB and ECA, which fixed city electricians' hourly rate at 2s. for a forty-four-hour week, forty-seven outside Dublin. Country electricians would earn 3s. 11d. an hour for a fifty-three-hour week. The IEIU was also party to the agreement which did not include 'operational electricians' within the ESB. The ETU had a long and bitter struggle to gain recognition of this category from the Board.[131]

Table 31: ETU membership, 1929-39.[132]

Year	Membership	Year	Membership
1929	240	1935	300
1930	240	1936	300
1931	260	1937	530
1932	300	1938	530
1933	300	1939	1,200
1934	300	-	-

The rise of the Inchicore Union

Throughout the 1930s, the IGREU/IEFU experienced spectacular augmentation as it reaped the bounty of its rival's monetary plight. Between 1930 and 1938, its membership grew by a whopping 531 per cent as it spread across Dublin and into the provinces from its Inchicore base. Its centre of organisation moved from railway craftwork to general engineering and foundry work. By the decade's end, it had affiliated to the Dublin Trades Council (after two years of failed attempts) and was actively seeking membership of the ITUC. More significantly, it was the largest Irish engineering union. To reflect the change, as well as its new-found strength in the foundries, it renamed itself the more encompassing IEFU in 1933. The Foundry Union's aggressive poaching of the IEIU deprived its rival of some of their most able members. It was such a successful tactic that the IEIU was forced to withhold benefits to anyone who joined the IGREU/IEFU.[133] Pugnaciousness was a conscious decision, as noted by the Foundry Union itself:

> Young members, on finishing their apprenticeship, could not get a job on the (union) card ... This called for very grave discussions at the then Executive Council meetings... Finally, it was decided to step out boldly, to extend the union's ramifications, to defy all laws governing affiliated unions ... until a position would be created whereby the union would be respected as a force to be reckoned with in the engineering trades and the labour movement generally.[134]

In 1935, having established itself as the Dublin's iron moulders' union of choice, the Foundry Union began organising labourers in a drive to become an industrial union. The following year, it opened a Limerick branch, which mainly catered for GSR shopmen, and took over several IEIU men in Carlow. In 1937, it opened its doors to plumbers.[135] However, the Foundry Union experienced some losses to its rival. In 1938, it expelled the committee of its Dublin No. 9 Branch after they flouted their executive's authority and broke union rules. The men took legal action against the IEFU. Their case reached the High Court, which ruled that the union's action was illegal and that it had to pay the men's legal fees but did not impose an injunction on the resolution expelling the men. By then, they had joined the IEIU.[136] Growth gave the Foundry Union the funds to purchase a more spacious headquarters. After an attempt to purchase Colmcille Hall fell through, it bought a beautiful Georgian building at 33 Gardiner Place for £1,550.[137] By 1939, the IEFU was a national union that both employers and labour leaders had to take seriously, having spread from Dublin to Tuam and south to Mallow. The union had 75 percent of the locomotive shop and the GSR workshop in Limerick and 85 per cent of skilled men at the Tuam factory.[138] It also solidified its domination of the Inchicore and established a strong presence at the Post Office factory.

The IEFU's biggest dispute was not with an employer but with the British-based Operative Plumbers' Society, a continuation of the plumbers'-heating engineers' conflict. In 1935-36, the IEFU led demarcation-based strikes against the Operative Plumbers at the Office of Public Works at Leinster House, at Britain's garage and at Hadden's foundry.[139] In early 1936, an uglier manifestation of the dispute took place at the National Museum when the Plumbers' Society demanded that heating engineers there join their union or be paid off. The company capitulated and sacked them, prompting the rest of the Foundry Union men there to withdraw their labour. When the men refused to leave, police were called to escort them out. The plumbers threatened to strike themselves if the men were brought back. Beattie, who had kept his position as secretary of the Heating Engineers' Section after their transfer to the IEFU, was one of those who was sacked. His dismissal demonstrated the sheer determination of the Operative Plumbers to see off the heating engineers. As the museum's manager told the IEFU, 'he regretted to have to let him (Beattie) go, but the Plumbers held a pistol to his head, and he was forced to dismiss him.'[140] The situation risked spiralling out of control when the ITGWU and the Irish Seamen's and Port Workers' Union blacked goods to and from the museum. The IEFU feared that this would provoke the sending in of the army to break the strike, which would prompt over four thousand to come out in sympathy. Arbitration took place before anything like this could happen: the dismissed men were reinstated, but this did nothing to end the war between plumbers and heating engineers.[141]

The dispute, which been ongoing since 1886 when the first central heating plant was built in Dublin, was constant throughout the 1930s.[142] It spread from the capital to several centres across the state.[143] The Dublin Trades Council failed to resolve it, one of 'several efforts extending over may years to effect a reconciliation' in this 'old and outstanding' dispute.[144] This was not unique to Ireland as the two groups had also locked horns in the UK and the US. The Operative Plumbers believed that the only solution was for heating engineers and plumbers to join the same union, as had happened in the US and as was currently being negotiated in Britain.[145] It did not envisage this taking place on equal terms and sought to subsume the Foundry Union – but there was no chance of this happening. The Operative Plumbers accused the IEFU of 'carrying on a campaign of intense recruitment' that explicitly targeted plumbers.[146] Even attempts to affect a temporary settlement failed.[147] The battle, whether in Ireland or abroad, is symptomatic of how constant technological advancement was tormenting established trades. The introduction of acetylene welding in the early twentieth century caused many conflicts because it reduced the need for riveters, drillers and others. As welding served the same purpose as the old methods, several established crafts claimed it as their work. Likewise, the development of new industries, such as motorcar and aeroplane construction and maintenance, raised questions about whether the likes of fitters and coachbuilders should do the work or if new, specialised crafts should be formed.[148]

Table 32: Percentage of IEFU members at Inchicore Workshop, 1935.[149]

Workers/Department	Percentage
Iron founders, brass founders, patternmakers, loco. smiths, wagon shop smiths, iron machinists	100
Boilermen	50
Erecting shop (fitters)	90
Fitting shop (fitters & turners)	80
Brass finishers	33.33
Running shed	78
General stores	95

Table 33: IGREU/IEFU Membership and Branches, 1930-39.[150]

Year	Branches	Members
1930	Dublin nos. 1-4, Inchicore	381
1931	Dublin nos. 1-4, Inchicore, Dundalk	436
1932	Dublin no. 1-6, Inchicore, Dundalk	766
1933	Ibid	1,136
1934	Dublin nos. 1-7, Dundalk, Inchicore	1,466
1935	Dublin nos. 1-8, Dundalk, Inchicore	1,571
1936	Dublin nos. 1-8, Dundalk, Inchicore, Limerick, Waterford	1,877
1937	Dublin nos. 1-9, Dundalk, Inchicore, Limerick, Waterford	2,345
1938	Dublin nos. 1-9, Limerick, Inchicore, Dundalk, Enniscorthy, Waterford, Cork, Tuam	2,405
1939	Ibid	2,375

The apprenticeship system in the 1930s

The early 1930s saw the only change that the apprenticeship system would experience for a generation. Technical education had heretofore been voluntary, which created major problems. Getting apprentices to attend evening classes after a hard day's work proved insurmountable, especially during the summer months. Attendance during daytime depended on the goodwill and interest of both employers and apprentices, even when they had been released with pay. Apprentices made up as much as half the workforce of small firms, making employers reticent to release them for classes. Nevertheless, progress had been made in the 1920s. By 1932, the Department of Education was successfully operating the City of Dublin Technical Instruction Scheme, a two-year, fulltime course to train future tradesmen. The IEIU had an interest in many of the programmes it offered, which included plumbing; metal-plate, motor mechanical and electrical work; brass finishing; and watch and clockmaking. In Cork, a thriving day class for motor engineering apprentices had been set up with the cooperation of the garage owners. Similar innovations had taken place in Limerick and Waterford, where enrolment and attendance had gone up dramatically. The Department was also awarding medals and scholarships for excellence in craftwork and had a scheme where it covered three-quarters of the cost of training apprentices. In 1933, 276 mechanical engineers attended technical classes in Dublin, as did 160 motorcar engineers and one hundred workshop engineers.[151]

The report of the Commission on Technical Education, published in 1927, formed the basis of the Vocational Education Act 1930 and the Apprenticeship Act 1931. As per the report's recommendations, the 1930 Act established thirty-eight publicly funded Vocational Education Committees (VECs) which represented employers and trade unions with an independent, government-appointed chairman. The VECs were modelled on the Dublin Day Apprenticeship School on Bolton Street, which the IEIU had long lobbied to facilitate its apprentices.[152] They were responsible for technical education and 'general and practical training in preparation for employment in the trades.'[153] But the Cumann na nGaedheal government remained committed to laissez-faire. While the Act enabled VECs to provide training, it did not compel the use of their facilities. But pressure from employers – most of whom strongly supported Cumman na nGeadhael – ensured that the government conceded greater state regulation of apprenticeships. Apprentices would now have to attend a maximum of 180 hours a year at 'continuation classes.' In certain circumstances, the minister could now prosecute employers who failed to provide details of employees eligible to attend the VECs. Employers who refused to release apprentices without loss of pay to attend prescribed courses now faced criminalisation and a 20s. fine.[154]

The 1931 Act was more influenced by laissez-faire, much to the detriment of the apprentice. It established voluntary apprenticeship committees comprised of employers and trade unionists to establish ground rules for a trade. The committees were obliged to determine the following: who would be regarded as apprentices; the period of apprenticeship and the probationary period; the rates of pay; and the working hours. When rules were made and confirmed by ministerial order, a breach of these rules was unlawful. But there was little in the bill that benefited the apprentice metalworker. Unions could be prosecuted and fined if they tried to stop employers from taking on the number of apprentices specified by a committee, even if that number violated union rules. There was also no ban on the payment of apprenticeship premiums. As with most of the regulation of apprenticeships, this issue came under the remit of the committee. Under the Act, committees were encouraged, but not obliged, to regulate the area of premiums. There were five other such areas: educational entry qualifications, age of entry to apprenticeship, training rules, the number of apprentices per employer and overtime rates. Committees could also release both parties from an apprenticeship agreement, modify the arrangement or transfer the apprentice to another employer.[155]

The Act was poorly constructed and suffered from the worst of both voluntarism and criminalisation. Voluntarism ensured that there was little incentive for employers to participate. Why would they when apprentices were a source of cheap, easy labour? With the force of law, a committee might decide to increase pay, decrease numbers or alter an exploitative working arrangement which only benefited employers. The threat of legal sanction deterred unions from partaking in the committees. Craft unions like the IEIU were especially hostile to any limitation of their authority in the workplace. They would never surrender, or even share with employers or the state, their prerogative to choose who could become an apprentice. Doing so would abrogate their right to choose who could become a member of their union, a privilege more important now than ever in a depressed economy where tradesmen and unions were competing against each other for scarce employment. Union control was consistent with the nineteenth-century concept of the 'apprenticeship of the trade.' Craft unions believed that little could be gained by a legislative approach to apprenticeships, which tended to be slow, cumbersome and costly. The issue was better dealt with at the negotiating table where the threat of industrial action often ensured quick concessions.[156] The Act was ineffective in alter the quality of Irish apprenticeships and did little to improve life for apprentices, who continued to suffer exploitation and derision from both man and master. It remained the chief legislation governing apprenticeships until 1959, and the poor quality of the system remained a labour grievance as a result. Some unscrupulous profiteers exploited the situation for their own gain. In 1932, the ETU stopped taking on apprentices because parents were paying high fees to have their sons serve their time under 'people who were not in any sense competent to impart even an elementary knowledge of the electrical trade to their apprentices', which had reduced the trade to a 'blind alley occupation.'[157]

By 1934, the Department of Industry and Commerce had tried to encourage the formation of apprenticeship committees in the engineering trades only to face opposition from employers. Some craft unions were also cold to the idea. The Operative Plumbers' request that their work be designated a trade under the Apprenticeship Act was immediately shot down by the IEFU.[158] O'Hagan implicitly highlighted the heating engineers' Achilles heel – a poorly defined trade – when he told the department that the IEFU was 'at a loss to know what is the exact meaning of plumbing, glazing and domestic engineering.'[159] The department suspected the British union of wanting statutory inclusion of heating operations in the definition of the plumbing trade for sinister, 'alien purposes.'[160] It knew better than to involve itself in inter-union disputes where there was little hope of getting any agreed definition of the trade and the left the matter slide as a result. By 1940, the dispute was still unresolved, even though the Operative Plumbers were persisting with their demand. But the matter ended shortly thereafter when the department firmly rejected the union's proposal.[161] No apprenticeship committees were ever instituted in the engineering trade under the 1931 Act.

Chapter Notes and References

1 McCarthy, *Trade Unions*, pp. 98-99.
2 Ferriter, *Transformation*, p. 359.
3 Ibid., p. 358.
4 Devine, *Organising History*, p. 143.
5 O'Connor, *Labour History of Ireland* (2nd Ed.), pp. 129-130, 143-144.
6 Devine, *Organising History*, p. 143.
7 Kieran Allen, *Fianna Fáil and Irish Labour, 1926 to the Present* (London: Pluto Press, 1997), p. 47.
8 Ibid., p. 4.
9 O'Connor, *Labour History of Ireland* (2nd Ed.), pp. 143-144
10 Ferriter, *Transformation*, p. 398.
11 Allen, *Fianna Fáil*, p. 48.
12 Ferriter, *Transformation*, pp. 362-363.
13 O'Connor, *Labour History of Ireland* (2nd Ed.), pp. 129-130
14 IEIU REC minutes, 1, 6 Oct. 1930; IEIU NEC minutes, 19, 20, 21 June 1930.
15 IEIU REC minutes, 10 Oct. 1930.
16 Ibid., 1, 6, 10 Oct. 1930.
17 Ibid., 1, 6, 10 Oct. 1930, 25 Jan. 1932.
18 IEIU annual returns, 1930-40, T358, RFS records, NAI.
19 IEIU NEC minutes, 19, 20, 21 Nov. 1930; IEIU REC minutes, 23 Feb. 1931.
20 IEIU REC minutes, 23 Feb. 1931.
21 Ibid., 3 Mar. 1930.
22 Ibid., 7 May 1931, 4 Nov. 1935.
23 Ibid., 27 May, 2, 6 June 1932.
24 Ibid., 29 Mar. 1933.
25 Ibid., 10 July 1930, 8 Oct. 1931, 7 Jan., 16 June, 27 Oct., 24 Nov., 11 Dec. 1932, 9 Feb., 9 Mar., 19 Apr., 18 May, 1 June, 20 Sept. 1933, 30 Aug., 6, 10 Sept. 1934.
26 Ibid., 20 Sept. 1933.
27 Ibid., 7 Dec. 1933.
28 Ibid., 25 May 1933, 30 Aug., 6, 10 Sept. 1934.
29 Ibid., 3 Mar. 1931.
30 IEIU Dublin membership minutes, 30 Mar., 17 Aug. 1931.
31 Ibid., 30 Mar. 1931.

32 Ibid., 1, 8 June, 6, 13, 20 July 1933.
33 Ibid., 14 Apr. 1932.
34 Ibid., 1 Dec. 1930, 17 Aug. 1931.
35 IEIU Dublin membership minutes, 17 Aug. 1931.
36 Ibid., 1 Mar 1931; IEIU REC minutes, 19 May 1932.
37 IEIU REC minutes, 25, 27 May 1932.
38 Ibid., 14 Apr. 1932.
39 IEFU AGM minutes, 23 Mar. 1941; minutes of the meeting of the IEFU branch officers and shop stewards, 25 Mar. 1943; IEFU half-yearly meeting minutes, 8 Oct. 1944, all found in Box 1D, TEEU collection, ILHM; Ward-Perkins, *Trade Union Records*, p. 202.
40 IEIU REC minutes, 31 Jan. 1934.
41 Ibid., 9 Aug., 4 Oct. 1934.
42 Ibid., 29 Dec. 1931, 2 Nov. 1933, 5 Sept., 4 Nov. 1935, 17 Aug. 1936; ITUC executive minutes, 12 Sept. 1935, 14, 28 May, 19 June, 9 July 1936, ICTU/Box 101, ICTU collection, NAI.
43 J. O'Flanagan to Lord Mayor of Dublin, 22 Sept. 1936, TU27/13 (70), United Stationary Engine Drivers' collection, UCD Archives. The United Stationary Engine Drivers' Union was formed in 1932 when boilermen split from the ITGWU because they felt that a general union could not cater to their needs.
44 IEIU REC minutes, 4 Nov. 1935, 17 Aug. 1936.
45 ITUC executive minutes, 13 Mar. 1936, ICTU/Box 101, ICTU collection, NAI.
46 Ibid., 4, 25 July, 31 Oct., 28 Nov. 1935, 13, 26 Mar., 14 May, 19 June 1936, ICTU/Box 101, ICTU collection, NAI.
47 IEIU REC minutes, 7 May 1936.
48 IEIU Dublin membership minutes, 20 May 1935. For more internal discussion about the union's improved financial position, see IEIU REC minutes, 4, 15 Apr., 16, 20 May 1935.
49 IEIU REC minutes, 4, 14, 21 Nov. 1935.
50 Ibid., 14, 24, 28 Apr. 1932.
51 Ibid., 24 Apr. 1932.
52 Ibid., 15 Sept. 1932. The agreement was as follows:
    1) All ordinary heating work supplied from low pressure boilers was heating engineers' work.
    2) All heating work from high pressure steam was fitters' work.
    3) The maintenance, repair and upkeep of plants and institutions is fitters' work.
    4) All heating work on the installation of low-pressure steam plants for cooking is fitters' work.
    5) All heating work on laundries from low-pressure boilers is heating engineers' work, but the erection, repair and maintenance of pulleys and machinery is fitters' work.
53 Ibid., 30 Apr., 9, 23 Oct., 26 Nov. 1930, 11, 5 May, 16 June, Feb. 1932, 30 Aug. 1934.
54 Ibid., 8 Jan. 1931.
55 Ibid., 23 Apr. 1931.
56 Ibid., 30 July, 10 Dec. 1931, 5 Jan. 1933.
57 Ibid., 12 May 1932.
58 Ibid., 30 Nov. 1933.
59 Ibid., 12 Jan., 7, 14 Dec. 1933, 28 Feb., 22 Mar., 13 Apr. 1934; IEIU Dublin heating engineers' section minutes, 8, 9 Oct., 8 Nov. 1933.
60 IEIU REC minutes, 9 Aug. 1934; IEIU Dublin heating engineers' section minutes, 9 Sept. 1934.
61 IEIU Dublin heating engineers' section minutes, 9 Sept. 1934.
62 J. Cassidy to J. O'Brien, 21, 30 Sept. 1934, IEIU Dublin heating engineers' minutes, 8 Nov. 1933, 13 Feb., 28 May, 25 June, 2, 9, 16, 19 July, 15 Aug. 1934; *Irish Independent*, 9, 10, 12 Nov. 1934; IEIU REC minutes, 1, 9 Aug., 15 Nov. 1934.
63 Mary E. Daly, *Industrial Development and Irish National Identity, 1922-1939* (Dublin: Gill & Macmillan, 1992), pp. 63-70.
64 *Irish Press*, 13, 23 Apr. 1932.
65 Ibid., 21 July 1932.
66 *Irish Independent*, 2, 3 Aug. 1928, 7 May 1932.
67 Allen, *Fianna Fáil*, p. 147.
68 O'Connor, *Labour History of Ireland* (2nd Ed.), pp. 141-142.
69 Allen, *Fianna Fáil*, pp. 20-63
70 McCarthy, *Trade Unions*, pp. 142-167.

71   O'Connor, *Labour History of Ireland* (2nd ed.), p. 150.
72   McCarthy, *Trade Unions*, p. 123.
73   The IEFU's application was supported by the AEU, NUR, ATGWU and ITGWU, who had no objection if the Foundry Union confined its activities to the engineering industry. See ITUC executive minutes, 25 July, 12 Sept., 11 Oct. 1935, 14, 28 May, 19 June, 9 July 1936, 10 Feb. 1938, 25 May, 29 Dec. 1939, 25 Apr., 1 Aug., 26 Sept., 31 Oct. 1941, ICTU/Box 101, ICTU collection, NAI; IEFU REC minutes, 9 Jan. 1935, 23 Mar. 1936.
74   Cited in McCarthy, *Trade Unions*, p. 107.
75   Ibid., pp. 108-110.
76   The Friends of Soviet Russia (1927), The League Against Imperialism (1927), The Labour Defence League (1928), The Connolly Workers' Club (1928), Workers' Revolutionary Party (1930), Revolutionary Workers' Group (1930) and Soar Éire (1931) are examples of these groups. See Milotte, *Communism in Modern Ireland*, pp. 96-121.
77   Cited in Richard English, 'Socialism and republican schism in Ireland: the emergence of the Republican Congress in 1934', *Irish Historical Studies*, Vol. 27, No. 105, May 1990, p. 48.
78   O'Connor, *Labour History of Ireland* (2nd Ed.), pp. 136-138; Milotte, *Communism in Modern Ireland*, pp. 150-157.
79   Cited in English, 'Socialism and the republican schism in Ireland', p. 51. Seán Redmond subsequently wanted to travel to Spain to fight on the Republican side of the country's civil war, but Peadar O'Donnell prevented him from doing so.
80   O'Connor, *Labour History of Ireland* (2nd Ed.), p. 136; Emmet O'Connor, 'Anti-communism in twentieth-century Ireland', *Twentieth Century Communism*, Vol. 6, No. 6, Mar. 2014, pp. 59-81.
81   The ban effectively covered any organisation more left-wing than the Labour Party and more republican than Fianna Fáil or Sinn Féin. The ban included Saor Éire, the IRA, Fianna Eireann, Cumman na mBan, the Labour Defence League, the Friends of Soviet Russia, the Irish Working Farmers' Committee, the Workers' Research Bureau, the Irish Tribute League, the Women's Prisoners' Defence League, the Workers' Defence Corps and the Workers' Revolutionary Party. See Milotte, *Communism in Modern* Ireland, pp. 106-113.
82   Cited in Ibid., p. 101
83   *Cork Examiner*, 5 June 1929; *Irish Independent*, 12 Feb., 14 Mar. 1930. The 'Labour League Against Fascism', founded in early 1934, was another communist front group. See Purséil, *The Irish Labour Party*, pp. 53-54.
84   IEIU REC minutes, 13 Feb. 1930.
85   Ibid., 20 Feb. 1930.
86   Ibid., 5 Mar. 1930.
87   For Irish communist groups in the 1920s and early 1930s, see Emmet O'Connor, 'Bolshevising Irish Communism: The Communist International and the Formation of the Revolutionary Workers' Groups, 1927-31', *Irish Historical Studies*, Vol. 33, No. 132, Nov. 2003, pp. 452-469.
88   Ibid., pp. 101-102; *Cork Examiner*, 5 June 1929
89   Milotte, *Communism in Modern* Ireland, pp. 106-113.
90   *Irish Independent*, 11 Apr. 1935.
91   IEIU REC minutes, 21 Jan. 1932; *Irish Press*, 18 Jan. 1932.
92   IEFU, *Fourth Half-Yearly Report, July to Dec. 1938*, Box 103, TEEU collection, p. 28.
93   IEIU REC minutes, 2 Jan. 1931; *Cork Examiner*, 2 Jan. 1931.
94   *Irish Independent*, 2 Aug. 1932; *Irish Press*, 8 Aug. 1932; IEIU REC minutes, 25 July, 3 Aug. 1932.
95   *Evening Herald*, 4, 5, 6, 9, 10, 11, 12 Aug. 1932; *Irish Independent*, 17 Aug. 1932; *Irish Press*, 19 Aug. 1932.
96   *Irish Press*, 9 Jan., 19 Sept., 8, 29 Oct. 1932, 7 June 1933; *Irish Independent*, 17, 24, 29 Oct., 17, 23 Dec. 1932, 8 June 1933.
97   IEIU REC minutes, 11 May 1933, 14 Feb. 1934, 18 July, 5, 12 Sept., 27 Nov. 1935; *Evening Herald*, 2, 3, 4 Jan. 1933; *Irish Press*, 28 Jan. 1933; *Cork Examiner*, 30 Jan. 1933.
98   *Irish Press*, 18 June 1937, 7 Jan., 2 Feb., 20 Apr. 1938; *Irish Independent*, 18-20 Jan. 1938; *Evening Herald*, 18 May 1938.
99   *Irish Press*, 14, 19 Feb., 12, 30 Dec. 1935, 6, 14 Jan., 24 Apr., 21 May 1936.
100 *Evening Herald*, 30 Oct., 4, 11, 13, 23, 24 Nov., 18 Dec. 1937. The shopmen secured a 6s. increase, making pay 90s. 1d.

101 *Irish Independent*, 5 May 1938; *Cork Examiner*, 7, 12 Sept. 1938.

102 *Irish Independent*, 14, 15, 17, 19-24 Sept., 27 Oct. 1938; *Evening Herald*, 28 Sept. 1938; *Irish Press*, 29 Sept. 3 Oct. 1938; IEFU, *Third Half-Yearly Report, Jan. to June 1938*, Box 103, TEEU collection, ILHM, pp. 29-32.

103 *Irish Press*, 29 Aug., 6-27 Sept., 4, 8, 26 Oct., 14-26 Dec. 1932, 3, 12 Jan. 1933.

104 *Evening Herald*, 5, 6, 12 Mar., 8 Apr. 1937. Under the terms of settlement, meter readers and collectors were required to drive cars as usual, as were installation inspectors, sub-station inspectors, supervisors, foremen and electricians on emergency work.

105 Department of Industry and Commerce, *Statistical Abstract* (Dublin: Stationary Office, 1942).

106 *Irish Independent*, 3, 11 Aug. 1932.

107 *Irish Press*, 16-26 Oct. 1934.

108 'Statement by President on Sugar Beet Position', TSCH/3/S9293A, Dept. of An Taoiseach records, NAI.

109 'Sugar factories strike', TSCH/3/S9293A, Dept. of An Taoiseach records, NAI.

110 IEIU REC minutes, 25 Oct. 1934.

111 ITUC, *Forty-first annual report*, 1934-35, ILHM, p. 63; ITUC executive committee minutes, 8 Feb. 1935, ICTU/Box 100, ICTU collection, NAI.

112 IEIU REC minutes, 27 Feb. 1936; ITUC, *Forty-first annual report*, 1934-35, ILHM, pp. 62-65.

113 ITUC executive committee minutes, 8, 21 Feb., 5 Apr. 1935, ICTU/Box 100, ICTU collection, NAI; IEIU REC minutes, 14 Feb. 1935.

114 Department of Industry and Commerce, *Census of Industrial Production* (Dublin: Stationary Office, 1937).

115 IEIU REC minutes, 19 Aug., 2 Sept, 15 Oct. 1936; ITUC executive minutes, 29 Oct., 27 Nov., 17 Dec. 1936, ICTU/Box 101, ICTU collection, NAI; *Irish Press*, 15 Oct. 1935, 12-29 Oct. 1936, 20 Jan. 1937; *Irish Independent*, 16 Oct. 1935, 4, 15-29 Oct., 12 Nov. 1936. Specifically, the court heard from the 'Thurles Sugar Workers' Protection Association', which was comprised of members who broke away from the IEIU and ITGWU.

116 *Evening Herald*, 2, 5 Oct. 1937; *Irish Press*, 4 Oct. 1937; IEIU REC minutes, 30 Sept., 7, 14, 21 Oct., 2 Dec. 1937. Despite its strong presence at the Tuam factory, the IEFU was excluded from the board. See IEFU AGM minutes, 23 Mar. 1941, Box 1D, TEEU collection, ILHM.

117 *Irish Press*, 26 Apr., 2 May 1938, 10, 11 Oct. 1939; *Tuam Herald*, 30 Apr. 1938; IEIU REC minutes, 13 Jan., 28 Apr, 5 May, 9 June 1938. The strike was caused by the firing of six employees, with whom the IEIU and ITGWU struck in sympathy.

118 IEIU REC minutes, 25 Apr., 16 May 1935. For accounts of the 1935 tram strike, see Bill McCamley, *Dublin tram workers, 1872-1945* (Dublin: Labour History Workshop, 2008); and Bill McCamley, *The role of the rank and file in the 1935 Dublin tram and bus strike* (Dublin: Labour History Workshop, 1981).

119 Allen, *Fianna Fáil*, p. 48.

120 *Irish Independent*, 17, 27, 30 Apr., 14, 15 May 1937; *Evening Herald*, 22 Mar. 1937; IEIU REC minutes, 7 Jan., 18 Mar., 8, 22, 29 Apr., 6 May 1937.

121 IEIU REC minutes, 12 Mar. 1936-1 Sept. 1938.

122 Ibid., 4 Nov. 1935, 16, 29 Apr., 14, 28 May, 4 June, 11 Aug. 1936, 20 Feb., 15, 29 Apr. 1937; *Cork Examiner*, 20 Apr., 11 May 1936, 9, 10, 14 Apr., 1 May 1937.

123 Donal Nevin (ed.), *Trade Union Century* (Cork: Mercier Press, 1994), p. 396.

124 *Irish Independent*, 11 Aug. 1932; ETU REC minutes, 1 Sept., 27 Oct. 1937.

125 *Evening Herald*, 20 Dec. 1930; *Irish Press*, 9 Mar. 1933. Alfred Septimus Orpen, Application for MSP, DP6564, MSP Collection, MA.

126 *Irish Press*, 6 Apr. 1934, 20, 22 July 1942.

127 *Irish Press*, 16, 17 Aug., 16 Sept. 1939.

128 Peter Cassells & Finbarr Flood, *Dispute between the TEEU and employers in the electrical contracting industry*, (Dublin: Department of Enterprise, Trade and Employment, 2009), p. 8

129 *Irish Press*, 16 Feb., 16 July 1934; *Irish Independent*, 2 Nov. 1934.

130 *Irish Independent*, 7 Mar. 1929; *Irish Times*, 22 July 1931; *Irish Press*, 31 Jan. 1936.

131 TEEU, *Michael Mervyn, 1900-1960* (Dublin: TEEU, 2016), p. 15; Ward-Perkins, *Trade Union Records*, p. 119.

132 ITUC, annual reports, 1929-39, ILHM.

133   IEIU REC minutes, 2, 16 July 1931. In 1936, the union purported to represent 85 per cent of Broadstone's signalling and telegraph department.

134   IEFU, *First Half-Year Report, Jan. to June 1937*, Box 103, TEEU collection, ILHM, p. 2.

135   IEFU REC minutes, 23, 30 Jan., 3 Nov. 1935, 29 Apr. 1936; *Limerick Leader*, 13 June 1936; *Labour News*, 20 Nov. 1937.

136   *Irish Independent*, 3 Nov. 1938, 1, 2 Mar. 1939.

137   IEFU REC minutes, 30 Oct., 4 Nov. 1935.

138   IEFU AGM minutes, 23 Mar. 1941, Box 1D, TEEU collection, ILHM.

139   *Irish Independent*, 26 Sept. 1935, 11 Mar. 1936; *Irish Press*, 20, 22 Jan., 15, 26 Feb. 1936; *Evening Herald*, 22 Feb. 1936; ITUC executive committee minutes, 31 Oct. 1935, ICTU/Box 101, ICTU collection, NAI; IEFU REC minutes, 9 Jan., 30 Sept. 1935, 9 Jan., 5, 19, 26 Feb., 4 Mar. 1936.

140   IEFU REC minutes, 19 Jan. 1936.

141   Ibid., 29 May, 17, 31 July, 21 Aug. 1935, 9, 19, 22, 29 Jan., 26 Feb. 1936.

142   The 1886 Health Exhibition was held in Dublin. The construction of the central heating plant was plagued by a clash between the fitters and the plumbers over the division of work, the first of many to come. See *Irish Press*, 8 Dec. 1948.

143   IEFU REC minutes, 20 Nov. 1935; ITUC executive committee minutes, 31 Oct. 1935, 26 Mar., 27 Nov., 17 Dec. 1936, 9 July 1937, 25 May 1939, ICTU/Box 101, ICTU collection, NAI. For example, the IEFU reported its existence in Thurles in November 1935 and ITUC reported the same in Sligo in November 1936.

144   Ibid., 31 Oct. 1935, ICTU/Box 101, ICTU collection, NAI. See also *Irish Press*, 28 Feb., 4, 25 Mar. 1936.

145   ITUC executive committee minutes, 9 July 1937, ICTU/Box 101, ICTU collection, NAI; *Irish Press*, 21 Jan. 1936; IEFU REC minutes, 9 Jan., 11 Dec. 1935.

146   ITUC executive committee minutes, 17 Dec. 1936, ICTU/Box 101, ICTU collection, NAI.

147   For instance, in mid-1936, the ITUC and Dublin Trades Council proposed a six-month ceasefire. They hoped that this would give them enough time to negotiate an amalgamation of both unions, which they agreed was the only solution to the conflict. But neither side accepted this, and the ceasefire never happened. See IEFU REC minutes, 16, 29 Apr. 1936; *Irish Press*, 24 Apr., 1 May 1936.

148   John Henry Richardson, *An Introduction to the Study of Industrial Relations* (London: Allen & Unwin, 1954), pp. 198-199.

149   *Irish Press*, 5 Mar. 1935.

150   IGREU/IEFU, 1930-39, T357, RFS collection, NAI.

151   Ryan, Apprenticeships in Ireland', pp. 224-229.

152   Ibid., pp. 164-167; IEIU REC minutes, 25 May 1928.

153   Cited in Ryan, Apprenticeships in Ireland', pp. 193-194.

154   Ibid., pp. 194-196; McCarthy, *Apprenticeships in Ireland*, pp. 5-6.

155   Ryan, Apprenticeships in Ireland', pp. 203-215.

156   Ibid., pp. 212-215, 243-246.

157   *Irish Independent*, 10 May 1932.

158   IEIU REC minutes, 10, 24, 30 Apr. 1930.

159   Cited in Ryan, 'Apprenticeships in Ireland', p. 236.

160   Cited in Ibid., p. 237.

161   Ibid., pp. 234-238.

5

Emergency and Post-Emergency, 1939-46

Emergency and Post-Emergency, The impact of the Second World War – still known in Ireland as the Emergency – on Irish workers has been underappreciated. After the government declared a state of emergency in September 1939, the relationship between labour and the state began to fundamentally change, with trade unionism radically altered as a result. In 1939, one-sixth of the Irish workforce was in industry and 150,000 workers unionised.[1] Until then, the struggle for survival defined labour: with only 25 per cent of workers unionised, success depended on militancy. Like many countries, wartime hardship, poverty, unemployment and inequality swung public opinion to the left during the war. Irish neutrality had overwhelming public and political support. Strict censorship was introduced to cocoon the public from the war, making subsequent revelations of Nazi atrocities and the Holocaust even more shocking to Irish eyes and ears. The government hoped that censorship would protect neutrality by not providing ammunition to the few who wanted intervention on the Allied side. Censorship could only go so far, however, and British newspapers and newsreels circulated freely. Nothing could stop the Irish public learning of the 1942 Beveridge Report, the blueprint for Britain's extensive post-war welfare state, and the achievements of Clement Attlee's Labour Party government. With memories of the war and the grinding poverty of the Great Depression still raw, Irish workers shared Europe's hopes for a more equal society after 1945.[2]

The Emergency was a time of experimentation in labour-state relations. It was a pivotal period when the long-standing clash of ideologies between British and Irish unions climaxed and when the foundation for the post-war industrial relations system was laid. A cabinet reshuffle at the outbreak of war led to Lemass being replaced as Minister for Industry and Commerce by Seán McEntee. It was a turning point for the unions' relationship with Fianna Fáil. Whereas Lemass was a labour sympathiser who sought consensus, McEntee was an acerbic, uncompromising right-winger who made no secret of his disdain for trade unionism. Embodying the conservative nationalism of Belfast's Catholic middle class, McEntee was a fierce anti-communist. He became a notorious hammerer of the left who led Fianna Fáil's red scares during the 1943 and 1944 general elections. During his tenure in Industry and Commerce, he extended state regulation to wages and trade unionism itself. In 1941, Lemass returned to his old portfolio and took a softer line. Nevertheless, he welcomed McEntee's wartime controls as laying the groundwork for subsequent economic policy.

State intervention was a direct challenge to the traditional voluntary mode of industrial relations and organisation championed by the amalgamateds. The role of the state in labour affairs became another fault-line in the enduring dispute between British and Irish unions. The ITUC's handing of this manifestation of the Anglo-Irish conflict was disastrously self-damaging. Irish unions in the private sector reacted warmly to state intervention and increasingly turned to the state, rather than Congress, as the vehicle for progress. This was because statutory wage orders yielded some increases for the poorly paid who were chiefly represented by these unions. For both ideological and practical reasons, the amalgamateds clung to their laissez-faire outlook. Having organised the workforce in the nineteenth century, British unions tended to represent the better off – wage militants who suspected an incomes policy behind state intervention. Their frenzied response to the 1941 Trade Union Act convinced Irish labour leaders that the amalgamateds – the font of Anglicisation and mental colonisation – were a hindrance to the evolution of a national labour policy, a view reinforced by the prevailing political climate.[3] The conflict reached a crescendo in 1945 and was the primary reason for the split that took place in the ITUC that year.

War abroad, hardship at home

Although the Irish public were thankful for neutrality, the Emergency's social and economic consequences were inescapable and severe. In September 1939, the Oireachtas passed the Emergency Powers Act, giving the government extensive powers in matters of state security, public order and the provision and maintenance of supplies. Like the First World War, inflation quickly became a chronic grievance for workers. Prices went up immediately and many complained bitterly about insufficient prices controls, profiteering and the growth of the black market. Because most food consumed in Ireland was locally produced, the basic problem for workers was food price, not scarcity. Inflation led to a spike in industrial unrest in late 1939 and 1940. The government introduced selective rationing of imports (such as petrol) incrementally from 1939 and belatedly issued general ration books to the public in June 1942. As in the First World War, German U-boats decimated the Anglo-Irish shipping trade. When the government denied the British access to trans-shipment facilities at Irish ports, they retaliated by restricting vital exports to Ireland. By 1943, petrol supplies were 20 per cent of pre-war levels, gas was 16 per cent and textiles 22 per cent. The cost of imports rose dramatically compared to the prices gained for exports. The building trade virtually shut down and factories closed for want of fuel and raw materials. A lively black market in scares goods developed as a result. Industrial output fell by 27 per cent between 1938 and 1943, making unemployment and emigration working-class norms again. At the height of the Emergency, ninety-six thousand Dubliners were unemployed, four times the figure in 1939 (23,250). The cost of living rose by 70 per cent during the war while wages increased by only one-third. Labour's share of domestically generated national income fell from 51 per cent in 1938 to 44.3 per cent in 1944. The poor economic performance led to a large rise in the gap between British and Irish wages. Between 1936 and 1946, 187,000 Irishmen took the boat to Britain, whose war economy was far more generous. There were other tragic social corollaries to the penury. A 1941 government report estimated that 60 per cent of Dublin mothers were unable to breastfeed due to malnutrition, while infant mortality averaged 7 per cent of births, high by European standards. A 1938 inquiry found that 111,950 people were living in 6,307 tenement houses; 60 per cent of Dublin tenements, housing 64,940 people, were unfit for habitation. The slums remained scourged by diseases like tuberculosis, cholera, typhus and rickets (which afflicted 173 children per thousand in 1943).[4]

Government decisions compounded the poverty. From August 1940, McEntee argued in cabinet for a general pay freeze. He succeeded, but only with protected industries and essential services. Ministers were committed to avoiding an upward spiral of wages, fearing it would lead to price inflation in the short-term and undermine the competitiveness of exports to Britain in the long-term. On 7 May 1941, McEntee issued Emergency Order No. 83, commonly known as the Wages Standstill Order. It froze wages in protected sectors and removed legal immunity from unions should the order be violated. The Order was the result of a strike by the Irish Municipal Employees' Trade Union at Dublin Corporation for a wage increase in March 1940. The stoppage, which the IEIU supported by withdrawing stationary engine drivers, was effectively smashed by the government.[5] On 31 May 1940 – with Senator Eamon Lynch, ITUC secretary, in attendance – the IEIU held a national conference at 6 Gardiner Row to decry the Order, 'which took away the right of the worker for looking for better conditions or the securing an increased wage to meet the meet the ever increasing cost of living.'[6] A week later, just as France had fallen to the Wehrmacht, the IEIU announced that any member who left his trade to serve as a volunteer or in the civil service or military was ineligible to receive union benefits.[7] This stringent policy only lasted two years. The man who ensured it was changed:

> felt it was not right to debar a widow from drawing mortality benefit if anything happened to her husband while helping to protect his country. Any member may be killed in his workshop by a bomb falling and that member may be working for the state... if everyone ... did not do something for the state we would be in very serious trouble. Perhaps we would be invaded by some of those at war at the present time.[8]

Table 34: Cost of Living in the Irish Free State/Éire, 1940-45 (July 1914 = 100).[9]

Year (Feb.)	All Items
1940	197
1941	218
1942	237
1943	273
1944	296
1945	295

The 1941 Trade Union Act

After issuing the Wages Standstill Order, the government's focus moved from wages to industrial relations. It viewed employer calls for compulsory arbitration of strikes sympathetically. The Dublin Corporation strike dismayed McEntee, who seized the opportunity to convince his colleagues that a legislative solution was needed to deal with similar disputes. His draft bill, based on the UK's Emergency Powers Act 1920 and Trades Disputes and Trades Union Act 1927, empowered the government to declare a state of emergency if strikes upset public or essential services. A second draft followed shortly afterwards. Replete with economic penalties in cases of non-compliance, both were draconian pieces of legislation that the cabinet considered provocative and unworkable.[10] Secret meetings between officials from the Department of Industry and Commerce and William O'Brien produced a bill with a different focus: reorganisation of the labour movement. 'It was a neat mutual accommodation;

O'Brien nudged the state away from coercion of industrial relations, while allowing the government to say it was implementing a trade union agenda.'[11]

The Trade Union Bill 1941 was published on 30 April. It was, in Charles McCarthy's words, 'the most radical attempt that has so far been made to restructure, by legislative means, the trade union movement.'[12] The bill aimed to achieve this in three ways: to clarify the legal position of trade unions, to liquidate smaller unions and to eliminate union multiplicity. It stipulated that a union must have a licence to enjoy legal immunity and the right to negotiate wages and conditions. Otherwise, the extensive protections of the Trades Disputes Act 1906 would not apply. To obtain a licence, unions would have to be registered under the Trade Union Acts 1871-1935; be a union registered under the laws of another jurisdiction; maintain a registered office in Ireland; lodge a deposit of between £2,000 to £10,000 to the High Court; and submit detailed returns on rules, officers and members to the Minister for Industry and Commerce. The inclusion of a provision to restrict wages was especially controversial. O'Brien's fingerprints were evident in several parts of the bill, which was the ITGWU supported it. For example, the bill proposed to institute a tribunal which could grant one or more unions the rights to negotiate for a group of workers where that union or those unions represented most of those workers.[13] The suggestion to group unions in specific industrial categories in a manner highly advantageous to the ITGWU as the biggest Irish general union closely mirrored O'Brien's 1936 memorandum. Accordingly, Irish unions that stood to lose – like the IEIU and IEFU – joined with their British adversaries to campaign for the bill's demise, with the WUI leading the charge.[14]

The government's belief that the unions would support the changes was exposed within days of the bill's publication. On 6 May, the Dublin Trades Council condemned the legislation as an 'unwarranted invasion of the constitutional and historic rights of the trade unions', unleashing an avalanche of 'emphatic opposition.'[15] The IEIU agreed. On 3 June, the same national conference that denounced the Wages Standstill Order also unequivocally condemned the bill by passing the following resolution:

> That we, the members of the … Irish Engineering Industrial Union … solemnly protest in the strongest possible manner against the introduction of the Trade Union Bill 1941 and the Emergency Powers Order No. 83 … That we … demand the immediate withdrawal of such arbitrary and undemocratic measures, as the putting into operation of such acts will destroy the fundamental principles for which the common people of our country have so long striven; and will … militate against Irishmen organising on Irish national trade union lines in their own land. We further pledge our support to any measure which may be adopted by the trade union movement against the latest act of aggression against the workers of Ireland.[16]

The IEFU followed suit two weeks later.[17] In August, Leo Farrell, its general president, warned his comrades that if 'trade unionists did not get together' to oppose the bill and Emergency Order 83, then 'their destiny would be left in the hands of the employer for them to deal with in whatever way they thought fair.' Two days later, Farrell told his colleagues that labour is going through a 'crisis' 'owing to the Trade Union Bill and Emergency Order Number 83… if these Bills are put into operation, the whole working class would be undoubtedly left to the mercy of the employing class… They are very detrimental to the working class as a whole... As regards fighting against the Trade Union Bill and Government Order ... this union would never be found wanting if a fight was declared.'[18]

Things were about to get worse for some trade unionists. McEntee introduced two amendments to re-orientate the bill's thrust from the smaller unions to the British ones: the first allowed the minister to abate the deposit by up to 75 per cent, but only for Irish unions; the second reserved sole negotiation licences for Irish unions. It was an explicit attack on the amalgamateds, whom McEntee vilified as the root of industrial unrest and the obstacle to reform of the labour movement.[19] On 22 June, the day Axis troops poured into the Soviet Union, twenty thousand workers and fifty-three trade unions marched from Parnell Square to College Green to watch Jim Larkin dramatically burn a copy of the bill. It was the sturdiest display of working-class tenacity since 1923. In response, the Labour Party announced that it would oppose the bill in its entirely rather than put down amendments. With the notable exception of the ITGWU, the unions considered the bill a wider crypto-fascist plot to implement a corporatist model of government with the unions put firmly under state control. While this may seem hyperbolic, it must be seen in the context of the proliferation of fascism in Europe and widespread sympathy for Catholic vocationalism, rather than parliamentary democracy, at home. The government had appointed a Commission on Vocational Education in 1939 to examine the feasibility of reorganising the political structure of the country along vocational lines. Four trade unionists (including Larkin) sat on the commission which heard evidence from both the IEIU and AEU. It issued a detailed report in 1943 which the ETU supported and believed would form the basis of post-war labour legislation.[20]

The passionate opposition to the bill was not just a fear of being swamped by the ITGWU, it was also rooted in ideology. While class consciousness was not strong in the Irish labour movement in 1941, it was solid enough to inspire solidarity with the amalgamateds on a matter of principle rather than succumb to the xenophobia of the time. 'In the past ... nationalist sentiment ... rapidly overwhelmed international socialist ideals; but this was not the case here. There was ... a strong sense of working-class identity and solidarity ... powerful enough to challenge the nationalist position.'[21] Hostility was rooted in a sectionalism which mistook restraints on trade union freedom with an assault on trade unionism itself and conflated the bill with the Wages Standstill Order. More than anything, hostility sprung from a conviction that free trade unionism depended on a minimal engagement with the state. 'This last mentality, anchored philosophically in English liberalism, underpinned all ideological criticism and was pervasive enough to transcend the structural Irish-British or craft-general divide.'[22] There was no connection between the bill and Order No. 83, no desire to 'nationalise' labour and certainly no insidious fascist plot. The Commission on Vocational Organisation was merely a sop to the Catholic right and the trade unionists on it did not take it seriously. The campaign against the 1941 bill backfired and did more harm than good to labour. 'Instead of exploiting its consent to the bill as a bargaining chip in power play against the wage freeze, union leaders confronted the rationalization issue with such ineptitude as to make the government's case for it.'[23]

In August 1941, Industry and Commerce was added to Lemass' remit as Minister for Supplies, heralding a return to census between labour and Fianna Fáil. In April 1942, he relaxed the pay freeze with Emergency Powers Order

No. 166, which allowed tribunals to award cost of living bonuses in certain circumstances. But Lemass had no desire to undo McEntee's work, so only licenced unions would be considered for bonuses. His Trade Union Act 1942 made only minor amendments to the 1941 Act. The government, especially Lemass, refused to concede any direct involvement to either business or labour in policy making. While Lemass was anxious to consult with interest groups, he did not conceive of having employers or unions as social partners. His notion of political authority led him to concentrate power in the state as exercised through the civil service and legislation.[24] However, many Irish workers regarded the Trade Union Acts as simply tools for union busting, evidence that Fianna Fáil had abandoned its 'radical' roots.

The rocky road to one Irish engineering union

By 1941, the Foundry Union had been trying to affiliate to the ITUC for six years, with the IEIU blocking it at every opportunity. When the IEIU removed its objection, the Congress executive leaped at the opportunity to push for the reunification of both unions. In 1942, Congress rejected another attempt from the Foundry Union to affiliate because it wanted to see unity between the two rivals.[25] But the Foundry Union reacted sharply to the overtures. At a meeting of its NEC, one representative demanded to know if 'the members … were expected to bend down our knees to the IEIU? … we were a much stronger body, and that we should not stoop to do this.' Another man reminded his colleagues that, 'the IEIU were much inferior to this union' so they should 'consider the question very carefully.'[26] There was still much animosity between the two. At a Foundry Union meeting, one Corkman 'stated that the attitude of the IEIU in the south was becoming a trade union racket, they were giving cards to everyone … if they applied.'[27] Accordingly, the Foundry Union told the ITUC that it was 'not prepared to sit down and discuss the question of fusion with the IEIU unless we were on equal footing.'[28] Not everyone agreed, however. One such man was Meade, the old IEIU Limerick branch secretary who had caused so much trouble in his former union. He supported fusion – even though he did not trust the IEIU – to strengthen Irish unions against the AEU.[29] The 1941 Act aimed to reduce the number of unions in the state, forcing the IEFU to consider unity. Members were fiercely divided. Its Dublin No. 1 branch agreed 'to the principle … of one engineering union for the whole engineering industry of Éire' provided that the 'status and conditions' of IEFU members was protected.[30] However, former IEIU man Peter Coates strongly opposed unity, declaring that 'he was not prepared to crawl to the IEIU.' Farrell wanted greater cooperation, but not fusion, with the IEIU because 'we have been trying to do this for a long time, but it only resulted in the loss of members.' His was the majority opinion within the Foundry Union.[31]

In March 1944, IEFU general treasurer Thomas Fleming spoke of 'negotiations going on between Irish unions against this union and of the IEIU approaching the Irish Transport Union.'[32] It is not clear if the IEIU approached the ITGWU. Regardless, the Transport Union involved itself in the reunification question. The renewed animosity between British and Irish unions facilitated a soothing of tensions that facilitated talks between the IEIU and the IEFU. As both were Irish, William O'Brien took a direct interest in their reunification. That October, he wrote to both proposing a conference under his chairmanship to explore this possibility. His letter was prompted by the Commission on Vocational Organisation's recommendation, which O'Brien supported, that

British unions should be banned from operating in Ireland.[33] Negotiating with O'Brien was controversial and both unions were suspicious of his reasons for wanting unity. His involvement prompted a furious response from the rank-and-file of the Foundry Union who intensely disliked him for splitting the labour movement. Coates and several other organisers vowed to leave the union if it merged with the IEIU under O'Brien's auspices. Coates prophesied that 'the day we sit down with William O'Brien will mean the end of the IEFU.' Chris Ferguson agreed, arguing that 'we should work on our terms ... not on William O'Brien's.' Another member believed that 'O'Brien does not have the confidence of the Irish working class. It was a plan to get control of Irish unions, a dictatorial control.'[34] The IEFU's Dublin No. 8 (Stationary Engine Drivers) Branch – of which Coates and Ferguson were committee members – opposed unity unless the IEIU accepted its rival's terms. The Dundalk representative considered O'Brien 'a tool of the government, and a renegade.' Coates regarded O'Brien as a class traitor who was 'colluding' with employers.[35] Despite the animosity, the IEFU executive received O'Brien. At the conference, however, both unions rejected his amalgamation plan as a ploy to lure them into the ITGWU.[36] Although the talks collapsed, they set a process in motion. Feeling threatened, the AEU launched a major recruitment drive to increase its Irish membership (twenty-three thousand in 1944) by pressing for a forty-hour week without a wage cut.[37]

Further negotiations between the IEIU and the Foundry Union were, the ETU believed, 'very successful to a point.'[38] They took place under the auspices of the newly formed Congress of Irish Unions, which wanted to clearly define groups and to rationalise labour by preventing overlapping. The ETU supported the merger because it believed that one Irish engineering union would encourage IEFU and IEIU electricians to join it, which Congress was also pushing for. A unified union would have four thousand members – 2,500 from the Foundry Union and 1,500 from the IEIU. Though they were surprised and disappointed by the failure of the talks, ETU leaders predicted that there would once again be a single Irish engineering union in about a decade or so. While some executive members wanted the ETU to remain separate, many, including the general secretary, supported amalgamation with the engineering unions.[39] In October 1945, the IEIU and the Foundry Union reopened negotiations. The decision was controversial and many of the rank-and-file were strongly opposed. The following month, the Foundry Union attended a dinner at Clery's, O'Connell Street to celebrate the IEIU's twenty-fifth anniversary. IEIU general president Michael Connolly spoke of his desire to see both unions as one, to which his Foundry Union guests responded warmly. Rooney, still the IEIU's general trustee, claimed that his union had paid out over £70,000 in benefits since its establishment and had made 'the greatest effort that had been made to establish Irish unionism on a national industrial basis.' It was his last major union function. He died the following month.[40]

The Foundry Union's organisation of labourers triggered lingering craft snobbery among some members of the rival union. The IEIU's Limerick branch was nervous of a merger because the Foundry Union had 160 members in the city, only twelve of whom were tradesmen. The IEIU branch had one hundred members, all tradesmen, who feared that if fusion took place, then labourers 'would have power and ... skilled men would have no say in the running of the branch.' They proposed that there be two branches in Limerick should reunification take place, one for craftsmen and another for labourers. There were other hoops the IEIU had to jump through to get its rival back. The Foundry Union insisted that its benefits must remain after reunification, which alarmed the financially weaker IEIU (the Foundry Union paid double the IEIU's rate of superannuation benefit, for example). Any proposed terms of amalgamation would have to be approved by a five-sixths majority of IEIU members, a difficult figure to secure.[41]

Table 35: Membership of the Irish Engineering Unions, 1939-46.[42]

Year (31 Dec.)	IEIU	IEFU	ETU
1939	1,785	2,375	-
1940	1,758	2,233	980
1941	1,652	2,547	984
1942	1,690	2,677	1,038
1943	1,785	2,839	1,147
1944	1,929	3,049	1,281
1945	1,988	2,409	1,337
1946	1,981	2,579	1,590

The birth of the Congress of Irish Unions

The inequity of the Emergency led to a spike in support for the Labour Party, which secured 15.7 per cent of the vote in the 1943 general election, its highest since 1922. However, the party's vote sunk to 8.8 per cent a year later. The decline was exacerbated by a split in the party about alleged communist infiltration and ITGWU unhappiness about Larkin being put forth for election to the Dáil. In 1944, the ITGWU and the rest of the party's right wing broke away and formed the centrist National Labour Party, which took 2.7 per cent of the vote in that year's election.[43] The split precipitated the 1945 schism in the ITUC, a clash between two distinct outlooks formed by the contrasting material conditions of Ireland and Britain. The amalgamateds were Anglocentric and reflected a trade unionism born in the British Industrial Revolution. In contrast, Irish unions like the IEIU, IEFU and ETU espoused a blend of corporatism, nationalism, Catholicism and anti-Communism. Between 1937 and 1944, British membership of unions affiliated to Congress mushroomed from sixty-eight thousand to 108,000, allowing them to gain a majority on its executive; Irish unions could only muster eighty thousand in 1944. In 1943, the ITUC had elected its first Belfast-based president since Thomas Johnson in 1917. By then, a third of the ITUC's membership were northerners. In January 1944, the ITUC executive declined an invitation from the British TUC to attend a conference in London on the war economy and post-war reconstruction. The executive, with its Irish majority, believed that attending a conference that identified with the Allies would undermine Irish neutrality. The ITUC membership subsequently passed a motion regretting the decision and the incoming, British-dominated executive reversed it. It was too much for Irish unions to bear.[44]

On 25 April 1945 fifteen Irish unions – ten of them affiliated to Congress – formed a separate body, the Congress of Irish Unions (CIU). British control, they argued, could not represent 'the opinions and aspirations' of Irish workers whose native unions 'occupy an intolerable and humiliating position.'[45] British unions accounted for 23 per cent of the total number of trade unionists in the state that year, a high never to be replicated.[46] The ITGWU led the schism. The Irish-British clash was compounded by the personal hatreds that O'Brien and Larkin had for each other. After the ITGWU left, the WUI, whose application to the ITUC had consistently been blocked by the Transport Union, joined the ITUC. The new Congress claimed 60,445 members at its foundation.[47] Within months, this number jumped to seventy-five thousand, surpassing the ITUC's seventy-two thousand members. The split immediately reversed the fortunes of British unions in the twenty-six counties, in contrast to their simultaneous growth in the North. As the amalgamateds stayed with the ITUC, 60 per cent of that Congress's membership was now north of the border. However, apart from the WUI, several Irish unions remained loyal, such as the bakers, postal workers and national schoolteachers. The CIU, on the other hand, was entirely comprised of southern-based bodies; the IEIU and ETU were two of its fifteen founder unions. The idea of having a Congress solely for Irish unions had a long history: several of the IEIU's founders had tried to establish a Federation of Irish Trades Unions in 1920.[48]

Owens presided over the CIU's inaugural meeting and John O'Brien was appointed to the provisional executive committee. Owens had little affinity to the new role but, 'unfortunately for himself', was appointed the first president of the new Congress. His reticence was shared by the rest of his union, who were 'not happy about the break', but believed that it was 'imperative as far as our members' aims and conditions are concerned. We have the right to strive for a wage which will provide us with enough money to live in frugal comfort.' Its Drogheda branch was the only one to oppose the breakaway. The ETU leadership, who donated £100 towards the CIU's inauguration, believed that the split, 'whilst very regrettable, was ... inevitable.' The union assumed joining the CIU would not harm its relationship with the British ETU which, although previously fractured, had improved of late. 'A new time has come, and such a state of affairs does not now exist, they recognising us as the representative body here and vice versa.' The ETU (Ireland) viewed the CIU as the logical conclusion of its own formation.[49] The IEIU agreed. One NEC delegate reflected the majority feeling when he argued that 'after twenty-three years of freedom in our native country ... it was ... time that such an organisation as was about to be formed had our wholehearted support.'[50] Connolly told the CIU's first annual meeting that his union 'had been longing for years past for something like this, some organisation free from the domination and dictation of the amalgamated unions.'[51] But the decision was not universally accepted within the IEIU. Paddy Bergin, a cook at the Carlow sugar factory and local branch chairman, believed that they 'would be doing a wrong thing in accepting the proposal of the Irish Transport and General Workers' Union' to form an 'Irish Council of Unions' because

> it threatens to disrupt the entire trade union and labour movement. If successful it will create divisions not alone in the ITUC but also individual unions, branches, trades councils and Labour Parties. It will not create an 'Irish Council of Unions', but only a council of sections of the trade union movement. The method of introducing the proposal tends to create disunity rather than create an all-Irish Trade Union Council. It seems that clear that the establishment of the body will be followed by legislation to outlaw the Amalgamated Unions, thus creating further bitterness between trade unionists.[52]

Shortly afterwards, the membership of the Foundry Union voted 20-1 to join the new Congress 'to break the domination of England.' As in the IEIU, the five per cent of dissentients were scathing. Citing loyalty to the ITUC, Coates abhorred that his union sent delegates to the CIU's inauguration meeting before it was even affiliated to it. He proclaimed that he had 'led' the Dublin No. 8 branch 'into the union and led them since they came in, and now I will lead them out with my head up and my hands clean … We will have nothing to do with the Congress of Irish Unions and will have nothing to do with the IEIU.' Coates then informed his colleagues that his branch was considering joining the AEU or 'two other unions.'[53] In the end, Coates' branch defected to the WUI, which would now compete with the three engineering unions. Coates became 'financial secretary' of the WUI's new Engineering Branch while Ferguson became its 'industrial secretary.'[54] They were not the only ones to disapprove of the CIU. Bro. Walsh, another prominent IEFU organiser, also opposed joining it, suspecting that Lemass was behind its creation via his 'renegade' stooge O'Brien to split and weaken labour. He argued that 'Ireland should march with the workers of the world' and denounced the IEFU leadership as 'wreckers.' Similarly, the union's Dundalk representative argued that it should join the ITUC and that the split was 'a political angle to control the trade union movement.'[55] No. 8's transfer was not the last to the WUI. In June 1946, another Foundry Union branch – this one catering for boilermen, fitters' helpers and other semiskilled engineering workers – went over to Larkin's union.[56]

In November 1945, nine CIU affiliates on the Dublin Trades Council – including the ETU and Foundry Union – received orders to break away and form the Dublin Council of Irish Unions, once again giving Dublin two trades councils. A month later, an equivalent council was launched in Cork with IEIU official and local branch secretary Seán Ó Murchú as chairman.[57] Catholicism was, after nationalism, a powerful motivator for the successionists. The objects of the Dublin Council of Irish Unions committed it to 'direct activities towards obtaining social justice for workers, in accordance with the teachings of the great Papal Encyclicals.'[58] For the IEIU, joining the new council was an easy decision. The union had already disaffiliated from the DTC in 1944 because it was unhappy with how it had handled a five-month, unofficial strike of members of the Boilermakers' Society against an IEIU man at the Liffey Dockyard. For others, however, joining the new councils was a tougher conundrum. In 1946, one of the ETU's two Dublin branches was attached to the original Dublin trades council. The union decided to sever this connection by only one vote.[59]

Labour historiography has presented the split as one between as right-wing nationalists and left-wing internationalists, but there was more to it than this simplistic characterisation.[60] Ideologically, both Congresses were enmeshed in a web of contradictions that the left-right spectrum cannot fully explain. The 'reformist' CIU combined anti-imperialism with nationalism, Catholicism and anti-communism; the 'conservative' ITUC was more secular, liberal and internationalist. Structurally, the schism revealed a division between better-off unions seeking to preserve the status quo and those who felt a change in labour-state relations could help them augment their membership and bargaining power. Tellingly, fourteen of the fifteen unions that formed the CIU – including the IEIU and ETU – operated primarily in the private sector. One of the CIU's two founding aims was to establish a new industrial relations apparatus with both Irish states: a 'new machinery for new times and new conditions', as its founding document put it.[61] The other, which was inextricably linked to the first, was to establish a national movement. The CIU and its affiliates eschewed wage militancy as a strategic weapon. Instead, they agitated for legal change to be brought about by cosier labour-state relations. The amalgamateds had still not ridded themselves of the British industrial methodology that the IEIU had rejected since 1920. The British method was based on strong unions in a strong economy and a party system clearly divided along class, left-right lines. This enabled unions to make gains through a voluntary system of industrial relations and a powerful Labour Party, none of which applied in Ireland.[62] And yet the ITUC took no heed of this. Having 'creamed off the better paid workers in the late nineteenth century', the amalgamateds 'were well situated for wage militancy in free collective bargaining', fearing that any move from the voluntary principle would constitute an attack on their British roots.[63]

The IEFU and the National Struggle

Until his departure, Peter Coates was one of the IEFU's most left-wing members from one of its most militant branches. As a socialist, he wanted his union to forgo nationalism for class politics by affiliating to the Labour Party. But class politics stood little chance of success during the Emergency. The popularity of neutrality spurred the growth of a brand of nationalism that stood for the defence of the state. For the first time, the war had mobilised Irish public opinion to consider the twenty-six-county state, rather than the partitioned island, as the primary unit of national loyalty.[64] Despite the hostile climate, Coates persisted. During a speech at a union meeting in which he urged his colleagues not to seek a negotiating licence under the 1941 Act, he veered off and 'continued by referring to the Blueshirts, etc.' The chairman intervened by telling Coates that he 'should not throw slurs on members, whether they were Blueshirts or Greenshirts.'[65]

Coates had always been a radical. Having joined the Irish Citizen Army in 1915, he fought at Liberty Hall and Stephen's Green during the Rising under the command of Markievicz and Michael Mallin. Coates later claimed that Connolly told his fellow ICA men to 'hold onto your guns, for when you are finished beating the enemy, you will want them for your friends.'[66] He re-joined the Citizen Army following his release from prison in December 1916. 'For his courage and coolness', he 'was always picked for any dangerous actions.'[67] He continued his ICA service during the War of Independence, taking part in the famous attack on the Custom House in 1921. Like most ICA men, Coates fought with the anti-Treatyites during the Civil War. He was a casual worker on the quays before finding employment as a boilerman at Dublin Corporation's abattoir where he worked until his death in late 1951 aged sixty-one.[68]

Ferguson was a close associate of Coates who had a strong republican pedigree himself. As a teenager, Ferguson took 'an active part' in the War of Independence with A Coy., 2nd Batt., Na Fianna, having joined in October 1919. In August 1921, he was transferred to the IRA – A Coy., 1st Batt., Dublin Brigade. Strongly opposed to the Treaty, he was arrested at the Inchicore works (where he was an apprentice boilermaker) on 15 August 1922 for shouting 'Up the Republic!' on the job. During his internment in Wellington (later Griffith) Barracks, his interrogator verbally and physically abused him and threatened to execute him. Ferguson was subsequently interned at Newbridge Camp (from which he escaped) and Mountjoy Prison. After his release, the IRA appointed him to the ASU and made him captain of A Coy., 1st Batt. In 1924, he was arrested again after going out in sympathy with the WUI during its strike at Inchicore. He later emigrated to England but returned to Ireland to work as a boilerman for the Department of Defence and joined the IEFU. After Larkin's death in 1947, he was appointed national organiser of the WUI. Though a communist in his youth, Ferguson's politics softened as he got older, and he was active in the Labour Party in his later years. Plagued by several years of ill-health, he died in 1957 aged fifty-three.[69] In 1949, the IEFU lost another veteran of the national struggle when James Keeley died. Born in Scotland to Irish parents, Keeley was an iron moulder by trade. During the War of Independence, he served as quartermaster of A Coy., 1st Batt. of the IRA's Scottish Brigade. He regularly shipped arms and hand grenades (which he assembled himself) from Glasgow to Dublin. In 1922, he returned to Ireland and took the anti-Treaty side in the Civil War, operating an IRA grenade foundry at Ballymun. He lived in Dublin until his death.[70]

The wages movement, 1939-46

The Wages Standstill Order and the statutory removal of immunity inevitably had a chilling effect on labour during the Emergency. Nevertheless, inflation ensured that the number of strikes and working days lost was surprisingly high. The index of hourly industrial wages (using 1953 as one hundred) rose from 47.9 in 1939 to 55.3 in 1945. Tight government control notwithstanding, the unions squeezed concessions from the complex tribunal system established to maintain industrial peace. To better combat wage claims, employer federations across the country came together and established the Federated Union of Employers (FUE) in 1942. The new body complemented the existing Confederation of Irish Industry established in 1932.

Railway shopmen were among the most militant engineering craftsmen during this period. In 1940, the GSR failed to give its shopmen the raise recently granted to those in the outside engineering shops and terminated the February 1935 agreement, which guaranteed payment based on a forty-seven-hour week. The unions resolved to take out 1,500 Dublin shopmen before postponing the action after McEntee intervened. The dispute persisted and erupted in mid-1943 when the three Irish engineering unions brought out three hundred shopmen for a £5. 17s. 6d. wage, a huge increase on their present rate of 79s. 1d. The higher rate was already being paid to pieceworkers. The district rate was 86s. 6d. A government-sponsored conference persuaded the men to accept a compromise and they returned to work.[71] Citing the Wages Standstill Order, the GNR refused applications for wage increases for its shopmen. The unions had pushed for an increase to offset the effect that their short week – 42½-hours – had on wages. The men had been on the shorter week since the late 1920s. In 1941, the GNR granted the shopmen the forty-seven-hour week they had long agitated for, thereby increasing their pay. Given the scale of inflation, it was a necessary trade-off.[72] The sugar factories were the other major centres of industrial conflict for the engineering unions during the Emergency, especially during harvesting season. In October 1943, IEIU sugar cooks went on unofficial strike at all four factories for a £50 bonus and two weeks' annual holiday. At Mallow alone, over 190,000 tons of beet were suspended. The cooks were already well-paid relative to other Irish workers. They earned £6. 1s. with a 15s. bonus for a fifty-six-hour week during the campaign and 97s. for a forty-eight-hour week during the rest of the year. Tradesmen's pay at the factories was similarly impressive – £5. 4s. – the least the cooks would settle for. Work was resumed when John O'Brien persuaded the cooks to submit their claim to the Joint Industrial Council.[73]

Table 36: Disputes and workdays lost in Éire, 1939-45.[74]

Year	Disputes	Workdays lost
1939	99	106,000
1940	89	152,000
1941	71	77,000
1942	69	115,000
1943	81	62,000
1944	84	38,000
1945	87	244,000
Average:	82.5	113,428

Table 37: Census of Fitters & Turners Employed at the Inchicore Works, 1937.[75]

Department	IEFU	IEIU	AEU	NUR	Total
Erecting shops	55	-	29	1	85
Millwright shop	11	-	3	-	14
Running shed	9	-	6	-	15
Machine shop	71	1	19	1	92
Lifting shop	5	-	4	-	9
Total	151	2	61	1	215

Chapter Notes and References

1 Ferriter, *Transformation*, p. 412.
2 O'Connor, *Labour History of Ireland* (2nd Ed.), pp. 137-138, 170.
3 Ibid., pp. 137-138.
4 Ibid., pp. 138-140; Ferriter, *Transformation*, pp. 372-374, 394-398; Brown, *A Social and Cultural History*, p. 186.
5 *Irish Press*, 29 Feb. 1940. For the 1940 Dublin Corporation strike, see Seán Redmond, *The Irish Municipal Employees' Trade Union, 1883-1983* (Dublin: IMETU, 1983), pp. 104-107.
6 *Irish Press*, 4 June 1941; IEIU NEC minutes, 31 May 1943.
7 IEIU NEC minutes, 7 June 1940.
8 Ibid., 25 June 1942.
9 Department of Industry and Commerce, *Statistical Abstract* (Dublin: Stationary Office, 1945).
10 O'Connor, *Labour History of Ireland* (2nd Ed.), pp. 141-143; McCarthy, *Trade Unions*, pp. 181-206; Finbarr Joseph O'Shea, 'Government and Trade Unions in Ireland, 1939-1946: The Formulation of Labour Legislation' (UCC: MA, 1988), pp. 36-80.
11 O'Connor, *Labour History of Ireland* (2nd ed.), p. 142.
12 McCarthy, *Trade Unions*, p. 181.
13 O'Connor, *Labour History of Ireland* (2nd Ed.), pp. 142-143; McCarthy, *Trade Unions*, pp. 200-206

14 McCarthy, *Trade Unions*, p. 206.
15 Cited in Ibid., p. 209
16 IEIU NEC minutes, 31 May 1941.
17 *Irish Press*, 4, 19 June 1941.
18 IEFU NEC minutes, 29, 31 Aug. 1941, Box 1D, TEEU collection, ILHM.
19 O'Connor, *Labour History of Ireland* (2nd Ed.), pp. 144-150.
20 Commission on Vocational Organisation, *Report* (Dublin: Stationary Office, 1943); ETU
    NEC minutes, 3, 4 Jan. 1945. The report advocated the creation of six vocational
    chambers – agriculture, industry, commerce, transport finance and the professions –
    which would elect a National Vocational Assembly to operate in tandem with existing
    political institutions.
21 McCarthy, *Trade Unions*, p. 210.
22 O'Connor, *Labour History of Ireland* (2nd ed.), p. 145.
23 Ibid., p. 146.
24 Girvin, 'Trade Unions and Economic Development', p. 121.
25 Minutes of the meeting of IEFU branch officers and shop stewards, 26 Feb. 1942, Box
    1D, TEEU collection, ILHM.
26 IEFU NEC minutes, 31 Aug. 1941, Box 1D, TEEU collection, ILHM.
27 IEFU AGM minutes, 23 Mar. 1941, Box 1D, TEEU collection, ILHM.
28 Ibid., 1 Mar. 1942, Box 1D, TEEU collection, ILHM.
29 Ibid., 28 Mar. 1943, Box 1D, TEEU collection, ILHM.
30 IEFU Dublin No. 1 branch minutes, 6 Nov. 1944, Box 1D, TEEU collection, ILHM.
31 IEFU, undated minutes, Box 1D, TEEU collection, ILHM.
32 IEFU, AGM, 26 Mar. 1944, Box 1D, TEEU collection, ILHM.
33 *Irish Times*, 5, 6, 14 Oct. 1944.
34 IEFU, half-yearly meeting, 8 Oct. 1944, Box 1D, TEEU collection, ILHM.
35 IEFU AGM minutes, 21 Oct. 1945, Box 1D, TEEU collection, ILHM.
36 *Irish Press*, 6 Oct. 1944; *Irish Independent*, 12 Oct. 1944.
37 *Irish Times*, 1 Sept., 27 Nov. 1944.
38 ETU (Ireland) NEC minutes, 5, 6 June 1945.
39 Ibid., 26, 27, 28 June 1946.
40 *Irish Independent*, 23 Nov. 1945; *Irish Press*, 14, 15 Dec. 1945.
41 IEIU NEC minutes, 29 Oct. 1946; IEFU AGM minutes, 3 Nov. 1946, Box 1D, TEEU
    collection, ILHM.
42 IEIU, IEFU & ETU annual returns, 1940-47, RFS records, NAI.
43 Brian Girvan, *The Emergency: Neutral Ireland, 1939-45* (London: Macmillan, 2006), pp. 243-
    246.
44 O'Connor, *Labour History of Ireland* (2nd Ed.), pp. 164-69.
45 IEIU NEC minutes, 22 Apr. 1945.
46 Between 1950 and 1970, the percentage of members of British trade unions in the state
    fluctuated between 13 and 17 per cent. The number of craftsmen as a percentage of the
    total number of trade unionists fell slightly from 10 per cent in 1945 to 8 per cent by
    1970. See McCarthy, *Trade Unions in Ireland*, pp. 622-623.
47 O'Connor, *Labour History of Ireland* (2nd Ed.), pp. 150-153; *Irish Press*, 22 Mar. 1945. For
    a thorough account of the split, see Ibid., pp. 229-280
48 O'Connor, *Labour History of Ireland* (2nd Ed.), pp. 173-174; McCarthy, *Trade Unions*, pp.
    277; *Evening Herald*, 12 June 1920; *Freeman's Journal*, 5 July 1920.
49 ETU (Ireland) NEC minutes, 5, 6 June 1945.
50 IEIU NEC minutes, 22 Apr. 1945.
51 *Report of the proceedings of the first annual meeting of the CIU*, 1945, ILHM, p. 57.
52 IEIU NEC minutes, 22 Apr. 1945.
53 IEFU AGM minutes, 21 Oct. 1945, Box 1D, TEEU collection, ILHM.
54 *Irish Press*, 22 Mar., 26 Apr., 9 May, 9 Nov. 1945; Devine, *Organising History*, p. 450.
55 IEFU AGM minutes, 21 Oct. 1945, Box 1D, TEEU collection, ILHM.
56 Devine, *Organising History*, p. 374.
57 *Irish Independent*, 31 Oct. 1945; *Irish Press*, 14 Nov. 1945; *Irish Times*, 19 Dec. 1945. Ó
    Murchú was born in Derry but raised in Cork.
58 Cited in Cody, O'Dowd & Rigney, *The Parliament of Labour*, p. 195.
59 *Irish Press*, 4 Oct., 11, 15, 27, 28 Nov. 1944; ETU (Ireland) NEC minutes, 5, 6, 7 Mar. 1946.
    Cork, Dublin No. 1, Tralee and Portlaoise voted in favour of disaffiliation while Waterford,
    Athlone and Limerick vote against; Sligo and Drogheda abstained.

60 For this view, see McCarthy, *Trade Unions*, p. 292.
61 Fergus A. D'Arcy & Ken Hannigan (eds.), *Workers in Union: Documents and Commentaries on the History of Irish Labour* (Dublin: Stationary Office, 1988), p. 212. See pp. 209-212 for a copy of the document.
62 O'Connor, *Labour History of Ireland* (2nd edition), pp. 168-169, 293.
63 Ibid., p. 168.
64 Allen, *Fianna Fáil*, p. 64; Browne, *Ireland*, pp. 215-216.
65 IEFU AGM minutes, 28 Mar. 1943, Box 1D, TEEU collection, ILHM. The Greenshirts were the paramilitary wing of the National Corporate Party, an openly fascist political party founded by Eoin O'Duffy in June 1935. By 1937, however, the party was defunct having been damaged by O'Duffy's retirement from politics following his return from Spain that year. See Martin White, 'The Greenshirts: Fascism in the Irish Free State, 1935-45' (University of London: PhD, 2004).
66 Ibid., 25 Mar. 1945, Box 1D, TEEU collection, ILHM.
67 'James O'Shea to Mr. Burke, 24 June 1936', Peter Coates' MSP Application, MSP34REF615, MSP Collection, MA.
68 Peter Coates, MSP Application, MSP34REF615, MSP Collection, MA; *Irish Press*, 31 Dec. 1951, 2, 4 Jan. 1952; 1911 Census.
69 Christopher Ferguson, military pension application, MSP34REF20609, military pension collection, MA; *Irish Independent*, 5 Feb. 1957; Yeates, *A City in Civil War*, pp. 224-225.
70 *Irish Press*, 12 Jan. 1949.
71 *Irish Independent*, 14 Oct., 2, 7, 14 Nov. 1940, 4 Jan. 1941; *Irish Times*, 13-26 Apr., 4-10 May 1943.
72 *Irish Independent*, 8 Aug. 1941.
73 *Irish Times*, 7-18 Oct. 1943.
74 Devine, *Organising History*, p. 332.
75 IEFU, *First Half-Year Report, Jan. to June 1937*, Box 103, TEEU collection, ILHM, p. 13.

6

Development and Decline, 1947-59

Between 1945 and 1950, the unions experienced a renaissance as membership exploded from 172,000 to 285,000. Irish unions grew at the expense of the amalgamateds, whose proportion of membership in the state fell from 22.9 per cent to 16.6 per cent over the same period. Union density – the proportion of workers in unions – exploded from 27.7 per cent in 1945 to 45.7 per cent in 1955.[1] There were two reasons for this. Firstly, Lemass brought a greater sympathy to labour back to the Department of Industry and Commerce, as evidenced by the Industrial Relations Act 1946. The Act made unions part of the 'social furniture', which is why Emmet O'Connor believes 1946 to be 'a watershed' in Irish labour history.[2] It instituted the Labour Court to conciliate the clamour of wage claims from September 1946 after the detested Wages Standstill Order lapsed. The Court consisted of workers' and employers' representatives under a government-appointed chairman. It only recognised licensed trade unions and barred worker nominees being attached to foreign unions. Not only did these measures give Irish unions a new prestige but they encouraged workers to join them. And secondly, statutory wage control paved the way for joint agreements on wages via national pay rounds under the government's watchful eye. Impressive post-war economic recovery also facilitated labour's rebirth. Economic growth led to increased consumer spending and exports to Britain. By 1949, industrial output was double the 1943 rate. Unemployment fell from 93,100 in 1939 to 60,700 in 1945, the bulk of the decline coming after 1943.[3]

Like the Labour Court, the pay rounds encouraged an acceptance of unions and wage standardisation. Pay raises were the result as the unions endeavoured to recover what they had lost since 1941. The first national pay round took place in 1946-47 after the first wage formula had been agreed with employers. It set a pattern of regular agreements on pay at local and national level. The Labour Court policed the terms of these agreements, which encouraged the development of national bargaining units in several industries. Although the pay rounds often granted significant pay advances, the post-war years were inflationary ones in Ireland, meaning that working-class living standards regressed considerably. The harsh winter of 1946-47 was the coldest to hit Europe in over 150 years. It led to severe economic disruption in Britain, civil disorder in the Netherlands and Copenhagen, and even famine in Germany. In Ireland, factories were forced to close for want of fuel. In January 1947, the government declared that a state of emergency still existed, and that greater austerity lay ahead.

By the early 1950s, the post-war hardship in Britain and western Europe had given way to an unprecedented economic boom driven by reconstruction and the growth of international trade. It was the golden age of capitalism in the West. But the Irish economy severely struggled throughout the 1950s, a decade now synonymous with penury and deprivation as a crisis of national confidence swept the country. Real national income rose by only 8 per cent in Ireland between 1949 and 1956 when the increase in Europe was 40 per cent. Ireland was the only country in Europe where the total volume of goods and services consumed fell and had the continent's highest rates of infant and maternal mortality. According to the 1946 census, there were 310,265 houses without any sanitary facilities; eighty thousand people lived in one-room dwellings, twenty-three thousand in Dublin alone. Employment in industry fell by thirty-eight thousand, or 14 per cent of the industrial labour force, between 1951 and 1959. Between 1946 and 1961, unemployment fluctuated but averaged 60,500, peaking at 69,700 in 1957. Over the same period, 528,334 people emigrated, culling the state's population to an all-time low of 2.8 million in 1961.[4] Government austerity contributed to a financial hardship which sometimes provoked lengthy stoppages, such as the strike of electricians at Coras Iompair Éireann (CIE) from April 1951 to the summer of 1952.[5] Though union membership exploded from 147,000 to 411,840 between 1947 and 1959, the number of strikes per year declined. Unions often eschewed militancy, offering voluntary wage restraint in 1946-48 and 1952-55. Wages increased consistently throughout the decade, but the gains were eroded by inflation. Real wages were lower in 1957 than in 1939.[6]

Table 38: Wage Rounds, 1946-59.[7]

Year	Round	Outcome
1946-47	1st	Average wage increase of 25 per cent
1948	2nd	'11s. formula': average increases of 8s. to 10s. for men and 4s. to 5s. for women
1951	3rd	10s. to 19s. increase men; women receive about two-thirds of this
1953	4th	12s. 6d. increase for women; women receive about two-thirds
1955	5th	General increase of 11s. to 17s.
1957	6th	10s. for men, 5s. to 7s. 6d. for women
1959	7th	10s. to 15s. for men, 7s. 6d. to 10s. for women

Table 39: Cost-of-Living Index, 1947-59 (August 1947=100).[8]

Year	Percentage	Year	Percentage
1947	97	1954	126
1948	99	1955	131
1949	100	1956	134
1950	102	1957	143
1951	113	1958	146
1952	123	1959	144
1953	125	-	-

Stagnation and internal conflict: the IEIU, 1947-59

The IEIU experienced mixed fortunes in the post-Emergency years. While the number and spread of its branches continued to grow, membership expansion was sluggish. Its animus towards British unions persisted, as encapsulated by one NEC member who 'felt that the sooner we had nothing further to do with English unions the better for ourselves as they were only a menace to the trade union movement.'[9] In 1949, the union reported its Carlow and Thurles branches as being 'strong and virile.' Although Tuam 'was still in a weak position', its affairs were 'now handled by a competent secretary.'[10] The growth culminated in two remarkable, but unsuccessful, endeavours to organise north of the border. 'Unfortunately, in each case the initiative did not come from the skilled element.' Nevertheless, 'use was made of these contacts to distribute our literature both in Newry and Warrenpoint.' Despite the setback, the union undertook not to give up on organising in the Six Counties and was confident of success in the future.[11]

The IEIU had established a presence at Athy, Edenderry, Portarlington and, via the Erne hydroelectric scheme, Ballyshannon. However, it had not yet re-established its Sligo branch despite wanting to do so. Athy mainly catered for the Irish Wall Board Factory while Edenderry and Portarlington catered for Bord na Móna workers. As its youngest branch, Ballyshannon, was 'ample proof' that the union was progressing. Relations between it and local employers were 'very cordial' because of the 'very tactful' approach of J.K. Greene, the branch secretary.[12] Among other crafts, the Ballyshannon branch comprised engineers, fitters, electricians and electric welders. It remained small, with numbers peaking at forty-six in August 1947. Although pay on the Erne scheme was high by Irish standards, the work was hazardous, leading to several accidents and fatalities. In January 1948, Michael Tinney, a fitter from Letterkenny, was electrocuted at the fitting shop. The inquest into his death determined that he had incorrectly wired a plug on a drill he was using, which caused the electrocution. At least eight strikes took place during construction. In September 1948, the Irish Union of Distributive Workers and Clerks (IUDWC) struck for recognition and negotiating rights for the clerical and catering staff. The engineers tried, and failed, to perform cookhouse duties to keep the camp in operation. While the IUDWC accepted that the engineers had acted on 'humanitarian' grounds, it resented that they continued to act as timekeepers during the strike, which lasted until November. Though rare, the fitters were also willing to take industrial action to remedy grievances. In 1953, six of them unofficially downed tools after Cementation Company, who were contracted to complete the scheme, failed to grant a pay rise recommended by the Labour Court.[13]

While many trade unionists had been vocal Fianna Fáil supporters in the 1930s, the Wages Standstill Order had deeply alienated them. Some, like James Hannigan, IEIU general president from 1948 to 1957, found solace in Clann na Poblachta, formed in 1946 by former IRA Chief of Staff Seán McBride. With its origins in the republican prisoners' aid committees, the new party espoused the rhetoric of early 1930s Fianna Fáil. It combined opposition to partition with demands for state intervention in the economy, a break with Sterling and repatriation of capital invested abroad. Hannigan, whose father was the IEIU's first caretaker, was a founding member of the party and served on its ard comhairle until his death in November 1964. A friend of Constance Markievicz, James Hannigan had a long republican history. During the revolution, he served in Na Fianna and the 3rd Batt. of the Dublin Brigade. He was interned three times between 1922 and 1932 for IRA activities before being released from Arbour Hill by the first Fianna Fáil government. During the first internment, one of his fellow prisoners was future minister Michael Hilliard. He continued his involvement in the republican movement after 1932, leading to further arrests and him losing his job at the Corporation.[14] In the 1948 general election, Clann na Poblachta won 13.2 per cent of the vote. By then, the CIU's affinity to Fianna Fáil had been dented and it made the National Labour Party, which won 2.6 per cent, its unofficial political wing. The Labour Party had secured 8.7 per cent. With Fine Gael, it was enough to form the first inter-party government and keep Fianna Fáil out of office. While that government is primarily remembered for the debacle of the Mother and Child Scheme in 1951, it had some concrete successes via its Labour ministers, especially in housing. Between 1947 and 1951, social spending doubled. New Housing Acts improved loans for buyers and grants for private construction, as well as giving local authorities more power to deal with housing. The number of houses built with state aid increased from 3,418 in 1949 to 12,305 in 1951.[15] Both Labour Parties reunited in 1950.

Healthier finances allowed the IEIU to restore some of what it had lost during the 1930s. On 15 March 1948, it renamed itself the Irish Engineering, Industrial and Electrical Trade Union (IEIETU), reflecting a renewed drive to organise electricians. The addition of 'Electrical' provoked a furious response from the ETU, who maintained that its rival had no right to use the word because the vast majority of electricians belonged to the ETU. It complained to the CIU and the Registry of Friendly Societies about this but to no avail. The issue remained an ETU complaint until the 1960s. In May 1948, the IEIETU rehired an assistant general secretary on a sizable wage of £7, significantly above the average craft rate. A year later, his pay was upped to £8 The union could even offer five annual scholarships to boys to spent time in the Gaeltacht.[16] Although the union's crisis in the previous decade had thawed traditional craft suspicion of the labourer, the hostility re-emerged in the 1940s. In 1949, several labourers at the Ford's factory in Cork were reported as being 'anxious' to join the IEIETU instead of the ITGWU. Seán Ó Murchú maintained that the IEIETU should contact the Transport Union to agree to 'an exchange of members as we believe you can never carry on a union with unskilled and skilled workers meeting at the onetime.' The NEC agreed because 'if an agreement would be arrived at in this direction that harmonious relations would exist between the ITGWU and ourselves.' General secretary John O'Brien was 'very keen on this union not catering for any semiskilled or unskilled workers.'[17] The sentiment is even more extraordinary given that it experienced little real growth at a time when membership of other unions was on the rise.

And the IEIETU was performing poorly on the industrial front. In March 1948, members at the Carlow factory withdrew their labour when Irish Sugar announced changes to how sugar cooks would be trained. The action quickly spread to the other sugar factories. At Carlow, Gardaí issued forty summonses to IEIETU members who attempted to prevent men from scabbing. On 21 August, the cooks returned to work with their tails between their legs after twenty-two weeks on strikes, forced to accept the changes. But defeat did not end there. The company announced that it no longer recognised the union, ensuring that its presence at the factories – once the mainstay of its rural membership – quickly faded to insignificance.[18] By the early 1950s, the union was eager to regain its former power at Irish Sugar – but this would not be easy. The company's board had an autocratic style that deplored union attempts to challenge its authority, from the IEIETU especially. Its manager 'resented very much any interference from any outside body and stated most emphatically that no member of this union would be employed in the sugar factories if it could be avoided.' However, through 'peaceful penetration', the union surreptitiously organised six men at the Mallow factory via its Cork branch. The same tactic also secured it a presence at the Carlow factory. By 1952, it was strong enough to down tools at the Carlow factory, even though the NEC believed this action was 'uncalled for.'[19] Paddy Bergin orchestrated the strikes. In 1948, he had accused the ITGWU of canvassing workers to replace IEIETU men on strike at Thompson's engineering works. The Transport Union strenuously denied his claim and threatened legal action against him.[20] By 1954, the IEIETU was 'slowly gaining strength' at the sugar factories, with eight to twelve members at Mallow and one at Thurles.[21]

By 1953, even though the union had been organised on a cross-craft basis for over thirty years, tensions between different trades was still a hurdle it had not yet surmounted. The fitters were openly calling for greater representation on the executive and a greater say in the running of the union. They justified this demand by reference to their numerical strength – over 40 per cent of IEIETU men were fitters; the proportion was over 50 per cent in Dublin.[22] The NEC did not assent as it feared revolt from the other crafts who considered the claim an attempt by the fitters to dominate the union. But the fitters persevered, stepping on the toes of other groups in the process. In 1954, the NEC had to arbitrate a conflict between the fitters and the iron machinists. While iron machinists had been members of the union from its foundation, it was not until 1949 that they were given their own section and were placed in the union's Group 1 category with the most skilled trades. CIÉ did not agree with the union and, in a change of previous company practice, did not grant machinists the same wage increases it had recently given its craftsmen. The company also discontinued its apprenticeship scheme for iron machinists, who now applied for legal aid from the union to take a case against the company.[23]

Table 40: IEIU/IEIETU Membership, 1947-59.[24]

Year (31 Dec.)	Membership	Year (31 Dec.)	Membership
1947	1,981	1954	1,943
1948	1,945	1955	1,933
1949	1,941	1956	2,122
1950	1,983	1957	2,192
1951	1,949	1958	2,062
1952	1,962	1959	2,338
1953	2,017	-	-

It was all too much for the fitters, who denied that machinists had any right to do craftwork. 'The avowed intention of the Engineers' Section was to do away with … iron machinists and replaced by fitters' apprentices as part of their proper training.' 'We have no alternative but to suffer the existence of these men for the time being… The union should turn its attention to ridding CIÉ of iron machinists and vicemen, both of which constitute a menace to the future employment of fitters.' In response, the machinists accused the fitters of colluding with the AEU to 'sabotage the efforts of brother trade unionists to secure our legitimate rights as skilled tradesmen and condoned our ultimate exclusion from the skilled group (CIÉ).' This was 'unique in annals of trade unionism' and was done so with 'antagonism' and 'tenacity.' The NEC was anxious to find a solution as the status quo was 'not conducive to fostering a spirit of co-operation between members of the union.' It ruled that the machinists were entitled to Group 1 membership 'without prejudice to the claim of the Engineers' Section that the occupation of iron machinists is not in itself an independent trade' and that there were enough iron machinists to merit their organisation by the IEIETU. Although it believed that an apprenticeship scheme for iron machinists was 'understandable' should industry expand, the weak economy meant that it was not willing to spend union funds on a legal battle to re-establish it. The fitters accepted the decision, the iron machinists did not.[25]

The conflict led to the resignation of the committee of the Engineers' Section of the Dublin branches when the NEC refused to remove the fitters' representative, Christopher Fullerton, from the REC after the committee passed a motion of no confidence in him.[26] For the sake of peace, the NEC capitulated and gave the fitters the representation they desired. Four of the ten REC seats were now reserved for the Engineers' Section, compelling it to end the boycott it had imposed on the REC. The decision to grant unequal representation was controversial. Despite their best efforts, the iron machinists were not given any seat on the REC.[27] In 1957, Hannigan chaired his last NEC and 'took this opportunity to say that in the last year or so more harm has been done to the union by the internal bickering due to personalities. He laid it at the door of the NEC for their decision to increase representation on the REC.'[28] Two years later, he was further disillusioned by the union's stance on ICTU's support for retaining proportional representation in the runup to the 1959 referendum on the issue. The union executive believed that Congress had violated its own constitution by adopting a political position. Hannigan expressed his disagreement publicly in a letter to the press. The NEC was incensed at his violation of the grievance procedures of the union's rules and disciplined him accordingly.[29]

The ETU (Ireland): growth and rural electrification

The electrification of rural Ireland, a priority for successive governments, began in 1946 and dominated the ESB's post-war activities. It was first mooted in a 1926 government paper discussing the Shannon Scheme. In 1945, Ireland lagged way behind other European countries in terms of electrification: Only 2 per cent of the Irish countryside had electricity while in Denmark and the Netherlands the figures were 85 and 98 per cent, respectively.[30] The scheme would serve 1.75 million people, of which only thirty-five thousand (about 2 per cent) lived in small villages. The rest lived in the open countryside. Over the next thirty years, the quality of life increased exponentially for these communities who, in the 1940s, were still blighted by poverty and emigration. Rural life in Ireland had changed little since the demise of landlordism in the early 1900s; electrification would be the biggest change since. It was, as one commentator aptly described it, a 'quiet revolution.'[31]

The Emergency years had been kinder to electricians than others. The war had led to a spike in demand for electricians that kept many in constant employment either at home or in Northern Ireland or Britain. The ETU predicted that rural electrification would create 'a great rush' for electricians 'for a relatively short period leading to a scarcity of men for a little while and then a slump.'[32] Over 300,000 workers had left for Britain for work or to join the army. Post-war demobilisation in Ireland and Britain released large numbers of engineering craftsmen and electricians eager for work. Many brought with them from their army days 'not just skill and discipline but a sense of comradeship which was to be one of the outstanding and enduring characteristics of the whole rural operation. It was those characteristics which were to sustain the operation through some of its most difficult days and enable it to make such a positive impact on community after community as it moved through the country.'[33] Over seventy-five thousand miles of overhead lines were erected, a massive extension considering that only two thousand miles of lines existed before the project. By 1962, 96 per cent of the eight hundred areas designated for modernisation had electricity.[34] In the mid-1970s, the ESB brought electricity to the last eight to nine hundred households in Ireland without it.[35]

From the mid-1940s to the early 1960s, the ETU was at the vanguard of the social changes which took place in Ireland. For the average electrician, the effects were seismic. While technological advances in machinery continued to simplify the building tradesman's job, electrical work was becoming more complex and difficult with more by-products. Without inspectors to check on installations, which the ETU demanded from the ESB, the work could be hazardous. As one member put it, it was 'by sheer good luck that there are not more accidents ... due to insufficient earthing of electrical commodities ... he could quote one case where wires were bare – eaten by rats.'[36] By then, there were two types of electricians: area electricians and ordinary ones. The former was paid according to the number of consumers in their district. As electricity increased in importance in Irish economic and social life, so did the significance and bargaining power those who installed it. The level of sophistication and quality required for electrical work intensified in tandem with technological development, putting the ETU in a favourable position to negotiate. It began agitating for extra remuneration for those who worked on live lines of conductors due to the dexterity they needed and the potentially fatal risks they took.[37]

From 1947, rural electrification vastly amplified the electrical workers' importance in Irish industrial life. The result was a huge augmentation in their numbers. By the mid-1950s, many electricians worked in industry, a major development from the days when all worked in the electrical trade. In 1943, the ETU only had branches in Cork, Limerick, Waterford, Drogheda, Athlone and one in Dublin. Two years later, however, its NEC predicted a massive expansion in membership over the coming years. It expected its small Athlone branch to grow by 300-400 per cent and planned to establish geographic branches in Dublin, Galway, Dundalk and a separate branch for area supervisors. As Table 41 illustrates, the NEC was correct. The growth compelled the union to appoint a second fulltime official as the workload was too much for the general secretary. IEIU electricians were increasing leaving their union for the ETU, which began organising new categories such as radio servicemen.[38] Expansion continued in concert with the construction of several major infrastructural projects, such as the hydroelectric stations on the rivers Erne and Liffey and at Poulaphouca. Similar projects were also planned for the rivers Lee and Clady and on the Torc and Comeragh mountains.[39] In total, the ETU estimated that rural electrification would require two thousand electricians over a ten-year period. After the war, the popularity of cinema continued to swell. Theatres popped up across the country, giving another membership boon to the union. Although cinema electricians in Cork and Limerick were in the ETU, the ITGWU had a 'tight grasp on theatres and cinemas in Dublin.' The ETU was anxious to avoid a clash with the Transport Union and so did not poach these workers. Unlike the ETU, the ITGWU catered for the operators, the bulk of any cinema's staff. Consequently, the ETU changed its membership eligibility to allow other cinema workers into its 'auxiliary section.' It claimed to have 'cordial' relations with all unions bar 'one or two' which 'annoyed' it.[40] One such union was the ATGWU, which began poaching ETU electricians and enticing them with 'propaganda.'[41]

Table 41: ETU (Ireland) Membership, 1947-59.[42]

Year (31 Dec.)	Membership	Year (31 Dec.)	Membership
1946	1,590	1953	2,440
1947	1,659	1954	2,491
1948	2,134	1955	2,653
1949	2,178	1956	2,769
1950	2,369	1957	2,698
1951	2,526	1958	2,862
1952	2,590	1959	2,934

As electricity gradually became a feature of life outside the cities, so too did the ETU. Between 1944 and 1947, the number of branches expanded from seven to thirteen, reaching fourteen by 1958. More branches meant stronger finances. Although the union had incurred 'very heavy expenses' during the war years, it had a surplus of over £100 in 1945, and its monetary situation improved every year thereafter until at least 1962. In 1946, it tried to set up a Galway branch as it had organised every ESB centre except for Galway and Sligo: it was the first in a series of failed attempts to establish a presence by the Corrib. In 1947, membership was reported to be expanding 'steadily', and by the following year, the union was reporting 'very rapid' growth. Michael Mervyn, general president since 1942, was appointed to the role fulltime on a weekly salary of £12 to help manage the expansion.[43] Like many ETU men, Mervyn was a veteran of the national struggle. As a teenager, he took part in the 1916 Rising for which he was sentenced to death, later commuted to ten years' penal servitude. He was active in Sinn Féin following his release, sometimes addressing party meetings.[44] During the War of Independence, he served with the 3rd Batt., Dublin Brigade. Afterwards, he worked in Belfast for a brief period before moving back to Dublin.[45] By the early 1950s, the ETU had seen off the IEIU and established itself as the primary electricians' union with whom employers would negotiate.[46]

The ETU was also diversifying its membership. In 1948, it began organising supervisors and their assistants.[47] The growth of the electrical trade presented employers with an opportunity to employ more women, who could be paid below the going (male) rate without any union protest.[48] Women were first organised in Dublin's armature winding and repair shops. Although electricians were traditionally highly imbued with the craft union mentality, the introduction of women forced a change in outlook. The ETU was quite progressive on the issue, acknowledging that 'the problem of women in the industry, their wages, conditions and limitation of work ... would ... have to be tackled.'[49] The 'problem' did not go away. Owens, who first raised the possibility of unionising women, 'agreed that the question of women workers was a problem – whether they should organise them or not.' The union eventually agreed to organise them. That an Irish craft union in the 1940s would even consider accepting women as members is extraordinary. Simultaneously, it also considered organising labourers and semiskilled men.[50] In 1948, Owens resigned as general secretary after it was revealed that he had mismanaged union funds. He was then suspended ignominiously from the union he had helped to found and was replaced by Patrick Keogh.[51]

Throughout the 1940s, the ESB continued to demand that its electricians drive themselves to jobs, and electricians continued to resist. For over a decade, they had long fought to protect craft privilege against such an incursion, but it was a battle they were bound to lose. In 1946, the Board informed them that they would have to drive themselves. By then, some had warmed to the idea – if they got extra remuneration for it! However, the issue was still divisive and caused friction within the ETU between electricians and motor drivers (of the Auxiliary Section). The allowance an electrician received for driving himself to a job remained 7s. 6d. in Dublin, which the union now sought across the state.[52] Like most Irish unions during this period, moderation and a desire for class harmonisation, not class struggle, were the ETU's guiding principles when dealing with employers. Its rule book embraced the teachings of the Catholic Church and *Rerum Novarum*, which advocated a wage that allowed a worker to live in frugal comfort. In the union's own words, its raison d'être was to 'rise the standard of living for our members to a level that will conform to Christian principles.'[53] The IEIU was similarly inspired by and committed to the tenets of *Rerum Novarum*.[54]

From 1952, the ETU had a quiet life for the rest of the decade, interspersed with notable achievements. One was the signing of a new agreement at the ENJIC, the first to feature the Society of Electrical Traders (forerunners to the Association of Electrical Contractors of Ireland (AECI)) in May 1955.[55] The EIEITU was also a signatory to the agreement which set new hourly minimums of 4s. for city electricians and 3s. 11d. for country ones. Hours remained forty-four in Dublin and forty-seven outside the capital. The ETU lost some longstanding members in the late 1950s and early 1960s. In 1957, its general secretary Patrick Keogh died from illness and was replaced by George Lynch. In February 1960, Mervyn passed away. Full military honours were rendered at his funeral. Mervyn unfortunately bequeathed a financial irregularity to the ETU upon his death. In May 1957, he overdrew his salary, discovered during a subsequent audit of accounts. Mervyn was expecting a salary increase and told the auditor he would inform the trustees of what he had done. The figures were to be correctly adjusted at the 1960 audit (by reducing Mervyn's salary), but Mervyn died in the meantime. While the NEC did not believe that he committed fraud or embezzlement, they were nonetheless disappointed because they had 'implicit faith' in him. The affair led the union to reform how it handled its finances by defining the duties of the trustees, both of whom subsequently resigned in ignominy. From then on, trustees would serve a maximum term of ten years and would be obliged to retire at seventy. Lynch became acting general president before Patrick Murphy was elected to the position, which became parttime again, in 1961.[56]

Table 42: ETU (Ireland) Branches, 1944-47.[57]

Branches	Date
Dublin 1, Dublin 2, Limerick, Cork, Tralee, Drogheda, Waterford.	June 1944
Dublin 1, Dublin 2, Limerick, Cork, Tralee, Drogheda, Portlaoise, Waterford.	Jan. 1945
Dublin 1, Dublin 2, Limerick, Cork, Tralee, Athlone, Drogheda, Portlaoise, Waterford.	June 1945
Dublin 1, Dublin 2, Limerick, Cork, Tralee, Drogheda, Portlaoise, Waterford, Sligo.	Mar. 1946
Dublin 1, Dublin 2, Limerick, Cork, Tralee, Drogheda, Portlaoise, Waterford, Sligo, Ardnacrusha.	June 1946
Dublin 1, Dublin 2, Limerick 1, Limerick 2, Drogheda, Dundalk, Portlaoise, Waterford, Cork, Sligo, Roche, Tralee.	Jan. 1947
Dublin 1, Dublin 2, Dublin 3, Limerick 1, Limerick 2, Drogheda, Dundalk, Portlaoise, Waterford, Cork, Sligo, Roche, Tralee.	June 1947

Fighting the red menace: the ETU and anti-communism

After dogmatically defining the Assumption of Mary, Pope Pius XII declared 1950 to be a Holy Year. In Ireland, the occasion was marked with displays and ceremonies of Catholic devotion. Thousands trekked to Rome as pilgrims. The secretary and president of the CIU were among them, sent 'to convey to the Holy Father the loyalty and homage of the Irish working class.'[58] That year's CIU Congress had agreed that 'the blessing of Almighty God should be invoked on the proceedings at Divine Services to be held on the Opening Day.'[59] In October 1950, John O'Brien and Mervyn journeyed to Rome as representatives of their unions as part of a CIU delegation where they met His Holiness the Pope.[60] Mervyn regarded it as one of the greatest honours of his life:

> I consider one of the most important events of the year under review was the decision to send a representative of the union on the pilgrimage of trade union representatives to Rome. It was important in two ways. First it meant that this union was able to show in a practical way it holds allegiance to the faith of the people of the country, and secondly that it helped to remove a great many doubts that existed among various people and members as to the policy of the union.[61]

CIU representatives also visited Rome the following year to celebrate the diamond jubilee of Rerum Novarum.[62] Nothing demonstrated the ETU's commitment to Catholicism more than its fierce anti-communism, something it shared with its fellow CIU affiliates.

The onset of Cold War anti-communism deepened the ideological chasm between both Congresses. The CIU was the more anti-communist of the two, which boded well for it given the political climate. Pope Pius XII understood the importance of international media to advance his church's cause and threw Catholics into the frontline of struggle against the Red Anti-Christ. The arrest of clerics who had collaborated with fascism and fuelled the hysteria, allowing the Church's power to surge to unprecedented levels in Ireland. Catholic anti-communism focussed on direction of thought, spirituality and external devotion. Whereas in the 1930s the Church had used social action and vigilantism to combat communism, it now pursued education as the means to 'protect' workers from this poison. In 1946, UCC president Alfred O'Rahilly introduced lectures in Catholic social teaching for trade unionists, which later developed into a two-year diploma in social and economic science. With CIU backing, similar lectures were introduced in UCD. In 1951, the Jesuits established the Catholic Workers' College, later the College of Industrial Relations, in Dublin. Trade unionists were constantly bombarded with anti-communist propaganda from the press and pulpits, and were gripped by the prospect of a sordid, Moscow-directed conspiracy to infiltrate their unions as a result.[63] The intensity of anti-communism among the working class is easy to gauge. In 1948, John Charles McQuaid, Catholic Archbishop of Dublin and anti-communist extraordinaire, raised £40,000 in a matter of days to combat communism in the Italian general election. One year later, up to 150,000 marched in Dublin against alleged persecution of the Church by the regimes of the Eastern Europe with the platform dominated by trade unionists.[64]

Given the Catholic Church's suffocating power in Irish society, anti-communism invariably shaped the mentality of the Irish trade unionist. In June 1947, the ETU was engulfed by the anti-Soviet frenzy that characterised the early stage of the Cold War in the West. One NEC member, Bro. Dowling, embodied the paranoia:

> most of the members know that communism is prevalent among union officials. He proposed that they have a prohibitive clause so that no communist be elected official of the union. He stated that infiltration of communists into the union will be attempted. Bro. Boyd asked what is a communist. Bro. Dowling replied a member of the communist party... Bro. Dowling said communism has infiltrated other unions. Bro. Brown didn't think we would see that here. Chairman said there are probably plenty of members communistic in views but not members of the Communist Party. These people generally manage to keep it dark that they are communists. He stated that the only thing is that there is not so much infiltration of communists into this country, but how were they going to know about infiltration into the union. General secretary said the Communist Party have gone underground here... Bro. Dowling suggested that they put a fine of £10... Bro. O'Neill thought they should give publicity to the fact that our trade union is not communistic. Chairman ... believed there is a rule that the executive can remove an official if he is not fit for the position, and that they could use that rule.[65]

In 1945, the ETU claimed that its relations with its British equivalent were 'most cordial, and it was hoped that would long remain so.' But just two-and-a-half years later, it was a vastly different story. Soon after the war, communists seized control of the British ETU's executive, much to the horror of its Irish counterpart. When the British ETU opened branches in Dundalk (in 1940) and Dublin (which was 'very much underground'), the Irish union reacted furiously.[66] The ETU (UK) had violated its 1932 promise to not travel south of the border. Although the British had legally obtained a licence (albeit with only seven members in Dundalk), the ETU (Ireland) refused to work with it and had a series of adverts published in the press threatening sanction against any member who did so. Mervyn resented 'a trade union endeavouring to infiltrate into this country to cater for men in the electrical industry when we are the sole people who should look after them… our union will not have this … we would have to go to the government, and if it requires legislation that licence will have to be taken from the English union.'[67] The British deliberately chose Dundalk to launch their invasion because it was 'by the backdoor of the artificial border … the backdoor for any British infiltration into the country.'[68] The ETU (Ireland) sought assistance from the CIU to oppose any attempt by its British rival to affiliate to the ITUC. It would have gone to the government but for the fact that ministers had friendly relations with their colleagues at Downing Street, some of whom were former British ETU members. It was willing to collaborate with the ESB and Electrical Contractors' Association (ECA), and even the IEIU, to smash the British ETU. Should this fail, it had another trick up its sleeve: infiltration ('peaceful penetration'), exactly what it had accused the 'communists' of doing. 'There are two ways to handle this thing. One is to use our strength, and the other way is to coax this union into an industrial dispute. Coax them into a position where we will be on a job with them, and it is a case of their getting off the job or our getting off the job, and then put it on the minister's lap.'[69]

There were four reasons for the frantic response. The first was the prospect of Irishmen once again losing control of their trade to Englishmen, who had reneged on their previous commitment. The second was the enduring complaint by Irish trade unionists that British trade unionists were complicit in the partition of Ireland, as Mervyn made clear:

> The flag of England has been kept flying in this country by the aid of English unions… This union is non-sectarian, and they didn't want to introduce anything of that sort into the union… Let us be national first and international after. They would not have interference from Masonic lodges in Belfast. He stated that he was a member of a member of a Belfast branch for a number of years… He knew there was not at that time one Catholic on any one of the branch committees in Belfast. Committees are selected from Protestants. Committees are selected in the main from the Lodges. He stated that some of the finest national men in this country are Protestants, he is not against them, but that he is against men infiltrating into this country for international communist purposes.[70]

The third, and most powerful, was the horror of a global communist conspiracy in which the British ETU was an active participant. Its organiser in Belfast (Joe Lowden), general secretary (Walter Stevens) and general president (Frank Foulkes) were all communist party members with sinister 'tactics and affiliations.'

> Lowden's position in this country as ETU official is only secondary to the position he holds. He is a member of the Communist Party in England, so also is Foulkes… a man is a rogue when he uses trade unionism to cover other tactics… General secretary stated that he knows Foulkes personally. He is a very decent man and … a friend … He makes no bones of being a member of the Communist Party, but it is not our way of life… Foulkes and the NEC official from Northern Ireland are … members of the Communist Party, and that he has an idea that the

'Cominfern' is working this way. They are infiltrating ... our union believes in Christianity. These people will seek to infiltrate, and they have the long view as well.[71]

Lowden had to subsequently resign his position after the discovery of a £600 defalcation to his name. Herein was the fourth reason for the hostility. Throughout their time in office (1945-61), the British ETU's communist leadership engaged in corruption, intimidation and fraud to maintain power against right-wing efforts to take control of the union. The struggle culminated in the communists rigging the ballot for the election of general secretary in 1959. Unearthed two years later, the scandal prompted a High Court case and was a major embarrassment for the British labour movement.[72] The Irish ETU was undoubtedly aware of the allegations throughout the 1940s and 1950s, further souring the relationship between both unions.

Once again, Dowling led the Irish charge against the British Bolsheviks. He was convinced that infiltration was inevitable unless the rules were changed to explicitly prohibit communists from holding official positions in the union. It had to done because the red menace lurked around every corner:

> most members knew members in the unions who were communists ... he was going to prevent this union being used for any organisation... he was sure there are cells in every town in Ireland... there are communists in the ETU (Ireland). The communist endeavour in a trade union is to prevent progress, to prevent good relations with the trade unions and the employers. He stated that there are plenty of men who look on employers as enemies, and they are not communists... they would have to watch ... that we are not going to let control of the union get into these people's hands... it is not necessary to be a communist to have communistic ideas.[73]

By 1949, the threat had been seen off as the British union was forced to flee the twenty-six counties with its tail between its legs. But the ETU (Ireland) was ecstatic with the outcome, as Mervyn gleefully told the CIU. Like others before it, the British ETU had been forced to 'go underground', which the Irish exploited. 'The trouble is that they had to make an excavation. We filled in that while they were underground and we kept them there.'[74] It proposed a resolution to the CIU of 'indignant protest against the continued operation of foreign unions in Ireland', that called on 'the Government of Ireland and people to end the present intolerable situation which has no parallel in any other free country in the world.'[75] The experience with the British ETU ensured that Irish electricians led the CIU's charge against communism from the beginning. In 1948, Mervyn warned the Congress that 'the people who controlled international communism were endeavouring very hard to get control of the trade unions all over the world. He knew enough about communism to know that it always endeavoured to cause disruption and strife. That was what communism was aiming at in Ireland and they must not allow it to happen.'[76]

The ETU's paranoia was typical of the political climate in the 1940s and 1950s, not only in Ireland but across the world. The Eastern Bloc's invasion of Hungary in 1956 unleashed another bout of labour anti-communism. In his presidential address to the CIU that year, John O'Brien, still IEIU general secretary, made clear how his Congress felt about the Red Menace:

The constitution of our Republic guarantees the freedom of religion and the freedom of the right of association, but these rights are not enjoyed by the peoples in the communist-dominated countries. They are trying to oust God from the world He created and naturally as a Christian people, our sympathies are with those nations and peoples who are opposing Russia and her satellites. I feel that if we are to avert the greatest catastrophe which threatens the world today, a disaster which would deprive us of our personal freedoms, we must oppose every attempt at the infiltration of communistic tendencies into our unions and representative bodies. Is this too much to ask from a country that professes Christianity?[77]

Strikes and the moves movement

Given the ongoing growth in the cost of living, much of the unions' work in the early 1950s was taken up with wage demands. The IEIETU and the ETU were in better positions than most. In Dublin, electricians earned 85s. 9d. for a forty-four-hour week, an enviable rate compared to what other workers received. In 1950, the ETU put in a claim for an hourly advance of 9d. Things got 'rather complicated' when some craft unions accepted 4d. per hour and several others accepted the smaller, CIU-backed improvement of 12s. 6d. a week. This put the ETU in an awkward position because it was now compelled to seek more than what had been accepted by the engineering unions. It thus pursued a 36 per cent increase on its 1939 rate. The union did not get the full amount, but it got a higher weekly increase of than any other union, 20s.[78] Pay advances were desperately needed. Inflation was rampant and the government was openly contemplating removing food subsidies, which would cause the cost-of-living index to rise by another twenty-two points. Although half of pre-Emergency strikes concerned wages, the percentage was much lower in the 1950s. Unofficial strikes also became more common.[79]

After many years of financial struggle caused by the increased use of road transport, the government merged the GSR and Dublin United Tramway Co. under the Transport Act 1944. The legislation created CIÉ, which came into existence as a private company on 1 January 1945 and took over the state's rail and tram networks. In March 1946, CIÉ established its own internal Conciliation Board which replaced the Railway Wages Board established in 1923. Both the IEIU and IEFU were formally recognised by the new board. Although the government nationalised CIÉ in 1950, public ownership did little to improve its receptibility to union requests.[80] In April 1951, the ENJIC issued a 5½d. per hour increase to electricians after unions threatened strike. The agreement set hourly rates at 3s. 8½d. in cities and 3s. 7½d. in the countryside. But CIÉ was not attached to the ENJIC and was therefore not obliged to pay the new rate. Accordingly, fifteen unions – including the IEIU, Foundry Union and ETU – immediately put forward a claim for the 3,450 railway shopmen. Most sought a 4d. increase; the electricians, however, wanted the 5½d. CIÉ electricians in the cities were on 3s. 3d. an hour while their counterparts in the country were on 3s. 2d. In May, the unions met the company and rejected its offer of a smaller increase. The case was then submitted to the Labour Court, which recommended the 4d. increase all round, a 10 per cent advance, leaving the electricians without their 1½d. an hour differential over other craftsmen. Accordingly, over one hundred CIÉ electricians withdrew their labour on 15 June. Most were members of the ETU, but the IEIE and IEFU also had some members involved.[81]

The stoppage was one of the most enduring labour disputes of the period. As trains in early 1950s Ireland were still gaslit, the electricians were at a major disadvantage from the beginning as CIÉ could carry on largely unaffected. Although the IEFU took out its mechanics, other unions passed pickets. To sustain the battle, the ETU had to issue paltry strike pay – 60s. a week, later increased to £5 after much agitation from branches. After the ETU refused to call a general strike in the electrical trade, the IEFU ordered its members back to work in early November 1952. The ETU had lost a vital ally in the struggle. On 17 November, after seventeen months of strike and a series of failed conferences, the electricians conceded defeat and returned to work. Their rate was fixed at 3s. 7d. an hour, as had been recommended by the Labour Court.[82] It was a humiliating experience for the ETU. The strike had put an enormous financial strain on it, although no exact figure of cost has survived. The NEC noted that it had spent £11,548, but this figure excludes Cork's expenditure as well as Waterford's from September 1951 to the end of the strike, by which time the union's bank overdraft was £1,985. It was a bitter pill to swallow for the strike committee and union rank-and-file, who were critical of the support they received from their executive. In turn, the executive maintained that only the IEIU, the Foundry Union and the port unions had sufficiently supported the strike. As the country's largest union, the ITGWU came in for particularly strong criticism. The ETU's preeminent branch, Dublin No. 1, passed a resolution calling on the REC to resign in disgrace because of the strike.[83]

The CIU's support for the strike was poor, driving a wedge between it and the engineering unions. This dissatisfaction fuelled rank-and-file calls to disaffiliate and/or push for the reunification of both Congresses. The IEFU 'had learned a lesson, seeing how little was done by unions affiliated to the CIU' to help the strike.[84] The ETU agreed, having approached the ITUC for support during the stoppage.[85] Mervyn told the 1952 CIU annual conference that his union was not 'getting the support we expected when we made a claim for a fundamental principle of trade unionism, the securing of a district rate'; in contrast, he applauded the engineering unions for endeavouring 'to give all the support they could.'[86] He was correct. The IEFU closed the Dublin foundries to support the electricians, leading to cast-iron work being fabricated in the Inchicore shop by members of the Boilermakers' Society and the NUR. CIÉ also locked out members of the Foundry Union and the IEIETU.[87]

The IEIU/IEIETU engaged in few major strikes after the Emergency, a reflection of its weakness during the period. By the late 1950s, it had a smaller membership than either the IEFU or the ETU. Nonetheless, it could still take on employers and gain concessions. In October 1946, it concluded a wages agreement with the sugar company to fill the void after the rescinding of the Wages Standstill Order. But many members were unhappy with the agreement and the way it was foisted on the workers without the involvement of the Labour Court. Two weeks later, the Mallow branch went on unofficial strike with several other unions, which their officials condemned. Shortly afterwards, workers at the other factories went on sympathetic strike bringing the total number affected to two thousand. The IEIU executive struggled to contain the situation and called on the Labour Court to intervene. The strike lasted until 11 December and cost beet farmers £200,000 for which the sugar company compensated them.[88] The dispute was referred to the Labour Court, one of the many cases it received in the years following the Emergency. The court's purview was not restricted to clashes between workers and employers. In 1948 and 1949, it tried to find a solution to the Foundry Union's standoff with the Operative Plumbers' Society over the line of demarcation between plumbers and heating engineers. It ruled that 'a rigorously exclusive demarcation of the work … was neither practicable nor desirable' and recommended the following division of labour:

1) Installation of lead piping – plumbers' work.

2) Cold water supplies – plumbers' work, except on cold water pipes from tank to boiler, on which heating engineers may be employed.

3) Hot water supplies: installation of piping leading from the boiler to the appliance – heating engineering or plumbers or both; connections between hot water pipes and appliances – plumbers' work; installation of piping for combined hot water and heating system – plumbers or heating engineers or both.

4) Central heating installations – primarily heating engineers' work, but plumbers may be employed on it.

5) Other heating and cooking installations: ordinary household installations – plumbers' work; non-domestic or institutional installations – heating engineers or plumbers or both.

6) Ventilating and air conditioning installations – heating engineers' work.[89]

The dispute persisted throughout the 1950s, indicative of the length to which craftsmen would go to protect their work and the enduring power of craft identity.

By 1955, the employers were firmly on top – and the unions knew it. That May, the IEFU met to consider the forthcoming (fifth) pay round and the other unions' claim for an extra 9d. an hour. One high-ranking organiser believed that 'such a demand was irresponsible, and the day had long passed when one could look for 9d. per hour increase.' He argued that the best the unions could get was 3d. or 4d. an hour. 'The employers were now a well organised body and were very business-like in their negotiations.'[90] The IEIETU encountered the same resilience but could get something from employers. It obtained increases of 4d. for electricians and 4½d. for fitters after threatening strikes at the ESB and in the private sector.[91] In the previous round, the unions had originally sought 9d. an hour but had to reduce the claim to 6d. after experiencing intransigence from the employers.

By the late 1950s, work study was an increasingly common feature of industrial life. To the shopmen's horror, in mid-1958 CIE introduced it into its workshops with the approval of the engineering unions. Specifically, the company implemented a system whereby the men could be monitored via a system of time and motion study. On 9 January 1959, Inchicore shopmen unofficially downed tools for the abolition of the new regime.[92] An AEU shop steward participated in the action and was duly sacked as a result. A meeting of shop stewards to discuss the situation was, as reported by the IEIETU general president, 'broken up in confusion by the stampeding of the men in the Diesel No. 1 Shop, who had decided to withdraw their labour in protest at the dismissal of the shop steward. I can only describe the scene as mob law in command.'[93] The dismissal goaded the AEU into making the strike official, which the IEIETU shopmen demanded from their union. They did not get it. Although most stayed loyal to their union, Bro. Fay, an REC member, joined the strike committee after agreeing with the decision not to regularise the strike. Fay had therefore broken union rules. The general president believed that Fay had 'undermined the general integrity of the union' and therefore should not be on the REC. The troublesome Engineers' Section gave official sanction to the strike and censured the general president for 'his action in connection with Bro. Fay.'[94] The NEC sided with the REC and refused to make the action official. In the previous year alone, it had dealt with serious unofficial strikes in Pierce's foundry in Wexford, the Drogheda foundry and at Ford's factory in Cork. The NEC's decision was deeply unpopular. Afterwards, no member 'made application for re-employment through the Head Office.'[95] But the IEIETU's opinion of unofficial action was widely shared across the labour movement. Every union and both Congresses deplored unofficial strikes and had as policy not to support them. The government was even considering outlawing them.

Table 43: Strike and workdays lost in Éire/Republic of Ireland, 1946-59.[96]

Year	No. of strikes	Workdays lost	Year	No. of strikes	Workdays lost
1946	105	150,000	1953	75	82,000
1947	194	449,000	1954	81	67,000
1948	147	258,000	1955	96	236,000
1949	153	273,000	1956	67	48,000
1950	154	217,000	1957	45	92,000
1951	138	545,000	1958	51	126,000
1952	82	529,000	1959	58	124,000

Table 44: Index of hourly wages, 1946-59 (1953 = 100).[97]

Year	Percentage	Year	Percentage
1946	57.0	1953	100.0
1947	68.3	1954	100.3
1948	74.5	1955	100.4
1949	81.1	1956	108.8
1950	81.3	1957	110.8
1951	81.7	1958	112.7
1952	91.7	1959	116.6

The engineering unions and the CIU

The Irish engineering unions were central to the CIU throughout its existence, especially the IEIU/IEIETU and the ETU. Owens, Jack Cassidy, general secretary of the Foundry Union, and Ó Murchú, chairman of the Cork Council of Irish Unions, all served on the Central Council. By 1951, the CIU had twenty-four unions and had affiliated trades councils in Dublin, Cork, Limerick,

Waterford and Dundalk. In total, the CIU represented 181,040 workers. It always knew that it faced an uphill battle in smashing British trade unionism in Ireland. In 1948, had Mervyn admitted that the new Congress was experiencing 'growing pains' because many Irish workers remained members of the amalgamateds and was disappointed with its progress on its central goal – an Irish-based movement.[98] At its annual meeting the following year, he excoriated his fellow delegates for their softness towards British unions. Referring to the amalgamateds' Irish members, he declared that:

> My policy cannot be termed non-aggressive, but I would remind delegates that for five years or more we have been holding out the hand of friendship to those men and asking them to join us. I am afraid that I cannot be a true Christian in this matter any longer. I am not going to turn the other cheek. I do suggest that unions affiliated to this Congress should adopt this policy of non-cooperation.[99]

The following year, he again demanded that the CIU 'blacken' British unions and inform employers and the government of such. He cited his own union's crushing of the 'British-based, communist controlled electrical trade union', which was driven out by direct action.[100] His arguments were persuasive: at its 1951 annual conference, the CIU resolved to not cooperate with British unions or Irish unions attached to the ITUC.[101]

By establishing a close relationship with the government, the CIU was sowing the seeds of its own demise. It had also isolated itself by adopting a stringent policy of non-cooperation with ITUC unions despite the tensions that existed between some CIU affiliates. In May 1949, the IEIETU refused a CIU directive to affiliate to the Limerick Council of Irish Unions because Meade, the old IEIU Limerick official, was the council's secretary. The IEIETU had several complaints against the IEFU that soured its relationship with the CIU. At O'Mara's bacon curers in Limerick, the AEU tried to withdraw one of its fitters to protest the company's employment of a boilerman to maintain the refrigeration plant. The man refused to cease work and was expelled from the AUE. He then joined the IEFU. When the IEIETU protested the IEFU's action, the CIU refused to act until the IEIETU joined the Limerick CIU. The IEIETU believed that the CIU's feeble handling of the incident had given licence to other employers to dispense with fitters and employ labourers on lower wages instead.[102] The IEIETU accused the IEFU's Limerick branch, of which Meade was secretary, of having issued union cards to men who had not served apprenticeships, of having blacklegged and, worst of all, of having an 'unskilled man' as its chairman In demanding that it join its Limerick council, the IEIETU felt the CIU expressed 'a rather dictatorial method of dealing with trade unionism.'[103] 'While agreeing that they should be affiliated with an Irish organisation', the IEIETU 'felt that the IEFU was a hindrance to the trade union movement.' The Foundry Union's Limerick branch had 'little to talk about' as '99 per cent of their membership were unskilled workers and employed by CIÉ', while 'the chairman of that branch had scabbed it at a period when other men in Limerick were walking the streets for a trade union principle.' The IEIETU asserted that there was much 'bitterness and ill-feeling in Limerick'[104] towards the IEFU and that 'under no circumstance' would it affiliate to the council 'as they strongly resented having anything to do with that union.'[105] The IEIETU stayed loyal to the Limerick Trades Council which, unusually, was not aligned with the ITUC.

The CIU's desire to cooperate with Fianna Fáil inevitably brought it into conflict with constituent members when the government engaged in austerity. The IEFU denounced McEntee's 1952 budget, which heavily taxed consumer goods and withdrew food subsidies, as 'an attack on the workers' and abhorred that the CIU was 'prominent by their silence on it.' The ITUC's opposition to the budget impressed the union, which demanded that their own Congress resist it 'by every means at their disposal.'[106] The IEIETU was similar aggrieved and adopted working towards the establishment of a unified Congress as official policy.[107] Nevertheless, the Foundry Union clung to the founding principles of the CIU and voted overwhelmingly to remain affiliated to it in 1953.[108] In 1956, however, the CIU suspended the union – which had changed its name to the National Engineering Union (NEU) earlier that year – for supposed poaching. The dispute arose when the NEU took over ITGWU members at Smith & Pearson's ironworks. The CIU sided with the Transport Union and told the NEU to hand the men back to their former union. When it refused, it was duly suspended.[109] Consequently, the CIU ordered its affiliates to cease co-operating with the NEU.[110] Two years later, the CIU investigated and arbitrated a dispute between the ETU and ITGWU at Whitegate oil Refinery, Co. Cork after the former 'gave insufficient strike notice, placed pickets and slandered other unions' officials.'[111] The clash stemmed from an industrial dispute about productivity-related payments and the introduction of work study.

Anti-British sentiment remained strong in the breakaway Congress throughout the 1950s. In December 1956, citing recent events in Hungary and the Suez, an umbrella group representing both Congresses issued a report criticising the IRA's Border Campaign and rejecting the use of violence to achieve a united Ireland. But not everyone agreed. At the following CIU annual conference, Ó Murchú bitterly attacked the report. An IRA sympathiser, he considered the statement an affront to his union's republican origins:

> I feel I am expressing … not alone my own personal views but … the views of a large volume of the members of my own union … Insofar as this section of the report implies in any way a repudiation of what James Connolly did in 1916, then it is repugnant to every feeling which I hold dear. I suggest that if you … make a subscription to the principles of charity … the best thing that this Congress could do would be to agree to a proposition – that you mark this as read, pass it in silence and let it rest in peace with the spirit of James Connolly, a great labour leader who was also a great soldier.[112]

As a member of the Sinn Féin ard comhairle, Ó Murchú was deeply involved in the republican and Irish language movements. In 1955, he was elected for the party to Cork Corporation, which made him a Harbour Commissioner. He too had a strong republican pedigree. His uncle was Captain Cornelius Murphy of E. Coy. of the Cork No. 2 Brigade, who had participated in the Kilmichael Ambush in November 1920 and was subsequently executed by the British in Victoria (now Collins) Barracks on 1 February 1921.[113]

While the split may have looked irrevocable to an outsider, by 1946 events were already clearing the way for reunion. William O'Brien retired as general secretary of the ITGWU, and Larkin died the following year. In June 1947, IEIU and Foundry Union representatives attended a meeting of unions attached to both Congresses to begin reunification.[114] Internal tensions within the CIU between craft and general unions also facilitated reconciliation. Craftsmen were outraged when, led by the ITGWU, the CIU's Central Council recommended acceptance of the fourth pay round, which granted 12s. 6d., a pitiful advance after an austerity budget. The craft unions had lodged claims ranging from 30s. to 33s. and opposed the 12s. 6d. increase because of its effect on differentials. The IEIETU was among those who rejected the advance, facilitating a rapprochement between it and the ITUC, which vehemently attacked the CIU's obsequiousness.[115] However, progress remained slow. Frustrated by the labour's inertia, in April 1953 Lemass announced that if the unions could not bring about unity, then legislation might be the only option. Frightened by the prospect, both Congresses sprung to life and an inter-Congress correspondence opened on May Day. A unity conference followed that autumn and established a joint committee.[116] The CIU's one condition was that reunification could only take place if Irish labour were 'wholly Irish-based and controlled.'[117] Its rival Congress was open to the idea. The CIU's demand was nothing new and was no more than the ITUC had already conceded. The crux was how to define 'Irish controlled.'[118] The ETU, for example, mooted unity as early as 1950, but insisted on constituent unions of any reunified Congress being Irish based.[119]

In April 1954, a joint committee produced a memorandum that, technically, granted the CIU's demand; in practise, however, it endorsed ITUC caveats that any restructuring must be gradual and done with the consent of all involved. During their tenures as CIU president, unity was a priority for both John O'Brien (1955-56) and Mervyn (1956-57). In January 1956, under Mervyn's stewardship, both Congresses came together and formed the 'Provisional Trade Union Organisation' to facilitate the move towards reconciliation. Mervyn chaired the working party which drew up proposals to facilitate this.[120] A draft constitution followed a year later which, in theory, affirmed that the new Congress would be an all-Ireland, Irish-controlled body. But there were qualifications. The Northern Committee – established by the ITUC in 1945 – would be subordinate to national policy making structures. A clever compromise was reached on the amalgamateds, whose participation in the new Congress was reserved for their Irish-based delegates. British unions could affiliate only in respect of their Irish membership, who would have 'Home Rule' over Irish affairs. These unions were to create Irish Councils to that effect. Ten of the nineteen seats on the executive were reserved for Irish unions. It was an Irish solution to an Irish problem: the CIU had secured the principle of Irish control, but the ITUC had defined the terms. The CIU had also infused the new constitution – which had a mild social democratic flavour – with an ethos of linking labour to national development. On 10 February 1959, delegates of both Congress overwhelmingly approved the constitution's final draft. Seven months later, the Irish Congress of Trade Unions (ICTU) held its inaugural conference at the Mansion House, at which Mervyn was elected to its NEC. Labour's position by the late 1950s is perhaps the most compelling reason why those who had led the 1945 split were so eager to reconcile with their former adversaries. From 1951, union growth had slowed considerably and in some cases was reversed. Having rocketed from 146,000 to 211,000 between 1945 and 1951, ITUC membership was only 226,333 in 1958. The figures for the CIU are even more striking: 77,500 to 170,601 before levelling off at 187,969 over the same period.[121]

Table 45: Membership of the IEFU/NEU, 1947-61.[122]

Year	Membership	Year	Membership
1947	2,681	1955	3,999
1948	2,860	1956	4,002
1949	3,086	1957	3,612
1950	3,434	1958	3,610
1951	3,508	1959	3,633
1952	3,515	1960	3,840
1953	3,551	1961	4,029
1954	3,695	-	-

The apprenticeship system in the 1950s

By 1952, unemployment had become a chronic problem once again. It aggravated another malaise, one common to underdeveloped economies: the skills shortage. Lemass believed that part of the solution lay in modernising the archaic apprenticeship system, whose legal governance had remained unchanged for over twenty years and whose operation had remained unchanged for far longer than that. By then, it was widely accepted that the Apprenticeship Act 1931 had failed, and that new legislation was needed. Lemass needed the cooperation of the electrical and engineering unions on two important matters: a united approach to reform and a more liberal admissions policy to the trades. His hope of addressing the first question disintegrated in February 1953 when the CIU refused to attend a joint meeting with the ITUC on apprenticeships. All craft unions, irrespective of what Congress they were attached to, were acutely hostile to any attempt to open the trades.[123] By 1959, the government's patience with the unions on reforming the apprenticeship system had run out and the Oireachtas passed another Apprenticeship Act.

The legislation was not a radical or even a novel approach to apprenticeships. Rather, it sought to sought to correct the obvious defects of 1931 Act, which it repealed. But the new legislation was imbued with the same thinking as its predecessor: a desire to structure, rationalise and improve the traditional apprenticeship system. Both Acts looked to the past rather than the future. The 1959 Act did, however, decisively break from established practice in one crucial respect: it inaugurated an apprenticeship board, An Cheard Chomhairle, comprised five trade unionists, five employers and three from the education sector, with a government-appointed chairman. Cassidy was appointed a labour representative to the first Chomhairle. The state had finally instituted a body to regulate and oversee the operation of the apprenticeship system. The board had the power to designate a trade, to set up apprenticeship committees and to appoint staff to supervise its operations, and this is where its strength lay. Once a trade was designated and a committee appointed, An Chomhairle was tasked with ensuring appropriate education standards for entry to apprenticeship and measures governing the recruitment of apprentices; the release of apprentices from work to attend technical college; on-the-job training to impart acceptable levels of skill; and supervision of progress by a system of tests in theory and practice. Should a strike or dispute affect apprentices, An Chomhairle could act to safeguard their continued training and could arrange with VECs for suitable courses. Course attendance was mandatory and failure to do so could result in pay deductions; employers were required to release their apprentices to attend. Apprentices undertook two exams: a junior one midway through the apprenticeship and a senior one at the end of it. An Chomhairle issued certificates to those who satisfactorily completed their apprenticeships. Inspectors with wide-ranging powers could be appointed to ensure that rules were being complied with. Failure to do so could lead to fines of £10-20.[124]

The apprenticeships committees were obliged to formulate rules on the period of apprenticeship and training and to submit progress reports on apprentices to employers. They could also prohibit the taking of premiums. Any rule devised by a committee had to be confirmed by An Chomhairle, which could also modify them. Rules had the force of law and breaches of them could lead to prosecution. But unlike the 1931 Act, the committees were powerless to regulate minimum wages and hours of work because the government felt that an employer-union conference was the appropriate forum. The 1959 Act created two registers: one of candidates seeking apprenticeships and another of boys who were apprentices, both of which had to be maintained by the apprenticeship committees. Employers were obligated to choose apprentices from the second register. To maintain some union control over the ratio of apprentices to journeymen, employers needed the committee's consent before taking on an apprentice. Committees could also require an employer to take on additional apprentices if it thought that not enough numbers were being trained and could investigate disputes between apprentices and employers.[125]

Chapter Notes and References

1   O'Connor, *Labour History of Ireland* (2nd Ed.), p. 173.
2   Ibid., pp. 170, 173.
3   Ibid., pp. 170, 172, 175; McCarthy, *Trade Unions*, pp. 539-40, 633-34.
4   Ferriter, *Transformation*, pp. 463, 465-466, 497.
5   CIU, *Report of the Central Council for the Year 1951-52*, pp. 26-27
6   Devine, *Organising History*, pp. 335-339, 467.
7   Ibid., p. 336.
8   Ibid., p. 467.
9   IEIETU NEC minutes, 2 June 1948. Specifically, the NEC was referring to the Shipwrights' Association, who had recently come to an agreement with the Liffey and Ringsend Dockyards.
10   Ibid., 29 June 1949.
11   IEIETU NEC minutes, 29 June 1949.
12   Ibid.
13   Brian Drummond & Dessie Doyle, *The Erne Hydroelectric Scheme* (Dublin: The Lilliput Press, 2013), pp. 55, 63-66; *Cork Examiner*, 21 Mar. 1953. The building of the Erne hydroelectric station (1956-55) was the second biggest hydroelectric project in the history of the state, after the Shannon Scheme.
14   *The Irish Workers' Voice*, 5 Oct. 1935; *Irish Press*, 23 Nov. 1964. The IEIU threatened to strike unless the Corporation gave Hannigan his job back.
15   O'Connor, *A Labour History of Ireland* (2nd Edition), pp. 178-180.
16   IEIETU NEC minutes, 2 June 1948, 29 June 1949.
17   Ibid.
18   *Irish Press*, 13, 30, 31 Mar., 1, 14, 21 Apr., 14 Aug. 1948; *Irish Independent*, 15-17 Mar., 22, 27 Apr., 29 June, 23 July 1948
19   IEIETU NEC minutes, 29 June 1949, 30 Apr. 1952.
20   Devine, *Organising History*, p. 348.

21 IEIETU NEC minutes, 21-23 July 1954.
22 In Dublin, the Engineers' Section had over four hundred members; the Electricians' Section, 236; Brassfinishers', 171; the ESB Section, 67; the Stationary Engine Drivers' Section, 87; the Blacksmiths' Section, 31; and the Machinists' Section, 13. See Ibid., 26 Sept. 1953.
23 Ibid., 21-23 July 1954; *Evening Herald*, 27 Jan., 13, 27 Feb., 20 Mar. 1953; *Irish Press*, 8 Apr. 1953. The increases given to CIÉ were the result of a Labour Court recommendation. The unions appealed the machinists' case to the Labour Court, which ruled that machinists were semiskilled and therefore only entitled to lesser increases.
24 IEIU/IEIETU, annual returns, 1940-60, T358, RFS records, NAI.
25 IEIETU NEC minutes, 21-23 July 1954.
26 Ibid., 3 Dec. 1954.
27 Ibid., 7 Nov. 1959.
28 Ibid., 6 June 1957.
29 Ibid., 10 June 1959; *Irish Press*, 10 June 1959; *Irish Independent*, 17 June 1959.
30 Ferriter, *Transformation*, p. 425.
31 Michael J. Shiel, *The Quiet Revolution: The Electrification of Rural Ireland, 1946-76* (Dublin: O'Brien Press, 1984). Following the Land Wars of the 1880s and 1890s, the British parliament passed the 1903 Wyndham Land Act to incentivise landlords to sell their land and their tenants to buy it. It sounded the death knell for landlordism in Ireland.
32 ETU NEC minutes, 5, 6 June 1945.
33 Maurice Manning and Moore McDowell, *Electricity Supply: The History of the ESB* (Dublin: Gill and Macmillan, 1984), pp. 130-131.
34 Ferriter, *Transformation*, pp. 499-500.
35 Ibid., pp. 136-141.
36 ETU NEC minutes, 8, 9, 10 Jan. 1947.
37 Ibid., 4 June 1957 (and following days), 3, 4, 5 June 1959.
38 ETU REC minutes, 7, 17 Dec. 1943; Ibid., 5, 6 June 1945, 26, 27, 28 June 1946.
39 ETU NEC minutes, 8-10 Jan. 1947.
40 Ibid., 5-7 Mar. 1946.
41 Ibid.
42 ETU annual returns, 1940-57, T353, RFS records, NAI.
43 ETU NEC minutes, 8-10 Jan. 1947, 14-16 Jan. 1948; *Irish Press*, 7 June 1958.
44 *Cork Examiner*, 6 May 1916; *Evening Herald*, 15 June 1917. For example, in September 1917 he addressed a demonstration of Wicklow Sinn Féiners held at Rathdrum protesting the arrest and imprisonment of suspected republicans. See *Wicklow News-Letter*, 29 Sept. 1917.
45 Gerard Doyle, WS 1511, BMH, MA, p. 53-54; *Irish Press*, 22 Feb. 1960.
46 Ibid., 5-7 Mar. 1946, 8-10 Jan. 1947, 14-16 Jan. 1948, 14-16 June 1949.
47 Ibid., 23 June 1948, 23-25 June 1953.
48 Ibid., 5, 6 June 1945.
49 Ibid.
50 Ibid., 27-30 June 1950.
51 Ibid., 22 Oct., 12 Nov. 1948.
52 Ibid., 5-7 Mar. 1946.
53 Ibid., 14-16 June 1949.
54 *Cork Examiner*, 28 May 1945.
55 ENJIC National Agreement on Wages and Conditions of Employment, May 1955.
56 *Irish Independent*, 22-24 Feb. 1960; ETU (Ireland) NEC minutes, 1-4 June 1960, 16 July 1961, 7-9 Nov. 1962.
57 ETU (Ireland) NEC minutes, 1944-48.
58 Cited in McCarthy, *Trade Unions*, pp. 296-297.
59 Cited in Devine, *Organising History*, p. 443.
60 *Irish Press*, 10, 19 Oct. 1950; *Irish Independent*, 25 Oct. 1950.
61 ETU (Ireland) NEC minutes, 19-22 June 1951.
62 McCarthy, *Trade Unions*, pp. 296-297.
63 O'Connor, *Labour History of Ireland* (2nd Ed.), p. 175; McCarthy, *Trade Unions*, pp. 389-394.
64 Ferriter, *Transformation*, pp. 489-492.
65 ETU (Ireland) NEC minutes, 8-10 Jan. 1947.
66 Ibid., 5,6 June 1945, 14-16 Jan. 1948.

67 Ibid., 14-16 Jan. 1948.
68 *Sixth annual meeting of the CIU*, 1950, ILHM, p. 78.
69 ETU (Ireland) NEC minutes, 5, 6 June 1945, 14-16 Jan. 1948.
70 Ibid., 14-16 Jan. 1948.
71 Ibid.
72 Lloyd, *Light & Liberty*, pp. 289-457
73 ETU (Ireland) NEC minutes, 5, 6 June 1945, 14-16 Jan. 1948.
74 *Fifth annual meeting of the CIU*, 1949, ILHM, pp. 87-88.
75 ETU (Ireland) NEC minutes, 14-16 June 1949.
76 *Fourth annual meeting of the CIU*, 1948, ILHM, p. 47
77 *Eleventh annual meeting of the CIU*, 1956, ILHM, p. 68.
78 ETU (Ireland) NEC minutes, 19-22 June 1951; *Irish Press*, 19, 20 Mar., 5 Apr. 1951.
79 O'Connor, *Labour in Irish History* (2nd Ed.), p. 173.
80 *Irish Times*, 24 Sept. 1945.
81 *Irish Press*, 7-9 Apr. 1951; 'Undated memo on the CIÉ dispute', 2001/50/85, Dept. of Industry and Commerce records, NAI.
82 *Irish Independent*, 10, 15, 17, 26 Nov. 1952.
83 ETU (Ireland) NEC minutes, 22-24 Jan. 1953.
84 Ibid., 29 Mar. 1953, Box 1D, TEEU collection, ILHM.
85 Cody, O'Dowd & Rigney, *Parliament of Labour*, p. 198.
86 *Eighth annual meeting of the CIU*, 1952, ILHM, p. 101.
87 Ibid., p. 103; *Irish Press*, 22 Jan., 27 Nov. 1952; *Irish Independent*, 16 Jan., 20 Feb. 1952
88 *Cork Examiner*, 5 Oct.-12 Dec. 1946.
89 *Irish Press*, 5 Apr. 1949; *Irish Independent*, 5 Apr. 1949. The Labour Court had also tried to adjudicate the dispute when it occurred during the construction of an extension at Peamount Sanitorium. See *Irish Press*, 8 Dec. 1948.
90 IEFU AGM minutes, 15 May 1955, Box 1D, TEEU collection, ILHM.
91 *Irish Independent*, 18, 23 Sept., 1 Oct., 17, 20 Dec. 1955.
92 *Irish Press*, 10 Jan.-4 Feb. 1959.
93 IEIETU NEC minutes, 23 Jan. 1959.
94 Ibid.
95 Ibid., 10 June 1959.
96 Devine, *Organising History*, p. 339.
97 Ibid., p. 337.
98 *Fourth annual meeting of the CIU*, 1948, ILHM, p. 47.
99 *Fifth annual meeting of the CIU*, 1949, ILHM, pp. 88-89.
100 *Sixth annual meeting of the CIU*, 1950, ILHM, p. 78.
101 *Irish Independent*, 21 July 1951.
102 IEIETU NEC minutes, 25 Jan. 1950.
103 Ibid.
104 Ibid., 29 June 1950.
105 Ibid., 27 June 1951.
106 IEFU AGM minutes, 6 Apr. 1952, Box 1D, TEEU collection, ILHM.
107 *Irish Independent*, 17 Apr. 1953.
108 The vote was 602 for disaffiliation to 1,195 against. See correspondence on disaffiliation from CIU, 7 May-30 July 1953, file 1, box entitled 'NEETU Inchicore Branch', TEEU collection, ILHM.
109 *Thirteenth annual meeting of the CIU*, 1957, ILHM, pp. 13-15.
110 Committee of the Provisional Trade Union Organisation, *Third Report of the Committee*, 1957-58, p. 8.
111 Devine, *Organising History*, p. 412. The strike took place during the construction of the refinery when ETU men went out over 'wet time' conditions. Over a thousand other workers joined them in an unofficial action. See *Irish Press*, 1-26 Sept. 1958.
112 Cited in McCarthy, *Trade Unions*, p. 299.
113 *Cork Examiner*, 9 May 1955, 28 Apr. 1956, 9, 23 Jan., 18, 19, 25 Feb., 5 Mar. 1957, 3 Oct. 1959; *Irish Independent*, 26 Nov. 1957.
114 *Irish Press*, 18 June 1947.
115 Ibid., 17 Apr. 1952; *Irish Independent* 1 Jan. 1953. The engineering unions claimed a 33s. increase.
116 McCarthy, *Trade Unions*, p. 404.
117 Cited in Ibid., p. 429.

118 Ibid.

119 ETU (Ireland) NEC minutes, 27-30 June 1950, 22, 23, 24 Jan. 1953.

120 For an account of the reunification process, see McCarthy, *Trade Unions*, pp. 426-447. In 1957, the 'Provisional Trade Union Organisation' successfully negotiated with employers on a joint agreement for the sixth national pay round.

121 O'Connor, *Labour History of Ireland* (2nd Ed.), pp. 174, 184-186. Membership of the CIU peaked at 194,138 in 1953.

122 IEFU/NEC annual returns, 1947-61, T357, RFS records, NAI.

123 McCarthy, *Trade Unions*, p. 403

124 Ryan, 'Apprenticeship in Ireland', pp. 288-293; McCarthy, 'Apprenticeships in Ireland', pp. 6-7.

125 Ryan, 'Apprenticeship in Ireland', pp. 289-291.

John O'Brien, General Secretary of IEI & BETU, receiving a
presentation outside the old ATGWU offices.
(Credit: *Connect Archive*)

Early Executive
(Credit: *Connect Archive*)

IEI & ETU officers, circa 1964
(Credit: *Connect Archive*)

IEIETU Social Committee 1949
(Credit: *Connect Archive*)

IEI & ETU General Secretary A. P. Tuke,
leading a delegation.
(Credit: *Connect Archive*)

RTÉ Industrial Correspondent, Pat Sweeney, interviews union leaders.
(Credit: *Connect Archive*)

Successful applicants for Union's Gaeltacht Scholarships – 26 June 1950.
(Credit: *Connect Archive*)

Mechanical members Guinness Dublin

(Photographer Rex Roberts, image courtesy of the Guinness Archive, Diageo Ireland)

Photo of members in the Dublin Dockyard
(including future General Secretary, Frank O'Reilly)

(Credit: Connect Archive)

Former ETU
General Secretary
and 1916 veteran
Sean Duffy
(Credit: *Connect Archive*)

Mobile promotion unit ESB
(Credit: *ESB Archive*)

Electrical Trades Union

Head Office:

5 CAVENDISH ROW, DUBLIN 1.
TELEPHONE No. 747047

To the Secretary..*Branch*

APPLICATION FOR MEMBERSHIP
(APPRENTICE SECTION)

Dear Sir,

I wish to make application for Membership of above Union, and in doing so, I desire to give the following particulars which I am prepared to prove are correct in all details.

All applications to be accompanied by a fee of not less than £1

(QUESTIONS TO BE ANSWERED BY CANDIDATE)
PLEASE WRITE IN BLOCK CAPITALS ONLY

Name ....

Permanent Address ....

Proposer to hold current card, Bro. ....*Branch No.* ....

Seconder to hold current card, Bro. ....*Branch No.* ....

Age last Birthday ....*Date of Application* ....

Where are you serving your time? ....

Did you pay a Fee? ....*If so, what was the amount* ....

Can you produce Indentures? ....

Date of commencing Apprenticeship ....

State number of Apprentice Identity Card ....

Are you attending Technical Schools? ....

State what class of work is carried out in your employment ....

....

State Names of at least three Members with whom you worked.

1 ....*Branch No.* ....

2 ....*Branch No.* ....

3 ....*Branch No.* ....

Original ETU application form
(Credit: *Connect Archive*)

Presentation to John O'Brien to mark his 25th year as
General Secretary of the IEIETU.

(Credit: *Connect Archive*)

Attendees at ETU Conference circa 1970's.

(Credit: *Connect Archive*)

Fitters, Limerick, Locomotive works, 1960.

(Credit: *National Library of Ireland*)

ETU members on protest march Circa 1950's.

(Credit: *Connect Archive*)

Bord Na Mona Boora Works.
(Credit: *Seán Cain*)

Fords Cork.
(Credit: *Connect Archive*)

7

Industrialisation and Modernisation, 1960-67

Fianna Fáil returned to power in 1957 for another sixteen-year stint in what was arguably the most transformative period in Irish economic history. The party launched a 'conservative revolution' – revolutionary in that it involved a fundamental rearrangement of the economy and conservative in that the changes were explicitly capitalist. In 1956, T.K. Whitaker was appointed secretary general of the Department of Finance. Three years later, Lemass succeeded de Valera as Taoiseach. While the West boomed through capitalism's golden era, the Irish economy was mired in endless crises. Fianna Fáil, the architects of protectionism, showed their pragmatic streak by abandoning tariffs for free trade. No decision in Irish economic history is as well-known or as acclaimed for its imaginativeness and ingenuity. The truth, however, is more complex. The shift must be seen in the context of developments in Europe, which made its timing opportune. Policymakers on the continent concluded that the best way to avoid another catastrophic war was to integrate the European economies to make war not only undesirable but impossible. In 1957, the European Economic Community (EEC) had instituted a common market between its member states. To Lemass and Whitaker, free trade was the road to modernity, a chance for Ireland to finally catch up with its neighbours. Ireland applied for EEC membership in 1961 and signed a free trade agreement with the Britain in 1965.

Free trade, and the 'open-door' policy to foreign direct investment that accompanied it, transformed the economy from an agricultural to an industrialised one. The dismantling of protectionism led to the eclipse of native industry by multinationals, beginning an economic transition from an import- to an export-orientated economy. The results were immediate. The First Programme for Economic Expansion, launched in 1958, aimed to lift national incomes 2 per cent annually between 1959 and 1963. The aim was surpassed as real incomes rose by nearly a quarter. Between 1958 and 1973, industrial output rose by over 250 per cent. Manufacturing exports grew from 25 per cent of, to near parity with, agricultural exports. The percentage of manufacture exported grew from 5 in 1962 to 30 in 1972. By then, 30 per cent of the labour force worked in industry and 25 per cent in agriculture. Unemployment fell and involuntary emigration virtually halted, allowing the population to grow by 0.5 per cent a year. National output and purchasing power rose by over 20 per cent. The number of cars on Irish roads doubled in the 1960s. A Second Programme (1964-70) was launched on the assumption that Ireland would be an EEC member by 1970. But embracing the new model entailed some trade-offs. Growth was driven by interaction with external markets during international capitalism's greatest ever boom, making the new economy highly vulnerable to global downturns. Moreover, the gulf between rich and poor widened. This conservative revolution bequeathed modern Ireland and laid the basis for the subsequent hegemony of liberalism, both economic and social, in the Irish body politic.[1]

The growth of social liberalism was another manifestation of a broader trend in the West that even included the Catholic Church. The opening of the Second Vatican Council in 1962 by Pope John XXIII led to a softening of Catholicism's harder edges and a relaxation of clericalism. For Irish radicals, the most meaningful change was the weakening of the Church's uncompromising anti-communism, which had made bishops suspicious of even the most moderate of leftist politics. Young priests were increasingly concerned about poverty and the resulting social problems rather than threats to the Church's authority or the faith of the flock. Trade unionists experienced the changes first-hand. Words like 'socialism' and 'socialist' were detoxified and became common in labour parlance. Obsequious displays of public piety were replaced by a more liberal Catholicism that was often justified by explicit references to Vatican II. Liberal Catholicism helped to pave the way for secularism from the 1970s.[2]

Emmet O'Connor has compared the 1960s to the 1930s, calling both times 'of industrial expansion and strike waves; of political idealism, social reform, radical experiments, and passionate concern with international affairs; of fresh popular consumerism, novel entertainments for the masses, and a lessening of habits of obedience and conformity.'[3] While often incomplete or insufficient, progress was made on longstanding problems. From 1963, public services experienced expansion and investment after a decade of neglect and regression. There were major structural advances in the provision of healthcare, housing and, most of all, education. The most celebrated achievement was the implementation of free secondary school education in 1967, but community schools, regional technical colleges and university grants were also introduced in the late 1960s. Housing policy was also touched by the liberal agenda. Housing construction was revived with a greater emphasis on the private sector and the Housing Act 1966 encouraged tenant-purchase schemes.

Industrial relations, 1960-67

Ireland began the 1960s as a heavily unionised country. ICTU represented over 500,000 workers, 60 per cent of whom were in the Republic. But the multiplicity of unions weakened the movement: 123 operated in the country, of which eighty-four had a membership of less than a thousand. For Lemass, the move to free trade involved instituting tripartite consultative bodies on production and planning, and reform of pay determination and industrial relations. He had not abandoned his consensus-seeking style of negotiation and was keen for labour support. But the unions were cold to his other aims: pay restraint through bipartite bargaining and industrial relations reform, which he saw as interconnected. Lemass still believed that free collective bargaining by numerous unions encouraged destructive wage militancy. His answer was to centralise authority within unions and the industrial relations machinery. In 1961, the government instituted tripartism – a three-way agreement on pay and conditions involving ICTU, the FUE and civil servants – by appointing the Committee on Industrial Organisation, a precursor of social partnership. Social partnership is a corporatist style of organising the relationship between labour, employers and the state based upon collective agreements between the three. It emerged in several countries in the post-war years, including West Germany, the Netherlands, Switzerland, Italy, the Benelux and Scandinavia. Fianna Fáil initiated social partnership structures for two main reasons. The first was the perceived 'external threat' to the economy upon its integration into the world system. The second was the 'internal threat' of the growing rank-and-file militancy. It was hoped that social partnership would draw union leaders closer to the state and engage them in the process of economic planning on the proviso that they would discipline their members should agreements be violated.[4]

In 1963, the government founded the National Industrial Economic Council, bringing together the three sides to discuss the direction of economic policy. Lemass was getting his wish of a compliant labour movement. The unions' traditional hostility to working with employers began to soften. The FUE, on the other hand, was openly favourable to tripartism from the start. ICTU was willing to participate in it but not centralised wage bargaining, which it considered synonymous with pay restraint. When a 1963 white paper called for exactly that, Congress withdrew from the Employer-Labour Conference, formed in November 1961 to stop 'leapfrogging' wage increases. The Conference was supposed to take advice on the movement of pay and prices with which it could issue guidelines for wage negotiations. But as no capitalist economy has ever found a way to regulate the pricing policy of individual firms, pay was the only element that was controlled.[5] Tripartism suffered another setback with Jack Lynch's (appointed Taoiseach in 1966) steady discontinuation of economic planning. In 1967, tripartism was shelved following the meeting of targets of the Second Programme and a mild recession the previous year. The Second Programme was also ended.[6]

The unions did much soul searching in the 1960s, especially about how to establish a consensus on pay and economic planning. Most wage claims and strikes were caused by relativities in pay. Tensions were compounded by the degree of fragmentation within unions, as they sought to strike a balance between commitment to long-term planning and the immediate threat of loss of relativities. This was one of the reasons why the government decided to give labour more input into policy formation via bodies of social partnership. Economic growth gave labour a chance to flex its industrial muscle. Ireland remained a poor economy by European standards. Labour costs were high due to low productivity rather than high wages. Although ICTU membership had expanded from 432,000 members in 1960 to 551,000 in 1969, many workers had not yet recovered from the Wages Standstill Order. Nearly 60 per cent of industrial workers earned under £10 a week compared with less than 8 per cent in Britain.[7] Labour costs were high in Ireland by international standards due to low productivity, not high wages. From the mid to late 1960s, Ireland was among the most strike-ridden countries in Europe. As is usual in times of growth, most disputes were brief and selective. The average numbers of days lost in strikes doubled from 228,000 between 1960 and 1964 to 571,000 between 1965 and 1969. A nine-week building trade strike in Dublin accounted for 80 per cent of days lost in 1964.[8] Involving twenty thousand workers (fourteen thousand) of whom were craftsmen) and bringing £20 million worth of contracts to a standstill, it was one of the biggest industrial disputes in the state's history. The men secured their demand, the forty-hour week; they were the first to do so, setting in motion a series of reductions in hours that continued until the decade's end. By then, the forty-hour week prevailed across the country. Both the IEIETU and ETU partook in the 1964 strike.[9] A year later, maintenance men in the building trade – mainly carpenters, plumbers and plasterers – went out for the forty-hour week. Unlike the ETU, the IEIETU ignored the stoppage, provoking the former to wryly comment that 'the strike picket does not seem to be the almighty principle for the ... IEIETU.'[10]

Table 46: Strikes, strikers and strike days in Ireland, 1964-69.[11]

	1964	1965	1966	1967	1968	1969
Strikes	87	89	112	79	126	134
Strikers (000s)	25.2	38.9	52.2	20.9	38.9	61.8
Strike days (000s)	545.4	552.4	783.6	182.7	405.7	953.9

Table 47: Wage Rounds, 1961-70.[12]

Year	Round	Outcome
1961	8th	Increases of up to 14s. for most except electricians and building workers who receive 20s. to 25s.; women receive 10s. to 15s.
1964	9th	12 per cent advance with minimum increase of 20s. for men
1966	10th	General increase of about 20s.
1968	11th	Men receive 35s. to 40s. in two or three phases, women about 75 per cent of this
1970	12th	Increases of 80s. in two or three phases over eighteen months. Women get about 80 per cent of this.

The IEIETU, 1960-66: perseverance and unity

After a decade of sluggish growth, the IEIETU expanded rapidly from 1960. It recruited over a thousand members in the first half of the decade. By 1961, it had regained recognition from Irish Sugar, helping it to obtain improvements for many new rural members. Growth prompted the union to 'vigorously pursue' the 'complete re-organisation of the union on modern lines.'[13] It appointed a fulltime assistant general secretary and a fulltime official for Cork, and established research, providential and educational facilities such as a library with trade textbooks.[14] As the economy grew and industrialised, the union continued to expand. In 1960, it reported recently established branches in Athy, Boora, Allenwood and Edenderry, re-establishing in some cases. In early 1965, it opened branches in Naas and Navan for craftsmen at the Bord na Móna plants there. That summer, it initiated an 'Instrumentation Section' for instrument mechanics, makers and technicians, which the ETU regarded as an 'obvious' attempt to poach its members.[15]

The 1960s also brought personnel changes to the union, as well as some personnel losses. Joseph Toomey passed away in September 1960 and the following May, John O'Brien, general secretary since 1928, retired. Assistant general secretary and organiser A.P. Tuke replaced O'Brien. Later in May 1961, the union lost another founding member when general president Charles Shelley died in office. The son of a Citizen Army man, Shelley was a teenage participant in the Rising as a member of the 'National Guard', a small group of scouts trained in the use of arms. During the War of Independence, he initially served with G. Coy., 1st Batt. before being transferred to the 5th Batt. upon its foundation. Having opposed the Treaty, Shelly was in the Four Courts the night it was bombarded and was captured at the IRA surrender there. He was interned until December 1923.[16] Patrick Mahon replaced him as general president. The NEU was also losing members who participated in the national struggle. In 1966, Richard Joseph Tobin, secretary of its Waterford branch for many years, died aged sixty-four. He was a founding member of Fianna Éireann in Waterford and had been active in the War of Independence.[17]

In June 1964, there was another change to the IEIETU executive when Seán Ó Murchú resigned as assistant general secretary to take up a post with the ITGWU. That October, Michael Connolly, a founding member and general president from 1932 to 1948, died. A month later, the union lost another former general president, James Hannigan. A friend of Constance Markievicz, Hannigan had a long republican history. During the revolution, he served with Na Fianna and the 3rd Batt. of the Dublin Brigade. He was interned three times between 1922 and 1930 for IRA activities. During the first internment, one of his fellow-prisoners was future minister Michael Hilliard. He was a founding member of Clann na Poblachta and served on its ard comhairle until his death.[18] In 1967, the union lost two general secretaries in quick succession: O'Brien died that November and Tuke died in office the following month. Tuke was another veteran of the national struggle, having served with Fianna Éireann during the Rising and with the 5th Batt., Dublin Brigade during the War of Independence. He later joined the army's Supply and Transport Corps, retiring with the rank of captain. Afterwards, he worked for the Midland Great Western Railway and the Irish Lights Commissioners. His brother Edward Tuke was a founding member of Na Fianna who served with the ICA during the Rising and War of Independence and the National Army during the Civil War.[19]

Table 48: IEIETU Membership, 1960-67.[20]

Year	Membership	Year	Membership
1960 (1 Jan.)	2,338	1964 (31 Dec.)	3,354
1961 (1 Jan.)	2,409	1965 (31 Dec.)	3,294
1962 (1 Jan.)	2,896	1966 (31 Dec.)	3,300
1963 (31 Dec.)	3,371	1967 (31 Dec.)	3,500

One of the most noteworthy features of the IEIETU in the 1960s was its militancy, indicative of the growth of same within Irish labour. Heretofore, calls for militant agitation did not come from unions but from middle-class left-wing intellectuals. As Fergal Tobin rightly noted, unions had been 'conservative protest groups within the overall structure of Irish capitalism, suspicious of socialist ideologues because of the damage they could do to the movement in a country which shared the bishops' unflattering view of socialism.'[21] The new mood was exemplified by the explosion in the number of times unions rejected Labour Court recommendations. Whereas unions had accepted 98 per cent of its recommendations in 1958, they accepted only 49 per cent in 1966.[22] Unlike the 1950s, economic development was visible everywhere as Gross National Product (GNP) grew by 4.5 per cent annually. The unions felt that a healthier economy meant that long-standing grievances could finally be dealt with and that Irish workers could catchup with their British counterparts. An early manifestation of the shift was a resolution passed at ICTU's first annual conference in 1959 demanding a forty-hour week throughout industry. A shorter week was harder to win than a pay rise and so unions only pursued it when they felt strong enough to do so. In January 1961, the engineering unions came together and held a conference at which they made the implementation of a forty-hour week official policy.[23] For the first time since the early 1920s, it made substantial progress on the question. After the 1964 building trade strike, the week began to be fixed at five days across the country. Working hours would be reduced from forty-four to 42½ or forty in Dublin and from forty-seven to forty-five or 42½ in the provinces.[24] The union had to down tools or threaten to do so several times for the shorter week, doing so at the Dublin Port and Docks Board in 1964 and 1965, for example.[25] By the decade's end. the forty-hour week was the norm in Dublin, allowing for 'eight hours' work, eight hours' leisure, eight hours' sleep.'[26]

Pay rounds continued throughout the 1960s and appeared to be yielding dividends for workers. Mahon told his union's 1964 annual delegate conference that 'in the field of industrial relations there was a noticeable improvement all round.' However, he denounced that many in the public sector had no right to strike and criticised the arbitration process for these workers as skewed in favour of the state.[27] Pay rises given under the rounds system were often insufficient and had an inflationary effect, the ninth round, which sparked a cascade of price rises in the first half of 1964, being a case in point. Although the IEIETU thought the awards were insufficient, it had no choice but to fall in line after ICTU accepted it.[28] Labourers often received proportionately higher pay increases than craftsmen under the rounds, bridging the gap between the two which the latter bewailed. During the negotiations for the ninth round, Fullerton complained that 'craft rates were ludicrous by present standards' and bemoaned the lack of a national engineering rate. Others protested that similar craftsmen in England had twice as much as their Irish counterparts and felt that ICTU was a 'stumbling block' to getting better wages. Craftsmen were also frustrated that their acceptance of work study and greater productivity drives from employers was not translating into material benefits.[29] The IEIETU decided to approach other craft unions to establish a substantial difference between craft and general rates. Craftsmen earned £13-10-1 (6s. 4¼d. an hour) for a 42½-hour week, a 'tragic state of affairs.' As one IEIETU official put it, 'wages throughout the country were far in excess of the craftsmen's rate and it was disgraceful that the status of craftsmen was not recognised.' Increase given under the round were 'twenty years too late. If we had percentage increases since 1938, the general workers would not have £12 a week and the craftsmen £17-4-0 per week.' However, not everyone viewed the labourer's betterment with such alarm. Jimmy Hynes believed that everyone in the engineering trade 'was entitled to the service of the union' because the IEIETU was an industrial union; most of his colleagues, however, strongly opposed organising labourers. Another NEC member complained that 'we were the only country where barmen, postmen and policemen had more money than toolmakers, electricians, blacksmiths and brass finishers.' Another believed that the apprenticeships 'would fall apart if we did not do something about the position where the semiskilled and unskilled man was going home with more money than the tradesman.'[30]

The IEIETU was at the heart of one of the decade's most prolonged dispute, which took place at the Cobh shipyard. The union had 650 of the yard's 750 workers, which it felt entitled it to go over the heads of the unions in dealing with the company. In 1960, after months of arduous negotiations, the Verolme Company, which had recently purchased the Cobh yard, agreed a closed shop with the union; only the IEIETU and the ETU would supply craftsmen to yard. The agreement also provided for workers to go to the Netherlands to take short, concentrated courses in modern production methods. The amalgamateds were enraged by the new arrangement, which the ICTU executive also 'deplored.'[31] It was only a matter of time before conflict arose. In April 1961, the AEU, the Amalgamated Society of Woodworkers and the Operative Plumbers withdrew their labour at the yard. The IEIETU opposed the strike and ordered its members to pass pickets. Seven members refused to do so and were disciplined by the Cork branch. ICTU intervention ended the strike. From then on, all unions would be able to participate in agreements with the company.[32] The *Irish Times* captured the strike's significance:

> There is something of an ideological conflict, or indeed several ideological differences, behind the strike at Verolme shipyard in Cork... this particular dispute arises from a difference the outlook of those unions which cling to an outmoded craft attitude to production and those which believe that ... labour should be ... able to turn to any of the numerous job that building a ship ... calls for... The firm's bilateral agreement with the IEIETU and ETU implies an acceptance ... of the European principle of industrial unionism, or one union for each industry, in place of the multilateral system of several unions and numerous agreements that operates in British and the majority of Irish industries.[33]

In late 1962, IEIETU pipefitters at Verolme went on an unofficial strike after being ordered to do work not applicable to their trade.[34] The REC strongly opposed the strike and demanded the men end it. The executive was determined to protect the agreement with the dockyard which the men had violated, as well as union rules. The strikers, the REC believed, had placed their employment 'in jeopardy' and had played 'into the hands of unfriendly elements.'[35] The strikers passed a resolution demanding their immediate re-employment; when the dockyard did not comply, the picket was re-imposed. The REC did not recognise the resolution and duly expelled several Cork members.[36] The incident reflected a broader trend in the labour movement. The number of unofficial strikes soared as the rank-and-file grew frustrated that economic development was not reaping more rewards. As Tobin observed, a 'dangerous gap opened up between the leadership and the ordinary members' during the 1960s.[37] IEIETU members went out in major unofficial stoppages at Bord na Móna (1960), Unidare (1963), Aer Lingus and the Drogheda cement factory (1965), and Goulding's (1965 and 1966).[38]

Unofficial stoppages occurred for many reasons, usually for higher pay or shorter hours. The perseverance of the craft mentality – the desire to protect the trade at all costs – also inspired unofficial action. In the early 1960s, the IEIETU refused to participate in the Bord na Móna 'group of unions' because it included labourers whose wages would, it feared, be used to depress the craft rate. The union eventually relented, but only on the condition that the group would not negotiate for tradesmen. In 1965, IEIETU foundrymen walked out when they were told that they must join the ITGWU after their transfer from Pierce's to the Star. Their union won a major victory that year when it forced the ITGWU to open its closed shop at the Star.[39] Tensions continued to exist between craft and semiskilled men within the IEIETU. In late 1964, its 'Allied Trades Section' complained that its AGM for that year was invalid 'because of the obvious intention of the semiskilled members to take complete control of the section.'[40] It told the REC that it would have no further dealings with or on behalf of any semiskilled group in the section because these men were 'endeavouring to take over the operation of the section.'[41]

Given its strategic and sectoral importance to the Irish economy, the IEIETU could issue strike notices that could have serious economic consequences. In August 1966, it secured a sizable increase for 1,670 CIÉ shopmen after threatening to go out. Early the following year, both it and the ETU secured an increase for electricians after resolving to cease work on the £9½ million Ballymun housing estate.[42] Conditions at the site were appalling as Hayden's, an English building firm, cut corners in constructing the massive project which employed 1,200-1,500 people. The ETU reported that 'safety precautions had not been observed, no handrails had been provided; a marquee had collapsed; a plank had fallen and burst a water main.'[43] 'Our members have to work out in the open twelve to fifteen stories from the ground. The men objected to working on flat roofs without a second guard rail as they considered the situation to be dangerous to life and limb.'[44] Hayden's responded by calling in men from other jobs and sacking them if they refused to work.

Fusion: NEETU is born

By the early 1960s, relations between the IEIETU and NEU had thawed considerably as they began to work together more often on the industrial front. In 1961, for example, both sought the forty-hour week for Wexford fitters and foundrymen. Both served joint strike notice on Dublin Corporation in 1963 and the Dublin Port and Docks Board a year later. In 1965, both ordered an overtime ban at the ESB.[45] In 1962, reunification was mooted for the first time that decade, leading to the initiation of formal talks for such the following year. Both unions changed their rules to facilitate fusion and held ballots on the issue.[46] The IEIETU changed its constitution to allow amalgamation if ratified by a simple majority. The Electrical Section opposed this and unsuccessfully tried to mandate that fusion only happen if a two-thirds majority supported it. It was the beginning of an ugly conflict between the IEIETU and its electricians. Both union memberships voted overwhelmingly in favour of unity: the IEIETU 1,228-293 and the NEU 1,592-334. The following month, the IEIETU confidently predicted that fusion was 'forthcoming.'[47]

This assessment was overly optimistic, even though fusion was officially announced in January 1965. Negotiations dragged on and required another ballot. In 1965, the IEIETU voted 1,802-267 in favour of amalgamation and the NEU 1,940-291 in favour.[48] The following year, after two years of work, both agreed upon the rules of the post-merger union. The IEIETU was especially anxious for unity. It was conscious of its smaller membership, especially in the capital where the NEU surpassed its 1,700 members (national NEU membership averaged three to four thousand in the 1960s). In June 1966, the talks concluded successfully: the result was the ten thousand-strong National Engineering and Electrical Trades Union (NEETU), just under 4,500 of whom came from the IEIETU. Five months later, the merger was made public at a celebratory dinner dance at the Imperial Hotel in Cork where the memory of Terence MacSwiney's opening of the IESFTU's Cork branch was invoked. At the tail end of 1966, the Registrar of Friendly Societies granted a certificate of registration for NEETU, officially finalising the merger.[49] A transitional REC was appointed: Cassidy was made industrial general secretary and Tuke financial general secretary. The position of general president would be shared between Fullerton (IEIETU general president since 1965) and Christopher Duffy (NEU general president).

Any hope that the merger would be conducted smoothly were quickly dashed. The negotiating teams had agreed that every district would have one seat on the REC – but not everyone accepted this premise. Several sections had been left without any representation. The Electrical Section was especially unhappy about the REC's constitution. They complained that fitters dominated the executive and that electricians – who had lost two-thirds of their representation from the IEIETU – were inadequately catered for given their numbers. They wanted NEETU to appoint a fulltime official solely for electricians because, in the words of Patrick Dunne, secretary of the Electrical Section, 'this union, to many people, meant a fitters' union; the electricians want to maintain their identity.' Dunne wanted his section to comprise three branches: apprentice, contract and maintenance. The electricians were critical of how the union was managed, including the executives handling of disputes, and argued that the provinces had too much representation and power.[50] They also made charges of irregularities in the election of the REC and threatened legal action unless this was dealt with. A meeting between officials and the section descended into unruly scenes of heckling and violence, after which the REC suspended the section's committee.[51] Little progress was made in organising the new union; selling it to the fitters was nearly as disastrous as it had been to the electricians. At a meeting of the Engineers' Section, officials were 'taunted … shouted down by a noisy minority and eventually the meeting was closed.'[52] The Allied Trades Section was also unhappy about the way the REC was appointed. One IEIETU NEC member spoke for many when he expressed his dismay 'that at the heart of the union there was so much friction.'[53]

NEETU also encountered financial problems at the onset. It had inherited the IEIETU's poor monetary position and had only £2,000 to its name. It had protracted trouble getting the IEIETU's trustees to hand over assets to NEEETU which, after initially refusing on legal grounds, they eventually agreed to do.[54] It took a year for the NEU to sell its assets (including 33 Gardiner Place) to NEETU and for a joint bank account to be opened, which was set up with a loan from the WUI.[55] NEETU felt it had no choice but to reduce expenditure and forcibly collect arrears, the non-payment of which was a major problem. The REC could not impose any more levies (as all strikes had already been levied for) and was unable to meet its liabilities, so it agreed to take out a £1,000 loan.[56] The timing of the merger was unfortunate as a national bank strike prohibited the new union from paying its debts. In July, the REC reported that it was 'in the red' fiscally and that 'there was no finance to meet any other expenses at this time.' Its car could not be taxed that quarter, its phone had been cut off the previous week and its electricity was threatened, just some of its many outstanding bills. The general treasurer told his colleagues that contributions were low and unpaid bills were worth more than their holdings in cheques and money orders. Compounding matters, NEETU had exhausted its overdraft.[57] A strike at Bord na Móna in the spring of 1968 also drained its limited finances. NEETU could not afford its ICTU affiliation fees, which were paid for by a loan from the Marine, Port and General Workers' Union.[58]

At an early meeting of the REC, a motion to revoke the new executive was defeated by the chairman's casting vote. An electricians' representative told his colleagues that his section 'would fight the matter vigorously.'[59] Indeed they did. In July 1967, the IEIETU's Electrical Section received a High Court injunction against the transfer of IEIETU funds or property to NEETU. It had successfully argued that the July 1965 ballot was illegal because at least thirty members received no ballot papers. In 1968, the High Court reiterated its rulings: the first ballot had not been conducted in accordance with statute and the second ballot took place after the unions had fused. As the merger had no legal basis, the old unions still technically existed; NEETU existed only on paper, even though it had a functioning executive that met regularly.[60] As NEETU was not an officially registered union, it had no negotiating licence. The IEIETU's Tuam branch condemned the section for its 'great disservice to our union, and to the cause of trade unionism in general.'[61]

Why did the Electrical Section react so furiously to joining a union that would have given them a stronger hand vis-à-vis the employers? The answer lies in the power of craft insecurity. In December 1967, a delegation from the Electrical Section addressed an IEIETU NEC meeting and spoke candidly about how they felt about the merger:

> We are here to defend our trade… This was a rigged ballot for election to the REC, our solicitor has sworn testimony on this matter… We were guaranteed full autonomy for our section; only electricians have a right to look after electricians. There were 2,000 coming across the road, nice gentlemen but not craftsmen. We must protect our craft position in power… We cannot accept the principle that any ruling body can take away the craft protection of our members. We joined the union for protection, all we got was repression… you are opposed to electricians… The trade is going down. We are now earning less than truck drivers… We are the weakest members in the union which is now being run by a power pack… We must have our whole trade absolutely protected. The fitters took over the union and now the officials are all fitters.[62]

Edward Hoare, section chairman, told the meeting that 'a ruse was entered into to remove them from office to allow itinerants to take over' and that 'Mr. Cassidy and his gang … are squatters and not paying rent.' He also claimed that the electricians had been locked out of their room and that their correspondence had been removed.[63] Within days, the dissidents went behind the executive's back and advertised a meeting of the section in the *Evening Herald*. The NEC was outraged by this 'intimidation from the Electricians' Section' and the 'appalling reports about rumours … that some kind of conspiracy was being perpetuated on the members.'[64] The section also disputed that the NEC was properly comprised and that Fullerton occupied his position as general president legitimately, leading to Hoare to denounce him as a 'lying dictator.'[65] Another electrician claimed that he was made 'sick' by the thought of 'educated men on the NEC trying to ruin the union. We are the weakest members in the union which is now being run by a power pack.'[66] The dissidents had also opposed the outcome of the 1968 strike, claiming that the union had 'sold out the electricians' by accepting it.[67]

Despite its early problems, NEETU grew at a steady pace. By 1969, it had thirty-eight branches across the country, with twelve in Dublin. By then, it had spread to towns as disparate as Kilkenny, Castlebar and Tobercurry.[68] It did its best to function as a properly constituted union. One of its first industrial actions took place at Dublin Corporation when councillors refused to implement the maintenance craftsmen's agreement, concluded in October 1966, which gave hourly rates of 7s. 4¼d. (the typical tradesman's rate was 6s. 10d.). The union's push was part of its campaign for the application of the rate across Dublin. The Corporation was willing to give it for a forty-hour week, but not a 42½-hour week, which would result in reduced pay. Thus, NEETU men downed tools for four days in June 1967, ensuring that two thousand tons of rubbish was not collected. Pickets were placed on city depots despite a High Court injunction against them. The settlement was an outstanding victory for the union. It obtained an even higher wage than what it had struck for because the Corporation agreed to a forty-hour week without loss of pay. Afterwards, the Corporation unsuccessfully took legal action against the union.[69]

Table 49: Consumer Price Index, 1965-69 (Base: mid-November 1953 = 100).[70]

Year (mid-November)	All Items
1965	144.8
1966	150.4
1967	154.3
1968	162.7
1969	175.1

Table 50: NEETU Dublin Branches, 1967.[71]

Dublin Branch No.	Membership
One	Public bodies
Two	Firms with head office north of the Liffey
Three	Firms with head office south of the Liffey
Four	Electrical workers
Five	Structural steel workers
Six	Foundrymen (skilled)
Seven	Heating engineers and laggers
Eight	ESB telegraph communication and installations
Nine	Semiskilled
Ten	Welders

The ETU, 1960-67

Like the IEIETU, the ETU experienced a boom in both membership and militancy during the 1960s. Rural electrification had given the electrician an indispensable importance to country life, a status he had long held in the cities. Industrialisation and the liberalisation of the Irish economy increased the number of electrical workers, as did the ongoing process of technological development. By the early 1960s, the ETU catered for over 90 per cent of the country's electricians.[72] But greater number did not always translate into greater success. The state's 2,500 electricians began the decade in a pay dispute with the ECA and ESB. The ETU heavily watered down the claim during negotiations, much to the ire of its three Dublin branches.[73] Its rank-and-file rejected the employers' offer by only eighteen votes (904-886), but their executive was forced to accept it as 49.5 per cent of members had voted in favour of it. The offer was less divisive among IEIETU electricians, who voted 93-66 to accept it. Having brought the country to the brink of power outages, the electricians had secured an increase of 4¼d. an hour in January 1960.[74]

An old enemy re-emerged in 1962, this time at Ardmore Studios in Bray. Since Ardmore's opening in 1958, the ETU (Ireland) had been the sole supplier of electrical workers there. It had hoped to retain this honour for the filming of *Term of Trial* and *The Very Edge* but was disgusted to learn that the respective production companies had an existing arrangement with the ETU (UK). The British union exploited this loosely worded agreement to demand that it provide a significant proportion of electricians to Ardmore. Although both films were completed as planned, relations between the two unions were in freefall. The situation deteriorated further when the ETU (UK) demanded that half of the eighteen electricians due to work on *The Running Man* (1963) be theirs. Because films produced at Ardmore qualified for a grant from the British Film Financing Company, the British union felt it stood on solid ground and refused its Irish rival's offer of 10 per cent representation. Filming continued as planned despite the dispute. Eventually, the Irish union was victorious. In a settlement negotiated by the film's director Carol Reed, two Britons joined the ETU (Ireland) and the seven who refused to do so were replaced by Irishmen. The British union was furious. Its executive instructed its British branches to ban Irish citizens from membership, prohibited the handling of equipment on hire due for Ardmore, and threatened to 'disrupt' the activities of British producers doing business in 'Southern Ireland.'[75] It pursued its original demand even more vigorously and refused to supply of its members to Ardmore, leading to the studio's closure with two hundred redundancies. The filming of *Five and a Half Detectives* was also affected. William Norton TD intervened but could not find a solution. After talks in London, both unions agreed to allow both British and Irish electricians to service a re-opened Ardmore Studios.[76]

The issue resurfaced in early 1963 when the British ETU insisted that at least eighty-five of its members be employed on *Of Human Bondage* (1964). The dispute nearly cost Ardmore the production after Seven Arts – who initially sided with the Irish and condemned the British union's demands as extortionate – considered shooting in Hollywood instead. The threat may have prompted the ETU (Ireland) to relent. It now waivered its objection to the presence of its British counterpart and reinstated the offer of 10 per cent representation, which the British rejected. Talks failed to reproduce a settlement that the ETU (Ireland)'s executive was willing to ratify. But this did not matter in the end. On 30 January 1963, the company announced that production would proceed because it had (secretly) brokered a deal with Congress, the ETU (UK) and the IEIETU which stipulated that the British would provide half the electricians and the two Irish unions a quarter each. Outraged at this betrayal, the ETU (Ireland) picketed the set, which Ardmore had injuncted by the High Court on several occasions, although the court eventually conceded the union's right to picket. The ETU (Ireland) lobbied the Minister for Industry and Commerce to intervene, but to no avail.[77] The affair poisoned relations between the two Irish electrical unions, already strained because of the ETU's complaints about the ease at which the IEIETU (and later NEETU) was issuing cards to electricians. The ETU, who had withdrawn from the Ardmore Studio Group of Unions the previous year, asserted that it would 'find it hard to forgive' the IEIETU for its role in the affair. In turn, the IEIETU complained that its rival was 'subjecting' it 'to a propaganda campaign.' The dispute also exacerbated the ETU's hostility to Congress, whose behaviour it denounced as 'despicable' and 'an act of sabotage.'[78] After the ETU (Ireland)'s departure from Ardmore, the IEIETU entered into a 50:50 agreement with the British union on the provision of electricians.[79]

In 1964, Ardmore concluded new agreements with the unions of the Studio Group, excluding the ETU (Ireland). Consequently, none of its members were employed on *Ballad in Blue*, which starred American R&B legend Ray Charles. The union mounted another picket which the other unions once again passed and which the High Court once more injuncted. Five years later, another dispute, this one involving NEETU, about the employment of British electricians at Ardmore erupted. This time, it concerned the filming of *Ryan's Daughter* by the Irish Film Production Group.[80]

The ETU was as opposed to unofficial action as any other union. In July 1963, it expelled fourteen members for an unofficial strike at Dromoland Castle, Co. Clare where an American firm was building a luxury hotel. One of the strikers took the union to the High Court seeking damage for conspiracy and loss of earnings, claiming that he had been unlawfully expelled. The man lost his case in the High Court.[81] It was an important victory for the union. 'If we did not go ahead with this case, our members would have been completely demoralised and it would give other union a chance to gloat, particularly the IEIETU... our enemies would be laughing.'[82] Although some ETU members wanted closer relations with the IEIETU, most feared that their rival union was out to subsume them. The Dromoland project was beset by labour relations problems from the start, which impelled the Americans to hand it to a Limerick contractor. The ETU and the contractor had agreed that men on site would earn £16. 9s. excluding subsistence and travel allowances for a forty-seven-hour week. However, the shop steward secured additional concessions for the men after threatening to withdraw labour. George Lynch and the Limerick branch secretary rewarded him by colluding with the employers to expel him from the union. In July 1963, the men downed tools in solidarity with their shop steward.

Some in the union suspected that the episode, like all unofficial action, was not simply the folly of grassroots militancy. A union trustee believed that the strike was a communist plot led by 'rejects of the English ETU' who were 'now returning to this country. The Communist Party had messed up that union over there, and these people were coming here trained to do a job.'[83] He reported that a union member who had picketed Ardmore without instructions was 'known as a leading communist.' Some on the executive feared that communists could infiltrate the union as former members of its British namesake, emigrants who had been lured home by the improved economic conditions, increasingly joined. The general president agreed that sinister forces were behind the flush of spontaneous action:

> the number of unofficial and threatened disputes ... leave little doubt that these disputes are not spontaneous but the result of organisation...
> there is among us a small group whose primary allegiance is not to the

union, and they are actively engaged in encouraging members to defy their executive and branch officials in the mistaken belief that there are shortcuts to achieve their wishes.[84]

Many branch members agreed with him. In June 1964, the NEC unanimously backed a Cork branch resolution for an inquiry into how many ETU men were communists.[85] But such an inquiry was unnecessary. By then, the communists had lost power in the ETU (UK), disgraced and discredited by the 1961 ballot rigging scandal.

As the economy grew, the scale of increases the unions secured continued to augment. After the ninth pay round in 1964, hourly rates in the cities for contract shop electricians were 6s. 5½d. for electricians, 7s. for chargehands and 7s. 7d. for foremen; outside the cities, they were 1d. less. All were now entitled to 84s. country money. In total, about three thousand electricians worked in the contracting trade. The ETU was also winning battles in the semi-state sector. Despite not being an affiliate, it helped the Civil Aviation Group of Unions to extract significant pay improvements for five hundred maintenance craftsmen at Dublin Airport in July 1966, having brought Aer Lingus and Aer Rianta to the brink of strike the previous December. Through incremental top-ups, salaries would reach £24. 8s. a week (€516 in 2017 terms) in April 1968 at the peak of the scale. Later in 1966, the Civil Aviation Group negotiated the first ever productivity agreement between craft unions and Aer Lingus, which Murphy described as a 'major step forward in industrial relations in Ireland',[86] and another one the following year which extended the terms of the 1966 agreement to other tradesmen at Dublin, Cork and Shannon airports.[87] Productivity agreements were novel in Ireland in the 1960s – being the result of the drive to make Irish industry more competitive on global markets – and were becoming increasingly commonplace across the economy. Although the new arrangements were yielding fruit for workers, many felt inhibited by national agreements and deplored stipulations that froze wages until the next round. There grew a feeling among the rank-and-file that the labour leadership had grown too close to the establishment via corporatist bodies that were a long way from the shop/factory floor. Paradoxically, the same process of industrialisation that had unleashed proletarian militancy across the country was also drawing union leaders into a closer relationship with Fianna Fáil.[88]

The 1961 electricians' strike

The craft militancy of the 1960s was especially apparent at the ESB. Whereas the ESB experienced only eight strikes in its first thirty years (none of which interrupted supply), thirty-eight strikes took place there between 1961 and 1968.[89] By the decade's end, the ESB employed ten thousand. As an employer, the ESB compared well to private contractors. It had a sophisticated internal system of conciliatory machinery comprised of two statutory tribunals: one for manual workers (set up in 1942) and one for salaried staff (set up in 1949). However, it was difficult for ESB electricians to negotiate for themselves because the Board fixed its wages on the local prevailing rates. In the early 1960s, the Board had four hundred operations electricians and the same number of contract electricians. The former was engaged in power supply and the latter's work related to the private sector. As such, contract electricians' wages at the ESB tracked those in the industry under the NIJC. When those wages were agreed, operations electricians' pay was negotiated. There was an advantage to this method: if there was a dispute about prevailing wage rates, then only the contracts men, not the operations men, would be involved, which kept power supply constant. It was nevertheless a flawed system, which had become obvious by 1961.

Electricians had serious grievances with the ESB which were exacerbated when the clerks received a substantial increase. They resented what they considered to be a policy of discrimination in favour of the clerks, which triggered the psychological insecurity ingrained in them as craftsmen. The ETU sought from a grading system for electricians, as existed for clerks, and less restrictive working conditions.[90] 'A point sourly remarked on at the time was that they saw the clerical people breezing out to mass on a holy day or to the shops from time to time, while the electricians were obliged to check in and out.'[91] In mid-1961, the ETU and IEIETU put in a claim for an upward revision of wages and a shorter week from the ECA and ESB. It was a significant move that altered the paradigm of the wages movement in the electrical trade: for the first time, operations and contracts men had submitted a claim together. Electricians were well paid compared to other Irish workers – the ECA paid 3d. to 8d. above minimum rates and an electrician typically earned 1½d. an hour more than a building tradesman. But all Irish workers had fared poorly since the Emergency: electricians' pay had only increased by 136 per cent compared to the 166 per cent jump in the cost of living.[92] Wages were 6s. 3d. an hour in Britain compared to 4s. 11d. in Irish cities and Irish contractors were determined to discourage an exodus to the UK. Accordingly, the ETU sought an extra 1s. 3d. an hour and the IEIETU 1s. The employers and the Labour Court offered rates of 5s. 5d. for city electricians and 5s. 4d. for provincial ones as well as a reduction of hours by 1½ in Dublin and two outside the capital. The unions rejected the offers.[93]

When no settlement was reached by 21 August, 2,600 electricians – eight hundred of them employed by the ESB – withdrew their labour. The decision to go on strike was, in Lynch's words, the most important in the history of the union up to the moment.'[94] It was the Republic's first power strike and the third national strike of 1961. As such, it created a political and media panic. The ICTU executive was similarly dismayed and strongly opposed the stoppage. The ETU had wanted to take out others in the industry, but Congress confined the action to electricians, prompting the union to resign from the ESB Group of Unions.[95] Workers widely ignored the directive from ICTU and the group to pass the picket, meaning that the supervisory staff had to man the stations. Electricians placed pickets on the contract shops and, more significantly, on the ESB's twenty-three generating stations. Manual workers set up a strike committee independent of ICTU structures. The Oireachtas was recalled so that the government could pass emergency legislation introducing compulsory arbitration into the ESB in some circumstances. On the surface, the strike resembled a typical industrial dispute caused by a demand for higher wages. But this was only part of the reason and there were deeper-rooted, structural reasons for the strike. As the 'boom' of the Lemass era got underway, workers sought to assert themselves after the despondency of the 1950s. As one ESB worker later explained:

> I started my apprenticeship in 1960, the beginning of the boom period, but I was always being told about the hard times of the previous decade. With the shortage of work in contracting, employers could pick whom

they wanted and treat them as they wanted. The boat to England was the only alternative … There were stories of people being paid less than the trade union rate, of non-union labour being used, of men having to queue … for a vacancy. As the boom continued, the attitude of the lads was to 'screw' the employers for as much as they could, as after the boom they would start 'screwing' the workers again.[96]

The legislation's threat of compulsory arbitration undoubtedly compelled the unions to negotiate. This, along with several other stringent components, were removed by government amendments. The venue for negotiation was never revealed for fear of demonstrations by the unofficial strike committee. The Electricity (Temporary Provisions) Act 1961 was innocuous and left only an obligation to establish a commission to inquire into industrial relations in the ESB. This reported in 1962 and recommended that the ESB disaffiliate from the ENJIC (which it did in 1967) and that a comprehensive national agreement be negotiated.[97] The final settlement was an astounding victory for the electricians which granted the following increases: 31s. 8d. in Dublin; 33s. 7d. in Cork, Limerick and Waterford; and 30s. in the provinces. Hours were cut from forty-four to 42½ in Dublin and from forty-seven to forty-five everywhere else.[98] The increases were very sizable for the time. They were more than double that of the concurrent eight round talks which granted 14s., the amount recommended by the Labour Court. Electricians' hourly rates were now 5s. 9d. in the cities and 5s. 8d. everywhere else, making weekly wages over £12 Employers granted the increases with the utmost reluctance, only doing so after extensive pressure from the government and the Labour Court. As they told the Minister for Industry and Commerce, they were terrified by the precedent it would set:

> The employers said that if this figure were imposed it should be made impossible for the electricians to hold the country to ransom again. They had been so successful in the present dispute that it was inevitable that they would pursue the same tactics again unless some procedure to prevent it were devised.[99]

The stoppage, which nearly bankrupted the ETU, illustrates how the removal of the fear of unemployment created a new confidence among rank-and-file trade unionists who were determined to improve their standard of living. The labourers, who had doggedly supported the electricians, also received a substantial increase. The ETU reaped the benefits. Many trade unionists were outraged by the lack of support for the strike and so there was a flurry of transfers to the ETU. The ITGWU was particularly intransigent, resulting in fifty of its members in Galway leaving and establishing an ETU branch in violation of ICTU rules. Other unions also accused the ETU of 'poaching.' However, the union was unperturbed by the allegations. Its membership had exploded from two thousand members at the beginning of the stoppage to three thousand by mid-1962: by the end of that year, it had nearly four thousand members. By then, the union needed three fulltime officials and had established a fourth Dublin branch to deal with the increased membership. The Dublin No. 3 Branch had reached seven hundred (with 250 auxiliary members) and Dublin No. 1 had jumped from four hundred to six hundred members.[100]

The ITGWU transfers went before the Congress Disputes Committee, which sided with the Transport Union and ordered that the ETU return the men.

When the ETU refused, they were suspended from Congress and remained so until 1967. ICTU ordered its affiliated unions and trades councils to cease co-operation with the ETU.[101] The hostility was mutual. Many ETU members were sickened by ICTU's lack of support for the strike, which exposed the 'true colours' and 'Tammany Hall methods' of the 'despicable' Congress.[102] Hostility lingered for many years thereafter and the union refused to seek reaffiliation. Relations between the two were further damaged by an electricians' strike at CIÉ in 1962. Like 1959, the stoppage began at Inchicore when an ETU shop steward was sacked for refusing to carry out an instruction, which the union considered a breach of its work study agreement with the company. The ETU then took out all CIÉ electricians. The strike, which lasted a month, was called off after the Labour Court intervened.[103] The ETU concluded that 'political inspiration' was the reason for ICTU's inaction during the dispute.[104]

The 1966 fitters' strike

While other ESB workers were making progress by 1965, the mechanical fitters were languishing behind. Once again, the discrepancy in pay between the clerks and the manual workers caused tension between the Board and the latter group. The ETU won a major victory that year at the ESB when it secured the implementation of a system of proficiency payments for electricians without prejudice to their claim for grading. The fitters, who were not even receiving the prevailing rates in the private sector, demanded the same scale as the clerical staff in mid-1965, who earned a maximum of £1,385 a year.[105] After threatening strike, six thousand manual workers received an increase from the Board, even though it was less than the 7 per cent they had sought.[106] By February 1966, with discontent at boiling point, the unions imposed an official ban on overtime. The ESB, which did not appreciate the seriousness of the situation, refused the claim. To its dismay, over one hundred mechanical fitters were called out on 29 April.[107]

Though most ESB fitters were organised by the AEU, the IEIETU and NEU had a considerable number between them. They earned just under £14 a week for the first two years, rising to just over £15 after five years' service.[108] The prospect of a national blackout terrified the union leadership as much as the public and political and media establishments. Pickets were placed on sixteen of the ESB's twenty-seven generating stations before being withdrawn to facilitate negotiations. On 9 May, there were widespread power outages across the country, affecting industry, customers and vital public services such as hospitals, which the ESB blamed on the unions. The IEETIU retorted that the outage had nothing to do with the strike and abhorred that the electrical current was cut off, suspecting that someone within the ESB was irresponsible.[109] The strike dragged on until 21 June when, after protracted negotiations at the Labour Court, the fitters secured a favourable settlement – an ample increase and a scale system of payment. They would now start off on £14-10-5 before rising to £19-5-0 after twenty years' service.[110] Shortly afterwards, they threatened strike for, and secured, a shorter week, a week's holidays, sick pay and a pension scheme. The stoppage would have embroiled eight thousand men in the cities.[111] The strike had a knock-on effect across the economy. The following year, fitters at the Dublin Port and Docks Board threatened to withdraw their labour for an incremental salary scale instead of being paid by the hour.[112]

In response to the strike, the Oireachtas passed the Electricity (Special Provisions) Act 1966 to make it more difficult for ESB employees to withdraw their labour or picket in certain circumstances. ICTU and the Labour Party both fiercely opposed the legislation. It also outraged the ETU rank-and-file, as did their union's feeble opposition to it. Several wrote irate letters to head office demanding an aggressive campaign for repeal of this 'infamous Act.' The Limerick No. 2 Branch wanted the executive to declare a one-day national strike in defiance of the law. An officer from the branch contended that there was 'growing unrest with the union's inactivity to the legislation' and reported that:

> some of our most valued members are appalled at what appeared to be tacit acceptance of this notorious Act … that if we were not prepared to lead now, we would disintegrate in many areas. That we gave that lead in 1961 with beneficial results but we cannot bask in the glory of five years ago. That the lack of leadership in our union was being harped on by our own members as well as other trade unionists. That the ETU should be purged of government supporters. That the legislation is a denial of human rights as it is both oppressive and coercive and can never be accepted by the workers. That members are being canvassed by other unions.[113]

In response, the ETU executive had resolved to test the legislation by threatening to take out thirteen hundred electricians out on national strike for a wage increase and a shorter week. The plan worked: that July, the ENJIC granted a week of forty hours in Dublin and 42½ in the provinces, additional holidays and a wage increase.[114] Despite their mutual estrangement, the executive opted to work with Congress to campaign against the Act. The ICTU executive paid lip service to its affiliates by condemning the Act but quickly accepted the government's invitation to discuss a voluntary no-strike agreement in return for new legislation. Workers soon experienced the draconian nature of the Act. In 1968, ESB labourers were imprisoned after striking for a pay rise. The ICTU leadership panicked at the prospect of a general strike at the ESB and negotiated with the government for the men's release. Soon afterwards, the Oireachtas quietly repealed the Act. Fianna Fáil dropped its plan to remove legal protection from unofficial strikes and re-established the Department of Labour in 1966. The government trundled on in its bid for statutory control of strikes and wages, with Congress vacillating between pacifying criticism and retraining its affiliates.[115]

The apprenticeship system in the 1960s

In April 1960, An Cheard Chomhairle was launched under the 1959 Apprenticeships Act. Craft unions were unhappy with its composition from the start, claiming that ICTU had used its nominees to overrepresent general unions. In its first annual report, An Cheard Chomhairle commented upon the severe pitfalls of a system based upon the goodwill of employers:

> arrangements in Ireland for the recruitment and training of apprentices are haphazard… little attempt has been made … to ensure that boys … have a proper educational background, or to provide for the systematic training of apprentices in practical skills or for their release from work to attend appropriate technical school courses. The importance of testing the progress of apprentices by examinations … is not adequately

recognised... the effectiveness of present arrangements ... depends mainly on the outlook of individual employers.[116]

The report proposed a pass standard in certain subjects in either Group Certificate or Intermediate Certificate examinations for entry into apprenticeship. It also enunciated the board's philosophy:

1) To foster a spirit of co-operation between workers, employers and educationalists on the subject.

2) To stimulate the formation of representative National Apprenticeship Committees and local Advisory Committees to help in regulating and controlling apprenticeship.

3) To ensure, by promoting reasonable arrangements for the intake of apprentices and by requiring an educational qualification for entry, that sufficient numbers of suitably qualified young persons enter on apprenticeship in the craft trades.

4) To ensure that apprentices are given not only an adequate opportunity to acquire the necessary practical skills and technical knowledge but also an opportunity for moral and cultural development.

5) To supervise the progress of the apprentices by, inter alia, a system of examinations in trade practice and theory, during and at the end of apprenticeship.

6) To ensure that there is adequate enforcement of rules laid down by An Cheard Chomhairle concerning apprenticeship.[117]

In 1961 and 1962, a voluntary apprenticeship committee covering the entire state was instituted in the engineering and metal trades. Localised committees were established for the building trade. An Chomhairle selected the motor mechanic and electrical trades for statutory examination under the 1931 Act, which were completed in March 1962. Examinations took the form of questionnaires sent out to employers. Following this, these trades were designated under the 1959 Act and National Apprenticeship Committees were set up in 1963. That September, An Chomhairle instituted a statutory apprenticeship scheme for the electrical trade. Rules governing entry into an apprenticeship in the electrical and motor mechanical trades followed shortly thereafter. There were one thousand apprentices in the electrical trade, with 200-250 being taken on every year. There were thirteen metal and engineering trades apprenticing 2,167 boys, 1,152 of whom were fitters. Although three to four hundred boys were taken on annually, there was still a skills shortage, the result of a low population, emigration, closed trades and inadequate housing facilities.[118]

In 1964, An Chomhairle concluded that the current apprenticeship system could not sufficiently provide for the needs of a growing economy. It recommended the formation of a new state body 'for industrial training needs in general, including training by way of apprenticeship' because 'the needs of industry for skilled workers could not be met by means of apprenticeship training alone.'[119] It turned its attention to bringing the engineering and metal trades (thirteen in total) and construction trades (twelve in total) under statutory control, which it achieved in 1964 and 1965 respectively In 1966, responsibility for An Chomhairle was transferred from the Department of Industry and Commerce to the newly-established Department of Labour. The following year, An Chomhairle was replaced by the Industrial Training Authority, An Chomhairle Oiliuna (AnCo), as per the Industrial Training Act 1967 which repealed the 1959 Act. The 1967 Act changed little, however. AnCo was given powers similar to those of its predecessor: to make legally enforceable rules governing the recruitment and training of apprentices. However, any industrial training committees (which replaced the apprenticeship committees) the new body established could only advise and assist, not make rules. It had six members: two employers, two trade unionists (one craft and one general union), one educationalist and one representative of the Minister for Labour. Cassidy was appointed as the craftsmen's representative. While An Cheard Chomhairle had put in place a rather competent national apprenticeship system that covered over forty trades, it was a hostage to deep-rooted craft tradition and made no radical changes. It only optimised the positive elements of the established system of apprenticeship. Crucially, it failed in the vital area of testing and certification. Certificates of completion were issued without the requirement that apprentices pass the senior trade exam.[120]

Chapter Notes and References

1   O'Connor, *Labour History of Ireland* (2nd Ed.), pp. 218-219, 221; Fergal Tobin, *The best of decades: Ireland in the nineteen sixties* (Dublin: Gill & Macmillan, 1984), p. 95.

2   O'Connor, *A Labour History* (2nd Ed.), pp. 218-219.

3   Ibid., p. 219.

4   Allen, *Fianna Fáil*, p. 115.

5   Ibid., p. 116.

6   O'Connor, *Labour History of Ireland* (2nd Ed.), pp. 221-223.

7   Brian Girvan, 'Industrialisation and the Irish working class since 1922', *Saothar*, No. 10, 1984, p. 35.

8   O'Connor, *Labour History of Ireland* (2nd Ed.), p. 223; p. Cody, O'Dowd & Rigney, *The Parliament of Labour*, p. 222

9   *Irish Press*, 22, 24 Aug., 15-17 Oct. 1964; Tobin, *The best of decades*, pp. 96-97; IEIETU REC minutes, 24 Aug., 21 Oct. 1964.

10   ETU REC minutes, 9 Dec. 1965.

11   O'Connor, *A Labour History of Ireland* (2nd Ed.), p. 223.

12   Devine, *Organising History*, p. 336.

13   IEIETU NEC minutes, 25, 26 Sept. 1964.

14   Ibid., 21 Oct. 1961, 25, 26 Sept. 1964, 6 July 1965. In 1965, the NEC heard that the union was losing potential recruits in Cork and Kerry to the AEU and ITGWU due to insufficient attention being given to Munster.

15   IEIETU, 'Organiser's Report, Jan. 1959-Mar. 1960; IEIETU REC minutes, 6, 11 Jan. 1965; *Evening Herald*, 25 May 1965; ETU REC minutes, 27 May 1965.

16   *Irish Press*, 14 Sept. 1960, 30 May 1961; IEIETU REC minutes, 2 May 1961; 'Sworn statement made before advisory committee by Charles Shelly on 31 Oct. 1935', Charles Shelly, MSP Application, MSP34REF2248, MSP Collection, MA; Charles Shelley, WS 870, BMH, MA. Toomey had worked for the Office of Public Works until his retirement.

17   *Irish Press*, 8 Apr. 1966.

18   IEIETU REC minutes, 5 June, 23 Oct. 1961, 22 June 1964; *Irish Press*, 27 Oct., 23 Nov. 1964; *Irish Independent*, 1 May 1965.

19   NEETU REC minutes, 6 Dec. 1967; *Irish Independent*, 14 Nov., 4, 5 Dec. 1967. See also Edward Tuke, MSP Application, 24SP3528, MSP Collection, MA; Frank Robbins, WS 585, BMH, MA, pp. 59, 77, 94, 95; Thomas O'Donoghue, WS 1,666, BMH, MA, pp. 26, 30; and *Irish Press*, 3 May 1960.

20   ICTU, annual reports, 1961-66, ILHM; IEIETU annual returns, 1960-66, T358, RFS records, NAI & Companies Registration Office (CRO).

21 Tobin, *The best of decades*, p. 49.
22 Allen, *Fianna Fáil and Irish labour*, p. 132.
23 IEIETU REC minutes, 22 Jan., 3 Mar. 1960.
24 Ibid., 18 Apr., 2 May 1961.
25 *Irish Press*, 7 Oct., 19 Dec. 1964, 20 Feb., 27 Mar. 3, 5 Apr. 1965.
26 IEIETU NEC minutes, 25, 26 Sept. 1964.
27 *Irish Independent*, 28 Sept. 1964.
28 Ibid., 15, 22 Apr. 1963; Tobin, *The best of decades*, p. 96; Charles McCarthy, *The decade of upheaval: Irish trade unions in the nineteen sixties* (Dublin: Institute of Public Administration, 1973), p. 253; IEIETU REC minutes, 6, 13, 20, 27 Jan., 2, 11, 16, 23 Mar., 13, 20 Apr. 1964.
29 IEIETU NEC minutes, 21, 23 Oct. 1963.
30 Ibid., 25, 26 Sept. 1964.
31 ICTU executive committee minutes, 24 Feb. 1961, ICTU/Box 103, ICTU collection, NAI.
32 IEIETU REC minutes, 8 Feb., 25 May, 25 July, 3 Nov. 1960, 11, 17, 18, 19 Apr., 7 June, 18, 27 July, 21 Oct., 11 Dec. 1961; *Irish Times*, 17 Apr., 2, 22 June, 27, 31 July, 15, 19 Aug. 1961; Ibid., 26 May 1961, ICTU/Box 103, ICTU collection, NAI.
33 *Irish Times*, 22 June 1961.
34 Ibid., 6, 9, 12 Oct. 1962.
35 IEIETU REC minutes, 8 Oct. 1962.
36 Ibid., 15 Oct., 5 Nov. 1962; IEIETU NEC minutes, 21 Oct. 1961.
37 Tobin, *The best of decades*, p. 96.
38 *Irish Independent*, 25 May, 2 June, 30 Sept. 1965.
39 ICTU executive committee minutes, 1 July, 28 Oct., 25 Nov. 1960, 24 Feb. 1961, ICTU/Box 103, ICTU collection, NAI; *Irish Independent*, 14, 15 May 1965; IEIETU NEC minutes, 6 July 1965.
40 IEIETU REC minutes, 29 Dec. 1964.
41 Ibid., 4 Jan. 1965.
42 *Irish Times*, 19 Jan. 8 Mar., 1-8, 13 Apr., 12, 25 Aug. 1966, 3-10, 14, 21, 24 Jan. 1967; NEETU REC minutes, 16, 23 Nov. 1966, 25 Jan., 1 Mar., 8 May 1967.
43 ETU (Ireland) REC minutes, 17 Nov. 1966.
44 ETU (Ireland), NEC minutes, 19, 20 Nov. 1966.
45 IEIETU REC minutes, 18 Jan., 3 May, 26 Sept. 1960, 3 Mar. 1961, 4 Mar., 30 Apr., 16 Dec. 1963, 28 Sept., 12 Oct. 1964, 27 Sept. 1965, 14 Feb., 11 May, 25 June, 11 July 1966.
46 IEIETU NEC minutes, 21, 23 Oct. 1963.
47 IEIETU REC minutes, 27 May, 5 June 1963; *Irish Times*, 15 May 1968; *Irish Independent*, 13 Sept. 1971.
48 Ibid., 3 Aug., 30 Sept. 1965; *Irish Independent*, 20 Jan. 1965; *Irish Press*, 21 Jan. 1965.
49 Ibid., 17 Aug. 1964, 9 Aug. 1965, 7 June 1966; *Cork Examiner*, 14 Nov. 1966; *Irish Times*, 30 Dec. 1967, 15, 31 May 1968.
50 IEIETU NEC minutes, 11 Oct. 1966.
51 Ibid., 5 Jan., 22 June 1967; 'IEIETU Unity Progress Report', File: NEC 1970.
52 'IEIETU Unity Progress Report', File: NEC 1970.
53 IEIETU NEC minutes, 22 June 1967.
54 Ibid., 7 Mar., 22 June, 5, 27 July 1967.
55 NEETU REC minutes, 1 Feb., 7, 11, 12, 14 June, 5 July 1967; Devine, *Organising History*, p. 557.
56 Ibid., 29 Dec. 1965, 10 Jan. 1966; *Irish Independent*, 21 Jan. 1965.
57 Ibid., 4, 16 July 1966.
58 Ibid., 10 Feb., 10 Mar. 1969.
59 Ibid., 27 June 1966.
60 Ibid., 26 July, 11 Oct. 1967; IEIETU NEC minutes, 7 Mar., 27 July, 26 Nov., 10, 17 Dec. 1967, 25 June 1968; *Irish Times*, 29 July 1967, 15, 31 May 1968; memo on NEETU, 3 Feb. 1969, 2007/28/622, Attorney General's Office records, NAI.
61 IEIETU REC minutes, 23 Sept. 1968.
62 IEIETU NEC minutes, 10 Dec. 1967.
63 Ibid
64 *Evening Herald*, 15 Dec. 1967; Ibid., 17 Dec. 1967.
65 IEIETU NEC minutes, 7 Nov. 1970.
66 Ibid., 10 Dec. 1967.
67 IEIETU REC minutes 11 Nov. 1968; Ibid., 7 Nov. 1970.

68   NEETU REC minutes, 12 May 1967, 10, 17 July, 25 Sept., 2, 9 Oct. 1938.
69   *Irish Times*, 14, 16 Feb., 10 Mar., 8-21 June 1967; Ibid., 15 Feb., 8, 22 Mar., 8, 17 May, 7-14 June 1967.
70   Central Statistics Office (CSO), *Statistical Abstract of Ireland, 1974-82* (Dublin: Stationary Office, 1983).
71   NEETU steering committee minutes, 5 Mar. 1967.
72   *Irish Press*, 3 June 1961.
73   *Irish Independent*, 9 Jan. 1960.
74   *Irish Press*, 6-21 Jan. 1960; ETU (Ireland) minutes, 19 Jan. 1960; IEIETU REC minutes, 6, 18 Jan. 1960.
75   Denis Murphy, 'Ardmore Studies, film workers and the Irish state: creative labour in the 'Decade of Upheaval", *Saothar*, No. 43, 2018, pp. 73-75; *Irish Press*, 10-13 Sept. 1962.
76   *Irish Press*, 6 Oct., 8-20 Nov. 1962.
77   *Irish Independent*, 22-26 Jan., 8 Feb., 2 Mar., 17-24 July 1962.
78   ETU (Ireland) NEC minutes, 27, 28 June 1963; IEIETU REC minutes, 25 Feb. 1963; interview with Owen Wills, 2 Mar. 2020.
79   IEIETU REC minutes, 18, 20 Feb., 20 Mar. 1963, 2 Aug. 1967.
80   *Irish Press*, 1, 9, 10, 19 June, 4, 23, 28 July 1964, 9, 16 Apr. 1969; *Irish Independent*, 7 Oct. 1964, 25 Mar. 1969; Ibid., 8, 24, 31 Mar. 1969; Murphy, 'Ardmore Studios', pp. 76-80.
81   *Irish Independent*, 17 Aug. 1963, 6, 9, 10, 11 Nov. 1964; ETU (Ireland) NEC minutes, 10 July 1964.
82   ETU (Ireland) NEC minutes, 10 July 1964.
83   Ibid., 24 Jan. 1964.
84   Ibid., 27, 28 June 1963.
85   Ibid., 27, 28 June 1964.
86   *Irish Press*, 26 Oct. 1966.
87   ETU REC minutes, Dec. 1965-Aug. 1966; ibid., 22, 25, 29, 30 Dec. 1965, 14 May 1966, 17 Nov. 1967; *Irish Independent*, 26 May, 9, 11, 13, 28 July 1966. This wage was reserved for a new grade of workers: 'approved tradesmen'. For the rest, the maximum rate from April 1968 would be £22-11-6.
88   Allen, *Fianna Fáil*, p. 113.
89   Department of Labour, *Final report of the Committee on Industrial Relations in the Electricity Supply Board* (Dublin: Stationary Office, 1969).
90   McCarthy, *The decade of upheaval*, p. 112.
91   Ibid., pp. 103-104.
92   *Irish Press*, 4 May 1960.
93   Ibid., 4-21 Jan. 1960, 16-21 Aug. 1961.
94   ETU (Ireland), NEC minutes, 19 Aug. 1961.
95   *Irish Press*, 23 Aug. 1961. Lynch had been as honorary secretary of the ESB group until his union pulled out.
96   Cited in McCarthy, *The decade of upheaval*, pp. 104-105.
97   Ibid., pp. 105-112. The ESB withdrew from the ENJIC in 1967 after granting their contract electricians the same rate as operations electricians. As the ENJIC only fixed down-town rates for electricians, the ESB could no longer remain affiliated.
98   *Irish Press*, 31 Aug. 1961.
99   'Report of meeting', 30 Aug. 1962, DIC/2001/50/53, Department of Industry and Commerce records, NAI.
100   *Irish Press*, 5 Sept. 1961, 7 Feb., 27 July 1962; *Connacht Sentinel*, 5 Dec. 1961; ETU (Ireland) NEC minutes, 7-9 Nov. 1962.
101   *Irish Independent*, 25 May, 27, 30 June, 3, 10, 27 July 1962, 8 Feb. 1963; *Irish Press*, 16 Sept. 1967.
102   ETU (Ireland) NEC minutes, 7-9 Nov. 1962, 27, 28 June 1963.
103   *Irish Press*, 28 Mar.-1 May 1962.
104   ETU (Ireland), NEC minutes, 27, 28 June 1963.
105   McCarthy, *The decade of upheaval*, p. 112.
106   *Irish Times*, 6 Feb., 6, 23 Mar., 24, 28-30 Apr., 1-29 May 1965; IEIETU REC minutes, 8 Mar., 5 Apr. 1965.
107   *Irish Independent*, 18-30 Apr. 1966.
108   *Irish Press*, 10 May 1966. In Dublin, ESB fitters were on just under £13-10-1 a week for the first two years and £15-0-2 after five years; outside Dublin, the scale was £14-4-11 to £15-7-10.

109 IEIETU REC minutes, 9 May 1966; *Irish Press*, 10 May 1966.
110 *Irish Independent*, 2 May, 14, 21, 22 June 1966.
111 *Irish Times*, 13 Aug.-2 Sept. 1967.
112 Ibid., 14-27 Feb. 1968.
113 ETU REC minutes, 30 June 1966.
114 *Irish Independent*, 2, 7-9 July 1966.
115 Allen, *Fianna Fáil*, pp. 131-132; O'Connor, *Labour History of Ireland* (2nd Ed.), p. 224.
116 Cited in McCarthy, *Apprenticeships in Ireland*, p. 7.
117 Cited in Ibid., p. 8.
118 Ryan, 'Apprenticeship in Ireland', pp. 305-310.
119 Cited in Ibid., p. 312.
120 Ibid., pp. 311-322, 328-360

8

Militancy and Inflation, 1967-76

NEETU's founders picked a fortuitous time to launch their union. In terms of the percentage of workers organised, Ireland had 'one of the strongest trade union movements outside the communist world.'[1] The figure was 56 per cent in the Republic compared to 49 per cent in Britain and 23 per cent in France.[2] Irish labour was justifiably optimistic that the coming decade would be fruitful for workers, as exemplified by Labour Party leader Brendan Corish's bold declaration that the 'seventies will be socialist.' The enthusiasm was wildly misplaced. Instead, the new decade brought political and economic tumult that destabilised Ireland and scuppered hopes of further advances. By 1970, Ireland had overtaken Britain in the number of days lost to industrial disputes and was second only to Italy in a European context. The following year, Ireland did one better and topped the league once more: the figure was double the British one and multiples of the German or Dutch rates. The 1967-76 period was characterised by political and industrial turmoil all over the world, comparable only to the international strike waves of 1869-1875 and 1910-24.[3]

On 1 January 1973, after a decade of preparation and two failed bids, Ireland joined the EEC. Jack Cassidy had served as a Congress representative on several government committees to prepare for accession.[4] The left claimed EEC membership would raise food prices, diminish democracy and result in major job losses in native industries. While right-wing nationalists opposed the EEC, neoliberals maintained it would complete Irish integration into the European economy and lead to booms in agriculture and foreign direct investment. Both sides were correct. The Labour Party opposed ascension, its final act of radicalism. That year, it joined a Fine Gael-led coalition which governed until 1977.[5] EEC membership made Ireland even more vulnerable to global economic shockwaves. In October 1973, in response to Western support for Israel during the Yom Kippur War, the Organization of Arab Petroleum Exporting Countries declared an embargo on the exportation of oil to the West, which sent global oil prices soaring. The crisis engulfed the West in its first post-1945 recession as mass inflation led to a spike in unemployment in many countries, including Ireland. Closer to home, the outbreak of the Northern Ireland Troubles in 1969 forced ICTU to once again grapple with the national question. But labour also had more immediate problems. There were still too many unions with too much overlap, which led to conflict among unions. In 1970, Congress had eighty-seven affiliates, many of them vying for the same workers.[6] Irish law, which was clear about how unions could break away but unclear about how they could legally merge, exacerbated the situation and confined NEETU to legal limbo. The Trade Union Act 1975 clarified matters and facilitated the union's legal birth the following year. For NEETU, it was the Labour Party's greatest achievement in government during its coalition with Fine Gael.

The unions found themselves in a changed environment. Between 1960 and 1974, the growth of American multinationals and plant-level bargaining complicated industrial relations: the foreign industry sector expanded 21.4 per cent annually compared to 5.6 per cent for all industry. ICTU continued its trajectory towards centralised bargaining. In 1970, it concluded its first National Wage Agreement (NWA), a system of pay regulations like what other European countries had. A strike of maintenance craftsmen, in which NEETU was central, was also a major factory in convincing Congress of the need to negotiate national wage claims. Whereas previous national agreements only set guidelines for decentralised bargaining, the NWAs marked a real departure that laid the foundations for Social Partnership from 1987. The economy grew by 4 per cent a year in the 1970s, allowing the NWAs to issue sizable increases: by 1979, Irish industrial wages were almost equal to UK levels. But inflation – which peaked at 21 per cent in 1975, the highest in the EEC – eroded these gains. Between 1973 and 1975, the price of milk jumped by 60 per cent, butter by 70 per cent and the price of meat doubled. While the workforce grew by 1 per cent per annum in the 1970s, unemployment rose with it, peaking in 1975 when it passed the 100,000-mark for the first time (101,734). At 8 per cent, Ireland's unemployment rate was the second highest in Europe. Although EEC membership had decimated certain local industries (such as textiles), unemployment was a worldwide problem. The US was suffering its worst unemployment rate since 1941 and West Germany its worst since 1959.[7] Working-class anger expressed itself in an explosion in the number of strikes, both official and unofficial, one of the decade's defining features.

NEETU: towards fusion

The IEIETU's legal fight to establish NEETU was compounded by its internal difficulties. Nevertheless, NEETU was spreading across the country. In December 1968, the REC agreed to allow the Irish Union of Scalemakers to join NEETU as a section. Eighteen months later, NEETU opened a supervisors' branch in Cork.[8] The IEIETU had twenty-two branches and 1,800 members in Dublin. Its REC was comprised of one representative each for the allied trades, aviation, brass finishers and ESB workers; two for the Electrical Section; and four for the Engineers' Section. The electricians refused to take their seats until May 1970 in demand of a third seat. That February, the REC had to sack Donal O'Sullivan, its provincial secretary for Cork, after head office received a litany of complaints from Cork and Limerick about his performance as an official. He had mishandled the election for the representative to the NEC and misallocated strike pay by giving some to people who 'could not be traced.'[9] The NEU had 4,500 members; two years later, it had 4,736 members and the IEIETU 4,050.[10]

However, the battle to establish NEETU was making progress. In April 1971, 'after five years of court battles and expenditure of thousands of pounds', the union had finally obtained 'the stamp of legal recognition.'[11] The Supreme Court upheld NEETU's appeal of the High Court's 1967 decision and ruled the merger of the IEIETU and the NEU legal under the Trade Union (Amendment) Act 1876. It also declared that NEETU now legally existed under the terms of its rulebook issued on 28 December 1966. It no longer had to pursue its activities under the IEIETU's and the NEU's separate negotiating licences. Cassidy became the new union's official industrial general secretary and Kevin McConnell its financial general secretary. 'The new 10,000-member union has set a headline for trade union rationalisation but the legal and financial snags it hit have also put many unions on their guard.'[12] However, NEETU still did not officially exist because Irish law remained ambiguous. For instance, it was unclear whether both the IEIETU and NEU (which still technically existed) needed simple or two-third majority votes from their respective members for amalgamation. In May 1972, NEETU's founders established a steering committee comprised of members of both the IEIETU and the NEU to oversee the amalgamation, but it achieved nothing. Despite meeting intermittently for two years, it had still not filled every union position or compiled a register ready for delivery to a solicitor. Progress was so frustratingly slow that one committee member asked his colleagues, 'do we want to proceed with fusion or let it lapse? All of the delays are on the IEIETU side.'[13]

On New Year's Eve 1974, NEETU held a dinner to mark Cassidy's retirement, ending an extraordinary fifty years of service to the labour movement. At the time of the dinner, his union had 12,942 members.[14] Cassidy was one of the country's best-known and most influential trade unionists, having served on the ICTU executive nearly every year since reunification. He had also been a member of the boards of AnCo and the Redundancy Appeals Tribunal. A native of Cork, Cassidy moved to Dublin to apply his trade as a fitter and had lived there ever since. His retirement marked the passing of the Grand Old Man of Irish trade unionism. Though he had cut his teeth in the 'old school' of conservative craft unionism, he had transitioned seamlessly into the modern age. He had therefore straddled two periods in Irish labour history: before and after industrialisation in the 1960s, having been a steadfast moderate throughout. A central figure in the negotiations that had established NEETU, he had overseen its impressive growth from nine thousand at its foundation to fifteen thousand members by the mid-1970s. Larry O'Neill – assistant general secretary, vice-president and DCTU president – succeeded him as industrial general secretary. On 29 September 1977, Cassidy died. Head office and branch offices everywhere remained closed on 1 October as a sign of respect for one of Ireland's most foremost trade unionists, whom the *Cork Examiner* described as 'a popular and courteous official.'[15]

Notwithstanding the progress made, the NEETU was still not a registered trade union by early 1976. Nevertheless, both the IEIETU and the NEU were firmly on track to finally complete the exhaustive process of amalgamation. In January 1976, the NEETU REC lodged another deposit for a negotiating licence by having the trustees of the three unions transfer the existing lodgements to NEETU's name. Five months later, IEIETU and NEU trustees transferred their combined assets to NEETU's bank account, which had opened on 1 October 1972.[16] On 19 June 1976, the NEETU officially held its first NEC meeting, a decade after its foundation. The IEIETU's property and assets had been transferred to NEETU, with the NEU's to follow at the end of the month. NEETU had ten Dublin branches. New branches had recently been opened in Thurles, Wicklow and Kilkenny, and one would soon open in Sligo. Navan also had a branch which catered for craftsmen at Tara Mines, Europe's largest lead and zinc mine, producing 10-eleven thousand tonnes of ore daily. Fullerton, NEETU's general president, opened the meeting by explaining to delegates that amalgamation had become protracted due to legal wrangling.[17] By October, however, the process was still not fully complete, and the two old unions still existed on paper. NEETU had not submitted any annual returns for 1969-75, resulting in the Registrar of Friendly Societies threatening to withhold issuing a negotiating licence. McConnell resolved the issue soon afterwards, and the IEIETU and NEU were finally laid to rest.

Table 51: IEIETU Membership, 1963-70.[18]

Year (31 Dec.)	Membership	Year (31 Dec.)	Membership
1963	3,371	1967	3,500
1964	3,354	1968	3,800
1965	3,294	1969	4,050
1966	3,300	1970	4,500

The 1969 maintenance strike

From January to March 1969, Irish industrial life was completely shut down by a strike of three thousand maintenance craftsmen. It was a watershed in Irish labour history that forever changed the structure and dynamics of industrial relations in Ireland. One of the most significant strikes since the foundation of the state, it is as controversial now it was then. Charles McCarthy decried it as 'the most devastating and cruel strike which we had yet experienced'; the *Irish Independent* denounced it 'the most disastrous in the history of the state.'[19] Both assertions are overly simplistic and do not do justice to the strike's complexity and mixed legacy. It gained substantial concessions from the employers and accelerated the trend towards national wage agreements across sectors. But it also exposed the extant of the divisions between 'trade and spade' and helped the ICTU executive to sell a system of two-tier picketing to its affiliates that remains in place to this day.

The maintenance strike has its origins in the 1964 building trade strike. When those workers were granted a reduction of hours, the unions immediately tried to obtain the same for craftsmen employed at maintenance work. The FUE strongly opposed the application. In 1965 and 1966, the Labour Court also rejected the claim, asserting that maintenance craft wages should be based on rates in the industry concerned, not on what craftsmen in other industries were getting. The lessening of hours for electricians in 1966 further galvanised the unions to achieve the same for the maintenance men. That October, after the tenth pay round negotiations had concluded, the FUE and the National Group of Maintenance Craft Unions – representing eighteen unions – reached an agreement which provided for flexibility on hours and a single national rate where firms followed the downtown rate.[20] It was 'an extraordinary example of centralised bargaining.'[21] The FUE was the driving force behind the agreement. Employers liked centralised, national agreements because they believed they would allow them to better plan their costings. The FUE saw wage negotiations as a straightforward bargain with unions. This perception sprang from a misunderstanding of industrial relations in other European countries and the FUE's desire to prepare the Ireland for EEC membership. The Group of Maintenance Craft Unions, of which Cassidy was vice-chair, had no formal relationship with ICTU. Fifteen of the eighteen unions were not very representative of maintenance workers: most had only a few such men while others had none. NEETU and the Amalgamated Union of Engineering and Foundry Workers (AEF), the AEU's successor since 1968, represented most maintenance craftsmen. The ETU came after that. It was not a member of the Maintenance Group and had strained relationships with some of the affiliates. It was ambivalent about the talks because it had rejected the 1966 agreement for not granting a week's holidays or a week of forty-hours in Dublin and 42½-hours in the provinces[22]

By 1968, the ETU was not alone in its opposition to the 1966 agreement, which contained some significant flaws. The flat rate was distorted by reductions in hours given in the meantime, creating discrepancies between men in different locations. When the Maintenance Group met again in September 1968, it was unanimous on the need for a wage increase. Maintenance men earned 7s. 9¼d. an hour. While the unions were happy to maintain pay differentials, they wanted to standardise the week at forty-hours.[23] From the beginning, there was a disjointed approach to negotiations. The group initially sought a 35 per cent increase; the FUE offered 12 per cent. While the employers were unified and simultaneously building a national organisation, the unions had little cohesion. NEETU had originally wanted an hourly rate of 12s. 6d.; the AEF wanted less than that while the Amalgamated Society of Woodworkers wanted more. The group eventually decided on a 70s. a week improvement, which would give a weekly wage of £18 from 1 January 1969 and £18 15s. from 1 July. The group used electricians as the benchmark for a 22 per cent advance. In November 1968, electricians had been granted an hourly rate of 9s. 9d. per after a four-week strike by NEETU.[24] Before that, only electricians and fitters at Aer Lingus and the ESB received that rate; the rest earned 7s. 4½d. The electrical agreement inadvertently drew the battle lines for the maintenance workers. Contract shop electricians had been organised by both NEETU and the ETU, ensuring that neither would settle less than 9s. 9d. Whereas previous generations of fitters and electricians defined their trade in relation to labourers, they now did so against their fellow craftsmen. The fitters insisted on an hourly rate while the building tradesmen wanted a weekly wage. The size of the advance sought reflected a major insecurity among the maintenance men – that their skill was being underappreciated. Industrial production workers, who were often on incentive payments, earned as much if not more than the craftsmen who maintained their machines – a major grievance for craftsmen.

> This recognition of skill was of great importance to the engineering workers and the electricians ... they had little time for a national agreement which treated them the same as painters and plasterers ... their reaction was to regard themselves as the essential group, letting the others tag along if the wished to gain from it.[25]

Unions snubbed the FUE's offer of a 10d. per hour increase. The Labour Court then intervened, but the unions refused to attend the hearing – a clear breach of the 1966 agreement – because they feared that the court would simply recommend an eleventh round. The stoppage was poorly coordinated from the start. The Maintenance Group's comportment was shoddy. It had not given Congress enough information about the strike and not even consulted other unions who may be affected by it, which infuriated ICTU. The strike began on 24 January 1969 but was suspended five days later to facilitate talks at the Labour Court. Unofficial pickets from NEETU members continued in the meantime, however. Meanwhile, an agreement of sorts was reached in the Labour Court. But hopes were dashed when, at a highly acrimonious meeting of the group, NEETU and the AEFU rejected the deal and broke away from the Maintenance Group, which effectively disappeared from the dispute. While NEETU agreed to lift pickets, it could not end the strike without the sanction of the executives of the Maintenance Group unions. NEETU violated the agreement within thirty minutes of leaving the Labour Court by resuming pickets. On 28 January, it made the strike official and issued a week's notice. It suspended pickets pending consideration of a new claim for an hourly rate of 10s. The group's chairman resigned in protest. The AEF and the ETU supported NEETU, as did the 100,000-strong ITGWU (who refused to pass pickets) and the Maintenance Group's Cork branch.[26]

On 5 February, after exhaustive talks ended in deadlock, the maintenance men officially withdrew their labour from 193 firms.[27] The strike committee formed by NEETU and the AEFU – who had two thousand of the three thousand strikers – became the effective authority coordinating action, which it did with 'a Cromwellian intensity.'[28] Relations soured between Congress and NEETU, leading the union to reject ICTU's plea for it to suspend the strike. NEETU even called for ICTU president Jimmy Dunne to resign, which he refused to do.[29] Divisions emerged everywhere as labour unity crumbled: 'executive committee against strike committee, amalgamated against national, building against engineering and, within the same union, representative against representative.'[30] Careless picketing caused widespread disruption. Some firms not affiliated to the FUE were picketed while some affiliates were not picketed. More ominously, firms with many labourers were picketed. 'In other words, the eighteen unions were threatening the livelihoods of large numbers of their fellow trade unionists, while minimising their own inconvenience.'[31] General unions became convinced that the craftsmen's real goal was to cause them maximum disruption, leading them to mount counter-pickets in response. The employers saw the strike in simpler terms: as an attack on the FUE. Not every NEETU member supported the strike. The Waterford No. 2 Branch went on protest marches to show that they were 'not sheep' blindly led by 'irresponsible people', much to the ire of their national executive. That branch, which catered for labourers and semiskilled workers, had been unhappy at its treatment by the executive for several years.[32]

 Disharmony and disorganisation manifested in bizarre spectacles. In late February, the executives of the NEETU and the AEFU accepted an enhanced offer by the FUE. However, a joint ballot of both unions rejected it by a 6-1 margin; the ETU rejected it 3-1. The employers appealed to the Taoiseach to intervene to no avail. Realising that their backs were against the wall, the employers capitulated. On 10 March, the strike ended when they conceded a 20 per cent raise (1s. 9d. an hour or 70s. a week). Maintenance craftsmen would now be on 9s. 0¼d. per hour. Having secured one of the biggest wage increases in the history of the state, NEETU celebrated a stunning victory.[33] Although more than thirty-one thousand were out of work and two hundred firms picketed at the height of the dispute, NEETU had only 483 (with another 534 indirectly affected) on strike and the ETU only 127. The stoppage had paralysed the economy: £13.4 million worth of industrial production was lost while £7 million was lost in export orders. Factories across the country had shut, halting the production of everything from chocolate to textiles to electronics to cement. Supermarkets had their stocks cleared as a frenzied public feared a prolonged dispute. In Waterford alone, fifteen firms closed, laying off three thousand. In Cork, sixty firms were involved. In Limerick, one thousand were affected while the figure at the Shannon industrial estate was five thousand.[34] Over £1.6 million in wages and 636,000 workdays were lost, while it cost the unions involved least £440,000. The stoppage accounted for 70 per cent of strike days in 1969.[35]

The strike galvanised others to put in wage claims. The National Industrial

Economic Council concluded that the 'round' system, wherein wage increases had a knock-on effect, was unmanageable. In 1970, it recommended guidelines to determine pay. Lynch reconvened the Employer-Labour Conference and, after Congress rejected centralised bargaining, introduced a bill which restricted increases to 6 per cent and banned all other claims until late 1971. ICTU was horrified and promptly concluded the first NWA on 21 December 1970. In return, the government withdrew the bill and appointed a commission chaired by Trinity College political science professor Basil Chubb to report on the maintenance workers' place in industry. Fullerton served on the commission. Its interim report recommended that the maintenance agreement be extended until 31 December 1970 and that the basic hourly rate be increased from 9s. 6d. to 10s. The AEF accepted these proposals, but NEETU did not, and instead a 10 per cent increase as part of the twelfth round. Offers and rejections ensued before the FUE suggested an extra 1s. per hour, which NEETU accepted.[36]

Disorganised and inconsistent picketing during the strike caused considerable friction between unions. Congress responded by recommending a new, two-tier picketing system. The first would apply to workers and unions directly affected; the second, an 'all-out' picket, could only be launched with ICTU approval. The picket had a special place in the hearts of Irish workers, having been the supreme manifestation of proletarian solidarity since the Larkinite era. The plan to introduce circumstances allowing one to pass a picket generated much controversy and soul-searching. In May 1970, however, an ICTU conference voted to accept the executive's proposal by 173-123.[37] McConnell told the conference that NEETU 'totally opposed' the change, which they considered 'the backwash of the 1969 maintenance dispute' that 'would be to the detriment of ... all industrial workers.'[38]

Unofficial strikes

As Table 52 demonstrates, the 1970s was a decade of working-class militancy in Ireland. The discontent was embodied by the 1974 strike at Guinness, the first in its 215-year history, when 1,200 labourers went out for a pay rise. Craftsmen at the brewery were often embroiled in demarcation disputes. NEETU fitters there had conflicts with plumbers over the laying of pipes and with coppersmiths over the modification of brewing vessels, which nearly led to unofficial stoppages.[39] The NWAs were centralising collective bargaining – taking power away from shop stewards and giving it to union executives and ICTU. The rank-and-file responded by taking matters into its own hands. Between 1973 and 1978, unofficial disputes accounted for over two-thirds of strikes, almost two-thirds of strikers and over one-third of strike days.[40] NEETU's experience was no different as the grassroots regularly took matters into its own hands. Some of the most significant strikes the union experienced in the 1970s were unofficial.

Table 52: Strikes, strikers and strike days in the Republic, 1970-79.[41]

	1970	1971	1972	1973	1974	1975	1976	1977	1978	1979
Strikes	134	133	131	182	219	151	134	175	152	140
Strikers (000s)	28.8	43.8	22.3	31.8	43.5	29.1	42.3	33.8	32.6	49.6
Strike days (000s)	1,007.7	273.8	207.0	206.7	551.8	295.7	776.9	442.1	634.4	1,465.0

Unofficial stoppages did not always stem from or result in tensions between the grassroots and the leadership, who sometimes endorsed shop floor militancy. When NEETU men went out at Unidare in Finglas in March 1971 against the sacking of chargehands, the executive quickly gave its blessing. ICTU then sanctioned an all-out picket which shut down the plant and brought out 1,500 men. After a fourteen-week stoppage, both sides agreed to a compromise based on a Labour Court recommendation in which some men were rehired.[42] Despite the solidarity shown at Unidare, inter-union relations were often volatile in the 1970s, creating rivalries with potentially dire consequences. Poaching remained common. In 1973, NEETU accused the Marine, Port and General Workers' Union of poaching three hundred of its members at Ericsson IM Ltd., the Irish subsidiary of the Swedish telephone and communications firm. The ICTU Disputes Committee ordered that the workers be returned to NEETU. The Marine Workers rejected the ruling as 'undemocratic' and withdrew from Congress as a result. NEETU did not back down and called strike at the company's premises at Upper Mount Street, Dublin, but was forced to concede defeat after the men stayed with the Marine Workers.[43] Employers sometimes resorted to the courts to deal with unofficial action. In December 1973, NEETU members employed by H. A. O'Neill – an electrical firm subcontracted by the Guinness brewery to help construct a new ale plant – struck for 15p. an hour 'dirty money' (compensation for working in unsanitary conditions). The High Court granted an injunction banning pickets. DTUC intervention settled the dispute.[44]

Some unofficial disputes yielded results after the executive regularised them. On 13 February 1974, NEETU members at Dublin Corporation launched one of the decade's most significant strikes their union experienced. That day, the Shop Stewards' Committee of the thirteen Corporation craft unions instructed their unions to submit a claim for wage parity with ESB tradesmen. At the same meeting, three hundred of the seven hundred workers involved decided that if the claim was not submitted, then the shop stewards should serve two weeks' notice on the Corporation. No official claim was forthcoming. Thus, thirty-nine craftsmen at the Stanley Street vehicle maintenance depot withdrew their labour without their union's sanction. Their stoppage had severe consequences for public life: central heating boilers were put out of commission in working-class housing estates such as Ballymun and Coolock; rubbish collection and street cleaning services were halted; public lights went out; and the Corporation's abattoir and transport fleet were affected. Army technicians were put on stand-by to man the Corporation pumping station at Ringsend which was being picketed. By then, six hundred men were affected, later to be 950.[45]

The NEETU executive amplified the situation by making the strike official from 7 March. The union had put ICTU's picketing rules to the test. The Congress executive issued a statement directing the union to confine its strike solely to its own members. Under the new rules, no union could give strike pay to employees who refused to pass a picket other than an all-out picket authorised by ICTU.[46] The strike was, therefore, 'a single union strike which, in accordance with Congress picketing policy, applies only to members of NEETU.' The statement appalled the strike committee, who were 'disgusted to note that the ICTU statement was one of solidarity with the employers rather than one of solidarity with the men who pay their wages.'[47] The Irish Municipal Employees' Trade Union, ETU and WUI took their cue from Congress and ignored NEETU's pickets. Frustrated and angered by their isolation, strikers blocked the entrances of four Corporation depots to prevent refuse-disposal lorries from leaving, leading to confrontations with Gardaí. The dispute then became even more serious after the ETU served strike notice.[48] The stoppage ravaged Dublin: by late March, over three thousand tonnes of rubbish had built up throughout the city. The Corporation employed hauliers to deal with the refuse, provoking a picket of its boiler house at Ballymun. The accumulation of refuse nearly had heart-breaking consequences.[49] On 18 April, uncollected rubbish stored in the basement of an eight-storey block of flats in Ballymun caught fire, sending smoke and flames throughout the building. The entire complex had to be evacuated and nine children – the youngest of whom was only two weeks old – had to treated in hospital for smoke inhalation. The tragedy may have helped to convince the two unions to accept the Corporation's latest offer: the same salary scale rates as previously offered (£32 rising to £37) extending over a period of 11½ years instead of twelve. On 22 April, the men resumed work.[50]

In November 1973, an old dispute re-emerged: NEETU electricians picketed Kilmainham Jail, the scene of the filming of 1973's Mackintosh Man, to oppose the ratio of Irish-British electricians employed by Warner Brothers. The pickets were successful and resulted in new Irish electricians being employed. But relations remained tense on the set and the Irishmen subsequently refused to work with their British colleagues.[51] On 10 June 1974, members of NEETU and other craft unions placed an unofficial work-to-rule and an overtime ban on the CIÉ workshops for pay parity with grade three clerical officers. A month later, the company served dismissal notices to five hundred shopmen. The workshops employed about 1,600 tradesmen who were organised by fourteen different unions. The industrial actions, which the NEETU executive called on their members to end, put 250 vehicles out of services for want of maintenance. But direct action yielded results as CIÉ suspended its redundancy notices. As a result, the men called off their action and negotiations between the company and the unions began. A new salary scale financed by three hundred voluntary redundancies emerged from the talks. Craft wages would now start at £35 rising with annual increments to £47.50.[52] NEETU also helped to obtain a weekly wage of £48.23 (£5 higher) for the one thousand craftsmen employed by Irish Sugar after bringing the company to the brink of strike on the eve of the 1975 beet harvesting campaign.[53]

Unofficial actions often deepened the chasm between the leadership and the rank-and-file. In April 1976, members at Sanbra Fyffe nearly left NEETU for the Marine Workers because their recent strike had not been made official. Two months later, NEETU and ETU maintenance craftsmen at Bord na Móna downed tools in an unofficial action in solidarity with the Amalgamated Union of Engineering Workers' (AUEW) demand for a shortening of the incremental pay scale, the effect of which would be a £7 pay raise. The claim was based on craft rates at the ESB and Aer Lingus. In total, 550 men were involved. By the end of June, the dispute was costing NEETU £1,535 a week. The stoppage was called off in late July when the Labour Court brokered a settlement.[54] Sometimes the NEETU executive struggled to control its branches even when their actions were made official. In late 1976, the Dublin No. 3 Branch threatened to leave the union or appoint its own fulltime officials, which 'would be contrary to rule and would not be allowed.' It had longstanding complaints about the 'lack of service from fulltime officials in attending meetings requested by this branch', citing its disputes with Weatherglaze, Roofcram, Gaelite Signs, P. Maye & Sons. The branch had previously threatened to resign because of its unhappiness with how the REC had handled its clash with Weatherglaze.[55] The executive held firm and regularly rejected branches' claims to serve strike notice. However, it did sometimes regularise actions taken at branch level, such as the fourteen-week strike at the Irish Cement factory in Drogheda in 1976 (for which an injunction was placed on NEETU picketers).[56]

An unofficial dispute at the ESB's new £7½ million turf burning station at Shannonbridge, Co. Offaly threatened to cause a national power outage over the Christmas period in 1976. It began when twenty-seven shift workers rejected the ESB's proposed levels of manning for the station, leading the company to remove them from its payroll on 9 December. Consequently, the demand for a £400 back payment became the primary cause of the dispute, which spilled over into the New Year. Initially, the shift workers, who were organised by NEETU, received little support from their colleagues at the other stations, but this changed after 9 December. Shift workers at every power station except Shannonbridge implemented a work-to-rule, leading to national blackouts on 10 January 1977 that cost Irish industry over £1,200,000 an hour.[57] The executive did not support their action and ordered they resume normal working conditions, which they did when the dispute was submitted to the ESB's Joint Industrial Council. The council offered 60 per cent of the men's claim, which they rejected; however, the executive overruled them by accepting the award. The decision was controversial considering the desire for strike was strong among the rank-and-file.[58] It was not the first episode of militancy among the shift workers. They had withdrawn their labour in April 1972 without executive sanction for a salary structure instead of a weekly wage. They received little sympathy from either the public or the government, who asserted that ESB shift workers were 'the best paid and have the best hours, allowances and conditions of employment.'[59]

Table 53: Percentage of members in different types of unions in the Republic, 1965-75.[60]

Year	General	White-collar	Craft	Other manual
1965	55.8	22.0	13.6	8.6
1970	52.9	24.9	13.7	8.5
1975	48.6	31.3	11.5	8.6

The Irish Electrical Technicians' Association

While most Irish electricians supported the establishment of NEETU, some could not bear the prospect of being in a union dominated by fitters. In early 1970, some of the IEIETU's Electrical Section broke away and established the Irish Electrical Technicians' Association (IETA). Despite the grandiose name, the secessionists were not electrical technicians but regular electricians, albeit with notions of themselves. Beginning with just eight members, their union was officially registered on 19 March 1971 and received its negotiating licence five weeks later. Its rules committed it to organising all electrical and communication workers. On 12 June, the IETA was formally launched from its headquarters at 39 Westland Row. Two years later, it moved to 2 Berkeley Street. Patrick Dunne became general secretary upon its foundation and John Bell, also from the IEIETU Electrical Section, its general president. Hoare was elected general president in 1976; both he and Dunne retained their positions for the rest of the union's existence. At its launch, Dunne claimed the IETA had 250 members including forty-five at the ESB.[61] Table 54 debunks this assertion.

Table 54: IETA Membership 1971-79.[62]

Year (31 Dec.)	Membership	Year (31 Dec.)	Membership
1971	116	1976	103
1972	202	1977	102
1973	206	1978	100
1974	147	1979	98
1975	106	-	-

The secessionists had a baptism of fire when, after only a month in existence, they took out ESB electricians in a one-day lightning strike against 'over-supervision' by supervisors and assistants. It presaged a more significant action. On 7 September, the Association took out its members at the construction site of the ESB's new £15 million 'B' generating station at Ringsend. The dispute was provoked by the Board's refusal to recognise the IETA, but it also involved issues of continuity of employment, site money for apprentices, travelling allowances and other matters. The ESB maintained that its hands were tied by the binding agreements it had with the ETU, NEETU and ATGWU, which gave those unions the sole right to negotiate for ESB electricians. The Board was in an unenviable position: if it refused recognition, then there would be a stoppage; if it granted recognition, it would violate its agreement with the three other unions who would then be forced to enter official dispute with the company. The IETA was isolated from the beginning: it had only ten of the ESB's one thousand electricians and most unions there vigorously opposed it as a troublesome, breakaway organisation; ICTU refused to recognise it for the same reasons. The ETU was horrified by 'the sheer callousness and irresponsibility of ... the IETA ... any organisation that fails to balance the consequences of its actions against ... the common good is not worthy of recognition by committed trade unionists.'[63] Only one of the eighteen unions at the ESB – the Shift Workers' Association, an unofficial body – ordered their members not to pass the IETU's pickets.[64] Nevertheless, its action reportedly received 'massive support' from ESB workers on the ground.[65] The IETA subsequently extended its picketing to the 'A' generating station at the Pidgeon House and the North Wall station. At the Pidgeon House, one hundred workers refused to pass pickets despite being ordered to do so by their unions, leading to serious power cuts across the country.[66] When the IETA extended its pickets to four provincial stations, it threatened to create a 'national power emergency.'[67] At its peak, over 450,000 people were affected as 60 per cent of the country's electricity supply was cut off, grinding the economy to a halt. ICTU intervention brought a resumption of work on 13 September. The IETA had suspended, but not terminated, its strike at the ESB.[68]

Immediately afterwards, however, the skirmish between the NEETU and ETU on the one hand and the IETA on the other spilled over into the new Bank of Ireland site on Baggot Street. Sixty NEETU and ETU electricians withdrew their labour after the IETA tried to recruit there.[69] Inter-union talks under the auspices of ICTU collapsed when the IETA demanded immediate recognition from Congress and the ESB Group of Unions, which neither could accept. The IETA's pugnaciousness elicited a strong response from both the FUE and the government. The latter revived the defunct 1966 Trade Union Bill, albeit without the most controversial elements, by making it the basis of the Trade Union Act 1971. The Act sought to deter the establishment of breakaway unions by making it more difficult to obtain a negotiating licence. Unions would now have to deposit a minimum of £5,000 to the High Court, certify at least five hundred members and wait eighteen months after application before a licence could be issued. The FUE criticised the legislation as insufficiently stringent.[70]

As well as seeking recognition, the IETA also demanded that the ESB revoke the redundancies of eight IETA members. The dispute continued into 1972 and brought the country to the brink of more national power outages. On 15 June, having threatened to down tools the previous month, the IETA went on a one-day strike and picketed nine ESB generating stations to secure recognition. This 'damp squib strike' was ineffective because the shift workers passed the pickets. The IETA had been the only organisation to support the shift workers' April 1972 strike and had refused to scab (which ICTU had allowed). The Association assumed that the solidarity would be reciprocated.[71] Lack of recognition crippled the IETA – even its apprentices were being let go by the ESB when they finished their time. The union knew it needed allies. In late 1972, it balloted its members on joining forces with the National Busmen's Union, the Post Office Officials' Association, the Psychiatric Nurses' Association and the ESB Shift Workers' Association to create an unofficial federation of unions outside ICTU control. In November 1973, talks between these unions culminated in the formation of the Irish Trade Union Federation without the IETA as a founding member.[72] To make matters worse, the shift workers – whom the Association had hoped to recruit – disbanded their union in favour of joining NEETU. NEETU's gain was also a defeat for the ATGWU, who had been hopeful of enlisting the shift workers. The ATGWU withdrew from the ESB Group of Unions in protest, complaining to ICTU that the transfer did not conform to Congress rules. Congress dismissed the complaint. No employer ever recognised the IETA which faded into obscurity from 1973 as a result. In 1981, it caused another power outage at the ESB for recognition, the last sting of a dying wasp. After another period in the wilderness, the IETA quietly dissolved itself in 1994.[73]

Table 55: IETA Membership, 1980-92.[74]

Year (31 Dec.)	Membership	Year (31 Dec.)	Membership
1980	97	1987	25
1981	96	1988	25
1982	87	1989	30
1983	60	1990	33
1984	29	1991	33
1985	27	1992	33
1986	26	-	

The ETU. 1967-76

The 1967-76 period was transformative for the ETU. Industrialisation and economic expansion continued to produce a sturdy growth in the number of electricians, which led it to embrace a more inclusive definition of electrical workers. It branched out to organise telephone and service engineers, instrument mechanics, electronic technicians and others.[75] Consequently, ETU membership expanded by an impressive 55.5 per cent during these years. Growth forced the executive to re-evaluate how the union was structured and how it could best meet the rapid changes taking place in electrical work. It concluded that it needed more officials. In 1967, it appointed a second fulltime official, an assistant general secretary, to be paid the same as a senior ESB electrician plus 12.5 per cent. In June 1973, the REC appointed another assistant general secretary, Frank O'Reilly, to look after the Dublin branches.[76] The Dublin branches had previously revolted when the NEC proposed to employ a fulltime general president to be appointed by the NEC rather than elected by the members. Branch officials called the move 'a takeover', the result of 'a small group' not 'acting in the union's best interest' who had 'gone power crazy under the illusion they can sweep all opposition off the road.'[77] Lynch believed suspected that the proposal would 'split the union in two and cause chaos.'[78] The opposition convinced the NEC to quietly drop the plan. The branches also opposed the REC's decision to accept the ESB Officers' Association's affiliation to the ETU because it was comprised of clerical workers.[79] Members did, however, support their union's readmittance to Congress in 1967. There was an element of cynicism in re-joining ICTU. As one REC official put it, 'we are being stymied by the ... IEIETU and by being in Congress we may be able to do something about it.'[80] By then, the ETU had eighteen branches, six of which were in Dublin. James McConway was elected general secretary in 1966 and James Egan became general president in 1969.[81]

The NEC toyed with the idea of organising the union around each branch being an area of operation: FUE, ENJIC, ESB, instrumentation and telecommunications, supervisors and auxiliary.[82] The proposal was popular among the rank-and-file, with one notable exception. One branch was outraged by the formation of the 'Auxiliary Branch' and demanded that its name be changed to 'General Workers' Branch' because 'in the course of our history' the word auxiliary was 'repugnant to the vast majority of our people ... and the majority of our branch members.'[83] In 1976, the NEC resolved to geographically diffuse the union and strengthen its provincial branches. It invested more resources into the Kilkenny branch as it was being 'heavily neglected' and expanded the Tralee branch to include all of Co. Kerry. The investment yielded dividends: Table 56 illustrates the extent to which membership expanded over this period. To assist the recruitment drive, the NEC appointed another assistant general secretary and a fulltime Cork-based organiser for the southern area.[84] Growth also encouraged a friendlier view of NEETU: in 1972, the ETU explored for the first time the possibility of establishing a 'federation of engineering unions.' The following year, the NEC tried to 'initiate strenuous efforts to re-organise and unite the trade by entering into negotiations with other unions catering for electricians and, if necessary, change the name of the union to achieve unity under one heading.'[85] The union's name did indeed change in 1974, but not because of union unity. That year, the British ETU became part of the Electrical, Electronic, Telecommunications and Plumbing Union (EETPU), allowing the Irish union to drop '(Ireland)' and become the 'Electrical Trades Union.' The Irish union could now completely distinguish itself from its British rival.

Table 56: ETU Membership, 1968-77.[86]

Year (31 Dec.)	Membership	Year (31 Dec.)	Membership
1967	4,620	1972	6,516
1968	4,727	1973	6,743
1969	5,104	1974	7,541
1970	5,903	1975	7,611
1971	6,500	1976	7,949

Relations with the ITGWU were also improving. In 1976, both unions signed a joint agreement recognising the other's right to organise in the electrical trade: the ETU would organise electricians and the ITGWU the operatives. Both agreed not to poach the other's members. Tom Heery, general secretary since 1969, was impressed with the ITGWU's sincerity and willingness to honour the commitment. Others were more sceptical, citing previous incidents of ITGWU poaching. George Swan, secretary of the Dublin No. 1 branch, pointed out that 'the policy of the ITGWU is OBU and, whatever they say, this remains their policy.' Some wanted an agreement with the ITGWU because 'what is at stake … is the existence of the ETU as a separate entity.'[87] Negotiations were prompted by the ITGWU's closed shop agreements – which the ETU's Waterford branch decried as 'the menace facing our union' – after a February 1976 membership dispute between the two at Braun's in Co. Carlow led the ETU to blacken the factory.[88] The ETU was the only craft union not to operate closed shops, which the NEC was determined to change. It insisted on clauses in the agreement protecting its 'special position' in organising electricians. Both unions would negotiate together on issues of joint interest but would do so separately on issues specific to each union (e.g., productivity deals for electricians). But it was not enough to convince some of the ETU's more craft conscious leaders. 'Bro. Richards felt that in negotiations members of a general union were a hindrance to craft unions, that semiskilled workers were getting as much as skilled electricians.' The NEC subsequently debated a resolution to 'adopt in principle a decision to amalgamate with another craft'; an amendment sought a merger with the ITGWU.[89] Although both were heavily defeated, they indicated that some at the grassroots were questioning their union's future. Closed shops remained a contentious issue for the rest of the decade. Richards had previously argued that 'if we do not amalgamate with a union of our choice in the near future, we will be swallowed up... We will have no choice in the future.'[90]

Despite technological development, electrical work remained hazardous in the 1970s. In late 1973, the executive endorsed the ESB electricians' refusal to connect electricity to three to four hundred new houses because the wiring work was being done by non-union, and therefore poor quality, labour. The ETU had long pressed for tighter control over electrical installation work to ensure that safety standards were complied with, which is why it wanted a register of electricians.[91] As it warned the public:

> The installation standards in this country over recent years have declined so alarmingly as to constitute a public danger. There have never been mandatory standards or testing requirements relating to electrical installations in this country and this, coupled with the fact that non-qualified people are engaging in electrical work, has brought about the present action by electricians... The introduction of competition certificates from 1 January 1974 will not in itself rectify the appalling situation which has grown up, but nevertheless, it is welcomed by the ETU.[92]

The dispute continued well into 1974. Two years later, the union undertook to organise other workers in the electrical industry – such as those dealing with instruments and electronics – 'to maintain its numerical strength with the advancement of electrical technology in industry.'[93]

Managing unofficial strikes was as difficult for the ETU executive as it was for NEETU. In late 1970, a dispute between shop floor militants and a cautious executive nearly crippled the country's economy during its busiest period. That November, ETU men at Fleet Street staged a 'stay-at-home' strike against unsuitable lunchbreak conditions. The following month, electricians issued an unofficial work-to-rule at the ESB station in Sligo against having to perform clerical duties. Over two hundred electricians in five major ESB regions soon followed suit. The men – whom the ESB suspended – then demanded that their union submit a wage claim for parity with the clerks, for which they would down tools if necessary. The executive refused to do so. At the height of the dispute, electricians in Sligo, Galway, Drogheda, Dundalk, Athlone, Waterford and Limerick were involved. Chaos over the New Year period was avoided when the men's leader, Tom Gilmartin, convinced them to return to work and pursue their grievances through the usual channels. Discontent dragged on into 1971, further imperilling national power supplies.[94] The wage discrepancy with clerks remained an abiding grievance for electricians for many years thereafter.[95]

The sluggish economy nudged the ETU to the left and convinced it the adopt a programme of greater state intervention in the economy. The initiative of employers, many of whom were taking advantage of the recession by using apprentices to do journeymen's work, could not be relied upon to reduce unemployment. In 1976, the union attacked the government's proposals on worker participation in the running of state enterprises as 'totally ineffective and likely to lead to a situation where the workers' representatives would be used as 'fall guys' for decisions which would not be in the interests of the workers in the semi-state industries.' Instead, the union wanted to see companies run by boards of management two-third of whom were elected by and from trade unionists with the rest appointed by the government. It also campaigned for the reintroduction of protective tariffs to maintain jobs and reduce unemployment. But there were limits to the radicalism: the NEC opposed calls from branches to adopt as official policy the nationalisation of the electrical contracting industry.[96]

The national wage agreements

Between 1970 and 1978, ICTU concluded seven annual wage agreements through the Employer-Labour Conference. While the first five NWAs were bipartite, the last two were tripartite.[97] The 1975 and 1977 agreements framed fiscal policy to supplement awards in pay, blurring the lines between bipartism and tripartism. The tripartite 'National Understanding for Social and Economic Development' of 1979 sought to integrate government economic policy and wage formation, further accelerating the drive towards Social Partnership. It was novel in being a two-tier agreement, the first pertaining to pay and the second to specific objectives in policy on taxation, education healthcare and housing.[98] Though Congress backed every agreement, the structure of the Irish labour movement was decentralised, giving the ICTU executive little authority over individual unions. While large, general unions like the ITGWU and the WUI supported the national wage agreements system, smaller craft unions like the EETPU and the Irish Union of Woodworkers opposed them, as did the ATGWU. The ETU supported only two NWAs (1970 and 1978) and NEETU only one (1978). Employers were similarly divided on the NWAs. While the Confederation of Irish Industry (a loose umbrella body for employer groups) supported the NWAs, it had no direct influence over its affiliates and its support for centralised economic agreements was often not shared by its constituent members. The FUE, the dominant employer organisation, resisted the agreements. The FUE did not have a coherent strategy in the 1970s. Instead, it was a resource for individual employers to promote their version of industrial relations. The diverse nature of Irish industry, which included a spectrum of high and low technological sectors, also mitigated against the ability of employers to adopt a common front.[99] The number of cases referred to the Labour Court quadrupled under the NWAs as both sides were infuriated by the regular violations of the agreements.

Congress ratified the first NWA without a vote from affiliates. The ETU nonetheless supported the agreement because the 'wages of craftworkers have moved very little in the past ten years. Semiskilled categories were earning as much and, in some cases, more than craftworkers.'[100] But it was so outraged by the next NWA that it considered withdrawing from ICTU because Congress had 'foisted' the agreement upon it, thereby frustrating 'the expressed will of the members and executive of this union.' A supporter of disaffiliation asserted that the ETU was 'just a voice in the wilderness in Congress. We do not need Congress. The electricians' wages are a disgrace. We have our identity.'[101] NEETU's Dublin members rejected the second NWA by a massive 85 per cent margin and revised terms 10:1. The rejections caused considerable surprise in the media because Cassidy was one of the ICTU representatives on the Employer-Labour Conference responsible for the draft.[102] NEETU's leadership had no choice but to reject the plan. There was internal disunity on the NWAs. Although Cassidy told the 1972 Congress that NEETU supported the principle of the NWA system, McConnell told delegates that it 'was opposed to a series of agreements per se. Hours and conditions of work should be negotiated freely.'[103] By the mid-1970s, the NWAs were coming under pressure as inflation soared and employers pressed for wage restraint at a time when real incomes per capita were growing by just 1 per cent a year.[104] The 1974 agreement was rejected by every ETU branch because the wages increases it contained were inadequate.[105] 'There are general workers sweeping the floor on a better rate than electricians', one member claimed.[106] NEETU's sixteen Dublin branches (whose combined membership was six thousand) rejected the agreement by a three-to-one margin. At its REC's instigation, NEETU members also rejected the 1976 agreement.[107] ETU men did likewise even though their REC had recommended acceptance 'in view of the numbers unemployment in the country and the number of our members on fixed incomes.'[108] By then, both unions had become critical of the system. NEETU had concluded that the NWAs 'depressed living standards' while the ETU accused them of 'creating further disparities between groups of workers.'[109]

Table 57: Consumer Price Index, 1969-81 (mid-November 1968=100).[110]

Year (mid-November)	All Items	Year (mid-November)	All Items
1969	107.6	1976	265.2
1970	118.4	1977	293.8
1971	128.6	1978	317.1
1972	139.2	1979	367.7
1973	156.8	1980	434.7
1974	188.2	1981	536.1
1975	219.9		

Table 58: National Wage Agreements, 1971-80.[111]

Year	Outcome
1971	Two phases over eighteen months: first, £2 a week, with women on minimum of £1.70; and second, 4 per cent, with automatic adjustment for increase in consumer price index (CPI)
1972	Phased agreement over seventeen months: first, 9 per cent on basic pay up to £30, 7 per cent on next £10 and 4 per cent on remainder; second, 4 per cent after twelve months on basic pay with automatic adjustments for increases in the CPI
1974	First phase, 9 per cent on first £30, 7 per cent on next £10, 6 per cent on next £10; min. hourly wage of £2.40; second, 4 per cent plus 60p.
1975	First phase, 8 per cent with min. of 2 per cent plus quarter of 1972 NWA; second, 5 per cent, minimum increase of £1; third, no increase except a quarter of second phase of 1972 NWA; fourth, 2.8 per cent
1976	3 per cent on basic pay plus £2 subject to max. of £5 a week or £3 if greater

Year	Outcome
1977	First phase, 2.5 per cent plus £1, min. increase of £2 a week, max. £5; second, same increases as first phase, giving max. increase of £4.23
1978	First phase, 8 per cent, min. increase of £3.50 a week; second, 2 per cent
1979	First National Understanding: First phase, 9 per cent, min. increase of £5.50; second, 2 per cent plus amount relating to movement in the CPI, min. increase of £3.50
1980	Second National Understanding: first phase, 8 per cent plus £1 a week; second, 7 per cent

NEETU and the Northern Troubles

In the 1960s, a cohort of young Marxists seized control of the republican movement and pushed it to the left. Marxism-Leninism and contemporary anti-imperialist struggles, they argued, provided a roadmap to finally end British rule in Ireland. Their goal was to transform the IRA from a 'bourgeois nationalist' force into a class-conscious proletarian army able to unite workers from across the sectarian divide. To achieve this, the IRA and Sinn Féin needed to embrace class politics by involving themselves in social agitation of which trade unions were a perfect crystallisation. The turn encountered fierce opposition from 'traditionalists' who opposed any move from armed struggle and towards socialist politics. In December 1969 and January 1970, the movement split into Official (Marxist) and Provisional (traditionalist) wings. It was a bitter schism that impacted all strands of the left, including the unions.[112] From the early 1970s, the ferocity of the Troubles caused many in the Republic to publicly question the moral character of militant Irish republicanism. Horrified by the carnage, labour was inevitably influenced by this intellectual trend. Union commemoration of the Irish revolution became noticeably less militant. In 1972, the Dublin Council of Trade Unions (DCTU) abandoned the firing-party at its annual Connolly Commemoration. This was partly because of the declining number of 1916-23 veterans, but also reflected increased state security measures on the use of firearms and the increasingly toxic association of physical force republicanism with the Provisional IRA.[113]

The Troubles gave Congress and thirty-two-county unions an unenviable task in maintaining working-class unity in the North amid ethno-sectarian conflict. With its several political factions, NEETU was heavily impacted by the Troubles and occasionally diverged from ICTU's silence on it. Like the rest of Irish society, the union deplored 'the catastrophe that befell the people of Derry' on Bloody Sunday in 1972. It closed head office for a day as a mark of respect to the victims and to participate in the protest march from the Garden of Remembrance to the British Embassy.[114] The ETU was more measured, asking its members to contribute an hour's pay to ICTU's Northern relief fund to protest the 'circumstances under which British troops operated against the people of Northern Ireland.'[115] Two years later, NEETU called on ICTU to campaign for the return of the Price sisters from Britain and signed an open letter to Prime Minister Harold Wilson demanding British 'disengagement' from the North.[116] On 4 October 1975, NEETU and ETU representatives participated in a march through Limerick protesting the IRA's kidnapping of Tiede Herrema the day prior. Herrema was a Dutch industrialist who owned Ferenka, a wire factory that was the city's biggest employer with 1,400 workers. Both unions signed a statement demanding Herrema 'immediate release and return to his wife and family unharmed' as he was 'regarded in the highest esteem by all.'[117] A few days later, Limerick shop stewards travelled to Dublin to hold an all-night protest vigil outside ICTU's headquarters for Congress to demand his safe return.[118] Herrema's popularity resulted from his kidnap rather than his charity as employer: conditions at Ferenka were notoriously poor and its regime rigidly authoritarian. Ferenka closed in 1977 after a seven-week strike over working conditions.[119]

In January 1975, Danny Ryan, national organiser for Clann na hÉireann, Official Sinn Féin's counterpart in Britain, was deported from Britain to Ireland under the Prevention of Terrorism Act 1974 'for his socialist republican activities.'[120] The deportation resulted from the British government's heavy crackdown on Irish republican organisations after the Birmingham Bombing. After his deportation, he joined NEETU's Dublin No. 1 Branch and was appointed an internal auditor of union accounts. Kevin McConnell denied Ryan had been legitimately appointed and refused to pay his expenses for union work. It was part of a broader struggle McConnell was waging (see Chapter 10). As a young man, McConnell had participated in the 1956-62 Border Campaign and was very sympathetic to the Provisionals. Ryan's politics were therefore an anathema to him, and they undoubtedly coloured McConnell's perception of him.[121] McConnell worked indefatigably as a republican campaigner. He and Jimmy Hynes, also an NEC member, served on the Committee of Trade Unionists Against the Criminal Law (Jurisdiction) Bill 1975. This controversial bill – which had been agreed as part of the 1974 Sunningdale Agreement – allowed for trial in the Republic for crimes committed in the North and vice versa.[122]

The apprenticeship system in the 1970s

The apprenticeship system experienced seismic changes during the 1970s, as government and employer-led calls to reduce the period of apprenticeship became overwhelming. AnCo was highly dissatisfied with the Irish apprenticeship system. While the number of craftsmen had grown from 17,942 in 1945 to 32,485 by 1970, an 81 per cent increase, the economy was suffering a skills shortage by the early 1970s. Although the number of electrical apprentices had expanded from 1,686 in 1966 to 2,723 in 1974, and the number of engineering apprentices had grown 1,759 to 3,012 over the same period, the intake of apprentices was simply insufficient to cater for the anticipated economic development.[123] In 1973, AnCo released a discussion document that proposed reducing apprenticeships to three years, opening them to adults and females, and intake quotas. The unions opposed these measures because they would increase the supply of craftsmen, control over which would be taken away from the unions. The ETU told AnCo that specialised training over three years would produce operatives rather than craftsmen and that it was placing too much emphasis on moulding the man for industry instead of developing him as an individual.[124] The unions were warmer to the AnCo's ideas for apprentice education, which included mandating apprentices to attend fulltime off-the-job training in their first year in specialised areas. This could happen in vocational schools, in industry or in

AnCO training centres. Industrial conditions and disciplines would apply in these centres and the emphasis would be on training and not on production. Training centres were an increasingly common part of the apprenticeship process and AnCo now sought to expedite this development. Apprentices would follow a holistic planned training syllabus with an educational component including testing procedures. They would spend the remainder of their time acquiring 'on-the-job' experience. There would be a system of compulsory testing and certification to national standards for apprentices, after which AnCo would issue a National Craft Certificate. AnCo issued a National Apprentice Curricula for fitters in November 1981.[125]

The ceding of control was too much for the ETU and it thus opposed the proposals. So too did the construction unions, the teachers' unions and the VECs, but NEETU, the AUEW and the employers supported it. AnCo was proposing to open the crafts to people other than the sons of craftsmen. Many were horrified at the prospect, viewing it as another example of how modernity was degrading their trade. The ETU was especially vituperative. At a 1974 NEC meeting to discuss the plans, one delegate called the proposals 'a subtle attack, concerted and continuous on the craft unions ... the status of the craftworker is being whittled away, and eventually people are going to say that if you can train a craftsman in three years then you should be able to train a craftsman in two years, and what is a craftsman anyway? I think we should stand our ground, and not join with the enemy.' Three-year apprenticeships already existed in Germany and France. Another believed that AnCo would enforce the three-year apprenticeship 'if they could get away with it' so that they could 'flood the industry' – 'this is the whole idea.' 'We will be going back to the 1930s and 1940s where an employer ... can come along and pick his men.' Swan agreed but acknowledged that the public would not.[126] There were murmurs of acceptance in some quarters from those who realised that the battle had been lost. Their argument was simple: However unpalatable, state operation of the apprenticeship system was now a reality, and it was inevitable that the trades would have to cede more control. The conflict between modernisers and conservatives manifested itself vividly in the ETU, whose NEC and REC clashed on the issue.

In October 1975, AnCo announced that the four-year apprenticeship would commence from 1 September 1976 with full implementation by 1981. By then, apprentices would work a 34¾-hour week instead of a forty-hour one, which employers opposed. In May 1976, the ETU NEC met to discuss the new situation. Bro. McLeod informed his colleagues that, 'while they were discussing a four-year apprenticeship, the three-year apprenticeship was already in Britain. He had no doubt that the same thing would come in here unless we 'put the boot in' now.' The British craft unions, he noted, had already notified the FUE that they would enter official dispute with it unless it supported the four-year apprenticeship. Swan believed that they would have to contend with a three-year apprenticeship because 'we would be taking on society. We would be seen as the people who would not contribute.'[127] One delegate wanted the ETU to affiliate to a political party to regain control of apprenticeships. Another believed that union should stand up to and say, 'no to ANCO because 'we ... are the people who ultimately train these apprentices... we are the custodians of the craft.' The ETU and AnCo also clashed over the 3:1 ratio of apprentices to journeymen in the electrical industry: the union wanted to see that ratio in every industry, which ANCO resisted. The ETU's Cork branch had adopted a policy of non-cooperation with AnCo and had closed the trade for twelve months, which many on the NEC admired. Christopher Kidd even argued that the union should call a national strike if necessary. The NEC mandated the REC to 'urgently initiative whatever action is necessary' to combat the four-year apprenticeship.[128]

The REC refused to carry out the order because it felt that the NEC needed to 'recognise the realities of the situation in the trade, having regard to government legislation regarding the shorter apprenticeship period.' The REC accepted the four-year apprenticeship 'to safeguard the best interests of our members and the electrical industry.'[129] AnCo introduced a voluntary three-year apprenticeship for leaving cert holders from 1 March 1977. The new system quickly proved popular among apprentices. In a 1977 study, only 5 per cent of apprentices trained under the new system felt that they would have been better trained under the old one, while 52 per cent of the 'traditional' apprentices would have liked to have gotten off-the-job training.[130] Apprentices continued to be paid a percentage of the basic craft rate: 30 per cent in the first year, 45 per cent in their second, 65 per cent in the third and 80 per cent in the fourth.

Chapter Notes and References

1   Cited in Diarmaid Ferriter, *Ambiguous Republic: Ireland in the 1970s* (London: Profile Books, 2012), p. 462.
2   Ibid.
3   Ernesto Screpanti, 'Long Cycles in Strike Activity: An Empirical Investigation', *British Journal of Industrial Relations*, Vol. XXV, No. 1, 1987, pp. 99-124; Mary E. Daly, *Sixties Ireland: Reshaping the Economy, State and Society, 1957-1973* (Cambridge: Cambridge University Press, 2016), p. 77.
4   *Irish Press*, 8 Dec. 1973.
5   O'Connor, *Labour History of Ireland* (2nd Ed.), p. 231.
6   Ferriter, *Ambiguous Republic*, pp. 460-464, 468-470, 480.
7   Eamonn Sweeney, *Down Deeper and Down: Ireland in the 70s & 80s* (Dublin: Gill & Macmillan, 2010), pp. 58-59.
8   NEETU REC minutes, 31 July, 4 Dec. 1968; NEETU Cork supervisors' branch minutes, 22 June 1970, TU/TE/1/8, TEEU collection, Cork City and County Archives.
9   'General secretary's report, 3, 4 June 1970', file: NEC 1970. See also NEETU REC minutes, 26 May, 22 Sept., 6 Oct., 3, 24 Nov. 1969, 16, 31 Mar. 1970.
10   Patrick Lalor, Dáil Éireann debates, 4 May 1972, Vol. 260, No. 11.
11   *Irish Independent*, 16 Apr. 1971.
12   Ibid.
13   Undated, unsigned notebook, NEETU steering committee minutes, 1972-74, File 14, box, TEEU collection, ILHM.
14   *Irish Press*, 1 Jan. 1975; Gene Fitzgerald, Dáil Éireann debates, 8 Nov. 1977, Vol. 301, No. 3.
15   *Irish Independent*, 30 Sept., 1 Oct. 1977; *Cork Examiner*, 30 Sept. 1977.
16   NEETU REC minutes, 9 June 1976, TEEU collection, ILHM; Kevin McConnell to branch secretaries, 19 May 1972, NEC 1970.
17   NEETU NEC minutes, 19 June 1976, TEEU collection, ILHM.
18   IEIETU, annual returns, 1964-70, T358, RSF records, CRO.
19   McCarthy, *The decade of upheaval*, p. 150; *Irish Independent*, 27 Jan. 1969.
20   *Irish Independent*, 14, 19, 27, 29 Oct. 1966.
21   McCarthy, *The decade of upheaval*, p. 154.
22   *Irish Independent*, 29 Oct. 1966.
23   Ibid., 27 Jan. 1969.
24   *Irish Times*, 1, 10 Oct.-6 Nov. 1968. The ETU did not support the strike.
25   McCarthy, *the decade of upheaval*, p. 156.

26 *Irish Independent*, 20 Jan.-6 Feb. 1969.
27 Ibid., 24-26 Jan., 5, 6 Feb. 1969
28 Tobin, *The best of decades*, p. 209.
29 *Cork Examiner*, 8 Feb. 1969; *Irish Press*, 11 Feb. 1969.
30 McCarthy, *the decade of upheaval*, p. 165.
31 Tobin, *The best of decades*, pp. 208-209.
32 *Irish Independent*, 12-14 Feb. 1969; NEETU REC minutes, 20 Nov. 1968, 29 Jan., 12 Feb. 1969.
33 *Irish Press*, 21 Feb.-15 Mar. 1969; NEETU REC minutes, 20, 28 Feb., 12, 19, 26 Mar., 2 Apr. 1969.
34 *Irish Press*, 27 Jan., 6 Feb. 1969; O'Connor, *A Labour History of Waterford*, pp. 317-319.
35 O'Connor, *Labour History of Ireland* (2nd Ed.), p. 223; Con Murphy, *Dispute between FUE and maintenance craft unions: report of inquiry* (Dublin: Stationary Office, 1969), pp. 34-36.
36 NEETU REC minutes, 3 Dec. 1969; *Irish Independent*, 6 Feb., 16, 23, 29 Apr., 29 May, 26 June 1970; *Irish Press*, 4 Feb., 17, 22 Apr., 1, 6 May, 29 June, 1 July 1971; ETU NEC minutes, 1, 2 Nov. 1971.
37 O'Connor, *Labour History of Ireland* (2nd Ed.), pp. 224-225.
38 *Irish Press*, 10 July 1970.
39 Ibid., 15 Feb. 1974, 12-14, 17 May 1977; NEETU REC minutes, 12, 18 May 1977.
40 O'Connor, *Labour History of Ireland* (2nd Ed.), p. 234.
41 O'Connor, *Labour History of Ireland* (2nd Ed.), pp. 223, 234.
42 *Irish Independent*, 9 Mar.-14 June 1971
43 *Cork Examiner*, 22, 24 Mar. 1973; *Irish Press*, 24 Mar., 8-11 May, 3 July 1973; *Evening Herald*, 26 Mar., 10, 23 May 1973; *Irish Independent*, 27 Mar., 4 July 1973.
44 *Irish Independent*, 21 Dec. 1973, 8, 15, 25 Jan., 21 Feb. 1974; *Irish Press*, 28 Feb. 1974
45 *Irish Press*, 4-15, 16 Feb., 1, 5 Mar. 1974.
46 Ibid., 5, 6 Mar. 1974.
47 Ibid., 7 Mar. 1974.
48 Ibid., 14, 16, 20, 21 Mar. 1974; ETU REC minutes, 7-21 Mar. 1974.
49 *Irish Press*, 26 Mar. 1974.
50 Ibid., 16-23 Apr. 1974; ETU REC minutes, 4-21 Apr. 1974.
51 *Irish Press*, 10, 14 Nov. 1972.
52 Ibid., 12 July-13 Aug., 28 Nov. 1974.
53 *Irish Independent*, 31 Oct.-6 Nov. 1975.
54 NEETU REC minutes, 10, 24 Mar., 2 Apr., 26 May, 2, 9, 23, 30 June 1976, TEEU collection, ILHM; *Irish Press*, 26, 29, 30 June, 2, 19, 24 July 1976; *Irish Independent*, 1, 6, 9 July 1976; *Evening Herald*, 5, 8 July 1976.
55 NEETU REC minutes, 17 Oct. 1979, TEEU collection, ILHM. Also see the same minutes for 8 Apr., 14 July, 15, 27 Sept., 13, 17 Oct. 1976.
56 *Irish Independent*, 9, 15 Apr. 1976; *Irish Press*, 19 July 1976.
57 *Irish Press*, 21, 22 Dec. 1976; *Irish Independent*, 23, 29-31 Dec. 1976, 4-14 Jan. 1977.
58 *Irish Press*, 13, 14 Jan., 3 Feb. 1977; *Cork Examiner*, 15, 31 Jan. 1977; *Evening Herald*, 21 Jan. 1977; *Irish Independent*, 2 Mar. 1977. NEETU REC minutes, 12 Jan., 2, 16 Feb. 1977, TEEU collection, ILHM.
59 Cited in Ferriter, *Ambiguous Republic*, p. 517.
60 Allen, *Fianna Fáil and Irish labour*, p. 125.
61 *Irish Independent*, 7 Apr. 1971; *Irish Press*, 13 June 1971.
62 IETA, annual returns, 1971-80, T553, RSF records, CRO.
63 ETU REC minutes, 14 Sept. 1971.
64 *Irish Independent*, 16 July 1971; *Irish Press*, 21, 23, 30, 31 Aug. 1971.
65 *Irish Independent*, 23 Sept. 1971.
66 *Irish Press*, 1-10 Sept. 1971.
67 Ibid., 11 Sept. 1971.
68 Ibid., 13, 15 Sept. 1971.
69 *Irish Independent*, 17 Sept. 1971.
70 Ibid., 8 Oct. 1971.
71 Ibid., 5 Feb., 29 Mar., 12, 17 Apr., 2, 3, 8-19 May, 9-16 June 1972.
72 *Irish Independent*, 11 Sept., 30 Oct., 12 Dec. 1972; *Irish Press*, 31 Oct., 4 Nov. 1972, 21 Nov. 11, 17 Dec. 1973; *Cork Examiner*, 15, 17, 18 Dec. 1973.
73 *Irish Independent*, 14 Nov., 19 Jan. 1973, 15 Feb. 1994; *Irish Press*, 8 Dec. 1973; *Cork Examiner*, 23 Sept. 1981.

74   IETA, annual returns, 1980-92, T553, RSF records, CRO.
75   John B. Smethurst & J.P.H. Carter (eds.), *Historical Directory of Trade Unions: Vol. 6: Including Unions in Building and Construction, Agriculture, Fishing, Chemicals, Wood and Woodworking, Transport, Engineering and Metal* (Farnham: Ashgate Publishing Company, 2009), p. 214
76   ETU NEC minutes, 6, 7 Nov. 1972, 26, 27 Apr. 1973; ETU REC minutes, 29 June 1973, TEEU collection, ILHM.
77   ETU REC minutes, 2 Mar. 1967.
78   ETU NEC minutes, 9 Apr. 1967, 12-14 Nov. 1969, 23-25 Oct. 1970.
79   Ibid., 4, 5 Feb., 26, 27 Aug. 1967.
80   ETU REC minutes, 9 Feb. 1967.
81   Ward-Perkins, *Trade Union Records*, p. 199; ETU NEC minutes, 12-14 Nov. 1969. In 1967, F. Maguire had defeated Patrick Murphy in the election for general president but could not take up the position because he was offered a job as a supervisor at Players, allowing Murphy to remain as president. See ETU REC minutes, 12, 26 Oct. 1967.
82   ETU NEC minutes, 23-25 Oct. 1970.
83   Ibid., 5, 6 Nov. 1973.
84   Ibid., 3, 4 May, 16 Nov. 1976.
85   Ibid., 6, 7 Nov. 1972, 26, 27 Apr. 1973, TEEU.
86   ETU annual returns, T453, RFS records, CRO.
87   ETU NEC minutes, 3, 4 May, 14-16 Nov. 1976.
88   Minutes of the first regional meeting of ETU southern branches, 22 Feb. 1976.
89   ETU NEC minutes, 16 Nov. 1976. For the dispute at Braun's, see *Irish Press*, 9 Feb. 1976; and *Cork Examiner*, 11 Feb. 1976.
90   ETU NEC minutes, 17-19 Nov. 1974.
91   *Irish Press*, 14 Dec. 1973, 30 July 1974. See also *Cork Examiner*, 14 Aug. 1974.
92   *Irish Independent*, 16 Dec. 1973.
93   Ibid., 16 Nov. 1976, TEEU collection, ILHM.
94   *Irish Independent*, 21 Aug.-5 Sept., 9-24 Dec. 1970, 15, 26 Jan. 1971.
95   *Irish Press*, 10 July 1974.
96   ETU NEC minutes, 5 Dec. 1976, TEEU collection, ILHM.
97   O'Connor, *Labour History of Ireland* (2nd Ed.), p. 233. For a thorough analysis of the NWAs, see James F. O'Brien, *A Study of National Wage Agreements in Ireland* (Dublin: ESRI, 1981). See also Noel Harris, *Challenge to Irish Trade Unionism: National Wage Agreements* (Dublin: Association of Scientific Technical and Managerial Staffs, 1973).
98   Andy Bielenberg & Raymond Ryan, *An Economic History of Ireland Since Independence* (London: Routledge, 2013), pp. 37-40; O'Connor, *A Labour History of Ireland* (2nd Ed.), p. 234.
99   Bielenberg & Ryan, *Economic History*, pp. 37-38.
100 ETU NEC minutes, 7 Feb. 1971.
101 ETU NEC minutes, 26, 27 Apr. 1973.
102 *Irish Independent*, 27 Jan., 19 June, 24 July 1972; *Irish Press*, 19, 20 June 1972.
103 *Irish Press*, 7, 27 July 1972; ICTU, *Annual Report for 1972*, ILHM, p. 495
104 O'Connor, *A Labour History of Ireland* (2nd Ed.), p. 234.
105 *Irish Press*, 26 Jan. 1974.
106 ETU NEC minutes, 17-19 Nov. 1974.
107 *Irish Press*, 9, 12, 26 Feb. 1974, 16, 21 June 1976; NEETU REC minutes, 16 June, 9 Sept. 1976, TEEU collection, ILHM.
108 ETU REC minutes, 10 Apr. 1975, 29 July 1976.
109 ICTU, *Annual Report for 1976*, ILHM, pp. 422-427.
110 CSO, *Statistical Abstract of Ireland* (Dublin: Stationary Office, 1975-83).
111 Devine, *Organising History*, p. 503.
112 For an excellent account of the split and its aftermath, see Brian Hanley & Scott Millar, *The Lost Revolution: The Story of the Official IRA and the Workers' Party* (Dublin: Penguin Ireland, 2009).
113 Cody, O'Dowd & Rigney, *The Parliament of Labour*, pp. 225-229. See also Brian Hanley, *The Impact of the Troubles on the Republic of Ireland, 1968-79: Boiling Volcano?* (Manchester: Manchester University Press, 2018); and Ferriter, *Ambiguous Republic*, pp. 120-215.
114 *Cork Examiner*, 2 Feb. 1972.
115 ETU (Ireland) REC minutes, 10 Feb. 1972.
116 *Evening Herald*, 1 Feb., 28 Jan. 1974.

117 *Irish Independent*, 4 Oct. 1975. NEETU and the ETU had the right to negotiate on behalf of the factory's craftsmen since 1973. See *Irish Independent*, 28 Aug. 1973.
118 *Irish Press*, 6 Oct. 1975.
119 Sweeney, *Down*, pp. 130-132.
120 NEETU NEC minutes, 16 June 1979, TEEU collection, ILHM.
121 Ibid; *Irish Press*, 31 Dec. 1974, 25 Jan. 1975.
122 *Irish Press*, 24 Nov. 1975.
123 ETU NEC minutes, 31 Oct.-2 Nov. 1981.
124 Ryan, 'Apprenticeship in Ireland', p. 418.
125 Ibid., pp. 398-456.
126 ETU NEC minutes, 17-19 Nov. 1974.
127 ETU NEC minutes, 3, 4 May 1976, TEEU collection, ILHM.
128 Ibid.
129 ETU REC minutes, 27 Mar. 1977, TEEU collection, ILHM.
130 Ryan, 'Apprenticeships in Ireland', pp. 469-476.

9

Chaos at 6 Gardiner Row, 1976-92

NEETU's experience between 1976 and 1991 mirrors that of the country. Initially brimming with optimism, its fortunes degenerated into unprecedented crises before experiencing an unlikely resurrection. NEETU underwent internal convulsions not experienced by any union since the split between Jim Larkin and the ITGWU executive in 1924. From the mid-1970s to the early 1990s, the NEETU executive was embroiled in a constant struggle with Kevin McConnell, its financial general secretary, fighting much of it in the courts. McConnell presented himself as a champion of integrity, battling corruption within the union and protecting it from crooked officials. The executive deplored both his claims and his refusal to accept its authority and did their utmost to get rid of him. The conflict did enormous damage to the union. Huge legal bills brought it to the brink of bankruptcy and members fled rather than support a dysfunctional organisation whose errant officials were as likely to be in the High Court as the Labour Court, all while employers were demanding redundancies and wage cuts. By the late 1980s, the executive was exasperated. Hamstrung by its own rules, which prohibited it from sacking McConnell, it was desperate for a way out. Unexpectedly, an old enemy provided the light to reach the end of a very dark tunnel.

The McConnell saga, part one

At its first official NEC meeting, Fullerton told his colleagues that establishing NEETU became a decade-long ordeal due to legal troubles 'and other difficulties.'[1] He was correct to mention the 'other difficulties' NEETU faced, difficulties that were far more costly and damaging than amalgamation. Any hope that the union would have a smooth birth was ruined by the legal and personal battles taking place between McConnell and the other members of its executive, the first of many. In December 1974, McConnell had been elected financial general secretary. Very shortly into his term, however, he began to regularly miss REC meetings, frustrating the running of the union and causing friction between him and the rest of the executive. And head office began to receive a litany of complaints from branches about the service they received from McConnell. By early 1976, his colleagues had had enough. On 4 February, after being absent at a meeting he had promised to attend, Joseph Carter, 'wished to be recorded as saying that he was totally dissatisfied with the attitude of the financial general secretary to this executive.' He moved, and Bro. Hurley seconded, that McConnell be removed from office 'for his non-compliance with the rules.' But Carter withdrew his motion after discussion. Eleven days later, however, McConnell was indeed removed from office for failure to obey union rules and carry out REC directives. Larry O'Neill took over as financial general secretary and Joe Moneley became acting industrial general secretary. As per the legal advice it had received, the REC ordered McConnell to vacate 6 Gardiner Row and to hand back the union property (minutes books for 1973-75) he had removed from office.[2] McConnell refused because he did not recognise his suspension as legitimate. Consequently, the union went to the

High Court to obtain an injunction removing him from the premises.[3] Fullerton told the High Court that McConnell 'had annoyed and incensed' NEETU members and was 'creating antagonism towards the union and its officers.' Justice McWilliams granted the union their injunction.[4]

Before the conflict could escalate any further, the ICTU executive intervened. McConnell undertook to carry out all duties of the office of financial general secretary and to hand back union property. Should disagreement arise, NEETU's general secretaries and general president would discuss the matter. Failing agreement, the issue would be referred to a third party. McConnell was reinstated as financial general secretary and Larry O'Neill became industrial general secretary again. Within days, however, the settlement nearly collapsed when McConnell refused to hand over the minute books. Although it is not recorded in the minutes, he appears to have handed back the books, probably because the union threatened him with more legal action.[5]

McConnell's reinstatement did not improve his poor relationship with the rest of the executive. In August, he aggravated his colleagues again when he took holiday leave without informing or getting approval from the REC, resulting in there being no money to pay staff that week. By mid-September, McConnell was still not attending REC meetings. Nobody knew where he was. *Independent Newspapers* had closed the union's account and was taking legal action against it to recoup unpaid bills. The REC accused McConnell of abusing his position after he placed a notice without authority on the door of the financial office stating that no expenses would be paid during the ongoing bank strike (28 June to 6 September 1976). The REC asked him to account for his actions, but he refused to do so. Its patience ran out and they initiated legal proceedings against him in accordance with the terms of the recent settlement.[6] It fined McConnell £5 for responding to the charges against him via a solicitor's letter rather than defend himself in person. On 20 October, McConnell returned to the REC, claiming to have answered the charges in writing even though nobody else had seen this letter. Afterwards, McConnell began to skip meetings again. Additionally, he still had union property in his possession. In December, the REC fined him again for not handing over correspondence addressed to the industrial general secretary to Moneley, who was filling in for Larry O'Neill while he was on annual leave.[7] But the row dissipated and so the REC kept McConnell as their financial general secretary. The following year, however, he would not be so lucky.

In February 1977, the REC had a new gripe with McConnell – expenses. Union officials complained that McConnell would not pay expenses and were unhappy that the financial office had to sign off on every item, arguing that expenses should be paid on submission of same. McConnell suspected that the expenses procedure was being abused and that many claims were illegitimate. His appearances at REC meetings were still sporadic and he was often not present when his performance as financial general secretary was discussed. There were also complaints about his inefficiency in producing contribution cards. Claiming dereliction of duty, the REC seized the opportunity to get rid of its troublesome financial officer once again. On 9 March, it suspended McConnell with pay after he failed to attend a meeting to which he had been summoned. Two days later, the NEC voted nine to five to remove him from office and temporarily appointed Tommy White in his place. McConnell had supporters and sympathisers throughout the union. O'Hanlon moved an amendment that

McConnell appear before the next NEC to answer the charges made against him. It was defeated by the same margin.[8]

McConnell had gone on holidays in early March, which is why, he believed, the REC waited until then to sack him. The REC maintained it had given him adequate notice of his summoning and that McConnell had not informed it of his intention to take a holiday, which he denied. McConnell did not recognise his suspension and arrived at 6 Gardiner Row every morning to administrate NEETU's financial business, thereby 'disrupting and hindering the management and conduct of the union's affairs.'[9] He retained keys and books belonging to the union and was forcibly preventing White from doing what the REC had directed him to do. Infuriated that McConnell was 'occupying' the financial office, the REC took the legal route once more. On 25 March, the High Court granted the NEETU's three trustees – Carter, Sylvester Sheridan and Eustace Connolly – an injunction restraining McConnell from 'trespassing' on the union's premises and from removing any property therein. This latest attempt was, McConnell suspected, a deliberate, pre-arranged attempt to sack him when the REC knew he was in no position to defend himself. Thus, he had been denied constitutional justice because he had not been allowed have a representative cross-examine those making the allegations. The injunction was lifted when McConnell agreed to return the keys and minute books in the presence of both his and the union's solicitors. McConnell immediately issued a counterclaim for reinstatement, claiming he had been denied natural justice. He was successful. In June, the High Court declared his suspension invalid and awarded him his lost wages in damages.[10]

McConnell's thriftful handling of his office continued to fuel conflict between him and the executive. Throughout 1977, members complained about his refusal to pay expenses. He had also taken another holiday in August which, the REC asserted, he had no right to do as he had made no request to do so. In October, it once again charged McConnell with dereliction of duty on three counts: absence without leave, failure to pay expenses and not supplying the Dublin No. 4 Branch with an up-to-date register despite being requested to do so. The following month, McConnell appeared before the REC to answer the allegations. He did so in a written reply having received legal advice not to respond verbally.[11] At a subsequent hearing, McConnell declared that one official had confessed that the executive wanted to sack their him and that they would 'make no mistakes this time.' McConnell was not the only one to suspect conspiracy. Christopher Duffy stated that he had heard the same official tell someone that 'McConnell would have to go.'[12]

In the spring of 1979, McConnell renewed his attacks against the union leadership in a letter of reply. On 23 March, the NEC met and, after having considered the letter, agreed that 'McConnell should be disciplined, and some felt even to go as far as dismissal... its contents were an insult to the delegates who ... had travelled long distances to ... find that there were no accounts available.'[13] The letter – which McConnell had circulated across the union – accused Fullerton of waging a campaign of intimidation and harassment against him. McConnell had not attended this meeting despite being summoned to it. On 7 April, he appeared before the NEC to answer the charges but left within minutes because the meeting decided to deal with a request from the fulltime officials for a salary increase first. In his absence, the NEC suspended him with pay, effective from 27 April 1979, and again appointed White to act in his place.[14] McConnell refused to accept its authority to dismiss him because, he alleged, the NEC was not constituted in accordance with union rules and there were members sitting on it who should not have been there. The conflict had become a struggle for control. As Pat O'Neill asked, 'who was running the union? … McConnell or the NEC?'[15] McConnell was not the only one to reject the NEC's constitution. Jim Rossiter, an NEC member for the Wexford branch, threatened to leave the union and take his branch with him as he believed that the Dublin delegates were not properly comprised. Executive meetings had become dysfunctional – and not just because of McConnell. Members regularly attended meetings with, and under the influence of, alcohol, especially Pat O'Neill. When one NEC man tried to prohibit this, Fullerton advised him that his motion to suspend anyone attending meetings intoxicated was unenforceable![16] O'Neill had previously worked as an electrician in England where he joined the ETU (UK), forming part of its Communist bloc. He was heavily implicated in the ballot rigging scandal and perjured himself in the High Court case on same, with the presiding judge calling him a 'inveterate liar.'

In May 1979, Hynes claimed that the saga with McConnell 'was affecting the running of the union which we had set out to make the strongest engineering union in the country.'[17] He was correct. That March, delegates from the EETPU's Irish membership had approached NEETU to discuss a merger, having long been unhappy with their union. Their Dublin official had spoken unofficially with the ITGWU about the Transport Union taking over the twenty-six-county membership, but the EETPU's Ireland Management Committee in Belfast had stopped this. There are several reasons why NEETU entertained the prospect of amalgamation, the strongest being the desire to increase membership and eliminate a rival. The enduring survival of craft consciousness was another reason, as Larry O'Neill demonstrated when he 'referred to the encroachment of general unions into the craft sector' and how 'a big union could combat this.' Another benefit was that the new card would be recognised in the UK, facilitating members who may need to emigrate for work.[18] Although they started well, the talks quickly fell apart. Tony Murray believed the EETPU was not interested in merging on equal terms with NEETU. Hurley felt that any merger at this time was highly inopportune 'due to our own internal problems' which 'the efforts of the NEC and REC should be directed at solving.' Connolly agreed. Duffy opposed merger with any British union because Irish members had to sever connection with their union before progress could be made. Hanlon gave the most colourful argument against the merger, asserting that 'the members who founded this union did so to set up an Irish union and would turn in their graves if they thought this union were to join with an English-based union.' Though Carter maintained that the goal of negotiations was not to 'sell out' members but 'to form a thirty-two county Irish-based engineering union', his colleagues did not buy it and the talks unravelled.[19]

In May, McConnell was reinstated and continued to not pay expenses he considered illegitimate.[20] The union's financial position was 'serious', he reported, and these 'expenses' were partially to blame. For example, £6,120 had been paid out in levies to support the strike at North Kerry Milk Products which had not been recorded, as well as an extra £1,040 in strike benefit. In June, an NEC report imputed McConnell of incompetence, criticising his preparation of accounts and slowness in issuing cards to branches. He ignored the charges. The following month, he was again fined £5.[21] Expenses remained the crux. McConnell answered the leadership's charges with counter-allegations of impropriety and accused Hurley and his branch of stealing union funds. By late 1979, the branches had become embroiled in the conflict. Four branches – Cork and Dublin Nos. 3, 7 and 9 – deliberately withheld a total of £6,000 from head office because they had not received annual balance sheets. McConnell was not compiling quarterly accounts because the branches were not sending on the necessary financial documentation. Nevertheless, support for McConnell within the union was strong and most members considered him competent and proficient. In December 1979, he was re-elected as financial general secretary, this time permanently, as per union rules, with an astounding 71 per cent of the vote. The other successful candidates were general president, Fullerton; general vice-president, Justin Fleming; industrial general secretary, Moneley; Provincial Secretaries, Seán Finnan (Limerick) and Harry O'Donovan (Cork). Larry O'Neill was subsequently elected assistant general secretary.[22]

Continued legal wrangling, 1980-82

McConnell's re-election exacerbated the conflict. By 1980, he was still not attending NEC or REC meetings or carrying out their instructions. Without authorisation, he wrote to Larry O'Neill to inform him that he had been sacked as assistant general secretary. The REC had to retract the letter, which McConnell had also circulated to every branch and to Congress. The NEC 'totally condemned' his 'disgusting' actions and retained O'Neill in his position until further notice.[23] But McConnell's behaviour was becoming increasingly reckless. As well as not providing proper financial statements for the union. he stopped paying O'Neill's salary and did not issue contribution cards for 1980 to Dublin Nos. 7 and 9 branches because they had withheld £2,000 worth of remittance. For this, McConnell was again fined £5. When he then failed to pay NEETU's ICTU affiliation fees, the NEC pulled the plug. On 16 February, it unanimously voted to suspend him with pay for not carrying out REC and NEC directives. White was appointed acting financial general secretary.[24]

Six weeks later, McConnell presented himself to the NEC to answer its twelve charges against him, saying he had nothing to add to his letter of response. In April, the NEC held another meeting to consider the charges. There were two hearings, one in the morning and another in the afternoon, followed by a vote on every individual charge later in the afternoon. After not being able to get into the building in the morning, a group of NEC members were present for the afternoon session, having gotten in during the lunch break. This change of composition would later prove profoundly consequential. Members voted to indict McConnell on eight charges, not to indict him on one, while three charges showed even voting. Afterwards, the NEC voted 7-3 to dismiss McConnell from office. Donnchadha MacRaghnaill, the Drogheda delegate, believed the motion was too lenient because it did not include barring McConnell from ever again holding office. But McConnell had his defenders. Hanlon spoke 'strongly on behalf of Brother McConnell' and Bro. Egan 'stated that we were all guilty of some misdemeanours', that 'those without sin should cast the first stone.'[25]

McConnell was not as forgiving. He and his family had been put in a perilous financial position, devoid of wages and social welfare benefit as the union refused to issue him his cards. As he did not recognise his sacking as legitimate, he continued to publicly call himself NEETU's industrial general secretary, even if it violated court orders.[26] He believed that the executive's action against him was a pretext for something far more sinister:

> An attempt is being made by the general president ... to hound me out of my union because of my political beliefs ... for my role and support for the H-Block campaign. He refuses to accept my re-election to office ... he is receiving active support from a small, unrepresentative clique, led by Donnachadha Mac Raghnaill of 'Sinn Féin' the so-called 'Workers' Party', within our union who are trying to seize control of our organisation and identify me as the one person in Head Office standing in their way.[27]

McConnell's assertion was partially true – several officials were deeply uncomfortable with his political involvement and feared he was allowing republican organisations to meet at 6 Gardiner Row.[28] The 1980-81 hunger strikes of republicans in the Maze prison convulsed NEETU as they convulsed Irish society. As many trade unionists supported the demands for political status, unions struggled to remain apolitical. By March 1980, trades councils in Dublin, Cork and Waterford had passed resolutions supporting the anti-H-Block campaign. NEETU was divided on the issue. Its Sinn Féin The Workers' Party faction, one of several political elements, were vocal opponents, but others were more sympathetic. In 1980, McConnell was appointed secretary of the National H-Block Committee and served on the executive of the National H-Block Trade Union Committee, which wanted Congress to call one-day general strikes in support of the hunger strikers. In these roles, he tirelessly toured Ireland and Britain to raise funds for the campaign. He was also in the campaign to free Nicky Kelly who had been wrongly imprison for the 1976 Sallins Train Robbery.[29] The NEETU executive was indignant at how McConnell referred to himself as the union's financial general secretary when signing letters to the press on behalf of both campaigns. Officially, NEETU supported ICTU's position on the hunger strikes – that the hunger strikes should be called off – but internal dissent was blatant and hard to suppress. In December 1980, for example, the Cork branch sent a motion to head office demanding that the NEC write to the British ambassador protesting his government's treatment of the prisoners. No vote was taken. MacRaighnaill, treasurer of a Sinn Féin The Workers' Party branch in Dublin, believed that the union should instead 'call on the Provos' to 'ask the strikers to call off their hunger strike and terrorism in Northern Ireland.' Five months later, the Dublin No. 9 Branch resolved 'that we support the five demands of the prisoners at the Maze.' In response, the REC 'informed' the branch of 'the union's position on the matter.'[30]

In April 1980, the High Court granted NEETU an injunction against McConnell entering the financial office, which it issued again on 20 June.[31] From early July, however, he began to violate the order. On one such occasion, White returned from union work to find McConnell in the financial office. When asked to leave, 'his reply ... was to tell him to get out of his office, 'scab', which he repeated ... to the point of hysteria.'[32] The police were called to remove him. McConnell still had his admirers. One such person was Mary Hargadon, his secretary in the financial office, much to the intense irritation of the NEC. A motion to sack her was seconded but withdrawn. McConnell had removed the office keys and filing cabinets which meant that the union could not pay staff and officials' salaries, Christmas bonuses or superannuation benefits to retired members. On 19 December, he was held in contempt of court after trespassing on 6 Gardiner Row. Justice McWilliams committed him to prison, although he withdrew this order a month later. McWilliams did, however, dismiss McConnell's claim that he had not received natural justice because he ruled that such was not applicable to disputes between employers and employees. McConnell had removed a large amount of union documentation pertaining to 1980, for which officials tried to have him jailed again for contempt of court.[33] McWilliams refused counsel for McConnell in his non-suit against NEETU in which he alleged that the union had not proven its case against him.[34]

Legal action was exerting a heavy financial burden on the union. Union contributions had to be raised by 60 per cent, making them much higher than other unions, which made members 'very upset.' The four Cork branches were especially resentful. Only one paid it and that branch warned that 'the services they were getting for such an increase could be obtained at a cheaper rate from a British-based union.' The union also had to raise rent on tenants at Gardiner Row.[35] The saga inevitably impacted the executive's ability to respond to branches' needs, especially in Dublin where finances were controlled by head office. As they were monetarily self-sufficient, branches outside of Dublin could pay their officials' expenses and were therefore less affected by the chaos. Their membership held relatively steady throughout the 1980s. But as Table 59 reveals, overall membership halved between 1978 and 1989, with Dublin accounting for most of the loss. In April 1981, the Scalemakers' Section of the Dublin No. 1 Branch passed a motion of no confidence in Moneley because of how 'he had attended to their business.' The section subsequently joined the AUEW.[36] The Dublin No. 3 Branch, which had several longstanding gripes with head office, also passed a motion of no confidence in the REC. It deplored the 'lack of service from fulltime officials' in attending branch meetings, citing disputes with Weatherglaze, Roofcram, Gaelite Signs and Maye & Sons as examples. It threatened to leave the union or appoint its own fulltime officials, which the REC would forbid as contrary to rule.[37] The branch's 1981 dispute with J.C. McGloughlin, which the executive referred to the Labour Court, deepened the wedge between it and head office. White could not attend the hearing because he had to be in court to testify against McConnell. The Dublin Nos. 1 and 5 and the Midlands branches also complained that their requirements were not being met.[38]

Table 59: NEETU Membership, 1976-89.[39]

Year (31 Dec.)	Membership	Year (31 Dec.)	Membership
1975	14,000	1983	12,610
1976	14,044	1984	10,700
1977	14,143[40]	1985	10,001
1978	19,600	1986	9,524
1979	18,000	1987	9,274
1980	18,450	1988	9,524
1981	14,950	1989	9,774
1982	12,976	-	-

Despite rank-and-file resentment, the NEC foolishly divided up McConnell's annual salary (£16,500) amongst themselves – a 100 per cent increase for fulltime officials. The REC opposed the increase because it was 'a very big claim on the union … when the financial position … is in such a bad way.' However, officials were poorly paid for a heavy workload. For example, Harry O'Donovan was paid £20 a week below the workers he represented.[41] The increase nonetheless infuriated the membership. While the could NEC justifiably claim that it was based on what officials in other unions got, it was a counterproductive move at a time when head office was never less popular and the union never more divided. At the December 1980 NEC meeting. a motion to rescind the decision was defeated.[42] But rank-and-file hostility to the officials paled in comparison to the complete breakdown in relations between the officials themselves. In January 1981, the Dublin No. 1 Branch committee fined White £50 for an altercation he had with McConnell. The REC later invalidated the decision as contrary to union rules. White strenuously denied the allegations and claimed that McConnell had assaulted him when he gave him his High Court notice.[43]

In early 1981, the executive concluded that it had no choice but to take legal action against McConnell. That February, Fullerton went to the High Court to have it uphold the 1980 decision, but the case was never heard. In response, McConnell lodged an appeal to the Supreme Court.[44] Sympathy for McConnell went beyond the rank-and-file and included some on the union executive.[45] In October, the REC discovered that McConnell was 'canvassing' members for financial support for his legal expenses – and that three REC men had signed a document pledging to do so. Joe Carter was furious and 'spoke very strongly at the attitude of members signing to support financially Brother McConnell to fight this union.' White declared that 'unless the members who had supported this action rescinded it, he would not continue to act in the financial office.'[46] The members concerned protested that they had signed the document 'merely to give financial support to Brother McConnell who is out of work for a long period' but received no sympathy. Another NEC man asserted that the signatories were 'well aware' of what they were doing and were not acting 'in the best interest of the union.'[47] They were disciplined after the NEC got legal advice that they had sullied union rules.[48]

The Supreme Court ruling

McConnell's appeal to the Supreme Court opened on 22 June 1982 and heard evidence until 17 December when it issued a verdict: McConnell had won. The court unanimously ruled that the proper procedures had not been adopted in April 1980 as McConnell had not received natural justice when sacked. Fullerton's decision to allow those who had not attended the morning session of McConnell's hearing to attend the afternoon one had grave consequences. The court believed that the votes on the charges against McConnell, which were taken in the afternoon, may have been inadvertently prejudiced by the body language, demeanour or comportment of the group that had not been there in the morning. Furthermore, those members had voted on charges even though they had not been there to hear McConnell's defence. The court struck down the 1976 judgement against McConnell, making the 1980 charges against him his first offence for which he could legitimately be fined, and awarded him damages. His total loss of earnings was £62,226 while his legal costs were £151,000.[49]

Fifteen minutes after the decision, a jubilant McConnell arrived in the financial office where an elated Hargadon was among the first to congratulate him.[50] From his desk, he boldly told the press that he was dismissed because he had 'campaigned against corruption', i.e., his refusal to carry out 'illegal' instructions given to him by the NEETU executive. In one instance, he claimed he was asked to pay wages to a former fulltime union official who had been ousted from that position by a vote of the membership. In another, he stated that he was asked to inflate NEETU's membership so that a certain individual could secure a seat on ICTU's executive council.[51] On 22 December 1982, the NEC met to discuss the judgement. McConnell was present, and his opponents spoke with their tails firmly between their legs. 'We should accept this and move to the way forward for NEETU and it would be up to everyone to work together for the good of the union', said Moneley. Bro. O'Mahony spoke in a similar vein, 'we should start to go forward and work together for the good of the union starting 1983 and make NEETU the great union that it could be.'[52]

Financial crisis and continuing trouble with McConnell

O'Mahony's optimism that the Supreme Court had ended NEETU's internal turmoil was wildly misplaced. At the first NEC meeting of 1983, McConnell told his fellow delegates that the NEC was not properly constituted because he had not had a vote in its election; because four members had not been properly elected to it; and because he had been illegally removed from office and therefore could not attend meetings or give input to same, which invalidated its decisions during his period of suspension. Therefore, the meeting should be abandoned. He based this opinion on 'the best legal advice' and claimed that they could not proceed with the meeting as any decisions reached would be invalid. The others disagreed and went ahead with the meeting, with Fleming, who presided over it, stating that he would not suspend the NEC unless ordered to do so by a High Court injunction. McConnell was enraged by what he considered the ongoing disregard for rule. MacRaighnaill fired back that 'the meeting was being intimated by a person with a loud and raucous voice whom the chairman was failing to call to order. To declare all decisions 'null and void' would be tantamount to dismembering the union.' McConnell retorted that MacRaighnaill was 'one of the main reasons the union lost the Supreme Court case, having seconded the motion to dismiss him' without hearing the evidence. MacRaighnaill had therefore 'disgraced himself.'[53]

The four men whom McConnell argued had no place on the NEC were Pat O'Neill, Jack Riordan, MacRaighnaill and Patrick O'Flynn. O'Neill, he alleged, was a lapsed member in arrears at the time of his nomination; Riordan had never been an officer of his branch; MacRaighnaill, as the vice-principal of a technical school, was not working at his trade; and O'Flynn had been nominated after nominations had closed. Furthermore, McConnell maintained that 'there are other members whose valid nominations are doubtful to say the least' and that Fleming was chairing meetings against rule.[54] Fullerton had died in February 1982 aged seventy-three.[55] Fleming had been acting general president ever since. NEETU's rules, which stated that the general president must preside over the NEC, had not been prepared to deal with a president dying in office and it was therefore unclear whether the general vice president could chair meetings. Plus, the union now lacked a general vice president who, according to rule, must be an NEC member. McConnell therefore stopped attending NEC meetings and did not recognise its authority. The NEC considered itself properly comprised, as did the REC which had established a subcommittee to examine the issue and received legal advice from Mervyn Taylor, a Labour Party TD and future Minister for Equality and Law Reform. The NEC resented the intrusion.[56]

From 1983, the mountain of legal bills begot an unprecedented financial crisis. McConnell blamed 'people withholding money' and the 'disastrous action against him' for the 'mess.'[57] Court cases aside, the union had been in a poor financial state for many years. McConnell estimated that the Dublin No. 11 Branch owed £10,000 while seven of the thirty provincial branches were withholding funds.[58] By March, both bank accounts had been overdrawn – by over £2,225 and £32,620, respectively. Bank of Ireland refused to cover cheques, including wages, and the union owed £50,000 in High Court costs.[59] In June, McConnell was forced to temporarily close the financial office because the union had run out of money, which meant that were no wages for officials or staff or strike pay for members that week. The union negotiated some leeway from the bank, but by October its patience had run out and they were no longer honouring cheques.[60] The REC imposed a £5 levy on members (bar apprentices) which caused uproar among the branches. The NEC scuppered the plan pending a financial report and 'valid reasons for explaining to members the necessity for the … levy.'[61] However, the NEC significantly increased contributions, recalled its assets and sold its premises in Dundalk for £55,000. Although McConnell made real progress in tackling the crisis, by the end of 1983 the union still had liabilities of £85,000; by September 1984, this figure had risen to over £106,000.[62]

The situation was so critical that the REC considered suspending all benefits, disposing of parttime employees and re-imposing the £5 levy. Its creditors, which included *Independent Newspapers* and Dublin Corporation, threatened legal action unless they received what they were owed. But just as the union was staring into the abyss, McConnell negotiated another bank overdraft that gave it some desperately needed breathing space. A substantial improvement in the flow of remittances also eased the pressure. The levy would have done much to clear the debts, but the NEC refused to implement it because McConnell was not attending its meetings and not providing it with financial information. The REC had previously overruled the NEC's deferral of the levy, which it should not have been able to do considering the latter was the union's supreme governing body.[63] Herein was a major administrative problem for the hapless NEETU – poorly drafted rules. When the NEC discussed how the REC could supersede its authority, a member admitted that 'certain rules in the book … are contradictory and lead to complete confusion.'[64] By July 1984, the union was still 'in a very bad financial position' and had been disaffiliated from both ICTU and the DCTU for not paying its affiliation fees.[65]

McConnell had an unenviable task in salvaging the wreckage of a union nearly bankrupted by the £140,000 in legal fees it had to pay out. Despite his tempestuous nature, McConnell was a highly intelligent man who was, as the NEC acknowledged, winning the war for NEETU's survival. Seán Fagan was 'satisfied that the job is being done in an excellent manner' and Duffy felt that McConnell had done an 'excellent job since he came back.'[66] There was a marked improvement in remittance, but the crisis limited the union's ability to pay superannuated members their entitlements or fulltime officials and branch members their expenses. But McConnell continued to polarise. He regularly sent 'offensive letters' to branches demanding that they remit, which alienated many branch officials.[67] In September 1983, he had alleged that Charlie Prizeman, chairman of the Dublin No. 1 branch, had threatened his family over the phone because Prizeman had not been allowed to attend a previous REC meeting. Prizeman forcefully denied the imputation and successfully sued McConnell for libel. Both the pro- and anti-McConnell factions of the fractured union gave conflicting evidence to the Dublin Circuit Court, which awarded Prizeman £3,000 in damages in June 1985.[68]

Despite its recognition of McConnell's abilities, the NEC remained deeply frustrated by his refusal to attend meetings, which had 'rendered the continued operation of the union impossible.'[69] He asserted that the 1984-85 NEC was, like its predecessor, improperly comprised. Apart from MacRaghnaill, McConnell also objected to the presence of Larry O'Neill, Tomás Ó Mordha and D. Carr, and maintained that the lack of an elected general president also invalidated the body. O'Neill should not have been on the NEC because he had lost an election for fulltime office; Ó Mordha because he was nominated after the closing date; and Carr because he was out of benefit at the time of nomination. McConnell also claimed that Moneley used the NEC to pass decisions which suited him personally, although it is unclear what he meant by this. The NEC strenuously rejected these contentions. McConnell abhorred the NEC's enlargement from twelve seats to fifteen, which he denounced as 'a blatant attempt' to gerrymander it. He claimed that the Dublin No. 1 District now had too much representation, the Cork No. 2 District too little and other branches in the Cork district no representation at all. Districts were allowed one seat for every thousand members. As the union's membership was just under thirteen thousand, fifteen NEC seats could not be justified.[70] Others on the REC also questioned the validity of some on the NEC, especially MacRaighnaill. The NEC had rejected legal advice that MacRaighnaill, a trade teacher, could not be described as 'working at his trade', a requirement for NEC membership.[71] Despite changing its rules to elect a new general president and general vice president, attempts to hold ballots for such had been recurrently postponed. In March 1985, Fleming had been re-elected acting general president until a ballot could be held on the position. Some REC members resisted Fleming's chairmanship and walked out of meetings. From this point, McConnell stopped recognising the REC as legitimately comprised and stopped attending its meetings.

The NEC regularly passed motions censuring McConnell for his 'deplorable' behaviour. By October 1985, it was 'exasperated' with him for 'openly flouting' union rules. Dealing with him had become 'an impossible task.' He had again stopped paying officials their expenses and was trying to force Larry O'Neill to retire on 31 December 1985 by deleting his name from the pension fund even though O'Neill did not yet want to retire. The union discussed charging him for 'gross subordination' by his 'continued failure to attend NEC meetings … and failure to submit financial information as required by the NEC.'[72] He continued to refuse to pay O'Neill's pension despite being ordered by both the NEC and REC to do so. Adding to its financial woes, a fire at head office caused severe damage and O'Neill sued the union for what it owed him because he 'had a pension imposed on him by Brother McConnell since September 1985 and had received nothing whatsoever since 28 December 1985.'[73] The NEC resolved that it would consider McConnell liable for any award and legal costs resulting from the case. McConnell also refused to pay ICTU or DTUC affiliation fees and his boycott of the NEC meant that it could not collect the £5 levy.[74]

Another High Court case and trouble with the office staff

NEETU's financial crisis was so severe that it not only affected its members but its employees, who were organised by the Irish Union of Distributive Workers and Clerks (IUDWC), as well. Their pay followed national trends and they always secured the increases given under national agreements. Though disputes regarding the staff's pay were quite common, relations between both unions remained amicable.[75] However, as chaos reigned in Gardiner Row, the rapport between NEETU and its staff plunged to extraordinary levels of nastiness.

The turn began in 1981 when the IUDWC accused Pat O Neill, Paul Murray and Prizeman of verbally abusing individuals in the financial office in separate incidents because of their handling of union work. The REC found the obdurate and unapologetic O'Neill guilty of the charges and 'severely reprimanded' him.[76] However, it rejected the allegations against Murray and Prizeman, prompting the IUDWC to serve strike notice for 10 October 1983.[77] While most of the REC took a conciliatory approach, Carter was hard-line. At a REC meeting on 8 October, he moved that the union fire any employee who struck; his motion fell as it was not seconded. Instead, the REC ordered that all officials report for work should a picket take place. At REC's next meeting, Armstrong expressed his outrage at Carter's motion. 'It inferred that people who go on strike should be sacked… he felt that Brother Carter should resign from this REC and his position in the union.' Carter replied that, as an elected member of the REC, 'it was his duty to protect this union … he was proud to do so and will continue to do so.' Armstrong's motion that Carter be expelled from the union was seconded. Two voted in favour, three against and four abstained.[78] Although the strike did not go ahead, the conflict with NEETU continued, becoming a general wage dispute.

During the negotiations for the twenty-third wage round in mid-1983, the IUDWC submitted a claim for the staff, whose weekly wages ranged from £95 to £157, which NEETU could not give because of its financial position. The dispute went to the Labour Court, which accepted NEETU's evidence but recommended a higher salary scale from 1985 when the union expected its finances to be stronger. The IUDWC accepted the Labour Court's recommendation. In the meantime, however, it was with 'extreme regret' that NEETU could not implement the scale because the union was still over '£100,000 in debt.'[79] Tensions between the unions worsened during the following two rounds. NEETU was very reluctant to fully concede claims as it was 'concerned' with 'financial plight.'[80] In early 1986, NEETU granted its staff an 18.5 per cent pay advance and five weeks' annual holidays after pressure from the Irish Distributive and Administrative Trade Union (IDATU, the IUDWC had changed its name in 1985). But due to its financial state, NEETU did not grant 'an old claim' of a £30 weekly increase to one of its employees. In response, on 9 May, IDATU took out the office staff and picketed 6 Gardiner Row.[81]

On 11 May, the REC met and ordered every official to report for work the following day. McConnell did not do so and was duly suspended without pay on 21 May for gross subordination of the union. The NEC backed the REC and ordered McConnell to return all union property in his possession. It again appointed White as acting financial general secretary. Fagan, a trustee who had also refused to pass the picket, was also suspended.[82] As the REC had suspended him without following procedure – to first inform him of the charges against him and then to hear his defence – McConnell lodged a case with the High Court. As such a procedure was mandated by rule, he did not attend NEC meetings to defend himself because only the REC could hear his defence. The executive had again denied him natural justice. McConnell also claimed his right to NEETU protection from victimisation from an employer for supporting another union's official picket, as per a REC decision of March 1982. Justice Hamilton, president of the High Court, agreed. Pending a proper hearing, on 22 July 1986, he granted McConnell's application for an order that the NEC not implement the 21 May resolution but did not grant his application for an injunction on anyone other than he from performing the tasks of financial general secretary.[83] On 3 December 1986, the High Court invalided the 21 May resolution, by which time NEETU had reinstated McConnell as financial general secretary.[84] The union needed McConnell's proficiency as Bank of Ireland had taken a civil case against it because the union's inability to pay off its overdraft.[85]

An ugly affair from the start, the strike of the office staff lasted until 27 May 1986. IDATU accused White of punching Marie Hayde, one of its officials, when she had her back to him as he arrived to pull down placards on the first day of the picket. The union reported the incident to ICTU and the Gardaí.[86] Moneley wholeheartedly rejected the allegations as 'totally unjustified ... only intended to bring the good name of the ... union into disrepute.' He further claimed that few of the picketers were NEETU members and that IDATU's intention was to prevent NEETU meetings from taking place. White, Moneley recounted, tried to leave head office after work but was prevented from doing so by a rowdy mob. Having asked the picketers to let him pass, an IDATU official called him a 'filthy f*****g scab' and swung a punch at him but missed. 'During the course of this disgraceful conduct Tommy White distinguished himself with the loyalty and dedication he displayed in his commitment to this union.'[87] NEETU later threatened legal action against IDATU for a 'disgraceful' article about the incident in its quarterly newsletter, *The Distributive Worker*.[88] The ICTU executive effectively sided with IDATU, expressing 'grave concern' at NEETU's behaviour and telling Moneley that it 'cannot see the position adopted by your union as supportive of Congress.'[89]

Relations between the two unions continued their downward spiral throughout 1987 and 1988, as did relations between NEETU and its staff. The officials justifiably maintained that NEETU's finances prohibited it from granting the desired concessions. Frustration at the state of the union sometimes boiled over into ill-treatment of employees. McConnell was especially aggressive and frequently stopped paying staff wages. In January 1987, IDATU complained that Moneley had verbally harassed Roseleen Kelly, one of its shop stewards, leading to her 'absence from work through illness.' Moneley retorted that Kelly was not paid because she was foul-mouthed, unpunctual and incompetent.[90] Kelly, he claimed, 'was not going to be paid ... for knitting wool garments in the industrial office' and he decried IDATU's pressing of the issue as 'a typical example of ... why the relationship between your union and ... NEETU are so strained.'[91] Relations soured further when Hargadon, a member of the IDATU executive, also alleged that Moneley had berated her, leading IDATU to accuse NEETU of being 'determined to scuttle any possible improvement in relationships … by continuing the practice of abusing our members in your employment.'[92]

IDATU was also aggrieved by NEETU's failure to grant the twenty-sixth round, fairly distribute overtime and provide adequate heating, toilet and canteen facilities. But NEETU could not even afford to give its own officials the increases conceded under the rounds. On 31 August 1987, the staff unofficially withdrew their labour to demand same. IDATU supported the action, which Moneley deplored as 'most unbecoming of a union when dealing with another union.'[93] IDATU was especially critical of White's treatment of the staff. White refused the imputation, which he considered nothing more than a 'filthy campaign of abuse' against him' by IDATU.[94] That October, IDATU implemented a work-to-rule and an overtime ban at 6 Gardiner Row after NEETU rejected its claim under the twenty-sixth round.[95] Negotiations to settle the dispute were acrimonious and were nearly derailed by a 'scurrilous' article about White's alleged chastisement of staff in *The Distributive Worker*. NEETU even considered derecognising IDATU because of its 'continued onslaught against this union and its officials.'[96] Relations had reached their nadir. The wages issue was finally resolved in late 1988 after Labour Court intervention, initiating a period of rapprochement between the two unions.[97]

Tensions subsequently resurfaced when NEETU refused to pay what it owed some of its employees. In January 1988, the Employment Appeals Tribunal awarded Eileen Harrison, a former clerk at the Cork office, £3,800 after NEETU had failed to pay her for nine weeks. On separate occasions in 1990 and 1991, McConnell again stopped paying wages. Vera Brady, an IDATU shop steward told the REC that 'she could not understand why Kevin McConnell should deceive staff by getting the wage cheque signed by the trustee and then not paying out wages. For two bank holiday weekends her members went without wages. This was incredible coming from a man calling himself a trade unionist.'[98] After IDATU threatened industrial action, the executive cleverly bypassed McConnell by getting the provincial branches to pay wages, expenses and benefits.[99] Sometimes the courts were needed to ensure that the staff received their full entitlements. In 1992, the Dublin Circuit Court ordered NEETU to pay Kelly the remaining £4,000 of the £11,000 compensation for unfair dismissal that the Employment Appeals Tribunal had awarded her in October 1990.[100] She claimed that she had left NEETU because McConnell had regularly locked her out of the financial office and that when she was allowed in, he often shouted at and harassed her.[101] Without his executive's consent, McConnell had employed someone else to replace Kelly after she took pregnancy leave, a flagrant breach of NEETU's agreement with IDATU.[102]

Continued problems

McConnell's reinstatement did nothing to quell his conflict with the officials, whose wages, expenses and pensions he once again stopped paying. Although union finances remained critical, McConnell countermanded a REC decision to open a £20,000 overdraft with Bank of Ireland, meaning that the union could not pay its debts because its cheques began to bounce. It faced more legal action from Dublin Corporation and the Department of Finance (to whom it owed £50,000) because McConnell had not paid rates or income tax on payments to officials and shop stewards. The executive was forced to increase contributions again and even considered selling Gardiner Row and to transfer head office to rented accommodation. O'Donovan warned of a 'serious reaction' if contributions were upped to the proposed £1.60, a rate which branches would struggle to enforce. As McConnell did not pay Congress affiliation fees for 1987 or 1988, NEETU had no vote on ICTU's crucial decision to endorse the first social partnership agreement; because he did not pay the premiums, Gaw's cancelled the union's insurance scheme. To compound matters, NEETU's accountants and auditors still could not establish how bad its finances truly were because of McConnell's constant absence from both NEC and REC meetings. Worst of all, the Circuit Court awarded Larry O'Neill £11,590 in unpaid pension entitlements which McConnell had still not paid. O'Neill died in 1993.[103] The union risked losing Gardiner Row. To prevent this, the NEC diverted branch money normally remitted to the general finances to settle debts that 'jeopardise the future of our head office.'[104] Its auditors encouraged it to sell the building because the union was on the brink of bankruptcy. As recently as 1990, the union needed a £6,000 overdraft because it was in a 'financial mess.'[105]

However, the leadership was making progress in other areas. In April 1988, NEETU finally elected a general president (Carter) and general vice president (Prizeman) under ICTU auspices despite McConnell's objections that the elections were not in order.[106] Carter was soon confronted with a major challenge to his authority in the new role. In November 1988, he indefinitely suspended the REC because three members were constantly disrupting the proceedings. They would protest an item on the agenda and subject 'members of the REC and the chairman in particular to a barrage of verbal abuse with venomous and slanderous remarks' before storming out, forcing the meetings to be abandoned due to lack of a quorum. White suspected that 'a co-ordinated campaign was taking place' to stop the REC from functioning.[107] REC meetings were being rendered farcical. In February 1989, White and Moneley stormed out of one after Fagan, who regularly subjected officials to 'filthy abuse', accused White of telling 'lies to the REC for so long you can't even remember them.' When Fagan started hurling insults at a subsequent meeting, the Gardaí had to be called to remove him. From mid-1991 to mid-1992, Damien Keogh, who was sympathetic to McConnell, launched a personal crusade to see Moneley sacked for his handling of a recent lockout at Irish Lights. Several meetings were reduced to 'pandemonium', with one having to be adjourned, as Keogh pursued the issue vigorously. He regularly attacked Moneley and White as grifters conspiring (with Prizeman) to prevent the REC from meeting. All three furiously denied his charges.[108] The executive acknowledged that 'crisis after crisis was being confronted daily' and that nothing would change unless McConnell attended meetings.[109] Although the executive's patience with him had long expired, its hands were tied because union rules allowed him to remain its permanent financial general secretary. The only way out was to lay NEETU to rest and launch a new union. When the opportunity arose to do just that, the executive grabbed it with both hands.

Chapter Notes and References

1   NEETU NEC minutes, 19 June 1976, TEEU collection, ILHM.
2   Ibid., 4, 15 Feb. 1976, TEEU collection, ILHM.
3   Ibid., 25 Feb., 13 Mar., 2, 7, 8 Apr., 5 May 1976 TEEU collection, ILHM.
4   *Irish Press*, 9 Mar. 1976.
5   NEETU REC minutes, 15, 17, 19 May, 2 June 1976, TEEU collection, ILHM; *Irish Press*, 19 May 1976.
6   Ibid., 25 Aug., 1, 9, 15, 22 Sept. 1976, TEEU collection, ILHM.
7   Ibid., 13, 20 Oct., 3 Nov., 1, 8, 22 Dec. 1976, TEEU collection, ILHM.
8   Ibid., 12 Jan., 23 Feb., 2, 9, 23 Mar. 1977; NEETU NEC minutes, 11 Mar. 1977, both found in TEEU collection, ILHM.
9   *Evening Herald*, 6 Apr. 1977.
10 *Irish Independent*, 26 Mar., 2, 7 Apr., 21 June 1977; *Evening Herald*, 6 June 1977.
11 NEETU REC minutes, 11, 18 Aug., 1, 22 Sept., 20 Oct., 10 Nov. 1977; NEETU NEC minutes, 15 Dec. 1977, both found in TEEU collection, ILHM.
12 NEETU REC minutes, 24 Nov. 1977, TEEU collection, ILHM.
13 NEETU NEC minutes, 23 Mar. 1977, TEEU collection, ILHM. See also minutes of same, 16 Feb. 1979.
14 Ibid., 24 Mar., 7 Apr. 1977; NEETU REC minutes, 25 Apr. 1977, both found in TEEU collection ILHM.
15 NEETU NEC minutes, 21 Apr., 12, 26 May 1977, TEEU collection, ILHM.
16 Ibid., 9 May 1977, 21 Apr. 1979, TEEU collection, ILHM.
17 NEETU REC minutes, 9 May 1979, TEEU collection, ILHM.
18 NEETU NEC minutes, 24 Mar. 1979, TEEU collection, ILHM.
19 Ibid., 21 Apr., 27 May 1979, TEEU collection, ILHM.
20 NEETU REC minutes, 9, 30 May, 6, 13 June 1979; NEETU NEC minutes, 16 June, 14 July 1979, both found in TEEU collection, ILHM.
21 Ibid 6, 30 June 1979; NEETU NEC minutes, 16 June 1979, both found in TEEU collection, ILHM.
22 NEETU REC minutes, 7 Nov., 29 Dec. 1979, TEEU collection, ILHM.
23 NEETU NEC minutes, 19, 20 Jan. 1980, TEEU collection, ILHM; NEETU REC minutes, 19 Jan.
24 Ibid., 2, 16 Feb. 1980, TEEU collection, ILHM.
25 Ibid., 29 Mar., 12 Apr. 1980, TEEU collection, ILHM. The charges were as follows: 1) Failure to attend REC meetings. 2) Failure to attend NEC meetings. 3) Refusal to pay Larry O'Neill his salary. 4) Refusal to issue 1980 contribution cards to Dublin Nos. 7 & 9 Branches. 5) Refusal to pay ICTU affiliation fees for 1980. 6) Failure to supply union accounts to the NEC or the REC in accordance with union rules or the High Court settlement. 7) Refusal to pay Pat O'Neill 'lost time' expenses. 8) Obstructing the union's internal auditor from carrying out his duties. 9) Refusal to pay the internal auditor his fees as authorised by the NEC. 10) Refusal to pay Moneley expenses for work done in Cork. 11) Failure to pay NEETU legal advisors as directed. 12) Constant refusal to carry out NEC and REC directions. Specifically, McConnell was found innocent of charge four whilst charges 7, 8 and 9 were ties.
26 NEETU REC minutes, 28 May 1981.
27 McConnell to branch secretaries, June 1980, file: 'Legal.'
28 NEETU NEC minutes, 2 Feb. 1980, TEEU collection, ILHM.
29 *Irish Press*, 31 Mar., 10 June, 22 July, 16, 26 Sept., 13 Nov. 1980; *Irish Times*, 13 May 1983.
30 NEETU NEEC minutes, 13 Dec. 1980; NEETU REC minutes, 20 May 1981, both found in TEEU collection, ILHM.
31 NEETU REC minutes, 30 Apr., 9 July, 10 Dec. 1980, TEEU collection, ILHM; *Irish Independent*, 20 Dec. 1980.
32 NEETU REC minutes, 10 Dec.1980, TEEU collection, ILHM.
33 NEETU NEC minutes, 13 Dec. 1980, TEEU collection, ILHM; *Irish Independent*, 20 Dec. 1980, 20, 27 Jan. 1981; *Meath Chronicle*, 26 Sept. 1981.
34 *Irish Press*, 25 June 1982.
35 NEETU NEC minutes, 13 Sept. 1980, TEEU collection, ILHM; See NEETU REC minutes, 27 Jan. 1982. The Union of Construction, Allied Trades and Technicians, the Coppersmiths' Union and the National Union of Sheet Metal Workers all rented from NEETU.

36   NEETU REC minutes, 15 Apr. 1981; NEETU NEC minutes, 12 Nov. 1988.
37   NEETU REC minutes, 17 Oct. 1979.
38   Ibid., 25 Mar., 1, 8 Arp., 24 June 1981, 13 July 1983, TEEU collection, ILHM.
39   NEETU, annual returns, 1976-89, T538, RSF records, CRO.
40   Although NEETU gave this figure as its membership for 31 December 1977, it is unlikely
      to be accurate as the union gave a figure of 18,100 for its membership at the beginning
      of 1978.
41   NEETU NEC minutes, 12 July 1980, TEEU collection, ILHM. See also NEETU REC
      minutes, 16 July 1980, TEEU collection, ILHM; McConnell to branch secretaries, Aug.
      1980, 'Legal.'
42   NEETU NEC minutes, 13 Dec. 1980, TEEU collection, ILHM.
43   NEETU REC minutes, 14, 21 Jan. 1981, 16 Feb. 1983, TEEU archives, ILHM.
44   Ibid., 11 Feb., 29 Mar., 1, 8 Apr., 28 May 1981.
45   Ibid., 14 Oct. 1981.
46   Ibid., 21 Oct. 1981.
47   NEETU NEC minutes, 21 Nov. 1981, TEEU collection, ILHM.
48   NEETU REC minutes, 28 Oct., 4 Nov. 1981; ibid., 13 Feb., 15 May 1982, TEEU collection,
      ILHM.
49   Interview with Donnchadha Mac Raghnaill, 27 Feb. 2020; *Cork Examiner*, 18 June 1983;
      NEETU REC minutes, 9 Mar. 1983.
50   *Irish Press*, 25 June, 18 Dec. 1982.
51   Ibid., 18 Dec. 1982.
52   NEETU NEC minutes, 22 Dec. 1982, TEEU collection, ILHM.
53   Ibid., 29 Jan. 1983, TEEU collection, ILHM.
54   McConnell to Moneley, 9 Nov. 83, 'Legal.'
55   *Irish Independent*, 26 Feb. 1982. Although they do not record what exactly happened, the
      NEETU REC minutes condemn 'the conduct of Kevin McConnell towards the Fullerton
      family at the funeral of the late Christopher Fullerton and to inform the family that we
      deeply regret that such an outrage occurred.' See NEETU REC minutes, 3 Mar. 1982.
      Fullerton had spent his working life as a foreman at Dublin Corporation as both a
      foreman and a supervisor. His father, George Fullerton, had served with the Citizen Army
      from 1916-23. He partook in the Easter Rising and fought the anti-Treatyites during the
      Civil War for which he was imprisoned from 1922 to December 1923. See George
      Fullerton, MSP Application, DP6810, MSP Collection, MA.
56   NEETU NEC minutes, 18 June 1983, 7 Dec. 1985, TEEU collection, ILHM; NEETU REC
      minutes, 15 June 1983.
57   NEETU REC minutes, 30 Mar. 1983.
58   Ibid., 30 Mar., 8 June 1983.
59   Ibid., 30 Mar., 13 July 1983.
60   Ibid., 22 June, 19 Oct. 1983.
61   NEETU NEC minutes, 18 June 1983.
62   NEETU REC minutes, 14 Apr., 19 Oct., 30 Nov., 10 Dec. 1983, 22 Feb., 7 Mar., 4 Apr., 14
      July, 8 Sept. 1984; ibid., 3 Dec. 1983, 28 July 1984, 23 Mar. 1985, both found in TEEU
      collection, ILHM.
63   NEETU REC minutes, 8 Feb., 21 Mar., 4 Apr. 1984, TEEU collection, ILHM.
64   NEETU NEC minutes, 30 June 1984, TEEU collection, ILHM.
65   Ibid., 30 June, 28 July 1984, TEEU collection, ILHM.
66   Ibid., 28 July 1984, TEEU collection, ILHM.
67   Ibid., 30 June 1984, TEEU collection, ILHM.
68   NEETU REC minutes, 14 Sept. 1983, 11, 14 July 1984, NEETU NEC minutes, 15 Sept.
      1983, both found in TEEU collection, ILHM; *Irish Independent*, 25 June 1985.
69   Ibid., 25 May 1985, TEEU collection, ILHM.
70   McConnell to Moneley, 31 Aug. 1984, 18 June 1986, 'Legal'; and NEETU NEC minutes,
      18 June 1986.
71   Ibid., 3, 10 Dec. 1983, 15 Sept., 3 Nov. 1984, 23 Mar., 20 Apr., 25 May, 5 Oct. 1985, TEEU
      collection, ILHM.
72   Ibid., 23 Mar., 20 Apr., 5 Oct. 1985, TEEU collection, ILHM.
73   Ibid., 8 Feb. 1986, TEEU collection, ILHM.
74   Ibid., 26 Apr. 1986, TEEU collection, ILHM.

75 NEETU REC minutes, 10 Nov., 8 Dec. 1976, 14, 21 Mar., 22 Aug. 1979, 27 Feb. 1980, TEEU collection, ILHM. Undated, unsigned memo entitled 'Staff pay claim for 22nd Wage Round', 'Legal.'

76 Ibid., 14, 21 Oct., 4, 11 Nov. 1981; NEETU NEC minutes, 15 May 1982, both found in TEEU collection, ILHM.

77 Ibid., 14, 21 Sept., 8 Oct. 1983, 25 Jan. 1984; NEETU NEC minutes, 24 Sept. 1983, both found in TEEU collection, ILHM.

78 NEETU REC minutes, 8, 19 Oct. 1983.

79 McConnell, submission to the Labour Court, 13 July 1984, File: NEETU-IDATU, 1984-1991, Box 144, TEEU collection, ILHM.

80 NEETU REC minutes, 12 Dec. 1984, TEEU collection, ILHM.

81 *Irish Press*, 10 May 1986; Unsigned letter to Moneley, 30 Jan. 1986, NEETU-IDATU, ILHM.

82 NEETU NEC minutes, 30 May 1986, TEEU collection, ILHM; Moneley to McConnell, 22 May 1986, 'Legal.'

83 NEETU REC minutes, 10 Mar. 1982; Tommy White to branch secretaries, 23 Mar. 1982, 'Legal'; 'Judgement delivered by the President of the High Court on the 22nd day of July 1986 between NEETU, Ignatius J. Moneley and Thomas White and Kevin M.P. McConnell', 'Legal'; *Irish Independent*, 19 July 1986. In March 1982, the REC decided to discontinue automatic strike pay for members engaged in sympathetic strike with other unions due to difficult negotiations during the 22nd Wage Round, the possibility of many official strikes and the union's financial ordeal.

84 NEETU NEC minutes, 6 Dec. 1986, TEEU collection, ILHM; *Irish Press*, 4 Dec. 1986.

85 Ibid., 5 Oct. 1985; 'list of civil cases at Trim District Court, 17 Oct. 1986, 'Legal.'

86 John Mitchell to Donal Nevin, 14 May 1986, NEETU-IDATU, ILHM.

87 Moneley to Nevin, 24 June 1986, ibid.

88 *The Distribute Worker*, Apr.-Oct. 1986; Moneley to Nevin, 2 Nov. 1986, ibid.

89 Nevin to Moneley, 22 Dec. 1986, NEETU-IDATU, TEEU collection, ILHM.

90 Brendan Archbold to Moneley, 7, 9 Jan. 1987; Moneley to Archbold, Ibid., both found in TEEU collection, ILHM.

91 Moneley to John Mitchell, ibid.

92 Archbold to Moneley, 31 Aug. 1987, ibid.

93 Moneley to Archbold, ibid.

94 White to Archbold, ibid.

95 Archbold to Moneley, 7 Oct. 1987, ibid.

96 NEETU REC minutes, 9 Mar., 20 Apr. 1988.

97 Following are terms of agreement: a 3 per cent interim increase from July 1987 to 30 June 1988; a 2 per cent increase from July 1988 to 31 Dec. 1988; and the implementation of the National Agreement from 1 Jan. 1989.

98 NEETU REC minutes, 20 Mar., 3 Apr. 1991.

99 Ibid., 24 Apr. 1990, 3, 27 Apr., 8 May 1991; NEETU NEC minutes, 11 May 1991.

100 Rosaleen Kelly to chairman of NEETU REC, 11 Feb. 1987, NEETU-IDATU, ILHM; *Irish Independent*, 14 Jan. 1988.

101 *Irish Press*, 25 July 1991

102 NEETU NEC minutes, 6 May 1989, 3 Feb., 12 May, 21 July 1990; NEETU REC minutes, 5 July 1989, 7, 21 Feb., 7, 21 Mar., 23 May, 1 Aug., 3 Oct., 15 Nov. 1990, 18 Sept. 1991, 11, 20 Mar., 10 June 1992; *Irish Press*, 25 July 1991.

103 NEETU REC minutes, 6 Sept. 1989, 3 Oct., 15 Nov. 1990, 24 June 1991; NEETU NEC minutes, 12 Nov. 1988, 6 May, 30 Sept. 1989.

104 NEETU NEC minutes, 30 Apr. 1988.

105 NEETU REC minutes 24 Jan. 1990.

106 NEETU REC minutes, 4 May, 16 June 1988.

107 NEETU NEC minutes, 12 Nov. 1988.

108 NEETU REC minutes, 23 Feb., 5 Apr., 5 July 1989, 19 June, 20 Nov., 4 Dec. 1991, 5 Feb., 11 Mar., 13 May, 10 June 1992.

109 NEETU NEC minutes, 3 Feb. 1990; NEETU REC minutes, 20 Mar. 1991.

10

The Crisis Years, 1976-92

By the time NEETU received its negotiating licence, Irish labour had lost the optimism that had characterised it at the beginning of the decade, sapped by a lethargic economy tormented by inflation, which reached 20 per cent. Fianna Fáil stormed the 1977 general election, winning their last ever overall majority. Its gamble that tax cuts and increases in public expenditure would lift the economy backfired spectacularly, creating a budgetary hole plugged by borrowing. The 1979 Iranian Revolution sent the oil prices skyrocketing again, plunging Western economies into another recession that compounded the domestic malaise. In Ireland, unemployment rose by 77 per cent between 1979 and 1982.[1] Nevertheless, Irish labour was in a strong position to combat the crisis: in the late 1970s, Ireland had the third highest rate of unionisation in the EEC. Inflation spurred industrial action. Working-class anger climaxed in 1979, the year when a record number of workdays were lost to strikes and the largest protest movement in the state's history, the tax marches, began. Militancy was an international phenomenon in the late 1970s: in 1978-79, Britain was consumed by its Winter of Discontent, a period of widespread strikes by public sector unions demanding pay rises.

The troubled 1970s gave way to the catastrophic 1980s, when unemployment and the national debt soared to historic levels. Averaging a respectable 4.7 per cent between 1961 and 1973, joblessness gradually rose to 8.1 per cent between 1974 and 1980. By 1986, however, it had exploded to 18 per cent. Between 1980 and 1985, the numbers out of work jumped from ninety-one thousand to 226,000, a 150 per cent increase. Nearly a third of the unemployed were under twenty-five. The unemployment disaster was primarily driven by the collapse of the manufacturing sector, which experienced a 25 per cent drop in employment between 1980 and 1987. Average earnings dropped by 7 per cent; the drop was 10.8 per cent in manufacturing and 16 per cent in construction. Joblessness ensured that emigration returned to levels not seen since the 1950s – 130,000 people left Ireland between 1983 and 1988. The government serviced budget deficits by borrowing heavily and imposing high levels of taxation. By late 1986, the national debt – which had tripled since 1980 – stood at 148 per cent of GNP. With Irish living standards at only 70 per cent of the EEC average, the country was mired in another crisis of self-confidence driven by economic failure.[2] Militancy declined from the early 1980s. The number of days lost to strikes in 1986 was the lowest in five years, partially aided by the reduction of unofficial stoppages.[3]

The West experienced another historic political paradigm shift in 1980s. The right had seized on the recessions and inflationary spirals of the 1970s to convince the public that Keynesianism was the root cause of Western economic woes. The elections of Margaret Thatcher in 1979 and Ronald Reagan in 1980 unleashed the forces of neoliberalism, sending social democracy into retreat. The global wave lifted its Irish counterpart. In 1985, an unapologetically neoliberal party, the Progressive Democrats (PDs), was founded. It would go on to exert a disproportionate influence on Irish policymaking over the course of its existence. In 1987, the unions responded to the neoliberal surge by accepting Charles Haughey's offer to re-establish national pay agreements – which had collapsed in 1980 – concluding that it was the best way to maintain their dwindling influence. The ETU continued to expand during these years despite the hostile climate; NEETU remained mired in crisis, however.

NEETU: development and decline

NEETU's growth was invariably stunted by the financial drain of the legal saga between it and its financial general secretary. But the union did experience some growth in the 1970s as rural Ireland continued to industrialise. In May 1977, its recently opened branch in Castlebar secured negotiating right at the new Asahi (a Japanese firm) synthetic fibre plant in Kilala, Co. Mayo after a month-long stoppage.[4] In May 1978, it created a supervisors' branch in Dublin. By the decade's end, NEETU also had branches in the Midlands, Newbridge, Athy and Portarlington, and was considering setting up shop in Portlaoise. Apart from diffusing itself geographically, the union was spreading to other trades. It opened sections for industrial pipefitters and domestic and heating engineers. By then, 'everyone accepted the need for a fulltime official' for Limerick and the mid-west region. A Limerick man told the NEC how membership in Limerick 'could be doubled in … two years if they had the services of a fulltime official.'[5] Instead, local officials were under severe pressure and members were threatening to leave because of the poor service received from head office. Nevertheless, it was not until 1982 that the NEC appointed a fulltime official for the Limerick area.[6] Rural branches also reported trouble: the Crossmolina branch, for example, reported that it was in 'financial chaos.'[7] It was eventually merged with Sligo to form the North-West branch. NEETU entered the 1980s numerically strong: in 1980, it had thirty branches, including eleven in Dublin.[8] However, the legal wrangling with McConnell throughout the decade sapped much time and resources that could have been invested in branches, which caused much friction between head office and the rank-and-file in Dublin. In 1989, the Dublin No. 8 Branch left en mass and joined the ITGWU and the Federated Workers' Union of Ireland (FWUI). The REC closed the branch and transferred its remaining seven members to Dublin No. 2.[9]

NEETU in the era of discontent

From the mid-1970s, there were major strikes in several crucial economic arteries, some of which lasted several months: the Dublin bus service (1974), the banks (1976) and the postal service (1979) to name but a few. NEETU did not call as many stoppages as other unions because, by the mid-1980s, its enormous legal bills had brought it to the brink of insolvency. Head office was understandably reluctant to add to its vast debts by sanctioning anything other than the most unavoidable of strikes. Nevertheless, the union engaged employers in some major actions. In June 1977, echoing the heyday of Irish syndicalism, NEETU and the ETU took part in a one-day local general stoppage at the Port of Cork in solidarity with craftsmen at Irish Steel who had been on strike for a pay rise since March. The strike ended in a compromise in September.[10]

The local authorities were another arena for wage militancy. On 1 September 1977, a major unofficial stoppage began when sixteen hundred maintenance craftsmen and their mates at twenty-two local authorities and five regional health boards downed tools for parity with rates at Dublin Corporation. NEETU and the ETU were among the eight unions involved. Hundreds of homes were left without water and several provincial hospitals were picketed. After two weeks, the men obtained their demands: a pay raise for craftsmen and their mates (who secured 80 per cent of the craft rate).[11] The discontent is also discernible by other forms of industrial action: work-to-rule was a cheaper alternative that could be quite efficacious. In April 1979, the long-standing dispute between NEETU and Dublin Corporation climaxed when nine hundred craftsmen at the Stanley Street depot went on work-to-rule and placed a ban on overtime for a £14 increase. Maintenance pay had long been stagnant, and NEETU had been trying to settle a £7 wage claim with the Corporation since 1973. Craft wages at Stanley Street were now amongst the lowest offered by the Corporation: refuse collection lorry drivers earned £4 more than craftsmen. In fact, local authority craftsmen were among the lowest paid craftworkers in the country. The government deployed the army to clear the large piles of rubbish that had built up. The men ignored recommendations from the executive to resume normal working practice.[12] Their cause was dealt a blow when the AUEW capitulated, leading to the unions accepting a smaller increase. A simultaneous strike of NEETU members at Wexford County Council for an increase caused similar scenes as tourists arriving at Rosslare Harbour were greeted by the ghastly sight of bags of rubbish piled up along the port.[13]

Later in 1979, the unions and the local authorities agreed to change the way public sector craftsmen were paid following a Labour Court recommendation. Wages would now be dictated by an analogue system examining nineteen comparable employments, both private sector and semi-state, and devise a wage at the local authorities and health boards based on general pay levels throughout industry. Reviews would take place after national pay rounds, usually every eighteen months, and increases would be given on top of national agreements. Introducing the analogue system granted significant pay rises and ended a decade of industrial unrest among local authority craftworkers.[14] That September, a NEETU-enforced work-to-rule and ban on welding at the ESB nearly caused major power outages. The union also banned moving from one station to another and the use of outside contractors. Its 180 fitters at the ESB rejected a 17 per cent increase (£16.40 a week) on their wage of £94 a week. The offer was an interim one until April 1980 when a new comprehensive agreement would be negotiated, the last one having expired on 31 December 1976. When NEETU men staged sit-ins in five generating stations and a walk-out at another, it provoked a wave of opposition from other workers who were afraid that Pope John Paul II's visit to Ireland would be imperilled. After ICTU intervention, NEETU referred the dispute to the ESB's Industrial Council, which gave one-off payments ranging from £70 to £280.[15]

The scale of the discontent is best illuminated by the proliferation of unofficial action. Between 19 October 1977 and 22 January 1978, NEETU men unofficially withdrew their labour at the ailing Liffey Dockyard for colleagues employed temporarily to be hired permanently. The executive subsequently sanctioned their action, while the strike committee called for the yard's nationalisation. On 2 January 1978, events took a sensational turn when six strikers broke into the B&I Line's offices on Westmoreland Street and replaced the company's flag with a Starry Plough. NEC men Danny Ryan, the chairman of the strike committee, and Belfast man Tony Murray, committee secretary, were among the occupiers. Gardaí arrested them after fighting broke out. Ten days later, NEETU men took over the company's offices again in a sit-in protest and hoisted the Starry Plough once more. They too were arrested.[16] By late 1978, unofficial action had driven employers to their wits' end. The Construction Industry Federation (CIF) advised its members to investigate their workers' backgrounds before employing to establish if they had led any 'wildcard strikes' so that 'potential trouble-makers could be weeded out.' Larry O'Neill denounced the call as 'nothing but S.A.S. tactics' and promised a vicious fight against any attempt to compile a blacklist.[17] On 27 August 1978, NEETU men went out unofficially at the Irish Cement factory in Drogheda against the company's plans to take on temporary workers. Two months later, men downed tools in a dispute about stand-by payments during emergencies. The executive sanctioned both actions. The disputes culled the Republic's production of cement by 65 per cent, leading to many layoffs in the building trade. Further unofficial action took place at Irish Cement two years later against the use of subcontractors.[18]

In 1978, Alcan – the Canadian aluminium giant – chose Aughinish Island as the site to build a new £330 million plant, the largest of its kind in Europe. It was the biggest industrial project in the history of the state and Europe's largest construction site at the time (one thousand acres), employing 3,600. Dan Miller, ETU assistant general secretary, served as the fulltime chairman of the group of unions on the site. He had a busy job. Alcan ran a strict regime and workers had grievances from the start, especially over bonus payments (which could double basic pay). The project was plagued by a rash of unofficial stoppages until its opening in 1983, prompting the government to consider legislating to curb such actions. From 3-9 January 1980, NEETU welders, riggers and general operatives took unofficial action against having to operate automatic welding machinery. Having defied their executive, the men had hit the site with its eleventh strike in eighteen months. Although a thousand others refused to pass the pickets, the NEETU men were forced to concede defeat and utilise the machines. From 1980 to 1982, NEETU locked horns with various contractors on the site in disputes over bonuses and allowances, the outcome of which was often the unofficial downing of tools. In 1986, there were more unofficial pickets after NEETU fitters allegedly intimidated colleagues.[19] Simultaneously, NEETU men also took unofficial action in pay disputes during the construction of the ESB's Moneypoint power station.[20] One of the largest capital projects in the state's history, Moneypoint was commissioned between 1985 and 1987 as the country's only coalfired power station. From the beginning of the Whitegate site in 1957 to the closure of Moneypoint site in 1984, there was always at least one major industrial project under construction, employing many mechanical and electrical craftsmen whom NEETU and the ETU were happy to provide.

NEETU's peak of militancy: the Irish Glass Bottles and Tara Mines strikes

On 11 March 1980, seventy NEETU fitters at the Irish Glass Bottle Company downed tools for the reinstatement of four suspended men who had refused to handle machinery blacked in a demarcation dispute. The REC officialised the strike two days later. The men had already implemented a work-to-rule because the firm would not concede a pay claim it considered a breach of the National Understanding. NEETU's chances of defeating an openly hostile employer suffered a major blow when the ITGWU refused to support the strike. NEETU did, however, receive the Marine and Port Workers' support, who blacked cargos of sand destined for the company. The union needed all the help it could get because Irish Glass Bottles had several weeks' supply of sand to continue manufacturing glass; NEETU, on the other hand, was forced to cut strike pay to £15 a week. In June, Gardaí had to escort lorries carrying two hundred tonnes of sand at the company's gates at Ringsend. Gardaí also intervened to clear picketers blocking lorries from entering a warehouse which the strikers believed was being used to transfer sand to the factory.[21] NEETU considered calling a one-day national stoppage on 19 August which the 100,000-strong National Federation of Craft Unions (NFCU) pledged to support. But the FUE and ICTU concluded an agreement in the meantime, which the fitters voted to accept. On 1 August, they returned to work after five months on strike.[22]

On 2 July 1981, 120 craftsmen at Tara Mines struck for equalisation of pay and bonuses with miners and against a new shift system. NEETU had seventy-eight of the fitters, but the ETU, AUEW and the Union of Construction, Allied Trades and Technicians (UCATT) also had a presence at the mines. Craft wages had been among the top three in the country when the mine opened in 1974 but soon fell to a much lower level due to inflation and the stagnation of bonuses. The relativity claim went back to 1977. By 1981, craft wages were £125 a week compared to £100 for miners; however, miners could supplement their pay with weekly bonuses of up to £104, while craft bonuses only reached £18. In May 1981, the fitters enforced an overtime ban after management and the Labour Court rejected their claim. The company then tried to outflank the unions by introducing four-cycle shifts. When the fitters refused to work the new shifts, the company suspended them. In response, the unions overwhelmingly voted for strike. The strike brought production at the mines to a standstill, leading to eight hundred other employees being laid off.[23] It turned ugly later that month when vandals burned down the rented wooden prefab used by the strikers as a headquarters, which Gardaí treated as malicious. NEETU was forced to pay £150 to the owner. Picketers damaged employer's property and slashed the tyres of suspected blacklegs – the supervisors. Afterwards, the High Court gave the company an injunction from being picketed. The strike ended on 3 February 1982 when both sides accepted a Labour Court recommendation to enlarge the craft bonus scale to £52. The craftsmen subsequently accepted a 16 per cent pay rise.[24] The strike was the longest in the history of Tara Mines and one of the most enduring NEETU experienced. It devastated the local economy, costing the town £1 million in lost business, a huge sum for a town with a population of only twelve thousand. The ESB also lost £3 million and the Dublin Port and Docks Board £210,000. The closure of the mines in December 1981 had led to the suffering of hundreds of others employed in ancillary industries.[25]

The strike had exacerbated NEETU's internal woes by amplifying rank-and-file hostility to head office. Inevitably, it became enmeshed with the conflict between McConnell and the rest of the executive. In September, controversy erupted when McConnell wrote to NEETU's branch secretaries alleging that the REC had not given the fitters any strike pay when the men were entitled £10,000 worth. To the chagrin of the executive, McConnell signed the letter as the union's financial general secretary despite his dismissal from the role. Paddy Lawless, Navan branch secretary, denounced the letter as a 'a complete tissue of lies and a figment of Mr. McConnell's imagination', and accused McConnell of 'trying to wreck the union because they sacked him.' White made similar accusations. Lawless secured six weeks' strike pay after sustained pressure from his branch, infuriated that it had not received strike pay.[26] In November, the strikers began picketing 6 Gardiner Row to demand payment. Lawless believed that McConnell was behind the pickets 'to make capital' from the men's grievances. Others alleged that McConnell 'was provoking the members to turn against this union and … the advice … Moneley had given them.'[27] McConnell and his supporters participated in the pickets, which interfered with staff and officials conducting their business, resulting in their dispersal by Gardaí. The NEC passed a motion of confidence in the Navan branch for its handling of the strike. By June 1982, the men were still picketing head office, claiming that had only received three months' strike pay when they were entitled to seven.[28] Sixteen appeared before the REC to state their case. Chaos ensued when Fullerton told them that the REC would summon the picketers to answer charges. The men refused to leave the meeting which the chair had to adjourn. They 'continued to protest in very loud voices and made accusations against the REC and the branch secretary, noisily voicing their protest … the REC tried to advise the members of procedure within the rules of the union, but the members continued with the outbursts and protests.'[29]

The rules in question mandated that each member partaking in an official strike was entitled to dispute pay for ten weeks before a review would take place. The REC had paid out for twelve weeks whereas the fitters claimed for thirty-one weeks, the full duration of the stoppage. They maintained that each fitter was owed £255 and threatened legal action to get it. Even Lawless advised them to stop remitting money to head office until they got their strike pay, when they should leave NEETU. The men continued to disrupt REC meetings and 'hound' officials for the money.[30] NEETU's concurrent financial crisis meant that the executive did not have the money to pay up. By late 1985, it owed over £14,000. By then, many had left the union. The NEC resolved that no 'ex-members of NEETU be paid strike pay' and instead 'be paid on the understanding that they remain loyal members of this union.'[31]

NEETU and industrial militancy, 1982-92

Inflation had spurred industrial militancy in the 1970s. Nonetheless, the unions could only secure modest improvements in real pay under the NWAs and National Understandings. Militancy cooled as inflation moderated, leading to a decline of strikes across the country from the early 1980s. Private sector strikes fell substantially while the incidence of stoppage in the public sector increased. Globalisation, a by-product of neoliberalism, directly impacted Ireland as firms fled to the Third World for cheap labour, throwing many craftsmen into the dole queues. Cork was hit especially hard. In September 1983, Dunlop's closed its tyre manufacturing plant, confining 680 to unemployment. The following July, the city suffered another blow when Ford's closed with 1,100 redundancies. That November, the Verolme Dockyard closed with the loss of 720 jobs, three hundred belonging to NEETU men. It was the Republic's last major shipyard. It had struggled financially for years and had been steadily shedding jobs: in 1983, for instance, it had employed one thousand. It had been profitable until 1978 but was hit hard by the slump in the Western shipbuilding industry as companies relocated to south-east Asia for cheaper labour. By 1984, Verolme depended entirely on state contracts. The government concluded that the yard was no longer viable and promptly ended its support. As it had lost affiliation due to non-payment of fees, NEETU was unable to partake in the DCTU's one-day stoppage on 16 November 1983 for the re-opening of the struggling Clondalkin Paper Mills, which the government had bought earlier that year after a sit-in by the workforce. In 1987, the mills shut their doors for the last time.[32]

Despite its financial troubles, NEETU could still sustain prolonged stoppages early in the decade. From June to November 1982, it conducted a strike of technicians at the Commissioners of Irish Lights for a pay rise far above the 16 per cent public sector deal offered by the Commissioners. Labour Court intervention gave the technicians most of their demand. NEETU subsequently recruited thirty-two members at Irish Lights from the ITGWU, who soon began to complain about the lack of service from head office.[33] Unofficial action still occurred occasionally and continued to sour relations with employers. In May 1984, Rowntree-Mackintosh threatened to close its Inchicore factory unless the workers sign an agreement promising not to take unofficial action.[34] Rapport between the ESB and the union were similarly tense. Throughout 1984, the Board conducted a rationalisation plan to reduce the workforce by over a thousand. That August, NEETU took out its shift workers at the Poolbeg station after eleven men were removed from the payroll for refusing to carry out instructions. The ESB had wanted unit operators' working arrangements to become more 'flexible.' NEETU spread the action to provincial stations and considered calling a national strike after its members voted for such. Having rejected the Industrial Council's recommendation, the union submitted the issue to the Labour Court, which backed the Board's actions.[35] There were few major strikes for the rest of the decade, reflective of members' awareness that, because of the union's financial position, strike pay may not be forthcoming should a dispute take place. One exception was the stoppage of office workers – whom NEETU had poached from the Association of Scientific, Technical and Managerial Staffs – at the CERDAC plant in Drogheda (formerly the Irish Cake and Oil Mills) from 2 September to 1 November 1985 over redundancy proposals. The strike ended when the plant closed, for which management blamed NEETU, never to reopen.[36]

Table 60: Strikes in Ireland, 1961-91.[37]

Years	No. of strikes	Workers involved	Workdays lost
1962-66	416	141,664	2,219,011
1967-71	606	194,100	2,805,715
1972-76	817	168,899	2,038,178
1977-81	712	174,968	3,424,294
1982-86	686	306,388	1,951,079
1987-91	272	68,415	766,519

Table 61: Consumer Price Index, 1983-90 (mid-November 1982=100).[38]

Year (mid-November)	All Items
1983	110.3
1984	117.7
1985	123.5
1986	127.4
1987	131.3
1988	134.8
1989	141.1
1990	144.9

The ETU: growth and development

The ETU was a far more functional union than NEETU between 1976 and 1992. It was better managed and lacked the vicious personality conflicts that nearly destroyed its rival in the 1980s. Hence, it was financially secure throughout this time and experienced impressive growth. Its expansion in Munster resulted in the appointment of a fulltime official for the region, Owen Wills (a fulltime branch secretary for Cork from 1983). Brendan O'Donoghue replaced Egan as president in 1981, with Gary Browne taking over in 1983. O'Reilly replaced Heery as general secretary in 1986. By 1985, it had fourteen branches: eight in Dublin, two each in Limerick and Kerry, and one each in Sligo and Galway. It continued to broaden its base to include technicians, electrical and electronic assembly workers and others. It was also becoming more politically active. Like NEETU, it endorsed ICTU's campaign against Apartheid and affiliated to the Irish Anti-Apartheid Movement in 1978, the United Nations International Anti-Apartheid Year. The ETU had previously rejected calls to organise both internally and within ICTU for a boycott of South African goods and services and ban members from taking up jobs in South Africa.[39] Growth allowed the union to provide additional perks to its members. In 1988, it introduced a comprehensive insurance scheme covering car and house insurance, life assurance and investment policies.[40] By 1992, it had grown to ten thousand members in twenty-two branches.[41] It had surpassed NEETU in membership, an extraordinary achievement considering that it only organised in the electrical trade whereas NEETU organised all engineering and mechanical craftsmen. But the ETU had internal conflicts of its own, especially concerning automation and demarcation. The number of self-employed electricians grew throughout the 1980s, which impacted union meetings at the branch level. As the NEC acknowledged:

at the most recent meetings, discussion has centred on matters such as pricing policies, unfair competition, looseness in the system completion certificates etc. rather than on the traditional topics, such as the rate, proficiency pay etc. It is clear that there is large-scale abuses in the industry. Work is being done by non-qualified people. Other work is being done by qualified electricians operating in the black economy.[42]

Table 62: ETU Membership, 1976-91.[43]

1976	7,949	1984	9,688
1977	8,241	1985	10,286
1978	8,615	1986	10,269
1979	8,879	1987	10,288
1980	9,542	1988	10,425
1981	9,662	1989	10,718
1982	9,710	1990	10,562
1983	9,541	1991	10,813

Table 63: Composition of ETU Dublin Branches, March 1987.[44]

Branch	Industry
No. 1	Private sector maintenance
No. 2	Local authorities, lift & escalator, auto electrical
No. 3	ESB
No. 4	Private telephone companies & security
No. 5	Supervisors
No. 6	General workers
No. 7	Public service
No. 8	Contracting

The ETU and automation

In the run-up to the negotiations for the 1978 NWA, the ETU's NEC resolved that agreement with employers or government should be conditional on it containing a plan to expand state companies into extraction and exploit the country's natural resources to reduce unemployment. It wanted the government to launch a state smelter company to process minerals from the Tara Mines and it condemned the export of lead and zinc ore from Navan. It supported the Resources Protection Campaign, a civil society group agitating for state ownership of natural resources so that profits accruing from their exploitation could benefit the Irish people.[45] Electricians were being severely impacted by the economic malaise of the late 1970s, from suffering pay cuts to losing their jobs. In April 1978, the union deplored that 'our membership, in common with the majority of the working class, have borne the brunt of the economic crisis of the last few years' and committed to 'organise members in a common campaign for a thirty-five-hour working week and a national minimum wage of £100 a week for all electricians.'[46] Six months later, however, Heery informed members that:

Given the conditions under the terms of the NWA and the national climate in industrial relations ... some real or imaginary substantial

235

concession would have to be part of a deal that had £100 basic payment for a thirty-five-hour week. The two possibilities … are: 1) A thirty-five-hour week with an agreed output where additional hours without payment would be worked to reach that agreed output… 2) To set fabrications against the reduced hours and additional rate. Neither of these possibilities are being recommended by the officials as sound judgements.[47]

His letter sparked serious debate among ETU leaders about technological development and the resulting automation of electrical work. Richards felt making concessions on automation could help the union achieve better wages and hours. 'The dockers have done that, they are an example … where a big ship comes in, she goes for containerisation, they get compensated with big sums of money.' Kidd agreed, 'machinery has developed and improved… it is creating greater output and shorter working weeks for everybody… the shorter working week would be a counterbalance to the productivity and … increased unemployment.' Bro. Ó Ruairc, however, highlighted that automation would inevitably shed jobs and he would therefore not countenance a situation 'where men's jobs are going to be sacrificed for a few pounds.' For the same reason, Swan believed that automation would be disastrous for the electrical trade. He agreed with Richards that the docks were an example of automation relevant to the ETU, but not as an example to follow. The Port of Dublin, he declared, had been 'ruined' by containerisation, which had decimated the number of dockers on Dublin's quays from 1,500 to 450; soon, there would only be 350.[48]

The same meeting also debated whether to organise electricians' helpers and mates, and what, if anything, was the difference between the two. The latter question was unclear even to senior official of an electrical trade union: O'Ruairc, for example, could not see any difference. Bro. Maloney argued that there was a difference, that a mate was a 'most useful animal' who 'opened and stripped the cores and left them ready for jointing.' On the other hand, a 'helper' only erected the ladder and held it in place while the electrician worked. The roles of both helper and mate were poorly defined and varied from company to company. The discussion explored the essence of the union. Bro. Coyle acknowledged as much when he opined that the NEC had opened 'the question of whether we are becoming a general union or remaining a craft union.' Even more revealing was his fellow delegates' use of language redolent of the craft snobbery of old: 'It grieves me to hear delegates here use the term labourer. The day is long gone when you brought a labourer into the field and gave him a shovel and said, 'you dig a hole here.' Everybody requires a skill to some degree.'[49] Kidd wanted the union to enrol mates and helpers because 'if they were in the ETU, we could monitor what they do, but if they are in another union, we will have no control whatsoever over them.' Maloney countered that, 'if we introduce mates … you would be taking a step backwards… The English ETU had … a long battle to get rid of mates because they are a danger. They outshine the apprentice because they are more useful than an apprentice.' The Irish union had tried for years to eliminate the position of mates because they knew 'as much or a little less than an apprentice after five or six years.' Earlier in 1978, it had signed an agreement abolishing the role in the lift industry, where mates had traditionally graduated to become craftsmen.[50]

The meeting appointed a subcommittee to explore the issues, which reported the following year. Regarding closed shops, it affirmed that 'it is imperative that we move quickly ... to ensure that we control the electrical industrial section.' Industrial unionism and modern technology had combined to produce 'specialised, non-apprentice skills ... in the electrical industry' which risked 'creating second-class members.' The report concluded that closed shops were a 'fact of life to which we have no input at present' and it envisaged 'an amalgamation of craft/engineering forces to combat this. The other craft unions are ... actively closing shops against the ETU.' It advocated no change in policy on closed shops. The NEC agreed. 'The atmosphere was changing... The legal status of closed shops has been raised in Britain and ... this would, in turn, influence the Irish situation. Closed shops had caused problems for the unions operating them.'[51] The report also argued that the union should 'come to an understanding with the large general unions for the ETU to supply a pool of skilled electrical workers. We agree that this would mean honouring commitments to those unions to the exclusion of other craft unions ... that are actively excluding us.'[52] It was a thinly veiled reference to NEETU who had negotiated several closed shops at major companies, like the Verolme Dockyard. Closed shops were contentious issues for unions that could damage relations between them. NEETU had many closed shops with the ITGWU (at Howmedica and Beckon Dickinson, for example) and would subsequently negotiate others to exclude rivals like the AUEW and the ETU, as it did at Arklow Pottery after its takeover by Japanese firm Noritake. NEETU was not afraid to picket firms to secure negotiating rights with other unions, doing so at Maguire and Paterson in Dublin in 1976 (an AUEW closed shop) and at the new Asahi plant in Killala the following year (an ITGWU closed shop).[53]

Throughout the 1970s and 1980s, employers tried to use technological advancement to alter how electricians worked and were paid to gain control of the methods of production. Since the 1960s, they had developed the strategy of 'productivity bargaining' to try and rescind protections and informal rules of work and to implement stricter management control. In response, the ETU resolved that it 'rejects management work methods such as measured day work, work recording, that take control of the work situation from our members.'[54] The importance of craft had remained undiminished for over a century – skilled workers would still protect their trade, their livelihood, at any cost. Resistance to the encroachment was fierce, as ETU observed:

> Some of the productivity deals ... over the past few years, have given management the prerogatives and unilateral authority on work performance, manning levels and allocation of work, backed up by pseudo-scientific methods of assessment under managerial control, linked with new pay systems based on job evaluation, again giving union control over the wage structure to management... The pace and pressure of modern industrial life, together with increasing remote and technocratic control of the process of production, make protective practices ... more necessary to workers than ever they have been... We have our own rules on the recruitment and entry into the trade and apprenticeship ratios. These are controls we have, and we must guard them dearly.[55]

The ETU and the struggle for control

Demarcation disputes were another enduring manifestation of the craftsman's need to control his work. Modern technology had made engineering more significant to the economy than ever, which made demarcation disputes in the trade ruinous to society. In 1974, for example, one thousand electricians withdrew their labour from the ESB for five weeks because of a demarcation dispute with the linesmen, preventing the connection of four hundred newly built houses to the national grid.[56] In June 1979, a conflict between electricians (organised by the ETU) and instrument technicians (organised by the AUEW) at the ESB's Poolbeg power station blacked out over 800,000 homes and industries. The dispute, which had been ongoing for the previous six months, was over who carried out work on the station's new 270 megawatt generating unit. The electricians refused to carry out directives from the Board which they considered technicians' work. Seven men were laid off as a result. Events took a bizarre turn when Desmond O'Malley, the Minister for Industry, Commerce and Energy, foolishly called the ETU a British union in a thundering invective against it in the Dáil, to which the union reacted furiously. ICTU arbitration produced a temporary settlement, but not before more power cuts. The peace was fragile from the beginning and there were more strikes of AUEW members that November.[57] The incident provoked the government to again consider legislating against unofficial strikes.[58] The secretary of the ETU's Dublin No. 3 Branch was incensed by the executive's handling of the dispute and was highly critical of how his union was run. 'If this trend continues, the union will be left with very few members indeed… It is the sad opinion of this branch committee that over the last two years, the service this union is providing to our members is nothing short of deplorable.' The No. 5 Branch agreed. It was 'completely despondent with the delay in handling the few cases that are on our minute book.' Having concluded that 'our activities are a complete waste of time', its committee resigned at the end of that year.[59]

Demarcation disputes continued between mechanical fitters, electricians and instrument technicians at the ESB and damaged the ETU's relations with NEETU and the AUEW. In 1980, an inter-union clash erupted into a five-week strike at Nitrigin Eireann Teo's fertiliser plant at Marino Point, Cork Harbour. From August to November 1981, the ETU and NEETU withdrew their labour at Dunlop's tyre plant in Cork over the suspension of two craftsmen who had refused to repair a boiler because labourers had previously repaired it. During the dispute, the ETU launched a localised twenty-four-hour general strike in solidarity with the men. RTÉ was the centre for demarcation rows between electricians and technicians. The ETU organised electricians, rigger-drivers, installers among others at the national broadcaster. One such conflict nearly prevented coverage of Regan's May 1984 visit to Ireland. The ETU withdrew notice the day the strike was due to begin after the Labour Court brokered a settlement. In February 1988, however, the ETU took out its members at RTÉ for eighteen days in a dispute with lighting operators.[60] The strike was part of the union's struggle against automation. In November 1986, it had determined to 'take immediate steps to halt the increasing leakage of members from the ETU due to the redefinitions of job description which accompanies the expansion of electronic systems.' It specifically targeted RTÉ, 'where automation of studio systems may lead to an upgrading of jobs, which will no longer be defined as appropriate to the union.'[61]

The ETU: strikes and the wages movement

Healthy finances allowed the ETU to pursue industrial grievances more vigorously, giving it a competitive edge over NEETU. In January 1980, the ETU entered official dispute with the ESB over category agreements between the Board and its drivers. The union took out two hundred drivers in a series of one-day stoppages in the Spring of 1980, threatening power supplies in the process. The conflict escalated in January 1981 when the union took the drivers out again, this time for two months. With the threat of national power outages looming, the ESB conceded wage increases worth £40,000 to its employees, which settled the dispute.[62] However, some branches were unhappy about how head office had handled the strike. The committees of the Area Supervisors' and Dublin No. 4 Branches both nearly resigned in protest at the settlement. Concurrently, the Dublin No. 2 Branch committee resigned when the REC refused its request to make its strike at Kirwan's electrical contractors in Cabra official after the firm had sacked and blacklisted a member of staff. The tensions were mutual as officials felt 'resentful' towards grassroots criticism. One NEC man believed that the rank-and-file felt they were being 'pushed to the background' because 'NEETU run most of the agreements in the engineering shops' as they had 'organisations in all the small towns where we only have one branch for a much larger district.'[63] The drivers' dispute reopened a long-standing dilemma for the ETU: was it a craft union or an industrial union in the electrical trade? It was both – an industrial union in the ESB and a craft union outside it. It even considered organising more non-craftworkers (such as cleaners) but rejected the idea due to fear of conflict with the general unions.[64]

On 30 May 1980, just as holiday season was about to commence, ten unions took out Aer Lingus's 950 maintenance craftsmen in a relativity pay claim first submitted in 1976. Disputes over relativities had become common in Aer Lingus due to its decision in 1966 to introduce salary scales for craftsmen. Before that, only clerks were on incremental scales. The strike lasted four-and-a-half weeks and cost the airline £5.5 million and the tourist industry £2.4 million. It ended when the men accepted a £6 increase. The strike had a knock-on effect: within hours of the settlement, the general operatives started agitating for the increase.[65] In November 1980, the Construction Group of Unions (representing fifty-five thousand) concluded an agreement with the CIF (to which the ECA was now affiliated). The agreement was controversial. Although it gave better allowances and working conditions, the group had conceded peace clauses and a three-month pay pause on all future increases due under national wage agreements. The ETU was unhappy with certain parts of the agreement. 'The intrusion of the CIF into the affairs of the ENJIC continues to be a problem... They represent a serious barrier to the development of wages and conditions for electricians.'[66] Labourers had narrowed the wage gap in the construction sector now 92 per cent of the craft rate. Their success galvanised the ETU to reiterate its demand for a minimum wage of £3.50 an hour for a thirty-five-hour week, with those working above ground level to be paid even more on a graduated scale (10ft to 40 ft).[67]

The tax marches

In the late 1970s, Fianna Fáil's hope of securing industrial peace through economic expansion unravelled because of sluggish rates of private sector job growth. Between 1971 and 1981, the workforce swelled by 126,000 as ninety-seven thousand new jobs were added to economy, half of which were in the public sector. The state's contribution to national output grew from 43 to 63 per cent. The surge that in consumer spending that Fianna Fáil had hoped for never materialised. The 1977 'giveaway' budget (which abolished domestic rates and motor tax) required heavy state borrowing.

The government serviced the debt with heavy taxes on labour: between 1970 and 1981, the contribution of the Pay As You Earn (PAYE) and Pay Related Social Insurance schemes to the total tax take rose from 30 to 45 per cent. By 1978, 87 per cent of income tax came from PAYE, making heavy tax rates on labour a chronic grievance. Although workers were being granted high nominal wage awards, they experienced little increase in real disposable income as inflation ensured that wages entered higher tax bands. From 1970 to 1977, Irish consumer prices rose by 13.8 per cent a year, 4 per cent above the EEC average, while gross national product increased by only 25 per cent over the same period. Workers especially resented the fact that famers paid little tax, even though real per capita income in agriculture rose by 72 per cent between 1970 and 1978. The fury exploded into unofficial strikes when the government capitulated to the Irish Farmers' Association and dropped a 2 per cent tax on farmers in the 1979 budget. The ICTU leadership initially opposed direct action but was forced to delegate responsibility for coordinating a response to trades councils, which became focal points of the revolt.

On 11 March 1979, fifty thousand people marched through the streets of Dublin to demand tax equity in the biggest protest Dublin had ever experienced, surpassed by a march of 150,000 nine days later. In Cork, forty thousand took to the streets.[68] 'It dwarfed any other action the workers' movement had taken and was the first general strike in the history of the Republic of Ireland.'[69] The revolt peaked in January 1980 when 700,000 PAYE workers across the country – 350,000 in Dublin alone – took to the streets to demand tax justice. Unfortunately for NEETU, the protests took place during the executive's dispute with McConnell. The union banner was not available for the January 1980 march because it was locked in the financial office and McConnell had not turned up.[70] The DCTU called a third stoppage for 1 May, when another thirty thousand turned up to a rally in Dublin city centre. The militancy frightened the government into incorporating even greater promises on employment, health and housing into the first National Understanding, which was negotiated during the tax strikes. The ETU smelled blood and urged ICTU 'to escalate the 'tax reform now' campaign beyond 'petition signing" into mass industrial action for a fairer tax system.[71]

The marches were watersheds in Irish labour history, partially because they crystallised the widening chasm between its political and industrial wings. The Labour Party refused to back the marches, or any other mass movement on the streets, another indication of its drift to the centre. The party had some achievements during the 1973-77 coalition. Over 100,000 new houses were built (double the previous rate of construction), several new allowances were introduced, and the rates and eligibility of existing social welfare schemes were improved. Overall, spending on welfare rose from 6.5 per cent to 10.5 per cent of GNP, which was partially funded by new taxes on wealth, farmers, capital gains and acquisitions, and the mining of natural resources. The party also produced an impressive quantity of labour law. Legislation was passed to protect workers from unfair dismissals, end gender-based discrimination in pay and to introduce worker directors on the boards of semi-state companies. Although ICTU's fingerprints were visible on these laws, the next Fine Gael-Labour coalition was determined to reduce union influence on public policy.[72]

National Agreements, wage rounds and social partnership

In March 1978, ICTU endorsed that year's NWA by a mere twenty-five votes (240-215). Though the country's two biggest unions, the ITGWU and the ATGWU, opposed the agreement, the votes of the WUI and the craft and public sector unions were enough to see it through. Both the NEETU and ETU votes (twelve and ten respectively) were crucial. NEETU's support was especially significant, and surprising, given that its REC had recommended rejection. It was the last NWA. Like Congress, both NEETU and the ETU opposed the first National Understanding but supported the second one. The National Understandings introduced tax concessions on top of the increases outlined in Table 64. The ITGWU, FWUI and ATGWU supported the agreements, which was crucial to ICTU's endorsement of them.[73]

Wage increases given under the twenty-second round were dictated by the 1981 public sector pay deal which granted advances of 15-16 per cent. In 1982, Aer Lingus craftsmen received a phased 13 per cent pay rise and ESB granted its craftsmen a 17 per cent rise.[74] In August 1982, NEETU affiliated to ICTU's Public Services Committee to combat the public sector wage embargo recently imposed by the government.[75] Inevitably, the economic crisis severely impacted the unions' ability to keep pay in line with inflation. During the twenty-third round, for example, the ETU sought a 25 per cent rise. Employers asked the union to defer all claims for six months so they could assess the state of the electrical trade. The ETU rejected this and balloted their members, but the response was so poor they did could not enter official dispute. Employers then offered a 10 per cent increase which the union accepted because 'the state of the industry made it impossible to fight for more.'[76] The union was also 'very disappointed' with the 9.5 per cent increase the ESB's Industrial Council offered – the second round in a row where ESB workers received an advance below the average. The recommendation 'emerged in an atmosphere of ESB bashing and vilification of trade unions in the media which has been orchestrated by government and other vested interests in the private sector.'[77]

Table 64: National Wage Agreements and the National Understandings, 1977-80.[78]

Year	Outcome
1977	First phase, 2.5 per cent plus £1, min. increase of £2 a week, max. £5; second, same increases as first phase, giving max. increase of £4.23
1978	First phase, 8 per cent, min. increase of £3.50 a week; second, 2 per cent
1979	First National Understanding: First phase, 9 per cent, min. increase of £5.50; second, 2 per cent plus amount relating to movement in the CPI, min. increase of £3.50
1980	Second National Understanding: first phase, 8 per cent plus £1 a week; second, 7 per cent

Table 65: Price and Wage Inflation, 1979-85.[79]

Year	Price inflation (%)	Wage inflation (%)
1979	13.2	15.7
1980	18.2	21.4
1981	20.4	16.7
1982	17.1	14.7
1983	10.5	11.5
1984	8.6	10.9
1985	5.4	8.0

During the twenty-fourth round, the dispute nearly led to national power shortages. The union presented the ESB with a claim for a 15 per cent raise over a fifteen-month period; the Industrial Council offered 5 per cent over twelve months, which was rejected. By then, the ETU had two thousand of the ESB's 12,500 employees – 1,500 electricians and five hundred supervisors – giving it real economic leverage during negotiations. The union resolved to bring out its Dublin members on 19 February 1985 followed by a national strike from 11 March. This was called off when it accepted a 7 per cent rise over fifteen months.[80] In February 1985, craftworkers at the local authorities and health boards received a 9 per cent pay hike from the Labour Court, the highest increase given to public sector workers in this round, after threatening strike. It was a major victory considering the government had tried to impose a 6 per cent rise across the public sector.[81]

In 1981, NEETU also helped to conclude a 'comprehensive agreement' with the ESB which gave workers a 15 per cent pay rise in addition to increases given under national pay pacts until 1 April 1984. A 'peace clause' gave another 3 per cent as a lump sum in exchange for no industrial action. Although that section was controversial, the unions accepted the agreement because the Board had previously wanted binding arbitration in the event of a strike.[82] On 30 September 1981, the second National Understanding expired for tradesmen. There would be no third agreement. It was a setback for centralised bargaining and Irish wage negotiations reverted to the 'free collective bargaining' of the pre-NWA rounds. The FUE refused to sit down with the NFCU to discuss a new national agreement as employers wanted a return to industry-by-industry bargaining for craftsmen. On 14 January 1982, the NFCU brought out forty thousand workers in a one-day strike to force the bosses to negotiate with it about its claim for a 25 per cent increase for a twelve-month period.[83] When the employers continued to snub it, the federation planned another one-day strike for late February pending a ballot from its affiliates. As its secretary told a frightened press, 'the men are in a militant mood.'[84] Horrified by the prospect of another 1969, the media took him seriously. But it need not have worried. Although NEETU members voted in favour of strike, they did not do so by the two-thirds majority required by union rules. Under such circumstances, the REC had the final say and it unanimously agreed to vote against another strike at the coming NFCU meeting. Five unions voted for strike and seven against. The federation capitulated and agreed that its affiliates should negotiate shop by shop and should not accept less than the 16 per cent given to public sector workers. Electricians secured a 22 per cent improvement.[85]

In February 1987, Fianna Fáil returned to power in a minority government, the last time the party has governed on its own. Like 1959, a change of government heralded a fundamental shift in economic policy. That October, ICTU, farmers' organisations and employer federations concluded the Programme for National Recovery (PNR). Social partnership was born, bringing Irish corporatism to a new level. Partnership deepened over the following two decades and became a principal component of Irish macroeconomic policy until its demise in 2009. It impelled a partial recovery of union membership in the 1990s, which had slumped to a low of 475,000 in 1990. Recovery was also aided by the increased numbers of those at work. Social partnership is often cited as one of the major reasons for the birth of the Celtic Tiger in 1994. The impetus for social partnership came from the National Economic and Social Council's 1986 paper *A Strategy for Development, 1986-90*, which implicitly suggested that only agreement between employers and unions could facilitate the fiscal austerity needed to ameliorate Irish economic woes. By 1987, ICTU had already backed entering national talks. Irish labour leaders had spent seven years watching Thatcher's crushing of union power in Britain with horror and were increasingly fearful a similar outcome in Ireland. It was not a misguided belief. The PDs were in the ascendancy, having won 11.9 per cent of the first preference vote in that year's general election, giving them fourteen seats. But their influence in the Irish body politic would far exceed their numbers.[86] From 1989, 'they would colour coalitions with Fianna Fáil like a drop of ink in a glass of water', helping to make privatisation, deregulation and tax cuts central to Irish political discourse.[87] Social partnership was how ICTU tried to ensure that the 'Celtic Tiger' would not mutate into a 'Celtic Thatcher.'[88]

Social partnership was the culmination of the experiments in corporatism stretching back to the first Dáil. It was also the institutionalisation of the paternalistic relationship between Fianna Fáil and the trade unions. Whereas the National Understandings were two-tier trade-offs on pay and specific policies, social partnership integrated pay deals into a comprehensive framework. Congress leaders championed partnership because, they argued, it would consistently increase wages, especially for low-paid workers; increase employment and labour influence over public policy; and institutionalise and legitimise unions as part of the political furniture. General and public sector unions supported early agreements but became more hostile with time. British unions maintained their longstanding opposition to centralised bargaining. Like other craft unions, NEETU and the ETU rejected the deals as they were better placed for militancy. Within unions, the strongest opposition came from shop stewards, whose traditional roll was being undermined by centralised bargaining. With much justification, many complained that deals did not do enough to raise the 'wage floor', to force employers to recognise unions and to translate partnership at national level to company level.[89] Moreover, unions doubted employers' commitment to partnership above the shop floor level.

The first agreement set out broad macroeconomic goals, including the maintenance of social welfare benefits, tax reduction, job creation and a pay hike. Discrepancies in pay between craft and non-craftworkers had inspired many pay claims in the 1980s. In late 1989, the ETU and NEETU sought a £30 a week rise from the electrical contractors, a claim first made in 1984. When they refused, both unions readied themselves for a national strike of 3,500 electricians – but preparations proved unnecessary. In early 1990, a settlement gave the electricians a £20 a week pay hike, a thirty-nine-hour week and three weeks' annual holidays. The victory had a knock-on effect and helped to inspire workers across the economy to agitate for a 4pm finish on Fridays. NEETU threatened strike for it at Irish Cement. The thirty-nine-hour week, the first reduction of hours since the 1960s, had been a major goal for the unions on entering talks for the PNR. Despite ferocious opposition to it in some quarters, employers had conceded it in most workplaces by 1990.[90] In 1991, ICTU concluded the Programme for Social and Economic Progress (PESP). It provided unions with the ability to bargain locally, which aimed to satiate workers' frustrations at being unable to exploit the profits' boom of 1989-90. The ETU rejected the PNR because of its unrealistic targets of job creation and tax relief, and because of how the peace clause 'would affect the rights of the trade union movement to take strike action when they deem it necessary.' The support of the ITGWU, FWUI and the public sector unions was enough to ensure its passage through Congress. NEETU had no vote on the deal. When its vote was returned, it rejected the second agreement.[91]

The ETU also rejected the PESP because it was too long in duration and gave insufficient wage increases. Relativity in pay was a major grievance at the ESB. From 22-27 April 1991, the ETU withdrew the labour of one thousand electricians against the Board's long-standing plan to regrade them, which would give them a heavier workload and reduce their numbers. Having cost the economy over £35 million, the stoppage ended on terms the union had previously rejected – a £10 a week rise and the receipt of a lump sum already due to electricians. The government viewed the strike as a threat to the PESP, whose success overall was premised its success in the semi-state sector. Although the ETU believed its claim had nothing to do with the PESP, ICTU, the FUE and the ESB all shared the government's view. The ICTU-arranged settlement ensured that the agreement remained intact and that there were no knock-on claims by other workers. Afterwards, the ETU sought pay increases above the national agreements in return for greater productivity. The government intervened to stop the ESB from making offers lest they endanger the PESP, prolonging the dispute for another three years and nearly provoking strikes in 1992, 1993 and 1994.[92] To better assert themselves in social partnership Ireland, the FUE and the Confederation of Irish Industry merged and formed IBEC in 1993.

Table 66: Wage Rounds, 1981-87.[93]

Year	Round	Outcome
1981	22nd	16.4 per cent average cumulate increase over 14.9 months in the private sector
1982	23rd	10.9 per cent average cumulate increase over 13.5 months in the private sector
1983	24th	9.3 per cent average cumulate increase over 14.9 months in the private sector

Year	Round	Outcome
1984	25th	6.8 per cent cumulative increase over twelve months in the private sector
1985	26th	6 per cent cumulative increase over twelve months in the private sector
1986	27th	6.5 per cent cumulative increase over 15.4 months in the private sector

Table 67: Summary of Social Partnership Agreements, 1988-1994.[94]

Agreement	Duration	Summary
Programme for National Recovery	1988-90	7.5 per cent wage increase, tax cuts of £225 million and special pay awards for public servants
Programme for Economic and Social Progress	1990-93	10.75 per cent wage increase, 3 per cent local bargaining and £400 million in tax cuts

The apprenticeship system, 1976-92

Between 1976 and 1982, the intake of apprentices expanded by 42 per cent before recession and automation sent numbers plummeting. The number of apprentices in the electrical trade grew from 2,767 in 1974 to 3,568 in 1980, while in the engineering trade numbers swelled from 3,163 to 5,559 during those years.[95] The number of apprentices in all trades had peaked at 21,498 in 1980, the final year of the old five-year apprenticeship, while first year intake under the new system reached a record figure of 14,219 in 1982. From then on, however, first year intake continuously declined, reaching a nadir of 2,445 in 1988. The number of apprentices declined to only 11,804. Thereafter, intake climbed to 2,919 in 1991 when there were 14,010 apprentices. Some significant reforms were made in the 1980s: AnCo introduced the National Craft Certificate in 1986 and the Dáil passed The Labour Services Act the following year. The Act merged AnCO, the Youth Employment Agency, the National Manpower Service to create An Foras Áiseanna Saothair (FÁS) from 1 January 1988. Its board contained four trade union members, only one of whom represented a craft union, and four employer members, a reduction of one each from AnCO's board. The change represented a significant diminution of the craft unions' influence over the new institution compared to what they exerted over An Cheard Chomhairle and AnCO. It signified that FÁS would lessen the emphasis placed on apprenticeship in its future operations.[96]

In 1989, FÁS proposed significant changes to the existing apprenticeship system, which it considered inefficient, by moving from a time-based to a standards-based model. It proposed in-house tests at the end of each period of off-the-job training and a progression of competency tests, the passing of which would culminate in the award of the National Craft Certificate. The apprentice would have to pass each test before the he/she could take the next one and would not achieve full craft status unless awarded the National Craft Certificate. FÁS would develop an industry-based assessment system, with the apprentice completing several core projects to be checked by a craft supervisor. Assessment of practical skills and related theoretical knowledge would be the main components of the testing procedures. Agreement between employers, unions, the Department of Education and FÁS would decide the standards to be achieved to obtain the National Craft Certificate. Apprentices would start their time aged sixteen and the length of time taken to attain the required competencies would determine the duration of apprenticeship. FÁS endorsed the new model in 1990, as did the government and the social partners during the talks for the PESP. In September 1991, FÁS established the National Apprenticeship Advisory Committee to oversee the transition and advise on all aspects of apprenticeship training, including curricula, testing, certification, duration, entry requirement and apprentice numbers. Five representatives of trade unions and five of employers sat on the committee. After delays, the new system commenced in 1993.[97]

The birth of the Technical Engineering and Electrical Union

Despite its monetary afflictions, which were well-known in labour circles, in 1988 several unions unofficially approached NEETU looking to amalgamate with it. The most alluring came from the Irish membership of Manufacturing, Science and Finance (MSF), a powerful British white-collar union.[98] When NEETU's NEC met to discuss the propositions that May, White told his colleagues that someone at ICTU asked him if NEETU would talk to the FWUI; later, the ATWGU and the EEPTU reached out. More significant were the overtures from the ETU, which was having merger discussions of its own with the EEPTU, MSF and the AEU. The MSF's history of poaching NEETU members meant it had enemies in Gardiner Row. Nonetheless, the question of merging with it opened a debate about the nature of NEETU. Some officials had travelled to London to visit MSF's headquarters and were amazed by the superb level of organisation and computerisation they saw. MacRaghnaill supported merging with MSF because he was conscious of the 'very bad financial position of NEETU' and was impressed with the MSF as a union. Finbarr Dorgan sympathised but saw two difficulties: an Irish union merging with a British one and 'the industrial problem of a craft hourly union joining with a largely white-collar and management union.' But the NEC knew it had to merge with someone because it was 'cognisant of … membership, finance and negotiating strength in the face of multinational employers.' Referring to Dublin's many unorganised building sites, Sheridan maintained that 'this union and all unions in this city are dead.' He argued that NEETU should 'talk to unions with similar categories of members, not unions with white-collars' and opposed amalgamating with a British union. Bro. Darcy believed that if it merged with MSF, 'many members would leave NEETU and join other unions – any union rather than join MSF.' Although MacRaghnaill's motion to negotiate with MSF was defeated, there was consensus that there had to be rationalisation of craft unions in Ireland. Most felt that the ETU was the most logical choice for a merger as both unions had similar memberships and the ETU's finances were healthy. NEETU was also anxious to strengthen its presence in the electrical trade. The meeting voted to enter negotiations with the ETU to amalgamate both unions.[99]

Relations between NEETU and the ETU had not always been cordial that decade. In Cork, for example, the ETU had previously refused to cooperate with NEETU in training apprentices. The Rebel City also the centre of another dispute between them when, in May 1980, the ETU took out its members at Capwell Garage over the employment of a NEETU man. The dispute, which severely curtailed the city's bus service for a month, was over demarcation. The ETU was on the verge of bringing out all its members at CIÉ before the unions and the company negotiated a settlement.[100] Like NEETU, the ETU's decision to enter merger talks were also driven by a desire for survival. In 1987, Dublin No. 1 called on its NEC to recognise that 'the ETU is facing a period of rapid economic, social, industrial and technological change' and that it had to change accordingly. The resolution acknowledged that 'rationalisation ... is now imperative' and called on the NEC to consider 'the possibility of seeking amalgamation, transfer of engagements, sharing resources or some other engagement with other trade unions that will ensure future viability.' Another motion unsuccessfully requested the NEC to discuss amalgamation because of 'the economic climate now existing and the poor state that unions now find themselves in.'[101] Arthur Hall, ETU assistant general secretary, made his calls for amalgamation public when addressing the ICTU Youth summer school in August 1988. He asserted that the multiplicity of craft unions prohibited them from making the necessary financial investment in 'recruitment, education, retraining, multiskilling, health and safety or research into new technology and its effects on members.' Without rationalisation, he argued, craft unions would not survive the 1990s. His colleagues agreed. The existence of traditional craft unions was imperilled by the 'new job definitions and training modes and the closed-shop arrangements typical of new industrial ventures.'[102]

Negotiations for amalgamation began smoothly and it soon 'became clear that there were no major issues which could not be resolved through future discussions.'[103] NEETU's NEC gave its REC no input into the talks, which the latter resented.[104] The ETU, who had already elected a committee to finalise proposals, 'pleasantly surprised' NEETU with its favourability to amalgamation. Despite some 'serious differences of opinion', talks were progressing satisfactorily. NEETU's ailing finances and the 'structure' of the merged union were the main obstacles to progress. It was inevitable that McConnell's behaviour would impede the talks, especially his refusal to provide his colleagues with vital information about NEETU. He did not reply to Carter's request for financial reports to advance the negotiations. The NEC vowed to obtain the information from McConnell 'through any means necessary,' including 'going legal.' Although the talks were making progress by March 1989, it had been 'very difficult' to get the necessary documentation from McConnell. While members were impressed by the ETU's commitment to amalgamation, Carter spoke for all when he contended that 'while a merger was very desirable, we were not in the business of being taken over by the ETU or any other organisation and were not going 'cap-in-hand.' It was up to our side to preserve the interest of NEETU members.' For the ETU, the main obstacles were NEETU's insolvency, McConnell's refusal to provide financial information, and how to convince some of its branch committees (especially Waterford) of the merits of mixing trades at local level. However, most ETU members strongly supported the merger.[105]

In June 1989, NEETU accepted the 'schedule for merger' as negotiated. But by May 1990, neither union had still not received the necessary financial documents because McConnell had not provided the audits for 1988 or 1989 or a proper register of NEETU membership. It was the greatest threat to success because 'on all other fronts the merger talks were progressing very well.'[106] Given the trouble that NEETU's rules had caused, negotiators agreed that, with amendments, the ETU rulebook would form the basis for the new union's rules.[107] McConnell strongly opposed the merger and wrote to the Registry of Friendly Societies formally objecting to it. He was not the only one impeding progress: many NEETU branches had also not sent registers or audits which also seriously delayed the outcome of negotiations. A successful conclusion was contingent on how much of NEETU's dysfunctionality the ETU could take; as NEETU itself acknowledged, 'the ETU have continued to show great patience … but this cannot go on forever.'[108] But take it they did, leading to the successful conclusion of talks in May 1991. Both would now ballot on the final proposals. The following month, NEETU's NEC unanimously endorsed the terms of merger. Duffy, the stalwart who had been seminal in creation of NEETU, felt that 'a historic decision was now being made.' MacRaighnaill stated that 'while everything in the rulebook is not perfect', and although the new union 'will not be strong financially initially', it could 'linkup to likeminded and stronger unions in a European context.' White considered the merger the only way to confine to finally 'emerge from the deep cloud hanging over us for many years.'[109]

However, McConnell had still not handed over the financial documents – and his colleagues' patience had been exhausted. They took him to the High Court, which ordered that he produce a register of paid-up NEETU members so that a ballot on the merger could take place on 4 October as planned. The court also awarded full costs to NEETU. When he failed to comply, he was nearly imprisoned for contempt of court, only escaping because he was too ill to attend the proceedings. He took legal action of his own to restrain the ballot, but the High Court dismissed his claim. McConnell still had some fight left and was determined that the merger would not happen. He locked himself into the financial office and barricaded the door when Frank O'Reilly and David Naughton arrived at Gardiner Row to acquire the relevant documentation. The police were called and tried to coax him out of the office. After several hours and a false promise to leave, their patience ran out. They brought in a locksmith who dismantled the steel frame McConnell had installed over the wooden door of the financial office and the Gardaí escorted him out of the building. He would never set foot in 6 Gardiner Row again. After acquiring the register, NEETU sent out 6,055 ballots of which only 2,101 (35.4 per cent) were returned. Of that number, 1,890 (90.3 per cent) supported the merger and 199 (9.5 per cent) were against. ETU members voted 2,029-568 in favour. Both unions appointed a transitional NEC comprised of their respective executives. The exhaustive process of amalgamation was nearly over.[110]

On 30 June 1992, the Registrar of Friendly Societies granted the new union its negotiating licence after protracted delays. The twenty-two thousand-strong Technical, Engineering and Electrical Union (TEEU) was born. The Department of Labour had financially supported the merger with a grant of £104,923.64.[111] It was part of a broader pattern, as unions fused to consolidate their diminishing strength against the neoliberal juggernaut. The Thatcherite Industrial Relations Act 1990, which repealed the Trade Disputes Act 1906, made secret ballots for strike action mandatory, curtailed the right to picket and take sympathetic action, and removed political strikes from the category of trade disputes. The number of unions fell from ninety-five in 1970 to sixty-eight in 1990, the year the ITGWU and FWUI were finally reunited as the Services, Industrial, Professional and Technical Union (SIPTU). SIPTU had 160,000 members and a quarter of ICTU membership. The SIPTU and TEEU mergers encouraged others to follow suit. By 1995, the number of unions had diminished to forty-six.[112]

Chapter Notes and References

1   Brown, *A Social and Cultural History*, p. 316.
2   Ferriter, *Transformation*, p. 672; Hastings, Sheehan & Yeates, *Saving the Future*, p. 116.
3   *Irish Independent*, 16 Feb. 1987.
4   NEETU REC minutes, 9 Mar., 20 Apr., 4 May, 18 May 1977, TEEU collection, ILHM; *Irish Independent*, 20 May 1977; *Evening Herald*, 27 Apr. 1976, 3 May 1977; *Cork Examiner*, 4 May 1976.
5   *Evening Herald*, 28 Apr. 1978; NEETU NEC minutes, 26 May 1979, TEEU collection, ILHM.
6   NEETU NEC minutes, 26 May, 16 June 1979, TEEU collection, ILHM.
7   Ibid., 6 Oct. 1979, TEEU collection, ILHM
8   'NEC Election, 1980', file: NEETU Executive Minutes, 1979-84, Box: NEETU, 1948-84, TEEU collection, ILHM. The non-Dublin branches were Allenwood, Athy, Ballydermot, Boora-Ferbane, Carlow, Castlebar, Cobh, Cork, Crossmolina, Drogheda, Dundalk, Edenderry, Enniscorthy, Galway, Kilkenny, Limerick, Navan, Newbridge, Passage West, Portarlington, Sligo, Supervisors', Timahoe, Thurles, Tuam, Wexford, Waterford Nos. 1 & 2, Wicklow, Cork Supervisors.'
9   NEETU REC minutes, 25 Oct. 1989.
10 *Cork Examiner*, 28 Mar. 1977; *Irish Independent*, 21 June, 12 Sept. 1977; NEETU REC minutes, 6, 13 Apr., 15 June, 23 July, TEEU collection, ILHM.
11 *Irish Independent*, 1, 5, 15, 17, 22, 31 Aug., 1-14 Sept., 10 Nov. 1977; NEETU REC minutes, 18 Aug., 20 Oct. 1977, TEEU collection, ILHM.
12 *Irish Press*, 19 Apr., 8 June, 26 July, 11, 14, 18 Aug. 1979; *Irish Independent*, 10 July 1979; NEETU REC minutes, 30 May 1979, TEEU collection, ILHM.
13 *Irish Independent*, 17 Aug. 1979.
14 *Evening Herald*, 18 July 1983
15 *Irish Press*, 12-26 Sept. 1979; *Irish Independent*, 26 Oct., 7 Nov. 1979; NEETU REC minutes, 26 Sept., 3 Oct. 1979, TEEU collection, ILHM; NEETU NEC minutes, 22 Sept., 6 Oct. 1979, TEEU collection, ILHM.
16 *Evening Herald*, 2, 12 Jan. 1978.
17 Ibid., 16 Nov. 1978.
18 *Irish Independent*, 1 Sept., 28 Oct.-4 Nov. 1978, 30 May, 11 June 1980.
19 Ibid., 5-10 Jan., 4-8 Nov. 1980, 19-23 Feb, 3 Apr., 4 July, 26 Sept. 1981, 29 Nov. 1986, 9, 29 Apr., 23 July 1987; NEETU REC minutes, 17 Sept, 22 Oct. 1980
20 *Irish Press*, 9 Sept. 1981.
21 *Irish Independent*, 14-26 Mar., 17 Apr., 20 May, 10, 21 June, 10 July 1980.
22 Ibid., 17, 26 July 1980; NEETU REC minutes, 9, 16, 30 July 1980. The NFCU was founded in 1973 and disintegrated in 1986.
23 *Irish Press*, 4, 10, 22 July 1981; NEETU REC minutes, 1 July 1981, TEEU collection, ILHM.
24 *Meath Chronicle*, 3 Oct., 7, 14 Nov. 1981, 6, 13 Feb. 1982; *Irish Independent*, 14 June 1982.
25 Ibid., 19 Dec. 1981.
26 Ibid., 26 Sept. 1981.
27 NEETU REC minutes, 25 Nov. 1981, TEEU collection, ILHM.
28 NEETU NEC minutes, 21 Nov. 1981, 15 May, 19 June 1982; ibid., 7, 21 Apr., both found in TEEU collection, ILHM.
29 NEETU REC minutes, 30 June 1982, TEEU collection, ILHM.
30 Ibid., 21 July 1982, TEEU collection, ILHM; *Meath Chronicle*, 12 June 1982.
31 NEETU NEC minutes, 24 Sept. 1983, 9 Nov. 1985, 8 Feb. 1986, TEEU collection, ILHM.
32 *Irish Independent*, 9 Feb., 1-17 Nov. 1983; *Cork Examiner*, 5 Aug. 1983, 8 Feb., 6 Sept. 1984; Miriam Nyhan, *'Are You Still Below?': The Ford Marina Plant, Cork*, 1917-1984 (Cork: Collins Press, 2007).

33 *Irish Independent*, 14 June, 27 Nov. 1982; NEETU REC minutes, 5 July 1989.
34 *Irish Press*, 22 May-7 June 1984.
35 Ibid., 28 July, 7, 14, 21 Aug., 20 Sept. 1984; NEETU REC minutes, 8, 19 Sept. 1984, NEETU NEC minutes, 28 July 1984, TEEU collection, ILHM.
36 *Drogheda Independent*, 23 Aug.-15 Nov. 1985.
37 Hastings, Sheehan & Yeates, *Saving the Future*, p. 3
38 CSO, *Statistical of Ireland, 1983-91*, (Dublin: Stationary Office, 1983-91).
39 ETU NEC minutes, 24-25 Apr., Oct. 1978, 20-22 May 1979, 30 Apr.-2 May 1983, 19 Jan. 1985, 26-28 Jan. 1986; ETU REC minutes, 17 Nov. 1983.
40 *Irish Independent*, 18 Nov. 1988.
41 'Financial Report, May 1991', file: NEC Report, ETU 1984-1996, TEEU collection, ILHM. Its non-Dublin branches were Athlone, Cork, Wexford, Waterford, Drogheda, Dundalk, Galway, Area Supervisors', Portlaoise, Limerick Nos. 1 & 2, Kerry North, Kerry South, Sligo.
42 ETU NEC minutes, 25-27 Apr. 1987.
43 ETU annual returns, T453, RFS records, CRO.
44 Frank O'Reilly to M. Keogh, 23 Mar. 1987, file: 'NEC April 1987', Connect archives.
45 ETU NEC minutes, 27-28 Nov. 1977, TEEU collection, ILHM.
46 Ibid., 24-25 Apr. 1978, TEEU collection, ILHM.
47 Ibid., Oct. 1978 (undated), TEEU collection, ILHM.
48 Ibid.
49 Ibid.
50 Ibid.
51 Ibid.
52 ETU NEC minutes, 20-22 May 1979, TEEU collection, ILHM.
53 NEETU REC minutes, 20, 27 Oct. 1976, 19 Jan. 16 Feb., 15 Sept. 1977, TEEU collection, ILHM; *Irish Press*, 20 Oct., 11 Nov. 1976, 20 May 1977.
54 ETU NEC minutes, 27 Nov. 1979, TEEU collection, ILHM.
55 Ibid.
56 *Irish Press*, 19 July 1974; *Cork Examiner*, 8, 15, 31 Aug., 3 Sept. 1974. The electricians alleged that the lines had violated the ESB's 1953 demarcation agreement, as amended in 1967.
57 *Irish Independent*, 19, 28 June, 18, 19 July, 22, 29, 30 Nov. 1979; *Irish Press*, 20 July, 16 Oct., 3-30 Nov. 1979.
58 *Irish Press*, 30 July 1979. The instrument technicians were members of the AUEW.
59 Dublin Branch No. 3 Secretary to ETU REC, 13 Sept. 1979; Dublin No. 5 Branch to Heery, 17 Sept. 1979, both found in ETU letters of correspondence, TEEU collection ILHM.
60 *Irish Press*, 16-18 Oct. 1979, 5 May 1980; *Cork Examiner*, 12 Oct., 18, 23 Nov. 1981, 26 May 1984; *Irish Independent*, 4 Dec. 1986, 1-19 Feb 1988.
61 ETU NEC minutes, 15-17 Nov. 1986.
62 ETU REC minutes, 31 Jan.-23 Mar., 6, 13 Nov. 1980, 8 Jan.-12 Mar. 1981.
63 ETU NEC minutes, 25-28 Apr. 1981; *Evening Herald*, 28 Feb. 1981.
64 Ibid., 31 Oct.-2 Nov. 1981.
65 *Irish Press*, 1 Feb., 1 June-5 July 1980.
66 'Report to the ETU NEC', April 1981.
67 Ibid.
68 O'Connor, *Labour History of Ireland* (2nd Ed.), pp. 220, 235.
69 Allen, *Fianna Fáil*, p. 155.
70 NEETU REC minutes, 23 Jan. 1980, TEEU collection, ILHM.
71 ETU NEC minutes, 25-27 Nov. 1979.
72 O'Connor, *Labour History of Ireland* (2nd Ed.), pp. 220, 235; Bielenberg & Ryan, *Economic History*, p. 38; Ferriter, *Ambiguous Republic*, pp. 507-509; Cody, O'Dowd & Rigney, *The Parliament of Labour*, pp. 231-240; Allen, *Fianna Fáil*, pp. 155-156.
73 *Irish Independent*, 22, 23 Mar. 1978; *Evening Herald*, 23 July 1979; ETU NEC minutes, 20-22 May 1979, TEEU collection, ILHM. *Evening Herald*, 25 Nov. 1980; *Irish Independent*, 27 June 1981; NEETU REC minutes, 16 Sept. 1981, TEEU collection, ILHM.
74 *Irish Press*, 11 Mar., 5 May 1982.
75 NEETU REC minutes, 18 Aug. 1982.
76 ETU NEC minutes, 12-14 Nov. 1983.
77 Frank O'Reilly to Thomas Heery, 30 June 1983, TEEU collection, ILHM.
78 Devine, *Organising History*, p. 503.

79   Tim Hastings, Brian Sheehan & Padraig Yeates, *Saving the Future: how social partnership shaped Ireland's economic success* (Dublin: Blackhall Publishing, 2007), p. 4.
80   *Irish Press,* 14 Jan.-19 Feb. 1985.
81   *Irish Independent,* 16, 28 Feb., 6, 9, 15 Mar., 13 Apr. 1985.
82   *Irish Independent,* 1, 10 Aug. 1981
83   Ibid., 8, 13, 14, 15 Jan. 1982.
84   *Irish Press,* 18 Jan. 1982
85   NEETU REC minutes, 16 Dec. 1981, 6, 17, 24 Feb., 3 Mar. 1982; ENJIC meeting minutes, 17 Feb. 1982.
86   Hastings, Sheehan & Yeates, *Saving the Future,* pp. 19-24; O'Connor, *Labour History of Ireland* (2nd ed.), p. 244.
87   O'Connor, *Labour History of Ireland* (2nd Ed.), p. 245.
88   Ibid., p. 244.
89   Ibid., pp. 246-248; Devine, *Organising History,* pp. 798-801
90   ETU REC minutes, 2 Nov. 1989-15 Nov. 1990; *Irish Independent,* 23 Nov. 1989, 26 Jan. 1990; Hastings, Sheehan & Yeates, *Saving the Future,* p. 51.
91   ETU NEC minutes, 22 Oct. 1987, 31 Jan., 20 Feb. 1991; NEETU REC minutes, 20 Feb. 1991.
92   *Irish Independent,* 18-27 Apr. 1991, 9-28 Oct. 1992, 25 Apr., 14-16, 28 May 1994; Hastings, Sheehan & Yeates, *Saving the Future,* p. 120; TEEU EMC minutes, 17 Sept., 12 Oct. 1992, 13 May 1993.
93   Devine, *Organising History,* p. 503.
94   Hastings, Sheehan & Yeates, *Saving the Future,* pp. 213-214.
95   ETU NEC minutes, 31 Oct.-2 Nov. 1981.
96   Ryan, 'Apprenticeships in Ireland', pp. 441-476.
97   Ibid., pp. 482-547.
98   NEETU NEC minutes, 6 Dec. 1986, 10 Oct. 1987, 27 Feb., 30 Apr. 1988.
99   NEETU REC minutes, 4 May 1988.
100   *Cork Examiner,* 24 Nov., 21 Dec. 1979, 21 Apr.-22 May 1980; ETU REC minutes, 28 Feb., 6, 27 Mar., 2, 10, 17, 24 Apr., 1, 8 May 1980.
101   ETU NEC minutes, 21-23 Nov. 1987.
102   *Irish Independent,* 15 Aug. 1988; ETU NEC, 12-14 May 1990.
103   NEETU REC minutes, 25 Jan. 1989.
104   Ibid., 21 Feb. 4 Apr. 15 Nov. 1990, 13 July, 11 Sept., 6 Nov. 1991, 13 May 1992.
105   NEETU NEC minutes, 28 May, 12 Nov. 1988, 4 Mar. 1989; ETU NEC minutes, 23-24 Apr., 25-26 Nov. 1989.
106   NEETU REC minutes, 22 Nov. 1989.
107   NEETU NEC minutes, 28 May, 12 Nov. 1988, 4 Mar., 6 May 1989, 12 May 1990.
108   Ibid., 25 Jan. 1989.
109   Ibid., 30 Sept. 1989, 3 Feb., 21 July, 15 Dec. 1990, 11 May, 14-16 June 1991.
110   Ibid., 2 Nov. 1991; ETU NEC minutes, 2 Nov. 1991; *Irish Independent,* 2-5, 18, 19 Oct. 1991.
111   NEETU NEC minutes, 27 June 1992; Tom Kitt, Dáil Éireann debates, 22 June 1999, Vol. 506, No. 5.
112   O'Connor, *Labour History of Ireland* (2nd Ed.), p. 250.

Connect dispute at Leibherr Kerry.
(Credit: *Connect Archive*)

Connect Presentation to the European Alliance for Apprenticeships.
(Credit: *Connect Archive*)

Connect Trade Union Banner first outing Limerick Soviet Centenary March.
(Credit: *Connect Archive*)

Connect Trade Union flag proudly flying at 6 Gardiner Row at Union launch.
(Credit: *Connect Archive*)

Craft Union Officials meet the Taoiseach Charlie Haughey at the
launch of Team Aer Lingus.
(Credit: *Connect Archive*)

Delegates voting at the TEEU 2014 BDC.
(Credit: *Connect Archive*)

Union participation in anti-austerity protest.
(Credit: *Connect Archive*)

First meeting of TEEU Women's Forum Committee.
(Credit: *Connect Archive*)

ETU Executive circa 1990.
(Credit: *Connect Archive*)

Former UCATT Executive Members, Officials and Staff at the launch of
Connect Trade Union.

(Credit: *Connect Archive*)

General Secretary addressing UA Convention 2016.

(Credit: *Connect Archive*)

Photo Section 34

General Secretary and President of Ireland Michael D Higgins
at the launch of TASC Report (2).

(Credit: *Connect Archive*)

General Secretary Paddy Kavanagh presentation to
IBEW General President Lonnie Stephenson at
IBEW 39th Convention 2016.

(Credit: *Connect Archive*)

Guest speaker Mary Lou McDonald (Sinn Fein) meets the
Nordic unions delegation along with General Secretary & General President.

(Credit: *Connect Archive*)

NEETU Executive, circa 1990.
(Credit: *Connect Archive*)

Officers at the first Global Power Unions meeting, Dublin 2013.
(Credit: *Connect Archive*)

Outgoing General Secretary Eamon Devoy welcomes incoming
General Secretary Paddy Kavanagh, 2016.

(Credit: *Connect Archive*)

Patricia King ICTU General Secretary unveiling the nameplate
for the new union Connect.

(Credit: *Connect Archive*)

Renewal of Federation Agreement with the
United Association Leinster House with Labour Senator, Ged Nash.
(Credit: *Connect Archive*)

TEEU Banner at Anti-Austerity March.
(Credit: *Connect Archive*)

TEEU delegation to ICTU BDC 2007.
(Credit: *Connect Archive*)

TEEU Green Isle dispute.
(Credit: *Connect Archive*)

TEEU picket line Dublin during the 2009 National Electricial Dispute.
(Credit: *Connect Archive*)

TEEU protest at Dublin construction site.
(Credit: *Connect Archive*)

TEEU Shop Stewards training.
(Credit: *Connect Archive*)

Union protest against Apprentice Fees.
(Credit: *Connect Archive*)

Youth forum team building outing BDC 2014.
(Credit: *Connect Archive*)

Facilitator Kieran Mulvey welcomes International Union leaders to
Connect BDC 2018.

(Credit: *Connect Archive*)

Trade Union Federation (TUF) Executive.

(Credit: *Connect Archive*)

11

The TEEU, 1992-2016

When the TEEU was founded, Ireland stood on the cusp of major economic, political and social change. By the end of the 1990s, the Celtic Tiger had been unleashed, secularism liberalism had triumphed over conservative Catholicism, and the Troubles had ended. The Celtic Tiger transformed Ireland from the 'poorest of the rich' in 1987 to the fourth richest country in the world according to GNP per capita in 2002. However, the country still had high levels of poverty by Western standards and the Celtic Tiger deepened inequality.[1] Economists have cited several reasons for the Celtic Tiger: a low corporate tax rate; the IDA's ability to attract IT investment; the devaluation of the Irish Pound in 1993; and a well-educated, English-speaking workforce. Though GNP grew by one-third between 1987 and 1993, unemployment rates remained stubbornly high. GNP growth exceeded 8 per cent between 1994 and 1999, adding over a thousand jobs a week to the economy and slashing unemployment to 3.6 per cent by 2001. The Celtic Tiger ended the long-time scourge of forced emigration. Net immigration reached its zenith in 2006 when the number of immigrants, mostly from central and eastern Europe, outstripped the number of emigrants by 71,800. By then, the number non-Irish citizens resident in the country had reached 419,733. Immigration contributed to the significant population growth in the Republic, which expanded from 3.52 million in 1991 to 4.24 million in 2006.[2] The Celtic Tiger crashed spectacularly in 2008, the result of economic and fiscal mismanagement and deregulation of finance and construction. The ensuing recession was the worst in the history of the state.

Three main forces lay behind the ascent and hegemony of liberalism, the most important of which was a change in the class structure brought about by deindustrialisation and globalisation. By the 1990s, Irish socialists' long-held goal of transforming society by modernising it had been realised, but not in the way they had envisaged. There would be no mass, class-conscious industrial proletariat, who were being rapidly replaced by the 'precariat.' This new working class was characterised by the absence of job security, intermittent employment and underemployment, and the resulting precarious existence. They were the product of a second wave of economic modernisation, this one driven by services rather than industry. In 1966, employment in industry peaked at 35 per cent of the workforce, while services accounted for 34 per cent and agriculture 31 per cent; in 1992, the proportions were 28 per cent, 59 per cent and 13 per cent. By 2009, services employed three-quarters of the workforce. Opening the economy had made workers less propertied. From 1961 to 1985, the percentage of working males classified as employers or self-employed fell from 44 to 30. The bourgeoisie was also changing as the growing service sector consolidated a new, suburban middle class. In the same period, the proportion of professionals and managers among working males rose from 8 to 17 per cent while the percentage of white-collar, lower middle-class employees jumped from 16 to 22. The two primary categories of the working class had swapped places: skilled manual workers grew from 12 to 20 per cent of the male workforce while semi- and unskilled workers fell from 21 to 12 per cent.[3]

The collapse in the Catholic Church's moral authority was second factor in the rise of liberalism in the 1990s. While the pace of secularisation had heretofore been slower than in other parts of the West, the trend was undeniable. The revelation of scandals within the Church from 1992, especially the disclosure of decades of coverup of sexual abuse of children from 1994, disgraced the institution and accelerated the trajectory. The success of the 1995 referendum to legalise divorce was the turning point when liberal Ireland established its dominance. The third factor was global: the 'fall of the wall' in 1989 and the Soviet Union's demise two years later ended the Cold War in a resounding victory for the West. The Celtic Tiger, Irish neoliberals argued, was irrefutable proof of the superiority of the capitalist system. Command economies would inevitably fail, while even mild manifestations of socialism were undesirable. Communist and Marxist parties across the world suffered splits led by social democratic factions who would soon abandon class politics. The Workers' Party, which had seven Dáil seats and an MEP, experienced such a split while Dick Spring effectively turned the Labour Party into a liberal party by moving so far to the centre.[4] This too was a global trend, as embodied by Bill Clinton's New Democrats and Tony Blair's New Labour.

The TEEU was more affected by the new milieu than most Irish unions. The Celtic Tiger gave engineering and electrical workers an importance to the economy that NEETU or the ETU could only dream of. It made good use of the new power by securing impressive pay rises for its members and combatting the exploitation of vulnerable foreign workers by unscrupulous employers. Its successes were widely recognised, resulting in its membership and financial strength reaching unprecedented heights. It made inroads in eliminating its long-time British rivals as its continued to establish itself as the union of choice for Irish engineering craftsmen and strengthened its presence in the building trade. The TEEU took a stand against the employers' assault on wages and conditions after the 2008 crash, inspiring other unions to do the same. The greatest economic disaster in the history of the state nearly led to the TEEU's implosion, but the determination and loyalty of its members saw it through the crisis. By 2016, its last year in existence, the TEEU had not only recovered but was larger and stronger than ever, a fitting farewell to a union that achieved so much in such a short period of time.

The TEEU, 1992-2000

The TEEU held its first executive meeting on 6 August 1992 after having 'taken possession' of 6 Gardiner Row from McConnell. Anxious to avoid the mistakes of the past, there would be no REC but an Executive Management Committee (EMC) to look after the union's pressing affairs on a biweekly, and later monthly, basis. In both NEETU and the ETU, REC members had to reside in Dublin, which caused consternation in both unions. In contrast, the EMC would be open to everyone. Major decisions would still be the prerogative of the NEC, which met once a year. In the meantime, the transitional NEC would remain in place. The NEETU and the ETU negotiating teams had been keen to ensure that no TEEU member perceived the merger as a 'takeover' by the other union: Browne and Carter would share the presidency; O'Reilly was the agreed general secretary; and Moneley and McConnell would serve as assistant general secretaries even though few believed that McConnell would co-operate. The executive put McConnell on leave of absence without pay after he failed to report for work. O'Reilly reported that McConnell had now 'accepted' the TEEU and was 'reflecting on his own position within the union.'[5] His reflection did not last long. O'Reilly had been negotiating a voluntary severance agreement with McConnell's solicitor, but McConnell rejected the package offered to him. The litigious McConnell once again took legal action, this time against the TEEU's officials and trustees for unlawfully conspiring to remove him from office. This was only a blip on what was otherwise an extraordinarily successful merger. O'Reilly deserves much credit for his vision of a single Irish engineering union and his leadership in convincing his ETU colleagues of its benefits despite NEETU's problems. This was his legacy, as Carter acknowledged when O'Reilly retired in 1998, when he asserted that the merger was 'more efficient and trouble-free … than any other amalgamation … due to the diligence of Frank O'Reilly.'[6] O'Reilly himself recognised as much in May 1993 when he told the NEC that 'it is widely perceived in the trade union movement that the amalgamation has been successful.'[7]

The TEEU was formally launched on 29 May 1993, by which point Moneley had retired. The executive opted to make 5 Cavendish Row the new union's head office instead of 6 Gardiner Row. Much progress had been made in combining and rationalising branches. Come amalgamation, NEETU had thirty-six branches and the ETU had twenty-two. The transitional NEC decided that there would be twenty-eight TEEU branches, as outlined in Table 68. Some branches were unhappy about being combined – the two Kerry branches, for example – and other did not initially cooperate with the executive. On 7 May 1994, the transitional NEC held its final meeting, having achieved its goal of establishing a solid bedrock on which the new union could thrive. A permanent NEC took the reins the following day. O'Reilly would remain as general secretary and Carter would be the sole general president, a position he kept until 2003 when Jimmy Nolan took over. Finn Lawless, Miller, O'Donovan, White, Wills and Finbarr Dorgan served as assistant general secretaries and David Naughton, John Kidd and Anthony Farrell as trustees. Finances were healthy from the mid-1990s. NEETU and the ETU had bequeathed £120,000 worth of assets to the TEEU at its foundation, helping to insure it against any unexpected financial upheavals. The NEC also improved its monetary situation by raising weekly contributions by 10p. to £2. A rapidly growing membership made the results instantaneous and bountiful. The union's first audit, which reported in May 1995, made for pleasant reading: finances for 1994 were excellent considering the merger had only recently taken place. In October 1995, a financial drain was plugged when McConnell ended his legal action. Having reached the High Court that March, both sides agreed to an out-of-court settlement when McConnell accepted a voluntary severance sum and a union pension. The Department of Enterprise and Employment covered the costs. O'Reilly had completed in one effort what NEETU officials had failed to do in several attempts. In June 1996, the TEEU reported its first budget surplus, which had reached £150,000 by the following year.[8]

Table 68: TEEU Membership, 1992-99.[9]

Year (31 Dec.)	Membership
1992	22,042
1993	22,645
1994	23,375
1995	24,206
1996	26,031
1997	27,400
1998	28,628
1999	30,396

Table 69: TEEU branches, March 1993.[10]

Branch	Workers catered for	Branch	Workers catered for
Dublin No. 1	Maintenance	Dublin No. 6	General Workers
Dublin No. 2	Local Authorities	Dublin No. 7	Aviation
Dublin No. 3	ESB	Dublin No. 8	NJIC
Dublin No. 4	Telecommunications	Dublin No. 9	Semi-state
Dublin No. 5	Supervisory	Dublin No. 10	Construction
Athlone	Geographical	Kerry	Geographical
Carlow	Geographical	Limerick No. 1	Non-ESB
Cork	Geographical	Limerick No. 2	ESB
Drogheda	Geographical	North-Western	Geographical
Dundalk	Geographical	Portlaoise	Geographical
Technical Supervisors	ESB	Tipperary	Geographical
Galway	Geographical	Waterford No. 1	Geographical
Kildare	Geographical	Waterford No. 2	General Workers
Kilkenny	Geographical	Wexford	Geographical

In November 1997, Wills was elected general secretary designate to facilitate O'Reilly's coming retirement. Having defeated White for the post, Wills took office in late 1998. He inherited a union in superb condition. In 2000, the union reported a bank surplus of £249,535 excluding its property portfolio. Healthy finances allowed the executive to renovate the union's head office, which Wills considers his proudest achievement as general secretary. In 1998, the executive agreed with Senator Donie Cassidy to swap 5 Cavendish Row for his hotel at 7 Gardiner Row, allowing both 6 and 7 Gardiner Row to be developed into a spacious head office. But this arrangement fell through, and so the executive decided to renovate 6 Gardiner Row instead. In 2004, the union applied for planning permission which it obtained the following year. Work began in May 2006. The refit was an expensive endeavour, costing €4.1 million. The union funded it by taking out a bank loan, raising contributions from €3.75 to €4.25, and selling 5 Cavendish Row and its premises in Drogheda and Limerick. The refurbishment was completed in 2009 and the impressive new building officially opened in January 2010 by President Mary McAleese.[11]

Growth continued at an impressive pace in the late 1990s as the TEEU consolidated its position as the primary union for engineering craftsmen. Some of the membership growth, however, was the result of expansion in the building trade where NEETU had only a toehold. In early 1999, UCATT wrote to complain that the TEEU Cork branch was organising carpenters, while SIPTU complained that the branch had taken in several painters. Wills ordered that they be returned to their old unions, claiming that retaining them would be 'contrary to good trade union practice.' The TEEU also held discussions with the National Union of Sheet Metal Workers of Ireland about merging, but that union opted to remain independent for another four years when it would review the situation again.[12] That April, the TEEU resolved to organise all workers in the technical, engineering and electrical fields. It knew it had to evolve because work involving modern technology and machinery was being done by 'groups outside the maintenance workforce.' 'If we are to be successful in organising these workers and gain control of the new maintenance work area, we will have to facilitate their integration into the maintenance workforce and allow for the type of flexible working arrangements that have evolved in the past between the traditional trades.'[13] The TEEU was also becoming increasingly political. In December 1999, it condemned Budget 2000, which controversially included measures benefitting working couples over single-income households, because 'it does not provide for those on low pay and … clearly discriminates against stay-at-home spouses.' ICTU shared the union's hostility.[14]

1996: The persistence of the Anglo-Irish conflict

From the beginning, the TEEU was anxious to establish better relations with other unions than NEETU and the ETU had. Although officials reached out to SIPTU and the Communication Workers' Union to find common ground, the most significant overtures were made to the Auld Enemy – the Amalgamated Engineering and Electrical Union (AEEU), the result of the AEU's 1992 merger with the EEPTU. The TEEU built strong relations with the AEEU, inside and outside the negotiating rooms, for which the Irish union had an ulterior motive. In 1994, the EMC began to 'explore' the possibility of merging with the AEEU via contacts it had in that union, including Eamon Devoy (Dublin district secretary) and Patrick Guilfoyle (district secretary for south-west Ireland). That year, O'Reilly and Wills met Devoy, Guilfoyle and Gavin Laird, AEEU general secretary, in Cork. Laird, a Scotsman, told the TEEU men that he could not understand why his union still existed in Ireland when there was an Irish alternative to it. Inter-union talks were going well until March 1995 when the issue of 'total autonomy as against some autonomy' for the TEEU became a sticking point. The TEEU wanted any new union to be a twenty-six-county body with full autonomy because 'that was the only way we would be able to control our destiny … it would be right and proper to have a single engineering union in the Republic of Ireland and we saw ourselves as the appropriate one.' The AEEU wanted the new union to be organised across the thirty-two counties. The TEEU was 'totally opposed to that' for fear of stoking sectarian tensions in the North and upsetting the ongoing political discussions (which culminated in the Good Friday Agreement in 1998). However, the TEEU was open to the proposed union being all-island sometime in the future. Negotiations broke down shortly after Ken Jackson, the right-wing former EEPTU president, replaced Laird as AEEU general secretary in the spring of 1995 and left the issue fall by the wayside by not responding to the TEEU's overtures.[15]

Jackson implemented the EEPTU's centralised structure in his new role and displayed a profound insensitivity to Irish needs. In early 1996, his executive council drafted a new constitution and rulebook for the AEEU based on those of his former union. Many Irish members, like Devoy and Guilfoyle, were horrified because the new rules took no account of the fundamental political, economic and industrial differences between Ireland and Britain. In fact, there was no mention of Ireland in it at all. The AEEU's Belfast-based, thirty-two-county Ireland Management Committee, comprised of fulltime officials and local district secretaries, had overseen its affairs in Ireland with much autonomy. The new rulebook proposed rationalising several Irish branches and replacing local representative structures with ones based on the British model. Guilfoyle called the new system 'a reflection of post-Thatcherite Britain rather than… the European model of social partnership which is a hallmark of the Irish trade union movement.'[16] There were also fears that the AEEU would accept the introduction of a British-style apprenticeship where, unlike Ireland, Thatcher had dismantled the unions' input into apprentice training.[17] Though the new structures were more democratic for British members, they abolished the Dublin District Committee. The new rules allowed for an Irish conference – which could put motions and send delegates to the biennial conference in Britain – but placed day-to-day management in the hands of fulltime officials, most of whom were based in the North where the union had most of its Irish membership. These officials were answerable to the executive in London, not the Ireland Management Committee, and Irish members complained that their right to call a strike was being taken away from them. Accordingly, they argued that the rulebook breached the Industrial Relations Act 1990, which states that Irish members of British unions in Ireland must have control over financial and political affairs.[18] On 11 March 1996, Devoy wrote a confidential letter to the TEEU stating that his committee supported going over to the Irish union, prompting the EMC to devise contingency plans for same. The conflict between Dublin and London 'developed to the point where it became necessary for the AEEU officials in the Republic of Ireland to make contact with the TEEU for accommodation' because they had been locked out of their offices.[19]

On 1 May, the rulebook came into effect, having received 90 per cent approval in a members' ballot on 18 March. The TEEU monitored the situation closely, later reporting that 'we were aware of friction between England and the Ireland section of the AEEU.' Devoy met Jackson and told him of the Dublin District Committee's 'total dissatisfaction' with the new rulebook's disregard for the 'Irish situation.' If the executive did not maintain the current structures for Irish members, the committee would release members to join Irish unions with 'a democratic base.' The committee also wanted the executive to re-commence and conclude the amalgamation talks with the TEEU, which the Irish membership strongly supported. The TEEU considered the rulebook an impediment to a merger, which is why O'Reilly rejected Jackson's attempt to informally revive talks in Cork on 29 May. When the AEEU executive did not progress matters, Irish members launched a petition demanding that their union negotiate with the TEEU. Devoy secretly met O'Reilly to plan a transfer. O'Reilly told Devoy that he could no longer keep the matter confidential and reported to his EMC, which gave him legal advice and advocated a change of rules to facilitate the influx of members.[20] Devoy then met his committee and told them of the TEEU's willingness to take them. On 9 June, the committee resigned from the AEEU and voted to join the TEEU. The following day, fifty-seven Dublin shop stewards, representing members in thirty companies, did likewise. Most of the AEEU's fitters went over but most of its plumbers stayed put. The following day, Devoy and Guilfoyle resigned and joined the TEEU, taking their personal secretaries with them. Both became 'fulltime officials' on the TEEU executive. The TEEU formed a 'transition branch' managed by Devoy and Guilfoyle to cater for AEEU members wishing to join.[21]

Enraged by the TEEU's actions, the AEEU parachuted Brendan Fenelon, a Carlow-born member of its executive, into Ireland to halt mass defections. Fenelon declared that his union was in official dispute with the TEEU. He invoked the ICTU disputes procedure and pleaded with Congress to intervene to prevent 'all-out war' between the two unions. The AEEU was even willing to take the TEEU through the courts, wherein it would rely on the Articles 2 and 3 of Bunreacht na hÉireann (subsequently amended as part of the Good Friday Agreement settlement). It was a bizarre spectacle: on one side was a British union, most of whose Irish membership were Northern loyalists, upholding the Republic's claim to all thirty-two counties; on the other was a union born of the national struggle whose defence was the law of the twenty-six-county state. Ironically, the AEEU accused its rival of 'playing the republican, sectarian card' for highlighting that it was an Irish union.[22] The desire to leave the AEEU was strong: by mid-July, the TEEU had received over a thousand applications. These were mainly from small Dublin firms, although 220 members at Thermo King had applied to join (who later returned to the AEEU). In total, about two thousand applied to join. However, the transfers were poorly co-ordinated and there were no adequate structures to facilitate them. The TEEU did not process the applications pending the decision of the ICTU subcommittee established to adjudicate on the dispute. Across the country, AEEU members arrived at TEEU offices with completed application forms only to be turned away. On 1 August, despite only hearing evidence from the AEEU, the subcommittee issued an interim ruling ordering the TEEU not to seek or accept any applications pending a final decision. Its final report, issued on 20 September, condemned the TEEU's transition branch and recent promotional document, 'Towards One Engineering and Electrical Union in the Republic of Ireland', as inducing AEEU members to swap unions. The report censured the TEEU for having 'acted in a manner contrary to the interests of the AEEU' and recommended that it stop providing special arrangements to encourage transfers. However, it did not conclude the transfers constituted poaching and therefore did not stop them. Rather, it reaffirmed the rules of Congress on the matter: where there were joint shops between the AEEU and the TEEU, members were free to transfer from one to the other; where there were closed shops, only a ballot with a minimum of 80 per cent support could authorise a transfer.[23]

The subcommittee allowed six hundred applicants to join the TEEU to do so if they wished. By then, however, the momentum was gone. That November, in a speech roundly attacking the TEEU, Fenelon told his union's first Irish conference that only 160 had transferred and that no more than two hundred would leave because many had decided to stay.[24] The TEEU had recently cut its subscription rate from £2.25 to £1.93 for AEEU members wishing to join. Fenelon considered this tantamount to poaching and lodged another complaint to ICTU. In response, the AEEU equalised its subscription rate across the island at £1.75 – which heretofore only Northerners paid – to undercut its rival.[25] In June 1997, the TEEU abolished the special rate after Congress disapproved of it. The rivalry had a lasting effect on how the TEEU conducted its financial affairs. In 1998, the NEC shot down a proposal to raise contributions because it would put the rate 'well above' the AEEU's.[26] Guilfoyle believes that the introduction of AEEU officials helped to move the TEEU away from being a 'negotiating union' – whose focus was defending members' pay and conditions – to becoming a 'recruiting' union that aggressively pursued new members, as the AEEU had done. He also argues that that these officials helped to politicise the Irish union, as their former union had never eschewed adopting political positions, even on controversial topics like a United Ireland.[27] Although it is difficult to ascertain just how many transferred, it is likely to be a far bigger number than Fenelon claimed. Devoy believes that about 2,000-2,500 joined over a period of several years. Nevertheless, the 1996 war was an opportunity lost by the TEEU, who had hoped to bring over at least three thousand members. Though wounded, the AEEU survived and still had eight thousand members in the Republic in 2000 compared to ten thousand in 1996. The TEEU could have wiped its powerful rival – which had 700,000 members in the UK and £60 million of assets compared to the TEEU's £1 million – and become the country's only engineering craft union.[28] Relations between the two had been irreparably damaged. When the AEEU was presented with a chance to hit back in 1998, it did so mercilessly.

Discontent in the Dublin No. 1 branch

The foundation of the TEEU meant that that the two largest group in maintenance craftwork, fitters and electricians, would now be in the same union – a tremendous change for both. NEC officers have recalled some initial tension between the two groups, although this dissipated in most branches shortly afterwards as most realised unity was in the interests of both. This was not the case in the Dublin No. 1 branch, however, where there was persistent animosity. The trouble began immediately after amalgamation when a group of former ETU men on the branch committee – most of whom worked at Cadbury's chocolate plant in Coolock – began agitating for the executive to split Dublin No. 1 into separate branch for electricians and fitters. Within the ETU, this group had fought vigorously against the merger because they feared that fitters would dominate the resulting union. George Swan led the charge. Though he retained his position as secretary of the Dublin No. 1 branch in the TEEU, he had strongly advocated that the ETU amalgamate with SIPTU instead of NEETU. The TEEU executive struggled to resolve the situation. It opposed the men's demand, fearing that 'Cadbury's may be used as a catalyst for a future fragmentation of the branches between fitters and electricians' and abhorred 'giving members a separate branch under threat.'[29] The EMC established a subcommittee to make recommendations on how best to cater for the electricians. The group objected to the decision, but the EMC held firm. It replied by highlighting 'the fundamental concept behind the amalgamation' – that there would not be two 'separate organisations masquerading as one union.'[30] While the group's demand did not reflect the majority opinion of Dublin No. 1, there were tensions between electricians and fitters on the ground. In late 1993 and early 1994, head office had to settle a demarcation dispute between them at Irish Glass Bottles and Cadbury's, respectively. The electricians were unhappy about head office's rulings on demarcation as well as the branch's heavy workload.[31]

Trouble continued throughout 1994 and 1995. In May 1994, the branch committee denounced the executive's plan as 'totally unworkable', claiming that the interests of both fitters and electricians would be best served by separate branches. The NEC again rejected the plea because it would 'set an unacceptable precedent for the union.' That December, the subcommittee reported. It proposed dividing Dublin No. 1 into two integrated branches with sectional subcommittees for both crafts, not separate branches. Although many expressed reservations about doing this, the NEC accepted the report as an interim measure.[32] But this was not enough for Swan and co. and so the report was never implemented. Unsurprisingly, tensions between fitters and electricians were the deepest at Cadbury's where Swan had a base. In January 1996, fitters there unofficially walked out when the firm suspended a colleague who refused to operate new machinery it had installed. They objected to the electricians preparing metal strips to secure electrical panels to the factory floor – the culmination of a four-year row between the two groups over who operated the new technologies the company was introducing. Ironically, these new machines eventually simplified and clarified the work at Cadbury's, which ended the dispute – the last demarcation dispute before ICTU's Disputes Committee.[33] Technological development also helped to rationalise the number of industrial crafts, thereby reducing the possibility of conflict over demarcation. At Becton Dickinson, for example, there had been a hierarchy of four crafts – production fitters, maintenance fitters, toolmakers and electricians – each with a 5 per cent pay differential over the other. The introduction of new machinery had helped NEETU to eliminate grades and equalise craft pay.[34]

In August 1996, Swan reiterated the group's demand. He wrote to the EMC to deplore its 'jackboot tactics', 'dictatorial manner' and 'arrogant, supercilious attitude' after officials attended a meeting of the committee of the Electrical Section of the Dublin No. 1 branch without invitation.[35] The following month, the EMC received a branch delegation comprised of Swan, David Grant, David Drinkwater and Paul Bedford to hear their unhappiness about the current arrangement. Swan informed the EMC that 'the relationship between the fitters and electricians is not good.' Grant was more vituperative, telling officials that he wanted a separate branch 'to deal with the question of multiskilling' and that electricians in Dublin were being 'attacked' daily by fitters and were going to be 'swamped' by them. The group's anger was boiling over. The union had recently started teaching fitters how to do electrical work and electricians how to do fitters' work, which Swan deplored. He accused head office of training fitters to take electricians' jobs. Bedford reported that electricians across the country were 'dissatisfied with the amalgamation.' He threatened that Cadbury's members 'will have their own branch one way or the other', even if it meant forming their own union, or they would stop paying contributions. If the EMC did not relent, then the electricians would join SIPTU or the AEEU if they were given their own branch.[36]

Relations between Dublin No. 1 and the executive, and between the fitters and electricians within the branch, continued their descent throughout 1997. Attendance at branch meetings dwindled as the fitters had stopped going. Prizeman, the branch's chairman, alleged that this was because an electrician had remarked at a 1995 meeting that 'it was bad enough the amalgamation took place' even though 'he was not aware of any electricians voting for it. But an even bigger insult was for the electricians to be forced into a branch with fitters, which was like being placed into a barrel of slop.' Prizeman believed that Swan's group was 'carrying over from the ETU bitter and entrenched grievances, and that the order of the day was revenge ... if you agreed with the amalgamation you were treated with suspicion if not contempt. There was a totally hostile reaction to anyone who promoted the principle of the TEEU.' Swan and others were also unhappy with how Devoy and Guilfoyle had filled the vacancies left on the EMC left by Moneley and McConnell's departure. He maintained that the appointments were undemocratic and broke union rules because they were not ratified by the membership.[37] The electricians started only attending the branch's final weekly meeting of the month, boycotting the others. They quickly broke their promise to the executive that they would obey union rules and started privately meeting to establish their separate branch.

The conflict reached its apex at the Dublin No. 1's shambolic 1998 AGM, held in January. Swan and co. demanded that the branch's NEC officer be an electrician; otherwise, the union's supreme governing body would have no electrical representative. Fears of being 'swamped by fitters' were intensified by the allocation of an NEC seat to the 'transition branch' which was mainly composed of fitters. The electricians wanted Prizeman, the branch's sole nominee for the NEC, to withdraw in favour of Bedford; afterwards, the electricians would nominate Prizeman to the post of union president. When Prizeman refused this proposition, Swan subjected him to a tirade of abuse and proclaimed that he would not accept the legitimacy of the branch committee, which was returned unopposed. But Swan was still technically the branch secretary and was thus mandated to attend committee meetings, which he stopped doing.[38] In March, the EMC suspended him from office, which he decried as 'a tactic one would associate with an employer who attempts to victimise a worker.'[39] Swan and his cohorts had had enough. That July, he resigned as branch secretary and his men joined the AEEU after it promised them their beloved electricians' branch. In total, forty-one went over: thirty-nine from Cadbury's, one from Millennium Control and one retired member, Swan. Many electricians and some fitters at Irish Glass Bottles also went over.[40] The following month, the AEEU's Ireland Conference introduced Swan as the man who was going to bring electricians into their union. It was beginning of another vicious conflict between the TEEU and AEEU.

Spheres of influence: the Cadbury's dispute, 1998-2007

The turmoil within the Dublin No. 1 branch had given the AEEU a chance to recover from 1996 and satisfy its thirst for revenge. It cynically exploited the Cadbury's situation to undermine the TEEU. As every electrician at Cadbury's had gone over, the AEEU was happy to use the TEEU's own logic against it: that if 80 per cent or more vote to transfer to another union, ICTU could not stop them. But the crafty TEEU had a secret weapon – spheres of influence. The labour movement had always operated on the basis that, in the absence of explicit agreements, custom and practice delineated who unions could organise and who they could not. This was a 'sphere of influence', which everyone was obliged to respect. In the twenty-six counties, the AEEU and its predecessors had never organised electricians, as this sphere of influence belonged to the ETU and NEETU. The TEEU went to the Disputes Committee claiming that the AEEU had violated its sphere of influence (engineering) and therefore poached. It argued that this sphere was established in 1922 by the foundation of the Irish state, within which electricians had always been organised by an

Irish union. In 1932, the ITUC reinforced this informal arrangement when it allowed the ETU (UK) to affiliate on the understanding that it confined its activities to the North. Electricians in the Free State came under the sphere of influence of Irish unions which the AEEU and its predecessors confirmed on several subsequent occasions, most recently in 1995.

The AEEU told the Disputes Committee that the transfers were in accordance with ICTU rules because over 80 per cent had applied to join and both unions were rivals. The committee, however, was not convinced. In October 1998, it ruled in favour of the TEEU and ordered the AEEU not to accept the electricians. The AEEU appealed the verdict, which the Disputes Committee heard in October 1999. It was another defeat for the union as the committee upheld its original decision.[41] As the committee observed, 'relationships between the two unions have deteriorated rather than improved since ... 1996. This dispute is largely due to residual tensions and distrust arising from those events.'[42] The AEEU ignored the ruling. It brazenly tried to poach more TEEU electricians, this time at Lufthansa Airmotive, and accepted the Cadbury's men in March 2000. Its logic for doing so was simple: the TEEU had been 'trying to destroy the AEEU in the Republic of Ireland since 1996.' Thus, the British union terminated all agreements and understandings with its rival which, it claimed, never existed in the first place.[43] It took a more legalistic line with Congress, arguing that implementing the Disputes Committee's report would violate the electricians' individual rights under Bunreacht na hÉireann, the Good Friday Agreement and the EU's Charter of Fundamental Rights.[44] The AEEU wrapped itself in the tricolour by blasting ICTU's 'narrow, partitionist view on union recruitment and interaction.'[45] Neither Congress nor its affiliates were impressed. ICTU had intended to suspend the AEEU that July but deferred doing so for two months at Jackson's request. On 20 September, however, Congress suspended the union for failing to comply with the Disputes Committee's directive.[46] In response, the TEEU declared that it would not co-operate with the AEEU 'at any level within the Irish trade union movement.'[47] Suspension had serious consequences for the AEEU. It was now excluded from representation on ICTU groups in many major companies including Bord na Móna, CIÉ, the Construction Industry Committee, the ESB, government departments, health boards, Irish Cement and the local authorities. It was also prohibited from participating in public bodies where Congress had representation, such as FÁS. The debacle convinced the ICTU executive to tighten its anti-poaching rules.[48]

Nevertheless, the AEEU still refused to hand back the electricians throughout 2001. That July, ICTU gave it until the end of the year to comply or face expulsion. It refused. Accordingly, the AEEU was expelled from Congress on 31 December 2001. Afterwards, the TEEU determined not to negotiate or hold multi-union meetings with the AEEU and advised other ICTU-affiliated unions to do likewise. In early 2002, over four hundred plumbers, pipefitters and mechanical service craftsmen, including shop stewards and committee members, left the AEEU for the TEEU in one of the largest inter-union transfers in recent times. The influx continued well into 2003. To facilitate it, the NEC re-designated the Dublin No. 10 branch as the Construction, Plumbing and Mechanical Services Branch.[49] In 2001, the men had approached White 'due to their dissatisfaction' with the AEEU and their 'high opinion' of the TEEU after it negotiated major pay increases for plumbers from the CIF – €21 an hour or €820 for a thirty-nine-hour week.[50] Not everyone welcomed the newcomers: the chairman of Dublin No. 10 berated White for allowing the plumbers to 'takeover' the branch. Despite their suspension, the AEEU still refused to hand over the Cadbury's men.

The affair had soured relations between Congress and the TEEU. The union considered disaffiliating from ICTU because of its failure to implement its own rules and because of the 'underlying anti-TEEU attitude promoted within Congress.'[51] Nonetheless, it opted to remain affiliated, partially because Jack O'Connor, SIPTU president, promised to force Congress to get Amicus – the result of the 2002 merger between the AEEU and MSF – to comply. The introduction of former MSF officials, who had not been involved in the dispute, eased tensions between Amicus and the TEEU and provided an avenue to resolve the issue. In January 2003, John Tierney, former MSF Irish Secretary, informed Wills that Amicus now accepted the Disputes Committee's report, a prerequisite for affiliating the new union to Congress. The Cadbury's men revolted against being handed back, so Amicus reneged. Besides, accepting a report did not necessarily mean implementing it. In January 2004, Wills again met David Begg, ICTU president, and Tierney, who agreed to accept ICTU's findings; to not represent George Swan; to tell the Cadbury's men to return to the TEEU; to tell Cadbury's that Amicus would not represent its electricians; and to investigate if any Amicus branch existed solely to poach TEEU members and, if it did, to dissolve that branch. By December 2006, however, Amicus had still not fulfilled its commitments. The TEEU threatened Congress with legal action for not implementing its own rules and demanded that it expel Amicus. It was enough to force Congress to finally assert its authority, leading to a flow of Cadbury's men returning to the TEEU. In March 2007, the EMC reported that the last electricians had made his way back to Dublin No. 1, finally ending the affair.[52]

The TEEU, 2000-2008

Though the early 2000s were kind to the TEEU, they were not trouble-free. In 2000, conflict erupted between Finbarr Dorgan and the Waterford No. 1 Branch. The branch committee had undermined Dorgan in front of a firm with whom he was negotiating when it circulated a letter critical of him to shop stewards. The circular called on him to cease representing the branch until its autonomy, which head office had recently curtailed, had been restored. The branch had breached union rules by sending the letter, which it circulated because of previous grievances with Dorgan. The EMC warned the branch that it would be liquidated unless it stopped.[53] In April, the branch committee accused the EMC of 'persistent' attempts to 'humiliate and degrade' it.

> You as a committee have taken unilateral action against officials … to impose your will on them… by using the jackboot tactics… You should be thoroughly ashamed of yourselves. We belong to a trade union, not some form of 'sect' where blind obedience may be a requirement.[54]

After several meetings with the EMC, the branch agreed to withdraw the letter (tensions remained high between the executive and the branch for over a decade thereafter). Dorgan, however, was not happy with the outcome as he had wanted to see the branch sanctioned for its behaviour.[55] It was not the only example of destructive internal conflict during this time. In January 2005, the High Court ruled that the TEEU had contractually employed Philip Kirwan, secretary of the Drogheda branch, for work had had done on behalf of the union from 1992 to 2000. He was awarded €200,000 in lost time payments, a reimbursement for wages forgone while conducting union business. Kirwan had taken the case after the executive had determined that he was not employed under a contract of service insurable under Class A PRSI and was therefore not entitled to lost time. The union spent €161,195 appealing the case to the Supreme Court, which upheld the original verdict.[56]

In the early 2000s, after the destruction of its relationship with the AEEU, the TEEU turned to SIPTU to form a strategic alliance. In 2001, both signed a framework of cooperation to 'best enable them to resist any external threat.'[57] Though some TEEU members were fearful that the negotiations would pave the way for amalgamation with SIPTU, they culminated in something different. On 20 February 2003, both unions instituted the Trade Union Federation (TUF) to promote mutual interests, improve and share services, and optimise co-operation. Having access to SIPTU's vast research facilities was a boon to the TEEU. The new arrangement created joint negotiating groups, dampening the possibility of inter-union disputes with SIPTU and facilitating the TEEU's spread to new areas such as Kerry Foods. The TUF launched its Membership Services Scheme on 1 November 2004. The federation was part of the TEEU's efforts to consolidate union presence in the private sector. It had been instrumental in persuading ICTU to institute a Private Sector Committee in 2001. Devoy, then TEEU assistant general secretary, became the committee's first secretary.[58]

The union's increasing politicisation is evidenced by its opposition to local authority-imposed service charges. In 2001, it deplored the charges as a step towards privatisation of refuse services and condemned the jailing of Joe Moore, secretary of the Cork branch of the Communication Workers' Union and the president of the Cork Council of Trade Unions, for peacefully protesting them. It also participated in the 100,000-strong demonstration in Dublin on 15 February 2003 against the coming invasion of Iraq by the US-led coalition. Frank Keoghan, who was elected TEEU general president in 2010, served on the committee of the Trade Union Campaign Against the War. Up to thirty million people took part in co-ordinated rallies in sixty countries to oppose the war, the largest protest movement in world history. That Autumn, Dublin City Council and the three Dublin County Councils stopped collecting refuse in response to years of mass non-payment of bin charges. Protests and blockades of bin lorries ensued, leading to the imprisonment of Joe Higgins TD and left-wing activist and future TD and MEP Clare Daly. Although O'Connor and Begg denounced the protests, the TEEU supported them. Devoy condemned the imprisonments and called a meeting of shop stewards which decided to refuse servicing trucks.[59] The union's politicisation led to its participation in the campaign against the Lisbon Treaty in 2008 and the Fiscal Compact Treaty in 2012. This was despite ICTU's call to vote yes for Lisbon and the TEEU's silence on the Nice Treaty in 2001. Much of the growth of Euroscepticism in the intervening years is attributable to the infamous Laval Judgement in late 2007, when the European Court of Justice ruled that Laval, a Latvian company which sent workers to Sweden, was not obliged to obey collective agreements within the Swedish construction industry.[60] This 'attack by capital on the rights of workers' outraged the TEEU which undertook to 'campaign with like-minded unions both in Ireland and across Europe to maintain the right to strike and maintain national and collective agreements.'[61]

In the mid-2000s, the TEEU was to the fore in revealing the dark underbelly of the Celtic Tiger: rampant exploitation of non-national workers by foreign subcontractors. In March 2006, it gallantly exposed Zre Katowicz, a Polish energy company, for paying Polish workers below the minimum wage after the ESB contracted it to refurbish Moneypoint power station. The company had fired three Poles for highlighting their underpayment but was subsequently forced to rehire them. Under pressure from the TEEU, the ESB terminated Zre Katowicz's contract and gave it to a German firm. Zre Katowicz still owed two hundred Polish workers six weeks' unpaid wages, holiday and pension entitlements, however. After protracted talks at the Labour Relations Commission, the TEEU's threat of strike secured for the men what they were owed. Simultaneously, the union highlighted the case of Serbian workers contracted to work on the ESB's networks, who were paid as little as €3.20 an hour due to a work permits' loophole that allowed non-EU contractors to pay below the minimum wage. Since March 2006, hourly rates were €20.39 at the ENJIC and €18.67 for engineering craftsmen. These incidents impelled the union to tell the government that it would not partake in talks for the second phase of 'Sustaining Progress' unless ministers agreed to outlaw such exploitation. The government yielded and legislated to make contractors responsible for the rates offered by their subcontractors. The TEEU gained a sizeable number of foreign members because of its stand, especially from Poland. By 2007, the union had so many foreign members that it offered English language classes via ETOS, a training centre it had established in 2005 with Seán Heading, a former AEEU official from Belfast, as manager.[62] ETOS continues to provide courses in construction and manufacturing technical skills, among others.

TEEU membership continued to expand in the early years of the twenty-first century, enhancing the influence of the provinces at a national level. In 2001, it appointed a fulltime official in Galway. But many members were disappointed with the union's growth. In November 2006, the union's biennial delegate conference launched a renewed recruitment drive specifically targeting apprentices and migrant workers. In February 2007, the EMC held a special meeting which resolved to make the TEEU a union where 'organising and recruitment is the norm as opposed to an *add on* activity.' The union set itself the following goals:

- Aggressively recruit members and develop 'a mindset' conducive to organisation and recruitment.

- Target self-employed and agency workers, inactive members and those who have not completed an apprenticeship.

- Overcome the 'craft mentality' and organise and recruit a broader occupational membership.

- Encourage greater voluntary participation from in branches and from shop stewards.

To achieve these aims, the union decided to reaffirm the closed shop and to target new companies and construction sites, schools, Institutes of Technology, FÁS centres and the ENJIC. The EMC gave shop stewards a greater role in recruitment. Firstly, the union would focus on organising all apprentices and encouraging lapsed members to participate again. Then, it would create an 'Organising Unit' to target specific areas based on previous research. In

December 2009, the recruitment strategy culminated in the EMC's decision to actively organise the building trade, which brought it into conflict with the Building & Allied Trades Union (BATU).[63] But by then, the economy had crashed, and the unions were firmly on the defensive.

Table 70: TEEU Membership, 2000-2010.[64]

Year (31 Dec.)	Membership	Year (31 Dec.)	Membership
2000	32,065	2006	42,176
2001	33,065	2007	42,185
2002	35,684	2008	45,035
2003	36,882	2009	44,319
2004	38,944	2010	41,440
2005	40,827		

Social partnership, 1994-2009

The TEEU continued the precedent established by its antecedent unions in regularly opposing social partnership agreements, which continued to dictate Irish macroeconomic policy throughout the 1990s. The Programme for Competitiveness and Work (1994-96) contained stronger commitment to job creation than its predecessors, which was spurred by the 'jobless growth' of the early 1990s when economic expansion was not cutting unemployment. Having been reluctant participants at the beginnings, employers became the strongest advocates of centralised bargaining. For IBEC, partnership ensured pay stability and industrial peace and even granted tax concessions all in a period of low inflation. From 1997, partnership evolved from a bargaining to a problem-solving dynamic. Subsequent agreements incorporated a 'fourth pillar' – voluntary, community, rural and religious groups – and tried to address problems the Celtic Tiger had created such as soaring property prices and traffic gridlock.[65] Guilfoyle believes that employers never took partnership seriously and that it never existed above the shop floor. The TEEU was also critical of the general nature of the wages increases issued, which did not include a way to compel rich multinationals to give higher rises than small engineering firms. Partnership gave public sector workers generous increases, a major reason why their unions support the agreements, which the TEEU resented.[66] The recognition conundrum was pertinent for all unions and was an obvious failure of the process. Employers increasingly exploited partnership to not recognise and derecognise unions. Although ICTU membership rose from 670,000 to 832,116 between 1987 and 2007, union density – the proportion of workers in unions – nosedived. Having peaked at over 60 per cent in the late 1970s and early 1980s, density had contracted to 36 per cent by 2007.[67]

In 1997, the TEEU rejected the Partnership 2000 by an 8:1 majority.[68] O'Reilly joined with other trade unionists to agitate for Congress to reject the deal because 'under the previous agreement, profits rose twice as fast as wages and there is nothing fundamentally different about this proposal.'[69] Congress nonetheless endorsed Partnership 2000. O'Reilly told the *Irish Independent* that he was against the agreement because 'the concept of partnership ... was 'too shallow', a number of significant sectoral agreement had not been honoured to date by certain employers and the tax concessions proposed … fell far short of the tax reform pursued by the PAYE sector.'[70] While O'Reilly succeeded in getting the ATGWU and Mandate to oppose the deal, his view was a minority one among the crafts. Technological development had reduced the power of craftworkers within the labour movement by the 1990s. Their ability to pursue pay rises above the norm severely declined throughout the 1980s: between 1981 and 1987, the construction worker was the lowest paid craftsman in the private sector. Many craft unions, especially in construction, therefore supported the national agreements for pragmatic reasons.[71]

Although partnership did not kill labour the way its critics feared, it did not give labour the prestige its supporters claimed it would. Congress tried to address the unions' declining power in its 1995 document 'Managing Change', which advocated a system of aggregate ballots for Congress votes. The TEEU resisted the proposal because it would drown out the views of craft unions and thus make them irrelevant. The union criticised ICTU's propensity to refer industrial disputes to third parties, like the Labour Court, whose rulings generally favoured employers, and for ignoring the casualisation of craftwork in the maintenance sector. Combined with the national pay agreements, ICTU's failure in these areas would 're-enforce the impression that trade unions are no longer relevant.'[72] In 2000, the TEEU used its twenty-four votes at Congress to vote against the Programme for Prosperity and Fairness. The opposition was even more intense next time around. After its membership voted 87 per cent against it, the union was one of the strongest critics of 'Sustaining Progress', an agreement divided into two eighteen-month deals.[73] Wills denounced ICTU's ratification of it as 'another terrible mistake which is both anti-worker and anti-union.' He abhorred the deal's emphasis on control of labour relations and its emasculation of trade unionism by the imposition of binding decisions by the Labour Court and warned that the unions' concessions would not be easily reversed.[74] The TEEU executive strongly recommended acceptance of Towards 2016 due to the commitments to strengthen employment rights and prevent gross exploitation. Only former ETU official Jimmy Kelly voted against it. Members endorsed the deal by 82 per cent, the only time the union supported a social partnership agreement. The TEEU was not alone in making the change: the margin of acceptance for Towards 2016 was the highest of any deal, 242-84.[75]

In 2009, social partnership collapsed under the weight of the economic crisis. The Celtic Tiger's excesses had kept all participants happy: taxes were kept low to satisfy employer demands while workers' wages and government spending were drastically boosted. Reform of agricultural subsidies kept farmers on board and taskforces to improve social cohesion appeased the community and voluntary sectors. A mechanism based on consensus simply could not survive employer calls for wage cuts and union calls for tax increases to deal with the crisis. Did the pros of social partnership outweigh the cons for labour? Externally, it consolidated ICTU's authority and strengthened the idea of social solidarity as a trade-union principle. Other developments would have happened anyway in tandem with the economic change, irrespective of social partnership. Ireland was unique in that social partnership was not initiated by a social democratic party, which partially explains why the socio-economic values that suffused the process were a contradictory blend of neoliberalism and social solidarity.[76]

Table 71: Summary of Social Partnership Agreements, 1994-2007.[77]

Agreement	Duration	Summary
Programme for Competitiveness and Work	1994-96	8 per cent phased increase
Partnership 2000	1997-2000	7.25 per cent phased wage increase with 2 per cent local bargaining in private sector and 3 per cent in public sector
Programme for Fairness	2000-02	15 per cent wage phased increase Prosperity and and commitments to improving infrastructure
Sustaining Progress	2003-05	13 per cent phased wage increase.
Towards 2016	2006-07	10 per cent phased wage increase, commitments to delivering the National Development Plan, and protect and enforce employment rights

Strikes and the wages movement, 1992-2008

The number of strikes continued to decline from 1987. Unlike the NWAs and National Understandings, social partnership contributed to the relative industrial peace of its era. Its impact on pay disputes was especially pronounced. But partnership was not the primary factor for industrial peace: high unemployment and increasing competitive pressures – with the consequent threat to jobs – were also important in the dramatic decline in industrial disputes in the 1980s. Partnership strictly controlled wage growth as unemployment fell, periods when unions typically seek increases, and ensured that wage rises mirrored inflation. Between 1987 and 1996, however, there were times when increases slipped below the inflation rate. To offset this, the government provided modest tax relief to boost disposable incomes. Tax reductions were a major reason why workers' disposable income augmented considerably during the social partnership years when compared to the 'free for all' which preceded them. By the 2000s, income tax levels were nearly half the 1980s rates.[78] The TEEU took advantage of the PESP's local bargaining provision to make gains, albeit in exchange for increased productivity. In May 1993, craft unions at Dublin Bus took out their members after the company snubbed requests for a pay rise in return for generous promises of increased productivity. The TEEU had twenty-seven of the 247 maintenance men at Dublin Bus. The strike ended a month later after the union accepted the Labour Court's offer of a better productivity deal.[79]

Before relations between the two collapsed, the TEEU and AEEU often took joint action together. In 1996, both downed tools at Airmotive, Aer Lingus's engine maintenance plant, for a 10 per cent pay. The Labour Court successfully induced the men back to work. In mid-1997, 5,500 contract electricians nearly downed tools for an award due to them that employers did not pay. After the TEEU served strike notice, the Labour Court heard the case and awarded the union its full demand: electricians received a phased increase of £33 a week backdated to January when the award was supposed to have been implemented. A review of the ENJIC rate the following year gave a rise of 73p. per hour to £28.47 from 1 Apr. 1999.[80] Later in 1997 and 1998, four thousand craftworkers clashed with the local authorities, health boards and voluntary hospitals over a pay claim for which they were willing to strike. It would have been the first ever national strike of local authority and health board craftsmen. The TEEU recommended rejection of a Labour Court offer other crafts unions were willing to accept, which exacerbated inter-union tensions. TEEU members were among those to unofficially picket Waterford Regional Hospital on 11 May 1998. The dispute was resolved that July when members accepted an improved offer, giving them a £25 weekly wage increase.[81]

The TEEU remained willing to engage employers in prolonged battles in the late 1990s and early 2000s. On 13 July 1998, it brought out 250 lift and escalator craftsmen from thirteen maintenance companies across the country for a wage of £11.66 an hour. The media excoriated the union for the hardship the six thousand residents of the Ballymun housing complex, which had buildings of up to fifteen stories, had to endure. Even Seán Ó Cionnaigh – Workers' Party city councillor, chairman of the Ballymun Better Lifts Service Campaign and a SIPTU member – accused it of failing 'to understand the misery and hardship' it had caused and of using the residents as 'pawns to get at the employers.'[82] The TEEU was undeterred by such allegations which did not do justice to the merits of the strike. The stoppage made it to the High Court when tenants pleaded for a court order to direct Dublin Corporation to repair sixty of the seventy-three lifts in the flats, which the court refused to do. The residents then appealed their case to the Supreme Court, which overturned the High Court decision. The strikers had no choice but to repair some of the lifts. The TEEU was furious and accused IBEC of importing scabs from Britain to break the strike. When the Corporation recruited a company from the North to repair the elevators, the union panicked and called off the strike at Ballymun. On 22 September, the strike ended in a Labour Court-facilitated settlement that was not made public. The stoppage had forced the Corporation to reconsider its policy of contracting out services to private companies. The TEEU showed its value again the following year when, along with SIPTU, it negotiated a cost-cutting rescue package that saved 630 jobs at Tara Mines after Outokumpu declared that the mine was no longer profitable. Although the TEEU had fought off company demands for a ten-hour day, workers had to accept new working practices, cuts in productively bonuses and voluntary redundancies.[83]

Table 72: No. of Strikes and Workdays Lost, 1969-94.[84]

Year	Strikes	Days lost (to nearest 100)
1969	134	935,900
1979	152	1,427,000
1988	65	143,000
1989	38	41,000
1990	49	223,000
1991	54	86,000
1992	38	191,000
1993	48	65,000
1994	32	24,000

Year	Republic of Ireland	Northern Ireland	Great Britain
1997	69	24	10
1998	31	7	12
1999	167	10	10
2000	72	33	20

By the early 2000s, the unions' brief flirtation with neoliberalism was over. ICTU recoiled at high-profile instances of boardroom militancy encouraged by the Industrial Relations Act and resumed its opposition to privatisation in 2003, which it had accepted since 1990. The TEEU had been directly affected by employer aggression. In May 1997, for example, it was forced to defer the strike notice it had served on Coca-Cola after the company threatened it with legal action in a dispute over changes in work practices. The TEEU suffered another bout of boardroom militancy in late 2002, again at the Ballymun flats. When lift maintenance men struck after Pickering Lifts sacked a colleague, the company imported foreign workers with bodyguards to repair the elevators. The government sent in the army to supplement protection. After a two-month strike, arbitration reinstated the dismissed employee.[86] The number of days lost to strikes fell consecutively from 1979 (its peak) to 2000, periods of both free collective and centralised bargaining. This too was an international trend as neoliberalism disempowered unions across the West. While strikes do not necessarily reflect union power, they are manifestations of union confidence. Comparing the number of strikes in Ireland and the UK suggests that Irish unions were quite vibrant in the late 1990s and early 2000s. The TEEU was no exception. In mid-2004, it nearly took out six thousand contract electricians on national strike for a craft parity pay claim and against the employers' failure to give the once-off 1 per cent payment to offset inflation due under the Programme for Prosperity and Fairness. The union referred the issue to the Labour Court, which sided with the union. The employers granted a 5 per cent increase, 89c. an hour, making hourly electrical rates €18.23 and €18.98.[87]

Problems emerged within the ESB Group of Unions in early 2004 and continued to worsen until they reached crisis point in 2005. The group's affiliates had common demands for which they were willing to call strike: an 18.5 per cent pay rise, clearing the €530 million pension deficit and giving workers a 15 per cent share in the company. Different unions placed a different emphasis on what to prioritise. The disagreement soured relations between the TEEU, which wanted the group to pursue the deficit, and the ESB Officers' Association, which wanted employees to have a greater share in the ESB. Some of the animosity, it was alleged, also stemmed from the clerks' favourability to plant closures and privatisation of the ESB, from which they hoped to secure a generous windfall through their shareholding. The TEEU moved to have Patrick Reilly, general secretary of the ESBOA, removed as secretary of the Group of Unions at a coming meeting of the group. When Reilly learned of this, he sought a High Court injunction to prevent the meeting from taking place. It was the last straw for the TEEU. In February, its ESB members voted nine-to-one to leave the group. The ATGWU soon followed suit. Only a small SIPTU and ESBOA rump remained of the once powerful ESB Group of

Unions. It was not the only trouble the TEEU had at the ESB. In early 2005, the Board ousted Joe LaCumbre – a member of the union executive and a worker-director since 1990 – as deputy ESB chairman. TEEU members even threatened to strike unofficially unless the Board reinstate LaCumbre. Fragmentation hindered the unions' ability to provide a united front that September when the ATGWU took out its network technicians, the first official strike at the ESB since 1991, over the Board's outsourcing of work to outside contractors. Though the TEEU directed members to ignore the pickets, many members supported the ATGWU, and some even protested outside 5 Cavendish Row to demand that the union support the strike.[88]

Demarcation disputes occasionally re-emerged. By 1993, the longstanding dispute between electricians and instrument technicians (now represented by the MSF) had not been resolved. That May, 150 electricians staged an unofficial sit-in at twenty power stations across the country after the ESB determined that the fitting of burner management systems was technicians' work. The conflict was eventually resolved by an internal body. Disputes also took place within unions. In November 2007, the HSE suspended TEEU fitters, electricians and plumbers from its Munster hospitals after they implemented work-to-rule in a demarcation row before a settlement ended the affair.[89] Automation and the concentration of craftsmen in single unions (such as the TEEU) has made demarcation disputes rare since the mid-1990s.

The financial and economic crisis that began in 2008, the worst in the history of the state, hit the TEEU harder than most unions. The supposedly booming construction sector was in fact a housing bubble on which the state was far too economically and fiscally reliant. Successive Fianna Fáil-PD governments had fuelled the bubble by giving tax breaks to property developers and using the revenue generated from stamp duty to slash income tax. It was calamitously irresponsible and helped to open a €24.6 billion hole in the public finances. The burst of the bubble coincided with the worst global financial and economic meltdown since the Great Depression, with Ireland suffering more than most Western countries. Unemployment skyrocketed from 4.98 per cent in 2007 to 15.45 per cent by 2012. The national debt ballooned from 23.9 per cent of GDP to 120 per cent by 2013, driven in large part by the government's disastrous bank guarantee scheme in September 2008, which committed the state to covering the banks' enormous debts. The final cost to the state was €41.7 billion. The human cost of the crisis was also massive, with a staggering 397,500 people leaving the country between 2008 and 2013.[90]

Austerity across the public and private sectors became the order of the day as the government inflicted savage spending cuts and tax increases to stabilise the public finances. Employers tackled plummeting demand by slashing pay. The crisis frightened the TEEU into voting 80 per cent in favour of the 2008 transitional national wage agreement between the social partners, a voluntary accord which provided for increases of 6 per cent over twenty-one months. There would be a pay pauses of three months in the private sector and eleven months in the public sector. In December 2009, however, IBEC formally withdrew from the agreement, killing social partnership and plunging the economy into free collective bargaining for the first time since 1986.[91] The TEEU's twelve hundred members in the public sector would suffer redundancies, a pension levy and pay cuts of up to 15 per cent. In 2010, construction workers had their wages slashed by 7.5 per cent and their allowances reduced.[92] The crisis forced many members to emigrate for work, mostly to Australia, which the union facilitated via an agreement with the Australian Embassy. A battle loomed for those who stayed.

Table 74: Gross earnings for industrial workers, 1992-97 (September 1985 = 100).[93]

Year (Mar.)	All industries	Year (Sept..)	All industries
1992	146.1	1995	164.7
1993	155.8	1996	168.9
1994	159.5	1997	177.5

The 2009 electricians' strike

From 1990, pay increases in the electrical contracting trade had been determined by an analogue system. The analogue aggregated annual wage increases across a group of sixteen companies outside the contracting sector from September of the previous year to September of the current year. The average of these calculations was then applied to electricians in the contract shops as the minimum wage effective from 1 April each year. The system was written into a Registered Employment Agreement (REA). When registered by the Labour Court, REAs were legally binding, even to those who were not even a party to the deal. By 2009, there were sixty-eight REAs covering over 500,000 workers.[94]

The system had served electricians better than most. Excluding allowances and expenses, electricians' annual pay was approximately €42,000 by 2009 while the average industrial wage was €34,000. The rise due for 2008 was based on average increases for electricians in manufacturing between September 2006 and September 2007 – 5pc on top of the current €21.49 per hour. The Labour Court originally approved the increases, with the approval of both employers and unions, but when the contractors withdrew their support, it decided not to register the proposed increases. Employers withdrew from the REA, and so the electricians received no rise. By April 2008, the property bubble had burst sending the construction sector into recession months before the rest of the economy. Accordingly, employers argued that the increases were based on economic data no longer applicable by 2008. In June, a newly formed breakaway group, National Electrical Contactors Ireland (NECI), secured a High Court injunction against the Labour Court considering the 5 per cent advance. The new group represented 460 small contractors who resented being legally obligated to pay the REA rate. The ECA, on the other hand, represented fifty-one major contractors who employed 4,800, while the AECI represented 220 small and medium sized contractors. Months of legal wrangling in the High Court ensued before the TEEU succeeded in having the injunction lifted in October. But the contractors continued their legal war against the REA, leading the TEEU to ballot for industrial action.[95] For the TEEU, standing in defence of the electrical REA meant standing up for all workers. By November, the economy and financial system had crashed ignominiously, and employers sought to unravel the REAs in response. The CIF, for example, was demanding that their REA be altered to reduce wages by 10 per cent. Arguing that some wanted to slash rates down to minimum wage levels (then €8.65 an hour), Wills told the 2008 biennial delegate conference that the electrical contractors were presenting 'the most serious challenge to an agreement in our sector since 1920 and to collective bargaining in the history of the state.'[96]

Predictably, electricians did not receive a raise in April 2009 when the analogue increase was calculated at 6.73 per cent. By then, electricians were legally entitled to a 11.37 per cent pay rise (€2.49 an hour), which would bring hourly rates from €21.49 to €23.98. The TEEU put this claim before employers who, by then, were seeking a 10 per cent pay cut and a weakening of conditions guaranteed by the REA. Unsurprisingly, the contractors refused the union's claim. The union claimed that some employers threatened to cut rates to €19.34 and apprentice rates by 5 to 10 per cent, and to hire unqualified staff to work at cheaper rates. Intervention from the Labour Court, Labour Relations Commission and High Court could not resolve the dispute. In March, the Labour Court ruled to keep the REA in force and that the previously agreed 5 per cent increase (€1.05 an hour) be renegotiated to take account of the economic crisis. It also rejected an application from NECI and another unaligned group (who represented 541 contractors) to cancel the registration of the REA.[97] No agreement was reached between the union and the contractors, with an inevitable result.

On 5 July 2009, the TEEU took out 10,500 electricians from two hundred construction sites on national strike for the increase. It did so despite threats from the ECA that it would victimise 4,500 electricians by putting them on temporary notice should there be a strike. Several major infrastructural projects under construction were picketed, including Lansdowne Road stadium; Dublin Airport; the Luas lines; O'Connell Street, Dublin; Croke Park; the National Convention Centre; NUI Galway; the Corrib Gas Line; St. James's Hospital; Shannon Airport; the Ballymun Regeneration Project. Major firms such as Guinness, Pfizer and Intel, where contractors were working within the plant, were also picketed. Cadbury's and Irish Distillers obtained injunctions against pickets at their premises. The contractors had the support of the establishment press. The *Independent* informed the TEEU that its action flew 'in the face of reason' and that the 'average citizen' was 'utterly baffled' by it. The *Irish Examiner* denounced the claim as 'not only unrealistic but virtually immoral' and, in more classist terms, 'high stakes proletarian posturing.'[98] The strikers had their supporters too. SIPTU, Unite the Union, BATU and UCATT refused to pass pickets and announced they would support the TEEU's request from Congress for an all-out picket.[99] Reciprocating the solidarity, Devoy declared that the TEEU had to win the dispute for 'every worker in Ireland.'[100]

When the government directed the Labour Relations Commission to call intervene, the TEEU agreed to restart negotiations with the contractors. The breakthrough came when the ECA and the AECI to take the 10 per cent cut off the table, to comply with the REA and to refer the pay issue to the Labour Court. The union also accepted binding arbitration from the Labour Court. The result was an astounding victory for the TEEU: the court recommended a 4.9 per cent pay increase (€1.05 an hour). The stoppage ended on 12 July, with the electricians returning to work the following day. The ECA agreed to give the increase, but the AECI and the NECI did not, ensuring that the advance was never implemented. Nonetheless, the outcome ensured no cut for electricians, bucking the downward spiral of wages across the economy. The electricians' stoppage was part of a wider explosion of worker militancy against wage cuts and austerity. There were 329,593 days lost to strikes in 2009, more than any year since 1985, though this figure dropped by 98 per cent in 2010 to 6,602 days.[101]

The government commissioned an investigation to examine the adequacy of negotiating and collective bargaining arrangements in the electrical contract trade and the need, if any, for change in agreements and how they can be implemented. The union rejected its report, issued in December 2009, for several reasons. Primarily, the EMC feared that the proposals would dilute the trade and facilitate employers in decimating pay and conditions and not paying pension contributions. The executive also condemned the provisions that proposed a binding disputes resolution body, fearing it would harm the union's ability to call strikes.[102]

Table 75: Days Lost to Industrial Disputes in Ireland, 2002-2016.[103]

Year	Days Lost	Year	Days Lost
2002	21,257	2009	329,593
2003	37,482	2010	6,602
2004	20,784	2011	3,695
2005	26,665	2012	8,486
2006	7,352	2013	14,935
2007	6,038	2014	44,015
2008	4,147	2015	32,964

Becoming Connect, 2010-2017

The TEEU had no time to celebrate its victory in 2009 as it was simultaneously gripped by another financial crisis. The economic crash had brought emigration back to 1980s levels. TEEU membership had grown by 65 per cent between 2000 and 2010 but declined by 6.5 per cent in 2010. In total, about 9,500 members left the country, taking about €2.5 million worth of desperately needed union contributions with them. Total income for 2011 alone was down €160,280 on the previous year. Meanwhile, the union had to pay off the mortgage it had taken out to renovate head office at the peak of the Celtic Tiger housing bubble, with its grossly inflated property prices. The executive had hoped to finance the refurbishment by selling 5 Cavendish Row and its premises in Drogheda, which would have necessitated taking out only a small loan from the bank. But because of the economic crash – which had led to a collapse in property prices and ensured that the union had been unable to sell its properties – it now required substantial borrowing from the bank. Having previously been able to make the repayments, it severely struggled to pay back the mortgage and risked insolvency as a result. At its nadir, the TEEU was €5.3 million in the red and was facing repeated threats from the bank to foreclose 6 Gardiner Row.[104]

But the union reacted swiftly and decisively to the crisis. In early 2010, the EMC formed a subcommittee (which Wills chaired) tasked with devising solutions. Its report was a stark crystallisation of how perilous the situation was. It recommended a reduction of staff of eight over a period of thirty months and upping union contributions to €6 per member per week (a 30 per cent increase) by 2019 in five separate instalments. With the survival of the TEEU at stake, the EMC adopted the report's recommendations in February 2010, and the staff did likewise the following month. As well as significantly reducing union expenditure, the EMC rented out rooms at 6 Gardiner Row, introduced a more flexible system for members in arrears, cut the number of TEEU delegates to Congress and mandated fulltime officers to spend a week out of every month focussing exclusively on recruiting. To assist in this, it appointed another subcommittee to oversee a renewed recruitment drive to alleviate the union's financial woes. That subcommittee's work soon yielded results as well: in the first quarter of 2011, union membership grew for the first time in eighteen months.[105] That summer, the EMC reported that a 'considerable reversal of the trend over the last two years' was taking place, with the adoption of a 'no arrears culture' being credited for the revival.[106] In total, 12,069 people joined the TEEU between 2011 and 2016.

Perhaps most significantly, the executive began the painstaking process of negotiating to restructure its €4.5 million debt with AIB, against which the deeds of its properties had been lodged as collateral. The talks were exhausting and often fraught. In 2013, after the union stopped paying interest on the mortgage, the bank sent a receiver to foreclose and sell its properties. In response, the TEEU threatened to use its contingency fund to launch a media campaign against the bank. In the context of widespread public outrage at the greed and recklessness of banks during the Celtic Tiger, which were major reasons for the economic catastrophe tormenting the country, the union knew that going public 'would be like lighting a fuse to a volatile banking sector'.[107] Realising this as well, AIB took the threats seriously and appointed a senior manager to resume negotiations with the union. Finally, in 2014, after three arduous years, both sides reached an agreement. AIB would restructure the TEEU's debt to make it a five-year financial arrangement followed by a fifteen-year mortgage. The bank also wrote off of €105,000 and gave the TEEU two years to yield €950,000 through the sale of properties. The deal gave the union enough breathing space to allow the concurrent recovery of the property market to make its impact felt. It sold its offices in Drogheda (for €250,000) and Cork (for €245,000) in 2014 and 5 Cavendish Row (for €650,000) the following year. It also sold its premises in Limerick and Galway, but not Waterford, and struck a deal to lease rooms from IMPACT (now Fórsa) in Cork in lieu of offices of its own.[108]

Table 76: Annual Increase in TEEU Membership, 2011-2016.[109]

Year (31 Dec.)	Membership Gain	Year (31 Dec.)	Membership Gain
2011	3,535	2014	1,870
2012	1,077	2015	1,444
2013	1,675	2016	2,468

The resolution of the crisis was, of course, not solely down to the executive. As in times past, members and staff put their shoulders to the wheel for the sake of their union. The staff – who had to take on extra work without being paid overtime – had their salaries frozen for five years and had to make greater contributions to their pensions. The TEEU could not afford to hire new employees to help with the additional workload and had to stop buying stationery and diaries and spending money on promotional material for several years.[110] But the sacrifices helped to turn things around. In April 2014, the EMC felt confident enough to predict a coming budget surplus of €10,000. And the following year, Devoy (general secretary of the union since 2010) could accurately tell the NEC that 'the TEEU was never in a stronger position than it is today … Our membership is growing significantly, our finances are on a sound footing and our relationship with other unions at home and across the globe has strengthened our organisation exponentially'.[111] That the union went from the brink of bankruptcy to a position of unprecedented financial stability was a testimony to the loyalty and commitment of its leadership, staff and members.

Given the economic crisis, the TEEU's survival was vital if craftworkers were to stand any chance of defending pay and conditions against a renewed employer onslaught. It was a hectic period for the union. The EMC served forty-eight notices of industrial action between 2008 and 2010 (twenty-four in 2009 alone), ten of which resulted in strike with a satisfactory outcome. It sanctioned twelve disputes during 2011, seventeen during 2014, six during 2015 and eight during 2016.[112] The TEEU was also active in fighting austerity in the public sector and was among the minority of unions that rejected the Croke Park (2010) Agreement, which focussed on redeployment in the public service rather than cutting pay or issuing redundancies. The TEEU did, however, accept the Haddington Road (2013) and the Lansdowne Road (2015) agreements. The former reduced the earnings of better-paid public servants and introduced additional, unpaid working hours for most, while the latter extended the provisions of Haddington Road but partially restored pay on a phased basis.[113]

On 31 August 2009, forty TEEU members at the Green Isle Foods frozen pizza-making plant in Naas, Co. Kildare walked off the job in solidarity with three workers who had been sacked the previous month whom the company had refused to reinstate or compensate. Green Isle claimed that the workers had breached the company's IT policy by downloading pornographic material, allegations the workers in question categorically refuted, insisting that they had been scapegoated after inadvertently accessing files from management detailing cutbacks the firm would soon issue. The TEEU mounted pickets through the unseasonably cold winter of 2009-10 and had its position vindicated when, in December, the Labour Court recommended that the workers be reinstated or compensated as their dismissals were unjustified. Two strikers even went on hunger strike after the company rejected the Labour Court's recommendation and employed scabs from the UK. Finally, in early March, nearly six months after the sackings had taken place, the dispute was brought to an end. Although the workers did not get their jobs back, they received significant financial compensation from Green Isle.[114]

The TEEU had a similarly prolonged fight with Pickerings Lifts. In early February 2010, the union brought out thirteen maintenance craftsmen after accusing Pickerings of unfairly dismissing seven employees and not paying them the redundancy payment to which they were entitled. The company refused to attend the Labour Court to find a resolution, with the people of Ballymun being left without lifts in the nine remaining eight-storey blocks and the one remaining fourteen-storey tower block. The strike led to Dublin City Council terminating its maintenance contract with Pickerings and seeking a

High Court injunction against the TEEU's pickets. However, the plan backfired when the union won the case in a significant judgement that established new protections of the right to strike under common law. Justice Mary Laffoy interpreted Section 11.1 of the Industrial Relations Act 1990 to allow for the picketing of client sites with immunity even after a company had had their contract terminated.[115] In July, both sides reached an agreement on redundancy packages that, although confidential, were 'in line with the industry norm for redundancy agreements in the industry', the union maintained.[116] Other major industrial actions the TEEU engaged in during the years of austerity included bringing out Bord na Móna workers in a dispute over a 3.5 per cent pay rise in the summer of 2012 and a ten-day strike in 2013 at St. James's Hospital over the suspension of three members.[117]

Not every major dispute devolved into a strike, however. Christmas 2013 was sparred what would have been the first stoppage at the ESB since 1991 over a long-running row about how the Board's €1.7 billion pension shortfall was to be addressed. The ESB and the Group of Unions had clashed over the company's insistence that, since 2010, its pension system was a defined contribution (rather than a defined benefit) scheme. This would have made the workers liable for the deficit and would have removed their guarantee of receiving a fixed pension upon retirement. But in early December, a settlement was brokered at the Labour Relations Commission: the ESB conceded that its pension was a defined benefit scheme and that, as a result, the company was solely responsible for plugging the deficit.[118] It was an impressive victory for the unions.

The ramifications of the 2009 electricians' strike were profound, creating a bitter industrial atmosphere in the electrical contracting trade with significant legal (and even constitutional) ramifications. In June 2010, employers were dismayed by the state's successful defence of the constitutionality of the Industrial Relations Act 1946 and the REA system before the High Court. But this setback did nothing to diminish their desire to the see REAs dismantled. By March 2011, the instances of employers not implementing the REAs had escalated massively and was continuing to grow. The TEEU had recorded 395 cases, 115 of which had been referred to the Labour Court and ten of which were before District Courts. In three recent District Court hearings, the TEEU had successfully secured prosecutions against electrical contractors who were not paying the €21.49 rate (i.e., 'non-compliant'). In May alone, eighteen non-compliant contractors were prosecuted. At its 2011 annual general meeting, the AECI (with ECA support) resolved to continue its campaign for the dissolution of the REA in the electrical contracting sector. The ECA's preference was for a revised agreement but, in the absence of that, it was willing to support the AECI's challenge. After unsuccessfully arguing its case before the Labour Court and the Labour Relations Commission, the AECI took its challenge to the Supreme Court in early 2012.[119] It was fateful decision.

On 9 May 2013, the Supreme Court dropped a bombshell, better known as the McGowan judgement.[120] It ruled that Part 3 of the Industrial Relations Act 1946, which gave the REAs their legal authority, was unconstitutional and struck it down accordingly. Hundreds of thousands of workers risked having their collective wage agreements cancelled as a result of the landmark judgement as there were approximately seventy REAs registered with the Labour Court.[121] Devoy decried the ruling as 'another dark day for employment in Ireland'[122] which had essentially 'heralded the end of national centralised collective bargaining' in the country.[123] Many employers were elated and felt emboldened to seek greater deregulation of the Irish industrial relations apparatus. Brendan McGinty, IBEC director of industrial relations, claimed that the judgement 'calls into question ... the Joint Labour Committee system and adds weight to the argument that the JLC system should be abolished entirely'.[124] The AECI announced that it was no longer bound by national collective agreements in the electrical contracting industry and that its only legal obligation was to pay the minimum wage of €8.65 an hour. It also recommended that contractors stop collecting contributions for the TEEU at source and actively discouraged electricians from remaining in the Construction Workers' Pension Scheme. The TEEU did, however, secure promises from the ECA and the Mechanical, Engineering and Building Services Contractors' Association (MEBSCA) that they would honour the terms of the old national agreements.[125]

However, in early 2014, the ECA announced its desire to cut pay by 10 per cent, from €21.49 an hour to €19.34, claiming that its competitors were paying less and that it needed to remain competitive. The TEEU would not accept any downward revision of wages, which the ECA claimed was effectively an endorsement of a free-for-all, where each individual contractor would have to come to an agreement with his electricians on a case-by-case basis. The union's response was equally dogged. After members voted 94 per cent in favour, the union served strike notice on the ECA and AECI for the 4.9 per cent increase foregone in 2009 (which would bring hourly rates to €22.56) and for the maintenance of existing conditions and benefits. It asserted that under former agreements and Labour Court recommendations, electricians were actually entitled to an hourly rate of €24.78 from 1 April 2014. Over five hundred sites and 6,500 electricians would be affected by the prospective strike. However, talks at the Labour Relations Commission delivered a tentative peace when both sides agreed to withdraw their respective proposals to alter existing wages.[126]

Although the TEEU had rescinded its strike notice, it reserved the right to mount 'strategic strikes' or blockades at sites where the contractor was non-compliant. On 7 May 2014, it exercised that right when it blockaded three of the biggest construction sites in the country: UCD, the Dublin Institute of Technology site in Grangegorman and St. Patrick's College in Drumcondra. Sherlock Recruitment was undertaking the electrical work at Grangegorman while Cosgrove Electrical Services and Precision Electric had been contracted at St. Patrick's and UCD, respectively. None of these firms were paying the €21.49 rate, the TEEU insisted. In fact, it alleged that Sherlock was paying as little as €14 an hour to agency workers, was withholding travel time, sick pay, pension and mortality benefits, and had sacked some electricians. Cosgrove, it asserted, was paying only €15 an hour and was similarly denying benefits. The rolling pickets and blockages yielded instant results. Thirty-one non-compliant contractors – some of whom were allegedly paying as little as €9 an hour – implemented the €21.49 rate.[127]

The union's success vitalised it to pursue a 5 per cent rise for all of its forty thousand members from late 2014, which it pursued vigorously throughout 2015. By then, the public finances had been stabilised and the economy was growing steadily again (GNP expanded by 36 per cent between 2013 and 2016), and the unions were determined to claw back at least some of what they had surrendered during the economic crisis. Wages for craftsmen in the electrical and mechanical contracting trades did not reflect rates across those industries, where the average was €24.79.[128] The TEEU also put forward once again the 4.9 per cent claim on the ECA and AECI which, when added to the 5 per cent increase the union was also demanding, would have given electricians in the contracting trade an hourly rate of €25.29. But the employers would not countenance any talk of wage increases until Sectoral Employment Orders (SEOs) had been signed into law. The AECI continued to deny the existence of a national collective agreement and stated that they would only pay what was to be mandated by an SEO. Because, the AECI claimed, most electricians were working for €13-14 per hour, it would support an SEO for a rate of €17-18. SEOs are statutory instruments issued by a minister that set pay, pensions or sick pay schemes in a particular industry following a Labour Court recommendation. They are a central feature of the Industrial Relations (Amendment) Act 2015, which the Fine Gael-Labour government passed to fill the lacuna left by the McGowan judgement.[129]

By the year's end, the TEEU's patience was wearing thin, and it once again threatened industrial action. Employers took the threats seriously and, for the first time, both the ECA and AECI accepted the €21.49 rate and agreed that any wage increase would apply to that rate. In early 2016, following months of negotiations at the Labour Relations Commission, they conceded hourly hikes of 2.4 per cent from 1 July 2016 and 2.5 per cent from 1 January 2017, the first wage improvements electricians had received since April 2007. The TEEU also helped to secure for craftsmen in the mechanical contracting trade a 10 per cent increase over the subsequent two years from the MEBSCA. The TEEU had argued that the amount sought (and eventually obtained) was 'ludicrously' low, but the more conservative voices on ICTU's Construction Industry Committee prevailed.[130]

The TEEU's struggles in post-Celtic Tiger, austerity Ireland were not restricted to the fight to protect and advance pay and conditions. It enthusiastically participated in the massive anti-water charges protests which took place across the country on 31 January 2015 and affiliated to the Right2Water campaign that August. Throughout 2014 and 2015, it led the charge against the apprenticeship fees announced by the government in Budget 2014, which would range from €833 to €1,466. Whereas the ten-week period apprentices had to spend in college had previously been covered by general taxation, it would now have to be paid by the apprentices themselves. And this was despite the fact that, under existing legislation, it was the employers who were liable to pay when SOLAS (establish in 2013 to succeed the scandal-ridden FÁS) provided courses about apprenticeship training. The TEEU had helped to defeat the last attempt to introduce such charges in 2004 when it organised a one-day stoppage at the nineteen Institutes of Technology across the country and threatened High Court proceedings against FÁS. By 2014, the economic crash and the austerity that followed had decimated the living standards of apprentices. From a high of 29,753 in 2007, their numbers had tumbled to 20,170 by 2010, 7,351 of whom were unemployed. However, as many employers had laid off apprentices without informing FÁS, the number of unemployed apprentices may well have been even higher. By 2012, the apprentice population had shrunk to 12,039, 4,626 of whom were unemployed.[131]

After a series of meetings between Devoy and Minster for Education Ruairí

Quinn could not clear the impasse Budget 2014 had created, the outraged TEEU launched its 'Axe the Tax' campaign. In June 2014, it summoned its twelve hundred apprentice members to meetings in Dublin, Cork, Waterford, Limerick and Galway. But the turnout was abysmal, with only thirty-two (2 per cent of the apprentices in the union) attending. In July 2015, the union initiated a campaign of agitation against employers who refused to pay the apprenticeship fee and announced its intention to conduct a one-day national strike on 2 November unless IBEC covered the charge. Once again, threats of direct action produced tangible results: IBEC recommended to its affiliates that they pay the fee, with the vast majority doing so by the year's end.[132]

Table 77: Annual Intake of Apprentices, 2006-2010.[133]

Trade	2006	2010
Engineering	448	138
Motor	808	272
Electrical	2,495	407
Printing	41	3
Construction	4,514	193
Total	**8,306**	**1,013**

The TEEU did much to deepen its international links during these years. In 2010, the EMC resolved to support a boycott of Israeli goods and to form an 'International Committee' to highlight the plight of trade unionists in countries where organising workers can incur state repression and vigilante violence.[134] The following year, Devoy attended the Electrical Trades Union of Australia's annual conference where he highlighted 'the need for the trade union movement to take a global view and establish global contacts', which was 'immensely important if the employers are to be confronted on the global stage'.[135] With this goal in mind, the TEEU affiliated to the IndustriALL Global Union – a newly established federation of various international federation, including the International Metalworkers' Federation – in June 2013 at a cost of €4,000 a year.[136] IndustriALL represents fifty million workers across 140 countries in the mining, energy and manufacturing sectors. But the internationalisation of the TEEU was only just beginning.

In August 2014, United Association of Journeymen and Apprentices of the Plumbing, Pipefitting and Sprinkler Fitting Industry of the United States and Canada (United Association or UA) – one of America's largest unions with 370,000 craftworkers in the US, Canada and Australia – wrote to the TEEU looking to establish fraternal ties. The EMC understood that the increasing monopolisation of the global economy by a small number of giant multinational corporations required an international trade-union response and so it jumped at the opportunity to deepen its links with sister unions abroad. To help with this, Devoy and Brian Nolan attended the UA's tripartite conference in Chicago that October. On 24 November, the TEEU met UA representatives to establish formal relations and federate under the guiding principles of the International Trade Union Confederation. The new relationship would facilitate the future training of members of each union and inaugurate a Joint Venture Training Company. The UA would build training facilities in Ireland and TEEU members could use UA training facilities in North America to upskill in areas such as welding, refrigeration, heating, ventilation and air conditioning. Both unions also committed themselves to setting up a joint bank account with a threshold of $50,000. The EMC ratified this agreement the following month. The same meeting also voted to take industrial action at OTIS Lifts (an Australian company) in support of OTIS workers in Australia whom the company had locked out. The dispute was resolved at the eleventh hour without the need for the TEEU to down tools, but the fact that it was willing to do so demonstrates the international links it was cultivating at this time.[137]

In January 2015, the TEEU signed what the *Irish Times* called an 'historic agreement' with the UA in the Irish Embassy in Washington in the presence of the US Secretary of Labor Thomas Perez. 'The first arrangement of its kind', the agreement allowed for the TEEU to bring American trainers to Ireland to upskill workers under a 'train the trainers' programme.[138] Both unions committed to opening a training centre (worth €1.5 million) in Ireland, with the TEEU entering into discussions with Kildare/Wicklow Education & Training Board to explore the possibility of using their facilities to open the centre. UA trainers visited Ireland at their own expense to upskill Irish fitters (at the Intel site in Leixlip, Co. Kildare, for example) and deliver instructional classes on welding for mechanical craftsmen. Representatives of the International Brotherhood of Electricians did likewise to train Irish electricians.[139]

Domestically, the TEEU continued to deepen its bonds with other unions, which helped it to reassert itself as a major force within Irish trade unionism. In 2014, the TEEU and SIPTU revived the TUF and promised to cooperate more closely in the future. The most vivid manifestation of the new arrangement was the establishment of a single-table bargaining protocol in the manufacturing sector, which included provisions for joint action on issues that affected both (threatened plant closures, redundancies or cuts in pay or remuneration) while respecting each union's right to negotiate separately with employers on matters that affected their individual members (operative-specific vs. craft-specific issues).[140]

Nevertheless, it was inevitable that the TEEU would clash with other unions who were similarly ambitious to recruit. The most bitter and lengthy dispute began in January 2012 when, in contravention of the ICTU constitution, Unite poached TEEU electricians in Merck and Sharpe and Dohme as well as mechanics in Limerick and electricians and plumbers on construction sites across Dublin, Drogheda, Clonmel, Clonskeagh and Carlow. Unite's contribution rates were lower than the TEEU's, which clearly appealed to some. The embittered TEEU took the issue to the ICTU Disputes Committee which ruled against Unite and ordered it to return the members it had admitted. Unite refused to do this.[141] That December, Begg issued a report asserting that the dispute would be difficult to resolve given the fundamental differences between the unions which, he believed, was akin to comparing oil with water. 'The TEEU position was one of supporting the industrial relations institutional architecture and … [its] reputation in this regard is well known, e.g., defending the REA in the courts and generally pursuing progress through the Labour Court and maintaining their agreements… Unite's position was to pursue an antagonist philosophy towards employers… no further attempt at conciliation would be helpful or in any way effective'.[142] Hence, the conflict dragged on well into 2013 and soured relations between the two unions. That May, Unite sought a meeting with the TEEU about the agreement governing wages in the mechanical contracting trade, but the TEEU refused to meet with it until it had implemented the Disputes Committee verdict and promised not to poach TEEU members again.[143] The TEEU was also angered by ICTU's reticence to enforce its own ruling. Unless Congress asserted itself, the TEEU would 'be left with no alternative but to use … means outside of the trade union movement to have Congress observe its own constitution.'[144] But thankfully it did not come to this. On 4 December 2013, both unions finally reached an agreement, with Unite recognising the TEEU as the sole union for electricians in the Republic of Ireland.[145]

Its dispute with Unite was not the most consequential interaction the TEEU had with another union during this period. In October 2012, the EMC heard that an Irish UCATT official had approached the TEEU floating the possibility of a future amalgamation of the two unions. Anxious to build its strength in the building trade, the TEEU wasted little time establishing channels of communication. By November of the following year, the EMC was told that the talks between the two were very proceeding smoothly, especially on the issue of the 'transfer of engagements', i.e., the transfer of UCATT's assets, liabilities, obligations and agreements with employers to the TEEU. In 2014, formal negotiations began between the TEEU executive on the one side and the Irish regional committee and the (London-based) national executive of UCATT on the other. Separately, the Operative Plasterers and Allied Trades Society of Ireland approached the TEEU to explore a potential fusion between the two. So did the Energy Services Union (formerly the ESB Officers' and Staff Association), but neither proposal advanced any further than that.[146]

When the EMC met in April 2016, it heard that feedback about the proposed merger with UCATT from TEEU branches across the country was 'all positive'. The process of amalgamation received a boon when junior minister Ged Nash pledged that the Department of Jobs, Enterprise and Innovation would cover the costs of the venture with a generous grant. A vote of TEEU members took place on 25 May 2016. All of UCATT's seven thousand Irish members across the thirty-two counties were balloted the following month, with voting wrapped up by 24 June. The results were overwhelming: 90 per cent of its 5,500 members in the Republic of Ireland – mainly carpenters, painters and sheet metal workers – voted to transfer their engagements to the TEEU (its fifteen hundred members in Northern Ireland joined Unite UK instead). Every single TEEU and UCATT branch in the Republic voted in favour of the amalgamation. In the meantime, both unions had signed a formal agreement of amalgamation on 2 June, including arrangements for the pensions and the pay of the fulltime UCATT staff members who were about to transfer. By November, the TEEU had received the last of the necessary legal documentation from UCATT, facilitating the full transfer of engagements to 6 Gardiner Row. On 1 January 2017, the twenty-four-branch, forty-six-thousand-member Connect Trade Union was formally launched at 6 Gardiner Row with Paddy Kavanagh as its first general secretary, Frank Keoghan as its first general president and Arthur Hall as its first assistant general secretary.[147]

Chapter Notes and References

1   Ferriter, *Transformation*, p. 663.
2   O'Connor, *Labour History of Ireland* (2nd Ed.), pp. 244-246; Bielenberg and Ryan, *Economic History*, p. 96.
3   O'Connor, *Labour History of Ireland* (2nd Ed.), pp. 244-246.
4   Ibid.
5   TEEU EMC minutes, 6 Aug. 1992.
6   TEEU NEC minutes, 26 Sept. 1998.
7   Ibid., 29, 30 May 1993.
8   Ibid., 29 May 1993-10 May 1997, 10, 11 May 2003.
9   TEEU annual returns, 1992-2001, T603, RFS records, CRO.
10 'General Secretary's Progress report on the Amalgamation, Mar. 1993', File: TEEU Branch Reports, 1987-1995, Box 166, TEEU collection, ILHM.
11 *Evening Herald*, 9 Dec. 2004; *Irish Independent*, 19 July 2009; TEEU NEC minutes, 12, 13 May 2001, 11, 12 May 2002, 13 May 2006, 15 May 2010; TEEU EMC minutes, 19 Nov. 1998, 20 Nov. 2003, 19 Feb., 21 Oct. 2004, 16 June, 20 Oct. 2005, 19 Sept., 19 Nov. 2009.
12 TEEU EMC minutes, 7 Jan., 2 Sept. 1999.
13 TEEU NEC minutes, 24 Apr. 1999.
14 TEEU EMC minutes, 9 Dec. 1999.
15 TEEU NEC minutes, 8, 9 June 1996.
16 Patrick Guilfoyle to Jackson, 11 June 1996.
17 Interview with Patrick Guilfoyle, 5 Mar. 2020.
18 TEEU NEC minutes, 23 May 1996; *Irish Times* 13 June 1996; interview with Devoy.
19 TEEU EMC minutes, 30 May 1996
20 TEEU NEC minutes, 8, 9 June 1996.
21 *Irish Times*, 13 June 1996; TEEU EMC minutes, 11, 20 June 1996.
22 *Belfast Newsletter*, 30 Apr. 2002.
23 *Irish Times*, 26 June, 15, 17 July 1996; ICTU, 'Report of the subcommittee appointed to investigate complaints by AEEU against TEEU', 20 Sept. 1996; interview with Eamon Devoy, 12 Feb. 2020; interview with Wills.
24 *Irish Times*, 27 Sept., 22 Nov. 1996.
25 Ibid., 25 Nov. 1996.
26 O'Reilly to Kevin Duffy, 26 June 1997, 'Cadbury's: AEEU/TEEU' folder; TEEU NEC minutes, 26 Sept. 1998.
27 Interview with Guilfoyle.
28 Interview with Devoy; interview with Prizeman; *Irish Times*, 26 June 1996.
29 TEEU EMC minutes, 14 Oct. 1993.
30 Ibid., 11 Nov. 1993.
31 Ibid., 14 Oct., 11 Nov. 1993, 7 Apr. 1994.
32 TEEU NEC minutes, 4, 5 Dec. 1993, 7 May, 17 Dec. 1994.
33 *Irish Independent*, 4-6 Jan. 1996; *Irish Times*, 28 May 1996.
34 Interview with MacRaghnaill.
35 George Swan to Frank O'Reilly, 27 Aug. 1996.
36 Report of meeting re. Dublin No. 1 Branch, 23 Sept. 1996.
37 Prizeman to O'Reilly, 1 Apr. 1997; interview with Charlie Prizeman, 20 Sept. 2020.
38 TEEU EMC minutes, 6 May, 5 June 1997, 5 Feb.-2 Apr. 1998; Prizeman to O'Reilly, 4 Feb. 1998.
39 Swan to O'Reilly, 31 Mar. 1998
40 Brendan Fenelon to O'Reilly, 16 July 1998; interview with Prizeman.
41 TEEU EMC minutes, 23 July, 20 Aug., 29 Oct. 1998, 29 Apr. 1999
42 ICTU Disputes Committee Report 99/1, 27 Oct. 1998.
43 TEEU EMC minutes, 27 Jan., 24 Feb., 9 Mar. 2000; Peter Williamson to Wills, 10 Jan. 2000.
44 Eddie Miller to Tom Wall, 6 July 2000.
45 *Irish Independent*, 1 Aug. 2000.
46 TEEU EMC minutes, 13, 27 July, 21 Sept., 12 Oct. 2000.
47 Ibid., 5, 19 Oct. 2000.
48 *Irish Times*, 29 Sept. 2000; *Irish Independent*, 18 May 2001.
49 TEEU EMC minutes, 23 Nov. 2001, 17 Jan., 21 Feb. 2002; *Irish Independent*, 25, 30 Apr. 2002.

50   TEEU NEC minutes, 11, 12 May 2002.

51   TEEU EMC minutes, 20 Nov. 2003.

52   Ibid., 15 Jan., 19 Feb. 2004, 15 Mar. 2007; Wills to Begg, 8 Sept. 2004, 11 Dec. 2006, ICTU Disputes Committee folder; interview with Devoy.

53   TEEU EMC minutes, 30 Sept. 1999, 10, 24 Feb., 9 Mar. 2000

54   Ibid., Apr. 2000

55   Ibid., 15, 29 June, 13 July 2000

56   Ibid., 23 Nov. 1995, 8 Jan., 4, 19 Feb. 1998, 20 Jan., 17 Feb. 2005, 19 June 2008, 24 June 2010; TEEU NEC minutes, 12 Mar. 2005; Judgment of Justice Laffoy, Philip Kirwan vs Technical, Engineering and Electrical Union, 14 Jan. 2005, https://www.courts.ie/acc/alfresco/afac54d0-e3b3-498d-8eef-dd485c3d09ca/2005_IEHC_5_1.pdf/pdf#view=fitH (retrieved 2 Mar. 2020).

57   TEEU EMC minutes, 19 July 2001.

58   *Irish Independent*, 20 Feb. 2003; Devine, *Organising History*, p. 839; ibid., 13 Dec. 2001.

59   *Irish Examiner*, 17 May 2001; TEEU EMC minutes, 21 June 2001, 15 Feb., 20 Mar., 17 July 2003; *Irish Independent*, 20, 25 Sept. 2003, 27 Apr. 2012. ICTU made no recommendation on the Fiscal Compact Treaty.

60   TEEU EMC minutes, 21 Feb., 17 Apr. 2008.

61   Ibid., 17 Jan. 2008.

62   *Irish Independent*, 14-17, 28 Mar., 4 Apr., 15 May 2006, 7 July, 22 Oct.-1 Nov. 2007; TEEU EMC minutes, 15 Sept. 2005, 15 Feb. 2007.

63   TEEU NEC minutes, 12, 13 May 2001; TEEU EMC minutes, 22 Mar., 15 Feb., 19 July 2007, 17 Dec. 2009, 26 Feb., 20 May, 24 June, 16 Sept. 2010. The ICTU Dispute Committee sided with BATU and censured the TEEU for organising building trade workers.

64   TEEU annual returns, 2000-2010, T603, RFS records, CRO.

65   O'Connor, *Labour History of Ireland* (2nd Ed.), pp. 246-248.

66   Interview with Guilfoyle.

67   O'Connor, *Labour History of Ireland* (2nd Ed.), pp. 246-248; Devine, *Organising History*, pp. 798-801

68   TEEU EMC minutes, 10 Mar. 1994, 23 Jan. 1997.

69   *Examiner*, 17 Jan. 1997.

70   *Irish Independent*, 11 Jan. 1997.

71   Hastings, Sheehan & Yeates, *Saving the Future*, pp. 47-48.

72   TEEU EMC minutes, 19 Oct. 1995.

73   *Irish Independent*, 19 Mar. 2003; Devine, *Organising History*, p. 853.

74   Ibid., 27 Mar. 2003.

75   *Examiner*, 11-17 Jan. 1997; ibid., 26 June, 31 July, 21 Aug. 2006.

76   O'Connor, *Labour History of Ireland* (2nd Ed.), p. 252.

77   Hastings, Sheehan & Yeates, *Saving the Future*, pp. 213-216.

78   Ibid., pp. 68-70, 115.

79   *Irish Press*, 11, 24, 29 May, 2, 18 June 1993; TEEU EMC minutes, 27 May 1993.

80   *Irish Independent*, 16 Mar.-28 Apr. 1996, 16 May; TEEU EMC minutes, 5 June-24 July 1997, 3 Dec. 1998.

81   *Examiner*, 17 Sept. 8 Nov. 1997, 24 Apr., 13 June 1998; TEEU EMC minutes, 11 May, 25 June, 9 July 1998; *Munster Express*, 22 Oct. 1999.

82   *Examiner*, 23 Sept. 1998.

83   *Irish Independent*, 13 July, 11, 15, 18, 19 Aug., 1, 10 Sept. 1998, 21 Apr., 1-5, 11, 29, 30 June, 1-19 July 1999.

84   Hastings, Sheehan & Yeates, *Saving the Future*, p. 70.

85   O'Connor, *Labour History of Ireland* (2nd ed.), p. 251.

86   TEEU EMC minutes, 20, 27 Mar., 6 May 1997; *Drogheda Independent*, 5-26 Dec. 1997; ibid., 6, 10 Dec. 2002, 25 Jan. 2003.

87   TEEU EMC minutes, 6 Apr., 3 May 2004.

88   *Irish Independent*, 5 May, 26 June, 10 July 2004, 12 Jan-25 Feb., 2, 16, 27 June 2005; TEEU EMC minutes, 24 Mar. 2005.

89   *Irish Independent*, 20, 21 May 1993, 1-15 Nov. 2007.

90   These figures have been gathered from CSO reports found at https://www.cso.ie/en/statistics/ (accessed 5 Apr. 2022); *Irish Times*, 5, 6 Jan. 2010, 30 Sept., 2 Oct. 2019; and *Financial Times*, 29 Aug. 2013.

91 TEEU EMC minutes, 18 Sept., 1 Oct. 2008; *Irish Times*, 18 Sept., 10 Oct., 18 Nov. 2008, 26 Nov., 24 Dec. 2009.

92 TEEU EMC minutes, 25 Mar., 16 Sept. 2010, 20 Jan. 2011; *Irish Times*, 3 July, 29 Sept. 2010, 21 Nov. 2012. The CIF had originally sought a 20 per cent cut.

93 CSO, *Statistical Abstract* (Dublin: Stationary Office, 1999), p. 111.

94 *Irish Independent*, 10 July 2009. The introduction of the analogue system into the electrical contracting trade resulted from NEETU and the ETU serving pay claims upon the expiry of the twenty-fifth pay round on 1 January 1987. It was subsequently agreed that the national collective agreement would be submitted to the Labour Court for registration. Any outstanding claims would also be referred to the Labour Court to be argued on their merits.

95 TEEU EMC minutes, 19 June 2008-18 June 2009; *Irish Times*, 28 June 2008.

96 *Irish Times*, 24 Nov. 2008.

97 *Irish Independent*, 4, 13 Mar., 20 June 2009.

98 Ibid., 7 July 2009; *Irish Examiner*, 6 July 2009.

99 Unite was formed 1 May 2007 by the merger of Amicus and the ATGWU.

100 *Irish Independent*, 10 July 2009.

101 Ibid., 6-13, 23-25 July, 3, 6, 7 Aug. 2009, 26 Aug. 2010; TEEU EMC minutes, 12, 16 July 2009.

102 TEEU EMC minutes, 17 Dec. 2009, 14 Jan. 2010.

103 CSO, 'quarterly reports on industrial disputes in Ireland', https://www.cso.ie/en/statistics/labourmarket/archive/ (accessed 15 Mar. 2022).

104 General secretary's address, TEEU BDC 2010, Biennial Delegate Conferences (BDC) file; TEEU NEC minutes, 26 May 2012; interview with Frank Keoghan, 16 Sept. 2020.

105 TEEU EMC minutes, 21 Jan., 26 Feb., 25 Mar., 15 Apr., 16 Sept., 16 Dec. 2010, 20 Jan., 21 Apr. 2011.

106 Ibid., 16 June 2011.

107 General secretary's industrial report to the NEC, Apr. 2016, BDC file.

108 TEEU EMC minutes, 17 Feb. 2011, 17 Feb., 8 Apr., 21 Aug., 22 Oct., 20 Nov. 2014, 20 Aug., 15 Oct. 2015.

109 TEEU annual returns, 2011-2016, T603, RFS records, CRO.

110 Interview with Keoghan.

111 TEEU EMC minutes, 8 Apr. 2014; TEEU NEC minutes, 25 Apr. 2015.

112 TEEU NEC minutes, 25 May 2010, 26 May 2012; general secretary's reports to the NEC, Apr. 2016, May 2017, BDC file.

113 TEEU EMC minutes, 15 Apr. 2010, 7 Mar., 12 June 2013; *Irish Times*, 15 Apr., 28 May 2010, 26 Mar., 12 Apr. 2013, 28 July 2015, 13 Nov. 2016. The TEEU also rejected the Croke Park II (2012) agreement, as did most unions. The rejection of Croke Park II paved the way for the Haddington Road agreement.

114 *Irish Examiner*, 26 Aug. 2009; ibid., 22, 24 Feb., 1 Mar. 2010; *Irish Times*, 4 Mar. 2010; TEEU NEC minutes, 25 May 2010; general secretary's address to TEEU BDC 2010, BDC file.

115 *Irish Examiner*, 20 Mar. 2010; *Irish Times*, 10 June, 2010; general secretary's address, TEEU BDC 2010. BDC file; TEEU EMC minutes, 25 Mar. 15 Apr. 2010.

116 *Irish Times*, 19 July 2010.

117 *Irish Independent*, 6 Mar., 13 Apr., 6, 12, 30 June 2012; *Irish Examiner*, 19 Feb. 2013; TEEU EMC minutes, 7 Mar. 2013.

118 TEEU EMC minutes, 15 Sept. 2011, 18 July, 22 Aug., 11 Dec. 2013; *Irish Independent*, 9 Sept. 2011, 23 Nov., 9 Dec. 2013; *Irish Examiner*, 19 Nov. 2013; *Irish Times*, 22 Nov. 2013. The unions had also threatened to down tools during the 2004 dispute at the ESB over how the pension deficit should be cleared. See *Irish Independent*, 4 Oct. 2004.

119 TEEU EMC minutes, 15 July 2010, 24 Mar., 21 Apr., 16 June, 3 Nov. 2011, 19 Jan., 23 Feb. 2012.

120 The official name of the judgement is 'Benedict McGowan and Others v Labour Court and Others.

121 Laura Graham, 'Supreme Court Declares Registered Employment Agreements Unconstitutional – How Does This Impact Your Business?', 19 Nov. 2016, https://reddycharlton.ie/insights/supreme-court-declares-registered-employment-agreements-unconstitutional-how-does-this-impact-your-business/#:~:text=The%20Supreme%20Court%20recently%20declared,the%20Supreme%20Court%20Case%E2%80%9D (accessed 30 Jan. 2022).

122 *Irish Independent*, 10 May 2013

123 General secretary's address, TEEU BDC 2014, BDC file.

124 *Irish Examiner*, 10 May 2013.

125 General secretary's address, TEEU BDC 2014, BDC file; TEEU EMC minutes, 12 June 2013. The other major employers' body in the mechanical contracting field was the Mechanical & Electrical Contractors Association (MECA).

126 TEEU EMC minutes, 16 Jan., 6, 17 Feb. 2014.; *Irish Independent*, 19 Jan., 7-14 Feb. 2014.

127 Various emails contained in 'File On Construction Claims (2014)'.

128 Brian Nolan to Tamara Harte, 15 Sept. 2015, 'File on Electrical Contracting Claims (2014)'.

129 TEEU EMC minutes, 25 June, 20 Aug., 15 Oct., 19 Nov. 2015.

130 Ibid., 12 June 2013, 25 June, 20 Aug., 17 Dec. 2015, 21 Jan., 16 Feb., 21 Apr., 19 May 2016; Nolan to Harte, 15 Sept. 2015; 'General secretary's industrial report to the NEC', Apr. 2016, BDC file.

131 TEEU EMC minutes, 17 Oct. 2013, 15 Jan., 20 Aug. 2015; TEEU NEC minutes, 25 May 2010, 26 May 2012; *Irish Times*, 25 Feb., 15 Nov. 2004; *Irish Independent*, !9 Apr. 2004. The outcome in 2004 was a compromise: the government agreed to pay the Student Service Charge and the TEEU agreed to accept introduction of an exam fee for apprentices. I am grateful to Eamon Devoy for this information.

132 TEEU EMC minutes, 16 Jan. 2014, 16 July, 15 Oct., 19 Nov. 2015; General secretary's address, TEEU BDC 2014, BDC file; *Irish Times*, 4 Nov. 2013, 10 Jan. 2014, 26 Apr. 2015; *Irish Independent*, 11 Jan. 2014.

133 General secretary's address, TEEU BDC 2010, BDC file.

134 TEEU EMC minutes, 21 Oct. 2010.

135 Ibid., 16 June 2011.

136 TEEU EMC minutes, 21 Feb., 12 June 2013; general secretary's address to TEEU BDC 2014, BDC file.

137 Ibid., 21 Aug., 18 Dec. 2014.

138 *Irish Times*, 27 Jan. 2015.

139 TEEU EMC minutes, 25 Apr., 20 Aug. 2015, 19 May 2016.

140 General secretary's address, TEEU BDC 2014; ibid., 17 July 2014.

141 TEEU EMC minutes, 19 Jan., 18 Oct., 19 Nov. 2012.

142 Ibid., 12 Dec. 2012.

143 Ibid., 28 May, 12 June 2013.

144 Ibid., 17 Oct. 2013.

145 Ibid. 11 Dec. 2013.

146 General secretary's address, TEEU BDC 2014, BDC file; ibid., 7 July 2016.

147 Ibid., 18 Oct. 2012, 7 Nov. 2013, 15 Oct., 19 Nov., 17 Dec. 2015, 21 Apr., 19 May, 7 July, 15 Sept., 1 Nov. 2016. Kavanagh had been elected TEEU general secretary in December 2015, became 'general secretary designate' in April 2016 and formally took over from Devoy that July.

12

Conclusion

The Connect Trade Union is the direct successor to the Irish Engineering, Shipbuilding and Foundry Trades Union, launched in May 1920 by a group of craftsmen imbued with an extraordinary sense of dedication to the cause of Irish independence in every sphere. Craft consciousness and conflict, and the interplay between the two, were constant themes throughout the history of Connect's predecessors; so too were conflicts with British unions, a manifestation of the Anglo-Irish conflict. The IESFTU was the result of the turbulence Ireland endured between 1907 and 1921. Big Jim Larkin helped to lay the groundwork for the establishment of the IESFTU. His arrival in Ireland in 1907 and his foundation of the ITGWU two years later were decisive breaks with the established (British) mode of trade unionism in Ireland. The creation of an independent, national union in Ireland not beholden to an executive council in London was a partial decolonisation of Irish labour. The ITGWU led the way for Irish workers to pursue a brand of trade unionism applicable to Irish political and material conditions. It was an inspiration to the men who launched the IESFTU, whose complaints that British craft unions had little sympathy with or understanding of Irish needs had much legitimacy by 1920.

Without the First World War, Ireland's first national engineering craft union would not have been established when it was, if at all. The carnage of the war, and the economic hardship it produced, thoroughly discredited Europe's ruling elites. In Ireland, the necessities of war unintentionally took the unions off life-support and back into the pulse of local life. Mandatory, binding arbitration forced the recognition of unions on the factory floor, while employers no longer had the luxury of surplus labour. The groundswell of anti-establishment sentiment among the working class was also directed at the British unions after the Labour Party entered government in December 1916, obliging it to support draconian policies widely loathed since the execution of the leaders of the Easter Rising. The war thus destabilised conservative politics, creating the space for radical ideologies like republicanism, socialism and syndicalism to flourish and become mainstream. Labour's embrace of syndicalism – a reprise of Larkinite militancy – also helped it to rise from the ashes of the 1913 lockout. Syndicalism gave workers the tools to combat the mass inflation that tormented the economy between 1914 and 1920. As the most popular revolutionary ideology until 1917, radicals widely discussed syndicalism in underground, revolutionary circles. No syndicalist idea was as mesmerising as the One Big Union, the vehicle for working-class power. Syndicalism provided the rationale for radical craftsmen within the IRB to dispense with insular 'craft consciousness' and plan the One Big Engineering Union. A product of revolution at home and abroad, syndicalism was a flexible ideology that moulded itself to the Irish context and easily integrated into a non-revolutionary labour movement. It achieved extraordinary, lasting gains for the working class that could not have happened without a redistribution of power and wealth. Its Irish iteration was Ireland's contribution to the social tumult Europe endured in 1919 and 1920. Irish syndicalism's ability to inspire discontent among workers and 'to generate and sustain action with a method of agitation' made Irish syndicalism 'a minor but brilliant illustration of syndicalist capacity.'[1]

The First World War vastly expanded the British engineering industry, deepening its differences with its Irish counterpart and putting craftsmen in both countries on different trajectories. This diluted the shared experiences of British and Irish engineering workers and intensified secessionist desire among the latter. Despite their underdevelopment, the Irish engineering and electrical trades had enough economic and strategic importance by 1918 to justify IRB plotters to choose them as the starting point in their quest to smash British unions in Ireland. From there, the IRB Labour Board intended to infiltrate other unions, like those in the building trade. The One Big Engineering Union would never have been established without the Labour Board, whose importance to the republican struggle even Collins recognised. The Board spearheaded the establishment of the IESFTU against extraordinary odds. This is its ultimate legacy, a testament to the ability of those who worked fulltime for it.

From its very beginning, the IESFTU gave vital assistance to the IRA during the War of Independence. Apart from housing the Dublin Brigade and the ASU, union members used their craft to construct and wire explosives for the struggle. The union's close links to the republican movement were vital to its survival from the powerful amalgamateds, who hoped to strangle it in the cradle. But like all Irish unions during this period, the IESFTU was unable to reconcile the inherent tensions between nationalism and class politics. From the Anglo-Irish truce, the alliance between the labour and republican movements disintegrated under the weight of their conflicting social outlook and class compositions. The IESFTU's feelings towards the republican movement, both pro- and anti-Treaty, began to mirror that of other unions: aloofness and hostility. What did labour get from investing so much in the revolution? Everything it asked for: self-determination, a Department of Labour, neutrality towards the wages' movement, a safe space for direct action, toleration of red flag radicalism and an extraordinary prestige for its officials. Whether it should have asked for more is another matter.[2] The paradox of the Irish revolution was that the seeds of reaction were sown into its modus operandi. Sinn Féin undermined British rule in Ireland not by smashing its institutions but by creating a shadow state with institutions modelled on those they sought to dislodge, which helped to ensure that the Irish revolution would be a conservative one. Republicanism could accommodate, even nurture, radical aims, but as a pan-class, nationalist movement led by the petit-bourgeoisie, Sinn Féin's goal was fundamentally conservative. The party viewed social radicalism as secondary to separatist aims and class-based politics as a threat that endangered national unity.[3]

The foundation of the IESFTU was both a throwback to the exclusivist craft unionism of the past and a reflection of contemporary syndicalism. Although firmly rooted in the nineteenth-century concept of craft, the new union anticipated developments in the late twentieth century by bringing together different trades across industrial lines for the common cause of protection. The War of Independence had generated a feeling of national unity that kept them together. But the experiment proved premature and was undone by the reassertion of craft exclusiveness among engineering workers, especially electricians, from the Truce. It took the rest of the century to reunite them, and some never accepted reunification. The splits reflect the perils of organising and maintaining disparate craftsmen, even within the same industry, in one union in the early twentieth century. They also demonstrate the strong internal divisions within the labour movement and how deeply stratified Irish society was along class lines. A craftsman was defined by his work, on which he based his worth as a human being. He had spent seven years of his life imbibing the value system imparted by the apprenticeship, which instilled craft, rather than class, consciousness into him. The attachment to work was so intense that any threat to it, real or perceived, from a different type of craftsman – or even from the same type of craftsman in a different industry – was enough to trigger deeply rooted feelings of insecurity. As a minority within a minority, electricians were especially infused with a craft consciousness that often amounted to little more than class snobbery. Upholding harmonious relations between the crafts, especially against electrician-led incursions, was a constant struggle for the union for most of its history. It is significant that neither the Inchicore men in 1921 nor the electricians in 1923 re-joined their old unions. The revolution had delegitimised all manifestations of the British presence in Ireland and syndicalism had broken Irish labour's dependency on its British counterpart, its most enduring legacy.

Labour endured a terrible decade under Cumman na nGaedheal. Kevin O'Higgins' 1923 quip that his colleagues were 'probably the most conservative-minded revolutionaries that ever put through a successful revolution' is both revealing and accurate. Said in the context of justifying draconian measures against the anti-Treatyites, it was as much a proud boast as a plea for understanding.[4] After defeating all threats to their hegemony between 1921 and 1924, the Treatyites cemented the 'conservative consensus' that dominated post-revolutionary Ireland. The interests of employers, not workers, would dictate government policy and the labour-republican alliance was replaced by an unofficial marriage between the Irish state and a reactionary, authoritarian Catholic Church. Herein lays the tragedy of the Irish revolution: those who invested so much in it, the working class, received little in return whereas those who invested little, the employers and the Church, received much.

Internal monetary mismanagement meant that the IEIU did not benefit from labour's resurgence in the 1930s as other unions did, as it limped into the decade embroiled in its second financial crisis in ten years. This crisis was even more intense and, coupled with the simultaneous growth of the IEFU, threatened the IEIU with extinction. The Foundry Union ripened into a national force to be reckoned with in the 1930s – a genuine alternative to the IEIU that took many of its most able officials. By the decade's end, the Foundry Union was the larger of the two. Nevertheless, the IEIU could claim real credit for overcoming its internal crisis and winning the battle for survival. Fianna Fáil's programme of industrialisation, which benefitted most unions, inadvertently saved the IEIU from implosion. The ensuing growth in industrial employment helped labour to claw back members, especially in rural areas and major towns. Industrialisation increased the unions' economic importance and enhanced their bargaining power, incentivising workers to join them. The IEIU recovered from its losses to the Foundry Union with a renewed recruitment drive, especially in the new industries like sugar manufacture, turf production and aviation, thereby broadening its geographic spread.

The Emergency years were characterised by another inflationary spiral and a profound alteration in labour's relationship to the state. Joint opposition to the Wages Standstill order and the 1941 Trade Union Act facilitated a rapprochement between the IEIU and the Foundry Union, as did their participation in the CIU. By then, age-old tensions between British and Irish unions had re-emerged as labour's primary fissure, further helping to improve relations between the IEIU and IEFU. Though talks between them broke down quickly, they were essential precursors to the successful talks of the early 1960s from which NEETU materialised. Poor management and infighting hampered the IEIU/IEIETU during the 1940s and 1950s, allowing the IEFU/NEU to maintain its numerical superiority. Nevertheless, the IEIETU held its own against its larger rivals on the wages front. The union was partially aided by the emergence of the pay rounds, the first examples of national, centralised wage bargaining, which culminated in social partnership. The system of rounds and the Labour Court both encouraged an acceptance of unions from 1946, further incentivising workers to join. The result was an impressive growth in the levels of unionisation. But the 1950s was a bleak decade for workers as the Irish economy struggled despite an unprecedented global boom, putting the employers firmly on top once again. The decade was kinder to the ETU, whose membership and importance grew exponentially consequent of the electrification of rural Ireland from 1946, one of the Irish state's great achievements. Rural electrification made the ETU a larger union than the IEIETU from 1948. Surpassed by both of its breakaway rivals and hamstrung by internal divisions and incompetence, the IEIETU suffered the same crisis of self-confidence as the country endured in the 1950s. The intense conservatism and anti-communism of Irish society that decade had a marked effect on all three unions, especially the ETU.

Industrialisation in the 1960s once again enhanced labour's bargaining position. The growth of modern industry with its need of constant maintenance had made craft unions especially important to the economy, which provided another opportunity for the IEIETU to expand. By then, relations between the IEIETU and the NEU had improved to such an extent that amalgamation was possible. Congress had recognised that labour was bedevilled by union multiplicity and supported fusion as empowering mechanical craftsmen against the growth of multinational employers. Even the employers and Fianna Fáil wanted to see fewer unions, the multiplicity of which they believed to be a major cause of disruptive militancy. But this meant little to many IEIETU electricians, who remained trapped in the sectionalist mindset of the nineteenth century, a reflection of the enduring power of craft consciousness. Industrialisation and modernisation vastly expanded and diversified the number of electrical workers in the country. In response, the ETU broadened its base and reaped the rewards with another surge in growth, filling it with a newfound confidence. Its 1961 strike was a turning point in its history: despite ICTU's disapproval, it had stood on its own two feet and won an outstanding victory.

The foundation of NEETU in 1966 was widely supported both inside and outside the labour movement. Unfortunately for labour, successive Irish governments had failed to provide legislation or a financial incentive for unions to fuse, which the legal wrangling to officially establish NEETU between 1967 and 1975 vividly illuminated. The confusion was a major reason for the passage of the remarkably successful Trade Union Act 1975, which remains the chief legislation governing union mergers. Despite its lack of legal recognition,

NEETU was a formidable force in Irish trade unionism from the start, as evidenced by its prominence in the 1969 maintenance strike, one of the most significant labour disputes in the history of the state. The strike crystallised how, despite modernity and industrialisation, the divide between 'trade and spade' remained salient within the Irish working class. It also reflected the new militancy of the craft unions, conscious of how recent industrialisation had increased the demand for maintenance work, thereby enhancing their bargaining position. While the maintenance strike was a short-term victory, its long-term results were more mixed – the deepening of centralised bargaining and two-tier picketing were direct outcomes of it. The outbreak of the Troubles in 1969 provided a fault line within labour between those who wanted to pursue 'pure' trade unionism and those who wanted the movement to take an overtly political line on the national question. With its origins deep in the republican movement, NEETU was more affected than most by this renewed debate over what labour's relationship to 'nationalism' should be.

NEETU's legal birth in 1976 should have signalled the end to its recurring appearances in the High Court. But the union was led by officials who, despite their obvious abilities, were a dysfunctional collective unit. Foremost among them was Kevin McConnell, one of the most intelligent and able trade unionists of his generation, whose clashes with his colleagues nearly destroyed the union he claimed to be defending. Though his early contentions that expenses were being abused may have had some justification, his subsequent behaviour is harder to defend. From 1976 to 1991, the legal sagas affected all aspects of the union's life. Officials had to invest so much time, energy and resources into them that their goal of building Ireland's largest engineering union degenerated into another fight for survival. The quality of service invariably decayed under the crushing weight of legal bills, leading to an exodus of members. Those who stayed loyal did so at a time of recession, when their union was less able to defend them from wage cuts and unemployment. McConnell's abilities were tempered by deep flaws that precipitated his downfall. After 1986, he became detached from the reality of his obligations as financial general secretary. His refusal to hand over NEETU's registers to facilitate its merger with the ETU, despite repeated requests to do so, was an easy case for the union to win. The ETU threw a lifejacket to the drowning NEETU by agreeing to enter amalgamation talks with it. Frank O'Reilly deserves more credit than anyone else for the merger. It was he who fronted efforts to initiate talks from the ETU side and his adroit handling of NEETU's internal problems overcame a major hurdle to a successful outcome. Despite its troubles, NEETU was not a failure. Its officials were skilled negotiators who maintained levels of pay for members that compared well to what other unions had secured. However, it did not fulfil its potential and was badly administered with poorly written rules, for which its legal advisors are partially to blame. The war between McConnell and his colleagues on the NEETU executive was the most prolonged episode of union infighting in Irish labour history and the most consequential since the 1924 split in the ITGWU.

The TEEU was, by any standard or definition, an effective trade union. Its creation was the most successful union merger until that point and remains one of the most successful of its kind. The TEEU was very professionally managed from the beginning, as evidenced by its excellent finances and the impressive levels of growth it sustained over a prolonged period. It benefitted massively from the introduction of the ETU's proficient officials and the removal of the personal conflicts that had nearly obliterated NEETU, whose former officials found a new lease of life and thrived in the TEEU. The timing could not have been better to launch an engineering and electrical craft union in Ireland. With the country's greatest ever economic boom just around the corner, the new union would soon obtain an importance to the economy that its predecessors would have envied. A flood of foreign direct investment and a construction boom (later a bubble) put the TEEU in an ideal situation to extract concessions for its members, which it did with considerable success. It consolidated its position as the country's premier craft union. In 2007, the Celtic Tiger roared for the last time. The TEEU's strength in the electrical contracting and construction sectors, had made it especially vulnerable to the ensuing collapse. Its disclosure of exploitation in the mid-2000s and the 2009 electricians' strike were outstanding displays of the continuing relevance of unions to workers, despite three decades of anti-union media narratives and neoliberal policies from successive governments.

What did Connect's forerunners achieve? Everyone born on or after 9 May 1920 within the twenty-six counties has been affected by them in some way, insofar as anyone has gained from the existence of an independent Irish state. The public has politically benefitted from the IESFTU's role in achieving Irish independence, while every craftsman who was a member of the IESFTU and its descendants has received additional material benefits. Redistributing wealth, improving workers' rights and living standards, combatting neoliberalism and campaigning for high quality, well-funded public services have benefitted all of society. Like all unions, the overwhelming majority of Connect's work is not documented because it takes places every day in the workplace. And this work is no less important. Thousands of claims – about wages, hours, conditions, treatment by employers, etc. – are resolved without recourse to industrial action or referral to a third party because union membership makes an individual part of a collective, giving workers some control over their own working and social lives.[5] It is fitting that, one hundred years after its establishment, Connect is closer to achieving the goal of its founders – being the One Big Union for Irish craft and Engineering workers – than any at any point in its history thus ensuring it remains "THE UNION FOR CRAFT AND SKILLED TECHNICAL, ENGINEERING, ELECTRICAL AND CONSTRUCTION WORKERS IN IRELAND".

Chapter Notes and References

1   O'Connor, *Syndicalism in Ireland*, p. 191.
2   Ibid., p. 94.
3   Ibid., p. 91.
4   Ferriter, *Transformation*, p. 296.
5   Francis Devine concluded similarly about SIPTU. See Devine, *Organising History*, pp. 881-882.

Bibliography

Primary sources

Connect archives
ETU Dublin No. 1 branch minutes, 1937-45
ETU REC minutes, 1937-46, 1962-92
ETU Rulebook (1941)
IEIU Rulebook (1922)
IGREU Rulebook (1922)
ETU NEC minutes, 1944-91
Biennial Delegate Conferences (BDC) file
File On Construction Claims (2014)'
File on Electrical Contracting Claims (2014)'
File: 'Legal'
File: 'NEC 1970'
File: 'TEEU-AEEU'
IESFTU REC minutes, 1920
Irish Engineering, Electrical, Shipbuilding and Foundry Trade Union REC minutes, 1921
IEIU Dublin membership minutes, 1931-35
IEIU Heating Engineers' Section minutes, 1933-34
IEIU/IEIETU REC minutes, 1921-23, 1926-38
IEIU/IEIETU NEC minutes, 1921-24, 1930, 1941-70
IESFTU, provisional executive and REC minutes, 1920
NEETU NEC minutes, 1986-92
NEETU REC 'decisions', 1982-87
NEETU REC minutes, 1981-83, 1987-92
TEEU EMC minutes, 1992-2010
TEEU NEC minutes, 1992-2010

Cork City and County Archives
IEIETU/NEETU/TEEU Cork branch minutes, 1955-
Liam de Róiste diaries
Terence MacSwiney Papers

Córas Iompair Éireann Archives, Heuston Station
GSWR board minutes

ESB Archives
Annual reports, 1929-2006

Guinness Archive
Labour and Industrial Relations Department records
Skilled Group of Unions papers

Interviews

Eamon Devoy, 12 February 2020

John McLoughlin, 17 February 2020

Donnchadha MacRaghnaill, 27 February 2020

Peter Lanigan, 27 February 2020

Owen Wills, 2 March 2020

Patrick Guilfoyle, 5 March 2020

Jimmy Nolan, 23 March 2020

Frank Keoghan, 16 Sept. 2020

Charlie Prizeman, 20 September 2020

Irish Labour History Museum

Annual reports of the CIU, 1946-59

Annual report of ICTU, 1959-92

Annual report of the ITUC, 1926-49

IEFU AGM minutes, 1941-55

IEFU Dublin No. 1 branch minutes, 1944

IEFU, *Fourth Half-Yearly Report, July to Dec. 1938*

IEFU/NEU REC minutes, 1955-60

IEFU NEC minutes, 1941

Minutes of the meetings of IEFU branch officers and shop stewards, 1942

NEETU NEC minutes, 1976-86

NEETU REC minutes, 1976-80

NEU NEC minutes, 1962-63

Irish Railway Record Society

GNR records

GSWR records

GSR records

Military Archives

Bureau of Military History Collection

Military Service Pension Collection

Modern Records Centre, University of Warwick

AEU, *Annual report for 1920*

National Archives of Ireland

1901 & 1911 Censuses

Chief Secretary's Office Registered Papers

Dáil Éireann Cabinet Minutes

Dáil Éireann Government Minutes

Department of An Taoiseach records.

Department of Industry and Commerce records.

Department of Labour records

Limerick Stationary Engine Drivers' and Firemen's Society minutes, TU/98/40/1.

ICTU collection

'Memorandum of discussion at conference of representatives of joint committee re. scheme for the formation of one Irish union compromising 'all branches of engineering trades in Ireland', DE 2/116, Dáil Éireann collection.

Memo on NEETU, 3 Feb. 1969, 2007/28/622, Attorney General's Office records.

Registry of Friendly Societies' records

Siemens collection

National Library of Ireland

Department of Industry and Commerce, *Census of Industrial Production* (Dublin: Stationary Office, 1937).

Labour Gazette, 1914-22

ITUC annual reports, 1913-25

ITUC, *Munitions of war fund: receipts and disbursements* (Dublin: Word Printing Works, 1921)

Statistical Abstract

Thomas Johnson Papers

William O'Brien Papers

Newspapers

Belfast Newsletter

Cork Examiner/Examiner/Irish Examiner

Drogheda Independent

Evening Herald

Freeman's Journal

Irish Independent

Irish Press

Irish Times

Limerick Leader

Meath Chronicle

Munster Express

Northern Whig

Voice of Labour

Watchword of Labour

Workers' Republic

Official Reports

Commission on Technical Education, *Report* (Dublin: Stationary Office, 1927).

Commission on Vocational Organisation, *Report* (Dublin: Stationary Office, 1943).

Dáil Éireann debates

Department of Labour, *Final report of the Committee on Industrial Relations in the Electricity Supply Board* (Dublin: Stationary Office, 1969).

Intercourse between Bolshevism and Sinn Féin, 1921.

Seanad Éireann debates

Reports on strikes and lock-outs in the United Kingdom, 1888-1913, 1889-1916.

Royal Commission on Labour, Minutes of Evidence, Appendices (Group A) Volume III. Mining, Iron, Engineering and Hardware, 1893.

Report on Standard Time-Rates of Wages in United Kingdom, 1900, 1900

Report on conciliation and arbitration, being particulars of proceedings under the Industrial Courts Act, 1919 [including the Wages (Temporary Regulation) Acts, as amended], the Conciliation Act, 1896, and the Restoration of Pre-War Practices Act, 1919, 1921.

Standard time rates of wages in the United Kingdom at 1st October, 1913, 1914.

Standard time rates of wages and hours of labour in the United Kingdom at 31st December, 1920, 1921

UCD Archives

Patrick McGilligan Papers

Ricard Mulcahy Papers

United Stationary Engine Drivers' collection.

UCC Archives

Murphy's brewery collection

Indenture of Henry Marsh to the Painting Trade, June 1916, U233, UCC Manuscripts Collection

Secondary Sources

Contemporary Books and Pamphlets

Bates, Richard Dawson, *Red Terror and Green: The Sinn Féin Bolshevist Movement* (London: Murray, 1920).

Bowley, A.L., *Prices and Wages in United Kingdom, 1914-1920* (Oxford: Oxford University Press, 1921).

Bowley, A.L., *Wages and Income in the United Kingdom since 1860* (Cambridge: Cambridge University Press 1937).

Coakley, D.J., *Cork: Its Trade and Commerce* (Cork: Incorporated Chamber of Commerce and Shipping Booklet, 1917).

Cassells, Peter & Flood, Finbarr, *Dispute between the TEEU and employers in the electrical contracting industry*, (Dublin: Department of Enterprise, Trade and Employment, 2009).

Conroy, J.C., *A History of Railways in Ireland* (New York: Longmans, Green and Co. Ltd, 1928).

Harris, Noel, *Challenge to Irish Trade Unionism: National Wage Agreements* (Dublin: Association of Scientific Technical and Managerial Staffs, 1973).

Jeffreys, James B., *The Story of the Engineers, 1800-1945* (London: Lawrence & Wishart Ltd., 1945).

MacSweeney, A.M., *Poverty in Cork* (Cork: Purcell & Co., 1917)

Murphy, Con, *Dispute between FUE and maintenance craft unions: report of inquiry* (Dublin: Stationary Office, 1969).

O'Brien, James F., *A Study of National Wage Agreements in Ireland* (Dublin: ESRI, 1981).

O'Brien, William, *Forth the Banners Go: Reminisces of William O'Brien* (Dublin: Three Candles Ltd, 1969).

Riordan, E.J., *Modern Irish Trade and Industry* (London: Methuen and Co. Ltd, 1920).

Smellie, John, *Shipbuilding and Repairing in Dublin: A Record of Work Carried Out by the Dublin Dockyard Co., 1901-1923* (Glasgow: McCorquodale & Co., 1935),

Wolfe, Humbert, *Labour Supply and Regulation* (Oxford: Clarendon Press, 1923).

Books

Allen, Kieran, *Fianna Fáil and Irish Labour, 1926 to the Present* (London: Pluto Press, 1997).

Augusteijn, Joost, *From Public Defiance to Guerrilla Warfare: The Experience of Ordinary Volunteers in the Irish War of Independence, 1916-1921* (Dublin: Irish Academic Press, 1996).

Bew, Paul, Hazelkorn, Ellen, Patterson, Henry, *The Dynamics of Irish Politics* (London: Lawrence & Wishart, 1989).

Bielenberg, Andy & Ryan, Raymond, *An Economic History of Ireland since Independence* (Oxford: Routledge, 2013).

Bielenberg, Andrew, *Cork's industrial Revolution, 1780-1880: Development and Decline?* (Cork: Cork University Press, 1991).

Bielenberg, Andrew, *Ireland and the Industrial Revolution: The Impact of the Industrial Revolution on Irish Industry* (London: Routledge, 2009).

Borgonovo, John, *The Dynamics of War and Revolution: Cork City, 1916-1918* (Cork: Cork University Press, 2013).

Boyd, Andrew, *The Rise of the Irish Trade Unions* (Dublin: Anvil Books, 1972).

Boyle, John W., *The Irish Labour Movement in the Nineteenth Century* (Washington D.C.: The Catholic University of America Press, 1988).

Cahill, Liam, *Forgotten Revolution: Limerick Soviet 1919* (Dublin: O'Brien Press, 1990).

Carey, Tim, *Hanged for Ireland: 'the Forgotten Ten': Executed 1920-21: a Documentary History* (Dublin: Blackwater Press, 2001)

Clarkson, Jesse Dunsmore, *Labour and nationalism in Ireland* (New York: AMS Press, 1925).

Cody, Seamus, O'Dowd, John & Rigney, Peter, *The parliament of labour: 100 years of the Dublin Council of Trade Unions* (Dublin: Dublin Council of Trade Unions, 1986).

Coe, W.E., *The Engineering Industry of the North of Ireland* (Newton Abbot: David & Charles, 1969).

Cox, Ronald C. & Gould, Michael H., *Civil Engineering Heritage: Ireland* (London: Thomas Telford, 1998).

Cronin, Maura, *Country, Class or Craft? The Politicisation of the Skilled Artisan in Nineteenth Century Cork* (Cork: Cork University Press, 1994).

Cullen, Louis M., *An Economic History of Ireland since 1660* (London: B.T. Batsford Ltd).

Daly, Mary E., *Industrial Development and Irish National Identity, 1922-1939* (Dublin: Gill & Macmillan, 1992).

Daly, Mary E., *Sixties Ireland: Reshaping the Economy, State and Society, 1957-1973* (Cambridge: Cambridge University Press, 2016).

Daly, Seán, *Cork, a city in crisis: a history of labour conflict and social misery, 1870-1872* (Cork: Tower Books, 1978).

D'Arcy A., Fergus & Hannigan, Ken (eds.), *Workers in Union: Documents and Commentaries on the History of Irish Labour* (Dublin: Stationary Office, 1988).

Darlington, Ralph, *Radical Unionism: The Rise and Fall of Revolutionary Syndicalism* (Chicago: Haymarket Book, 2008).

Devine, Francis, *Organising History: A Centenary of SIPTU, 1909-2009* (Dublin: Gill & Macmillan, 2009).

Drummond, Brian & Doyle, Dessie, *The Erne Hydroelectric Scheme* (Dublin: The Lilliput Press, 2013).

Enright, Michael, *Men of Iron: Wexford Foundry Disputes of 1890 & 1911* (Wexford: Wexford Council of Trade Unions, 1987).

Ferriter, Diarmaid, *Ambiguous Republic: Ireland in the 1970s* (London: Profile Books, 2012).

Ferriter, Diarmaid, *A Nation and Not a Rabble: The Irish Revolution*, 1913-1923 (London: Profile Books, 2015).

Ferriter, Diarmaid, *The Transformation of Ireland, 1900-2000* (London: Profile Books, 2004).

Fitzpatrick, David, *Politics and Irish Life, 1913-21: Provincial Experience of War and Revolution* (Dublin: Gill & Macmillan, 1977).

Foster, Gavin, *The Irish Civil War and Society: Politics, Class and Conflict* (New York: Palgrave Macmillan, 2015).

Fox, R.M., *The History of the Irish Citizen Army* (Dublin: J. Duffy & Co., 1944).

Garvin, Tom, *Nationalist Revolutionaries in Ireland, 1858-1928* (Oxford: Clarendon Press, 1987).

Garvin, Tom, *The Evolution of Irish Nationalist Politics* (Dublin: Gill & Macmillan, 1981).

Gaughan, J. Anthony, *Thomas Johnson, 1872-1963: first leader of the Labour Party in Dáil Éireann* (Dublin: Kingdom Books, 1980).

Girvan, Brian, *The Emergency: Neutral Ireland, 1939-45* (London: Macmillan, 2006).

Geary, Dick, *European Labour Politics: From 1900 to the Depression* (London: Macmillan, 1991).

Hanley, Brian, *The Impact of the Troubles on the Republic of Ireland, 1968-79: Boiling Volcano?* (Manchester: Manchester University Press, 2018).

Hanley, Brian & Millar, Scott, *The Lost Revolution: The Story of the Official IRA and the Workers' Party* (Dublin: Penguin Ireland, 2009).

Hart, Peter, *The I.R.A. and its Enemies: Violence and Community in Cork, 1916-1923* (Oxford: Clarendon Press, 1998).

Hart, Peter, *The I.R.A. at War, 1916-1923* (Oxford: Oxford University Press, 2003).

Hassan, Gerald, *Thunder & Clatter: The History of Shipbuilding in Derry* (Derry: Guildhall Press, 1997).

Hastings, Tim, Sheehan, Brian & Yeates, Padraig, *Saving the Future: how social partnership shaped Ireland's economic success* (Dublin: Blackhall Publishing, 2007).

Hinton, James, *The First Shop Stewards' Movement* (London: George Allen & Unwin, 1973).

Hobsbawm, Eric, *Labouring Men: Studies in the History of Labour* (London: Weidenfeld & Nicolson, 1964).

Holton, Bob, *British Syndicalism, 1900-14: Myths and Realities* (London: Pluto Press, 1976).

Hopkinson, Michael, *Green Against Green: The Irish Civil War* (Dublin: Gill & Macmillan, 1988).

Hume, John R., and Moss, Michael S., *Shipbuilders to the World: 125 Years of Harland and Wolff, Belfast, 1861-1986* (Belfast: Blackstaff Press, 1986).

Irish, Bill, *Shipbuilding in Waterford, 1820-1882: a historical, technical and pictorial study* (Bray: Wordwell, 2001).

Johnstone, Kevin, *In the Shadows of Giants: A Social History of the Belfast Shipyards* (Dublin: Gill & Macmillan, 2008).

Keogh, Dermot, *The Rise of the Irish Working Class: The Dublin Trade Union Movement and Labour Leadership, 1890-1914* (Belfast: Appletree Press, 1982).

Kissane, Bill, *The Politics of the Irish Civil War* (Oxford: Oxford University Press, 2005).

Kostick, Conor, *Revolution in Ireland: Popular Militancy, 1917-1923* (London: Pluto Press, 1996).

Laffan, Michael, *The Resurrection of Ireland: The Sinn Féin Party, 1916-1923* (Cambridge: Cambridge University Press, 1999).

Leddin, Jeffrey, *The 'Labour Hercules': The Irish Citizen Army and Irish Republicanism, 1913-23* (Dublin: Irish Academic Press, 2019).

Lee, Joseph, *Ireland, 1912-1985: politics and society* (Cambridge: Cambridge University Press, 1989).

Lloyd, John, *Light & Liberty: A History of the EETPU* (London: Weidenfeld and Nicolson, 1990)

Lyons, F.S.L., *Ireland Since the Famine* (London: Weidenfeld & Nicolson, 1971).

Manning, Maurice and McDowell, Moore *Electricity Supply: The History of the ESB* (Dublin: Gill and Macmillan, 1984).

Matthews, Ann, *The Irish Citizen Army* (Cork: Mercier Press, 2014).

McCamley, Bill, *Dublin tram workers, 1872-1945* (Dublin: Labour History Workshop, 2008).

McCamley, Bill, *The role of the rank and file in the 1935 Dublin tram and bus strike* (Dublin: Labour History Workshop, 1981).

McCarthy, Charles, *The decade of upheaval: Irish trade unions in the nineteen sixties* (Dublin: Institute of Public Administration, 1973).

McCarthy, Charles, *Trade Unions in Ireland, 1894-1960* (Dublin: Institute of Public Administration, 1977).

McCarthy, Michael, *High Tension: Life on the Shannon Scheme* (Dublin: Lilliput Press, 2004).

Meenan, James, *The Irish economy since 1922* (Liverpool: Liverpool University Press, 1970).

Milne, Ida, *Stacking the Coffins: Influenza, War and Revolution in Ireland, 1918-19* (Manchester: Manchester University Press, 2018).

Milotte, Mike, *Communism in Modern Ireland: The Pursuit of the Workers' Republic since 1916* (Dublin: Gill & Macmillan, 1984).

Mitchell, Arthur, *Labour in Irish politics, 1890-1930: the Irish labour movement in an age of revolution* (Dublin: Irish University Press, 1974).

Mitchell, Arthur, *Revolutionary Government in Ireland: Dáil Éireann* (Dublin: Gill & Macmillan, 1995).

Mitchell, B.R., *British Historical Statistics* (Cambridge: Cambridge University Press, 1988).

Mitchell, Brian, *The Making of Derry: An Economic History* (Derry: Genealogy Centre of Derry, 1992).

Morgan, Austen, *Labour and partition; the Belfast working class, 1905-23* (London: Pluto Press, 1991).

Morrissey, Thomas J., *William O'Brien 1881-1968: socialist, republican, Dáil deputy, editor, and trade union leader* (Dublin: Four Courts Press, 2007).

Nyhan, Miriam, *'Are You Still Below?': The Ford Marina Plant, Cork, 1917-84* (Cork: The Collins Press, 2007).

O'Connor, Emmet, *A Labour History of Ireland, 1824-1960* (Dublin: Gill & Macmillan, 1992).

O'Connor, Emmet, *A Labour History of Waterford* (Waterford: Waterford Trades Council, 1989).

O'Connor, Emmet, *Big Jim Larkin: Hero or Wrecker?* (Dublin: University College Dublin Press, 2015).

O'Connor, Emmet, *Derry Labour in the age of agitation, 1: New unionism and old, 1889-1906* (Dublin: Four Courts Press).

O'Connor, Emmet, *Derry Labour in the age of agitation, 1889-1923, 2: Larkinism and syndicalism, 1907-23* (Dublin: Four Courts Press, 2016).

O'Connor, Emmet, *James Larkin,* (Cork: Cork University Press, 2002).

O'Connor, Emmet, *Reds and the Green: Ireland, Russia and the Communist International* (Dublin: University College Dublin Press, 2004).

O'Connor, Emmet, *Syndicalism in Ireland, 1917-1923* (Cork: Cork University Press, 1988).

Ó Drisceoil, Donal, *Utter Disloyalist: Tadhg Barry and the Irish Revolution* (Cork: Mercier Press, 2021).

Ó Gráda, Cormac, *Ireland: a new economic history, 1780-1939* (Oxford: Oxford University Press, 1994).

Ó Gráda, Cormac, *A Rocky Road: The Irish Economy since the 1920s* (Manchester: Manchester University Press, 1997).

O'Halpin, Eunan, *Defending Ireland: The Irish State and its Enemies since 1922* (Oxford: Oxford University Press, 1999).

O'Mahony, Colman, *In the Shadows: Life in Cork, 1750-1930* (Cork: Tower Books, 1997).

O'Mahony, Colman, *The Maritime Gateway to Cork: A History of the Outports of Passage West and Monkstown, 1754-1942* (Cork: Tower Books, 1986).

Patterson, Henry, *Class conflict and sectarianism: The Protestant working class and the Belfast labour movement, 1868-1920* (Belfast: Blackstaff Press, 1980).

Patterson, Henry, *The Politics of Illusion: A Political History of the IRA* (London: Serif, 1997).

Prunty, Jacinta, *Dublin Slums, 1800-1925: a study in urban geography* (Newbridge: Irish Academic Press, 1998).

Puirséil, Niamh, *The Irish Labour Party, 1922-73* (Dublin: University College Dublin Press, 2007).

Redmond, Seán, *The Irish Municipal Employees' Trade Union, 1883-1983* (Dublin: IMETU, 1983).

Regan, John M., *The Irish Counter-Revolution, 1921-1936: Treatyite Politics and Settlement in Independent Ireland* (Dublin: Gill & Macmillan, 1999).

Roche, William K., *British unions in Ireland: aspects of growth and performance* (Dublin: University College Dublin Press, 1994).

Rubin, Gerry, *War, Law and Labour: The Munitions Acts, State Regulations and the Unions, 1915-1921* (Oxford: Oxford University Press, 1987).

Rumpf, E. and Hepburn, A.C., *Nationalism and Socialism in twentieth-century Ireland* (Liverpool: Liverpool University Press, 1977).

Share, Brendan, *In Time of Civil War: The Conflict on the Irish Railways, 1922-23* (Cork: Collins Press, 2006).

Shiel, Michael J., *The Quiet Revolution: The Electrification of Rural Ireland, 1946-76* (Dublin: O'Brien Press, 1984).

Smethurst, John B. & Carter, J.P.H. (eds.), *Historical Directory of Trade Unions: Vol. 6: Including Unions in Building and Construction, Agriculture, Fishing, Chemicals, Wood and Woodworking, Transport, Engineering and Metal* (Farnham: Ashgate Publishing Company, 2009).

Stearns, Peter N., *Revolutionary Syndicalism and French Labor* (New Jersey: Rutgers University Press, 1971).

Sweeney, Eamonn, *Down Deeper and Down: Ireland in the 70s & 80s* (Dublin: Gill & Macmillan, 2010).

Sweeney, Pat, *Liffey Ships and Shipbuilding* (Cork: Mercier Press, 2010).

Thorpe, Wayne, *The Workers Themselves: Syndicalism and International Labour, 1913-1923* (Dordrecht: Kluwer Academic Press, 1989).

Tobin, Fergal, *The best of decades: Ireland in the nineteen sixties* (Dublin: Gill & Macmillan, 1984).

Van der Linden, Marcel, *Transnational Labour History: Explorations* (Aldershot: Ashgate Publishing Ltd., 2003).

Van der Linden, Marcel & Thorpe, Wayne (eds.), *Revolutionary Syndicalism: An International Perspective* (Aldershot: Scolar Press, 1990).

Ward-Perkins, Sarah, *Select Guide to Trade Union Records: With Details of Unions Operating in Ireland to 1970* (Dublin: Irish Manuscripts Commission, 1996).

Webb, Sidney & Webb, Beatrice, *The History of Trade Unionism* (London: Longman, 1894)

Wright, Arnold, *Disturbed Dublin: The Story of the Great Strike of 1913-14* (London: Longman, 1914).

Yeates, Pádraig, *A City in Civil War: Dublin, 1921-4* (Dublin: Gill & Macmillan, 2015).

Yeates, Pádraig, *A City in Turmoil: Dublin, 1919-21* (Dublin: Gill & Macmillan, 2012).

Yeates, Pádraig, *A City in Wartime: Dublin, 1914-18* (Dublin: Gill & Macmillan, 2011).

Yeates, Pádraig, *Lockout: Dublin 1913* (Dublin: Gill & Macmillan, 2000).

Book Chapters

Bielenberg, Andy, 'The Industrial Elite in Ireland from the Industrial Revolution to the First World War', in Fintan Lane (ed.), *Politics, Society and the Middle Class in Modern Ireland* (London: Palgrave Macmillan, 2010), pp. 148-169.

Borgonovo, John, 'Republican Courts, Ordinary Crime and the Irish Revolution, 1919-1921', in de Koster, Margo, Leuwers, Hervé, Luyten, Dirk & Rousseaux, Xavier, (eds.), *Justice in wartime and revolutions: Europe, 1795-1950* (Brussels: Algemeen Rijksarchief, 2012).

Broadberry, Stephen and Howlett, Peter, 'United Kingdom During World War One: Business as Usual?', in Broadberry, Stephen and Harrison, Mark (eds.), *Economics of World War One* (Cambridge: Cambridge University Press), pp. 206-234.

Cronin, Maura, 'Place, Class and Politics', in Crowley, J.S., Devoy, R.J.N., Linehan, D. and O'Flanagan, P (eds.), *Atlas of Cork City* (Cork: Cork University Press, 2005), pp. 202-214.

Cronin, Maura, 'Work and Workers in Cork City and County, 1800-1900', in O'Flanagan, Patrick and Buttimer, Cornelius G. (eds.), *Cork History and Society* (Dublin: Geography Publications, 1993), pp. 721-754.

Farrell, Brian, 'Labour and the Political Revolution', in Nevin, Donal (ed.), *Trade Union Century* (Cork: Mercier Press, 1994), pp. 42-53.

Farrell, Michael, 'The Establishment of the Ulster Special Constabulary', in Morgan, Austen & Purdie, Bob (eds.), *Ireland: Divided Nation, Divided Class* (London: Ink Links, 1980), pp. 125-137

Brian Girvin, 'Trade Unions and Economic Development', in Donal Nevin (ed.), *Trade Union Century* (Cork: Mercier Press, 1994), pp. 117-132.

Gourvish, T.R., 'The Standard of Living, 1890-1914', in Alan O'Day (ed.), *The Edwardian Age: Conflict and Stability, 1900-1914* (London: Archon Books, 1979), pp. 13-34.

Gribbon, H.D., 'Economic and social history, 1850-1921', in Vaughan, W.E. (ed.), *A New History of Ireland: VI, Ireland under the Union, II, 1870-1921* (Oxford: Clarendon Press, 1996), pp.

Hanley, Brian, "The Layers of an Onion': Reflections on 1913, Class and the Memory of the Irish Revolution', in McNamara, Conor & Yeates, Pádraig (eds.), *The Dublin Lockout 1913: New Perspective on Class War & its Legacy* (Newbridge: Irish Academic Press, 2017).

Hart, Peter, 'Class Community and the Irish Republican Army in Cork, 1917-1923, in O'Flanagan, Patrick and Buttimer, Cornelius G. (eds.) *Cork History and Society* (Dublin: Geography Publications, 1993), pp. 963-986.

Kennedy, Liam, 'The Cost of Living in Ireland, 1698-1998', in Dickson, David and Ó Gráda, Cormac (eds.), *Refiguring Ireland: Essays in honour of L.M. Cullen* (Dublin: Lilliput Press, 2003), pp. 249-276.

Johnson, D.S., 'The Belfast boycott, 1920-1922', in J.M. Goldstrom and L.A. Clarkson (eds.), *Irish population, economy, and society: essays in honour of the late K.H. Connell* (Oxford: oxford University Press, 1981), pp. 287-307.

Laffan, Michael, "Labour must wait': Ireland's conservative revolution', in Corish, P.J. (ed.), *Radicals, Rebels and Establishments* (Belfast: Appletree Press, 1985), pp. 203-222.

Laffan, Michael, 'Politics in Time of War', in Crowley, John, Ó Drisceoil, Donal, Borgonovo, John & Murphy, Mike (eds.), *Atlas of the Irish Revolution* (Cork: Cork University Press, 2017), pp. 459-467.

Lee, David, 'The Munster Soviets and the Fall of the House of Cleeve', in Lee, David and Jacobs, Debbie (eds.), *Made in Limerick: History of Industries, Trade and Commerce*, vol. 1 (Limerick: Limerick Civic Trust, 2003), pp. 286-306.

Lynch, John, 'Labour and Society, 1780-1945' in Liam Kennedy and Philip Ollerenshaw (eds.), *Ulster since 1600: Politics, Economy, and Society* (Oxford: Oxford University Press, 2013), pp. 195-210.

Lynch, John, 'The Belfast Shipyards and the Industrial Working Class', in Devine, Francis, Lane, Fintan & Purséil, Niamh (eds.), *Essays in Irish Labour History: A Festschrift for Elizabeth and John W. Boyle* (Dublin: Irish Academic Press, 2008), pp. 135-156.

Martin Maguire, 'The Church of Ireland and the problem of the Protestant working class of Dublin, 1870s-1930s', in Alan Ford, James McGuire & Kenneth Milne (eds.) *As by Law Established: The Church of Ireland since the Reformation* (Dublin: Lilliput Press, 1995), pp. 195-203.

Moriarty, Theresa, 'Work, warfare and wages: industrial controls and Irish trade unionism in the First World War', in Adrian Gregory & Senia Pašeta (eds.), *Ireland and the Great War: 'A War to Unite Us All'?* (Manchester: Manchester University Press, 2002), pp. 73-93.

Morris, R.J., 'The labour aristocracy and the British class structure', in Anne Digby & Charles Feinstein (eds.), *New Directions in Economic and Social History* (London: Gill & Macmillan, 1989), pp. 170-181.

Murphy, Maura, 'The Economic and Social Structure of Nineteenth-Century Cork', in Harkness, David and O'Dowd, Mary (eds.), *The Town in Ireland* (Belfast: Appletree Press, 1981), pp. 125-154.

O'Connor, Emmet, 'Labour and Politics, 1830-1945: Colonisation and Mental Colonisation', in Lane, Fintan and Ó Drisceoil, Donal (eds.), *Politics and the Irish Working Class, 1830-1945* (New York: Palgrave Macmillan, 2005), pp. 27-43.

O'Connor, Emmet, 'True Bolsheviks? The Rise and Fall of the Socialist Party of Ireland, 1917-21' in George Boyce & Alan O'Day (eds.), *Ireland in Transition, 1867-1921* (London: Routledge, 2004), pp. 209-222.

O'Connor, Emmet, 'War and Syndicalism, 1914-1923', in Nevin, Donal (ed.), *Trade Union Century* (Cork: Mercier Press, 1994), pp. 54-65.

O'Connor, Emmet, 'Sheep in Wolves' Clothing: Labour and Politics in Belfast, 1881-1914', in Devine, Francis, Lane, Fintan & Purséil, Niamh (eds.), *Essays in Irish Labour History: A Festschrift for Elizabeth and John W. Boyle* (Dublin: Irish Academic Press, 2008), pp. 65-82.

Ó Drisceoil, Donal, 'Losing a War it Never Fought: Labour, Socialism and the War of Independence', in Crowley, John, Ó Drisceoil, Donal, Borgonovo, John & Murphy, Mike (eds.), *Atlas of the Irish Revolution* (Cork: Cork University Press, 2017), pp. 487-494.

O'Rourke, Kevin, Boyer, George & Hatton, Timothy J., 'The impact of emigration on real wages in Ireland, 1850-1914', in Timothy J. Hatton & Jeffrey G. Williamson (eds.) *Migration and the international labour market, 1850-1993* (London: Routledge, 1994), pp. 221-239.

Patterson, Henry, 'Industrial labour and the labour movement', in Kennedy, Liam & Ollerenshaw, Phillip (eds), *An Economic History of Ulster, 1820-1939* (Manchester: Manchester University Press, 1987).

Patterson, Henry, 'The Irish Working Class and the Role of the State, 1850–2016', in Biagini, Eugenio F. & Daly, Mary (eds.), *The Cambridge Social History of Modern Ireland* (Cambridge: Cambridge University Press, 2017), pp. 145-160.

Pimley, Adrian, 'The working-class movement and the Irish Revolution', in Boyce, D.G. (ed.), *The Revolution in Ireland, 1879-1923* (London: Macmillan Education, 1988), pp. 204-215.

Puirséil, Niamh, 'War, work and labour', in Horne, John (ed.), *Our War: Ireland and the Great War* (Dublin: Royal Irish Academy, 2008), pp. 181-208.

Stack, Ellis, 'Victorian Cork', in Jeffries, Henry Alan (ed.), *Cork Historical Perspectives* (Dublin: Four Court Press, 2004), pp. 172-191.

Walker, Graham, 'The Protestant working class and the fragmentation of Ulster Unionism', in Busteed, Mervyn, Neal, Frank & Tonge, Jonathan (eds.), *Irish Protestant Identities* (Manchester: Manchester University Press, 2008), pp. 360-372

Journal Articles

Boyd, Black, 'Reassessing Irish industrial relations and labour history: the north-east of Ireland up to 1921', *Historical Studies in Industrial Relations*, Vol. 14, Autumn, 2002, pp. 45-85.

Comerford, RV, 'Patriotism as pastime: the appeal of Fenianism in the mid-1860s', *Irish Historical Studies*, Vol. 82, No. 86, Sept. 1980, pp. 239-250.

Fitzpatrick, David, 'Strikes in Ireland, 1914-1921', *Saothar*, no. 6, 1980, pp. 26-39.

Foster, Gavin, 'Class dismissed? The debate over a social basis to the Treaty split and the Irish Civil War', *Saothar*, no. 33, 2008, pp. 73-88.

English, Richard, 'Socialism and republican schism in Ireland: the emergence of the Republican Congress in 1934', *Irish Historical Studies*, Vol. 27, No. 105, May 1990, pp. 48-65.

Garvin, Tom, 'The Anatomy of a Nationalist Revolution: Ireland, 1858-1928', *Comparative Studies in Society and History*, Vol. 28, No. 3, July 1986, pp. 484-491.

Geary, Frank & Stark, Tom, 'Examining Ireland's Post-Famine Economic Growth Performance', *The Economic Journal*, Vol. 112, No. 482, Oct. 2002, pp. 919-935.

Geraghty, Hugh & Rigney, Peter, 'The Engineers' Strike in Inchicore Railway Work, 1902', *Saothar*, Vol. 9, 1983, pp. 20-31.

Hanley, Brian, 'The Irish Citizen Army After 1916', *Saothar*, Vol. 28, 2003, pp. 37-47.

Hart, Peter, 'The Social Structure of the Irish Republican Army, 1916-23', *The Historical Journal*, Vol. 42, No. 1, Mar. 1999, pp. 207-231.

Hatton, Timothy J. and Williamson, Jeffrey G., 'After the Famine: Emigration from Ireland, 1850-1913', *The Journal of Economic History*, Vol. 53, No. 3, Sept. 1993, pp. 575-600

Jacobson, D.S., 'The Political Economy of Industrial Location: The Ford Motor Company at Cork, 1912-1926', *Irish Economic and Social History*, vol. IV, 1977, pp. 36-65.

MacSweeney, A.M., 'A Study of Poverty in Cork City', *Studies*, vol. IV, 1915, pp. 92-104.

Maguire, Martin, 'A socio-economic analysis of the Dublin Protestant working class, 1870-1926', *Irish Economic and Social History*, 1993, Vol. 20, 1993, pp. 35-61.

Maguire, Martin, 'The Organisation and Activism of Dublin's Protestant Working Class, 1883-1935', *Irish Historical Studies*, Vol. 29, No. 113, May 1994, pp. 65-87.

Malone, A.E., 'Irish Labour in war time', *Studies*, vol. VII, 1918, pp. 319-327.

McCabe, Conor, 'The Irish Labour Party and the 1920 Local Elections', *Saothar*, no. 35, 2010, pp. 21-31.

Murphy, Denis, 'Ardmore Studies, film workers and the Irish state: creative labour in the 'Decade of Upheaval'', *Saothar*, No. 43, 2018, pp. 69-82.

Murphy, Muara, 'The working classes of nineteenth-century Cork', *Journal of the Cork Historical and Archaeological Society*, vol. 85, 1980, pp. 26-51.

O'Connor, Emmet, 'Active Sabotage in Industrial Conflict, 1917-23', *Irish Economic and Social History*, vol. 12, 1985, pp. 50-62.

O'Connor, Emmet, 'Anti-communism in twentieth-century Ireland', *Twentieth Century Communism*, Vol. 6, No. 6, Mar. 2014, pp. 59-81.

O'Connor, Emmet, 'Agrarian unrest and the labour movement in County Waterford, 1917-1923', *Saothar*, no. 6, 1980, pp. 40-58.

O'Connor, Emmet, 'Bolshevising Irish Communism: The Communist International and the Formation of the Revolutionary Workers' Groups, 1927-31', *Irish Historical Studies*, Vol. 33, No. 132, Nov. 2003, pp. 452-469.

O'Connor, Emmet, 'Problems of Reform in the Irish Trade Union Congress, 1894-1914', *Historical Studies in Industrial Relations*, Vol. 23-24, Apr. 2007, pp. 37-59

O'Connor, Emmet, 'Old Wine in New Bottles? Syndicalism and 'Fakirism' in the Great Labour Unrest, 1911-1914', *Labour History Review*, Vol 17, No. 1, 2014, pp. 19-36.

O'Connor-Lysaght, D.R., 'September 1921, Month of Soviets', *The Plough*, no. 1 (1972).

O'Connor-Lysaght, D.R., 'The Rake's Progress of a Syndicalist: The Political Career of William O'Brien, Irish Labour Leader', *Saothar*, no. 9, pp. 48-62.

Ó Gráda, Cormac, 'Migration as disaster relief: Lessons from the Great Irish Famine', *European Review of Economic History*, Vol. 1, No. 1, Apr. 1997, pp. 3-25.

O'Rahilly, Alfred, 'The Social Problem in Cork', *Studies*, vol. VI, 1917, pp. 177-188.

O'Rourke, Kevin, 'Emigration and Living Standards in Ireland since the Famine', *Journal of Population Economics*, Vol. 8, No. 4, Nov. 1995, pp. 407-412.

O'Rourke, Kevin, 'Did the Great Irish Famine Matter?', *The Journal of Economic History*, Vol. 51, No. 1, Mar. 1991, pp. 1-22.

Pickering, Paul A., '"Irish First": Daniel O'Connell, the Native Manufacture Campaign, and Economic Nationalism, 1840-44', *Albion: A Quarterly Journal Concerned with British Studies*, Vol. 32, No. 4, Winter, 2000, pp. 598-616.

Screpanti, Ernesto, 'Long Cycles in Strike Activity: An Empirical Investigation', *British Journal of Industrial Relations*, vol. XXV, no. 1, 1987, pp. 99-124

Thompson, William J., 'The Census of Ireland, 1911', *Journal of the Royal Statistical Society*, June 1913, Vol. 76, No. 7, pp. 635-671.

Townshend, Charles, 'The Irish railway strike of 1920: Industrial action and civil resistance in the struggle for independence', *Irish Historical Studies*, vol. 21, 1978, pp. 265-282.

Turner, John D., 'Wealth concentration in the European periphery: Ireland, 1858-2001' *Oxford Economic Papers*, Vol. 62, No. 4, Oct. 2010, pp. 625-646.

Williamson, Jeffrey G., 'Economic convergence: placing post-famine Ireland in comparative perspective', *Irish Economic and Social History*, Vol. 21, 1994, pp. 5-27.

Yeates, Pádraig, 'Craft workers during the Irish Revolution, 1919-1922', *Saothar*, no. 33, 2008, pp. 37-56.

Magazine Articles

McGuire, Charlie, "The strike that 'never should have taken place'? The Inchicore rail dispute of 1924', *History Ireland*, Issue 2, Vol. 17, Mar/Apr. 2009.

Online Articles

Brennan, Cathal, 'The Postal Strike of 1922', 8 June 2012, *The Irish Story*, https://www.theirishstory.com/2012/06/08/the-postal-strike-of-1922/ (accessed 11 Mar. 2019).

Central Statistics Office, 'quarterly reports on industrial disputes in Ireland', https://www.cso.ie/en/statistics/labourmarket/archive/ (accessed 15 Mar. 2022).

Central Statistics Office, https://www.cso.ie/en/statistics/ (accessed 5 Apr. 2022);

Graham, Laura, 'Supreme Court Declares Registered Employment Agreements Unconstitutional – How Does This Impact Your Business?', 19 Nov. 2016, https://reddycharlton.ie/insights/supreme-court-declares-registered-employment-agreements-unconstitutional-how-does-this-impact-your-business/#:~:text=The%20Supr eme%20Court%20recently%20declared,the%20Supreme%20Court%20Case%E2%80 %9D (accessed 30 Jan. 2022).

Ó Maonaigh, Aaron, 'The death of Volunteer Seán Doyle: 'A conflict of testimony", 7 June 2019, *The Irish Story*, https://www.theirishstory.com/2019/06/07/the-death-of-volunteer-sean-doyle-a-conflict-of-testimony/#_ednref12 (accessed 29 Mar. 2020).

Pamphlets

Quinlivan, Aodh, *Dissolved: The remarkable story of how Cork lost its Corporation in 1924* (Cork: Cork City Library, 2017).

TEEU, *Michael Mervyn, 1900-1960* (Dublin: TEEU, 2016).

Yeates, Pádraig, *Irish Craft Workers in a Time of Revolution* (Dublin: TEEU, 2016).

Unpublished Theses

Crean, Thomas, 'The Labour Movement in Kerry and Limerick, 1914-21', (TCD: PhD, 1994).

Fitzpatrick, Claire, 'Labour, ideology and the states in Ireland, 1917-32' (University of Cambridge: PhD, 1993).

Harding, Keith, 'The Irish Issue in the British Labour Movement, 1900-1922' (University of Sussex: PhD, 1983).

Judge, Jerome Joseph, 'The Labour movement in the Republic of Ireland: an analysis of the major trends which have affected the development of labour in Ireland since 1894' (PhD: UCD, 1955).

Lahiff, Edward, 'Industry and Labour in Cork, 1890-1921' (UCC: MA, 1988).

Linehan, Thomas Anthony, 'The Development of Cork's Economy and Business Attitudes, 1910-1939', (UCC: MA, 1985).

MacSweeney, A.M., 'Poverty and the Wage-earning classes', (UCC: MA, 1914).

Maguire, Martin, 'The Dublin Protestant working class, 1870-1932: Economy, Society, Politics' (UCD: MA, 1990).

McCabe, Conor, 'The Amalgamated Society of Railway Servants and the National Union of Railwaymen in Ireland, 1911-1923' (University of Ulster: MLitt., 2006).

McQuay Reddick, Stephen, 'Political and Industrial Labour in Cork, 1899-1914' (UCC: MA, 1984).

Murphy, Denis, 'A Labour History of Irish Television and Film Drama Production, 1958-2016' (DCU: PhD, 2017).

Murphy, Maura, 'The Role of Organised Labour in the Political and Economic Life of Cork City, 1820-1899' (University of Leicester: PhD, 1979).

O'Connor-Lysaght, D.R., 'Class Struggle during the Irish War of Independence and Civil War, 1916-1924' (UCD: MA, 1982).

O'Shea, Finbarr Joseph, 'Government and Trade Unions in Ireland, 1939-1946: The Formulation of Labour Legislation' (UCC: MA, 1988).

Rigney, Peter, 'Trade Unionism on the Great Southern and Western Railway, 1890-1911,' (TCD: BA, 1977).

Ryan, John Gerard, 'Apprenticeship in Ireland: An Historical Analysis' (Maynooth: PhD, 1993)

White, Martin, 'The Greenshirts: Fascism in the Irish Free State, 1935-45' (University of London: PhD, 2004).

Index

Amalgamated Engineering and Electrical Union (AEEU), 257 - 266, 269, 284

Amalgamated Engineering Union (AEU), 46,48, 52, 75, 81, 101, 106, 152, 188, 257

Amalgamated Society of Engineers (ASE), 6, 8, 19, 21, 23, 24, 28, 29, 34, 35, 38, 43, 46, 59

Amalgamated Transport and General Workers' Union (ATGWU), 75, 90, 107, 142, 195, 196, 200, 241, 268, 271, 272

Amicus, 264, 286

Apprenticeships, 4, 5, 6, 17, 84, 85, 92, 112, 117, 152, 155, 156, 159, 166, 178, 183, 203 - 204, 208, 251

Arbitration, 22, 25, 33, 34, 48, 49, 51, 54, 56, 62, 73, 75, 77, 79, 90, 116, 126, 137, 198, 207 - 208, 270, 274, 319, 322, 337, 346

Army Council, 23, 30, 31, 43, 45, 58, 69, 80, 102, 110

Artisans, 3, 4, 6, 15, 20, 24,

Associated Society of Locomotive Engineers and Firemen, 31, 56

Australia, 24, 273, 281, 282

B

Bakers, 3, 4, 127

Barry, Tadhg, 30, 38

Belfast, xii, 3, 5, 6, 8 - 19, 23, 25 - 28, 34, 35, 36, 37, 39, 42, 44 - 46, 49, 50, 51, 52, 54, 57, 59, 60, 62, 81, 119, 126, 142, 146, 212, 229, 258, 266, 284

Blacklegging, 23

Blacksmiths, 4, 13, 26, 39, 43, 47, 50, 51, 54, 61, 88, 157, 166

Boilermakers, 6, 13, 81, 26, 29, 43, 51, 59, 61, 69, 73, 74, 79, 128, 149

Bourgeoisie, 6, 15, 68, 253, 290

Browne, Gary, 234, 254

Brush makers, 4

Building and Allied Trades Union (BATU), 267, 274, 285

Building tradesmen, 3, 75, 189

C

Cabinetmakers, 4, 45

Capitalism, 1, 4, 21, 24, 33, 53, 100, 135, 161, 165

Carpenters, 4, 9, 13, 17, 88, 163, 257, 283

Carter, Joseph, 209, 211, 212, 216, 220, 223, 247, 254, 255

Cassidy, Jack, 97, 151, 155, 169, 170, 180, 185, 186, 187, 188, 200

Casualisation, 3, 268,

Catholic Church, 102, 143, 144, 145, 162, 254, 291

Catholics, 8, 10, 17, 26, 44, 60, 144

Celtic Tiger, 243, 253, 254, 266, 267, 268, 275, 276, 280, 294

Child mortality, 12, 136

City and County of Dublin Conservative Workingmen's Club, 28, 38

Civil War, ix, 20, 21, 27, 32, 38, 45, 62, 63, 64, 67 - 71, 72, 74, 80, 84, 88, 89, 100, 129, 133, 165, 225

Class conflict, 7, 8, 11, 18, 19, 20, 21, 27, 33, 37, 38, 41, 48, 49, 51, 67, 72, 73, 75, 88, 89, 118, 119, 135, 136, 223, 234, 337, 338, 347, 348, 350, 351, 354, 355

Class consciousness, 9, 15, 24, 60, 76, 98, 114, 123, 139, 337, 339

Closed shop, 167, 198, 199, 236, 237, 266

Clydeside, 8, 9, 23, 42, 51, 68, 73, 74

Coachbuilders [coachmakers], 3, 4, 26, 49, 73, 75, 100, 110

Collins, Michael, ix, 30, 31, 34, 38, 42, 43, 45, 59, 60, 69, 81, 84, 153, 290

Combination, 5, 7

Commission on Prices, 14

Committee on Production, 22, 73

Communication Workers' Union, 257, 265

Mechanics' Union, 28

Irish Congress of Trade Unions (ICTU), 115, 154, 175, 176, 178, 185, 186, 190, 192, 193, 196, 200, 202, 203, 214, 243, 244, 263, 267, 268, 283, 292

Irish electrical workers, 6, 26, 30, 58, 63, 83, 84, 85, 105, 108, 138, 141, 142, 143, 152, 171, 172, 175, 186, 192, 195, 198, 200, 203, 230, 234, 235, 237, 244, 254, 257, 271, 278, 279, 290, 292, 294

Irish Engineering and Foundry Union (IEFU), iv, 97, 98, 99, 101, 103, 109, 110, 111, 113, 122, 124, 125, 126, 129, 130, 148, 149, 150, 152, 153, 155, 291, 292

Irish Engineering, Shipbuilding and Foundry Trades Union (IESFTU), 35, 289

Irish General Railway Engineering Union (IGREU), 80, 81, 82, 83, 95, 96, 97, 103, 104, 109, 110

Irish Independent, 30, 37, 38, 39, 54, 61, 62, 63, 88, 89, 90, 91, 92, 114, 115, 116, 117, 132, 133, 156, 157, 158, 180, 181, 182, 183, 188, 205, 206, 207, 208, 210, 218, 224, 225, 226, 249, 250, 251, 267, 274, 284, 285, 286, 287

Irish Labour Party, 7, 30, 32, 39, 42, 48, 56 - 60, 62, 64, 67, 71, 72, 74, 89, 94, 100, 101, 103, 108, 115, 119, 123, 126, 129, 130, 133, 137, 138, 153, 154, 161, 173, 178, 185, 202, 218, 227, 240, 243, 254, 268, 270, 289, 290

Irish Press, 38, 58, 64, 91, 92, 114, 115, 116, 117, 131, 132, 133, 156, 157, 158, 180, 181, 182, 183, 205, 206, 207, 208, 224, 225, 226, 249, 250, 251, 285

Irish Republican Army (IRA), iv, ix, 27, 28, 29, 30, 31, 35, 37, 38, 42, 44, 45, 46, 47, 52, 58, 59, 61, 62, 64, 69, 70, 71, 80, 102, 108, 115, 129, 130, 137, 153, 165, 202, 203, 207, 289

Irish Republican Brotherhood (IRB), 15, 16, 29, 30, 31, 34, 38, 41, 44, 58, 59, 64, 289, 290

Irish Stationery Drivers' Society, 31, 43, 44, 45, 61, 97, 98, 103, 114, 121, 125, 157

Irish Times, 89, 90, 116, 132, 133, 167, 282, 286, 287

Irish Trades Union Congress (ICTU), 7, 37, 47, 48, 53, 76, 82, 89, 98, 106, 119, 124 - 128, 140, 151, 152, 162, 163, 165, 166, 167, 169, 175 - 178, 185 - 193, 195, 196, 197, 200, 202, 203, 210, 213, 214, 217, 218, 219, 221, 223, 224, 229, 234, 238, 240, 241, 243, 244, 246, 247, 249, 257, 259 - 265, 267, 268, 271, 280, 282, 283, 292

Irish Transport and General Workers' Union (ITGWU), 11, 14, 24, 30, 43, 46, 47, 48, 52, 57, 61, 62, 64, 68, 73, 74, 75, 76, 81, 82, 90, 97, 98, 101, 105, 106, 107, 110, 114, 115, 116, 122, 123, 124, 125, 126, 127, 138, 139, 142, 149, 153, 158, 165, 167, 176, 180, 190, 198, 200, 209, 212, 228, 230, 233, 237, 241, 244, 249, 289, 293

Iron, 1, 2, 3, 6, 9, 19, 32, 39, 43, 48, 54, 55, 61, 79, 81, 82, 91, 109, 110, 130, 139, 140, 149, 153

Iron Moulders' Society, 6, 32, 39, 44, 52, 54, 55, 61, 70, 79, 82, 97, 107, 109, 130

J

Jackson, Ken, 257, 258, 263

Journeymen, 4, 5, 6, 58, 75, 156, 199, 204, 281

K

Kavanagh, Paddy, vii, ix, 283, 287

Knutsford, 29

L

Labourers, 1, 5, 7, 8, 9, 10, 11, 18, 21, 23, 24, 25, 27, 28, 47, 49, 50, 58, 67, 73, 75, 82, 85, 86, 96, 98, 104, 105, 109, 125, 138, 143, 152, 166, 167, 176, 178, 189, 190, 191, 238, 239

Laird, Gavin, , 257

Laissez-faire, 4, 22, 68, 112, 120

Larkin, James (Big Jim) , 7, 11, 24, 36, 82, 84, 91, 103, 123, 126, 127, 128, 130, 153, 191, 209, 289

Larkinism, 7, 11, 36, 62, 65

Larkinites, 7, 82

Lawless, Finn, 255

Lawless, Paddy, 231

Leahy, Thomas, 29, 38, 58, 62, 64